The Unpublished Opinions of the Rehnquist Court

The Unpublished Opinions of the Rehnquist Court

The Unpublished Opinions of the
REHNQUIST COURT

BERNARD SCHWARTZ

New York Oxford
OXFORD UNIVERSITY PRESS
1996

Oxford University Press

Oxford New York
Athens Auckland Bangkok Bombay
Calcutta Cape Town Dar es Salaam Delhi
Florence Hong Kong Istanbul Karachi
Kuala Lumpur Madras Madrid Melbourne
Mexico City Nairobi Paris Singapore
Taipei Tokyo Toronto

and associated companies in
Berlin Ibadan

Published by Oxford University Press, Inc.
198 Madison Avenue, New York, New York 10016

Library of Congress Cataloging-in-Publication Data
The Unpublished opinions of the Rehnquist court
[compiled by] Bernard Schwartz.
p. cm.
ISBN 0-19-509332-1
1. Judicial opinions—United States. I. Schwartz, Bernard, 1923– .
II. United States. Supreme Court.
KF101.8.S377 1996
347.73′26—dc20 [347.30735] 94-23862

1 2 3 4 5 6 7 8 9

Printed in the United States of America
on acid-free paper

As Always,
for Aileen

Contents

The Unpublished Opinions of the Rehnquist Court

Introduction

Almost twenty years ago, Nina Totenberg wrote in the *New York Times:*

> There is probably no more secret society in America than the Supreme Court. Its nine Justices are among the most powerful, yet least visible, men in the United States. It is unheard of for a Justice to reveal anything specific about the Court's case work; law clerks, too, are sworn to secrecy. The Court's written decisions are supposed to speak for themselves. It is the least accountable branch of Government.[1]

When Totenberg wrote this, about the only things publicly known about the Supreme Court's functioning were the briefs, the oral arguments, and the published judgments and opinions. Everything else in the Court took place behind the scenes—as removed from the public gaze as the decision process in the Kremlin under Stalin or Brezhnev.

The Totenberg description is, however, no longer accurate. Starting with *The Brethren* in 1979,[2] there have been a number of books describing the internal functioning of the Court—including seven by myself,[3] giving an inside picture of the Warren and Burger Courts in operation. These books provide an unprecedented view of what happens behind the red curtain after the oral arguments that conclude the public proceedings in a case. For better or worse, the Court's curtain of secrecy has been lifted to reveal what goes on during the Justices' deliberative process.

A major reason for the recent insights into the behind-the-scenes operation of the Court has been the willingness of Justice William J. Brennan to make his papers available to serious researchers. Other members of the Court have, however, been disturbed by Brennan's actions in this respect. This is shown by a December 19, 1990, Memorandum to the Conference circulated by Justice Brennan both to the other Justices and to retired Chief Justice Warren E. Burger and Justice Lewis F. Powell.

"Sandra and the Chief," began the memo, referring to Justice Sandra Day O'Connor and Chief Justice William H. Rehnquist, "have expressed to me the concern—shared, they tell me, by others of you—that researchers who examine my official papers thereby gain access to memoranda written to me by other Justices. They have suggested that, to avoid embarrassment to any of our colleagues, I should not grant access to files that may include any written material from Justices who are still sitting on the Court."

"I appreciate your concerns," the Brennan memo stated. It then confirmed that the Justice had, indeed, given researchers access to his "collection of official papers in the Manuscript Division of the Library of Congress," which consist primarily of files on the cases decided by the Court: "About a decade ago, I began to grant permission to study these files to certain academic researchers, and that practice has continued. . . . Virtually all of the researchers who received permission have been affiliated with an institution of higher learning (typically, a law school or political science department)."

Brennan assured his colleagues, "My decision to allow selective access to my papers was not taken lightly." However, the Justice went on, "I ultimately concluded that scholarly examination of the Court's workings would serve the public interest. That belief was strengthened by the record of published work utilizing collections of other Justices' papers, which seemed to have promoted awareness and understanding of the Court. My experience in the subsequent decade has confirmed this view. Works published by scholars who have used my papers among other collections have been uniformly substantive and, on the whole, worthwhile. To my knowledge, there have been no irresponsible uses of this material."

"While I recognize—and indeed share—many of your concerns," the Brennan memo concluded, " I continue to believe that this arrangement will foster responsible scholarship about the Court."

Publication of this book shows my agreement with Brennan's view that it is in the interest of both the country and the Court itself for the public to learn as much as possible about the operation of the highest tribunal. With Justice Brennan, I believe that the claims of history are more important than those of judicial secrecy.

This book is a companion to *The Unpublished Opinions of the Warren Court*[4] and *The Unpublished Opinions of the Burger Court*.[5] Like those volumes, it contains the draft opinions that were prepared by the Justices in the cases that are included. Such draft opinions are, of course, private Court papers. They have not been published until this book. They are, however, now available in the Thurgood Marshall papers in the Library of Congress, except for the first drafts of the Stevens draft opinion of the Court and the Marshall draft concurrence and dissent in *Hodgson* v. *Minnesota* (reprinted in Chapter 7).[6] The post-1986 communications among the Justices, which are referred to throughout the book, are also from the Marshall papers. Those before 1986 are identified or were made available on a confidential basis.

In presenting the draft opinions in this work, I have followed the format of my Warren and Burger Court opinions books. Before the reproduced opinions, there is a statement containing a short history of the case as well as the setting in which the different drafts were circulated. After the opinions, there is an analysis of what happened after the drafts were sent around to the Justices. As in the earlier books, I try to explain why the drafts were not issued as the final opinions or concurrences and dissents in these cases. In particular, I try to show what would have happened if the draft opinions had come down as they are reprinted here. The contrast between the drafts and the final opinions has made for a substantial difference in the law in the various fields involved. The law and even our society might be very different today if the original draft in *Webster* v. *Reproductive Health Services* (reprinted in Chapter 6), which virtually overruled *Roe* v. *Wade*, had been issued as the final opinion of the Court.

Once again, I should stress that I have not reproduced these unpublished draft opinions and told what happened in the Court in these cases in an effort to produce a mini-*Brethren*.[7] Rather, my purpose is to give students of the Supreme Court further insight into the Court's largely unrevealed decision process in the cases covered. My discussion and the draft opinions reproduced will show what too few realize, that the decisions of the highest Court are basically collaborative efforts in which nine supreme individualists must cooperate to bring about the desired result. The burden is, of course, greatest on the Chief Justice, who must lead the majority when he is in it, and the Justice he calls upon to write the opinion—one who must command the support of at least four other strong-willed lawyers, with their own definite views on the law and the Constitution. It is my hope, as in my Warren and Burger Court opinions books, that the actual operation of the Court's decision process will be made clearer by my account of these ten cases and the opinions that never came down.

Mr. Right as Chief Justice

Just before he became Chief Justice, William H. Rehnquist gave an interview to the *New York Times* in which he compared the Warren and Burger Courts. Justice Rehnquist stated that the impact of the Court had been diminished under Chief Justice Warren E. Burger. "I don't think that the Burger Court has as wide a sense of mission. Perhaps it doesn't have any sense of mission at all."[8]

What he said of the Court then was emphatically not true of Justice Rehnquist himself. If any Justice had a "sense of mission" it was the Justice whom *Newsweek* had dubbed "The Court's Mr. Right."[9] In fact, Rehnquist was one Justice who came to the Court with a definite agenda. In his *Times* interview he noted that he joined the Court with a desire to counteract the Warren Court decisions. "I came to the court," Rehnquist said, "sensing . . . that there were some excesses in terms of constitutional adjudication during the era of the so-called Warren Court." Some of that Court's decisions, the Justice went on, "seemed to me hard to justify. . . . So I felt that at the time I came on the Court, the boat was kind of keeling over in one direction. Interpreting my oath as I saw it, I felt that my job was . . . to kind of lean the other way."[10]

In his first years on the Court, however, Justice Rehnquist was scarcely able to secure his desired repudiation of the Warren jurisprudence. On the contrary, the intended counterrevolution served only as a confirmation of most of the Warren Court jurisprudence. It can be said that no important

Warren Court decision was overruled by its successor. Worse still, from the Rehnquist point of view, the Burger Court went even further than the Warren Court in some cases—notably in its *Roe* v. *Wade* abortion decision.[11]

True, Justice Rehnquist repeatedly spoke out against the Court's direction during the Burger tenure. During his early Court years, nevertheless, the majority remained largely unsympathetic to Rehnquist's entreaties from the right. It was then that he received a Lone Ranger doll as a gift from his law clerks, who called him the "lone dissenter" during that period. During his fourteen years as an Associate Justice, Rehnquist dissented alone fifty-four times—a Court record.

Rehnquist's extreme views did not prevent him from being on good terms with the other Justices. Even his ideological opposites, like Justice William J. Brennan, have remarked on their friendly relations with the categorical conservative. To the others, Rehnquist was as well known for his good nature as for his rightist acumen. On a Court where, as Justice Blackmun once lamented, "[t]here is very little humor,"[12] Justice Rehnquist stood out because of his irreverence and wit. When the Burger Court sat, one of Rehnquist's clerks would every now and then pass notes to the Justice. These were not legal memos but Trivial Pursuit-style questions. Rehnquist would answer them and then hand them to Justice Blackmun for that Justice to try his hand.[13]

Rehnquist's wit was almost proverbial in the Burger Court. He was the only Justice in recent memory to begin opinions with a Gilbert and Sullivan lyric[14] or the limerick, "There was a young lady from Niger."[15] In a December 1986 argument, the counsel said that his opponent "wanted words to mean what he says they mean. That didn't fool Alice and I doubt very much that it will fool this Court." "Don't overestimate us," came back Rehnquist's riposte.

Another illustration of Rehnquist's wit may be seen in a 1973 Rehnquist memorandum: "In going over some material which had been stored for a long period of time in my present Chambers, I came across a manuscript poem entitled 'To a Law Clerk Dying Young,' written by someone named A. E. Schmaussman, or Schmousman (the handwriting is not too good), who was apparently a law clerk here at one time." (This was an obvious take-off of A. E. Housman's once-famous poem "To An Athlete Dying Young.") Justice Rehnquist wrote, "I found the poem very moving and emotional, and thought that a public reading of it would be a suitable occasion for a gathering of present and retired members of the Court and their law clerks to toast a departing Term with sherry."

Rehnquist's memo concluded with a satiric allusion to Chief Justice Burger's obsession with Court secrecy: "P.S. I debated circulating the actual text of the poem with this invitation, but decided that there was too great a chance that it might be leaked to the newspapers before the party."

Rehnquist's sense of humor sometimes degenerated into practical jokes. On April Fool's Day, 1985, Chief Justice Burger was his victim. Rehnquist had a life-size photo cutout of Burger produced and sent a street photographer to a corner outside the Court with a sign, "Have your picture taken with the chief justice, $1." To make sure he wouldn't miss Burger's reaction, the Justice called him at home, saying he needed a ride to Court on April 1. Rehnquist was laughing loudly when he drove past the scene that day with the overdignified Chief Justice.[16]

Before his appointment as Court head, Rehnquist also had anything but the appearance of a Justice. Well over six feet tall, he looked like an overage college student with his long sideburns, lumbering around the Court in his thick brown glasses, mismatched outfits, and Hush Puppies shoes. "In the marble halls of the Court, he looked more like a refugee from a small college math department than a justice of the Supreme Court."[17]

Despite his robust appearance and weekly tennis with his law clerks, Justice Rehnquist has had health problems. In 1982, he was hospitalized with back pain and suffered a period of mental confusion and slurred speech, when the heavy dosage of a powerful pain killer, Placidyl, was reduced. In 1977, Rehnquist had written in reply to a letter comment on his draft opinion in a case: "It may be that my adverse reactions to your letter of March 7 are partially induced by my doctor's insistence that I take valium four times a day."[18]

Since becoming Chief Justice, Rehnquist has restrained both his appearance and his wit. Gone are his sideburns, and his disheveled attire has been replaced by more appropriate conservative dress. Rehnquist has also exhibited something of his predecessor's emphasis on the dignity of his office. In a February 16, 1990, memorandum on the instructions given to counsel arguing before the Court, he noted that "they are told: 'A member of the Court should be addressed as "Justice"—not judge.'" Rehnquist pointed out "that this is not, strictly speaking, correct so far as The Chief Justice is concerned." Therefore, Rehnquist wrote, "I suggest we replace this sentence with the following: 'A member of the Court should be addressed as "Chief Justice" or "Justice" as the case may be—not as "judge."'"

At times, however, the old Rehnquist appears beneath the Chief Justice veneer. In a May 2, 1991, memorandum transmitting a fourth draft opinion in *Barnes* v. *Glen Theatre*,[19] Rehnquist wrote, "[It] is my great hope that the enclosed draft will dispel some of the confusion about the case which has, unfortunately, been engendered by the dissenting and concurring opinions." The Chief Justice then asserted, "The theme of this fourth draft is a very positive one, and it can be summed up in the following verse from a once popular song:

> Accentuate the positive
> Eliminate the negative
> Latch on to the affirmative
> Don't mess with Mr. In Between."

In his October 26, 1990, memorandum inviting Court personnel to that year's Christmas party, Chief Justice Rehnquist urged, "Please join us and bring your 'best singing voice.'" More often than not, the Chief Justice would lead the party in belting out his old favorites. Even the Justices feel the pressure to join the Rehnquist caroling. Before the 1991 Christmas party, a law clerk asked Justice David H. Souter if he would sing along with the Chief Justice. Souter replied, "I have to. Otherwise I get all the tax cases." Some Justices have said that they would rather volunteer to wash windows than be assigned the chore of writing tax opinions.

Typically, by the way, Justice Thurgood Marshall would reply to the Rehnquist invitations to the annual party with a "Dear Chief" note, such as the one he sent on November 1, 1990: "As usual, I will *not* attend the Christmas Party. . . . I still believe in the separation of church and state." Later that same day, Justice John Paul Stevens wrote to Rehnquist: "Like Thurgood, I will not be able to attend the Christmas Party, . . . but my excuse is perhaps less principled and more secular than his."

Rehnquist and Compromise

As Chief Justice, Rehnquist has trimmed more than his sideburns. In a 1976 article, Justice Rehnquist had discussed the role of a Chief Justice, using Chief Justice Charles Evans Hughes as his model.[20] "Except in cases involving matters of high principle," a book on Hughes points out, "he willingly acquiesced in silence rather than expose his dissenting views. . . . Hughes was also willing to modify his own opinions to hold or increase his majority."[21]

Rehnquist too has realized that a Chief Justice who does not have a majority has failed in his primary function of leading the Court. More than is known, Chief Justice Rehnquist has modified his position to retain a Court, even though it meant compromising his extreme rightist views. Thus, in a November 28, 1990, letter to Justice White on a pending case, the Chief Justice wrote, "I believe I voted to affirm at Conference in this case, but in the interests of getting a solid Court opinion I am prepared to join your present draft vacating and remanding if you would make some minor changes."[22]

Earlier the same month, on November 13, Chief Justice Rehnquist circulated a Memorandum to the Conference. In it, he informed the Justices, "Nino [Scalia] has shown me a copy of a proposed concurrence in this case[23] which he will circulate this morning. The concurrence takes the position that the same presumption of equitable tolling should apply to statutes of limitations applicable to government suits as is applicable to private suits."

Rehnquist wrote, "I prefer the position taken in the most recent circulation of my proposed opinion for the Court, but want very much to avoid a fractionated Court on this point." Therefore, the memo went on, "[i]f a majority prefers Nino's view, I will adopt it; if I can get a majority for the view contained in the present draft, I will adhere to that. If there is some 'middle ground' that will attract a majority, I will even adopt that."

In the end, Rehnquist did adopt the Scalia position. This enabled him to issue his opinion as that of the Court; a strong majority joined his opinion including Justice Scalia, who withdrew his proposed concurrence.

The Liberal Holdovers

Even with the tendency to compromise just noted, William H. Rehnquist has proved to be a strong Chief Justice, more in the Warren than the Burger mold. It was said that Chief Justice Burger's discussion of cases at conference left the Justices with the feeling that he was "the least prepared member of the Court."[24] In a comment on Chief Justice Rehnquist, Justice Marshall said, "He has no problems, wishy-washy, back and forth. He knows exactly what he wants to do, and that's very important as a chief justice."[25] There is little doubt that Marshall was contrasting the Rehnquist performance with that of his predecessor.

In particular, Rehnquist has been an efficient leader of the conference. He goes through cases briskly, focusing on the key issues raised and how the lower court ruled on them. He keeps the discussion moving at a rapid pace, usually with minimal discussion and no haggling. The Rehnquist conference presentation has been described by a Justice as "honest." "The Chief Justice does not slant his comments or leave out key facts so as to put a conservative spin on the issue."[26]

More than that, Chief Justice Rehnquist came to his position with a definite agenda. From his first appointment to the Court, Rehnquist has sought what he called "a halt to . . . the sweeping rules made in the days of the Warren Court"[27]—and not only a halt, but a rollback of much of the Warren jurisprudence. The Rehnquist conservative program has included enlargement of government authority over individuals, a check to the expansion of criminal defendants' rights, limitations on access to federal courts, and increased emphasis on protection of property rights. As Chief Justice, he has finally been in a position to advance his conservative agenda.

That was not, however, true during Rehnquist's first years as Chief Justice. Before the retirement of Justice William J. Brennan in 1990 and of Justice Thurgood Marshall in 1991, there were four Justices who made up a strong liberal bloc in the Rehnquist Court. In addition to Brennan and Marshall, Justices Harry A. Blackmun and John Paul Stevens would usually vote against the Chief Justice on important constitutional issues.

The liberal bloc was led by one of the great names in Supreme Court history, William J. Brennan Jr. He served on the Supreme Court from 1957 to 1990; only five members of the Court have served longer. He wrote about twelve hundred opinions and often noted that he had sat on the bench with one-fifth of all the Justices ever appointed. In terms of influence, Brennan was the most important Justice since Oliver Wendell Holmes; he served as the catalyst for some of the most significant decisions during his tenure. He was the leader of the Court's liberal wing under Chief Justices Warren, Burger, and Rehnquist. More important, the Brennan jurisprudence set the pattern for much of American legal thought as the century drew toward its end. So pervasive was Brennan's influence that an English periodical headed its story on his retirement "A Lawgiver Goes."[28]

Before his 1956 appointment by President Eisenhower, Brennan had been a judge in New Jersey for seven years, rising from the state trial court to its highest bench. He was the only Justice on the Warren and Burger Courts to have served as a state judge before Justice Sandra Day O'Connor's appointment.

"One of the things," Justice Felix Frankfurter once said, "that laymen, even lawyers, do not always understand is indicated by the question you hear so often: 'Does a man become any different when he puts on a gown?' I say, 'If he is any good, he does.'"[29] Certainly Justice Brennan on the highest bench proved a complete surprise to those who saw him as a middle-of-the-road moderate. He quickly became a firm adherent of the activist philosophy and a principal architect of the Warren Court's jurisprudence. Brennan had been Frankfurter's student at Harvard Law School; yet if Frankfurter expected the new Justice to continue his pupilage, he was soon disillusioned. After Brennan had joined the Warren Court's activist wing, Frankfurter supposedly quipped, "I always encourage my students to think for themselves, but Brennan goes too far!"

Brennan is small and feisty, almost leprechaun-like in appearance; yet he has a hearty bluffness and an ability to put people at ease. Brennan's unassuming appearance and manner mask a keen intelligence. He was perhaps the hardest worker on the Court. Unlike many Justices with strong views, Brennan was always willing to mold his language to meet the objections of his colleagues, a talent that would become his hallmark on the Court.

On the Warren Court, Brennan soon became a member of a group of four Justices (with the Chief Justice and Justices Black and Douglas—those whom Judge Learned Hand once referred to as "the Jesus Quartet")[30] who favored activist solutions to constitutional issues. In 1962, with the retirement of Justices Frankfurter and Charles E. Whittaker and their ultimate replacement by Justices Arthur J. Goldberg, Abe Fortas, and Thurgood Marshall, a majority for the Four's position was secured. It was then that our law entered its most important period of development since its formative era—remaking much of the constitutional corpus in the process. Justice Brennan was a leader in this development.

After Chief Justice Warren's retirement, Brennan was no longer the trusted insider. Instead, he became the Justice who tried above all to keep the Warren flame burning and serve as leader of the Burger Court's liberal wing. Even under Chief Justice Burger, Brennan was able to secure the votes for his position in many important cases. In his last years, the Court, under Chief Justice Rehnquist, moved more toward the right, and Brennan spoke increasingly in dissent. However, in the Rehnquist Court also, Justice Brennan was able to gain notable victories, particularly in the areas of abortion, separation of church and state, freedom of expression, and affirmative action. He was primarily responsible for the decisions just before his retirement that flag burning was protected by the First Amendment and upholding broad congressional authority in the field of affirmative action.[31]

No account of Justice Brennan would be complete that did not touch upon the Justice as a human being. Even his ideological foes stressed, as one put it upon his retirement, that "you cannot dislike this man on a personal level." No Justice enjoyed more respect and affection among his colleagues. He had warm relations with everyone on the Court and always had a friendly word for everyone, from the Chief Justice to the maintenance staff.

What struck those who met Justice Brennan was that he remained unceremonious and unassuming, despite his reputation as the most influential Justice of the past half century. He once related to me with awe how, at a charity auction, someone bid several thousand dollars to have lunch with him and Mrs. Brennan.

Next to Brennan in the Rehnquist Court's liberal bloc was Justice Thurgood Marshall. His career added a racial dimension to the American success story. The first black appointed to the Court, Marshall was the great-grandson of a slave and the son of a Pullman car steward. Justice Blackmun tells how, "[w]hen we went up to Justice Marshall's native Baltimore for the ceremony in connection with the dedication of his statue up there in front of the Federal building, he and I were sitting next to each other and he said, 'Why do you think that fellow asked me what high school here in Baltimore I went to? Hell, there was only one I could go to!'"[32]

Tradition says that the junior Justice answers the conference door (one of them used to quip that he was the highest-paid doorman in the world). This led Justice Marshall to describe his first year on the Court, "Here I am, born in the ghetto, worked my way up to be special counsel for the NAACP, a judge on the 2nd Circuit, solicitor general, and now, what do I hear? 'You boy, open that door!'" Marshall was the first head of the NAACP Legal Defense Fund's staff and chief counsel in the *Brown* school segregation case. On the Court, he was always a firm member of the liberal bloc. In the Burger and Rehnquist Courts he served as a virtual judicial adjunct to Justice Brennan. The law clerks, it is said, took to calling Marshall "Mr. Justice Brennan-Marshall."

In a 1986 analysis of the divisions within the Court, Justice Harry A. Blackmun placed himself "in the middle."[33] In the Rehnquist Court, however, Blackmun was a firm member of the Brennan bloc. Blackmun himself had served eleven years on the U.S. Court of Appeals for the Eighth Circuit. He went to grade school with Warren Burger, and the two remained close friends thereafter. He was best man at Burger's wedding. After graduation from Harvard Law School, Blackmun served as a law clerk in the court of appeals, spent sixteen years with a Minneapolis law firm, and was counsel to the Mayo Clinic for almost ten years.

Because of his work as Mayo counsel, the others tended to consider Justice Blackmun a medical expert. Justice John Marshall Harlan once wrote to him, "I am consumed with admiration for your mastery of the medical lexicon, and . . . I am perfectly content to leave my legal conscience in your hands on this score."[34] That may be one reason why he was given the opinion in *Roe* v. *Wade*—the landmark abortion case.[35]

In his early years on the Court, few expected Justice Blackmun to be more than an appendage of the Chief Justice. He was then virtually Burger's disciple; they were on the same side in almost all cases. The press had typecast Blackmun as the subordinate half of the "Minnesota Twins," after the baseball team.

All this was to change. Blackmun's opinion in *Roe* v. *Wade* sounded his declaration of independence from the Chief Justice. "I am fairly positive," Blackmun himself says, "that [the Chief Justice] feels I have not been the supportive arm he would have liked me to be."[36]

In the later years of his tenure, Justice Blackmun was completely his own man. His opinions became as liberal as any that might have been written by the Justices on what Blackmun called "the left."[37] In addition, it may be said, as a 1983 *New York Times* article put it, "Justice Blackmun's evolution as a jurist and prominence on the Court represent one of the most important developments in the judiciary's recent history."[38]

Justice Blackmun's 1986 classification of the Justices also placed Justice John Paul Stevens "in the middle." Stevens, too, was a judge on the federal court of appeals when he was appointed to the Supreme Court in 1975. It has been even harder to classify Stevens than the others on the Court. "On a Court that everyone likes to divide into liberal and conservative, Justice Stevens has a list of labels all his own: enigmatic, unpredictable, maverick, a wild card, a loner."[39]

Justice Stevens was the Justice nearest the Burger Court's center, disagreeing equally with the Justices at the poles. Thus, in the 1981 term, Stevens disagreed with Justice Rehnquist in 35 percent of the cases and with Justice Brennan 33 percent.[40] In the Rehnquist Court, however, Stevens has tended to vote more often with the liberal holdovers than the increasingly conservative majority. Perhaps the best characterization of the Stevens jurisprudence, however, was that of a former law clerk, who described it as a "unique mix of radicalism and restraint."[41]

Justice Stevens has been a loner like Justice William O. Douglas, to whose seat Stevens was appointed, and, like Douglas, Stevens makes little effort to win over other members of the Court. What a law clerk once said about Douglas applies equally to Stevens: "Douglas was just as happy signing a one-man dissent as picking up four more votes." Stevens writes more dissents than any other member of the Court; he is often a lone dissenter. A book on the Court concludes that, while Stevens was once viewed as a potential leader of the Court, "the effect of his independence of mind often has been to fragment potential majorities and leave the state of the law indeterminate."[42]

Over the years, Justice Stevens has acquired something of the reputation of an iconoclast—albeit an idiosyncratic one. Stevens is idiosyncratic in more than his decisions. He hires only two law clerks instead of the usual four and drafts more of his own opinions than any of the others. He also deviates from the Court's unwritten conservative dress code; his constant bow tie (worn under the judicial robe) gives him a sophomoric appearance. In 1986, the Justices were hearing argument on whether Orthodox Jews, with their religious duty to wear yarmulkes, should be exempt from the military dress code's ban on hats indoors. Counsel for the government told the Justices, "It's only human nature to resent being told what to wear, when to wear it, what to eat." "Or whether you can wear a bow tie?" chimed in Stevens.[43]

The First Sister

When the Supreme Court was first established, the author of an opinion was designated, "Cushing, Justice." In 1820, the form was replaced by "Mr. Justice Johnson" as opinion author. This style lasted over a century and a half. Then, at a June 1980 conference, Justice Byron R. White suggested that since a woman Justice was bound to be appointed soon, they should avoid the embarrassment of changing the style again at that time. All the others agreed, and the manner of designating the author of an opinion became, simply, "Justice Brennan."[44]

The Court, however, tends to be a conservative institution and some of the Justices opposed the change proposed by Justice White. A November 17, 1980, "Dear Chief" letter from Justice Blackmun began, "If you are maintaining a permanent record on the vote to eliminate the use of 'Mr.,' please record me as in opposition."

"It seems to me," Blackmun's letter asserted, "that of late we tend to panic and to get terribly excited about some other inconsequential things. I regard this as one of them. . . . So far as I am concerned, I think it would have been far better to let the present system, in force for many decades, continue until a woman is on the Court and her particular desires are made known. We seem to be eliminating, step by step, all aspects of diverseness, and we give impetus to the trend toward a colorless society."

Justice Powell also sent a November 17 letter to Chief Justice Burger. The letter was headed "*Confidential*" and stated, "I must say that I agree with Harry as to the change at this time in the traditional reference to a sitting member of this Court."

Powell's letter noted, "It is as certain as anything in this life can be that one of us will be replaced by a woman. In my view, this not only will be desirable; the choice of a woman may well be overdue, given the glacial changes in our society over the past two decades."

His view in this respect did not, however, lead Justice Powell to support the nomenclature change. Instead, his letter concluded, "it does seem more dignified, and perhaps less anticipatory of a political judgment, to defer making a change at this time. It certainly will be appropriate when a 'Sister' joins us."[45]

A "sister" did, of course, join the Court when Justice Sandra Day O'Connor was appointed in 1981. Her career dramatically illustrates the changed place of women in the law. Though O'Connor graduated third in her class at Stanford Law School (Rehnquist had been first), only one California law firm would hire her: a Los Angeles firm offered her a job as a legal secretary. She turned them down. Ironically, Attorney General William French Smith, one of the partners in the firm that had refused to hire her as an associate, recommended O'Connor for the Supreme Court.[46]

After law school, O'Connor returned to Arizona, where she combined legal work with political activity. She became assistant attorney general and then a member, and ultimately leader of the Republican majority of the state senate. She was elected to the Arizona Superior Court, where she served for five years. In 1979, she was appointed to the Arizona Court of Appeals. O'Connor was the second Burger-Rehnquist Court member (after Justice Brennan) to have served as a state judge.

Soon after O'Connor took her seat, a *Time* headline read "And Now the Arizona Twins: Justice O'Connor Teams Up with Court Conservative Rehnquist."[47] There is no doubt that Justice O'Connor has been more conservative than her predecessor, Justice Potter Stewart. "I think it is fairly clear," said Justice Blackmun during the last Burger term, that O'Connor "is on the right."[48] She typically voted opposite Justice Rehnquist only about 10 percent of the time, while disagreeing with Justices Brennan and Marshall in over 45 percent of cases.[49]

It is, however, not accurate to picture Justice O'Connor as only a Rehnquist clone. She has tended to be as conservative as the latter in criminal cases and was, in fact, the author of opinions limiting *Miranda*[50] during the last two Burger terms.[51] She has also sided with her fellow Arizonian, Rehnquist, on the importance of recognizing state powers[52] and the need for judicial restraint vis-à-vis the legislature.[53] But she has been more moderate in a few areas—most notably (in view of her own experience with sex discrimination) in cases involving sexual bias,[54] but also in cases involving affirmative action[55] and the First Amendment.[56]

Even those who disagree with her recognize that O'Connor has been an above-average Justice, who has become an effective conservative voice. She has not been hesitant in expressing her views both in conference and from the bench. Her opinions have been characterized by clear analysis and focus on the points at issue. But they have at times been lightened by a little-credited gift for language. In a case involving the right of a defendant to represent himself, the O'Connor opinion of the Court noted, "We recognize that a . . . defendant may wish to dance a solo, not a pas de deux."[57]

The Other Conservatives

In the Burger Court, the balance of power was held by the Justices who were, in Justice Blackmun's phrase, "in the middle." In Chief Justice Burger's last terms, however, the center's grip started to weaken. As Justice Blackmun put it just after Burger retired, "I think the center held generally . . . [but] it bled a lot. And it needs more troops. Where it's going to get them, I don't know."[58]

As it turned out, it was not the center but the right that received the additional troops during the period covered by this book. The first of them, Antonin Scalia, was appointed in 1986 to fill the vacancy created by Justice Rehnquist's elevation to the Chief Justice's chair. Scalia had been a law professor (primarily at the University of Chicago), a government official, and a judge of the D.C. Circuit Court of Appeals. As a Justice, Scalia has been a doctrinaire conservative—even more extreme in his rightist views than the Chief Justice himself—though he has also exhibited a libertarian streak that has led him to resist some governmental intrusions.[59]

It was expected by many that Justice Scalia's intellectual brilliance would enable him to perform a leadership role on the Rehnquist Court. So far, it has not worked out that way. Instead, the Justice has persisted in extreme positions that have not been accepted even by a conservative majority that might be willing to accept a properly tempered Scalia posture.

Justice Scalia is the first noted law professor to be elevated to Olympus since Felix Frankfurter. Scalia has not, however, confined himself to the relatively restrained judicial role assumed by his predecessor. Instead, he has been a judicial activist, not hesitating to import his own academic theories into our public law. But if Justice Scalia seems unduly rigid in his approach, at least he is always interesting in his opinions. This should make him the professoriate's favorite Justice. Both for those who agree and those who disagree with them, the Scalia opinions should provide grist for the academic mills for years to come.

Another vacancy occurred on the Rehnquist Court when Justice Lewis F. Powell retired in 1987. Anthony M. Kennedy, then a circuit judge, was chosen in Powell's place. After graduation from Harvard Law School, Kennedy was in private practice for fifteen years (six of those as a sole practitioner) and also taught part-time at the McGeorge School of Law in Sacramento. Justice Powell had been a leader in the Burger Court's centrist core. Justice Kennedy has, more often than not, been a vote for the Rehnquist Court's growing conservative majority. He has, however, been anything but a doctrinaire conservative in the Scalia sense. He has displayed a willingness to listen to opposing views and an openness to dialogue that contrast with Justice Scalia's often inflexible posture.

Perhaps the most notable thing about Justice Kennedy is the number of opinions he has written, particularly in critical cases. The unusually high number assigned to Kennedy as a junior Justice indicated the Chief Justice's immediate confidence in him. This confidence has been justified by Justice Kennedy's general adherence to Rehnquist's jurisprudence.

The Kennedy appointment meant that Chief Justice Rehnquist now had a five-Justice conservative core (the Chief Justice and Justices White, O'Connor, Scalia, and Kennedy). But the conservative majority was still a fragile one, which often saw defections by one or more members. That situation did not change until President Bush was able to select replacements for Justices Brennan and Marshall, the last liberal holdovers from the Warren Court, who retired in 1990 and 1991 respectively.

Of the two replacements, only Justice David H. Souter sat on the Court during the time covered by this book, and only when the cases in the last two chapters were decided. His vote switch was the decisive factor in the last case discussed in this book, the *Ford Motor Credit* case. It should, however, be noted that Justice Souter did not assume an active role in the Court until after the cases covered here. In the last few terms, he has become one of the Justices (along with Justices Scalia and Ruth Bader Ginsburg) who have virtually dominated oral arguments. In addition, Justice Souter has been taking a more positive part in the Court's decision process; it was he who was most responsible for the eloquent 1992 opinion refusing to overrule *Roe* v. *Wade*.[60]

Justices Powell and White

For the period covered by this book, Justice Lewis F. Powell was the converse of Justice Souter. Powell served only during the first year of the Rehnquist Court, though he was, by then, one of the Court's most important members and did play an important part in the decision process in *Missouri* v. *Blair*, the first case discussed in this book (Chapter 1).

By the time he retired in 1987, Justice Powell had developed the reputation of a model conservative who avoided doctrinaire positions and hard-edged ideological decisions. His judicial approach was reminiscent of that followed by Justice John Marshall Harlan during the early Burger years. Like Harlan, Powell believed in following precedents that he may have disapproved of, until they were overruled. Thus, he voted to decide cases in accordance with the *Mapp* and *Miranda* decisions,[61] even though he might well have voted against those decisions had he been on the Court when they were handed down. In the conference on a 1983 case,[62] Powell said, about a prior decision,[63] "It's bad law. I would want to limit it to its own facts, without overruling it in so many words."[64]

The remaining Justice, Byron R. White, is harder to classify. He tended to take a lawyerlike approach to individual cases, without trying to fit them into any overall judicial philosophy, and was considered one of the more conservative Justices in the Burger Court's center, particularly in criminal cases. "In the criminal field," as Justice Blackmun put it, "I think Byron White is distinctly a conservative."[65]

In one area, however, Justice White tended to vote with the liberal bloc—civil rights. "One gets into racial problems . . . ," says Blackmun, "and Byron is distinctly to the left of center. I think it's the old John F. Kennedy influence, if you like."[66] As President Kennedy's Deputy Attorney General, White had personally gone to Montgomery, Alabama, to restore order during the Freedom Riders' protest in May 1961. In a confrontation with the Alabama governor, when the governor sarcastically asked, "Where are all those Freedom Riders?" White replied that they were in the hospitals to which the Governor's men had sent them.[67] In the Rehnquist Court, White often voted with the Brennan wing in civil rights cases, particularly in the *Metro Broadcasting* case[68] where Justice Brennan secured his last victory in the field.

It is fair to say that White was more respected among his colleagues than outside the Court—in part because of his gruff bluntness and no-nonsense manner. When loyalty oath cases were still part of the Court's agenda, he curtly told a conference, these oath cases are a "pain in the neck."[69] When he did not think much of a case, he termed it "this pipsqueak of a case."[70] And once, when an attorney was doing a particularly bad job in oral argument, White was heard saying in a stage whisper, "This is unbelievable."[71]

How the Court Operates

To understand how the Supreme Court dealt with the cases covered in this volume, one must understand how the Court itself operates. The Justices sit from the first Monday in October to late June or early July, in annual sessions called terms, with each term designated by the year in which it begins. Cases come to the Court from the lower federal courts and the highest state courts, either by appeals or petitions for writs of certiorari. Technical rules govern whether an appeal or certiorari must be sought. The Justices have virtually unlimited discretion in deciding whether to take an appeal or grant certiorari (or "cert," as it is usually called in the Court). Each year the Justices decide to hear only a fraction of the cases presented to them. Thus, in the 1988 term, when the appeal to the Supreme Court in the *Webster* case (discussed in Chapter 6) was filed, the Court reviewed and issued opinions deciding 170 cases out of 4,806 on its docket. In 1955, Justice Felix Frankfurter had asked another Justice, "Wouldn't you gladly settle for one in ten—such is my proportion—in granting petitions for certiorari?"[72] By the time the *Webster* case arose, the proportion granted had declined to one in almost thirty.

Following an unwritten rule, when at least four of the nine Justices vote to take a case, certiorari is granted or the appeal is taken. However, if the case elicits fewer than the required four votes, the case in question is over, and the last decision of the state court or lower federal court becomes final. In recent years, some Justices have urged that changes be made in the Rule of Four, on the ground that it results in the Court agreeing to hear too many cases.

Thus, Justice John Paul Stevens has proposed that five votes be required to grant certiorari.[73] That would certainly cut down on the number of cases taken by the Court. But it would also eliminate important cases which the Court should decide. If a five-vote rule had been in effect during the Warren Court years, at least one of the Court's most important decisions, *Baker* v. *Carr*,[74] the famous legislative apportionment case which Chief Justice Earl Warren once described as "the most important case of my tenure on the Court,"[75] would never have been decided. Though it was not made public by the Court, only four Justices voted to hear that case.[76]

For those few cases the Supreme Court agrees to take, written briefs will be submitted by the opposing lawyers, and then the attorneys for both sides will appear for oral argument in which they present arguments in favor of affirming or reversing the lower court decision. The arguments are presented publicly in the ornate courtroom. Each side usually has half an hour, and the time limit is strictly observed—though, in important cases some additional time may be allowed.

It is said that Chief Justice Charles Evans Hughes was so strict in enforcing the time limits that he cut off an attorney in the middle of the word "if." Chief Justice William H. Rehnquist has a similar reputation; he, too, has been known to stop counsel in the middle of a word when the red light goes on signaling expiration time. Once counsel saw the light come on and stopped on his own. Justice Antonin Scalia interposed, "He wasn't watching. I think you could have gotten away with the end of that sentence." Chief Justice Rehnquist then noted, "Even Homer nodded."

What makes argument most difficult for counsel is the fact that the sessions are characterized by incessant interruptions from the bench. The days of the great advocates of the past, when Daniel Webster or William Wirt would give virtuoso performances extending over several days, have long since gone. Supreme Court arguments now are less solo presentations than Socratic dialogues in which bench and bar play an almost equal part.

All too often, indeed, the bench may all but take over the argument. This has been notably true of former law professors, such as Justices Antonin Scalia and Felix Frankfurter. The latter in particular used to treat oral argument as the equivalent of a Harvard Law School class, with himself displaying the professor's mastery of the Socratic method. "Some of us," writes Justice William O. Douglas in his autobiography, "would often squirm at Frankfurter's seemingly endless questions that took the advocate round and round and round."[77] Above all, Justice Frankfurter could never shed the professorial need to get in the last word, whether in conference or repartee from the bench. About the only time he failed to do so occurred when a lawyer from the Midwest arguing his case did not answer a series of Frankfurter's questions to the Justice's satisfaction. His patience exhausted, Frankfurter testily asked, "Counsel, before you go any further, I want to know how did you get to this Court?" The answer came back, "I came on the Pennsylvania Railroad." For once, the normally irrepressible Justice was speechless.[78]

In the Rehnquist Court, the participation by the Justices in oral arguments has, if anything, intensified. There are times, in fact, when the Justices have so much to say that the attorneys can hardly get a word in edgewise. In a racent argument, as soon as the counsel began her case, Justice Scalia interrupted. Before she could reply, other Justices chimed in. The exchange among them went on until the red light on the lectern flashed, signaling that the attorney's thirty minutes were up. "Thank you, Ms. Foster," said Chief Justice Rehnquist, "I think you did very well in the four minutes that the Court allowed you."[79]

The *Webster* case provides another illustration of how argument before the Court proceeds. In this case, the argument took place on April 26, 1989. Like all Supreme Court sittings, the session began at precisely 10 AM. When the hands of the clock behind the bench indicated the hour, the nine black-robed Justices stepped through the red draperies and took their places. At the sound of the gavel, all in the packed courtroom rose and remained standing while the Court crier intoned the time-honored cry, "Oyez! Oyez! Oyez! All persons having business before the Honorable, the Supreme Court of the United States, are admonished to draw near and give their attention, for the Court is now sitting. God save the United States and this Honorable Court."

The Court Chamber itself is the most impressive room in the Supreme Court building. It measures 82 by 91 feet and has a ceiling 44 feet high. Its twenty-four columns are of Siena Old Convent marble from Liguria, Italy; its walls are of ivory vein marble from Alicante, Spain; and its floor borders are of Italian and African marble. Above the columns on the east and west walls are carved two marble panels depicting processions of historical lawgivers. Of the eighteen figures on the panels only one is famous as a judge, and he is the one American represented: John Marshall. His symbolic presence strikingly illustrates the Supreme Court's role as a primary lawgiver in the American system.

The room is dominated by the Justices' long, raised bench. It used to be the traditional straight bench, but in 1970 Chief Justice Warren E. Burger had it altered to its present "winged," or half-hexagon, shape. In a February 4, 1971, Memorandum to the Conference, Burger informed the others that everyone was in favor of the "change with the possible exception of Justice Black whose position can probably be described as 'take it or leave it'." Like all the furniture in the courtroom, the bench is mahogany. In back of the bench are four of the room's massive marble columns. The large clock hangs on a chain between the two center ones. In front of the bench are seated, to the Court's right, the pages and clerk, and, to the Court's left, the marshal. Tables facing the bench are for counsel. Behind the tables is a section for members of the bar and a much larger general section for the public, with separate areas for the press and distinguished visitors.

Goose-quill pens are placed on counsel tables each day that the Justices sit, as was done in the earliest session of the Court. The practice had been interrupted by World War II, when the prewar supply ran out, and then again in 1961, when the quills were temporarily replaced by more modern writing instruments. But traditions die hard at the Supreme Court. The quills soon found their way back to the counsel tables, and there are still spittoons behind the bench for each Justice and pewter julep cups (now used for their drinking water).

The *Webster* argument began just after the Justices sat down in their plush, high-back, black-leather chairs. The audience also sat down, and Chief Justice Rehnquist began, in his bass, "We will hear argument now in No. 88-605, *William L. Webster* v. *Reproductive Health Services.* By General Webster."

At this, William L. Webster, the Missouri attorney general, who argued the case for the appellant, stepped to the lectern and began with the traditional opening, "Mr. Chief Justice, and may it please the Court."

After the other attorneys had presented their arguments, the session concluded with a rebuttal by Webster. Chief Justice Rehnquist then leaned forward and said, "Thank you, Mr. Webster. The case is submitted."

"Whereupon," the official transcript concludes, "at 11:00 a.m., the case in the above-entitled matter was submitted."

Conference and Decision

Oral arguments in the Supreme Court are often dramatic events, participated in by leading attorneys. That was certainly true of the *Webster* argument, which had all the drama associated with the landmarks of Supreme Court jurisprudence. Yet it was not the headlined argument that played the significant part in the Court's decision. Indeed, it can be said that, like the report of Mark Twain's death, the typical reports on the value of Supreme Court oral argument are greatly exaggerated. True, virtually everyone who has written on the subject, including the Justices themselves, has stressed the importance of the argument to the Court's decision process. A lifetime's study of the high bench has, however, convinced me that the principal purpose of the argument before the Justices is a public relations one—to communicate to the country that the Court has given each side an open opportunity to be heard. Thus not only is justice done, but it is also publicly seen to be done.

But the cases are rare when the arguments of counsel—brilliant though they may appear to the courtroom audience—really influence the decision in an important case. The oral argument in *Webster* itself well illustrates the point. It may be doubted whether the statements by counsel influenced even one vote on the Court. Instead, as Justice Robert H. Jackson once put it, the Court's argument begins where that of counsel ends.[80] The crucial argument in a case takes place among the Justices in their conference that meets after the public oral argument is concluded.

As far as the public is concerned, the postargument decision process in the Court is completely closed. The next time the outside world hears about the case is when the Court is ready to announce its decision publicly; simultaneously, the majority opinion and any dissents or concurrences are distributed. But in that interim period between oral argument and the announcement of the Court's decision, much has gone on. First, the Justices have "conferenced." These conferences used to be held only on Fridays. More recently, Wednesday sessions have been held as well. The privacy of the conference is one of the most cherished traditions at the Court. It began over fifty years ago when the Justices mistakenly thought that a clerk, secretary, or page had leaked a decision.[81] Since then, only the nine Justices may attend. In addition to the conference discussion, ideas are exchanged by the Justices through the circulation of draft opinions and memoranda. Such a memo, sent to all the Justices, is usually titled "Memorandum to the Conference."

The *Webster* conference, like all those held by the Justices, took place in the Court's conference room—a large, rectangular chamber at the rear of the Court building, behind the courtroom. One of the longer walls has two windows facing Second Street. The other, with a door in the middle, is covered with bookshelves containing reports of decisions of the Supreme Court and federal courts of appeals, as well as copies of the *United States Code* and *U.S. Code Annotated.* Along one of the shorter walls is a fireplace, above which hangs a Gilbert Stuart portrait of Chief Justice John Marshall in his robes.

In the center of the conference room ceiling is an ornate crystal chandelier, and at one end of the room stands a rectangular table around which the Justices sit, with the Chief Justice at the head and the others ranged in order of seniority, the most senior opposite the Chief Justice, the next at the Chief Justice's right, the next at the Senior Associate Justice's right and so on. In the ceiling above the chandelier are bright fluorescent lights—one of the improvements installed by Chief Justice Burger.

At the conference, the Justices discuss the cases that have been argued and decide how to dispose of them. The discussion sometimes becomes heated, reflecting the controversial nature of the case or personal differences among the Justices. The Warren years, for example, saw heated exchanges between Justice Felix Frankfurter and Chief Justice Earl Warren. According to one account, when Warren took exception in conference to a Frankfurter sermon, the furious Frankfurter retorted, "You're the worst Chief Justice this country has ever had!" The Justices who sat during the Warren years told me that no such Frankfurter outburst occurred. But none denies that Frankfurter came to have a poor opinion of Warren. Once, during a heated conference session, according to a law clerk, Frankfurter was overheard screeching at the Chief Justice, "Be a judge, God damn it, be a judge!" Use of the verb "screeching" is not an exaggeration. As Justice Potter Stewart described it to me, once Frankfurter would "get going . . . his voice would rise to a pretty high decibel content and pretty high on the scales."

After the vote is taken at the conference, the case is assigned by the Chief Justice, if he is in the majority, either to himself or to one of the Justices for the writing of an opinion of the Court. If the Chief Justice is not in the majority, the senior majority Justice assigns the opinion. Justices who disagree with the majority decision are free to write or join dissenting opinions. If they agree with the result but differ on the reasoning, they can submit concurring opinions. Opinions are usually issued in the name of individual Justices. Sometimes per curiam (literally, "by the court") opinions are issued in the name of the Court as a whole. That is what happened in the so-called Pentagon Papers Case[82]—where the Burger Court refused to stop the *New York Times* and *Washington Post* from publishing a classified Defense Department history of the Vietnam War—though each of the Justices there also wrote an individual opinion explaining the decision from his own point of view.

The last stage is the public announcement of decisions and the opinions filed by the Justices. The custom used to be to have decisions announced on Mondays (a tradition that began in 1857); hence, the press characterization of "decision Mondays." In 1965, this was changed to announcing decisions when they were ready.

When decisions are announced, the Justices normally read only a summary of their opinions, especially when they are long. But some insist on reading every word, no matter how much time it takes. On June 17, 1963, Justice Tom C. Clark was droning through his lengthy Court opinion in the case involving the constitutionality of Bible reading in public schools. Justice William O. Douglas, who could stand it no longer, passed Justice Hugo L. Black a plaintive note: "Is he going to read all of it? He told me he was only going to say a few words—he is on p. 20 now—58 more to go. Perhaps we need an antifilibuster rule as badly as some say the Senate does."[83]

Sorcerer's Apprentice?

In a review of a recent biography of Justice Oliver Wendell Holmes, a Washington lawyer who had been a Supreme Court law clerk stressed that in Holmes's day the judges "considered it their personal duty to explain in writing . . . why they reached a particular result." That is no longer true. "Not so today. Even highly respected federal judges routinely assign opinion writing to . . . law clerks." In the Supreme Court, the "clerks spend their time drafting the lengthy decisions that are issued in the Justices' names."[84]

A few weeks later another lawyer, who had been a fellow law clerk, wrote challenging the reviewer's statement as "the hyperbole of an advocate [that] inflates the preceived importance of law clerks." Referring to his own experience clerking for a Justice, the attorney asserted, "Even if the Justice did not write every 'and' and 'the,' or turn phrases with Holmes's facility, it was the Justice who voted on the cases, the Justice who determined the legal theory for his vote and for his opinion, and the Justice who took the entire responsibility for the final opinion he signed."[85] This has also been the case with regard to the other Justices.

The dispute between the two former law clerks brings to mind a congratulatory letter that Justice Douglas wrote to Justice Rehnquist upon Rehnquist's 1971 appointment to the Court. "I realize that you were here before as a member of the so-called Junior Supreme Court."[86] Douglas was referring to Rehnquist's service as a law clerk to Justice Robert H. Jackson. Once upon a time, Douglas's characterization of the clerk corps might have been taken as one made in jest. The exchange between the two former clerks shows that that is no longer the case. When we talk today about the drafting of Supreme Court opinions, we are dealing with a subject in which there is a sharp difference between appearance and reality and one that brings us to the controversial question of the role of the law clerks in the Court's decision process. Indeed, the use the Justices now make of their law clerks means that "no one knows what, if anything, the Justices themselves have written.'"[87]

Justice Louis D. Brandeis was once asked why people respected the Supreme Court. His short answer was, "Because the Justices are almost the only people in Washington who do their own work."[88] The legend that this remains true is still prevalent, and in his book on the Court, Chief Justice Rehnquist, too, tells us that "the individual justices still continue to do a great deal more of their 'own work' than do their counterparts in other branches of the federal government."[89]

Before the Court moved into its present Marble Palace in 1935, what Justice Brandeis said was entirely true. The Justices then had no office facilities in their old Capitol Court space. They did their work at home, helped only by a messenger or a secretary or law clerk. Dean Acheson, who clerked for Justice Brandeis later nostalgically recalled, "Poindexter, the messenger, and I constituted the whole office staff; and Poindexter, half the household staff as well.[90]

The practice of having law clerks started with Justice Horace Gray, who hired (at first at his own expense) a Harvard law graduate each year to assist him in his work. In 1886, Congress provided each Justice with funds to pay for a secretary or clerk, with provision for law clerks in addition to secretarial assistance in 1919. Under Chief Justice Fred M. Vinson, the number increased to two. In the Burger Court, the number grew to three and then to four, with the Chief Justice having a fifth senior clerk.

It may be assumed that Justices such as Holmes or Brandeis used their clerks as little more than research assistants. Charles Evans Hughes later recalled that, when he was an Associate Justice early in the century, "I kept them busy with dictation, hating to write in longhand," and, referring to research, "whatever was necessary in that line I did myself."[91] Hughes writes that he worried that if the clerks were used too much "it might be thought that they were writing our opinions."[92] That, however, is what has actually happened. In recent years the Justices have given their clerks an ever larger share of responsibility in the drafting of opinions. "In the United States," notes a 1986 London *Times* article, "judges have 'clerks', i.e., assistants who prepare and frequently write judgments which their masters often merely adopt and which a qualified observer can easily recognize as the work of a beginner."[93]

Chief Justice Rehnquist has candidly described his opinion-writing process. "In my case," Rehnquist said, "the clerks do the first draft of almost all cases to which I have been assigned to write the Court's opinion." Only "when the case-load is heavy" does Rehnquist sometimes "help by doing the first draft of a case myself." Rehnquist concedes that the "practice . . . may undoubtedly . . . cause raised eyebrows." Still, the Chief Justice asserts, "I think the practice is entirely proper: The Justice must retain for himself control not merely of the outcome of the case, but of the explanation of the outcome, and I do not believe this practice sacrifices either."[94]

It is, of course, true that the decisions are made by the Justices—though, even with regard to them, the weaker Justices have abdicated much of their authority to their clerks. In most chambers, the clerks are, to use a favorite expression of Chief Justice Earl Warren, not "unguided missiles." The Justices normally outline the way they want opinions drafted. But the drafting clerk is left with a great deal of discretion. The Justices may, in Rehnquist's phrase, "convey the broad outlines," but they "do not invariably settle exactly how the opinion will be reasoned through."[95] The details of the opinions are left to the clerk, in particular the specific reasoning and research supporting the decision.

To be sure, the Justices themselves go over the drafts, and, said Chief Justice Rehnquist, "I may revise it in toto." But, he also admits, "I may leave it relatively unchanged."[96] Too many of the Justices circulate drafts that are almost wholly the work of their clerks, doing little more than lend their names to their clerks' product. "These days," a recent book sums up the situation, "a Court opinion is, probably put together by a clerk, relying mostly on language from earlier opinions. . . . The clerks draft most of the majority and dissenting opinions for most of the justices."[97]

The result is that the drafting process in the Court is that recalled by one of Justice Stanley Reed's clerks: "The clerk had the first word, and he had the last word." This means that most of the opinions reproduced in this book were originally drafted by law clerks, with the Justice in whose name they were issued performing essentially an editing function.

The law clerks' "first word" has had a most unfortunate effect upon the Supreme Court product. Most obviously, it has led to an increase in the length, though plainly not the quality, of opinions. What Justice Douglas once wrote about Court opinions has become increasingly true: "We have tended more and more to write a law-review-type of opinion. They plague the Bar and the Bench. They are so long they are meaningless. They are filled with trivia and nonessentials."[98]

As Justice Ruth Bader Ginsburg notes, the law clerks may be "highly intelligent. . . . But most of them are young and in need of the seasoning that experiences in life and in law practice afford."[99] Law clerks have similar academic backgrounds and little other experience. For three years they have had drummed into them that the acme of literary style is the law review article. It is scarcely surprising that the standard opinion style has become that of the student-run reviews: though there are exceptions, most are bland and bloodless, prolix, platitudinous, always erring on the side of inclusion, full of lengthy citations and footnotes—and above all dull.

The individual flair that makes the opinions of a Holmes or a Cardozo literary, as well as legal, gems has become a thing of the past: "[T]hese days no one confuses Court opinions with literature."[100] There is all the difference in the world between writing one's own opinions and reviewing opinions written by someone else. It is hard to see how an editor can be a great judge. Can we really visualize a Holmes or a Cardozo coordinating a team of law clerks and editing their drafts?

According to a federal appellate judge, "We need to reduce our dependence on the system of judicial apprenticeships and on a mass production model that will soon swallow us up."[101] In the Supreme Court, as in most institutions, the balance of power has shifted increasingly to the bureaucrats and away from the nominal heads. The Justices have become the managers of a growing corps of law clerks, who increasingly write the opinions even in the most important cases. The swelling system of judicial apprenticeships threatens to repeat the story of the sorcerer's apprentice—though not necessarily with its happy ending.

Shooting the Piano Player?

In a 1988 case, Justice Scalia wrote an opinion of the Court that reversed a Ninth Circuit Court of Appeals decision granting certain naturalization petitions.[102] Justice Blackmun was noted as concurring in the result. Blackmun explained his action in a letter to Scalia stating that "the tone of the opinion" had disturbed him. "I am frank to say," Blackmun wrote, "that what concerns me is the repeated criticism of the Ninth Circuit and its Judges. As the old saying goes, 'Don't shoot the piano player; he is doing the best he can.'"[103]

My intention in publishing this book has been anything but to shoot the judicial piano player. On the contrary, my purpose has been only to show how he, too, does the best he can. In addition, I have used the cases covered to illustrate how the final tune may often be different from the one originally chosen.

There are those, however, who assert that, while a book such as this may not shoot the piano player, it may affect the way in which he plays. Thus, Anthony Lewis has argued that a book such as this, which reveals what goes on during the Justices' decision process, may make if difficult for the Court to perform its crucial function effectively. Speaking of the notes, documents, and discussions revealed in *The Unpublished Opinions of the Warren Court*, a predecessor to this volume, Lewis asks: "What effect will such disclosures have on the work of the Court? Will the justices be able to argue among one another with the candor that may change minds if they think their words will soon be retailed to the public? Or will their conferences degenerate into posturing, like most Congressional debates?"[104]

"It is," Lewis goes on, "no doubt old-fashioned to worry about such things. But the Supreme Court is one institution that works in this country, and I think scholars should be wary of distorting the conference that is so essential to its work."[105]

Erwin N. Griswold, former Solicitor General and Harvard Law School Dean, has voiced a similar concern. "One wonders," he wrote, "what effect this sort of presentation of documents, interviews and so on, so soon after the events, has on freedom of exchange, frankness, trust, common understanding, even bonhomie, among present and future justices." Griswold then posed the question, "Is there not an appreciable risk that there may be a similar chilling effect in interchange even among Supreme Court justices? Sunshine can be carcinogenic as well as antiseptic."[106]

My own view on the matter is similar to that of Justice Brennan in his 1990 answer to his colleagues' objections to the access he has provided to his Court papers—"that scholarly examination of the Court's workings would ultimately serve the public interest."[107] My primary purpose in this book and its predecessors is to show how the highest Court operates. The documents published—the drafts and internal memoranda, the extracts from letters and conference notes—these all help to explain the workings of the Court: how the Justices vote and change their votes and how opinions are drafted and redrafted before they are finally issued. The Court's decision process is made clearer by this sort of material than it possibly can be by analysis, acute though it may be, of only the opinions published in the *United States Reports*.

The public has the same right to know how the highest Court operates as it has with regard to other governmental institutions. The right of the people to know does not degenerate into a mere slogan where the work of the Justices is concerned. The country has the same right to information on how the Supreme Court operates as it has with regard to other governmental institutions. Contrary to Lewis's claim, dissemination of such information will help more than it will hinder the work of the Justices.

Ultimately, as Justice Brennan put it in his 1990 memorandum, books such as this "utilizing collections of . . . Justices' papers seemed to have promoted awareness and understanding of the Court."[108] Not too long ago, Justice Felix Frankfurter complained to a law professor, "What strikes me increasingly, in writing on the work of the Court is their unrelatedness to actuality."[109] What Brennan's memo called "responsible scholarship about the Court"[110] can help the country to find out how the highest bench actually operates. That in turn can only increase understanding of the Court and its crucial role in our constitutional polity.

The Supreme Court is more than the usual law court; it is primarily a political institution, in whose keeping lies the constitutional destiny of a mighty nation. My hope is that students of the Court will learn from this book and its predecessors that the Justices' decision process itself is essentially a political process (in the nonpejorative use of that word). Yet all the "lobbying" and efforts at persuasion that go on—the infighting, the drafts and memoranda back and forth among the Justices, the changes made in opinions as part of the bargaining process—all this is done for the purpose of reaching what the individual Justice considers the best result. There is, to be sure, politicking, compromises, and horse-trading in the often complex negotiations and compromises needed to attain a working majority, yet all for the purpose of advancing not the Justices themselves but the judicial doctrines in which they believe.

Once again, my intent was to use the draft opinions to show what actually happened behind the red curtain and let the chips fall where they may. Once again, they do fall in a way that reflects favorably on the Court. One privy to the Court's decision process is bound to be impressed by the willingness of Justices to change their views after consideration of the intellectual arguments made by their colleagues. No other governmental institution could be subjected to comparable scrutiny of its internal processes and come out so well.

The reader may conclude from this book and its predecessors that the Court does not work at all in the cold, purely logical way that most people think it does; but it does work, and through the constant give and take between the Justices, in a way that ultimately serves the best interests of the country. Surely, it is better for Court and country that this be made known than for it to be kept concealed in the Marble Palace.

Notes

1. *New York Times Magazine*, March 16, 1975, p. 15.
2. Bob Woodward and Scott Armstrong, *The Brethren: Inside the Supreme Court* (1979).
3. *Super Chief: Earl Warren and His Supreme Court* (1983); *Inside the Warren Court*

(1983); *The Unpublished Opinions of the Warren Court* (1985); *Swann's Way: The School Busing Case and the Supreme Court* (1986); *Behind* Bakke: *Affirmative Action and the Supreme Court* (1988); *The Unpublished Opinions of the Burger Court* (1988); *The Ascent of Pragmatism: The Burger Court in Action* (1990).

4. Supra note 3.
5. Supra note 3.
6. Two pages are missing from my copy of the Stevens (p. 16) and Marshall (p. 7) *Hodgson* drafts. Fortunately, the omitted pages do not contain important portions of the opinions.
7. Woodward and Armstrong, supra note 2.
8. *New York Times Magazine*, March 3, 1985, p. 35.
9. *Newsweek*, July 23, 1979, p. 68.
10. Supra note 8, at 33.
11. 410 U.S. 113 (1973).
12. *Time*, October 8, 1984, p. 28.
13. *New York Times*, October 8, 1986, p. A32.
14. *Richmond Newspapers* v. *Virginia*, 448 U.S. 555, 604 (1980) (dissenting).
15. *Corporation Commission* v. *FPC*, 415 U.S. 961 (1974) (dissenting).
16. David Savage, *Turning Right: The Making of the Rehnquist Supreme Court* 16 (1992).
17. Id. at 47.
18. William H. Rehnquist to William J. Brennan, Re: No. 75-1064 *Kremens* v. *Bartley*, March 8, 1977.
19. 501 U.S. 560 (1991).
20. See William H. Rehnquist, "Chief Justices I Never Knew," 3 *Hastings Constitutional Law Quarterly* 637, 643 (1976).
21. Charles Evans Hughes, *The Autobiographical Notes of Charles Evans Hughes* xxvi (1973).
22. *Cheek* v. *United States*, 498 U.S. 192 (1991).
23. *Irwin* v. *Veterans Administration*, 498 U.S. 89 (1991).
24. David O'Brien, *Storm Center: The Supreme Court in American Politics* 189 (1986).
25. *New York Times*, December 13, 1987, p. 37.
26. Savage, supra note 16, at 53.
27. Supra note 8.
28. *Economist*, July 28, 1990, p. 20.
29. Felix Frankfurter, *Of Law and Men* 133 (1956).
30. Learned Hand to Felix Frankfurter, June 2, 1960. Frankfurter Papers, Library of Congress.
31. *Texas* v. *Johnson*, 491 U.S. 397 (1989); *Metro Broadcasting* v. *FCC*, 497 U.S. 547 (1990).
32. *New York Times Magazine*, February 20, 1983, p. 20.
33. *New York Times*, March 8, 1986, p. 7.
34. John Marshall Harlan to Harry A. Blackmun, Re: No. 108-*Richardson* v. *Perales*, April 21, 1971.
35. Supra note 8.
36. Supra note 32.
37. Supra note 33.
38. Supra note 32.
39. *New York Times*, July 23, 1984, p. 8.
40. Galloway, "Who's Playing Center?" 74 *American Bar Association Journal* 42 (1988).

41. *8 Men and a Lady: Profiles of the Justices of the Supreme Court* 179 (1990).
42. *The Burger Court: The Counter-Revolution That Wasn't* 252 (Blasi ed., 1983).
43. *New York Times*, January 7, 1986, p. A14.
44. William H. Rehnquist, *The Supreme Court: How It Was, How It Is* 302 (1987).
45. The Blackmun and Powell letters are in the Thurgood Marshall Papers, Library of Congress.
46. Elder Witt, *A Different Justice: Reagan and the Supreme Court* 29 (1986).
47. *Time*, April 19, 1982, p. 49.
48. *New York Times*, March 8, 1986, p. 7.
49. Galloway, supra note 40, at 45.
50. *Miranda* v. *Arizona*, 384 U.S. 436 (1966).
51. *Moran* v. *Burbine*, 475 U.S. 412 (1986); *Oregon* v. *Elstad*, 470 U.S. 298 (1985).
52. *Garcia* v. *San Antonio Metropolitan Transit Authority*, 469 U.S. 528, 580 (1985) (dissenting).
53. *Metropolitan Life Insurance Co.* v. *Ward*, 470 U.S. 869, 884 (1985) (dissenting); *Akron* v. *Akron Center for Reproductive Health*, 462 U.S. 416, 453 (1983) (dissenting).
54. *Mississippi University for Women* v. *Hogan*, 458 U.S. 718 (1982).
55. *Wygant* v. *Jackson Board of Education*, 476 U.S. 267, 284 (1986).
56. *Minnesota Star Co.* v. *Commissioner of Revenue*, 460 U.S. 575 (1983).
57. *McKaskle* v. *Wiggins*, 465 U.S. 168, 187-88 (1984).
58. *New York Times*, September 25, 1986, p. B10.
59. See, e.g., *National Treasury Employees Union* v. *Von Raab*, 489 U.S. 656 (1989); *Texas* v. *Johnson*, 491 U.S. 397 (1989); *R.A.V.* v. *St. Paul*, 112 S.Ct. 2538 (1992).
60. *Planned Parenthood* v. *Casey*, 112 S.Ct. 2791 (1992).
61. *Mapp* v. *Ohio*, 367 U.S. 643 (1961); *Miranda* v. *Arizona*, 384 U.S. 436 (1966).
62. *Guardians Association* v. *Civil Service Commission*, 463 U.S. 582 (1983).
63. *Lau* v. *Nichols*, 414 U.S. 563 (1974).
64. Schwartz, *The Ascent of Pragmatism* 26 (1990).
65. *New York Times*, March 8, 1986, p. 7.
66. Ibid.
67. Schwartz, *Super Chief: Earl Warren and His Supreme Court* 429 (1983).
68. *Metro Broadcasting* v. *FCC*, 497 U.S. 547 (1990).
69. Commenting on *Communist Party* v. *Whitcomb*, 414 U.S. 441 (1974).
70. Schwartz, *The Unpublished Opinions of the Burger Court* 412 (1988).
71. Schwartz, *Behind* Bakke: *Affirmative Action and the Supreme Court* 53 (1988).
72. Felix Frankfurter to Sherman Minton, September 19, 1955, Frankfurter Papers, Harvard Law School.
73. Stevens, "The Life Span of a Judge-Made Rule," 58 N.Y.U.L. Rev. 1, 21 (1983).
74. 369 U.S. 186 (1962).
75. Earl Warren, *The Memoirs of Earl Warren* 306 (1977).
76. Schwartz, supra note 67 at 411.
77. William O. Douglas, *The Court Years 1939–1975: The Autobiography of William O. Douglas* 181 (1980).
78. Earl Warren, "Address to California State Bar," 109 *Congressional Record* 19849 (1963).
79. *Wall Street Journal*, January 17, 1994, p. A10.
80. Westin, *The Anatomy of a Constitutional Case* 125 (1958).
81. See Witt, supra note 46, at 742.
82. *New York Times Co.* v. *United States*, 403 U.S. 713 (1971).

83. Schwartz, supra note 67, at 65.
84. *New York Times Book Review*, November 21, 1993, p. 22.
85. *New York Times Book Review*, January 2, 1994, p. 23.
86. William O. Douglas, *The Douglas Letters* 146 (Urofsky ed., 1987).
87. Supra note 84.
88. Wyzanski, *A Judge's Premises: Essays in Judgment, Ethics, and the Law* 61 (1985).
89. Rehnquist, supra note 44, at 261.
90. Dean Acheson, *Morning and Noon* 41 (1965).
91. Alexander Bickel and Benno Schmidt, *History of the Supreme Court of the United States: The Judiciary and Responsible Government 1910–21* 82 (1984).
92. Ibid.
93. *Times* (London), July 11, 1986.
94. Rehnquist, supra note 44, at 299–300.
95. Id. at 300.
96. *Harvard Law School Bulletin*, Winter 1986, p. 28.
97. Savage, supra note 16, at 73, 74.
98. William O. Douglas, Memorandum to the Conference, October 23, 1961. Black Papers, Library of Congress.
99. *New York Times*, January 7, 1994, p. B11.
100. Savage, supra note 16, at 74.
101. *A Dialogue about Legal Education as It Approaches the 21st Century* 29 (Kelso ed., 1987).
102. *INS* v. *Pangilinan*, 486 U.S. 875 (1988).
103. Harry A. Blackmun to Antonin Scalia, June 9, 1988.
104. *New York Times Book Review*, December 29, 1985, p. 20.
105. Ibid.
106. Griswold, Book Review, 69 *American Bar Association Journal* 1506 (1983).
107. Supra p. 4.
108. Ibid.
109. Felix Frankfurter to Jerbert Wechsler, September 27, 1954. Frankfurter Papers, Library of Congress.
110. Supra p. 4.

1

Missouri v. *Blair* (*1987*): *Traffic Arrests and Homicide Evidence*

May the police use evidence in a homicide case that has been obtained after an arrest for a traffic violation, where the police lacked probable cause to arrest the defendant for homicide, and the traffic arrest was made at the request of the police homicide unit? This was the question presented in *Missouri* v. *Blair*,[1] where the Court had granted certiorari on January 13, 1986, during Chief Justice Burger's last term.[2]

The *Blair* case arose out of a murder that had been committed in Kansas City. The only clue was a palm print in the victim's truck. An informer implicated the defendant. The police did not arrest the defendant for homicide because of lack of probable cause. They knew, however, that a municipal court had issued a bench warrant for her arrest in connection with a minor traffic violation, that is, for failure to pay a fifteen-dollar parking ticket. They arrested her, informing her that they were arresting her on the municipal court warrant. She was taken to the police station and her finger and palm prints were taken. The defendant posted bond and was released. When it was found that her palm print matched that taken at the scene, the defendant was again arrested, and, after interrogation, she confessed to the murder. The Missouri courts granted a motion to suppress, on the ground that the arrest on the traffic warrant was a mere subterfuge and that the palm print and the statements taken from her were the fruits of an illegal arrest for homicide and should accordingly be suppressed.

At the postargument conference presided over now by Chief Justice Rehnquist, the Justices voted to reverse the lower court decision by a bare majority, with Justices Brennan, Marshall, Powell, and Stevens dissenting. The opinion was assigned to Justice White, who circulated a January 9, 1987, draft opinion of the Court, reprinted on p. 32. After stating the facts and the holding below, the draft stated, "the issue comes down to whether the police violated Blair's Fourth Amendment rights when they acquired her palm print to investigate the killing of Carl Lindstedt. We hold that they did not."

Though the police lacked probable cause to arrest the defendant for homicide and take her to the station house and secure her palm print, she was, according to the White draft, "the subject of a valid bench warrant issued by the municipal court and authorizing her custodial arrest at any time." Had the respondent "been arrested and booked on that warrant, independently of any desire to investigate the homicide, the Fourth Amendment would not forbid taking her finger and palm prints and retaining them in police files." Indeed, the White draft concludes, "[h]ad Blair's palm print been taken in this manner, its use in the homicide investigation would have raised no question under the Fourth Amendment."

Such would be the case, Justice White's draft goes on, even if the palm print had been taken at the request of the homicide unit. As the draft put it, "The testimony was that such requests were honored while traffic arrestees were in custody, and since the State in such cases would be doing no more than the Constitution allowed, there would be no occasion to apply the exclusionary rule, which is designed to deter unconstitutional conduct."

Nor should the result be changed "if Blair's arrest on the traffic warrant was triggered by the need to get her palm print to investigate the homicide." Even in such a case, the White draft asserts, "There would have been a valid arrest, a valid temporary custody and the taking of identifying prints in connection therewith, which is no more than the Constitution permits."

The basic principle according to Justice White's draft opinion of the Court, is that, "When a valid custodial arrest occurs and the police take fingerprints or gather other evidence incident to that arrest that proves relevant in investigating another crime, the Federal Constitution does not forbid using such evidence for that purpose, even if it could be proved that the impetus for the immediate arrest was the interest in investigating the other crime. The Fourth Amendment does not require inquiry into the motives of the police officers in such situations." In this case, "assuming a valid arrest on the traffic warrant, taking Blair's palm print was legally permissible and consistent with standard procedures when a request for a palm print is made."

1st DRAFT

SUPREME COURT OF THE UNITED STATES

No. 85–303

MISSOURI, PETITIONER *v.* ZOLA BLAIR

ON WRIT OF CERTIORARI TO THE SUPREME COURT OF MISSOURI

[January ——, 1987]

JUSTICE WHITE delivered the opinion of the Court.

On November 24, 1981, the Kansas City, Missouri, police discovered that Carl Lindstedt had been murdered. The only clue to the murderer was a palm print found in the victim's pickup truck. Two months later, an informer implicated respondent, Zola Blair, and her family in the murder.[1] The police had on file palm prints of all members of the family except respondent, but none of these prints matched that found at the scene. On January 28, 1982, a homicide detective requested that respondent be "picked up" for homicide but did not seek an arrest or search warrant for lack of probable cause. The police, however, knew that a municipal court had issued a bench warrant for her arrest in connection with a traffic violation,[2] and on February 5, 1982, arrested Blair at her home. The police informed respondent that they

[1] The informant also stated that the Blairs routinely stored stolen property at their residence. Three days later, the police observed what appeared to be Lindstedt's sofa inside the residence of James Blair. They obtained a warrant to search the house and found the sofa and other property which had been stolen from Lindstedt.

[2] Respondent had been ticketed by the Kansas City, Missouri, police on November 10, 1981 for parking a vehicle displaying license plates registered to another vehicle, in violation of Kansas City Municipal Ordinance 34.276. She failed to pay the $15.00 fine or to appear in court, and on January 8, 1982, the Kansas City Municipal Court issued a bench warrant for her arrest. Record, Doc. 6, pp. 5–6.

MISSOURI *v.* BLAIR

were arresting her on the municipal warrant.[3] She was taken to the Homicide Unit at police headquarters and then to the Detention Unit where, with a permission slip from the Commander of the Homicide Unit, she was booked on a homicide charge.[4] The Record of Arrest form showed that she was being held for the Crimes Against Persons Division and for the Warrant Service Unit. Record, Doc. 6, p. 51. Her finger and palm prints were taken. She was questioned about the homicide but denied any knowledge of it. She was released the next morning at 10:45 but was immediately booked on the municipal court warrant. Her right index finger was printed. She posted bond on that charge and was released at 12:55 p. m.

Two days later, after the police learned that respondent's palm print matched the print found at the scene, a warrant issued, and she was arrested. Interrogation led to a confession when respondent was confronted with a match-up of the palm prints. Respondent filed a pretrial motion to suppress, asserting that she was arrested both for homicide and on the traffic warrant, that the latter arrest was a mere subterfuge, and that the palm print and the statements taken from her were the fruits of an illegal arrest for homicide and should accordingly be suppressed. The motion was granted, but there were no findings of fact or conclusions of law. The Missouri Court of Appeals, agreeing that the arrest on the warrant was "but a subterfuge or pretext for the purpose of gathering evidence of the entirely separate crime of homicide," affirmed. App. to Pet. for Cert. A–24. The Missouri Supreme Court, in a 4–3 decision, also affirmed. *State* v. *Blair*, 691 S. W. 2d 259 (Mo. banc 1985). After stating that the question before it was "whether, in the circum-

[3] Respondent alleged in her motion to suppress that the police arrested her on the pretext of an outstanding municipal court warrant for a parking violation so that they could take her to the Homicide Unit for booking and interrogation. App. 7.

[4] "Booking" is the administrative recording of an arrest.

MISSOURI *v.* BLAIR

stances of this case, defendant's initial arrest was pretextual and rendered her subsequent detention unlawful and evidence obtained incident thereto inadmissible," it observed that the evidence was in conflict on whether Blair was arrested on the outstanding traffic violation warrant and that the trial court had resolved the conflicts in favor of Blair. 691 S. W. 2d, at 260, 261–262. The court went on to hold that, "Assuming an arrest for the parking violation, the arrest, in the circumstances of this case, was at best a pretext employed to gather evidence on an unrelated homicide, and this Court cannot say, on this record, that the trial court erred in suppressing the evidence so seized."[5] 691 S. W. 2d, at 262.

We granted certiorari. 474 U. S. —— (1986).

The Missouri Supreme Court opinion may be read as asserting alternative grounds for suppressing the palm print: first, that it was the product of an unlawful arrest for homicide; and second, that if it was the product of an otherwise valid arrest on a municipal warrant, that arrest was unlawful because it was a pretext to gather evidence on the homicide. On either approach, the issue comes down to whether the police violated Blair's Fourth Amendment rights when they acquired her palm print to investigate the killing of Carl Lindstedt. We hold that they did not.

The police suspected respondent of homicide and desired to compare her palm print with that found in the deceased's pickup truck. Had her print been on file in connection with some other case, as was true of the prints of other members of her family, obviously that print could have been used for

---

[5] The dissent asserted that respondent had been arrested on the traffic warrant on February 5 and was subject to finger and palm printing pursuant to that arrest. In any event, as the dissent saw it, respondent was booked on the warrant on February 6, and held until she made bond, and her prints could have been taken at that time. Since the police already had the decisive palm print, the dissent thought it absurd to require the police to take that print again.

MISSOURI *v.* BLAIR

comparison purposes without violating the Fourth Amendment. But the print was not on file; and lacking probable cause to arrest Blair for homicide, the police could not, without Blair's consent, take her to the station house and secure her palm print. *Davis* v. *Mississippi*, 394 U. S. 791 (1969).

Blair, however, was the subject of a valid bench warrant issued by the municipal court and authorizing her custodial arrest at any time.[6] If Blair had been arrested and booked

---

[6] Officer Stewart, one of the arresting officers, testified at the suppression hearing as follows:

"Q. Why was Zola Mae Blair arrested on the 5th of February, 1982?

A. For an outstanding city warrant violation.

Q. And what else?

A. She wasn't arrested at the scene for criminal homicide. She was arrested for the city warrant violation. . . .

Q. Let me ask you this. Do you go to people's homes and arrest them on parking warrants?

A. Yes, sir, we do.

Q. And do you do that on a regular basis when there's no other reason to pick them up?

A. Yes, sir.

Q. And you go out and serve city warrants?

A. Yes, sir, we do.

Q. For parking violations?

A. Yes.

Q. This was a parking violation in this case?

A. Yes, sir." Record, Doc. 4, p. 25.

Respondent concedes that Missouri law permits a custodial arrest upon the commission of a motor vehicle offense and does not contend that such an arrest violates the Fourth Amendment. A valid custodial arrest authorizes, in and of itself, a search incident to the arrest. *United States* v. *Robinson*, 414 U. S. 218 (1973); *Gustafson* v. *Florida*, 414 U. S. 260 (1973). And, as we state *infra*, a person in lawful custody may also be subjected to photographing and fingerprinting as part of routine identification procedures.

Respondent does argue in her merits brief in this Court that she was not validly arrested on the municipal warrant because the police did not have physical possession of the warrant at the time they arrested her. According to respondent, a warrant issued on the basis of a nonappearance to answer a parking violation must, under Missouri law, be in the possession of

MISSOURI *v.* BLAIR

on that warrant, independently of any desire to investigate the homicide, the Fourth Amendment would not forbid taking her finger and palm prints and retaining them in police files. The Fourth Amendment prohibits only unreasonable seizures. "Thus, the permissibility of a particular law enforcement practice is judged by balancing its intrusion on the individual's Fourth Amendment interests against its promotion of legitimate governmental interests." *Delaware* v. *Prouse*, 440 U. S. 648, 654 (1979). Fingerprinting is minimally intrusive and is a routinely conducted and commonly accepted procedure, not only in the context of law enforcement, but in employment and other contexts as well. As Chief Justice, then Judge, Burger stated in *Smith* v. *United States*, 324 F. 2d 879, 882 (CADC 1963), cert. denied, 377 U. S. 954 (1964), "it is elementary that a person in lawful custody may be required to submit to photographing, *United States* v. *Amorosa*, 167 F. 2d 596, 599 (3d Cir. 1948), and fingerprinting, *United States* v. *Krapf*, 285 F. 2d 647, 650–651 (3d Cir. 1961), as part of routine identification processes." In many criminal cases, as in this case, the only solid identification evidence is a fingerprint. The State's interest in maintaining files of fingerprints is legitimate and substantial. Balancing this need against the minimal intrusion on privacy, it is evident that taking fingerprints and palm prints incident to an arrest is reasonable, even if such fingerprints are not needed as evidence of the particular offense for which the person is being arrested.

Had Blair's palm print been taken in this manner, its use in the homicide investigation would have raised no question

---

the arresting officer to be validly executed. The State argues in response that the record is not clear as to whether the arresting officers had the municipal warrant in their possession, and in any event, Missouri law does not require physical possession in all circumstances. The State further argues that this issue of Missouri law is not properly before us because it was never presented to or passed upon by any of the State courts. We agree that the issue is not properly before us.

MISSOURI *v.* BLAIR

under the Fourth Amendment. Nor would it if the usual practice in Kansas City of taking only a single fingerprint in connection with arrests on traffic warrants had been departed from at the request of homicide and a palm print taken as well. The testimony was that such requests were honored while traffic arrestees were in custody,[7] and since the State in such cases would be doing no more than the Constitution allowed, there would be no occasion to apply the exclusionary rule, which is designed to deter unconstitutional conduct.

The same result under the Fourth Amendment would follow if Blair's arrest on the traffic warrant was triggered by the need to get her palm print to investigate the homicide. There would have been a valid arrest, a valid temporary custody and the taking of identifying prints in connection therewith, which is no more than the Constitution permits. A State is free to enforce a different rule under its own law and prevent a valid arrest on one crime from being used to investigate another. The court below, however, proceeded on Federal Constitutional grounds. It viewed the execution of the municipal warrant as a subterfuge or pretext to gather evidence of the unrelated crime of homicide. Accordingly, the arrest was actually an arrest for homicide without probable cause, and the palm print, the homicide warrant, and the confession were products of an illegal arrest that the Fourth Amendment required to be suppressed.

As we have indicated, the Amendment does not reach so far. When a valid custodial arrest occurs and the police take fingerprints or gather other evidence incident to that arrest that proves relevant in investigating another crime, the Federal Constitution does not forbid using such evidence for that purpose, even if it could be proved that the impetus for the immediate arrest was the interest in investigating the other

[7] A Detention Unit officer testified that on state charges a full set of prints is the rule but that in municipal warrant cases, palm prints are taken only when "ID asks for it." Record, Doc. 4, p. 46.

crime. The Fourth Amendment does not require inquiry into the motives of the police officers in such situations. Fourth Amendment claims such as these are to be evaluated by "objective assessment of an officer's actions in light of the facts and circumstances then known to him" and "without regard to the underlying intent or motivation of the officers involved." *Scott* v. *United States*, 436 U. S. 128, 137, 138 (1978).

In *Abel* v. *United States*, 362 U. S. 217 (1960),[8] a search incident to an arrest on an administrative warrant was held valid and the evidence seized admissible in a criminal proceeding even though the administrative arrest was plainly occasioned by the desire of law enforcement officers to investigate and prosecute for an unrelated crime. The conduct of the searching officers was legal and their good faith settled by the fact that they did no more than the administrative warrant entitled them to do. So here, assuming a valid arrest on the traffic warrant, taking Blair's palm print was legally permissible and consistent with standard procedures when a request for a palm print is made.[9]

---

[8] In that case the Federal Bureau of Investigation (F. B. I.) had obtained information that Abel was involved in espionage but believed that the evidence was insufficient to justify his arrest. The F. B. I. therefore brought Abel to the attention of the I. N. S. and supplied the I. N. S. with information regarding his status as an alien. On the basis of this information, the I. N. S. District Director determined that Abel was an alien subject to deportation and issued an administrative warrant for his arrest. F. B. I. agents accompanied I. N. S. agents to the hotel where Abel was residing. While the I. N. S. agents waited outside Abel's room, F. B. I. agents interrogated him about his activities as a spy. When Abel did not cooperate, the F. B. I. agents signaled the I. N. S. agents who then executed the administrative warrant. The I. N. S. agents thoroughly searched the hotel room and Abel's belongings, permitted Abel to pack his belongings, and departed with him. The F. B. I. agents remained in the hotel room after Abel checked out and seized the articles he had left behind. These articles were introduced at Abel's trial for espionage.

[9] Respondent asserts that if we do not hold her arrest on the municipal warrant unlawful, we will have given the police *carte blanche* to stalk a

MISSOURI *v.* BLAIR

In *United States* v. *Villamonte-Marquez*, 462 U. S. 579, 584, n. 3 (1983), we upheld, against a challenge under the Fourth Amendment, the boarding of a vessel by federal customs officers under the authority of 46 Stat. 747, as amended, 19 U. S. C. § 1581(a).[10] Upon boarding, the customs officers discovered bales of marijuana, and convictions on various drug offenses ensued. The respondents argued that the true purpose of the customs officers in boarding the vessel was not to examine documents but to search for marijuana; they were accompanied by a Louisiana state policeman and were following an informant's tip that a vessel in the ship channel was thought to be carrying marijuana. The respondents asserted that they therefore could not rely on the statute authorizing boarding for inspection of the vessel's documentation. We rejected this argument, noting that this line of reasoning had been rejected in a similar situation in *Scott* v. *United States*, 436 U. S. 128, 135–139 (1978).[11]

---

suspect until he or she commits, almost inevitably, a minor motor vehicle violation, at which point the police can arrest the suspect and conduct a search incident to the arrest for evidence of an unrelated offense. Obviously, we need not address the legality of such hypothesized conduct. Here, the police merely executed a preexisting valid arrest warrant. The need to obtain respondent's palm prints for the Lindstedt investigation hastened the execution of the warrant but the police eventually would have arrested her. It was no infringement of her Fourth Amendment rights to be arrested sooner rather than later.

[10] That statute provides that "[a]ny officer of the customs may at any time go on board any vessel . . . at any place in the United States or within the customs waters . . . and examine the manifest and other documents and papers . . . ."

[11] The Missouri Supreme Court relied upon the dictum in *United States* v. *Lefkowitz*, 285 U. S. 452, 467 (1932), that "[a]n arrest may not be used as a pretext to search for evidence." The Court in that case merely applied to a search incident to arrest the then extant Fourth Amendment doctrine that searches for "mere evidence," as distinguished from contraband and instrumentalities of crime, were unreasonable. That doctrine, however, and the cases following it, were overturned in *Warden* v. *Hayden*, 387 U. S. 294 (1967), and *Lefkowitz* was noted as being one of those cases. 387 U. S., at 296, n. 1.

MISSOURI *v.* BLAIR

We conclude that the Fourth Amendment is not violated by an arrest on a valid municipal warrant, issued before the police suspected the subject of involvement in another offense, nor by palm and fingerprinting incident to that arrest, even though the police may have hastened the time of the arrest so that they could obtain the fingerprints for use in another investigation.

The discussion so far has addressed the situation where there is a custodial arrest for one crime, evidence of another crime resulting from that custody, and then an arrest or charge on that other crime. We must also proceed on the hypothesis that respondent's palm print was the fruit of an illegal arrest for homicide, either at respondent's home or at the police station. The opinion of the Supreme Court of Missouri can arguably be read as concluding that the trial court found there was an arrest for homicide at respondent's home. However that may be, respondent was taken to police headquarters, booked for homicide, and detained on that charge as well as on the municipal warrant. There was police testimony that she was under arrest for homicide when she was booked on that charge. Record, Doc. 4, p. 32. The intermediate appellate court accepted that view, although it stated that the arrest initially was on the municipal court warrant; and the state supreme court indicated no disagreement with the idea that there was an arrest for homicide at least when respondent was booked and held on that charge. The state court may well have concluded that it was in connection with the homicide arrest, whenever it occurred, that the palm print was taken. Was the print therefore the forbidden fruit of an unlawful arrest that tainted the subsequent warranted arrest for homicide and the ensuing confession to murder? We think not in the circumstances present here.

The circumstances are that even if the police did not arrest respondent at her home on the traffic warrant, they were aware of it, could have immediately booked her on that warrant, detained her briefly and taken her palm print. Al-

MISSOURI *v.* BLAIR

though they did not forthwith formally book her on the warrant, the Record of Arrest shows that she was detained for the Warrant Service Unit as well as for homicide. In any event, within minutes after her release from homicide she was taken into custody on the warrant. Had her palm print been taken, either in connection with her detention on the warrant or in connection with her booking on that warrant, surely it would have been usable to identify respondent as the murderer and to furnish untainted probable cause for her custodial arrest. As it happened the print was not obtained in this manner but had it not been taken on February 5, it appears to us that it surely would have been taken when she was booked on the traffic warrant the next day.

In *Nix* v. *Williams*, 467 U. S. 431 (1984), we adopted the inevitable discovery exception to the exclusionary rule, concluding that the high social cost of the exclusionary rule is not justified when the illegally seized evidence would inevitably have been discovered by lawful means. The exclusionary rule is designed to put the police in the same position they would have been in without the Fourth Amendment violation. But we decided in *Nix* that the police should not be put in a *worse* position than they would have been in had no police error or misconduct occurred.

Here the homicide officers were plainly interested in the palm print, and there is little doubt that the unit detaining respondent on the traffic charge would have been requested to take the print and would have complied.[12] Since we have already held that taking the print in this manner does not vio-

[12] The Supreme Court of Missouri stated that the State had failed to carry its burden of proving that the palm print would inevitably have been discovered. This statement, however, seems to have addressed the question whether the palm print would have been taken had respondent been arrested and booked on the traffic warrant alone, without regard to the likelihood that homicide officers might have requested that her palm print be taken, and legally could have done so, even if the impetus for respondent's arrest on the warrant at that time was to obtain her palm print and to investigate a homicide.

late the Fourth Amendment, the print would have been available to those investigating the homicide.

Respondent's palm print, therefore, properly supported the warrant issued for her arrest on February 8, 1982, and is admissible at her trial. Her confession resulted from a lawful arrest, and assuming no violation of any other constitutional right, is admissible at her trial. The judgment of the Missouri Supreme Court is accordingly reversed, and the case is remanded for further proceedings not inconsistent with this opinion.

It is so ordered.

3rd DRAFT

SUPREME COURT OF THE UNITED STATES

No. 85–303

MISSOURI, PETITIONER *v.* ZOLA BLAIR

ON WRIT OF CERTIORARI TO THE SUPREME COURT OF MISSOURI

[February ——, 1987]

JUSTICE POWELL, with whom JUSTICE BRENNAN joins, dissenting.

The Missouri courts in this case found that the police arrested respondent Zola Blair on a municipal parking warrant and took her palm print solely because they lacked probable cause to arrest her on a charge of murder. This Court today finds that the evidence obtained by the police during this arrest need not be suppressed because the parking violation warrant could have justified obtaining the evidence. In my view, the police conduct was not objectively reasonable and was undertaken to evade constitutional restraints otherwise applicable to their conduct. Accordingly, I dissent.

I

On November 24, 1981, officers of the Kansas City, Missouri Police Department discovered the body of Carl Lindstedt in a Swope Park lagoon. The only evidence gleaned from the site of the murder was a palm print. On January 22, 1982, an informer implicated Zola Blair and her family in the murder. The prints of other family members were on file at the Department. A comparison of these prints with the print found at the site failed to produce a match.

On January 23, a police detective requested that Blair be "picked up" for homicide, but did not ask for a homicide arrest or search warrant because he "believed that there was not enough evidence to support a warrant." 691 S. W. 2d

MISSOURI *v.* BLAIR

259, 260 (Mo. 1985) (en banc). The police then discovered that Blair was subject to an outstanding municipal warrant for a parking violation. The warrant had been issued on January 8, 1982, but the police had made no effort to execute it. On February 5, 1982, the police used the warrant to arrest Blair at her home.[1] The arresting officer gave Blair the warnings required under *Miranda* v. *Arizona*, 384 U. S. 436 (1966), although such warnings usually are not given to individuals arrested for parking violations.

The Missouri Supreme Court found that the normal procedure for executing parking violation warrants called for taking Blair to the district station, booking her on the parking violation charge, and taking only a single fingerprint.[2] Under standard procedures, Blair then would have been allowed to remain at the station for four hours in order to post bond. In Blair's case, the police departed from each of the standard parking violation arrest procedures. They filed a report of the arrest under the homicide charge number as "investigation arrest-criminal homicide." They took her to the homicide unit at the police department's downtown station and booked her on the *state* charge of homicide. The police

[1] The Missouri Supreme Court noted that "[t]he evidence conflicts on whether the officers arrested defendant on the outstanding parking violation warrant" or solely on the murder charge. 691 S. W. 2d 259, 261 (1985) (en banc). Like the Missouri Supreme Court, we "[a]ssum[e] an arrest for the parking violation." *Id.*, at 262.

[2] The Court quotes from the trial court suppression hearing to support its assertion that the taking of a palm print for a parking violation arrest was normal police department procedure. See *ante*, at 6, and n. 7. Both state courts in this case, however, found as a fact that taking a palm print was *not* part of the normal booking procedure for a traffic violation. 691 S. W. 2d, at 262; App. to Pet. for Cert. A25 (opinion of the Missouri Court of Appeals). This Court generally does not review or supplement state court findings of fact. See *Hayes* v. *Florida*, 470 U. S. 811, 814–815, n. 1 (1985). The Court's use of testimony not noted in the decision of any state court to reach a result favorable to the State is particularly unusual in light of the Missouri Supreme Court's finding that "[t]he trial court resolved [the conflicts raised by the evidence] in favor of [Blair]." 691 S. W. 2d, at 262.

MISSOURI *v.* BLAIR

then took a complete set of Blair's palm and finger prints, interrogated her about the homicide, and detained her overnight. The next morning the police booked Blair on the *municipal* parking violation warrant for the first time. Several hours later, she posted bond on the parking violation and was released.

Three days later, on February 8, the police determined that Blair's palm print matched the print found at the murder site. They then sought and obtained a warrant to arrest Blair for the homicide. The police arrested her, and for the second time booked her for homicide. During an interrogation, Blair first denied knowledge of the killing. But after the officers confronted her with evidence of the matching prints, she admitted to being in the vicinity of the victim's truck at the time of the murder.

The State sought to use Blair's palm print and statement against her in a trial for first-degree murder. Blair filed a motion to suppress the palm print and statement, and to quash the homicide arrest warrant. The motion alleged that the first arrest for homicide was without a warrant and without probable cause and that the arrest on the parking violation warrant was "a 'sham' in order that defendant could be brought to the Homicide Unit for booking and interrogation." App. 7. The trial court granted Blair's motion without opinion. The Missouri Court of Appeals, and the Missouri Supreme Court sitting en banc, affirmed.

The Missouri Supreme Court found it "undisputed that the police lacked probable cause to arrest defendant on the homicide charge." 691 S. W. 2d, at 261. The court rejected the State's attempt to justify the arrest on the basis of the parking violation warrant:

> "The execution of the parking violation warrant was but a subterfuge or pretext, not pursued, to gather evidence of the unrelated crime of homicide. The palm and finger prints and statements obtained on February 5, 1982, were properly suppressed because they resulted from an

> unlawful arrest and search. Because the illegally seized evidence provided the sole basis for the arrest warrant for homicide of February 8, 1982, and led directly to [Blair's] statements on that day, the warrant and statement are also inadmissible as 'fruits of the poisonous tree.' *Wong Sun* v. *United States*, 371 U. S. 471 (1963)." *Id.*, at 263.

The court found that neither the "inevitable discovery" exception to the exclusionary rule established in *Nix* v. *Williams*, 467 U. S. 431 (1984), nor the "good faith" exception of *United States* v. *Leon*, 468 U. S. 897 (1984), applied to the evidence suppressed in this case. As to the former, the court found that the State had not established that the police inevitably would have discovered the evidence by lawful means. 691 S. W. 2d, at 264. As to the latter, the court found that the police in this case did not act with an objective good faith belief that their conduct was constitutional. Instead, "in the case at hand all of the evidence supports a conclusion that the officers acted in bad faith without a search warrant." *Id.*, at 264.

II

It is undisputed that the police lacked probable cause to arrest Blair for homicide on February 5. Absent probable cause to arrest, the police were without authority to detain Blair for the purpose of obtaining her palm prints for use in their investigation of the homicide. See *Hayes* v. *Florida*, 470 U. S. 811 (1985); *Davis* v. *Mississippi*, 394 U. S. 721 (1969). The question presented in this case is whether the pre-existing municipal warrant for a parking violation provided an independent justification for the police conduct.

A

The Fourth Amendment protects against "unreasonable searches and seizures." U. S. Const., Amdt. 4. To this end, the Amendment requires that "no Warrants shall issue, but upon probable cause." The warrant and probable cause

MISSOURI *v.* BLAIR

requirements represent "the best compromise that has been found" to accommodate the competing interests of the State and the individual. *Brinegar* v. *United States*, 338 U. S. 160, 176 (1949). See *United States* v. *United States District Court*, 407 U. S. 297, 316–317 (1972). The Amendment recognizes that the police must be given "fair leeway" to arrest and search individuals for the purpose of discovering evidence of crime. *Brinegar* v. *United States*, *supra*, at 176. At the same time, the probable cause and warrant requirements channel police discretion to gather evidence and thereby accomplish the "central purpose of the Fourth Amendment, [that is] to safeguard the privacy and security of individuals against arbitrary invasions by government officials." *South Dakota* v. *Opperman*, 428 U. S. 364, 377 (1976) (POWELL, J., concurring).

Whether an intrusion is reasonable is usually an objective inquiry. See *Scott* v. *United States*, 436 U. S. 128, 137 (1978). The test for determining reasonableness "generally means that searches must be conducted pursuant to a warrant backed by probable cause." *New York* v. *Class*, 475 U. S. —–, —– (1986). Where the Court has established exceptions to the warrant and probable cause requirements, the standard of reasonableness is still primarily objective: "[W]ould the facts available to the officer at the moment of the seizure or the search 'warrant a man of reasonable caution in the belief' that the action taken was appropriate?" *Terry* v. *Ohio*, 392 U. S. 1, 21–22 (1968).

B

The State contends that the outstanding parking violation warrant provided an objective legal basis for the police conduct in this case. Even a cursory review of the facts indicates that no such objective legal basis existed. The police requested that Blair be "picked up" on a homicide charge. The arresting officers did not even possess the parking vio-

MISSOURI *v.* BLAIR

lation warrant.[3] Upon Blair's arrest, the police gave her *Miranda* warnings, took her to the downtown station, booked her on a charge of homicide, took a full set of finger and palm prints, interrogated her as to the homicide, and detained her overnight. The police conduct deviated in every respect from the procedures standard for an arrest on a parking violation warrant. Thus, a reasonable police officer could not possibly have believed that any of these actions were appropriate. Because the police conduct fails the test of objective reasonableness, the palm print and inculpatory statement were obtained in violation of the Fourth Amendment.

C

The Missouri Supreme Court did not rest solely on a determination that the police conduct lacked objective reasonableness. It explicitly found that the arrest for the parking violation "was at best a pretext employed to gather evidence on an unrelated homicide." 691 S. W. 2d, at 262. On this ground, the court found Blair's arrest to violate the Fourth Amendment. This finding is consistent with statements by this Court, as well as individual Justices, suggesting that police conduct undertaken for the sole purpose of evading the probable cause or warrant requirements could render the police conduct unreasonable and therefore unconstitutional.[4]

---

[3] JUSTICE STEVENS finds this fact dispositive as a matter of state law of the validity of the arrest. The Missouri Supreme Court, which is presumably aware of its own decisions, noted this fact but did not find it dispositive. 691 S. W. 2d, at 261. Accordingly, neither do I.

[4] See *Arizona* v. *Hicks*, —— U. S. ——, —— (1987) (O'CONNOR, J., dissenting) ("[T]he officer did not '"know in advance the location of [certain] evidence and intend to seize it," relying on the plain view doctrine only as a pretext.' *Texas* v. *Brown*, 460 U. S. 730, 737 (1983) (plurality) (quoting *Coolidge* v. *New Hampshire*, [403 U. S. 443, 470 (1971)])); *South Dakota* v. *Opperman*, 428 U. S. 364, 376 (1976) ("[T]here is no suggestion whatever that this standard [inventory] procedure . . . was a pretext concealing an investigatory police motive"); *United States* v. *Robinson*, 414 U. S. 218, 221, n. 1 (1973) (reserving the question of a pretextual arrest); *id.*, at 238,

MISSOURI *v.* BLAIR

Although the focus in this case is appropriately on the lack of "objective reasonableness" and the deviations from "standard procedures," the finding of a constitutional violation can-

---

n. 2 (POWELL, J., concurring) (noting that the arrest in a similar case "would have presented a different question if the petitioner could have proved that he was taken into custody only to afford a pretext for a search actually undertaken for collateral objectives"); *Ker* v. *California*, 374 U. S. 23, 42–43 (1963) ("[A]n arrest may not be used merely as the pretext for a search without warrant"); *Abel* v. *United States*, 362 U. S. 217, 226 (1960) ("The deliberate use by the Government of an administrative warrant for the purpose of gathering evidence in a criminal case must meet stern resistance by the courts"); *Jones* v. *United States*, 357 U. S. 493, 500 (1958) (invalidating the entry and search of a house that might have been constitutional as an arrest because the federal agents' "purpose in entering was to search . . . not to arrest"); *United States* v. *Lefkowitz*, 285 U. S. 452, 467 (1932) ("An arrest may not be used as a pretext to search for evidence"). See also *New York* v. *Class*, 475 U. S. ——, ——, n. —— (1986) (POWELL, J., concurring) ("I do not suggest, of course, that the Fourth Amendment is inapplicable in [the context of Vehicle Identification Number inspections.] An officer may not use VIN inspection as a pretext for searching a vehicle for contraband or weapons"); *Michigan* v. *DeFillippo*, 443 U. S. 31, 41 (1979) (BLACKMUN, J., concurring) ("There is no evidence in this case . . . that the [stop-and-identify] ordinance is being used in [a] pretextual manner"); *id.*, at 46, n. 3 (BRENNAN, J., dissenting) (finding constitutional error where "[j]urisdictions so minded may avoid prosecuting under [stop-and-identify ordinances] and use them merely as investigative tools to gather evidence of other crimes through pretextual arrests and searches"); *Brown* v. *Illinois*, 422 U. S. 590, 611 (1975) (POWELL, J., concurring in part) (If "the evidence clearly suggested that [an] arrest was effectuated as a pretext for collateral objectives, [the fact that *Miranda* warnings were given would] rarely [be] sufficient to dissipate the taint").

The Court's treatment of two of the above cases requires comment. First, the Court implies that the Missouri Supreme Court erred in relying on *United States* v. *Lefkowitz*, *supra*. See *ante*, at 8, n. 11. Although the specific evidentiary doctrine relied upon in that case has subsequently been overruled, *Warden* v. *Hayden*. 387 U. S. 294 (1967), the more general statement quoted by the Missouri court remained, until today, good law: the police may not use an arrest as a pretext to evade constitutional restrictions on their conduct.

Second, as I read it, the Court's characterization of *Abel* v. *United States*, *supra*, is incorrect. The Court states that in *Abel*, "a search

MISSOURI *v.* BLAIR

not be divorced from its conceptual underpinnings. The purpose of the Fourth Amendment is to strike a balance between the interests of the State and the individual in the investigation of crimes. The crux of the balance is that arrests and searches designed to reveal evidence must be supported by probable cause. See *Henry* v. *United States*, 361 U. S. 98 (1959) (arrest); *Chambers* v. *Maroney*, 399 U. S. 42 (1970) (search). We accord the police substantial discretion in executing their investigative responsibilities. But this judicial deference is premised on the trust that the discretion will not be abused. Police conduct that evades the constitutional restraints on their evidence-gathering abilities is "flagrantly abusive" of Fourth Amendment rights and of this judicial trust. *Brown* v. *Illinois*, 422 U. S. 590, 610 (1975) (POWELL, J., concurring in part).

The reasonableness of police conduct depends upon an assessment of all the relevant facts and circumstances. A deviation from normal procedures is one fact to be considered in the reasonableness inquiry and does not independently constitute the type of "arbitrary" action prohibited by the Fourth Amendment. Otherwise even minor or inadvertent deviations would violate the Constitution. Instead, findings that police conduct was "objectively reasonable" and in ac-

---

incident to an arrest on an administrative warrant was held valid and the evidence seized admissible in a criminal proceeding even though the administrative arrest was plainly occasioned by the desire of law enforcement officers to investigate and prosecute for an unrelated crime." *Ante*, at 7. In contrast, the Court in *Abel* stated:

"We emphasize again that our view of the matter would be totally different had the evidence established, or were the courts below not justified in not finding, that the administrative warrant was here employed as an instrument of criminal law enforcement to circumvent the latter's legal restrictions, rather than as a bona fide preliminary step in a deportation proceeding. The test is whether the decision to proceed administratively toward deportation was influenced by, and was carried out for, a purpose of amassing evidence in the prosecution for crime. The record precludes such a finding by this Court." 362 U. S., at 230.

MISSOURI *v.* BLAIR

cord with "standard procedures" are relevant because they are highly probative, and possibly determinative,[5] that the police conduct did not exceed constitutional bounds.[6] The corollary of this principle is that deviations from standard procedures are highly probative of a Fourth Amendment vi-

[5] This case does not present the more difficult question of whether a pretextual purpose alone could render police conduct unreasonable. Neither *Scott* v. *United States*, 436 U. S. 128 (1978) nor *United States* v. *Villamonte-Marquez*, 462 U. S. 579 (1983) dispose of the question. *Scott* was not a pretext case. In *Scott*, government officials apparently intended to exceed Fourth Amendment restraints but did not in fact do so. In this context, the Court stated that "[s]ubjective intent alone . . . does not make otherwise lawful conduct illegal or unconstitutional." 436 U. S., at 136.

In *Villamonte-Marquez*, the Court relied on *Scott* to reject in a footnote respondents' argument that "because the [searching] officers were accompanied by a Louisiana state policeman, and were following an informant's tip that a vessel in the ship channel was thought to be carrying marihuana, they may not rely on the statute authorizing boarding for inspection of the vessel's documentation." 462 U. S., at 584, n. 3. In that case, there was no lower court finding of pretext. And, because the boarding policy was random, there could be no demonstrable deviation from standard procedures. Absent sufficient evidence to support an allegation of pretext, a Fourth Amendment claim is properly rejected.

[6] Where the possibility of a pretextual motivation has been raised, the Court has found the fact that the police abided by their normal procedures to be relevant to a determination that the challenged search was reasonable. See *United States* v. *Robinson*, *supra*, at 221, n. 1 ("Respondent argued below that [the officer] may have used the subsequent traffic violation arrest as a mere pretext for a narcotics search which would not have been allowed by a neutral magistrate had [the officer] sought a warrant. . . . We think it is sufficient for purposes of our decision that respondent was lawfully arrested for an offense, and that [the officer's] placing him in custody following that arrest was not a departure from established police department practice"); *South Dakota* v. *Opperman*, *supra*, at 374–375 ("[T]he protective search was carried out in accordance with *standard procedures* in the local police department") (emphasis in original); *Abel* v. *United States*, *supra*, at 227 ("[T]he proceedings taken by the Department differed in no respect from what would have been done in the case of an individual concerning whom no [additional] information was known to exist").

MISSOURI *v.* BLAIR

olation when they indicate a strong possibility that police discretion has been abused.[7]

Here, the state courts found more than a strong possibility of abuse; the state courts found that the deviations compelled the conclusion that the police arrested Blair on the parking violation warrant for the sole purpose of discovering incriminating evidence of a completely unrelated crime. Such pretextual conduct flouts the limits established by the Fourth Amendment on police investigative abilities. Accordingly, the state courts appropriately found the police conduct in this case to violate the Constitution.

III

A

Once a Fourth Amendment violation is found, the next question is whether the exclusionary rule requires that the evidence obtained be suppressed. The Court has held that the exclusionary rule is "a judicially created remedy designed to safeguard Fourth Amendment rights . . . through its deterrent effect." *United States* v. *Calandra*, 414 U. S. 338, 348 (1974). See *Stone* v. *Powell*, 428 U. S. 465, 486 (1976). Its remedial purpose is best served when "it can be said that the law enforcement officer had knowledge, or may properly be charged with knowledge, that the [challenged conduct] was unconstitutional under the Fourth Amendment." *United States* v. *Peltier*, 422 U. S. 531, 542 (1975). See *United States* v. *Leon*, 468 U. S., at 908–909 (The Court has never "seriously questioned . . . 'the continued application of the rule to suppress evidence . . . where a Fourth Amend-

[7] In other contexts, too, the Court has indicated that the lack of standard procedures presents an unacceptable possibility of abuse. See *United States* v. *Martinez-Fuerte*, 428 U. S. 543 (1976) (fixed checkpoints to search for illegal aliens obviate the "grave danger that . . . unreviewable discretion would be abused by some officers in the field"); *Deleware* v. *Prouse*, 440 U. S. 648 (1979) (finding random stops to check for drivers' licenses and vehicle registration unreasonable but suggesting that fixed checkpoints could appropriately limit officers' discretion).

MISSOURI *v.* BLAIR

ment violation has been substantial and deliberate'") (quoting *Franks* v. *Delaware*, 438 U. S. 154, 171 (1978)).

Here, the state courts found that the police intended to evade the constitutional limitations on their investigative powers. 691 S. W. 2d, at 264; App. to Pet. for Cert. A27 (opinion of the Missouri Court of Appeals). The exclusionary rule is most appropriately applied to such intentional and deliberate conduct. See *Brown* v. *Illinois*, *supra*, at 610–611 (POWELL, J., concurring in part). Thus, the products of Blair's illegal arrest and detention—the palm print and the inculpatory statement—were properly suppressed.

B

The State argues that the exclusionary rule should not apply because the palm print evidence fits within the "inevitable discovery" exception to the exclusionary rule established in *Nix* v. *Williams*, 467 U. S. 431 (1984). The State asserts that the outstanding parking violation warrant eventually would have led to Blair's arrest. The Missouri Supreme Court, however, explicitly found that the State had failed to establish "'by a preponderance of the evidence that the information ultimately or inevitably would have been discovered by lawful means.'" 691 S. W. 2d, at 264 (quoting *Nix* v. *Williams*, *supra*, at 444). There is no reason for this Court to overturn the factual findings of the state courts.[8] The Missouri Supreme Court reasonably concluded that the State would not inevitably have obtained the palm print or the inculpatory statement.[9]

---

[8] The Court bases its decision on its view that "the police eventually would have arrested [Blair]" on the parking violation warrant, *ante*, at 7, n. 9, and that normal police department practice for a parking violation arrest could include taking a palm print, *ante*, at 6, and n. 7. As I read the Missouri Supreme Court decision, it made contrary findings of fact on both of these points. See n. 2, *supra*. The Court's attempt to recast the Missouri Supreme Court's conclusions, see *ante*, at 10, n. 12, is unconvincing.

[9] The Court's view that the police "eventually would have arrested [Blair]", *ante*, at 7, n. 9, is in fact sheer speculation. The parking violation

MISSOURI *v.* BLAIR

C

The State also argues that even if the palm print was illegally seized, Blair's subsequent confession should not be suppressed because the connection between the print and the confession is sufficiently attenuated that the confession can be deemed "an act of free will unaffected by the initial illegality." *Brown* v. *Illinois*, *supra*, at 603. But the Missouri Supreme Court found that the palm print "led directly" to Blair's confession. 691 S. W. 2d, at 263. Specifically, Blair first declined to talk, and only changed her mind after being confronted with the matching prints. *Id.*, at 260. Blair's confession thus was obtained "by exploitation of [the] illegality," *Wong Sun* v. *United States*, 371 U. S. 471, 488 (1963), and should be suppressed.

IV

The Missouri Supreme Court found that the police in this case suspected Blair of homicide but knew that they lacked probable cause to arrest her on that charge. The court further found that the police relied on a theretofore unexecuted municipal parking violation warrant as a pretext to arrest Blair for the sole purpose of obtaining evidence of the homicide. In my view, this was a clear violation of the Fourth Amendment. Accordingly, I dissent.

---

warrant was issued on January 8, and remained unexecuted for almost a month, until February 5. Moreover, if at some future date the police had sought to execute the traffic warrant, they might not have found Blair. Even if the police had found Blair and lawfully arrested her for the parking violation, normal department procedure was to take only a single fingerprint. 691 S. W. 2d, at 262. Finally, we cannot assume that under different circumstances Blair would have made the incriminating statement.

3rd DRAFT

SUPREME COURT OF THE UNITED STATES

No. 85-303

MISSOURI, PETITIONER *v.* ZOLA BLAIR

ON WRIT OF CERTIORARI TO THE SUPREME COURT OF MISSOURI

[February ——, 1987]

JUSTICE STEVENS, with whom JUSTICE MARSHALL joins, dissenting.

In my opinion, the record unambiguously demonstrates that respondent was unlawfully arrested on a homicide charge and that her palm print was the product of that unlawful arrest. The report of her arrest was filed under a homicide charge number. When she was arrested, she was taken to the Homicide Unit, booked on a charge of criminal homicide, interrogated about the homicide, and detained at the police station overnight. Moreover, the officers could not have lawfully arrested her for a traffic offense because they did not have a warrant in their possession.[1] Because it

[1] When respondent was arrested on February 5, 1982, state law required that the arresting officer possess a warrant issued on the basis of nonappearance to answer a parking violation in order to make a valid arrest. The arresting "officer must inform the defendant by what authority he acts, and must also show the warrant if required." Mo. Rev. Stat. § 544.180 (1986). Construing this statute, the Missouri Supreme Court determined that the officer's possession of the warrant was a "clear prerequisite to the officer's ability to display the warrant to a person being arrested . . . ." *Rustici* v. *Weidemeyer*, 673 S. W. 2d 762, 771 (1984) (en banc). Yet the arresting officer testified that he possessed no warrant. Tr. 35 ("I did not have physical copy of any warrant"). The absence of such a warrant in this case, while obviously not dispositive of the question whether probable cause for any arrest existed, indicates that the arrest for the municipal violation, even assuming that it was made for that purpose, was invalid.

MISSOURI *v.* BLAIR

is undisputed that the arrest of respondent on a homicide charge was not supported by probable cause to believe that she was guilty of a felony,[2] or by a warrant authorizing her arrest on a homicide charge,[3] the police conduct was plainly unreasonable within the meaning of the Fourth Amendment.[4] Accordingly, I would affirm the judgment of the Supreme Court of Missouri.

It is of no relevance to this case that Missouri law no longer requires an officer executing a municipal traffic warrant to possess the warrant at the time of the arrest. Mo. Sup. Ct. Rule 37.46 (effective Jan. 1, 1986); Mo. Rev. Stat. § 544.216 (1986).

[2] 691 S. W. 2d 259, 261 (Mo. 1985) (en banc).

[3] The suppression hearing testimony of the officer who arrested respondent is illuminating:

"Q: [D]id you have a warrant for [respondent's] arrest for criminal homicide that you booked her on later that day?

"A: No, sir, I did not have physical possession of a warrant for the party's arrest for criminal homicide.

"Q: Did you know of any warrant existing for the arrest of Zola Mae Blair for criminal homicide? Did you know about any warrant whether you had it with you or not?

"A: I had no knowledge that a warrant had been issued by the Jackson County court." Tr. 35–36.

[4] The Court maintains that, if the evidence had not been taken at the time of the homicide booking, it "surely would have been taken when she was booked on the traffic warrant the next day." *Ante*, at 10. The Court thus concludes that the palm print would inevitably have been discovered by lawful means. I reject this conclusion for the reasons stated in Part III of JUSTICE POWELL's opinion.

1st DRAFT

SUPREME COURT OF THE UNITED STATES

No. 85-303

MISSOURI, PETITIONER *v.* ZOLA BLAIR

ON WRIT OF CERTIORARI TO THE SUPREME COURT OF MISSOURI

[January ——, 1987]

JUSTICE O'CONNOR, dissenting.

The question in this case is whether the detention and search of Zola Blair can be justified either as an arrest on a municipal parking violation warrant or as an arrest for homicide. The Court concludes that the police officers' conduct is supported by the municipal traffic warrant, or alternatively that the evidence fits within the "inevitable discovery" doctrine established by *Nix* v. *Williams*, 467 U. S. 431 (1984). Because I disagree with the Court on both grounds, I respectfully dissent.

The State's primary argument in this case is that the police officers arrested Blair pursuant to the municipal warrant, and that her palm print was taken incident to that custodial arrest. The State acknowledges that the police officers "hope[d] the arrest [would] further their investigation into the more serious crime," Brief for Petitioner 14, but it argues that this subjective hope should not taint an otherwise lawful traffic arrest. *Ibid.* To evaluate the State's claim, it is necessary to review the facts in this case. As found by the courts below, the normal procedure under Missouri law for executing parking violation warrants is to take the individual to a district police station; fill out a form (Form 85 PD) calculating the bond amount; and obtain one fingerprint from the person. The person arrested is allowed to remain at the district station for four hours in order to post bond. The police do not give the warnings required by *Miranda* v. *Ari-*

zona, 384 U. S. 436 (1966) when individuals are arrested for minor parking violations. The violation in Blair's case was for failure to pay a $15 parking ticket.

As found by the courts below, the conduct of the police officers in arresting Blair departed from these procedures in every respect. When Blair was arrested at her mother's home, she was advised of her constitutional rights as required by *Miranda*. She was then driven to the downtown police station, where she was taken to the homicide unit and booked on the state charge of homicide rather than on the municipal warrant. Once she was booked for homicide, she was under arrest upon that charge. The jail detention officer proceeded to take a complete set of palm and fingerprints as part of the standard procedure for processing homicide arrests (he was unaware of the outstanding search warrant for Blair's palm print). Blair was interrogated regarding the homicide and detained overnight. She was released at 10:45 the next morning because the police did not have probable cause to hold her for homicide. A quarter of an hour later, she was booked for the first time on the parking violation warrant. Blair's right index fingerprint was taken on the back of Form 85 PD, she posted bond two hours later, and she left the police station.

The officers' conduct clearly demonstrates that they did not initially execute a municipal parking violation arrest. The Court interprets the Missouri Supreme Court as assuming, as an alternative basis for its holding, that Blair's palm print was taken pursuant to "a valid arrest on the traffic warrant." *Ante*, at ——. I read the Missouri Supreme Court's decision differently, however. The state court concluded that execution of the traffic warrant was, in its words, at best an alternative "not pursued." See *State* v. *Blair*, 691 S. W. 2d 259, 263 (Mo. 1985) (en banc). Indeed, any other conclusion would have been inconsistent with the Missouri Supreme Court's factual findings. Whatever the officers' intent may have been at the time they arrested Blair, see *ante*, at ——,

MISSOURI *v.* BLAIR

n. 6, an "objective assessment of [the officers'] actions in light of the facts and circumstances then known to [them]," *Scott* v. *United States*, 436 U. S. 128, 137 (1978), shows that their conduct was flatly inconsistent with a municipal traffic violation arrest. Based upon the lower court's findings, it is clear that, if the officers were aware of the traffic warrant as an alternative basis for arresting Blair, they failed to act upon it. The traffic warrant, therefore, does not provide an independent basis for their conduct.

To justify an officer's actions under the Fourth Amendment, it is not sufficient simply to rely on the label the police choose to give their conduct; it is necessary to inquire whether, viewed objectively in light of the facts and circumstances known to the officer at the time, the officer's conduct conforms to the Fourth Amendment theory invoked to justify it. Thus, before a search could be justified as an inventory search under *Illinois* v. *Lafayette*, 462 U. S. 640 (1983), it would have to *be* an inventory search. If an officer searches a suspect's purse during an encounter on the street without either listing or securing the contents, the officer simply has not engaged in an inventory search, even if the search is no broader than what *could* have been done if it *had* been undertaken pursuant to an inventory. It might be, if the officer subsequently makes a valid arrest of the suspect, that the evidence inevitably would have been discovered when a proper inventory search was made at the station house. But that does not convert the previous search into conduct justified under *Illinois* v. *Lafayette*; it is sustainable, if at all, only under the inevitable discovery rule of *Nix* v. *Williams*.

Similarly, in this case most of the Court's argument is directed at determining whether the officers *could* have obtained a palm print pursuant to a traffic warrant arrest. But unless, viewed objectively, this *was* a traffic arrest, that argument is relevant only to the inevitable discovery question. The decisions relied upon by the Court are consistent with this view. In *United States* v. *Villamonte-Marquez*, 462

MISSOURI *v.* BLAIR

U. S. 579 (1983), we upheld a statute that authorizes customs agents to board a vessel and inspect the vessel's documentation. In a footnote, the *Villamonte-Marquez* Court rejected the respondents' argument that authorities may not make a document-inspection boarding if they do so hoping to make a plain view observation of narcotics. Nothing in the Court's opinion, however, suggests that its holding would justify a warrantless search of a vessel where the officers neither make a document inspection nor follow a course of action suggesting that they would have made such an inspection if their plain view observations of incriminating evidence had not intervened.

The decision in *Abel* v. *United States*, 362 U. S. 217 (1960), likewise does not support the Court's holding today. Federal agents investigating Abel for espionage learned that he was an alien subject to deportation. After the Federal Bureau of Investigation provided the Immigration Naturalization Service (INS) with this information, the INS issued an administrative warrant for Abel's arrest. The Court determined that the INS agents' subsequent execution of the arrest warrant and search of Abel's room were valid in light of the District Court's factual finding that the conduct of the INS agents "differed in no respect from what would have been done in the case of an individual concerning whom no such [espionage] information was known to exist." *Id.*, at 227. Viewed objectively, therefore, the search in *Abel* was indeed an administrative search: it was executed as "a bona fide preliminary step in a deportation proceeding." *Id.*, at 230. By contrast, the state court's factual findings here belie any claim that the evidence in this case was seized as a bona fide step in the execution of a traffic warrant. If the traffic violation warrant provides a justification for the officers' conduct in this case, it can only be because the officers *could* and *would* have obtained the palm print pursuant to the municipal warrant; it cannot be because they *did*.

MISSOURI *v.* BLAIR

Turning to the Court's alternative holding, I am not persuaded that the inevitable discovery doctrine recognized in *Nix* v. *Williams*, 467 U. S. 431 (1984), can be extended to cover this case. The Court finds it inevitable that if the officers had not taken the palm print while processing the unlawful homicide arrest, they would have thought to do so when they booked Blair for the municipal violation. I do not think that the record supports this conclusion. At the time the officers released Blair for lack of probable cause on the homicide arrest, they had every reason to believe that they had obtained the palm print unlawfully: they had known when they issued the homicide "pick up" order that they did not have probable cause to arrest Blair for homicide, see *State* v. *Blair*, 691 S. W. 2d 259, 260 (Mo. 1985) (en banc), and ultimately they had to release her for lack of probable cause. At the time of Blair's release, the officers also were aware of the outstanding municipal parking violation warrant, and they knew that Blair had not yet been processed on that charge. Thus, the officers in fact confronted the situation hypothesized by the Court— the possibility of obtaining the palm print as incident to a lawful arrest at a time when they had every reason to believe that they had obtained the first print unlawfully. Yet the officers did not do what the Court views as inevitable: they proceeded to book her on the traffic warrant, but they did not try to obtain the palm print incident to that lawful arrest. Thus, this is far from the kind of "inevitable" discovery that we found in *Nix*, where an independent, systematic search already was underway that was proceeding apart from the officer's unlawful conduct. The burden is on the State to show, by a preponderance of the evidence, that the information inevitably would have been discovered by lawful means. See *Nix* v. *Williams*, *supra*, at 444. The Missouri Supreme Court found that the State failed to make this showing, and I see no basis, on this record, for disturbing that finding.

MISSOURI *v.* BLAIR

If the officers had lawfully arrested Blair on the traffic warrant, taken her to the district police station, filled out form 85 PD, taken her finger *and palm* print, and then released her after she posted bond, this case would raise the difficult question of "pretext" discussed at length in the briefs. The question then would be whether departure from normal identification procedures, and "hasten[ing] the time of . . . arrest," see *ante*, at ——, render an arrest unlawful when these deviations are motivated by the desire to obtain evidence of another crime. See generally 1 W. LaFave, Search and Seizure § 1.4 (2d ed. 1987); Haddad, Pretextual Fourth Amendment Activity: Another Viewpoint, 18 U. Mich. J. L. Ref. 639 (1985); Burkoff, The Pretext Search Doctrine: Now You See It, Now You Don't, 17 U. Mich. J. L. Ref. 523 (1984). There is no need, however, to reach the pretext issue in this case. Although an alternative basis for detaining and searching Blair was available to the police, that alternative was not pursued. The evidence was taken incident to an unlawful homicide arrest, and the police would not inevitably have discovered it by some other means. Accordingly, I would affirm the decision of the Missouri Supreme Court.

Justice White's draft opinion of the Court would have given the police a virtual license to use arrests for minor offenses, such as traffic violations, to obtain evidence of other crimes, "even if it could be proved that the impetus for the immediate arrest was the interest in investigating the other crime." However, the majority that voted to reverse the lower court decision in *Blair* did not hold, and White's draft was not only not issued as the opinion of the Court—it was never issued at all.

The conference vote to reverse had been by a bare majority. The dissenters circulated draft dissents soon after they received the White draft opinion of the Court. The draft dissent, reprinted on page 43, was sent around by Justice Powell (whom Justice Brennan joined) and a two-page dissent, reprinted on page 55, was circulated by Justice Stevens (whom Justice Marshall joined). The dissenters urged that the defendant had really been illegally arrested on the homicide charge and that the traffic arrest was a mere pretext. As the Powell draft dissent put it, "the police arrested respondent Zola Blair on a municipal parking warrant and took her palm print solely because they lacked probable cause to arrest her on a charge of murder. . . . In my view, the police conduct was not objectively reasonable and was undertaken to evade constitutional restraints otherwise applicable to their conduct."

According to Justice Powell, the police conduct here was both objectively unreasonable and a mere pretext to evade the constitutional requirement: "[T]he police arrested Blair on the parking violation warrant for the sole purpose of discovering incriminating evidence of a completely unrelated crime. Such pretextual conduct flouts the limits established by the Fourth Amendment on police investigative abilities."

The Powell draft's conclusion was that "the police relied on a theretofore unexecuted municipal parking violation warrant as a pretext to arrest Blair for the sole purpose of obtaining evidence of the homicide. In my view, this was a clear violation of the Fourth Amendment. Accordingly, I dissent."

Powell's dissent led Justice O'Connor to rethink her position. On January 27, 1987, she sent a "Dear Byron" letter. "This has been a difficult case for me," Justice O'Connor wrote. "You have written as well as could be done in support of the State's position, but I find myself at the end of the day agreeing with Lewis that the judgment should be affirmed."

O'Connor's letter went on, "I disagree with Lewis, however, that it is open in all cases to explore the subjective motives of the police. In my view, if an officer's actions are objectively reasonable and in accordance with standard procedures, the accused has not suffered any additional invasion of privacy by reason of the improper motivation and there has been no Fourth Amendment violation. I agree with Lewis that the officers' actions in this case were not objectively reasonable." Justice O'Connor wrote that she would "circulate something concurring in part with Lewis' dissent in due course."

The promised O'Connor circulation was sent around on February 18. It is the draft dissent reprinted on page 57. In it, Justice O'Connor disagreed with White's conclusion "that the police officers' conduct is supported by the municipal traffic warrant." Instead, she found that the officers' conduct was objectively unreasonable. The facts here, O'Connor concluded, "belie any claim that the evidence in this case was seized as a bona fide step in the execution of a traffic warrant. . . . The evidence was taken incident to an unlawful homicide arrest, and the police would not inevitably have discovered it by some other means."

With O'Connor's switch, there was now a bare majority to affirm the suppression of the evidence. By now, however, the Justices were dissatisfied with that result as well. Their view was expressed in a letter from Justice Blackmun to Justice White. "I continue to rest uneasy about this case." Blackmun wrote, "You will recall that I so expressed myself at conference and that I then stated that I could go along with a DIG"—that is, dismiss as improvidently granted.

This was the solution adopted by the Court. On March 25, 1987, a per curiam was issued (drafted by the Chief Justice) stating simply, "The writ of certiorari is dismissed as improvidently granted."[3] Nor has the issue avoided by this disposition of *Blair* been dealt with since that case. In 1991, the Court refused to grant certiorari in *Cummins* v. *United States*,[4] where the petitioner alleged that the police used a traffic stop as a pretext for conducting a narcotics search. Justice White, the author of the putative *Blair* opinion, wrote a short dissent urging that certiorari should be granted "to address this recurring issue."[5] The issue would, of course, have been addressed if White's draft *Blair* opinion had been issued as the opinion of the Court. As it turned out, however, instead of the important Fourth Amendment case it would have been had the White draft come down as the opinion of the Court, *Missouri* v. *Blair* became not even a footnote in recent Supreme Court jurisprudence.

Notes

1. 480 U.S. 698 (1987).
2. 474 U.S. 1049 (1986).
3. Supra note 1.
4. 502 U.S. 962 (1991).
5. Ibid.

2

Hodel v. *Irving* (*1987*): *Regulation, Takings, and Just Compensation*

For over half a century, our public law has been based upon a dichotomy between property rights and personal rights, with the judges far more ready to find legislative invasion when personal rights were involved than in the sphere of economics.[1] As a critic summarizes it, "The Court generally observes this hierarchy of rights: At the top are the rights of expression, religion, sexual privacy, and voting: at the bottom are economic rights."[2]

Supreme Court jurisprudence has thus been based on the view that the Constitution gives a preferred status to personal, as opposed to property rights. The result is a double standard in the exercise by the Court of its review function. The tenet of judicial restraint does not rigidly bind the judge in cases involving civil liberties and other personal rights. The presumption of validity for laws gives way far more readily in cases where life and liberty are restrained. In those cases, the legislative judgment is subject to "a . . . more searching judicial inquiry."[3]

From a historical point of view, the subordinate status of property rights in the constitutional scheme is a relatively recent development. During the first part of this century, the emphasis in the law was on the rights of property. All this, of course, has changed over the past sixty years. Merely to repeat the 1922 statement of a federal judge "that of the three fundamental principles which underlie government, and for which government exists, the protection of life, liberty, and property, the chief of these is property"[4] is to show how far out of line such a statement is with the present scale of legal values. If, at the turn of the century, unrestricted acquisition and use of property was at its broadest, it became progressively narrowed as the century went on. Some years ago, Rudolf von Ihering, one of the greatest of modern jurists, formulated the matter thus: "Formerly high valuing of property, lower valuing of the person. Now lower valuing of property, higher valuing of the person."[5]

Since the accession of Chief Justice Rehnquist, however, the pendulum has started to swing the other way. The changing emphasis of the Rehnquist

Court in this respect may mark the beginning of a trend in favor of property rights. For the first time in years, the Court has relied upon the constitutional prohibition against takings of property without compensation to invalidate governmental action that did not involve public acquisition of property.[6] Noteworthy in those cases was the Rehnquist Court's use of heightened scrutiny to review the merits of land use regulations in order to decide whether a challenged regulation required judicial invalidation in the absence of compensation. Indeed, the Court has implied that claims of unconstitutional takings (whether by acquisition or regulation) now fall into a particularly sensitive constitutional category comparable to that in which freedom of speech claims fall.

Its decisions on takings without compensation may signal a fundamental shift in Bill-of-Rights jurisprudence, with a tilt by the Rehnquist Court in favor of protection of property rights and away from the strong preference given to personal rights by its predecessors. The increasing emphasis upon property rights is strikingly shown in the cases that expand the scope of the Takings Clause of the Constitution (prohibiting takings of private property for public use without just compensation) to include so-called regulatory takings. Though the constitutional prohibition seems to apply only to acquisitions of property by government, it has been urged that it should apply whenever a governmental regulation diminishes the value of property. More specifically, it has been claimed that regulation that results in a diminution in value should require compensation to the property owner.[7] Since government regulation inevitably limits the rights of those regulated, it may also diminish property values where property is being regulated. Thus, a zoning law, by restricting the uses to which property may be put, may reduce the value that the land might have without the restriction.

The law had always been that a regulation does not constitute a taking for which compensation has to be paid. The starting point for the change in Rehnquist Court jurisprudence in this area was the 1987 case of *Hodel* v. *Irving*.[8] But the case was originally decided on an entirely different basis, and one wonders about the "might have been" if the draft opinion of the Court prepared by Justice Stevens had come down as the final *Hodel* opinion. One may also speculate about the "might have been" if the "bright line" rule urged in a Scalia draft concurrence had been joined by two other Justices.

In *Hodel* v. *Irving*, Congress had attempted to deal with the problem of extreme fractionation of Indian lands that had been allotted to individual Indians, but had, through successive generations, been splintered into multiple undivided interests by descent or distribution. A federal law was passed providing that no undivided fractional interest in Indian lands should descend by intestacy or devise, but instead should escheat to the tribe, if it represented less than 2 percent of the tract concerned and earned its owner less than one hundred dollars per year.

As summarized in a November 5, 1986, letter from Justice Powell to Justice Stevens, "A clear majority at [the *Hodel*] Conference voted to affirm [the decision striking down the law], but there was considerable diversity of opinion as to the basis of the Court's decision." The opinion was assigned to Justice Stevens, who circulated a draft opinion of the Court early in November 1986, reprinted on page 68, holding the law invalid.

The government had argued that this case involved regulation, not a taking for which compensation had to be paid. "In this case," the Stevens draft pointed out, "the Secretary argues that no taking has occurred because the legislature had broad power to regulate the manner and terms upon which property may be transmitted at death, as well as the authority to prescribe who shall and who shall not be capable of inheriting it." Since the legislation was a reasonable exercise of Congress's power to regulate Indian property interests, the government claimed, it involved only regulation, not a taking.

The Stevens draft did not, however, deal with the question of whether or not a "taking" was effected. It avoided that issue by holding the statute invalid on the ground that it constituted a deprivation of property without due process of law. Due process, Justice Stevens asserted, requires "giving a property owner fair notice of a major change in the rules governing the disposition of his property." That is necessary to provide the property owner with an opportunity to avoid or mitigate the consequences of the deprivation.

The Stevens draft conclusion was "We hold that § 207 deprived decedents of due process of law by failing to provide an adequate 'grace period' in which they could arrange for the consolidation of fractional interests in order to avoid abandonment." Because of this holding, "we need not reach the ground . . . that the escheat of abandoned property would effect a taking of private property for public use without just compensation."

2nd DRAFT

SUPREME COURT OF THE UNITED STATES

No. 85-637

DONALD P. HODEL, SECRETARY OF THE INTERIOR *v.* MARY IRVING ET AL.

ON APPEAL FROM THE UNITED STATES COURT OF APPEALS FOR THE EIGHTH CIRCUIT

[November ——, 1986]

JUSTICE STEVENS delivered the opinion of the Court.

Appellees, the designated heirs and devisees of three deceased members of the Oglala Sioux Tribe, brought suit in District Court to enjoin a statutory "escheat" to the Tribe of their decedents' fractional land interests. The District Court held that the statute in question, § 207 of the Indian Land Consolidation Act of 1983, 96 Stat. 2517, 25 U. S. C. § 2206, does not infringe on any vested property right of the designated heirs and devisees. The Court of Appeals reversed, holding that § 207 violates the Fifth Amendment to the Constitution because it effects a taking of property without providing any compensation to the estate of the former owner.[1] *Irving* v. *Clark*, 758 F. 2d 1260 (CA8 1985). We noted probable jurisdiction of the Secretary of the Interior's appeal, —— U. S. —— (1986), and we now affirm.

I

Towards the end of the 19th century, Congress enacted a series of land Acts which divided the communal reservations of Indian tribes into individual allotments for Indians and unallotted lands for non-Indian settlement. See *Solem* v.

[1] The Fifth Amendment to the Constitution provides that no person shall "be deprived of life, liberty, or property, without due process of law; nor shall private property be taken for public use, without just compensation."

HODEL *v.* IRVING

Bartlett, 465 U. S. 463, 466–467 (1984). Two years after the enactment of the General Allotment Act of 1887, ch. 119, 24 Stat. 388 *et seq.*, Congress adopted a specific statute authorizing the division of the Great Reservation of the Sioux Nation into separate reservations and the allotment of specific tracts of reservation land to individual Indians. Act of Mar. 2, 1889, ch. 405, 25 Stat. 888 *et seq.* In order to protect the allottees from the improvident disposition of their lands to white settlers, the Sioux allotment statute provided that the allotted lands were to be held in trust by the United States. 25 Stat. 891. Until 1910 the lands of deceased allottees passed to their heirs "according to the laws of the State or Territory" where the land was located, 25 Stat. 891, and after 1910, allottees were permitted to dispose of their interests by will in accordance with regulations promulgated by the Secretary. Those regulations generally served to protect Indian ownership of the allotted lands.

As generations passed and Indian decedents' estates were divided among multiple heirs, the interests in many tracts of allotted lands were divided and subdivided into increasingly smaller fractional shares. The highly fractionated ownership of many tracts tended to diminish their value and to impose significant administrative burdens on the Bureau of Indian Affairs. To redress these problems as they affected the Devils Lake Sioux Tribe of North Dakota, the Senate in 1982 passed a special bill for the purpose of authorizing this tribe to adopt a land consolidation program with the approval of the Secretary of the Interior.[2] That bill provided that the tribe would compensate individual owners for any fractional interest that might be acquired; the bill did not contain any provision for escheat.[3]

[2] S. 503, 97th Cong., 2d Sess. (1982).

[3] The Report of the Senate Select Committee on Indian Affairs described the purpose of the Bill as follows:

"The purpose of S. 503 is to authorize the purchase, sale, and exchange of lands by the Devils Lake Sioux Tribe of the Devils Lake Sioux Reserva-

When the Senate Bill was considered by the House Committee on Indian Affairs, the Committee expanded the coverage of the legislation to authorize any Indian tribe to adopt a land consolidation program with the approval of the Secretary, and it also added § 207—the escheat provision at issue in this case—to the Bill. H. Rep. 97–908, 97th Cong., 2d Sess., 5, 9 (1982).[4] The report on the House Amendments does not specifically discuss § 207. In its general explanation of how Indian trust or restricted lands pass out of Indian ownership, resulting in a need for statutory authorization to tribes to enact laws to prevent the erosion of Indian land ownership, the Report unqualifiedly stated that, "if an Indian allottee dies intestate, his heirs will inherit his property, whether they are Indian or non-Indian." *Id.*, at 11.

The House returned the amended bill to the Senate, which accepted the House addition without hearings and without any floor discussion of § 207. 128 Cong. Rec. S. 15568–S. 15570 (Dec. 19, 1982). Section 207 provided:

---

tion, North Dakota. The bill is designed to allow the Tribe to consolidate land ownership with the reservation in order to maximize utilization of the reservation land base. The bill also would restrict inheritance of trust property to members of the Tribe provided that the Tribe paid fair market value to the Secretary of the Interior on behalf of the decedent's estate." S. Rep. 97–507, 97th Cong., 2d Sess., 3 (1982).

[4] The House additions were themselves an amended version of H. R. 5856, the Indian Land Consolidation Act. H. Rep. 97–908, 97th Cong., 2d Sess., 9 (1982). The House Committee on Interior and Insular Affairs had held hearings on H. R. 5856, but these hearings were not published. H. R. Legislative Calendar, Comm. on Interior and Insular Affairs, 97th Cong., 2d Sess., 72 (1982).

The purposes of the legislation were summarized by the House Committee on Interior and Insular Affairs as (1) to provide mechanisms for the tribes to consolidate their tribal landholdings; (2) to allow Indian tribes or allottees to buy all of the fractionated interests in the tracts without having to obtain the consent of all the owners; and (3) to keep trust lands in Indian ownership by allowing tribes to restrict inheritance of Indian lands to Indians. H. Rep. 97–908, *supra*, at 9–11.

HODEL *v.* IRVING

> "No undivided fractional interest in any tract of trust or restricted land within a tribe's reservation or otherwise subjected to a tribe's jurisdiction shall [descend][5] by intestacy or devise but shall escheat to that tribe if such interest represents 2 per centum or less of the total acreage in such tract and has earned to its owner less than $100 in the preceding year before it is due to escheat."

In the text of the Act, Congress took pains to specify that fractional interests acquired by a tribe pursuant to an approved plan must be purchased at a fair price. See §§204, 205, and 206. There is no comparable provision in §207. The text of the Act also does not explain why Congress made no provision of a grace period for consolidation of the fractional interests that "escheat" to the tribe pursuant to that section.

The statute was signed into law on January 12, 1983, and became effective immediately. On March 2, the Bureau of Indian Affairs of the Department of the Interior issued a memorandum to all its area directors to advise them of the enactment of §207 and to provide them with interim instructions pending the promulgation of formal regulations. The memorandum explained:

> "Section 207 effects a major change in testate and intestate heirship succession for certain undivided fractional interests in trust and restricted Indian land. Under this section, certain interests in land, as explained below, will no longer be capable of descending by intes-

[5] The word "descedent"—an obvious error—appears in the original text. The Act of Oct. 30, 1984, 98 Stat. 3171—which is not relevant to our consideration of this case—corrected the error by substituting the word "descend" for "descedent" in §207. The Senate Report accompanying the Act described how "descedent" made its way into the 1983 statute: "[T]he bill actually voted on by the House and Senate was garbled in the printing. It was this garbled version of Title II that was signed by the President." S. Rep. 98-632, 98th Cong., 2d Sess., 2 (1984).

HODEL *v.* IRVING

> tate succession or being devised by will. Such property interests will, upon the death of the current owner, escheat to the tribe.
>
> . . . . .
>
> "Because Section 207 of P. L. 97–459 constitutes a major change in Indian heirship succession, Area Offices and Agencies are urged to provide all Indian landowners under their jurisdiction with notice of its effects."[6]

The memorandum then explained how Indian landowners who wanted their heirs or devisees, rather than the tribe, to acquire their fractional interests could avoid the impact of § 207. It outlined three ways by which the owner of a fractional interest of less than two percent of a tract could enlarge that interest to more than two percent.[7]

The three appellees—Mary Irving, Patrick Pumpkin Seed, and Eileen Bissonette—are enrolled members of the Oglala Sioux Tribe. They represent heirs or devisees of members of the tribe who died in March or April 1983.[8] At the time of

[6] App. to Juris. Statement 38a–39a.

[7] The memorandum stated:

"To assure the effectiveness of a will or heirship succession under state law, any Indian owner within the above category (if he or she is concerned that the tribe rather than his or her heirs or devisees will take these interests) may purchase additional interests from coowners pursuant to 25 CFR 151.7 and thereby increase his/her ownership interest to more than two percent. Another alternative is for such an owner to convey his/her interest to coowners or relatives pursuant to 25 CFR 152.25 and reserve a life estate, thus retaining the benefits of the interest while assuring its continued individual, rather than tribal, ownership. A third alternative, if feasible, is to partition the tract in such a way as to enlarge the owner's interest in a portion of said tract.

"Indians falling within the above category and who are presently occupying, or in any other way using, the tract in question should especially be advised of the aforementioned alternatives." *Id.*, at 39a–40a.

[8] Mary Irving is the daughter of Chester Irving who died on March 18, 1983, see App. 18; Eileen Bissonette is the guardian for the five minor children of Geraldine Mary Poor Bear-Little Hoop Cross who died on March 23, 1983, see App. 21; and Patrick Pumpkin Seed is the son of Charles Le-

HODEL *v.* IRVING

their deaths, the decedents owned 41 fractional interests subject to the provisions of § 207. App. 20, 22–28, 32–33, 37–39. The size and value of those interests varied widely—the smallest was a 1/3645 interest in a 320-acre tract, having an estimated value of only $12.30, whereas the largest was the equivalent of three and one-half acres valued at $284.44. App. 22 and 23. If § 207 is valid, all of those interests "escheated" to the Tribe; if § 207 had not been enacted—or if it is invalid—the interests would have passed to the appellees.

Appellees filed suit in the United States District Court for the District of South Dakota, claiming that § 207 resulted in a taking of property without just compensation in violation of the Fifth Amendment. Although it expressed misgivings about the wisdom and the practical effect of the legislation,[9] the District Court concluded that the statute was constitutional. It held that the appellees had no vested interest in the property of the decedents prior to their deaths and that Congress has plenary authority to abolish the power of testamentary disposition of Indian property and to alter the rules of intestate succession. App. to Juris. Statement 21a–26a.

The Court of Appeals for the Eighth Circuit reversed. Although it agreed that the appellees had no vested rights in the decedents' property, it concluded that their decedents

---

roy Pumpkin Seed who died on April 2, 1983, see App. 34, and the nephew of Edgar Pumpkin Seed who died on June 23, 1983.

[9] "This Court is bound to apply the law as it finds the law. But, this Court does not agree, nor does it have to agree, with the policy that is implemented by the passage of legislation such as 25 U. S. C. § 2206.

"Following section 2206 to its logical conclusion, all trust or restricted land will escheat to the Oglala Sioux Tribe; it is only a matter of time. The argument that this result will benefit the Indian population as a whole is simply not valid in this Court's experience. The benefits derived from these lands do not filter down to the vast majority of the Indian people on the Pine Ridge Indian Reservation. In this respect, the system is not functioning as contemplated. Congress would be well-advised to examine closely the practical effect of legislation such as 25 U. S. C. § 2206." App. to Juris. Statement 25a.

had a right, derived from the original Sioux Allotment Statute, to control the disposition of their property at death. The court held that the appellees had standing to invoke that right and that its taking without compensation to decedents' estates violated the Fifth Amendment.

II

The Court of Appeals concluded that appellees have standing to challenge § 207. 758 F. 2d, at 1267–1268. The Government does not contest this ruling. As the Court of Appeals recognized, however, the existence of a case or controversy is a jurisdictional prerequisite to a federal court's deliberations. *Id.*, at 1267 n. 12. We are satisfied that the necessary case or controversy exists between the parties in this case. Appellees' particularized injury is that the operation of § 207 has deprived them of the fractional interests they would otherwise have inherited.[10] In light of the familial and testamentary relationships between appellees and their decedents, we conclude that appellees have alleged a sufficient economic injury in fact as a result of the challenged statute to satisfy the case or controversy requirement of Art. III of the United States Constitution. See *Singleton* v. *Wulff*, 428 U. S. 106, 112 (1976).

Beyond the limitations on standing imposed by the constitutional requirement that a case or controversy exist, we have recognized prudential limitations on the challenges that a federal court may hear. These prudential limitations can-

[10] Appellees demonstrate that, had Congress not enacted § 207, or if § 207 were to be struck down, they would have inherited fractional interests from their respective decedents. Appellee Mary Irving alleged that she would become an actual heir to her father, Chester Irving, absent the discovery of a will or contrary evidence bearing on her relationship to her father. Appellee Eileen Bissonette is the guardian of five minor children to whom their mother, Geraldine Mary Poor Bear-Little Hoop Cross, left all her worldly goods by will. Appellee Patrick Pumpkin Seed alleged that he was a potential heir of his father, Charles Leroy Pumpkin Seed, and of his uncle, Patrick Pumpkin Seed. App. 12–14.

HODEL *v.* IRVING

not be viewed as one unchanging set of hurdles which each litigant must clear regardless of the relationships among the parties, the non-parties, and the asserted rights. Prudential standing doctrines simply express in their various formulations "a healthy concern that if the claim is brought by someone other than one at whom the constitutional protection is aimed, the claim not be an abstract, generalized grievance that the courts are neither well equipped nor well advised to adjudicate." *Secretary of State* v. *Joseph H. Munson Co.*, 467 U. S. 947, 955 n. 5 (1984). Appellees rest their claim to relief primarily on the legal rights or interests of their decedents. Since practical obstacles obviously prevent the parties whose rights are at issue from asserting these rights on their own behalf, we inquire whether appellees "can reasonably be expected properly to frame the issues and present them with the necessary adversarial zeal." *Id.*, at 956.

We agree with the Court of Appeals' conclusion that appellees present the issues as concretely, and contest them as vigorously, as their decedents would have before their death. 758 F. 2d, at 1268. Appellees and their decedents are linked in an indissoluble identity of interest; the decedents' interest in disposing of their fractional interests by will or intestate succession to their heirs and devisees exactly coincides with those individuals' interest in receiving the property. A vindication of decedents' rights would ensure that the fractional interests pass to appellees; pressing these rights unsuccessfully would equally guarantee that appellees take nothing. The interests of decedents and appellees do not and will not diverge. We therefore find no constitutional or prudential barriers to our consideration of this case.

III

In this case, the Secretary argues that no taking has occurred because the legislature has broad power to regulate the manner and terms upon which property may be transmitted at death, as well as the authority to prescribe who shall

HODEL *v.* IRVING

and who shall not be capable of inheriting it. The Secretary does not, however, contend that this power is unlimited. Nor does he suggest that it is permissible to modify the individual's presently recognized right to dispose of his property at death without giving him a reasonable opportunity to make inter vivos dispositions that will avoid the consequences of a newly enacted change in the laws of intestacy and testamentary disposition. Rather, the Secretary argues that special features of this legislation make it a reasonable exercise of Congress' power to regulate Indian property interests.

The Secretary places great emphasis on the minimal value of the property interests affected by § 207, the legitimacy of the governmental purpose in consolidating such interests, and the fact that the tribe, rather than the United States, is the beneficiary of the so-called "escheat." A brief comment on each of these points is appropriate.

The value of a property interest does not provide a yardstick for measuring "the scope of the dual constitutional guarantees that there be no taking of property without just compensation, and no deprivation of property without the due process of law." *Texaco, Inc.* v. *Short*, 454 U. S. 516, 540–541 (BRENNAN, J., dissenting). The sovereign has no license to take private property without paying for it and without providing its owner with any opportunity to avoid or mitigate the consequences of the deprivation simply because the property is relatively inexpensive. *Loretto* v. *Teleprompter Manhattan CATV Corp.*, 458 U. S. 419, 436–437 & 438 n.16 (1982). The Fifth Amendment draws no distinction between grand larceny and petty larceny.

The legitimacy of the governmental purposes served by § 207 demonstrates that the statute is not arbitrary, see *Delaware Tribal Business Committee* v. *Weeks*, 430 U. S. 73 (1977), and that the alleged "taking" is for a valid "public use" within the meaning of the Fifth Amendment. Those facts, however, do not excuse or mitigate whatever obligation to

HODEL *v.* IRVING

pay just compensation is imposed by the Constitution. Nor does it lessen the importance of giving a property owner fair notice of a major change in the rules governing the disposition of his property.

The fact that § 207 provides for an "escheat" to the tribe rather than to the United States does not change the impact of the statute on an individual Indian who wants to leave his property to his children. Moreover, the use of the term "escheat" in § 207 differs in a substantial way from the more familiar uses of that term. At common law the property of a person who died intestate and without lawful heirs would escheat to the sovereign; thus the doctrine provided a mechanism for determining ownership of what otherwise would have been abandoned property. In contrast, under § 207 the statutory escheat supersedes the rights of persons who would otherwise inherit the property. Legislation has authorized the escheat of unclaimed property, such as real estate, bank accounts, and other earmarked funds, after an appropriate lapse of time and the provision of adequate notice to make sure that the property could fairly be treated as abandoned.[11] Section 207, in contrast, contains no mechanism to ensure

[11] For example, the Government both provides a grace period and bears an affirmative responsibility to prevent escheat in the distribution of funds to which enrolled members of the Peoria Tribe are statutorily entitled under 25 U. S. C. § 1222 (1982). See 25 U. S. C. § 1226 ("Any per capita share, whether payable to a living enrollee or to the heirs or legatees of a deceased enrollee, which the Secretary of the Interior is unable to deliver within two years after the date the check is issued . . . shall revert to the Peoria Tribe.")

State statutes governing abandoned property typically provide for a grace period and notice. See, *e. g.*, N. Y. Aband. Prop. Law §§ 300–302 (McKinney Supp. 1986) (property held by banking organizations); Ill. Rev. Stat., ch. 141, ¶¶ 102, 112 (1986) (property held by banking or financial organizations). Statutes governing the escheat of property of decedents intestate and without heirs also provide for notice and an opportunity for interested parties to assert their claims. See, *e. g.*, Cal. Civ. Proc. Code Ann. §§ 1420, 1423 (West 1982); Tex. Prop. Code Ann. §§ 71.101–71.106 (1984 & Supp. 1986).

that a fractional interest may fairly be considered abandoned before the "escheat" takes place.

Arguably, § 207 might be regarded as a statute imposing a duty on the owner of highly fractionated interests in allotted lands to consolidate his interests with those of other owners of similar interests. The method of enforcing such a duty is to treat its nonperformance during the owner's lifetime as an abandonment of the fractional interest. In turn, this abandonment might justify an escheat of the abandoned interest. Cf. *Texaco, Inc.* v. *Short*, 454 U. S. 516, 529 (1982). As we recognized in *United States* v. *Locke*, —— U. S. ——, —— n. 20 (1985), "[l]egislatures can enact substantive rules of law that treat property as forfeited under conditions that the common-law would not consider sufficient to indicate abandonment." These rules, however, are only reasonable if they afford sufficient notice to the property owners and a reasonable opportunity to comply. *Ibid.*

The Due Process Clause of the Fifth Amendment thus applies to § 207's determination of which acts and omissions constitute an abandonment as well as to the statutory escheat of property which is deemed abandoned. We hold that § 207 deprived decedents of due process of law by failing to provide an adequate "grace period" in which they could arrange for the consolidation of fractional interests in order to avoid abandonment. Because we find the statutory presumption of abandonment to be invalid under the precise facts of this case, we need not reach the ground relied upon by the Court of Appeals—that the escheat of abandoned property would effect a taking of private property for public use without just compensation.

In *Texaco, Inc., supra*, we sustained the constitutionality of Indiana's Mineral Lapse Act, a statute that extinguished an interest in coal, oil, or other minerals that had not been used for twenty years. Critical to our decision was the fact that an owner could readily avoid the risk of abandonment in

HODEL *v.* IRVING

a variety of ways,[12] and the further fact that the statute afforded the affected property owners a reasonable opportunity to familiarize themselves with its terms and to comply with its provisions. We explained:

> "The first question raised is simply how a legislature must go about advising its citizens of actions that must be taken to avoid a valid rule of law that a mineral interest that has not been used for 20 years will be deemed to be abandoned. The answer to this question is no different from that posed for any legislative enactment affecting substantial rights. Generally, a legislature need do nothing more than enact and publish the law, and afford the citizenry a reasonable opportunity to familiarize itself with its terms and to comply. In this case, the 2-year grace period included in the Indiana statute forecloses any argument that the statute is invalid because mineral owners may not have had an opportunity to become familiar with its terms. It is well established that persons owning property within a State are charged with knowledge of relevant statutory provisions affecting the

[12] "These decisions clearly establish that the State of Indiana has the power to enact the kind of legislation at issue. In each case, the Court upheld the power of the State to condition the retention of a property right upon the performance of an act within a limited period of time. In each instance, as a result of the failure of the property owner to perform the statutory condition, an interest in fee was deemed as a matter of law to be abandoned and to lapse.

"It is also clear that the state has not exercised this power in an arbitrary manner. The Indiana statute provides that a severed mineral interest shall not terminate if its owner takes any one of three steps to establish his continuing interest in the property. If the owner engages in actual production, or collects rents or royalties from another person who does or proposes to do so, his interest is protected. If the owner pays taxes, no matter how small, the interest is secure. If the owner files a written statement of claim in the county recorder's office, the interest remains viable. Only if none of these actions is taken for a period of 20 years does a mineral interest lapse and revert to the surface owner." 454 U. S., at 529.

HODEL *v.* IRVING

control or disposition of such property." 454 U. S., at 531–532.[13]

We may assume that the Congress has ample power to require the owners of fractional interests in allotted lands to consolidate their holdings during their lifetimes or to face the risk that their interests will be deemed to have been abandoned and still conclude that no such abandonment may occur unless the owners have a fair opportunity to avoid that consequence. In this case, it is palpably clear that they were denied such an opportunity.

This statute became effective the day it was signed into law. It took almost two months for the Bureau of Indian Affairs to distribute an interim memorandum advising its area directors of the major change in Indian heirship succession effected by § 207. *Supra*, at ——. Although that memorandum identified three ways in which Indian landowners could avoid the consequences of § 207, it is not reasonable to assume that appellees' decedents—who died on March 18, March 23, and April 4, 1983—had anything approaching a

[13] Earlier in the opinion we noted that in *Wilson* v. *Iseminger*, 185 U. S. 55 (1902), the Court had upheld a Pennsylvania statute that provided for the extinguishment of certain interests in realty "since the statute contained a reasonable grace period in which owners could protect their rights." *Id.*, at 527 n. 21. We quoted the following passage from the *Wilson* case:

"It may be properly conceded that all statutes of limitation must proceed on the idea that the party has full opportunity afforded him to try his right in the courts. A statute could not bar the existing rights of claimants without affording this opportunity; if it should attempt to do so, it would not be a statute of limitations, but an unlawful attempt to extinguish rights arbitrarily, whatever might be the purport of its provisions. It is essential that such statutes allow a reasonable time after they take effect for the commencement of suits upon existing causes of action; though what shall be considered a reasonable time must be settled by the judgment of the legislature, and the courts will not inquire into the wisdom of its decision in establishing the period of legal bar, unless the time allowed is manifestly so insufficient that the statute becomes a denial of justice."

HODEL *v.* IRVING

reasonable opportunity to arrange for the consolidation of their respective fractional interests with those of other owners. Whether the inclusion of a reasonable grace period would suffice to sustain the constitutionality of a statute like this is a question we need not decide on the present record.[14] With respect to these appellees' decedents "the time allowed is manifestly so insufficient that the statute becomes a denial of justice." *Wilson* v. *Iseminger*, 185 U. S., at 63.[15]

While citizens "are presumptively charged with knowledge of the law," *Atkins* v. *Parker*, —— U. S. ——, —— (1985), that presumption may not apply when "the statute does not allow a sufficient 'grace period' to provide the persons affected by a change in the law with an adequate opportunity to become familiar with their obligations under it." *Id.*, at —— (citing *Texaco, Inc.*, 454 U. S., at 532.) Unlike the food-stamp recipients in *Parker*, who received a grace period of over 90 days and individual notice of the substance of the new law, —— U. S. at ——, the Indians affected by § 207 did not receive a reasonable grace period. Nothing in the record suggests that appellees' decedents received the individual notice which the Bureau of Indian Affairs urged its area

[14] The legislative history of the Indian Land Consolidation Act of 1983 is mute with respect to § 207. See n. 4, *supra*. This silence is illuminating; it suggests that Indian landowners cannot reasonably be expected to have received notice about the statute before it took effect and to have arranged their affairs accordingly. The lack of legislative history concerning § 207 also demonstrates that Congress paid scant or no attention to whether, in light of its long-standing fiduciary obligation to Indians, it was constitutionally required to afford a reasonable post-enactment "grace period" for compliance.

[15] A statute which denies the affected party a reasonable opportunity to avoid the consequences of non-compliance may work an injustice similar to that of invalid retroactive legislation. In both instances, the party who "could have anticipated the potential liability attaching to his chosen course of conduct would have avoided the liability by altering his conduct." *Usery* v. *Turner Elkhorn Mining Co.*, 428 U. S. 1, 17 (1976) (citing *Welch* v. *Henry*, 305 U. S. 134, 147 (1938)). See also *United States* v. *Hemme*, —— U. S. ——, —— (1986) (following *Welch* v. *Henry*, *supra*).

directors to provide; nothing in the record contradicts the possibility that appellees only became aware of the statute upon receiving notices that hearings had been scheduled for the week of October 24, 1983 to determine if their decedents' tribe had a right through escheat to any lands that might otherwise have passed to appellees. 758 F. 2d, at 1262.[16]

Our conclusion that Congress has failed to provide appellees' decedents with a reasonable opportunity for compliance implies no rejection of Congress' plenary authority over the affairs and the property of Indians. The Constitution vests Congress with plenary power "to deal with the special problems of Indians." *Morton* v. *Mancari*, 417 U. S. 535, 551 (1974). We agree with the Secretary's own recognition, however, that the Government's plenary power over the property of Indians 'is subject to constitutional limitations.' Brief of the Secretary of the Interior 24–25. The Due Process of the Fifth Amendment required Congress to afford reasonable notice and opportunity for compliance to Indians that § 207 would prevent fractional interests in land from descending by intestate or testate succession.[17] In omitting any opportunity at all for owners of fractional interests to order their affairs in light of § 207, Congress has failed to afford the affected Indians the due process of law required by the Fifth Amendment.

The judgment of the Court of Appeals is

Affirmed.

---

[16] The notices were issued on October 4, 1983, after the death of appellees' decedents. This notice afforded no opportunity for decedents to comply with § 207 or for appellees to advise their decedents of the possibility of escheat.

[17] We need express no view on the constitutionality of § 207 as amended by the Act of Oct. 30, 1984, 98 Stat. 3171. All of the interests of appellees' decedents at issue in this case are governed by the original version of § 207. The decedents all died between January 12, 1983 and October 30, 1984, the period in which the original version of § 207 was in effect. The parties in this case present no case or controversy with respect to the application of the *amended* version of § 207.

4th DRAFT

SUPREME COURT OF THE UNITED STATES

No. 85-637

DONALD P. HODEL, SECRETARY OF THE INTERIOR, APPELLANT *v.* MARY IRVING ET AL.

ON APPEAL FROM THE UNITED STATES COURT OF APPEALS FOR THE EIGHTH CIRCUIT

[March —, 1987]

JUSTICE SCALIA, with whom THE CHIEF JUSTICE and JUSTICE POWELL join, concurring.

I do not believe the Court should decide whether § 207 of the Indian Land Consolidation Act of 1983, 96 Stat. 2517, 25 U. S. C. § 2206, violates the due process clause of the Fifth Amendment—a question not raised or argued at any stage of this litigation. To strike down an Act of Congress on a ground that the Secretary has not even had an opportunity to address displays, in my view, inadequate respect for both the coordinate branches of government. Conversely, it seems to me that we should decide the question the parties did brief and argue both here and below: whether § 207 effects a taking of property without just compensation, in violation of the Fifth Amendment.

I

Appellees contended below that by virtue of the statute they were themselves deprived of property protected by the Fifth Amendment. The Court of Appeals properly rejected that contention. When the statute was enacted, none of the members of the Tribe from whom appellees would have received the property by will or intestacy had died. Appellees' interest in the property was therefore entirely contingent, since the then-provided disposition could have been altered at any time by their decedents' making or changing their wills, see 25 U. S. C. §§ 373, 464 (1982), or by change in the gov-

HODEL *v.* IRVING

erning law of intestate disposition, see Act of Mar. 2, 1889, ch. 405, § 11, 25 Stat. 888, 891. Enactment of the statute, therefore, deprived appellees of "a mere unilateral expectation," *Webb's Fabulous Pharmacies, Inc.* v. *Beckwith*, 449 U. S. 155, 161 (1980), that does not constitute a property right within the meaning of the Fifth Amendment. *Ibid.* See *Irving Trust Co.* v. *Day*, 314 U. S. 556, 562 (1942); *Jefferson* v. *Fink*, 247 U. S. 288, 293–294 (1918).

Appellees attempted to argue that, even though potential heirs ordinarily do not have a property right, the trust patents given to the Oglala Sioux gave heirs a vested interest. As the Court of Appeals determined, the language of the statute providing for the patents will not bear that interpretation. *Irving* v. *Clark*, 758 F. 2d 1260, 1265 (CA8 1985). The Oglala patents were to declare

> "that the United States does and will hold the lands thus allotted . . . in trust for the sole use and benefit of the Indian to whom such allotment shall have been made, or, in case of his decease, of his heirs according to the laws of the State or Territory where such land is located . . . *Provided further*, That the law of descent and partition in force in the State or Territory where the lands may be situated shall apply thereto . . . ." Act of Mar. 2, 1889, ch. 405, § 11, 25 Stat. 888, 891.

That cannot reasonably be interpreted to create vested rights in any particular heirs, since the heirs are to be determined in accordance with "the law of descent and partition in force in the State or Territory where the lands may be situated." *Ibid.* See *Jefferson* v. *Fink*, *supra*, at 293–294. Moreover, as the Court of Appeals noted, vested rights in prospective heirs are inconsistent with the Oglala Sioux' power to make wills, see 25 U. S. C. §§ 373, 464, upon the validity of which the claims of Elaine Bissonette, one of the appellees, are premised. *Irving* v. *Clark*, *supra*, 758 F. 2d, at 1265.

HODEL *v.* IRVING

II

Although before this Court appellees no longer assert that the Indian Land Consolidation Act violates their own constitutional rights, they do seek to defend the Eighth Circuit's conclusion that it violates the property rights of their decedents. Before reaching the merits of that claim, it is necessary to determine that appellees have standing to assert the rights of third parties.[1] I believe that they do, but would rest that conclusion on narrower grounds than JUSTICE STEVENS.

For obvious reasons, it has long been recognized that the surviving claims of a decedent must be pursued by a third party. As the Court of Appeals stated, if there is a right protected by the Fifth Amendment to pass property after death, one feature of that right must be that a claim arising from its violation survives the testator's death; otherwise, the right would be nugatory. *Irving* v. *Clark*, *supra*, 758 F. 2d, at 1267.

At common law, a decedent's surviving claims were prosecuted by the executor or administrator of the estate, depending on whether the decedent died testate or intestate. For Indians with trust property, statutes require the Secretary of the Interior to assume that general role. 25 U. S. C. §§ 371–380. The Secretary's responsibilities in that capacity, however, include the administration of the statute that appellees claim is unconstitutional, see 25 U. S. C. §§ 2201–2210, so that he can hardly be expected to assert appellees' decedents' rights to the extent they turn on that point.

Under these circumstances, appellees can appropriately serve as their decedents' representatives for purposes of asserting the latter's Fifth Amendment rights. They are best situated to pursue the claims vigorously, since their interest in receiving the property is indissolubly linked to the dece-

[1] For the reasons stated by JUSTICE STEVENS, *ante*, at 7 and n. 10, I agree that appellees have suffered injury in fact as a result of the statute.

HODEL *v.* IRVING

dents' right to dispose of it by will or intestacy. See *ante*, at 8. The view that they are the appropriate representatives is consistent with the Uniform Probate Code (West), which provides that where a testator has failed to select an executor in his will, or where a decedent has died intestate, devisees and heirs have priority for appointment as personal representatives of the decedent. § 3–203. In recognizing appellees' standing to assert their decedents' rights, the Court of Appeals effectively made an appointment of a personal representative of the decedents for purposes of this suit, just as a probate court would be required to do where the decedent has failed to select one, or where his selection is defective. *Cf. Tooahnipah* v. *Hickel*, 397 U. S. 598, 600 (1970) (Court assumed that where statute provided that a will could be approved by the Secretary of Interior "before or after the death of the testator," beneficiaries were the appropriate persons to seek approval of a will after death). Such an appointment is a "settled practice of the courts" that is an exception to the general rule that a litigant cannot raise the rights of third parties. *Tyler* v. *Judges of the Court of Registration*, 179 U. S. 405, 406 (1900).

III

As to the merits of the claims appellees assert on behalf of their decedents, it should first be noted that § 207 affected appellees' decedents' dispositions of their property at death in two ways. First, it changed the law of intestate succession by providing that the property would no longer descend by intestacy according to the law of the State where the property was located, but instead would escheat to the Tribe. Second, it precluded the decedents from having their property descend by will. The combined effect of these restrictions is to deprive appellees' decedents absolutely of all ability to have their property descend even to their children or close relatives after their death.

The Secretary suggests (without quite arguing) that a legislature has unlimited power to revise the law of succession,

HODEL *v.* IRVING

since it is of statutory creation. I know of no authority for that proposition.[2] In several cases we have stated that the legislative power to regulate succession and testamentary disposition is very broad. See, *e. g.*, *Irving Trust Co.* v. *Day*, *supra*, 314 U.S., at 562; *Magoun* v. *Illinois Trust & Savings Bank*, 170 U. S. 283, 288–291 (1898); *United States* v. *Perkins*, 163 U. S. 625, 628 (1896); *United States* v. *Fox*, 94 U. S. 315, 320–321 (1876); *Randall* v. *Kreiger*, 90 U. S. (23 Wall.) 137, 148 (1874); *Mager* v. *Grima*, 48 U. S. (8 How.) 490, 492–493 (1850). None of those cases involved Fifth Amendment claims, however, nor did any involve the rights of the decedent. Rather they were brought by would-be heirs or devisees in their own right. Moreover the statutes considered in those cases did not eliminate heirship completely, but merely altered the identity of the prospective heirs or imposed inheritance taxes. Nor did they come close to eliminating entirely the power to direct property by will. I am confident that in making these statements the Court did not have in mind the complete elimination of all power to leave property to one's family; and even if it did, the statements are plainly dicta.[3]

---

[2] Its logic, of course—that any right conferred by statute can be withdrawn by statute—is erroneous. It has long been established, for example, that statutory land grants cannot be revoked without running afoul of the constitutional prohibition on impairment of contracts. *Fletcher* v. *Peck*, 10 U. S. (6 Cranch) 87, 135–36 (1810). They may be revoked or impaired where the statutory grant has reserved that right. See *United States* v. *Fuller*, 409 U. S. 488 (1973). But there is no basis for finding such a right of revocation implicit in the statutes giving the Oglala Sioux the right to pass property to their descendants. Even a statutory tax exemption—a privilege ordinarily assumed to be held at the grace of the legislature—has been held not subject to an implicit right of repeal where (as here) Indians have given up other claims to obtain it. *Choate* v. *Trapp*, 224 U. S. 665 (1912). The right to leave property to one's family at death is a much more traditional property right, as to which a right of repeal is even less likely to have been implicitly retained.

[3] In light of the careful distinction of these cases in the last five sentences, I am perplexed by JUSTICE O'CONNOR's statement that she "can-

HODEL *v.* IRVING

The Secretary argues that since the present case does not involve physical appropriation or destruction of property, the Fifth Amendment question must be decided on the basis of the "ad hoc, factual inquir[y]" that we conduct when a state regulates the use of property. Brief for Appellant 30, quoting *Connolly* v. *Pension Benefit Guaranty Corp.*, —— U. S. —— (1986). I disagree. We have applied the "regulatory takings" approach to laws that have an incidental effect on property rights, but whose primary purpose is not to reallocate property. In that context, as the Court explained in *Penn Central Transportation Co.* v. *New York City*, 438 U. S. 104 (1978), it is necessary to determine "whether the interference with [the claimant's] property is of such magnitude that '*there must be an exercise of eminent domain* and compensation to sustain [it].'" *Id.*, at 136, *quoting Pennsylvania Coal Co.* v. *Mahon*, 260 U. S. 393, 413 (1922) (emphasis added).

It would be a dangerous expansion, however, to extend that approach beyond the incidental effects of the government's exercise of its regulatory powers, to what is substantially the exercise of eminent domain itself—that is, to government action that has as its very purpose the transfer of property ownership. And that is the situation we confront here. The present statute does not seek to further the public health, *Mugler* v. *Kansas*, 123 U. S. 623, 668–669 (1887), preserve historically significant structures, *Penn Central*, *supra*, at 132, or prevent the destruction of a valuable national resource, *Andrus* v. *Allard*, 444 U. S. 51, 53 (1979). Rather, as the Secretary explains, its purpose is to *create a new structure of ownership of land interests* that Congress believes will be more beneficial to Indians. Brief for Appellant 9–10. While we held in *Hawaii Housing Authority* v. *Midkiff*, 467 U. S. 229 (1984), that such an objective was a "public purpose" for which the eminent domain power could

[not] join [me] in disapproving" them. *Ante*, at ——.

HODEL *v.* IRVING

be used, we assuredly did not hold that Congress could pursue it by regulation, *instead of* through eminent domain. To the contrary, our holding that the law was constitutional was expressly conditioned on the "assum[ption] . . . that the weighty demand of just compensation has been met." *Id.*, at 245. Where, as here, Congress has expressly stated that its objective is to create a new ownership structure for particular property, and where that is the public purpose that the government invokes to defend the statute in litigation, it would seem to me extraordinary not to require the eminent domain power, with its attendant safeguard of compensation, to be employed. See *Keystone Bituminous Coal Ass'n* v. *De Benedictis*, —— U. S. —— (1987) (the purpose of the action is critical in assessing whether the government is required to proceed by eminent domain).

In my view, the requirement of proceeding by eminent domain should apply in all cases where the reallocation of property rights is the acknowledged purpose of the government action, no matter how insignificant those rights may be. That should at least be the rule, however, where the government abrogates a property right that is as central to ownership as is the power to pass on property after one's death. Like the power to exclude others involved in *Kaiser Aetna* v. *United States*, 444 U. S. 164 (1979), it is a traditionally understood concomitant of ownership. In one form or another, the right to pass on property—to one's family in particular—has been part of the Anglo-American legal system since feudal times, even when property owners held their land by virtue of the grace of the King. See A. Simpson, An Introduction to the History of the Land Law 54–60, 171 (1961). In fact, as we have noted, "the general consent of the most enlightened nations has, from the earliest historical period, recognized a natural right in children to inherit the property of their parents." *United States* v. *Perkins*, *supra*, at 628. The Founding Fathers regarded the right to pass on property as so important that its elimination as a criminal penalty

HODEL *v.* IRVING

is proscribed by the Constitution, even as a penalty for treason. See Art. III, sec. 3, cl. 2 ("no Attainder of Treason shall work Corruption of Blood"). While we have long recognized the legitimacy of many forms of regulation of that right, its total abrogation withdraws from the owner "one of the most essential sticks in the bundle of rights that are commonly characterized as property." *Kaiser Aetna*, *supra*, at 176.[4] Thus, in *Choate* v. *Trapp*, 224 U. S. 665 (1912), this Court said, by way of exemplifying what would constitute a quintessential taking, that "[n]o statute would have been valid which reduced [the owner's] fee to a life estate." *Id.*, at 674. The statute at issue here does almost precisely that.[5]

The Secretary contends that the takings clause may be avoided because the land goes to the Tribe rather than to the United States. There is no authority for that proposition. The fact that appellees may benefit somewhat more from the land's reversion to the Tribe than they would from its appropriation by the government might, if proven, justify an offset in determining the level of compensation. But the "reciprocity of advantage" principle of *Pennsylvania Coal* v. *Mahon*, 260 U. S. 393, 415 (1922) and the dissent in *Penn Central*, 438 U. S., at 140, requires that the burden be spread as

[4] The Secretary also argues that appellees have not really been deprived of their right to transfer property at death, because they can convey the remainder *inter vivos* and retain a life estate. That is of course not equivalent to passing property at death, since the *inter vivos* transfer is effective immediately and irrevocably, whereas a devisor may change his mind and revoke his disposition until his death. In any event, the suggested transaction would have to be approved by the Secretary of the Interior, 25 CFR § 152.25, who would have ample grounds for disapproving it (indeed, might be compelled to disapprove it) on the ground that it would frustrate the policies of the statute at issue here.

[5] Since the owners of fractionated shares retain a limited right to convey more than a life estate, see 25 CFR § 152.25, as well as to engage in a few other complicated transactions that at least in theory may avoid escheat at their death, see 25 CFR §§ 151.7, 152.33, they have not lost all interest in the remainder. But that retained interest is negligible.

HODEL *v.* IRVING

broadly as the benefit, a state of affairs that nobody has contended is present here.

JUSTICE O'CONNOR criticizes the approach to appellees' claims advanced here as "creating a novel 'bright-line' rule." *Ante*, at ——. I will not remark upon the "bright-line" characterization, except to note my regret that it should be used as a term of reproach—particularly in this field, where clear rules are in such short supply that we have described our takings clause jurisprudence as a series of "essentially ad hoc factual inquiries." *Kaiser Aetna* v. *United States*, *supra*, at 175. But insofar as novelty is concerned, it seems to me that JUSTICE O'CONNOR's approach exemplifies that quality better than mine. For while it purports to adhere to traditional "regulatory taking" analysis, it effectively overrules without mention the unanimous decision of this Court in *Andrus* v. *Allard*, *supra*. In that case we held that an endangered-species regulatory statute forbidding owners of legally acquired bald or golden eagles or eagle parts from disposing of them by sale was not a sufficient restriction on property rights to constitute a taking because "appellees retain the right to possess and transport their property, and to donate or devise the protected birds." 444 U. S., at 66. Appellees here similarly retain the right to possess their property, as well as a limited right to transfer it *inter vivos* by gift or sale. It seems to me impossible to argue that abrogation of their right to transfer it after death is a greater interference with property than abrogation of the *Allard* appellees' right to sell it during life, or that the former right is constitutionally more significant than the latter. If *Allard* is to be overruled, it should not be done *sub silentio*, nor do I think it necessary to confront that question in the present case. The approach I have taken distinguishes *Allard* on the basis that, while the right there at issue was equivalently important, it was eliminated to effectuate environmental regulation, and not (as here) for the avowed purpose of transferring the property to someone else.

HODEL *v.* IRVING

The government's policies on Indian ownership have shifted with every political and intellectual breeze. One of the purposes of electing legislatures is to make such shifts possible, and there is nothing constitutionally suspect about their occurrence. But if the government's new policy requires the extinction of pre-existing property rights, justice and fairness require that the costs imposed by that policy be borne by society at large, and not by appellees. I would therefore affirm the Court of Appeals' ruling that Section 207 violates the Fifth Amendment.[6]

[6] I agree with JUSTICE STEVENS that the Court of Appeals erred in deciding the constitutionality of the amended statute. *Ante*, at 14, n. 17.

3rd DRAFT

SUPREME COURT OF THE UNITED STATES

No. 85-637

DONALD P. HODEL, SECRETARY OF THE INTERIOR, APPELLANT *v.* MARY IRVING ET AL.

ON APPEAL FROM THE UNITED STATES COURT OF APPEALS FOR THE EIGHTH CIRCUIT

[March ——, 1987]

JUSTICE O'CONNOR, with whom JUSTICE BRENNAN, JUSTICE MARSHALL, and JUSTICE BLACKMUN join, concurring in the judgment.

I agree with JUSTICE SCALIA that the Court should not examine the constitutionality of § 207 of the Indian Land Consolidation Act[1] under the Due Process Clause of the Fifth Amendment, since that issue has been neither briefed nor argued to the Court. I also agree that appellees have standing to mount a constitutional attack on § 207, and that § 207 as originally enacted effects a taking of property without just compensation in violation of the Just Compensation Clause. But I cannot join JUSTICE SCALIA in creating a novel "bright-line" rule prohibiting Government regulation without compensation:

> "in all cases where the reallocation of property rights is the acknowledged purpose of the Government action, no

[1] Pub. L. 97-459, Tit. II, 98 Stat. 2517-2519. Section 207 provided:

"No undivided fractional interest in any tract of trust or restricted land within a tribe's reservation or otherwise subjected to a tribe's jurisdiction shall descedent *[sic]* by intestacy or devise but shall escheat to that tribe if such interest represents 2 per centum or less of the total acreage in such tract and has earned to its owner less than $100 in the preceding year before it is due to escheat."

The law has been substantially amended and § 207 is codified in its amended version at 25 U. S. C. § 2206 (1982 ed., Supp. III).

HODEL *v.* IRVING

> matter how insignificant those rights may be . . . at least . . . where the Government abrogates a property right that is as central to ownership as is the power to pass on property after one's death." *Post*, at ——.

Nor can I join in disapproving the long line of cases recognizing the States', and where appropriate, the United States', broad authority to adjust the rules governing the descent and devise of property without implicating the guarantees of the Just Compensation Clause. See, *e. g.*, *Irving Trust Co.* v. *Day*, 314 U. S. 556, 562 (1942) ("Rights of succession to the property of a deceased, whether by will or by intestacy, are of statutory creation, and the dead hand rules succession only by sufferance. Nothing in the Federal Constitution forbids the legislature of a state to limit, condition, or even abolish the power of testamentary disposition over property within its jurisdiction"); *Jefferson* v. *Fink*, 247 U. S. 288, 293–294 (1918).

Rather, I simply find that a "taking" has occurred under the established balancing test set forth in such cases as *Pennsylvania Coal Co.* v. *Mahon*, 260 U. S. 393 (1922), *Penn Central Transportation Co.* v. *New York City*, 438 U. S. 104 (1978), and *Keystone Bituminous Coal Assn.* v. *DeBenedictis*, 480 U. S. —— (1987). *Penn Central* lists several factors of "particular significance" in determining whether regulation goes so far as to effect a taking:

> "The economic impact of the regulation on the claimant and, particularly, the extent to which the regulation has interfered with distinct investment-backed expectations are, of course, relevant considerations. . . . So, too, is the character of the governmental action." *Penn Central Transportation Co.* v. *New York City*, *supra*, at 124.

There is no question that the relative economic impact of § 207 upon the owners of these property rights can be sub-

HODEL *v.* IRVING

stantial. Section 207 provides for the escheat of small undivided property interests that are unproductive during the year preceding the owner's death. Even if we accept the Government's assertion that the income generated by such parcels may be properly thought of as *de minimis*, their value may not be. While the Irving estate lost two interests whose value together was only approximately $100, the Bureau of Indian Affairs placed total values of approximately $2700 and $1816 on the escheatable interests in the Cross and Pumpkin Seed estates. See App. 20, 21–28, 29–39. These are not trivial sums. There are suggestions in the legislative history regarding the 1984 amendments to § 207 that the failure to "look back" more than one year at the income generated by the property had caused the escheat of potentially valuable timber and mineral interests. S. Rep. No. pp. 98–632, pp. 7, 12 (1984); Hearing on H. J. Res. 158 Before the Senate Select Committee on Indian Affairs, 98th Cong., 2d Sess., 20, 26, 32, 75 (1984); Amendments to the Indian Land Consolidation Act: Hearing on H. J. Res. 158 Before the Senate Select Committee on Indian Affairs, 98th Cong., 1st Sess., 8, 29 (1983). Of course, the whole of these interests were not taken by § 207. Appellees' decedents retained full beneficial use of the property during their lifetimes. There is no question, however, that the right to pass on valuable property to one's heirs is itself a valuable right. Depending on the age of the owner, much or most of the value of the parcel may inhere in this "remainder" interest. See 26 CFR § 20.2031–7(f) (Table A) (1986) (value of remainder interest when life tenant is age 65 is approximately 32% of the whole).

The extent to which any of the appellees had "investment-backed expectations" in passing on the property, however, is dubious. Though it is conceivable that some of these interests had been purchased with the expectation that the owners might pass on the remainder to their heirs at death, the

HODEL *v.* IRVING

property has been held in trust for the Indians for 100 years and is overwhelmingly acquired by gift, descent, or devise. Because of the highly fractionated ownership, the property is generally held for lease rather than improved and used by the owners. None of the appellees here can point to any specific investment-backed expectations beyond the fact that their ancestors agreed to accept allotment only after ceding to the United States large parts of the original Great Sioux Reservation.

Weighing weakly in favor of the statute is the fact that there is something of an "average reciprocity of advantage," *Pennsylvania Coal Co.* v. *Mahon*, *supra*, at 415, to the extent that owners of escheatable interests maintain a nexus to the Tribe. Consolidation of Indian lands in the Tribe benefits the members of the Tribe. All members do not own escheatable interests, nor do all owners belong to the Tribe. Nevertheless, there is substantial overlap between the two groups. The owners of escheatable interests often benefit from the escheat of others' fractional interests. Moreover, the whole benefit gained is greater than the sum of the burdens imposed since consolidated lands are more productive than fractionated lands.

The character of the Government regulation here, however, is extraordinary. It amounts to virtually the abrogation of the right to pass on a certain type of property—the small undivided interest—to one's heirs.[2] As JUSTICE SCALIA notes, *post*, at ——, "in one form or another, the right to pass on property—to one's family in particular—has been part of the Anglo-American legal system since feudal times." See *United States* v. *Perkins*, 163 U. S. 625, 628 (1896). Even the United States concedes that total abrogation of the right to pass property is unprecedented and likely unconstitutional. Tr. of Oral Arg. 12–14. This statute ef-

[2] I say "virtually" because, as the United States points out, it is possible for the owners of these interests to effectively control disposition upon death through complex *inter vivos* transactions such as revocable trusts.

HODEL *v.* IRVING

fectively abolishes both descent and devise of these property interests even when the passing of the property to the heir might result in consolidation of property—as for instance when the heir already owns another undivided interest in the property. Compare 25 U. S. C. § 2206(b) (1982 ed., Supp. III). Since I do not accept the United States' submission that the escheatable interests are necessarily *de minimis*, nor its argument that the availability of *inter vivos* transfer is an adequate substitute for descent and devise, I see no way of upholding a *total* abrogation of these rights.

I recognize that the fractionation problem on Indian reservations is itself extraordinary and may call for dramatic action to encourage consolidation. The Sisseton-Wahpeton Sioux Tribe, appearing as *amicus curiae* in support of the United States, is a quintessential victim of fractionation. Forty acre tracts on the Sisseton-Wahpeton Lake Traverse reservation, leasing for about $1000 annually, are commonly subdivided into hundreds of undivided interests, many of which generate only pennies a year in rent. The average tract has 196 owners and the average owner undivided interests in fourteen tracts. The administrative headache this represents can be fathomed by examining Tract 1305, dubbed "one of the most fractionated parcels of land in the world." Lawson, Heirship: The Indian Amoeba, reprinted in Hearing on S. 2480 and S. 2663 Before the Senate Select Committee on Indian Affairs, 98th Cong., 2d Sess., 85 (1984). Tract 1305 is forty acres and produces $1080 in income annually. It is valued at $8000. It has 439 owners, one-third of whom receive less than $.05 in annual rent and two-third of whom receive less than $1. The largest interest holder receives $82.85 annually. The common denominator used to compute fractional interests in the property is 3,394,923,840,000. The smallest heir receives $.01 every 177 years. If the tract were sold (assuming the 439 owners could agree) for its estimated $8000 value, he would be entitled to $.000418. The administrative costs of handling this tract are estimated by the Bureau of Indian Affairs at $17,560 annually. *Id.*, at 86, 87. See also Comment, Too Little Land, Too Many Heirs—The Indian Heirship Land Problem, 46 Wash. L. Rev. 709, 711–713 (1971). Official investigators have deplored the situation for at least sixty years. L. Meriam, Institute for Government Research, The Problem of Indian Administration 40–41 (1928). Good, potentially productive, land has been known to lie fallow, amidst great poverty, because of the difficulties of managing property held in this manner. S. Rep. No. 1080, 73d Cong., 2d Sess., 2 (1934); see also 78 Cong. Rec. 11727–11728 (1934) (remarks of Rep. Howard) (fractionation of allotted lands bringing about "complete economic disintegration" on reservations).

This Court has given government considerable latitude to regulate property rights in ways that may adversely affect the owners when important public interests are substantially advanced by the regulation. See *Keystone Bituminous Coal Assn.* v. *DeBenedictis*, 480 U. S., at —— - ——; *Penn Central Transportation Co.* v. *New York City*, 438 U. S., at 124–128; *Goldblatt* v. *Hempstead*, 369 U. S. 590, 594–595 (1962). In *Andrus* v. *Allard*, 444 U. S. 51 (1979), this Court upheld as valid a regulation prohibiting the sale of eagles and eagle parts in order to conserve the dwindling populations of these birds. Obviously, this regulation implicated a different range of interests than the regulation at issue in this case. Of particular significance, in my view, is that the prohibition in *Allard* was narrowly tailored to addressing the important interest in preventing the killing of endangered species for commercial exploitation. As the Court noted, prohibition of sale of existing legally obtained artifacts was necessary to remove the incentive to poach since "there is no sure means by which to determine the age of bird feathers; feathers recently taken can easily be passed off as having been obtained long ago." *Id.*, at 58. Moreover, the payment of just compensation for the rights taken was not an available alternative in *Allard*; owners of illegally obtained feathers may have been

HODEL *v.* IRVING

happy to tender them to the government in return for compensation. Poaching, therefore, might have remained profitable absent an uncompensated prohibition against sale. Because of the very different context in which *Allard* arose, the different interests sought to be advanced by government regulation in that case, and the fact that the government regulation was narrowly tailored to solving the particular public problem at issue, it is distinguishable from the regulation in this case.

The question of whether a taking has occurred "necessarily requires a weighing of private and public interests." *Agins* v. *Tiburon*, 447 U. S. 255, 261 (1980). There is little doubt that the extreme fractionation of Indian lands is a serious public problem. In my view, it may well be appropriate for the United States to ameliorate fractionation by means of regulating the descent and devise of Indian lands. Surely it is permissible for the United States to prevent the owners of such interests from further subdividing them among future heirs on pain of escheat. See *Texaco, Inc.* v. *Short*, 454 U. S. 516, 542 (1982) (BRENNAN, J., dissenting). It may be appropriate to minimize further compounding of the problem by abolishing the descent of such interests by rules of intestacy, thereby forcing the owners to formally designate an heir to prevent escheat to the Tribe.

What is certainly not appropriate in my view is to take the extraordinary step of abolishing both descent and devise of these property interests even when the passing of the property to the heir might result in consolidation of property. Accordingly, I find that this regulation, in the words of Justice Holmes, "goes too far," *Pennsylvania Coal Co.* v. *Mahon*, 260 U. S., at 415. I therefore concur in JUSTICE SCALIA's conclusion that § 207 as originally enacted violates the Just Compensation Clause of the Fifth Amendment and in the judgment of the Court.

The lower court in *Hodel* v. *Irving* had ruled that the statute at issue violated the Fifth Amendment because it effected a taking of property without providing any compensation to the estates of the former owners of the Indian lands covered by the law. The Stevens draft opinion of the Court affirmed on the due process ground; it consequently did not have to consider whether the statute effected "a taking . . . without just compensation."

Stevens's avoidance of the takings issue proved to be unacceptable to the other Justices. On November 3, 1986, Justice O'Connor sent a "Dear John" letter: "Your draft opinion in this case goes off on a ground not raised by the parties—a Due Process ground. . . . The effect of your opinion seems to be that the Due Process Clause requires a grace period of reasonable length before a state may change the rules of intestate succession or laws governing disposition by will."

According to O'Connor's letter, the Stevens approach raised a serious problem: "Although you state the holding is limited to the Indian trust relationship, I do not see how the reasoning can be so confined. . . . The rationale strikes me as unduly broad and that it will throw into question a broad range of legislative changes."

Instead of taking the Stevens approach, Justice O'Connor wrote, "I am still inclined to affirm the judgment below . . . on the basis of the Takings Clause." The next day, November 4, Justice Scalia wrote agreeing with Justice O'Connor: "I also remain of the view that §207's elimination of the right to pass property . . . violates the takings clause." Justice Powell, who had tentatively voted at the conference to uphold the law, also wrote expressing doubt, as did Justice Blackmun.

At this point, Justice Scalia circulated a draft concurrence that strongly disagreed with the Stevens draft approach. "I do not believe," Scalia's draft began, "the Court should decide whether § 207 . . . violates the due process clause of the Fifth Amendment—a question not raised or argued at any stage of this litigation. To strike down an Act of Congress on a ground that the Secretary has not even had an opportunity to address displays, in my view, inadequate respect for both the coordinate branches of government." Instead Justice Scalia asserted, "we should decide the question . . . whether § 207 effects a taking of property without just compensation, in violation of the Fifth Amendment."

Scalia answered this question with a resounding affirmative. The draft explained the effect of the challenged statute: "First, it changed the law of intestate succession by providing that the property would no longer descend by intestacy according to the law of the State where the property was located, but instead would escheat to the Tribe. Second, it precluded the decedents from having their property descend by will."

According to Justice Scalia, "The combined effect of these restrictions is to deprive appellees' decedents absolutely of all ability to have their property descend even to their children or close relatives after their death." What the statute worked, in Scalia's view, was "the complete elimination of all power to leave property to one's family."

As the Scalia draft stated it, even though there was no physical appropriation or destruction of property here, the statute went "beyond the incidental effects of the government's exercise of its regulatory powers, to what is substantially the exercise of eminent domain itself—that is, to government action that has as its very purpose the transfer of property ownership." The statutory "purpose is to *create a new structure of ownership of land interests* that Congress believes will be more beneficial to Indians."

Such a purpose, the Scalia draft concluded, may not be pursued by regulation. "Where, as here, Congress has expressly stated that its objective is to create a new ownership structure for particular property, and where that is the public purpose that the government invokes to defend the statute in litigation, it would seem to me extraordinary not to require the eminent domain power, with its attendant safeguard of compensation, to be employed."

The Scalia draft then stated a broad general rule—what Justice O'Connor was to criticize as "a novel 'bright-line' rule": "In my view, the requirement of proceeding by eminent domain should apply in all cases where the reallocation of property rights is the acknowledged purpose of the government action, no matter how insignificant those rights may be. That should at least be the rule, however, where the government abrogates a property right that is as central to ownership as is the power to pass on property after one's death."

The Scalia draft concluded with an animadversion on Indian policies: "The government's policies on Indian ownership have shifted with every political and intellectual breeze." Still, Justice Scalia asserted, "if the government's new policy requires the extinction of pre-existing property rights, justice and fairness require that the costs imposed by that policy be borne by society at large, and not by appellees."

After he had received the Scalia draft, Justice Powell wrote a February 26, 1987, "Dear Nino" letter, "Although my Conference vote was the 'other way', I am persuaded by your fine concurring opinion." On March 3, Chief Justice Rehnquist sent Justice Scalia a similar note: "Although I voted to reverse at Conference, I find the second draft of your opinion in this case quite persuasive, and . . . I will join it."

Justice O'Connor also now circulated a draft concurrence, reprinted on p. 93, which agreed with Justice Scalia that the Court should not follow the Stevens draft and examine the constitutionality of the challenged statute under the Due Process Clause. "I also agree . . . ," O'Connor wrote, "§ 207 . . . effects a taking property without just compensation." But, she went on, "I cannot join JUSTICE SCALIA in creating a novel 'bright-line' rule prohibiting Government regulation without compensation."

"Rather," the O'Connor draft went on, "I simply find that a 'taking' has occurred under the established balancing test." In Justice O'Connor's view, "The question of whether a taking has occurred 'necessarily requires a weighing of private and public interests.'" Congress could have dealt with the problem of Indian land fractionation by appropriate regulation—for example, "to minimize further compounding of the problem by abolishing the descent of such interests by rules of intestacy, thereby forcing the owners to formally designate an heir to prevent escheat to the Tribe."

However, Justice O'Connor concluded, "[w]hat is certainly not appropriate in my view is to take the extraordinary step of abolishing both descent and devise of these property interests even when the passing of the property to the heir might result in consolidation of property. Accordingly, I find that this regulation, in the words of Justice Holmes, 'goes too far.'" Hence, O'Connor ended her draft, "I therefore concur in JUSTICE SCALIA's conclusion that § 207 . . . violates the Just Compensation Clause of the Fifth Amendment.

Justice Scalia came back with a redraft, reprinted on p. 83, that noted O'Connor's criticism of his approach as "a novel 'bright-line' rule." "I will not," Scalia countered, "remark upon the 'bright-line' characterization, except to note my regret that it should be used as a term of reproach—particularly in this field, where clear rules are in such short supply."

More important, Scalia accused the O'Connor draft itself of novelty in approach. "For while it purports to adhere to traditional 'regulatory taking' analysis, it effectively overrules without mention the unanimous decision of this Court in *Andrus* v. *Allard*."[9] *Allard* was a 1979 case which, as the Scalia redraft summarized it, "held that an endangered-species regulatory statute forbidding owners of legally acquired bald or golden eagles or eagle parts from disposing of them by sale was not a sufficient restriction on property rights to constitute a taking."

The statute at issue in *Allard* was the Eagle Protection Act. That law made it unlawful to "take, possess, sell, purchase, barter, offer to sell, purchase or barter, transport, export or import" eagle parts. Regulations prohibited sales of any objects containing eagle feathers, even those from birds legally killed before the act. Plaintiffs, who sold Indian artifacts containing eagle feathers, brought suit to have the statute and regulations ruled invalid. The district court held that the act and regulations violated plaintiffs' Fifth Amendment property rights because the prohibition wholly deprived them of the opportunity to earn a profit from their artifacts.

To Richard A. Epstein, a critic of the Supreme Court's *Allard* decision, the district court decision was plainly correct. Indeed, he writes, "On its facts the case is a simple one. The right of sale is part (perhaps the most valuable part) of the right of disposition. The loss of this right is not merely a diminution in value but is the deprivation of a property right, a partial taking for which compensation is prima facie required."[10] In other words, if government deprives plaintiffs of their right to sell their eagle feathers, that is a taking, even if the owners still have the rights to possess and use the feathers.

A unanimous Supreme Court rejected the Epstein reasoning in their *Allard* decision. The Court recognized that "a significant restriction has been imposed on one means of disposing of the artifacts." Indeed, concedes the opinion, "It is . . . undeniable that the regulations here prevent the most profitable use of appellee's property." But, said the Court, "that is not dispositive. When we review regulation, a reduction in the value of property is not necessarily equated with a taking." In this case, plaintiffs still retained all aspects of ownership, except the right to sell: "[A]ppellees retain the rights to possess and transport their property, and to donate or devise the protected birds." Hence, "it is not clear that appellees will be unable to derive economic benefit from the artifacts; for example, they might exhibit the artifacts for an admissions charge."[11]

In actual fact, the plaintiffs in *Allard* were deprived of the key right in the "bundle" of property rights that they had in the eagle feathers. Plaintiffs were in the business of selling Indian artifacts containing eagle feathers and they had purchased the artifacts only to be able to sell them at a profit. According to *Allard*, however, the regulation did not constitute a taking because all the beneficial interest in the property was not destroyed.

According to Scalia's redraft in *Hodel*, that case was comparable to *Allard*. In *Hodel*, his redraft stated, "[i]t seems to me impossible to argue that abrogation of their right to transfer it after death is a greater interference with property than abrogation of the *Allard* appellee's right to sell it during life, or that the former right is constitutionally more significant than the latter." Justice Scalia disagreed with *Allard*. Nevertheless, his redraft asserted, "[i]f *Allard* is to be overruled, it should not be done *sub silentio*, nor do I think it necessary to confront that question in the present case."

On April 21, 1987, Justice O'Connor notified the Justices, "I have redrafted my concurring opinion in this case as an opinion for the Court." Shortly afterwards, the Scalia draft concurrence was withdrawn after the Justice told Justice O'Connor that, as she explained it in a May 5 Memorandum to the Conference, "Nino has advised me that if I would return where I began—with only a brief reference to *Andrus* v. *Allard*—he would be able to join most of the opinion for the Court." Justice O'Connor removed her discussion of *Allard* from her draft and a revised version came down as the *Hodel* opinion of the Court on May 18, 1987. Justice Scalia issued a different one-paragraph concurrence.

Hodel has served as the foundation for subsequent Rehnquist Court expansions of the Takings Clause, culminating in the 1992 *Lucas* case holding that a zoning regulation that prevents beneficial use of property constitutes a taking.[12] Had Justice Stevens's original draft opinion come down as the opinion of the Court, it would have removed *Hodel* as a precedent on takings law. One may wonder whether the Court would have expanded the Takings Clause without the *Hodel* foundation. At a minimum at least, *Hodel* would have been an obscure due process case instead of the starting point for a significant emerging theme in Rehnquist Court jurisprudence.

On the other side, if Justice Scalia's draft had been issued as a *Hodel* concurrence, it might have strengthened the recent expansion of the Takings Clause. *Andrus* v. *Allard*[13] remains as the strongest decision rejecting the view supporting such an expansion. It would have been important for Justice Scalia and those who joined him to state that *Allard* was now definitely overruled. It is true that the one-paragraph Scalia concurrence actually issued in *Hodel* does imply that *Allard* was wrongly decided. But that is hardly the same as a flat statement that *Allard* was being overruled—even sub silentio. At present, at least, *Allard* is still the most substantial barrier to broadening of the Takings Clause to include all regulatory diminutions in property value.

Mention should also be made of the view indicated by Chief Justice Rehnquist during the *Hodel* decision process. On March 3, 1987, the Chief Justice, as indicated, sent a note to Justice Scalia joining his draft concurrence. However, Rehnquist's letter took issue with a sentence in the Scalia draft that, as Rehnquist put it, "suggests, at least to me, that there may be a distinction between a 'regulation' which does not involve a physical taking, even though all beneficial use is denied, and an outright physical taking."

Justice Scalia wrote back the same day to the Chief Justice, "I did not intend to suggest what you feared," and he deleted the offending sentence from his draft. The Rehnquist letter does, however, tell us that the Chief Justice thought at the time of *Hodel* that there was no difference, so far as the Takings Clause was concerned, "between a 'regulation' which does not involve a physical taking, even though all beneficial use is denied, and an outright physical taking." This was, of course, the view that the Court was to adopt in the 1992 *Lucas* case.

Notes

1. Compare *Kovacs* v. *Cooper*, 336 U.S. 77, 95 (1949).
2. Siegan, *The Supreme Court's Constitution* 41 (1987).
3. Stone, J., quoted in Bernard Schwartz, *A History of the Supreme Court* 281–282 (1993).
4. *Children's Hospital* v. *Adkins*, 284 Fed. 613, 622 (D.C. Cir. 1922).
5. Ihering, quoted in 1 Roscoe Pound, *Jurisprudence* 429–430 (1959).
6. *Dolan* v. *Tigard*, 114 S.Ct. 2309 (1994); *Lucas* v. *South Carolina Coastal Commission*, 112 S.Ct. 2886 (1992); *Nollan* v. *California Coastal Commission*, 483 U.S. 825 (1987).
7. See Bernard Schwartz, *The New Right and the Constitution*, chap. 4 (1990).
8. 481 U.S. 704 (1987).
9. 444 U.S. 51 (1979).
10. Epstein, *Takings: Private Property and the Power of Eminent Domain* 76 (1985).
11. 444 U.S. at 65–66.
12. *Lucas* v. *South Carolina Coastal Commission*, 112 S.Ct. 2886 (1992).
13. Supra note 9.

3

California v. *Rooney* (*1987*): *Garbage In*, *Evidence Out?*

California v. *Rooney*[1] would have been another leading Fourth Amendment case, if the draft circulated by Justice White had been issued as the opinion of the Court. The fact pattern in *Rooney* was strikingly summarized in a draft dissent prepared by Justice Marshall in the case:

> The picture presented . . . is somewhat humorous. The time is *2:30 a.m.*; the scene is the basement of a residential apartment house in Los Angeles. Half submerged in a five-foot high container of garbage are two Los Angeles police officers. Whether they are armed and in uniform the record does not disclose. Quietly, so as not to disturb the tenants peacefully slumbering above, they pursue their "investigation." The pile of garbage outside the bin grows larger as the pile inside grows smaller. Eureka! A brown paper bag, some letters, and a magazine. Success attends the labors of the patient.[2]

The search thus described took place in the communal trash bin, located in the subterranean garage, accessible to the public, of the apartment building in which the defendant lived. Still, as the Marshall draft dissent wryly put it, "this is unfortunately not the stuff of comedy; it is serious business."[3] The bag discovered by the police contained bookmaking notations and defendant was charged with bookmaking and associated crimes. After the trash search, the police had obtained a warrant to search the defendant's apartment and had obtained other evidence there. The California Court of Appeal had held the search warrant to be valid and the evidence seized under it to be admissible. However, the court also stated that the evidence seized from the trash bin was not admissible, since probable cause was lacking for the garbage search.

At the *Rooney* conference, the Justices decided by a bare majority to reverse the California court and hold that the evidence found in the bag taken from the trash bin was admissible. The opinion was assigned to Justice White, who on May 4, 1987 circulated the draft opinion of the Court reprinted on p. 107.

According to the White draft, "The question is whether the search of the trash bin and the seizure of some of its contents were unreasonable within the meaning of the Fourth Amendment." Justice White answered in the negative. He conceded that, under state law, the defendant "retained an ownership or posessory [*sic*] interest in the trash bag and its contents." That did not, however, "settle the matter for Fourth Amendment purposes." That was true, according to the draft, because "[t]he primary object of the Fourth Amendment is to protect privacy, not property, and the question in this case, as the Court of Appeal recognized, is not whether Rooney had abandoned his interest in the property law sense, but whether he retained a subjective expectation of privacy in his trash bag that society accepts as objectively reasonable."

The White draft conceded "that trash can reveal a great deal about the life of its disposer." But that did not mean that there was a legitimate expectation of privacy in domestic garbage. Moreover, Justice White declared, "A *hope* of privacy is not equivalent to an *expectation* of privacy."

In this case, the White draft notes, "the communal trash bin in which respondent placed his refuse was accessible to other tenants in the apartment building and their guests, to the owner and manager of the building, and to the public at large. It is common knowledge that trash bins and cans are commonly visited by animals, children, and scavengers looking for valuable items, such as recyclable cans and bottles, and serviceable clothing and household furnishings." Hence, "any expectation of privacy respondent may have had in the contents of the trash bin was unreasonable."

According to White, "Any distinction between the examination of trash by trash collectors and scavengers on the one hand and the police on the other is untenable. If property is exposed to the general public, it is exposed in equal measure to the police."

It follows, the White draft went on, "that the Fourth Amendment does not require the police to avert their eyes from evidence of criminal activity that any member of the public could have observed." Even if "a person minds an examination by the police more than an examination by an animal, a child, a neighbor, a scavenger, or a trash collector, . . . that does not render the intrusion by the police illegitimate." The draft conclusion was "that society is not prepared to accept as reasonable an expectation of privacy in trash deposited in an area accessible to the public pending collection by a municipal authority or its authorized agent."

1st DRAFT

SUPREME COURT OF THE UNITED STATES

No. 85-1835

CALIFORNIA, PETITIONER *v.* PETER ROONEY

ON WRIT OF CERTIORARI TO THE COURT OF APPEAL OF CALIFORNIA, SECOND APPELLATE DISTRICT

[May ——, 1987]

JUSTICE WHITE delivered the opinion of the Court.

The police obtained information that one Peter Ryan was accepting wagers on professional football games at 1120 North Flores Street, Apartment 8, West Hollywood, California. Two officers went to 1120 North Flores, a 28-unit apartment building with a subterranean garage which was accessible to the public, entered the garage, and searched the communal trash bin. In the bottom half of the bin they discovered a brown paper shopping bag which contained mail addressed to respondent at 1120 North Flores Street, Apartment 8, and papers bearing bookmaking notations. The police seized the bag. They used these items and the results of further investigation to support a search warrant of respondent's apartment, which was duly executed.

Rooney was charged with bookmaking and associated crimes. He moved to have the warrant quashed and the evidence obtained from the search of the trash bin excluded. The trial court granted his motion, the State declared that it could not proceed, and the case was dismissed. The State's appeal followed. The California Court of Appeal held that the State had failed to prove that Rooney had abandoned his property by putting it into the trash bin. Because the garage was accessible to the public, however, and the officers did not commit a trespass by entering the garage, the court also rejected Rooney's claim that the search of the bin was illegal because it occurred within the curtilage of his apart-

CALIFORNIA *v.* ROONEY

ment. In so ruling, the Court of Appeal relied on a holding of the California Supreme Court to this effect. *People* v. *Terry*, 61 Cal. 2d 137, 152, 390 P. 2d 381 (1964). The court went on to hold that under the decisions of the Supreme Court of California, the Fourth Amendment did not require a warrant for a trash bin search but did require probable cause, which the court found lacking here.[1] The search of the trash bin therefore violated the Fourth Amendment and the evidence seized from the bin was not admissible. The subsequent warrant, however, was itself valid, since it was supported by probable cause wholly aside from the trash-bin evidence. It is the former holding that the State challenged in its petition for certiorari after the California Supreme Court denied review. We granted the petition, —— U. S. —— (1986), and for the reasons that follow, we reverse.

We note at the outset that we have no reason to differ with the state court that the trash bin was not within the curtilage of Rooney's apartment, that the garage was open to the public and that the officers committed no trespass and were not invading any private zone when they approached the trash bin. The question is whether the search of the trash bin and the seizure of some of its contents were unreasonable within the meaning of the Fourth Amendment, which protects the right of the people to be secure "in their persons, houses, papers, and effects, against unreasonable searches and seizures."

---

[1] The court observed that the "Truth in Evidence" provision of the Victim's Bill of Rights (Proposition 8) abrogated a defendant's right to object to and to suppress evidence seized in violation of the California but not of the Federal Constitution. The Court of Appeal noted, however, that the California Supreme Court had held that under both the California and Federal Constitutions, a trash can outside the curtilage of a house could be searched without a warrant, but not without probable cause. *People* v. *Krivda*, 5 Cal. 3d 357, 486 P. 2d 1262 (1971), remanded, 409 U. S. 33 (1972), on remand, 8 Cal. 3d 623, 504 P. 2d 457, cert. denied, 412 U. S. 919 (1973).

CALIFORNIA *v.* ROONEY

The State submits that once Rooney placed the seized items in the trash bin, he abandoned them and lost any possessory or ownership interest in them that he may have had. Hence, they were no longer *his* papers or effects and were not protected by the Fourth Amendment.[2] The Court of Appeal rejected this submission; and for present purposes, we assume that under state law Rooney retained an ownership or posessory interest in the trash bag and its contents. Rooney's property interest, however, does not settle the matter for Fourth Amendment purposes, for the reach of the Fourth Amendment is not determined by state property law. As we have said, the premise that property interests control the right of officials to search and seize has been discredited. *Oliver* v. *United States*, 466 U. S. 170, 183 (1984); *Katz* v. *United States*, 389 U. S. 347, 353 (1967); *Warden* v. *Hayden*, 387 U. S. 294, 304 (1967). The primary object of the Fourth Amendment is to protect privacy, not property, and the question in this case, as the Court of Appeal recognized, is not whether Rooney had abandoned his interest in the property law sense, but whether he retained a subjective expectation of privacy in his trash bag that society accepts as objectively reasonable. *O'Connor* v. *Ortega*, —— U. S. ——, —— (1987); *California* v. *Ciraolo*, —— U. S. ——, —— (1986); *Oliver* v. *United States*, 466 U. S., at 177; *Smith* v. *Maryland*, 442 U. S. 735, 740 (1979); *Katz* v. *United States*, 389 U. S., at 361 (Harlan, J., concurring). We therefore proceed to that inquiry.

[2] The State emphasizes that the Fourth Amendment protects the "right of the people to be secure in *their* persons, houses, papers, and effects." It points to *Oliver* v. *United States*, 466 U. S. 170, 176–177 (1984), as an illustration of the plain language approach to the Fourth Amendment. In *Oliver*, we based our holding that the Fourth Amendment does not extend to an open field on the explicit language of the amendment. We held that an open field is neither a "house" nor an "effect." See also *id.*, at 184 (WHITE, J., concurring).

CALIFORNIA *v.* ROONEY

We acknowledge at the outset that trash can reveal a great deal about the life of its disposer.[3] As respondent eloquently phrases it, the domestic garbage can contains numerous "tell-tale items on the road map of life in the previous week." Brief for Respondent 15. A *hope* of privacy is not equivalent to an *expectation* of privacy, however. Respondent vigorously argues that he exhibited an expectation of privacy by taking the affirmative step of placing his bag of trash in the bottom half of the dumpster. Tr. of Oral Arg. 37–38, 43–44, 55–56. This argument is somewhat difficult to accept. Nothing in the record demonstrates that respondent actually buried his trash in the bin as opposed to simply throwing it in when the bin was nearly empty. In any event, assuming that respondent did have a subjective expectation of privacy, "steps taken to protect privacy [do not] establish that expectations of privacy . . . are legitimate." *Oliver* v. *United States*, 466 U. S., at 182. "Rather, the correct inquiry is whether the government's intrusion infringes upon the personal and societal values protected by the Fourth Amendment." *Id.*, at 182–183. A person may well intend not to relinquish all rights in personal property but nevertheless take action rendering this intent ineffective for Fourth Amendment purposes.

The State points out that the communal trash bin in which respondent placed his refuse was accessible to other tenants

[3]The Garbage Project of the University of Arizona, directed by archaeologists at the University, was founded upon the advice of archaeology pioneer Emil Haury: "If you want to know what is really going on in a community, look at its garbage." W. Rathje, "Archaeological Ethnography . . . Because Sometimes It is Better to Give than to Receive," in R. Gould (ed.), Explorations in Ethnoarchaeology 49, 54 (1978). In that project, Tucson Sanitation Division Personnel randomly selected refuse set out for collection by households throughout the city. Procedures ensured anonymity. The archaeologists sorted the refuse from each household into more than 150 categories in order to improve their understanding of contemporary society (as well as to refine techniques for understanding the material culture of earlier societies).

CALIFORNIA *v.* ROONEY

in the apartment building and their guests, to the owner and manager of the building, and to the public at large. It is common knowledge that trash bins and cans are commonly visited by animals, children, and scavengers looking for valuable items, such as recyclable cans and bottles, and serviceable clothing and household furnishings. Accordingly, California argues, any expectation of privacy respondent may have had in the contents of the trash bin was unreasonable.

Respondent argues in response that the probability that garbage collectors or the police will search the contents of a particular trash bin is extremely small, and that this minute probability, in and of itself, makes his expectation of privacy in the trash bin reasonable. According to respondent, the reality of domestic garbage collection is that the collectors move quickly from bin to bin, do not have time to look for valuable items, and probably would not recognize evidence of criminal activity. Garbage is promptly intermingled with other garbage in a truck such that its origin can no longer be identified. It is then "hauled to the dump, where it will be burned/destroyed/plowed under by Caterpillar tractors, to form the foundation for new housing developments." Brief for Respondent 16. Similarly, respondent asserts that there clearly are too few policemen in Los Angeles to conduct random searches of trash cans for evidence of crime. Respondent further argues that one may have a "differential expectation of privacy" with respect to animals, children, and scavengers and with respect to the police. *Id.*, at 18; see *Smith* v. *Alaska*, 510 P. 2d 793, 803 (1973) (Rabinowitz, C. J., dissenting). While it may not be totally unforeseeable that trash collectors or other third persons may occasionally rummage through one's trash, it may be quite unexpected that the police will conduct a systematic inspection for evidence of criminal activity. In any event, respondent states that the Fourth Amendment protects against the acts of the government, not private citizens.

CALIFORNIA *v.* ROONEY

We are unpersuaded. "What a person knowingly exposes to the public, even in his own home or office, is not a subject of Fourth Amendment protection. But what he seeks to preserve as private, even in an area accessible to the public, may be constitutionally protected." *Katz* v. *United States*, 389 U. S., at 351–352 (citations omitted). Respondent knowingly exposed his betting papers to the public by depositing them in a trash bin which was accessible to the public. Once they were in the bin, he no longer exercised control over them. While he may not have welcomed intrusions, respondent did nothing to ensure that his refuse would not be discovered and appropriated. Indeed, he placed his papers in the bin for the express purpose of conveying them to third parties, the trash collectors, whom he had no reasonable expectation would not cooperate with the police. In *Smith* v. *Maryland*, 442 U. S. 735 (1979), we held that the installation, at the request of the police, of a pen register at the telephone company's offices to record the telephone numbers dialed on the petitioner's telephone did not violate the Fourth Amendment. The petitioner had no legitimate expectation of privacy in the telephone numbers since he voluntarily conveyed them to the telephone company when he used his telephone. "This Court consistently has held that a person has no legitimate expectation of privacy in information he voluntarily turns over to third parties." *Id.*, at 743–744.

Respondent's reliance on the fact that the police do not ordinarily engage in random searches, or comprehensive city-wide searches, of trash cans is misplaced. A police department, like any organization with limited resources, allocates its resources to activities most likely to result in the detection or prevention of crime. The police in this case searched the trash bin after receiving a tip from an informant that a bookmaking operation was being conducted at the apartment house. It is not unforeseeable that police will investigate when they have information suggesting that an investigation will be useful. In *Smith* v. *Maryland*, for example, a Balti-

CALIFORNIA *v.* ROONEY

more woman was robbed and thereafter received threatening and obscene phone calls from a man identifying himself as the robber. When their investigation led the police to suspect that the petitioner was the perpetrator, they had the pen register installed and recorded a call from the petitioner's home to the victim. The petitioner would have been entirely justified in believing that the police would not likely have discovered his telephone call to the victim by means of a random search of telephone numbers dialed in the city, and that the police would not likely have undertaken a systematic search of all telephone calls made in the city. That fact, however, did not give petitioner a legitimate expectation of privacy in the telephone numbers he dialed. In *California* v. *Ciraolo*, —— U. S. ——, ——, n. 2 (1986), we expressly rejected the California Court of Appeal's position that a search, which it would have found permissible if conducted pursuant to a routine police patrol, violated the Fourth Amendment because information of illegality had led the police to focus on a particular place. We held in that case that the observation of a fenced backyard by police officers trained in marijuana identification from a private plane at an altitude of 1,000 feet did not violate the Fourth Amendment because the defendant had no legitimate expectation that his property would not be so observed:

> "The observations of Officers Shutz and Rodriguez in this case took place within public navigable airspace . . . in a physically nonintrusive manner; from this point they were able to observe plants readily discernable to the naked eye as marijuana. That the observation from the aircraft was directed at identifying the plants and the officers were trained to recognize marijuana is irrelevant. Such observation is precisely what a judicial officer needs to provide a basis for a warrant. Any member of the public flying in this airspace who glanced down could have seen everything that these officers observed. On this record, we readily conclude that respondent's expec-

CALIFORNIA *v.* ROONEY

> tation that his garden was protected from such observation is unreasonable and is not an expectation that society is prepared to honor." *Id.*, at ——.

Any distinction between the examination of trash by trash collectors and scavengers on the one hand and the police on the other is untenable. If property is exposed to the general public, it is exposed in equal measure to the police. It is clear from *Ciraolo* that the Fourth Amendment does not require the police to avert their eyes from evidence of criminal activity that any member of the public could have observed, even if a casual observer would not likely have realized that the object indicated criminal activity or would not likely have notified the police even if he or she had realized the object's significance. It may of course be true that a person minds an examination by the police more than an examination by an animal, a child, a neighbor, a scavenger, or a trash collector, but that does not render the intrusion by the police illegitimate.

The Court of Appeal noted the existence of municipal ordinances which prohibit persons other than authorized collectors from rummaging through the trash of another. Such ordinances, however, do not change the fact that the owner of the trash completely relinquishes control over the trash to a third party, the designated trash collector, who for all the owner knows, will cooperate with the police. Cf. *Lewis* v. *United States*, 385 U. S. 206 (1966); *Hoffa* v. *United States*, 385 U. S. 293 (1966). Moreover, it is not at all clear that such a municipal ordinance would evoke an expectation of privacy in trash. Respondent did not rely on any such ordinance here and it has been noted that the purpose of such ordinances is sanitation and economic protection of the authorized trash collector rather than privacy. See *United States* v. *Vahalik*, 606 F. 2d 99, 100–101 (CA5 1979), cert. denied, 444 U. S. 1081 (1980); *People* v. *Krivda*, 5 Cal. 3d 357, 368, n. 1, 486 P. 2d 1262 (1971) (Wright, C. J., concurring and dissenting), remanded 409 U. S. 33 (1972), on re-

CALIFORNIA *v.* ROONEY

mand, 8 Cal. 3d 623, 504 P. 2d 457, Cert. denied, 412 U. S. 919 (1973).

Every federal Court of Appeals that has addressed the issue has concluded that the Fourth Amendment does not protect trash placed for collection outside a residence and its curtilage. *United States* v. *Dela Espriella*, 781 F. 2d 1432, 1437 (CA9 1986); *United States* v. *O'Bryant*, 775 F. 2d 1528 (CA11 1985); *United States* v. *Michaels*, 726 F. 2d 1307, 1312–1313 (CA8), cert. denied, 469 U. S. 820 (1984); *United States* v. *Kramer*, 711 F. 2d 789 (CA7), cert. denied, 464 U. S. 962 (1983); *United States* v. *Terry*, 702 F. 2d 299, 308–309 (CA2), cert. denied, 461 U. S. 931 (1983); *United States* v. *Reicherter*, 647 F. 2d 397, 399 (CA3 1981); *United States* v. *Vahalik, supra*; *United States* v. *Crowell*, 586 F. 2d 1020, 1025 (CA4 1978), cert. denied, 440 U. S. 959 (1979); *Magda* v. *Benson*, 536 F. 2d 111, 112–113 (CA6 1976); *United States* v. *Mustone*, 469 F. 2d 970, 972 (CA1 1972). The Courts of Appeals had little difficulty reaching this conclusion. As the Third Circuit stated in *United States* v. *Reicherter*:

> "Defendant claims that . . . he had a reasonable expectation of privacy in the trash he placed in a public area to be picked up by trash collectors . . . . A mere recitation of the contention carries with it its own refutation. . . . Having placed the trash in an area particularly suited for public inspection and, in a manner of speaking, public consumption, for the express purpose of having strangers take it, it is inconceivable that the defendant intended to retain a privacy interest in the discarded objects. If he had such an expectation, it was not reasonable." 647 F. 2d, at 399.

This unanimity of opinion among the federal appellate courts supports our determination that society is not prepared to accept as reasonable an expectation of privacy in trash deposited in an area accessible to the public pending collection by a municipal authority or its authorized agent.

CALIFORNIA *v.* ROONEY

The judgment of the California Court of Appeal is reversed and this case is remanded for further proceedings not inconsistent with this opinion.

It is so ordered.

1st DRAFT

SUPREME COURT OF THE UNITED STATES

No. 85-1835

CALIFORNIA, PETITIONER *v.* PETER ROONEY

ON WRIT OF CERTIORARI TO THE COURT OF APPEAL OF CALIFORNIA, SECOND APPELLATE DISTRICT

[May ——, 1987]

JUSTICE MARSHALL, dissenting.

This Court does not sit to render advisory opinions on questions of law simply for the gratification of individuals stubborn enough to bring their abstract disagreements here. *Flast* v. *Cohen*, 392 U. S. 83, 96–97 (1968). The most important tool for determining the scope of the decision appropriate in a particular case is the record of the courts below. The record tells us what has previously been decided, and therefore what questions are presented for review. The record contains the facts upon which those decisions were based. Questions not presented in the record, and questions whose answers cannot be derived from the facts contained therein, are not questions upon which this Court should issue opinions.

Today, however, the Court demonstrates that the absence of a record is no longer a barrier to deciding broad propositions of federal constitutional law. Unable to convince its own courts, California has sought and obtained redress in this Court; the majority now ignores the glaring deficiencies in the record made by the State, and renders a sweeping decision in a hypothetical case. Were it not so obviously overbroad, the holding would be bad enough. The willingness of the Court to entertain the case at all is far more disturbing, and suggests that the pursuit of particular results has entirely eclipsed the prudential considerations which caution against the unnecessary decision of constitutional questions. See *Ashwander* v. *Tennesee Valley Authority*, 297 U. S. 288, 346–348 (Brandeis, J., dissenting in part).

The entire record in this case, amounting to one slim volume, comprises nine briefs and memoranda submitted by the parties, thirteen letters and declarations requesting extensions of time to file papers, and the opinion of the California Court of Appeal for the Second Appellate District. In addition, the record from the Superior Court contains 63 pages of motion papers, memoranda, and minute entries. There is also a 23-page transcript of the sole hearing held in this case, before a Magistrate on respondent's motion to suppress. No testimony was taken. The *only* evidentiary matter in this hardly extensive record is the four-page affidavit submitted in support of the original request for a search warrant. The validity of the warrant was upheld by the trial court, and the State now asks us to review only the propriety of the warrantless search of the trash receptacle, completed before the warrant application was made. The portion of the affidavit which describes that search is set out in the margin.[1] These are the only facts upon which this case can be decided.

[1] "On December 15, 1983, at approximately 0230 hours, your affiant and partner Officer Les Wyeth, #17223, drove to 1120 North Flores Street, West Hollywood and walked down the driveway to the apartment trash bin, which is a metal bin approximately 8 feet long by 4 feet wide by 5 feet high and is located in the subterranean garage at the southeast corner of the apartment building. Your affiant noticed that there was trash spilling out of the trash bin onto the ground. Your affiant and partner Officer Les Wyeth, #17223 searched the trash bin and noticed that there was trash from numerous different apartments co-mingled inside. As your affiant and partner Officer Les Wyeth, #17223, reached the bottom half of the trash bin, your affiant located a brown paper shopping bag with mail addressed to Pete Rooney, 1120 North Flores, #8, Los Angeles. Your affiant removed the bag of trash from the trash bin and recovered letters and a magazine addressed to Pete Rooney, 1120 North Flores, #8, Los Angeles. Also recovered were pieces of paper with sports wagers, pays and owes, and a tally sheet of wagers on different professional football teams (evidence booked on DR#83-9910022)." Record 29–30.

CALIFORNIA *v.* ROONEY

The picture presented by the affidavit is somewhat humorous. The time is *2:30 a.m.*; the scene is the basement of a residential apartment house in Los Angeles. Half submerged in a five-foot high container of garbage are two Los Angeles police officers. Whether they are armed and in uniform the record does not disclose. Quietly, so as not to disturb the tenants peacefully slumbering above, they pursue their "investigation." The pile of garbage outside the bin grows larger as the pile inside grows smaller. Eureka! A brown paper bag, some letters, and a magazine. Success attends the labors of the patient.

But this is unfortunately not the stuff of comedy; it is serious business and, according to the majority, entirely constitutional. Even the first-year student of criminal procedure might be pardoned for asking a few questions. Who owns the building and the trash bin? Is the garage locked at night? Did the police officers climb a fence or a barricade at the bottom of the driveway? What was the justification, if any, for police intrusion onto private property, by stealth, in the dead of night? Who came to carry away the garbage in due course: a municipal employee, or a private contractor employed by the owner of the property? The majority cannot answer these questions, of course, because the record is silent. Instead, the majority is compelled to ignore such questions, presumably on the ground that the answers would make no constitutional difference.

But if the record showed that respondent himself owned the entire apartment building and the trash bin, that there was a gate at the bottom of the driveway blocking access to the garage at the time the police arrived, and that respondent contracted with a private party to enter the basement to remove the accumulated trash, would the case be no different for Fourth Amendment purposes? Obviously it would be. The first ground alone, that respondent owned the apartment building, would in all probability have been decisive. As we have said, "in terms that apply equally to seizures of prop-

CALIFORNIA *v.* ROONEY

erty and to seizures of persons, the Fourth Amendment has drawn a firm line at the entrance to the house. Absent exigent circumstances, that threshold may not reasonably be crossed without a warrant." *Steagald* v. *United States*, 451 U. S. 204, 212 (1981) (quoting *Payton* v. *New York*, 445 U. S. 573, 590 (1980)). The majority's result, in short, depends upon assumptions concerning facts not in the record. The case the majority hypothesizes conveniently leads to the desired result, but it is a mirage.

Respondent met the burden imposed upon him to convince the trial court that the warrantless search of the trash container violated the Fourth Amendment. The State was then obliged to make a factual record upon which it could convince an appellate court that the trial court had made reversible errors of law. It simply has not done so. Indeed, it is hard to imagine a record providing less solid foundation for the decision of the Fourth Amendment issue the State seeks to raise.

Where the record is factually insufficient to permit decision of the claims presented, the writ of certiorari should be dismissed as improvidently granted. See *Minnick* v. *California Dept. of Corrections*, 452 U. S. 105, 127 (1981); *Gilbert* v. *California*, 388 U. S. 263, 269 (1967); *Mishkin* v. *New York*, 383 U. S. 502, 512–513 (1966); *Mitchell* v. *Oregon Frozen Foods Co.*, 361 U.S 231 (1960). The majority's unwillingness to apply this well-settled principle is directly traceable to its haste to overturn a decision of an intermediate state appellate court which the majority evidently believes provides more Fourth Amendment rights to citizens than they are entitled to have. This style of intervention in state court constitutional decisions at the request of the State has become lamentably popular in recent Terms. See *Connecticut* v. *Barrett*, —— U. S. ——, —— (1987) (STEVENS, J., dissenting); *Michigan* v. *Long*, 463 U. S. 1032, 1068 (1983) (STEVENS, J., dissenting).[2] Where constitutional questions are

[2] So far this Term, the Court has granted review, heard argument, and issued a decision in *Arizona* v. *Hicks*, —— U. S. —— (1987); *California* v.

CALIFORNIA *v.* ROONEY

squarely presented in the cases in which the Court rushes to judgment, the Court's eagerness is perhaps merely unwise; where, as here, the Court ignores the dictates of prudence to render decisions on hypothetical questions, the damage is far more severe. Is the community safer because the State of California will be permitted to introduce Peter Rooney's garbage as additional evidence of wrongdoing at respondent's forthcoming trial on bookmaking charges? The majority is evidently certain; I have my doubts. I would dismiss the writ of certiorari as improvidently granted, and accordingly I dissent.

Brown, —— U. S. —— (1987); *Colorado* v. *Bertine*, —— U. S. —— (1987); *Colorado* v. *Connelly*, —— U. S. —— (1986); *Colorado* v. *Spring*, —— U. S. —— (1987); *Connecticut* v. *Barrett*, —— U. S. —— (1987); *Illinois* v. *Krull*, —— U. S. —— (1987); *Maryland* v. *Garrison*, —— U. S. —— (1987); *Missouri* v. *Blair*, —— U. S. —— (1987) (writ dismissed as improvidently granted); and *Pennsylvania* v. *Ritchie*, —— U. S. —— (1987). Still awaiting argument or decision are *Arizona* v. *Mauro*, No. 85–2121; *Kentucky* v. *Stincer*, No. 86–572; *New York* v. *Burger*, No. 86–80; *Pennsylvania* v. *Finley*, No. 85–2099; and *Vermont* v. *Cox*, No. 86–1108.

2nd DRAFT

SUPREME COURT OF THE UNITED STATES

No. 85-1835

CALIFORNIA, PETITIONER *v.* PETER ROONEY

ON WRIT OF CERTIORARI TO THE COURT OF APPEAL OF CALIFORNIA, SECOND APPELLATE DISTRICT

[May ——, 1987]

JUSTICE STEVENS, dissenting.

As JUSTICE MARSHALL has demonstrated, it is unwise for the Court to decide this case on the basis of the limited record before us. There is also a serious procedural obstacle that the Court leaps over as it plunges into the alluring waters of constitutional adjudication. The California Court of Appeal held that the evidence suppressed by the Superior Court was admissible—the Court *upheld* the search of the apartment, which was the only issue before it. Thus, the State of California *won* below. 175 Cal. App. 3d 634, 221 Cal. Rptr. 49 (1985). Although the Court of Appeal, in the course of its opinion, determined that it would not rely on the evidence found in the trash bin to support the subsequent search warrant for the apartment, it did not, and could not, render a *judgment* suppressing the trash bin evidence, for neither the Magistrate nor the Superior Court had passed upon any motion to suppress that evidence. Given the lack of a state court judgment on the issue, our review is unquestionably premature.

The issue before the California Superior Court and Court of Appeal was whether the search warrant that the police executed for 1120 North Flores Street, apartment no. 8, was backed by probable cause. In support of the warrant, the police had submitted an affidavit stating that an informant told them that Peter Rooney was accepting wagers on professional football games over the telephone at a specified tele-

CALIFORNIA *v.* ROONEY

phone number, and that Rooney was there between 4:00 and 6:00 p. m. The police traced the telephone number to one Peter Ryan residing in Apartment no. 8. The utilities at that apartment were also registered to Ryan. A search of Rooney's police record, however, revealed that he had been arrested three years earlier for bookmaking activities at that apartment. The Police then decided to search the trash bin, and found evidence of gambling activity in a bag that also contained mail addressed to Rooney at apartment 8. Over a week later, the police conducted surveillance and saw Rooney enter the apartment during the time of day the informant indicated he would be there. The police dialed the number that was given to them by the informant and overheard a telephone conversation involving point spreads on professional football games. A search warrant for the apartment was issued based on this evidence, and incriminating evidence was found which led to Rooney's arrest.

Rooney brought a motion to quash the search warrant and to dismiss the felony charges against him. A magistrate granted the motion, reasoning that the evidence obtained from the trash bin could not be used to support the search warrant, and that the other evidence offered in support of the search warrant was insufficient to establish probable cause. The Superior Court agreed. Pursuant to California procedural rules, the State then informed the court that it could not prosecute the case without any of the evidence seized in the search of the apartment, and the case was dismissed, thus allowing the State to, in effect, *appeal the order quashing the warrant.*

The Court of Appeal reversed on the only issue before it—to use the State's words, "the sufficiency of the affidavit in support of the search warrant."[1] Although it concluded

[1]Appellant's Opening Brief in the Ct. App. Cal. 2d App. Dist., No. B006936. p. 2.

Throughout the proceedings it was clear that the courts were passing upon Rooney's motion to quash the search warrant and supress the evi-

CALIFORNIA *v.* ROONEY

that the evidence found in the trash bin could not be used to support the search warrant, the Court of Appeal examined the other evidence offered in support of the warrant under the standards set forth in *Illinois* v. *Gates*, 462 U. S. 213 (1983), and held that there was sufficient other evidence to establish probable cause in support of the warrant. The Superior Court's order dismissing the case was therefore reversed, allowing the prosecution to proceed. The California Supreme Court denied both petitioner's and respondent's petitions for review.

In light of the prosecution's complete victory on the only issue litigated below, one might reasonably ask why the State has sought review here, and even more to the point, why this Court granted review. The answer to the former question is relatively easy. First, the State has long desired to rid itself of the California courts' unique position that citizens have reasonable expectations of privacy in their trash.[2]

---

dence found in the apartment; there was no motion to suppress the evidence found in the trash. For example, the first thing the magistrate said after calling Rooney's case was: "This is before the Court on the notice of motion to quash the search warrant pursuant to Penal Code Section 1538.5." Clerk's Transcript 3. After hearing argument involving the different parts of the affidavit supporting the search warrant, the magistrate announced: "It is going to be the ruling of this Court that although this is a relatively close matter, but I feel that the notice of motion to quash the search warrant pursuant to Penal Code Section 1538.5 should be granted." *Id.*, at 21.

Again, when the case came before the Superior Court, the first thing the judge stated was: "The matter pending, motion to suppress evidence pursuant to Section 1538.5. At this point, to classify the issue, is directed at the sufficiency of the search warrant and challenges the affidavit on its face." App. 51.

[2] This Court granted the State's petition for certiorari in *People* v. *Krivda*, 5 Cal. 3d 357, 486 P. 2d 1262 (1971) *(en banc)*, but was unable to determine whether the California Supreme Court had rested its decision on state or federal grounds. 409 U. S. 33 (1972). On remand, the court announced that it had rested on both state and federal constitutional grounds. 8 Cal. 3d 623, 504 P. 2d 457 (1973), cert. denied, 412 U. S. 919 (1973). This prevented us from reviewing the case. In 1985, however, the people of

CALIFORNIA *v.* ROONEY

Since there is some discussion of that issue in the Court of Appeal opinion, the State believes that this case provides such an opportunity. Second, the State may eventually wish to introduce evidence of the trash search itself when, and if, it ever gets to trial on this case. If it does, the Court of Appeal decision will constitute law of the case on the trash-search issue, and the trial court will undoubtedly bar its admission. But while these two factors explain the State's seeking certiorari,[3] they do not justify this Court's action in reaching out to decide a constitutional question, especially in light on the inadequate record.

This Court "reviews judgments, not statements in opinions." *Black* v. *Cutter Laboratories*, 351 U. S. 292, 297 (1956); see also *Chevron, U. S. A. Inc.* v. *Natural Resources Defense Council, Inc.*, 467 U. S. 837, 842 (1984); *Williams* v. *Norris*, 12 Wheat. 117, 120 (1827). The fact that the Court of Appeal reached a correct decision through analysis differ-

---

California amended their constitution to bar the suppression of evidence seized in violation of the California, but not the Federal, Constitution. Cal. Const., Art. I, § 28(d); see generally *In re Lance W.*, 37 Cal. 3d 873, 694 P. 2d 744 (1985). Thus, the Court of Appeal was forced to rest its discussion of the trash-search issue in this case on the Federal Constitution.

[3] The Deputy District Attorney arguing the case before this Court candidly admitted that it is the first of these factors that primarily motivates the petition for certiorari:

"Q. So that everything you found under the search warrant is admissible.

"Mr. Guminski: That is correct, Your Honor. But the ruling . . . is a ruling that forecloses the use of what was discovered as far as the trash bag; that would be the rule of the case.

"Q. And you think you're really going to use that at this trial, or you think that you would really need to?

"A. Well, Your Honor, I think what we really want would be to . . . overrule *People* v. *Krivda*, which was here before the Court in 1972, and which was remanded then because there were independent state grounds.

"I mean, I wish to answer candidly to your question, Justice; there is an intention to use it, of course.

"But is it is a vehicle of review." Tr. of Oral Arg. 26–27.

CALIFORNIA *v.* ROONEY

ent than this Court would have used does not grant this Court a privilege to rewrite the California court's decision, any more than it grants the State a right to seek certiorari from it. Recently, in *Hewitt* v. *Helms*, —— U. S. —— (1987), we held that whether a party can be deemed a "prevailing party" for attorney's fees purposes depends upon the judgment issued—not the legal analysis employed in the opinion explaining the judgment. This reasoning should apply equally in this context. The Court of Appeal's use of analysis that may have been adverse to the State's long-term interests should not allow the State to claim status as a losing party for purposes of this Court's review.

The irony of today's decision is revealed by the Court's disposition of the case: it "reverses" the Court of Appeal. Of course, the judgment of the California Court of Appeal set aside the Superior Court's suppression order and remanded the case for trial. Presumably what this Court intends is that the opinion of the California court be rewritten in a way that will grant the State the right to use the trash bin evidence in the event that the State seeks its admission at an eventual trial of respondent. This is not our task. As the Court explained in *Hewitt*, that the Court of Appeal even addressed the trash bin issue is mere fortuity; the court could as easily have held that since there was sufficient evidence to support the search even without the trash evidence, it would not discuss the constitutionality of the trash search. "There is no warrant" for having this Court's jurisdiction "depend upon the essentially arbitrary order" in which lower courts "choose to address issues." *Id.*, at ——. Unless the State has the right to be here now to address the possibility that the Court of Appeal decision will bar it from introducing the trash evidence at trial, we have no right to hear this case.

It is painfully obvious that the State enjoys no such right, and that the Court's decision on the admissibility of the evidence at a possible future trial is wholly advisory. Not only do we not know whether this will be one of that small per-

CALIFORNIA *v.* ROONEY

centage of cases that culminates in an actual trial,[4] but we also do not know whether the prosection will seek to introduce the evidence found in the trash. If the evidence found in the apartment pursuant to the valid warrant is strong enough, the prosecution might not even be interested in presenting the more attenuated evidence found in the trash.

But, the State argues, *if* the case does come to trial, and *if* the State does wish to introduce the evidence, it will be barred from doing so because the reasoning in the Court of Appeal decision will constitute the law of the case. There are two too many "ifs" in that proposition to sustain our jurisdiction. Even if everything the prosecution fears comes to bear, the State will still have the opportunity to appeal such an order,[5] and this Court will have the chance to review it, with the knowledge that we are reviewing a state court judgment on the issue, and that the State Supreme Court has

[4] The overwhelming majority of criminal indictments in this country are disposed of without trial. In California, for example, only 10% of the felony and driving under the influence cases disposed of in 1984 involved a trial. See National Center for State Courts, State Court Caseload Statistics: Annual Report 1984, p. 145 (1986). Similarly, of the 50,040 defendants in United States District Courts whose cases were disposed of in the 12 month period ending June 30, 1986, only 13.3%, or 6,662, involved a trial. Administrative Office of the United States Courts, Annual Report of the Director, App. I, Detailed Statistical Tables, p. 56 (1986).

[5] Assuming that the respondent's motion to suppress the trash evidence will be granted, the prosecution will then have to decide whether it can prosecute without the evidence. If it cannot, then an order of dismissal will be entered, and the prosecution may immediately appeal. See Cal. Penal Code Ann. §§ 1238, 1538.5 (West 1982). Even if the prosecution can proceed without the evidence, however, it may still obtain immediate review through a writ of mandate or prohibition. § 1538.5(o). A writ of mandate could compel the superior court to admit the evidence and "must be issued where there is not a plain, speedy, and adquate remedy, in the ordinary course of law." Cal. Civ. Proc. Ann. Code § 1086 (West 1982). A writ of prohibition deals with jusridictional defects and would not appear to be relevant here. See Cal. Civ. Proc. Code Ann. § 1102 (West 1982). See generally B. Witkin, California Criminal Procedure §§ 869, 870 (1985 Supp., pt. 2).

CALIFORNIA *v.* ROONEY

passed upon or declined review in a case squarely presenting the issue. As it stands, we have no way of knowing what the California Supreme Court's position on the issue of trash searches currently is. Much has changed since its *Krivda* decision in 1969. A California Constitutional Amendment now requires the State to focus on the Federal Constitution alone in dealing with requests for exclusion of evidence. See n. 2, *supra*. The virtual unanimity of the Circuit Courts of Appeals in construing the Federal Constitution on the issue, see *ante*, p. 9, as well as this Court's many intervening precedents, see *ante*, pp. 4–8, might also have an effect on the California Supreme Court's position. It is no answer to say that the California Supreme Court already had its chance to review the matter and declined to do so when it denied the State's petition for review in this case. The denial of review may well have been based on that court's seeing a flaw in the prosecution's petition that this Court continues to miss: the prosecution won below. Giving the California Supreme Court an opportunity to consider the issue is a compelling reason for us to dismiss this petition.

The State of California "cannot irrevocably lose" the right to introduce the trash evidence "without having an opportunity to present that issue to this Court." *Pennsylvania* v. *Ritchie*, 480 U. S. ——, —— (1987) (STEVENS, J., dissenting). Of course, the prosecution may have no need for the evidence at trial, and the issue may therefore escape review, but that is surely a reason for avoiding today's decision, not a justification for it. See *id.*, at ——.

Notwithstanding the deficiencies in the record, and the dubious wisdom of providing judicial advice to a party who prevailed in the court below, this Court finds the case worthy of its attention. The Court's approach here is indicative of a greater evil, one that improperly magnifies our workload and erodes the quality of our work product. See *Connecticut* v. *Barrett*, 479 U. S. ——, —— (1987) (STEVENS, J., dissenting); *California* v. *Carney*, 471 U. S. 386, 396–397 (1985)

CALIFORNIA *v.* ROONEY

(STEVENS, J., dissenting). I wholeheartedly agree with JUSTICE MARSHALL that the writ of certiorari should be dismissed as improvidently granted.

On April 3, 1987, Justice Brennan sent a letter to Justice O'Connor: "Thurgood, John, you and I are in dissent. Will you dispose of this one?"

In her reply the same day, Justice O'Connor stated, "I am not at all sure I will dissent in this case." She took this position, she said, because she agreed "with the Chief that the case should be reversed on the theory that once trash is abandoned for pickup and public refuse disposal there is no further expectation of privacy which society should recognize as reasonable."

Nevertheless, Justice O'Connor indicated that she was troubled by application of Rehnquist's theory to the facts of this particular case. "My concern," she stated, "is with the curtilage concept and whether we should permit the police to enter the common area of the apartment building."

In other words, Justice O'Connor was troubled by the fact that the search here was not outside the curtilage (the house and its immediate surrounding area), but was conducted in the garage that was part of the apartment building itself. Justice Brennan, too, was uneasy about this. On April 6, he replied to Justice O'Connor, "I, too, am concerned about the curtilage problem." Brennan also wrote that, because of O'Connor's posture on the case, "I withdraw my request that you take on the dissent."

At this point, Justices Marshall and Stevens, who had voted against reversal of the state court's decision at the conference, delivered what amounted to flank attacks against the proposed decision. In draft dissents that they circulated, the two Justices urged that the Court should not decide the case, but should instead dismiss the writ of certiorari as improvidently granted.

On May 4 Justice Marshall circulated the draft dissent reprinted on page 117. It began by emphasizing the Court's refusal to render advisory opinions and the importance of "the record of the courts below" in enabling the Court to decide an actual case. Without an adequate record, the Court should not act: "Questions not presented in the record, and questions whose answers cannot be derived from the facts contained therein, are not questions upon which this Court should issue opinions."

What the majority was doing, according to the Marshall draft, was to write an opinion that "now ignores the glaring deficiencies in the record made by the State, and renders a sweeping decision in a hypothetical case." Indeed, Justice Marshall asserted, what the majority was doing "suggests that the pursuit of particular results has entirely eclipsed the prudential considerations which caution against the unnecessary decision of constitutional questions."

According to the Marshall draft, "The *only* evidentiary matter in this hardly extensive record is the four-page affidavit submitted in support of the original request for a search warrant." That was scarcely enough to enable the Court to answer the many questions that were pertinent to the decision. "The majority cannot answer these questions, of course, because the record is silent." In fact, the Marshall draft declared, "The majority's result . . . depends upon assumptions concerning facts not in the record. The case the majority hypothesizes conveniently leads to the desired result, but it is a mirage."

In such a case, according to Justice Marshall, "[w]here the record is factually insufficient to permit decision of the claims presented, the writ of certiorari should be dismissed as improvidently granted." Instead, the majority was acting in "haste to overturn a decision of an intermediate state appellate court which the majority evidently believes provides more Fourth Amendment rights to citizens than they are entitled to have."

At the end of his draft, Justice Marshall indicated his disagreement on the merits of the case: "Is the community safer because the State of California will be permitted to introduce Peter Rooney's garbage as additional evidence of wrongdoing at respondent's forthcoming trial on bookmaking charges? The majority is evidently certain; I have my doubts."

Soon afterwards, Justice Stevens sent around the draft dissent reprinted on page 122. It raised another obstacle to the majority decision on the merits. "There is," Stevens wrote, "also a serious procedural obstacle that the Court leaps over as it plunges into the alluring waters of constitutional adjudication. The California Court of Appeal held that the evidence suppressed by the Superior Court was admissible—the Court *upheld* the search of the apartment, which was the only issue before it." Thus, while the California court stated "that it would not rely on the evidence found in the trash bin to support the subsequent search warrant for the apartment, it did not, and could not, render a *judgment* suppressing the trash bin evidence, for [there had never been] any motion to suppress that evidence."

According to the Stevens draft, "the only issue" decided by the California court was "the sufficiency of the affidavit in support of the search warrant," and, on it, the prosecution had won below. The fact that the California court stated in its opinion that the trash bin evidence could not be used was not enough to justify Supreme Court review. "This Court," Stevens declared, "'reviews judgments, not statements in opinions.'"

The great "flaw in the prosecution's petition," Justice Stevens asserted, is that "the prosecution won below." It is "the judgment issued—not the legal analysis employed in the opinion explaining the judgment" that should be controlling. The need to adhere to this principle is shown by the White draft opinion of the Court's disposition of the case. "The irony of today's decision," Stevens's draft stated, "is revealed by the Court's disposition of the case: it 'reverses.' . . . Presumably what this Court intends is that the opinion of the California court be rewritten in a way that will grant the State the right to use the trash bin evidence in the event that the State seeks its admission at an eventual trial of respondent. This is not our task."

What the majority opinion was engaged in, Justice Stevens maintained, was "providing judicial advice to a party who prevailed in the court below." That, according to the Stevens draft, was not the business of the Court and the case should consequently be dismissed.

After he had read the Stevens draft dissent, Justice Scalia, who had been a member of the conference majority, circulated a May 19 Memorandum to the Conference that began: "I have reviewed the record in this case and reluctantly conclude that the new point John raises in his dissent is correct, and we are without jurisdiction."

As Justice Scalia now saw it, the only issue in the lower court "was whether the subpoena authorizing search of respondent's apartment should be quashed and the evidence obtained in that search suppressed." According to the Scalia memo, the constitutional issue dealt with in the White draft opinion of the Court "was involved in the case only because the State argued that the garbage seized from that dumpster, in combination with other evidence, provided probable cause for the warrant. The Court of Appeals concluded (after a lengthy and, as it turned out, unnecessary consideration of the trash issue) that probable cause existed even in the absence of the trash and reversed the trial court's suppression order. Thus, the State is asking us to review unfavorable dicta in a decision that granted the State all the relief it sought."

Hence, Justice Scalia concluded, "I change my vote to D.I.G. [dismiss as improvidently granted]."

With Justice Scalia's switch, White's draft opinion of the Court had lost its bare majority. Justice White tried to regain it by a May 19 letter to Justice Scalia that declared, "I am as confident as you are the other way that we have jurisdiction in this case." As White saw it, "The California court decided the federal issue because it thought it was raised and had to be decided. I would not second guess that court on what the issues were in the trial court, especially since we took the case to decide the federal issue and have had the case briefed and orally argued."

White's letter did not, however, induce Justice Scalia to rejoin the minority. Instead, as Justice Blackmun pointed out in a May 21 "Dear Byron" letter, "There now are five definite votes to DIG this case. I suppose the five prevail." Blackmun wrote that he "reluctantly would also vote to DIG and make a sixth."

On June 23, 1987, the Court issued a per curiam opinion in *California* v. *Rooney* drafted by Justice Stevens (itself an abbreviated version of the Stevens draft dissent) dismissing the writ as improvidently granted.[4] Justice White, joined by Chief Justice Rehnquist and Justice Powell, issued a dissent (a shortened adaptation of the White draft opinion of the Court) that disagreed with the Court's DIG disposition and also dealt with the merits of the case.

As it turned out then, the Court did not decide the constitutionality of garbage searches in *California* v. *Rooney*. However, as Justice Blackmun pointed out in his May 21 letter, "The issue, of course, remains a pertinent one and must be faced and resolved." It was resolved a year after the *Rooney* case in *California* v. *Greenwood*.[5]

In *Greenwood*, the police had asked the defendant's trash collector to turn over the plastic garbage bags that defendant had left on the curb in front of his house. Items indicative of narcotics use was found in the bags. The Court, in an opinion by Justice White, held that the Fourth Amendment did not prohibit the warrantless search and seizure of defendant's garbage.

The *Greenwood* decision did not, however, mean that the lacuna left in Fourth Amendment law by the DIGing of *Rooney* was now completely filled. In the first place, White's opinion in *Greenwood* was inferior to the draft that the Justice had prepared the year before in *Rooney*. More important, the *Greenwood* fact pattern did not present the curtilage problem that had concerned Justices O'Connor and Brennan in *Rooney*. Had White's *Rooney* draft come down as the opinion of the Court, it would have answered the question of whether the police could search an apartment building's communal trash bin in the affirmative. Since *Greenwood* did not deal with that question, it remains unanswered despite *Greenwood*'s resolution of the garbage search issue for trash left for collection outside the curtilage of a private home.

Mention should also be made of an interesting sidelight on the *Rooney* case. On June 12, 1987, Chief Justice Rehnquist sent around a Memorandum to the Conference that began, "It is with considerable unhappiness that I transmit to you the enclosed memorandum from Sheryl Farmer, Secretary to Toni House [the Court's public information officer], giving a narrative summary of an event which occurred yesterday afternoon in the Conference Room." The Justices had agreed to allow Tim O'Brien, of ABC News, to film the conference room. According to Farmer's memo, "About fifteen minutes into the filming, I noticed O'Brien was looking in the fireplace, leaned over to pick up sheets of paper and began looking through them. I immediately asked him to put them back, making him aware that he was there as a guest. A few minutes later I noticed that he was thumbing through a list of some kind that I didn't remember him bringing into the Conference Room. I noticed he was making notes but I couldn't determine if they were from the list or from the filming. When I asked him, he said they were notes on the filming."

Rehnquist's memo stated, "The 'list' which Tim O'Brien had apparently pulled out of the fireplace was the eight-page summary of circulating opinions which I distribute each week—this one for May 20, 1987." The Chief Justice concluded, "I think Tim O'Brien, if he did what he appears to have done, has committed a rather gross breach at least of courtesy if not of ethics, and that something should be done about it." Rehnquist asked the Justices to let him know how they felt about this.

All the Justices wrote to the Chief Justice criticizing O'Brien's conduct. Several, however, indicated that they were not overly disturbed—analogizing the situation to the *Rooney* case then pending before the Court. What O'Brien had done, Justice Scalia wrote to Chief Justice Rehnquist on June 15, was to conduct "a trash search in the Conference Room of the Supreme Court of the United States (an activity that we had some difficulty justifying in an apartment garage)."

A few days earlier, on June 12, Justice Blackmun had written to the Chief Justice, "I cannot get too disturbed about the [O'Brien] incident. . . . After all, it was 'trash' and reminiscent of the pending *Rooney* case. I do think that 'we' (including those who clean up the conference room) may tend to be a little careless in throwing complete papers into the fireplace. They ought to be torn up if they contain any information presumably confidential. . . . If we dispose of things that way, why should we be surprised if there is a leak?"

In other words, as Justice Powell put it in a June 15 letter to the Chief Justice, "[W]e place temptation in the way of others when confidential papers that have not been shreded [*sic*] are placed in wastebaskets or fireplaces." The obvious answer was given in O'Connor's June 12 reply to the Chief Justice, "[W]e should probably not leave confidential Court papers or documents in fireplaces or wastebaskets—only in the 'burn bags' provided for such material." Could the same answer not have been given in the *Rooney* and *Greenwood* cases? If defendants had intended the seized materials to remain confidential, why did they leave them in trash bins or garbage bags that were accessible to the public?

Notes

1. 483 U.S. 307 (1987).
2. Infra p. 119.
3. Ibid.
4. Supra note 1.
5. 486 U.S. 35 (1988).

4

Tompkins v. *Texas* (1989): *Race and Peremptory Challenges*

In addition to their right to challenge potential jurors for cause, both sides in a criminal case have a number of peremptory challenges, by which they can refuse to accept individuals as jurors without giving any reason. However, in *Batson* v. *Kentucky*,[1] decided in 1986 during Chief Justice Burger's last term, the Court held that the Equal Protection Clause prohibits a prosecutor from using peremptory challenges to exclude blacks from a jury. The lower court had held that the Sixth Amendment right to a jury drawn from a cross-section of the community had not been violated, relying on the 1965 decision in *Swain* v. *Alabama*.[2] That case had also held that racial discrimination might not be inferred merely from the prosecutor's use of peremptory challenges to dismiss blacks from the jury.

At the *Batson* conference, most of the Justices agreed that the case should be decided on equal protection rather than the Sixth Amendment. Chief Justice Burger, however, spoke for affirming the lower court decision. He said that the case should be decided "only [on] the Sixth Amendment cross-section" argument. "Our Sixth Amendment decisions don't suggest a different result from *Swain*."

The case the other way was led by Justice Brennan, as was usual by then in the Burger Court: "I think that we should overrule *Swain* and hold that a black defendant can establish an equal protection violation based on the prosecutor's racially motivated use of peremptory challenges to eliminate a significant number of blacks from the venire in the individual defendant's case. We should treat racial equal protection claims in the petit jury context basically the same way we treat other kinds of racial discrimination claims."

Justice Brennan stated the view accepted by the *Batson* majority. "I think that equal protection grounds are far preferable here to a 6th Amendment fair cross-section approach. . . . An equal protection approach to the problem would be narrower and more closely tailored to the problem. It would also avoid potentially serious difficulties in defining what groups should be cognizable under the fair cross section requirement. Because an equal protection theory would be available only to the singularly disadvantaged and distinct groups that receive special scrutiny, that approach should limit the number and types of challenges to the prosecution's use of peremptories."[3]

Only Justice Rehnquist supported Chief Justice Burger at the conference. The others agreed with Justice Brennan—rejection of the Sixth Amendment approach and reversal on equal protection. "I'd revisit *Swain*," said Justice White, "and say here that, contrary to *Swain*, if defendant can prove there's a striking [from the jury] on account of race, [he] can require the prosecutor to justify." Justice Blackmun declared, "It's discriminatory to assume blacks are acquittal-prone." Justice Stevens summed up the conference consensus: "The courts that have assumed Swain held [they] could use peremptories on racial [grounds are] wrong. We should say it's constitutionally impermissible."

The opinion written by Justice Powell for the majority in *Batson* followed the conference view, holding that the use of peremptory challenges to exclude blacks from the jury violated equal protection. Once a defendant shows such exclusion, the burden shifts to the prosecutor to come forward with a neutral explanation for challenging black jurors. Repeating the conference point made by Justice Blackmun, Powell's opinion points out that the prosecutor does not meet this burden by stating that he challenged the jurors on the assumption that they would be partial to the defendant because of their shared race.

Under *Batson*, peremptory challenges may not be used by the prosecution to exclude blacks from a jury. More than that, Justice Powell's *Batson* opinion adopted the view that he had stated at the conference, "We have to overrule *Swain*'s holding that won't permit inferences that striking causes an inference to arise of a racial basis." But *Batson* did not answer the question of what burden of proof the prosecutor had to meet to overcome the inference that the exclusion was racially motivated. That question was almost answered in the 1989 case of *Tompkins* v. *Texas*.[4]

Tompkins had been found guilty of an intentional killing during a robbery and kidnapping and had been sentenced to death. As stated in Justice Stevens's draft opinion of the Court, reprinted on page 139, "His case gives rise to two questions: (1) whether it was constitutional error for the trial judge to grant only one of petitioner's three requests for instructions on lesser included, noncapital offenses; and (2) whether the [lower court] erred when it affirmed the trial judge's determination that the prosecutors' use of peremptory challenges to exclude all blacks from the jury was based consistently on 'neutral, relative, clear and legitimate' reasons and 'was not racially motivated.'"

Tompkins came before an eight-Justice Court, Justice O'Connor having recused herself. The conference voted five to three to affirm on the first issue and reverse on the second. Justice Stevens prepared his draft opinion of the Court reprinted here. On the first issue, it ruled that a defendant was entitled "to have the jury instructed regarding not only capital murder and acquittal, but also one lesser included, noncapital offense suggested by the evidence at trial."

The defendant had argued that he had a constitutional right to have the jury instructed on *every* lesser included, noncapital offense that might be supported by the evidence. The Stevens draft rejected this claim. "It may well be," Justice Stevens wrote, "sound policy to instruct the jury on every lesser included offense supported by the evidence. But the Constitution requires no such rule. It mandates only that a jury be given a means to avoid a Hobson's choice between acquittal and capital murder. Because the instructions in this case afforded the jury such an option, they did not offend the Constitution."

The second question in *Tompkins* gave rise to what the Justices themselves called "the *Batson* issue." As we saw, *Batson* v. *Kentucky* invalidated the use of peremptory challenges by the prosecution to exclude blacks from a jury. Tompkins claimed that *Batson* had been violated in his case. He was black. All the jurors were white; the thirteen blacks on the venire, the panel from which the jury had been chosen, had all been excluded—eight by challenges for cause (for a reason) and five by peremptory strikes (without any reason). The Texas Court of Criminal Appeals had accepted the prosecutors' testimony of a neutral, nonracial reason for each of the peremptory challenges. As that court saw it, the finding of the trial judge, "which is supported by sufficient evidence, comports with that of a rational trier of fact."

According to the Stevens draft, the Texas court's "application of a sufficiency-of-the-evidence standard inadequately protected the important interests at stake." Hence, "[t]oday we reject the Texas criminal appeals court's standard for reviewing *Batson* claims." As Stevens's draft explains it, "The Texas court's sufficiency-of-the-evidence standard erodes *Batson*'s protection. Allowing reversal only when 'no rational trier of fact' would have ruled against a defendant asserting a *Batson* violation narrows the scope of review to a point that is virtually meaningless."

Instead, the trial court's decision must be reviewed under the clearly erroneous standard that normally governs appellate review in federal courts. As Justice Stevens explains, "[T]he clearly erroneous standard requires the appellate court, after locating record support for an explanation, to decide separately whether the trial judge was mistaken. . . . This extra step mandates more careful examination of the record and more considered evaluation of the validity of the trial court's findings. Thus a standard no less protective than clearly erroneous is essential to the faithful application of *Batson*."

"In this case," the draft concluded, "the process by which petitioner's *Batson* claim was assessed by the trial court and the Court of Criminal Appeals of Texas was inadequate." That was true because the Texas courts "seem to have assumed that any neutral explanation would suffice as long as the trial judge believed the prosecutor's testimony that the neutral reason prompted the peremptory challenge." However, the draft asserted, "[i]n addition to overlooking our admonition that the neutral explanation must be case-related, their assumption provides no protection against the danger that a facially neutral explanation may be nothing more than a proxy for racial bias, conscious or subconscious."

Also, "neither court heeded our admonition to 'consider all relevant circumstances.'" In particular, the Texas courts "made no comment on the dubious character of the questions put to the black venirepersons." As stated in the Stevens draft, "Courts must make sure that prosecutors are not permitted to circumvent our holding in *Batson* by requiring black venirepersons [those on the jury panel] to demonstrate an understanding of areas of the law—such as the 'law of parties'—that have no special relevance to the case at hand. Consideration of all relevant circumstances should encompass whether similar questions were propounded to white venirepersons and whether accepted jurors' answers differed significantly from those of the excused black jurors."

3rd DRAFT

SUPREME COURT OF THE UNITED STATES

No. 87–6405

PHILLIP D. TOMPKINS, PETITIONER *v.* TEXAS

ON WRIT OF CERTIORARI TO THE COURT OF CRIMINAL APPEALS OF TEXAS

[May ——, 1989]

JUSTICE STEVENS delivered the opinion of the Court.

A jury found petitioner guilty of an intentional killing in the course of a robbery and kidnapping and sentenced him to death. His case gives rise to two questions: (1) whether it was constitutional error for the trial judge to grant only one of petitioner's three requests for instructions on lesser included, noncapital offenses; and (2) whether the Court of Criminal Appeals of Texas erred when it affirmed the trial judge's determination that the prosecutors' use of peremptory challenges to exclude all blacks from the jury was based consistently on "neutral, relative, clear and legitimate" reasons and "was not racially motivated."

I

Early on the morning of January 27, 1981, the body of Mary Diana Berry, a 24-year-old hospital pharmacist, was found tightly bound to a tree near a remote road in the Houston area. A large wad of bedsheeting had been stuffed in her mouth, forcing her tongue deep into the rearmost part of her mouth and causing her to suffocate.

Berry had left work at about 11 p. m. on January 25. After an apparent collision with a car often driven by petitioner, Berry vanished, her car abandoned at the accident site. Two and one-half hours later, a night janitor at Berry's bank saw petitioner using an automatic teller card to withdraw $1,000 from her account; his testimony was corrobo-

TOMPKINS *v.* TEXAS

rated by photographs taken by an automatic camera. When petitioner was apprehended a few days later, the bank card, credit cards, and certain other items belonging to Berry were in his possession. A severed electrical cord in the trunk of his car matched the cord that had been used to bind Berry's ankles. In short, the record contains ample circumstantial evidence of petitioner's involvement in the crime. A Texas grand jury charged him with capital murder.[1]

In a written confession, petitioner stated that he had tied and gagged Berry solely to keep her from escaping and seeking help while he used her bank card. That confession, however, was not admitted into evidence and petitioner did not testify regarding the incident; in fact, the defense rested without introducing any evidence on petitioner's behalf.[2] Petitioner's attorneys nevertheless argued that it was reasonable to infer that the binding and gagging of Berry—rather than, for instance, strangling or stabbing her—demonstrated that he did not intend to kill her.[3]

---

[1] The Texas capital murder statute provides:

"(a) A person commits an offense if he commits murder as defined under Section 19.02(a)(1) of this code and:

. . . . .

"(2) the person intentionally commits the murder in the course of committing or attempting to commit kidnapping, burglary, robbery, aggravated rape, or arson . . . ."

. . . . .

"(c) If the jury does not find beyond a reasonable doubt that defendant is guilty of an offense under this section, he may be convicted or murder or of any other lesser included offense." Tex. Penal Code Ann., Art. 19.03 (Vernon 1974).

[2] Petitioner did testify briefly during the State's case in chief in an unsuccessful attempt to establish that his companion at the time of the incident was his common-law wife and thus disqualified under State law from testifying against him. Trans. 924–930.

[3] Trans. 1012. Petitioner's attorneys urged the jury to find a lack of intent to kill based on a number of circumstances, among them that: Berry was left close enough to a house to permit quick discovery, *id.*, at 1014–1015, 1043; the gag did not cover Berry's nose and the bonds were loose enough to demonstrate a lack of intent to kill, *id.*, at 1011, 1048; and

TOMPKINS *v.* TEXAS

To convict petitioner of capital murder the jury had to find both that he intentionally killed Berry and that he did so while engaged in robbing or kidnapping her.[4] Defense counsel asked that jurors be instructed that if they did not find that the State had proved capital murder, they could find petitioner guilty of any of three lesser, noncapital offenses. The judge gave the requested instruction on noncapital murder[5] but refused to instruct on either involuntary man-

---

Berry had a respiratory problem that aggravated an otherwise nonlethal gag, *id.*, at 1049. Counsel further argued that the State's evidence failed to prove petitioner robbed or kidnapped Berry. *E. g., id.*, at 1012–1013, 1041–1043. "[S]omeone much smarter and much meaner than Phillip Tompkins" was at fault, counsel suggested, and then laid the blame on petitioner's live-in female companion. *Id.*, at 1018–1021; see also *id.*, at 1047.

[4] The judge instructed the jury in part as follows:

"Before you would be warranted in convicting the defendant of capital murder, you must find from the evidence beyond a reasonable doubt not only that on the occasion in question the defendant was engaged in the commission or attempted commission of the felony offense of robbery and/or of kidnapping of Mary D. Berry, as defined in this charge, but also that during the commission of the robbery and/or kidnapping or attempted commission thereof, if any, the defendant suffocated Mary D. Berry by placing a cloth gag in her mouth with the intention of thereby killing her. Unless you find from the evidence beyond a reasonable doubt that the defendant, Phillip Daniel Tompkins, on said occasion, specifically intended to kill the said Mary D. Berry when he suffocated Mary D. Berry by placing a cloth gag in her mouth, if he so did, taking into consideration the foregoing instructions, you cannot convict him of the offense of capital murder." App. 36–37.

[5] Although the statute labels it "murder," we shall refer to the offense enumerated at Tex. Penal Code Ann., Art. 19.02(a)(1) (Vernon 1974), as "noncapital murder" to distinguish it from capital murder, *id.*, Art. 19.03. The judge instructed petitioner's jury regarding noncapital murder as follows:

"If you do not so find beyond a reasonable doubt, or if you have a reasonable doubt thereof, you will acquit the defendant of capital murder and consider whether he is guilty of the lesser offense of murder.

"If you find from the evidence beyond a reasonable doubt that on or about the 26th day of January, 1981, in Harris County, Texas, the defendant, Phillip Daniel Tompkins, did intentionally cause the death of Mary D.

TOMPKINS *v.* TEXAS

slaughter or criminally negligent homicide, neither of which requires an intent to kill. Having convicted petitioner of the capital offense, the jury, after a separate sentencing hearing, affirmatively answered the special questions that mandate a death sentence in Texas—in particular, that petitioner had acted "deliberately and with the reasonable expectation that . . . death . . . would result."[6] Thus, on two separate occasions, the jury found that petitioner intended to kill Berry.

On appeal petitioner argued that the refusal to instruct on involuntary manslaughter and criminally negligent homicide

---

Berry by suffocating her by placing a cloth gag in her mouth, and you have a reasonable doubt as to whether the defendant was then and there engaged in the commission or attempted commission of robbery and/or kidnapping of Mary D. Berry at the time of the suffocating, if any, then you will find the defendant guilty of murder, but not capital murder.

"If you find from the evidence beyond a reasonable doubt that the defendant is either guilty of capital murder or murder, but you have a reasonable doubt as to which offense he is guilty of, then you should resolve that doubt in the defendant's favor, and in such event, you will find the defendant guilty of the lesser offense of murder." App. 37.

The judge also charged the jury that it might exonerate petitioner: "If you have a reasonable doubt as to whether the defendant is guilty of any offense, then you should acquit the defendant and say by your verdict not guilty." *Id.*, at 38.

The instructions the jury received on capital murder and noncapital murder were substantially similar to those petitioner requested. See *id.*, at 24–27.

[6] Trans. 205. Texas law provides:

"(b) On conclusion of the presentation of the evidence, the court shall submit the following issues to the jury:

"(1) whether the conduct of the defendant that caused the death of the deceased was committed deliberately and with the reasonable expectation that the death of the deceased or another would result;

"(2) whether there is a probability that the defendant would commit criminal acts of violence that would constitute a continuing threat to society . . . .

. . . . .

"(e) If the jury returns an affirmative finding on each issue submitted under this article, the court shall sentence the defendant to death." Tex. Code Crim. Proc. Ann., Art. 37.071 (Vernon 1974).

TOMPKINS *v.* TEXAS

violated the Due Process Clause of the Fourteenth Amendment as construed in *Beck* v. *Alabama*, 447 U. S. 625 (1980).[7] The Court of Criminal Appeals rejected that argument because in this case, unlike *Beck*, the petitioner "did not testify or present any evidence from any source that he possessed only the intent to either rob or kidnap Berry." App. 88. Although we do not agree with the Texas court's basis for distinguishing *Beck*, we conclude that no constitutional error occurred because the trial judge did instruct the jury on the lesser included offense of noncapital murder.

In *Beck* we considered the constitutionality of Alabama's unique statutory prohibition against giving any lesser included offense instructions in capital cases.[8] Beck had been accused of an intentional killing in the course of a robbery, a capital crime. His own testimony established that he had participated in a robbery in which his accomplice unexpectedly had struck and killed the victim. If that testimony was true, Beck was guilty of noncapital felony murder, but not of the capital crime of robbery-intentional killing. The Alabama statute, however, prohibited the court from charging the jury on that lesser included offense. Thus the jury faced "the choice of either convicting the defendant of the capital crime, in which case it [was] required to impose the death penalty, or acquitting him, thus allowing him to escape all penalties for his alleged participation in the crime." *Beck*, *supra*, at 628–629.

We held that Alabama's refusal to allow the jury to consider any verdict between the two extremes was unacceptable in a capital case. We explained:

> "While we have never held that a defendant is entitled to a lesser included offense instruction as a matter of due

[7] Petitioner also argued that he was entitled to those lesser included offense instructions as a matter of state law. We, of course, do not review the Texas court's rejection of that argument. Cf. *Beck* v. *Alabama*, 447 U. S. 625, 630, n. 5 (1980).

[8] See *id.*, at 628, n. 3; 630, n. 5; 635, and 636, n. 12.

> process, the nearly universal acceptance of the rule in both state and federal courts establishes the value to the defendant of this procedural safeguard. That safeguard would seem to be especially important in a case such as this. For when the evidence unquestionably establishes that the defendant is guilty of a serious, violent offense—but leaves some doubt with respect to an element that would justify conviction of a capital offense—the failure to give the jury the 'third option' of convicting on a lesser included offense would seem inevitably to enhance the risk of an unwarranted conviction.
>
> "Such a risk cannot be tolerated in a case in which the defendant's life is at stake." *Id.*, at 637.

Thus Beck was entitled to have the jury instructed regarding not only capital murder and acquittal, but also one lesser included, noncapital offense suggested by the evidence at trial.

Petitioner interprets *Beck* to mean that the Constitution mandates lesser included offense instructions covering all possible permutations of juror determinations regarding elements of the capital crime. Contending that his jury, like the one in *Beck*, could have drawn conflicting inferences regarding his intent to kill, petitioner asserts that the trial court was required to give all requested unintentional homicide instructions.[9] The reason *Beck* ordered just one noncapital charge, he suggests, is that only one was requested.

Pretermitting this argument, the Court of Criminal Appeals attempted to distinguish *Beck* on the ground that there the defense had adduced evidence disputing intent to kill dur-

[9] The dissent agrees with this interpretation of *Beck* and suggests that it is reinforced by the "almost universal practice" of American courts. See *post*, at —— [slip op. at 4]. Neither petitioner nor the dissent, however, has cited a single appellate court case holding that the Constitution requires a judge to give multiple lesser included offense instructions. Moreover, it is noteworthy that petitioner's trial counsel did not request the court to instruct the jury on the lesser included offense of either kidnapping or robbery.

TOMPKINS *v.* TEXAS

ing its own case, whereas here petitioner rested without introducing any evidence.[10] Our reasoning in *Beck* would have been the same, however, if the evidence had been received during the prosecutor's case in chief. A defendant in a capital case is not required to waive his privilege against self-incrimination to obtain the benefit of a constitutionally required lesser included offense instruction.[11]

Nevertheless we are not persuaded that the right to one such instruction recognized in *Beck* entails a constitutional right to have the jury instructed on *every* lesser included, noncapital offense that might be supported by the evidence. As we explained in *Hopper* v. *Evans*, 456 U. S. 605, 609 (1982):

> "Our opinion in *Beck* stressed that the jury was faced with a situation in which its choices were only to convict the defendant and sentence him to death or find him not guilty. The jury could not take a third option of finding that although the defendant had committed a grave crime, it was not so grave as to warrant capital punishment. We concluded that a jury might have convicted Beck but also might have rejected capital punishment if it believed Beck's testimony. On the facts shown in *Beck*, we held that the defendant was entitled to a lesser included offense instruction as a matter of due process."

In this case, unlike *Beck*, the jury was given "a third option of finding that although the defendant had committed a grave crime, it was not so grave as to warrant capital punishment." *Ibid.* Thus, these jurors never faced the dilemma posed in *Beck*. From the outset they were given three options. They could have convicted petitioner of capital murder if that

[10] Ironically, the Texas Court of Criminal Appeals stated, "It appears that had appellant's written confession been admitted into evidence, the issue that appellant presents might call for a conclusion different from the one [we reach]." App. 85, n. 7.

[11] "No person . . . shall be compelled in any criminal case to be a witness against himself . . . ." U. S. Const., Amdt. 5.

TOMPKINS *v.* TEXAS

was warranted. They could have acquitted him if they decided that he had committed no crime. If their determination fell somewhere in between—if they found that petitioner had committed a serious, violent crime but did not believe he deserved to be executed for his act—they could have convicted him of noncapital murder.

On the record before us it is proper to presume that the jury followed the judge's instructions and was convinced beyond a reasonable doubt that petitioner did intend to kill Berry when he stuffed the gag and her tongue down her throat. The jury implicitly made such a finding when it returned the guilty verdict and expressly so found at the conclusion of the sentencing hearing.[12] If these jurors had doubted petitioner's intent to kill yet balked at exoneration, it is highly unlikely that they would have convicted him of capital murder, the more serious of the two types of murder on which they were instructed. Thus, on the facts of this case, petitioner was afforded the procedural safeguard mandated by our holding in *Beck*.

It may well be sound policy to instruct the jury on every lesser included offense supported by the evidence. But the Constitution requires no such rule. It mandates only that a jury be given a means to avoid a Hobson's choice between acquittal and capital murder. Because the instructions in this case afforded the jury such an option, they did not offend the Constitution.

II

Petitioner is black. All the jurors who convicted and sentenced him to death were white, as was his victim. There

---

[12] Petitioner does not question the sufficiency of the evidence supporting the capital murder conviction. It is therefore quite wrong for the dissent to conclude that petitioner "almost certainly" did not intend to kill his victim. See *post*, at —— [slip op. at 12]. The dissent bases its gratuitous factual finding on petitioner's self-serving comment in a statement to police, which was not admitted into evidence. Nor was the comment sub-

TOMPKINS *v.* TEXAS

had been 13 black persons on the venire from which the jury was chosen. After a lengthy *voir dire* examination, which included prolix hypothetical questions about the "law of causation," the "law of parties," and the "law of circumstantial evidence," as well as typical questioning about such matters as educational background and attitudes toward the death penalty,[13] the prosecutors successfully challenged eight of the black venirepersons for cause and used peremptory strikes against the other five. Petitioner moved unsuccessfully to quash the jury, arguing that the prosecutors systematically and purposely had excluded all members of the petitioner's race from the jury in violation of federal equal protection standards set forth in *Swain* v. *Alabama*, 380 U. S. 202 (1965).

Five years after petitioner's trial this Court found that *Swain*, interpreted by lower courts to require systematic exclusion in a series of cases, had "placed on defendants a crippling burden of proof. . . ." *Batson* v. *Kentucky*, 476 U. S. 79, 92 (1986). Thus we partially overruled *Swain*, and held that a defendant may rely solely on evidence regarding the use of peremptory challenges at his trial to prove discriminatory jury selection. *Id.*, at 95; 100, n. 25. A defendant asserting a *Batson* claim must prove prima facie that the prosecution purposefully discriminated in excluding blacks from the petit jury.[14] *Id.*, at 96. Upon such a showing "the bur-

---

ject to cross-examination, since petitioner elected not to testify about the crime. See *supra*, at n. 2.

[13] See App. to Brief of Respondent A-1 to A-37.

[14] "To establish such a case, the defendant first must show that he is a member of a cognizable racial group, *Castaneda* v. *Partida*, [430 U. S. 482,] 494 [(1977)], and that the prosecutor has exercised peremptory challenges to remove from the venire members of the defendant's race. Second, the defendant is entitled to rely on the fact, as to which there can be no dispute, that peremptory challenges constitute a jury selection practice that permits 'those to discriminate who are of a mind to discriminate.' *Avery* v. *Georgia*, 345 U. S. [559,] 562 [(1953)]. Finally, the defendant must show that these facts and any other relevant circumstances raise an

TOMPKINS *v.* TEXAS

den shifts to the State to come forward," *id.*, at 97, and "articulate a neutral explanation related to the particular case to be tried. The trial court then will have the duty to determine if the defendant has established purposeful discrimination." *Id.*, at 98.

Following our decision in *Griffith* v. *Kentucky*, 479 U. S. 314 (1987), that *Batson* applied to all cases on direct review when it was decided, the Court of Criminal Appeals of Texas abated petitioner's pending appeal and ordered

> "the trial judge to conduct an evidentiary hearing and determine whether appellant had made a prima facie showing of purposeful discrimination and, if so, whether the prosecuting attorneys in this cause could offer a racially neutral explanation for using their peremptory strikes . . . ." App. 62.

It is undisputed that at the *Batson* hearing petitioner established prima facie that the prosecutor had engaged in purposeful discrimination during jury selection. The record includes evidence that the prosecutors in this case, like their colleagues in other cases, were particularly careful about selecting black persons as jurors because of assumptions that many black persons "have preconceived notions about law enforcement and government"[14] and that as a group blacks are inclined to be sympathetic and lenient toward black defend-

---

inference that the prosecutor used that practice to exclude the veniremen from the petit jury on account of their race. This combination of factors in the empaneling of the petit jury, as in the selection of the venire, raises the necessary inference of purposeful discrimination." *Batson* v. *Kentucky*, 476 U. S. 79, 96 (1986).

Facts pertinent to assessment of a defendant's prima facie case include proof of systematic exclusion over time, *id.*, at 94; substantial underrepresentation of members of the defendant's race on the venire, *id.*, at 95; the extent and nature of prosecutor's use of peremptories to exclude black venirepersons in the particular case; *i. e.*, whether there is a pattern of strikes and the content of "the prosecutor's questions and statements during *voir dire* examination," *id.*, at 96–97.

[14] Trans. of *Batson* hearing 184.

TOMPKINS *v.* TEXAS

ants.[16] The trial judge made no reference to that evidence, instead basing her conclusion that a prima facie showing of discrimination had been made on three facts: (1) petitioner is black; (2) there were no blacks on the jury; and (3) the State exercised peremptory challenges against black venirepersons. App. 47. The state criminal appeals court affirmed her finding. *Id.*, at 62–63.

At the *Batson* hearing prosecutors testified to a neutral, nonracial reason for each of the five peremptory challenges. The trial judge accepted these reasons in her three-page list of findings of fact and conclusions of law. *Id.*, at 47–49. The reviewing court affirmed her judgment, invoking a state-law sufficiency-of-the-evidence standard that permits reversal "only if no rational trier of fact could have failed to find [the defendant's] factual allegation [of purposeful discrimination] true by a preponderance of evidence." *Id.*, at 65. Petitioner does not contest the state courts' approval of prosecutorial strikes against two venirepersons who had expressed concern about the death penalty. He does contend that the trial court's deference to the prosecutor and the appellate court's deference to the trial court draw into question the constitutionality of the challenges against venirepersons Thomas, Samuel, and Green. We proceed to examine those challenges.

Venireperson Thomas

Isabella Thomas was a 45-year-old woman who had been employed as a head cashier for 12 years. She was questioned at length about her ability to decide a case in which the evidence of guilt was entirely circumstantial. Toward the end of her examination, first in response to a question from the court and finally in response to a question by the prosecu-

[16] *Id.*, at 156, 162; see also *id.*, at 31, 181.

TOMPKINS *v.* TEXAS

tor, she unequivocally stated that she could apply the law of circumstantial evidence.[17]

At the *Batson* hearing six years later, one prosecutor testified that his "whole case" depended on circumstantial evidence and that he had struck Thomas as unable to follow the law on circumstantial evidence.[18] The trial judge found that because the prosecutor was "skeptical" about Thomas' ability to obey circumstantial evidence law, the "State's excusal of Ms. Thomas was neutral, relative, clear and legitimate as required by BATSON and was not racially motivated." *Id.*, at 48.

The Texas criminal appellate court devoted four pages of its opinion to the challenge of Thomas. It pointed out that while the trial judge eventually suppressed petitioner's confession, at the time of *voir dire* she had ruled it admissible. The prosecutor's testimony that the entire case was circumstantial thus was "a little shocking and totally not understandable." *Id.*, at 68. "Without more," the court added, "we would have to hold that only an irrational trier of fact

[17] "[THE COURT:] . . . If he proves his case to you beyond a reasonable doubt. Could you find the defendant guilty in any case based on circumstantial evidence or would you always require direct evidence before you could find somebody guilty.

"THE VENIREMEN [sic]: I am sure if I was shown all of the possibilities of beyond a reasonable doubt, I could." App. to Brief of Respondent A-19.

"[TRIAL PROSECUTOR:] Now, one of the tools so to speak in doing that, [is] the law of circumstantial evidence. And you are saying that you can apply that law to a given set of facts.

"A Yes I could." *Id.*, at A-20.

[18] "Q [*BATSON* HEARING PROSECUTOR:] Why was the law of circumstantial evidence so important at that particular time?

"A [TRIAL PROSECUTOR:] That was my whole case. We had no direct evidence." *Id.*, at A-21.

"Q The main reason you struck her then was she could not follow the law on circumstantial evidence?

"A She had problems in that regard, yeah." *Id.*, at A-24.

TOMPKINS *v.* TEXAS

could have accepted this reason as a 'neutral explanation'" for a peremptory strike. *Ibid.* The court instead made its own examination of the record. Concluding that admission of the confession would not have "completely rule[d] out an instruction by the trial judge on the law of circumstantial evidence," it held "that the prosecuting attorney exercised a peremptory on the venireperson rather than risk a hung jury." *Id.*, at 70.

Venireperson Samuel

Frank E. Samuel was examined at great length, as illustrated by the colloquy quoted in the margin, on "the law of causation" and "the law of parties."[19] At the *Batson* hearing

[19] "Q [TRIAL PROSECUTOR:] Good morning. As the Judge said, we have several questions to ask you. A lot of it is concerning certain applications of our laws; whether or not you can apply a law in a certain fact situation; whether or not you believe in that law; and, again, whether or not you sit on a jury and apply the law to the facts that you hear from the witness stand.

"One of the laws that we will be going over is the law of causation. The law of causation is a law that I anticipate the Judge— . . . —might give to you. In explaining the law of causation, let me first go through the piece of paper that charges Mr. Tompkins, this man right here, with the offense of capital murder.

"It alleges certain elements, certain things, that we must prove to you beyond a reasonable doubt. One of the things we must prove to you is the date that it happened; that on or about January 26, 1981, Mr. Tompkins committed capital murder. I must prove to you also where it happened, what jurisdiction; and I must prove just that it happened in Harris County, Texas. So the date, the Harris County, Texas—and then I must prove to you that the murder happened while in the course of committing or attempting to commit robbery. And I must prove to you, further, that during the course of that robbery, Mr. Tompkins had the intent to cause the death of Mary Berry, and I must prove to you what it means. Mary Berry died by suffocation, placing a cloth gag in her mouth. So I must prove to you that date, January 26, 1981; I must prove to you that the crime happened in Harris County, Texas; and I must prove to you that Mr. Tompkins, while in the course of committing the offense of robbery, intentionally caused the death of Mary Berry; and I must prove to you by what means.

TOMPKINS *v.* TEXAS

six years later, one prosecutor testified that he decided to excuse Samuel because his response to a jury questionnaire submitted before *voir dire* indicated that he might not be able

---

"Intent—if you notice, this piece of paper used the word 'intent.' Intent—I obviously can't open a man's mind up and say: Here it is. I can prove intent by either acts done or words spoken, by the witnesses that testify. Let's say that someone comes up to you and points a gun at you and says, 'Give me your money' and shoots you and kills you and someone witnessed that particular transaction. Someone saw that. Well, one, if those facts were testified to in court, one could come to the conclusion that person had the intent to rob you and also had the intent to kill you by what those people observed. The guy came up to you and he said a certain thing and he said, 'Give me your money' and he had a gun and pointed that gun at you and pulled trigger [sic]. With those facts, one could come to the conclusion that the person had the intent to commit capital murder—or had the intent to commit murder. Now, sometimes the law furnishes intent for us. It does so by the law of causation. Now, the law of causation says if the person has the intent of committing one felony and during the course of that felony, another felony is committed, then we are going to hold him responsible for that act, even though he never meant it.

"Let me give you and [sic] example. A goes into a bank with the purpose of robbing that bank. He goes up to the teller and pulls a gun and says, 'Give me your money.' The security guard that works in that bank sees what's going on and he pulls—that is, the security guard pulls—his gun or fires at the robber but misses him and kills B, a person who was there to cash their check. Now, we know A can be charged with capital murder because he was in the course of committing robbery where someone got killed. Now, he didn't intend to kill that lady; in fact, he wasn't the one that shot her. But the law says that if one has intent to commit a felony, like he had the intent to commit that robbery—he went in there with that intent—and, during the course of that robbery, someone else got killed, even though he didn't mean to cause that injury, then the Court is going to hold him responsible; and he can be charged with capital murder, be found guilty of capital murder, and the death penalty could be assessed.

"Now, the Judge said, if, for any reason, I don't explain myself to your satisfaction, please tell me.

"Now, my question to you is: Can you apply the law of causation in a capital murder case, in a proper case?

"A [VENIREPERSON SAMUEL:] Can I apply? Can I apply?

"Q Do you have any trouble with that law? The law of causation says that we are going to furnish the intent. We are going to hold you responsible

TOMPKINS *v.* TEXAS

to read.[30] When asked to read the text of the questions that the jury must answer at a capital sentencing hearing, however, Samuel had no difficulty doing so.[31] The trial judge,

---

for what you did but we are going to go a step further and hold you responsible for something you didn't do, because you start—it's like a snowball going down a mountain. That snowball accumulated more snow as it went down. And as a result of it—but for that person's action, that lady would not have been killed, you see.

"A (Juror nods head.)

"Q My question to you is: Can you find someone guilty of capital murder by applying the law of causation?

"A I think so.

"Q Now let's assume that we found someone guilty of capital murder. Capital murder is when someone, for our purposes,—while in the course of committing a robbery, he intentionally caused the death of somebody.

"Let me give you another example. A guy goes into a U-Totem with the purpose of robbing the place. He does so and he takes the customers of that U-Totem and places them in a cooler and locks them up and ties them up and leaves them. Now let's say the air-conditioning cuts off for some reasons and the people die. They suffocate. Now, air can't come in. Now, he comes in and he says: Well, I intended to rob the place but I didn't intend to kill them; the cooler was cool, and they could have stayed in there for a week without any harm coming to them. People come in and out of that store. Someone would have found them. The law of causations says we are going to hold him responsible for those people's death, even though he didn't mean to kill them, and he can be charged with capital murder and be found guilty of capital murder and the death penalty assessed.

. . . . .

"Another law that we have is the law of parties. The law of parties says if A and B go in the bank and they plan it—B's job is to take the money out—take the money out of the cash register. That's all; he doesn't have a gun. He doesn't mean to hurt anybody. A and B go into the bank. B goes up to the teller, takes the money, and leaves. A kills someone in the course of that robbery. Now, we know A can be charged with capital murder because he was in the course of committing that robbery and he caused someone's death. B can also be charged with capital murder because the law of parties says if you help—if B helps in the commission of that robbery/murder, then we are going to find him just as guilty; you see? And he can be charged with capital murder.

"Can you apply the law of parties? What I mean by 'apply'—do you agree with the law of parties?

TOMPKINS *v.* TEXAS

having remarked during the hearing that writing skill is not a prerequisite to jury service,[22] found that Samuel "obviously had extreme difficulty with legal concepts" and that "it was obvious" that the prosecutor's challenge "was motivated by what was perceived as Mr. Samuel's inability to understand and comprehend the issues . . . ." *Id.*, at 49. Accordingly, the State's striking of Samuel "was neutral, relative, clear and legitimate as required by BATSON and was not racially motivated." *Ibid.*

"A I think I would." *Id.*, at A-24 to A-30.

[20] On Samuel's questionnaire, introduced as State's Exhibit No. 1 at the *Batson* hearing, are short answers printed in capital letters and occasionally misspelled or abbreviated. Regarding Samuel, the prosecutor testified in part:

". . . . I really did think in all honesty that the man couldn't even read and I did ask him to read, I think, questions one and two, and to my surprise, he was able to read them, but even in that respect I was going to strike the man because of those reasons. I just didn't feel he could comprehend the issues or that he could read the charge and I made my mind up from the very beginning—probably when I saw the questionnaire." *Id.*, at A-36 to A-37.

If the prosecutor had made up his mind to excuse Samuel when he examined his questionnaire, it is difficult to understand the purpose of the inquiries quoted *supra*, at n. 17.

[21] "[TRIAL PROSECUTOR:] Now, let's assume we have found the person guilty of capital murder. We said you are guilty. What happens to him? Well, the Judge will submit two questions to you in deciding whether or not a person should be put to death. If you answer both questions yes—if all twelve jurors answer both questions yes—then the Judge will assess the death penalty. Those two questions are on the board. If you will, will you read Question No. 1 for us.

"[A VENIREPERSON SAMUEL:] It says 'whether the conduct of the defendant that caused the death of the deceased was committed deliberately and with a reasonable expectation that the death of the deceased or another would result.'

"Q And Question No. 2?

"A 'Whether there is a probability that the defendant would commit criminal acts of violence that would constitute a continuing threat to society.'" App. to Brief of Respondent A-29.

[22] Trans. of *Batson* hearing 141.

TOMPKINS *v.* TEXAS

In a brief discussion, the Court of Criminal Appeals placed no reliance on Samuel's supposed difficulty with legal concepts. Indeed, it indicated that venirepersons, including those accepted by the State, typically had manifested uncertainty about such concepts.[23] It pointed instead to the prosecutor's testimony that Samuel's reading and writing skills were poor, even though the record belies that testimony. Concluding that since the case "was expected to include detailed written jury instructions, the State evidently preferred to avoid literacy problems on the jury," the appellate court sustained the challenge to Samuel. *Id.*, at 70.

Venireperson Green

The trial judge's finding with respect to Leroy Green described certain aspects of his *voir dire* testimony but did not purport to state why the prosecutor excused him.[24] The Court of Criminal Appeals found no basis for objecting to Green in any of the testimony to which the trial judge had

[23] "[O]ur reading of the entire jury selection process in this case discloses widespread disagreement and uncertainty among the venirepersons, as it does in nearly every capital murder case, regarding legal definitions and concepts, which are usually alien to most venirepersons. Not surprisingly, it is not uncommon for those venirepersons to appear inarticulate, confused, and tentative under these conditions. We find that [Samuel's] answers to questions asked did not indicate an inability on his part, that was any greater or less than the unchallenged venirepersons['], to understand the law or to apply it impartially." App. 71.

[24] The relevant trial court findings were:

"17. Mr. Green testified that over the years he had frequently changed his opinion on the propriety of the death penalty and that his wife was opposed to the death penalty; he frequently made non verbal [sic] answers or 'yeahs'; there was no valid communication between the prosecutor and the juror. The juror had problems with and vascillated [sic] regarding his ability to follow the law of causation and indicated that he might require evidence of premeditation.

"18. The State's excusal of Mr. Green was neutral, relative, clear and legitimate as required by BATSON and was not racially motivated." *Id.*, at 49.

TOMPKINS *v.* TEXAS

referred; rather, it stated that "the sole reason given why the venireperson was struck was that he was an employee of the United States Postal Service." *Id.*, at 71. The court admitted

> "some difficulty understanding the relevancy of a venireperson's employment as a postman employed by the United States Government as far as his qualifications for jury service. Although the prosecuting attorney indicated that 'I have not had very good luck with postal employees', she did not elaborate upon her evident bias against such employees. Perhaps, indeed, federal postal employees share a common view of the criminal justice system antithetical to the interests of law enforcement. But if so, we are not aware of it, nor has the State undertaken to enlighten us further on the subject.
>
> "Notwithstanding what we have stated, we found that the prosecuting attorney's reasons that she gave constitute a racially neutral explanation, and it is not the office of this Court to judge her credibility. Explicit in *Batson* is that a prosecuting attorney is free to exercise his peremptory strikes, provided that they are non-race related. 'The challenge, after all, is still a peremptory one.'" *Id.*, at 71–72 (citations omitted).

Having considered petitioner's objections to each of the excluded venirepersons, the Court of Criminal Appeals concluded "that a rational trier of fact might have failed to find, by a preponderance of the evidence, an intentional discrimination on the part of the prosecuting attorneys in this cause . . . . Whether this Court would have made the same judgment as the trial judge did is unimportant," it continued, "because her conclusion, given a subjective belief in the truth of the prosecuting attorneys' explanations, which is supported by sufficient evidence, comports with that of a rational trier of fact." *Id.*, at 72–73.

The opinion of Texas Court of Criminal Appeals reflects conscientious and frank scrutiny of the record developed at

TOMPKINS *v.* TEXAS

petitioner's *Batson* hearing. Nonetheless its application of a sufficiency-of-the-evidence standard inadequately protected the important interests at stake. Our opinion in *Batson* states that "[s]ince the trial judge's findings in the context under consideration here largely will turn on evaluation of credibility, a reviewing court ordinarily should give those findings great deference." 476 U. S., at 98, n. 21. We cited as support *Anderson* v. *Bessemer City*, 470 U. S. 564 (1985), which held that a trial court's finding of intentional discrimination in violation of Title VII of the Civil Rights Act of 1964, 42 U. S. C. § 2000e *et seq.*, should be reversed only if clearly erroneous. "A finding is 'clearly erroneous,'" the Court had written in *United States* v. *United States Gypsum Co.*, 333 U. S. 364, 395 (1948), "when although there is evidence to support it, the reviewing court on the entire evidence is left with the definite and firm conviction that a mistake has been committed."

In accordance with the implication in *Batson*, most state appellate courts have applied a clearly erroneous standard to review appeals relying on that opinion.[8] The Texas Court of Criminal Appeals, however, has not followed this trend. Having applied the state-law sufficiency standard in this case without acknowledging any possible conflict with *Batson*, the court subsequently considered and rejected the clearly erroneous standard:

> "We believe that our focus, as well as that of the trial judge, should be on whether purposeful discrimination was established. We will of course consider the evidence in the light most favorable to the trial judge's rul-

[8] See, *e. g.*, *Stanley* v. *State*, 313 Md. 50, 84, 542 A. 2d 1267, 1283 (1988); *State* v. *Walton*, 227 Neb. 559, ——, 418 N. W. 2d 589, 592 (1988); *Ex parte Branch*, 526 So. 2d 609, 625 (Ala. 1987); *Gamble* v. *State*, 257 Ga. 325, 327, 357 S. E. 2d 792, 794 (1987), cert. denied, —— U. S. —— (1988); *Lockett* v. *State*, 517 So. 2d 1346, 1349–1350 (Miss. 1987); *State* v. *Antwine*, 743 S. W. 2d 51, 66 (Mo. 1987) (en banc), cert. denied, —— U. S. —— (1988).

TOMPKINS *v.* TEXAS

> ings and determine if those rulings are supported by the record. If the record supports the findings of the trial judge, they will not be disturbed on appeal." *Keeton* v. *State*, 749 S. W. 2d 861, 870 (Tex. Cr. App. 1988) (en banc).

This Court rarely and reluctantly interferes with a State's procedural rule. "By the same token, however, where state courts entertain a federally created cause of action, the 'federal right cannot be defeated by the forms of local practice.'" *Felder* v. *Casey*, —— U. S. ——, —— (1988) (quoting *Brown* v. *Western Railway of Alabama*, 338 U. S. 294, 296 (1949)). Thus 40 years ago we required that a complaint brought in state court pursuant to the Federal Employers' Liability Act, 45 U. S. C. § 51 *et seq.*, be construed according to federal law. *Brown, supra.* Last Term we invalidated a State's requirement that a plaintiff file a notice of claim before prosecuting a federal civil rights suit in state court.[36] *Felder, supra*, at ——. Today we reject the Texas criminal appeals court's standard for reviewing *Batson* claims.

This Court's commitment to ensuring that a State does not deliberately deprive a black defendant of an opportunity to have members of his race on his jury dates to 1880, when we held that a statute precluding black persons from jury service violated the Equal Protection Clause. *Strauder* v. *West Virginia*, 100 U. S. 303. We extended that concept to peremptory challenges in *Swain* v. *Alabama*, 380 U. S. 202 (1965), and most recently, in *Batson*, eased the defendant's burden

[36] We explained:

"Under the Supremacy Clause of the Federal Constitution, '[t]he relative importance to the State of its own law is not material when there is a conflict with a valid federal law,' for 'any state law, however clearly within a State's acknowledged power, which interferes with or is contrary to federal law, must yield.' *Free* v. *Bland*, 369 U. S. 663, 666 (1962)." *Felder* v. *Casey*, —— U. S. ——, —— (1988).

TOMPKINS *v.* TEXAS

of proving discrimination in order to secure the right to equal protection of the laws.[7]

Acknowledging that application of *Swain* had rendered "prosecutors' peremptory challenges . . . largely immune from constitutional scrutiny," we endeavored in *Batson* to strengthen equal protection guarantees in that context. 476 U. S., at 92–93. In addition to permitting a defendant to prove discrimination by reference to the facts of his case, *id.*, at 95, we stressed that only meaningful explanations by a prosecutor would rebut a prima facie inference of purposeful discrimination. *Id.*, at 97–98. Finally, we expressed confidence that trial courts would be "alert" for instances of invidious discrimination. *Id.*, at 99, n. 22.

The Texas court's sufficiency-of-the-evidence standard erodes *Batson*'s protection. Allowing reversal only when "no rational trier of fact" would have ruled against a defendant asserting a *Batson* violation, see App. 65, narrows the scope of review to a point that is virtually meaningless. The court's later statement that it "will of course . . . determine if [the trial court's] rulings are supported by the record," *Keeton*, 749 S. W. 2d, at 870, offers scant reassurance, since a record usually will include some support for any proffered explanation. In this case, for example, venireperson Samuel's answers to the jury questionnaire well may have provoked questions regarding his literacy. But for an appellate court to affirm the trial court's acceptance of this concern as a neutral justification for a peremptory challenge, without considering relevant factors such as the venireperson's reading of complex sentences during *voir dire*, saps *Batson* of its

[7] Sharing in this right are the defendant, who risks trial not by a jury of his peers but by a jury whose verdict may be infected by racial bias; the excluded venirepersons, who are barred from public service on account of their race, a factor "'unrelated to . . . fitness as a juror;'" and our democratic society, which seeks to eliminate racial prejudice and its ramifications. *Batson*, 476 U. S., at 86–87 (quoting *Thiel* v. *Southern Pacific Co.*, 328 U. S. 217, 227 (1946) (Frankfurter, J., dissenting)).

TOMPKINS *v.* TEXAS

force. In contrast, the clearly erroneous standard requires the appellate court, after locating record support for an explanation, to decide separately whether the trial judge was mistaken. See *United States Gypsum Co.*, 333 U. S., at 395. This extra step mandates more careful examination of the record and more considered evaluation of the validity of the trial court's findings. Thus a standard no less protective than clearly erroneous is essential to the faithful application of *Batson*.

The appellate court's application of its stated standard augmented the inadequacy of review of petitioner's *Batson* claim. Its opinion demonstrated that the trial judge's findings concerning venirepersons Samuel and Green were clearly erroneous, and that the finding concerning Thomas relied heavily on a misunderstanding about the extent to which the case rested on circumstantial evidence. Instead of setting aside the erroneous findings, the Court of Criminal Appeals—despite its avowal to the contrary, App. 65—substituted its own findings in an attempt to supply a permissible predicate for the challenges. This was error.[28]

In commenting in *Batson* on the burden to rebut a prima facie case of purposeful discrimination, we stated that "the prosecutor must give a 'clear and reasonably specific' explanation of his 'legitimate reasons' for exercising the challenges." 476 U. S., at 98, n. 20 (quoting *Texas Dept. of Community Affairs* v. *Burdine*, 450 U. S. 248, 258 (1981)).[29]

[28] In *Anderson* v. *Bessemer City*, 470 U. S. 564, 577 (1985), we were called upon to answer "not whether the Fourth Circuit's interpretation of the facts was clearly erroneous, but whether the District Court's finding was clearly erroneous." Likewise in this case we focus on the validity of the trial court's findings, not those of the appellate court.

[29] JUSTICE WHITE recognized that "[m]uch litigation will be required to spell out the contours of the Court's equal protection holding today . . . ." *Batson*, 476 U. S., at 102 (concurring opinion). Although this case represents our first opportunity to consider those boundaries, many lower courts and commentators already have done so. *E. g.*, *United States* v. *Alcantar*, 832 F. 2d 1175 (CA9 1987), *United States* v. *Wilson*, 816 F. 2d

TOMPKINS *v.* TEXAS

Although "the prosecutor's explanation need not rise to the level justifying the exercise of a challenge for cause," an intuition that a black venireperson might be biased in a particular case simply because the defendant is black cannot justify a peremptory challenge. *Id.*, at 97. We added:

> "Nor may the prosecutor rebut the defendant's case merely by denying that he had a discriminatory motive or 'affirm[ing] [his] good faith in making individual selections.' *Alexander* v. *Louisiana*, 405 U. S. [625,] 632 [(1972)]. If these general assertions were accepted as rebutting a defendant's prima facie case, the Equal Protection Clause 'would be but a vain and illusory requirement.' *Norris* v. *Alabama*, [294 U. S. 587,] 598 [(1935)]. The prosecutor therefore must articulate a neutral explanation related to the particular case to be tried." *Id.*, at 98.

As several state courts have remarked, *Batson* indicated that a prosecutor's explanation for striking a black venireperson is not sufficient simply because it appears neutral and nonracial; rather, scrutiny must prove it to be both genuine and related to the case on trial.[30] Indeed one Texas criminal appeals judge recently recognized that

421 (CA8 1987), *Keeton* v. *State*, 749 S. W. 2d 861 (Tex. Cr. App. 1988) (en banc), *Ex parte Branch*, 526 So. 2d 609 (Ala. 1987), and cases they cite; Comment, *Batson* v. *Kentucky*: Equal Protection, The Fair Cross-Section Requirement, and the Discriminatory Use of Peremptory Challenges, 37 Emory L. J. 755 (1988); Note, *Batson* v. *Kentucky* and the Prosecutorial Peremptory Challenge: Arbitrary and Capricious Equal Protection?, 74 Va. L. Rev. 811 (1988); Fisher, Batson v. Kentucky: Purposeful Discrimination in Jury Selection, 87 N. Y. L. J., Nov. 3, 1988, p. 1, col. 1, and Nov. 4, 1988, p. 6, col. 3.

Because it is uncontroverted that this petitioner made a prima facie showing of purposeful discrimination, see App. 62–63, we do not reexamine that aspect of the *Batson* inquiry.

[30] In a thorough examination of *Batson*'s requirements, the Missouri Supreme Court wrote:

TOMPKINS v. TEXAS

"if *Batson* is to be given any substantive meaning, a prosecutor should not be permitted to sustain his burden by giving what appear to be facially specious 'race-neutral' reasons . . . . These amount to nothing less than reasons for exercising a peremptory strike.

. . . . .

"It is imperative . . . if the prosecutor uses one of his peremptory strikes on a member of the same race as the defendant, he should couple his objectively stated reason with a reasonable explanation for his reasons. . . ." *Keeton*, 749 S. W. 2d, at 874, 879 (Teague, J., concurring).

Evidence of pretext may, but need not be, introduced by the defendant.[11] Either way, the trial judge must search for

---

"We do not believe . . . that *Batson* is satisfied by 'neutral explanations' which are no more than facially legitimate, reasonably specific and clear. Were facially neutral explanations sufficient without more, *Batson* would be meaningless. It would take little effort for prosecutors who are of such a mind to adopt rote 'neutral explanations' which bear facial legitimacy but conceal a discriminatory motive. We do not believe the Supreme Court intended a charade when it announced *Batson*." *Antwine*, 743 S. W. 2d, at 65.

See also, *e. g.*, *State* v. *Gonzalez*, 206 Conn. 391, 404, 538 A. 2d 210, 216–217 (1988); *State* v. *Slappy*, 522 So. 2d 18, 22–23 (Fla. 1988); *Gamble*, 257 Ga., at 326–330, 357 S. E. 2d, at 794–796; *State* v. *Goode*, 107 N. M. 298, ——, 756 P. 2d 578, 583 (N. M. App. 1988).

[11] Our sources for the guidelines set out in *Batson* were decisions pursuant to Title VII of the Civil Rights Act of 1964, 42 U. S. C. § 2000e *et seq.*, such as *McDonnell Douglas Corp.* v. *Green*, 411 U. S. 792 (1973), and *Texas Dept. of Community Affairs* v. *Burdine*, 450 U. S. 248 (1981). *Batson*, 476 U. S., at 94, n. 18; 96, n. 19; 98, n. 21. Indeed in *Batson*, *supra*, at 93, we embraced the theory of those cases that "[t]he ultimate burden of persuading the trier of fact that the [State] intentionally discriminated against the [defendant] remains at all times with the [defendant]," *Burdine*, *supra*, at 253, even though previous jury discrimination opinions resting exclusively on the Equal Protection Clause appeared to have transferred that burden to the State. *E. g.*, *Alexander* v. *Louisiana*, 405 U. S. 625, 631–632 (1972) ("Once a prima facie case of invidious discrimination is established, the burden of proof shifts to the State to rebut the presumption of unconstitutional action by showing that permissible racially neutral selection criteria and procedures have produced the

TOMPKINS *v.* TEXAS

pretext in evaluating an ostensibly neutral reason for a peremptory challenge. "'Rubber stamp' approval of all nonracial explanations, no matter how whimsical or fanciful, would cripple *Batson* . . . ." *State* v. *Butler*, 731 S. W. 2d 265, 268 (Mo. App. 1987), cert. denied, —— U. S. —— (1988). Just as "the trial court should consider all relevant circumstances" in deciding whether a defendant has established a prima facie case, *Batson*, 476 U. S., at 96–97, it also should examine proffered explanations in the context of the entire case. Pertinent, case-related factors may include the races of the defendant, victim, counsel, and prospective witnesses; the nature and thoroughness of the prosecutor's questioning of the prospective jurors;[32] the venirepersons' demeanor;[33] the

---

monochromatic result"); *Whitus* v. *Georgia*, 385 U. S. 545, 550 (1967) ("The burden is, of course, on the petitioners to prove the existence of purposeful discrimination. However, once a prima facie case is made out the burden shifts to the prosecution.") (citation omitted).

Since *Batson* declares that the State's burden is only that of coming forward with rebuttal evidence, 476 U. S., at 97, a court ought to permit the defendant "to demonstrate that the State's explanations are merely pretextual and, thus, not the true reason for the use of the State's peremptory challenges." *Antwine*, 743 S. W. 2d, at 64. Cf. *Burdine*, *supra*, at 256; *McDonnell Douglas*, *supra*, at 807.

Most courts reaching this issue have incorporated a pretext step. *E. g.*, *Alcantar*, 832 F. 2d, at 1180; *Wilson*, 816 F. 2d, at 423; *Gonzalez*, 206 Conn., at 398, 538 A. 2d, at 212; *Stanley*, 313 Md., at 62, 542 A. 2d, at 1272; *Branch*, 526 So. 2d, at 624; *Williams* v. *State*, 507 So. 2d 50, 53 (Miss. 1987). But see *United States* v. *Davis*, 809 F. 2d 1194, 1201–1202 (CA6), cert. denied, —— U. S. —— (1987). It is not, however, a necessary stage. *Gonzalez*, *supra*, at 399, n. 6, 538 A. 2d, at 214, n. 6. The trial court has an independent obligation to examine the prosecutor's neutral explanations to determine if purposeful discrimination has occurred. See *Batson*, 476 U. S., at 98; *Slappy*, 522 So. 2d, at 22.

In this case petitioner's counsel tried to show the prosecutor's neutral explanations were disingenuous by cross-examining the State's witnesses and by introducing as exhibits newspaper articles discussing exclusion of black jurors in Dallas County, Tex. See Trans. of *Batson* hearing and Defendant's Exhibits Nos. 1 and 2.

[32] "'[T]he prosecutor's demeanor may be relevant. Is the prosecutor "engaging in a process of careful deliberation based on many factors" during voir dire or has he failed to "engage these same jurors in more than

TOMPKINS *v.* TEXAS

presence or absence of a pattern of strikes;[34] and the nature of the crime, anticipated evidence, and possible punishment.[35] Of particular relevance are the treatment of black venirepersons in comparison with other venirepersons[36] and the strength of the defendant's prima facie case.[37] Considering all these circumstances in light of her own experience and

---

desultory voir dire or indeed to ask them any questions at all?"'" *Id.* (quoting *State* v. *Butler*, 731 S. W. 2d 265, 269 (Mo. App. 1987)) (citations omitted)).

See also *Branch*, 526 So. 2d, at 624.

[33] *Lockett*, 517 So. 2d, at 1352; cf. Note, 74 Va. L. Rev., at 828 ("[E]ven if there is evidence of a particular type of behavior, the prosecutor should be able to articulate his reasons for drawing a negative inference from it. Otherwise, general assertions that a prosecutor does not like the looks of a potential juror may present the appearance, if not the substance, of racism.").

[34] *Branch*, 526 So. 2d, at 623–624.

[35] *Antwine*, 743 S. W. 2d, at 65.

[36] According to the New Mexico appellate court, "[b]y far the most common factor noted by courts holding a state's explanations to be pretextual is a varying treatment of white and nonwhite panel members." *Goode*, 107 N. M., at ——, 756 P. 2d, at 582. See also *People* v. *McDonald*, 125 Ill. 2d 182, 199–201, 530 N. E. 2d 1351, 1358–59 (1988); *Stanley*, 313 Md., at 77–79, 542 A. 2d, at 1280–1281; *Walton*, 227 Neb., at ——, 418 N. W. 2d, at 593; *Antwine*, 743 S. W. 2d, at 65; *Branch*, 526 So. 2d, at 623–624; *Gamble*, 257 Ga., at 328–329, 357 S. E. 2d, at 796; *Lockett*, 517 So. 2d, at 1352.

[37] "The explanation offered for striking each black juror must be evaluated in light of the explanations offered for the prosecutor's other peremptory strikes, and, as well, in light of the strength of the prima facie case. The persuasiveness of a proffered explanation may be magnified or diminished by the persuasiveness of companion explanations, and by the strength of the prima facie case.

"A court charged with the duty of determining whether the prosecutor has rebutted a prima facie case may be less troubled by one relatively weak explanation for striking a black juror when all the remaining explanations are persuasive than where several of the prosecutor's proffered justifications are questionable. Similarly, a weak prima facie case may be rebutted more readily than a strong one." *Gamble*, 257 Ga., at 327, 357 S. E. 2d, at 795.

TOMPKINS *v.* TEXAS

direct observation of the *voir dire*, the trial judge must decide whether intentional discrimination has occurred.[38] She should detail her findings to facilitate appellate review.[39]

In this case the process by which petitioner's *Batson* claim was assessed by the trial court and the Court of Criminal Appeals of Texas was inadequate for at least three reasons.

First, both courts seem to have assumed that any neutral explanation would suffice as long as the trial judge believed the prosecutor's testimony that the neutral reason prompted the peremptory challenge. In addition to overlooking our admonition that the neutral explanation must be case-related, their assumption provides no protection against the danger that a facially neutral explanation may be nothing more than a proxy for racial bias, conscious or subconscious. Cf. *Batson*, 476 U. S., at 106 (MARSHALL, J., concurring). The prosecutor's purported intuition concerning postal workers, for example, may have been based on her experience with black postal workers and thus a manifestation of unwarranted racial prejudice. Otherwise, as the Court of Criminal Appeals recognized, it is extremely difficult to understand any relevancy in venireperson Green's status as a postal employee. To satisfy the case-relation requirement, an apparently nonracial reason for a challenge must be explained in terms of more substance than intuition.[40]

---

[38] See, *e. g.*, *Branch*, 526 So. 2d, at 624. Although this exacting inquiry may be difficult, it is essential to shield equal protection interests. See *Batson*, 476 U. S., at 99. See also *Antwine*, 743 S. W. 2d, at 64–65; *Branch*, *supra*, at 629, n. 16.

[39] "We emphasize here the need for the record to contain not only specific findings by the judge, but also information to support those findings; information such as the numbers of blacks and whites on the venire, the numbers of each stricken for various reasons, the reasons underlying the strikes for cause, pertinent characteristics of jurors excluded and retained, relevant information about the race of the defendant, the victim, and the potential witnesses, and so forth." *Stanley*, 313 Md., at 70, n. 11, 542 A. 2d, at 1277, n. 11.

[40] Cf. Note, 74 Va. L. Rev., at 827 ("The prosecutor should resolve any

TOMPKINS *v.* TEXAS

Second, neither court heeded our admonition to "consider all relevant circumstances." *Id.*, at 96–97. Petitioner's prima facie showing was powerful. A case in which the prosecutor succeeds in removing all 13 black venirepersons is surely more serious than one in which some blacks are rejected but others are accepted. The strength of the inference of discrimination based on the bare statistics should not be, but was, ignored. Moreover, since the record contained evidence that the prosecutors' office had taken race into account in striking venirepersons in other cases, evaluation of that evidence in relation to this case would have been appropriate.

Finally, although it acknowledged petitioner's argument that prosecutors had "fashioned their respective voir dire examination of the remaining black prospective jurors in such a manner so that all blacks would be prevented from serving as jurors in this cause," App. 57, the Court of Criminal Appeals made no comment on the dubious character of the questions put to the black venirepersons. Courts must make sure that prosecutors are not permitted to circumvent our holding in *Batson* by requiring black venirepersons to demonstrate an understanding of areas of the law—such as the "law of parties"—that have no special relevance to the case at hand. Consideration of all relevant circumstances should encompass whether similar questions were propounded to white venirepersons and whether accepted jurors' answers differed significantly from those of the excused black jurors.

The judgment of the Court of Criminal Appeals of Texas is reversed and the case is remanded for further proceedings not inconsistent with this opinion.

So ordered.

---

doubts concerning the potential juror's impartiality during voir dire. Courts should not permit the prosecutor's self-imposed ignorance to preclude a *Batson* claim.").

~~1st~~ 2d DRAFT

SUPREME COURT OF THE UNITED STATES

No. 87-6405

PHILLIP D. TOMPKINS, PETITIONER *v.* TEXAS

ON WRIT OF CERTIORARI TO THE COURT OF CRIMINAL APPEALS OF TEXAS

[April ——, 1989]

JUSTICE WHITE, concurring in part and dissenting in part.

This case presents two questions, first whether the Texas Court of Criminal Appeals properly applied *Beck* v. *Alabama*, 447 U. S. 625 (1980); and second, whether that court properly applied *Batson* v. *Kentucky*, 476 U. S. 79 (1986). Because I answer affirmatively both questions, and would affirm, I join Part I of the Court's opinion, concurring in the view that the *Beck* analysis was correct, but write to disagree with Part II's reversal on *Batson* grounds.

The Texas prosecutors successfully challenged 8 of 13 black venirepersons for cause, and, through peremptory strikes, dismissed the remaining 5. The defendant, petitioner here, Phillip Tompkins, who is black, commenced an equal protection attack based on *Swain* v. *Alabama*, 380 U. S. 202 (1965), alleging that Texas systematically and purposely excluded the black jurors because of their race. Subsequently on direct review, the Court of Criminal Appeals instructed the trial court to conduct an evidentiary hearing on the issue of discriminatory jury selection in light of this Court's decision in *Batson* v. *Kentucky*, *supra*, which as *Griffith* v. *Kentucky*, 479 U. S. 314 (1987), held, applies to cases on direct review when *Batson* was decided. The trial court held that Tompkins had made a prima facie showing of purposeful discrimination, which holding was not challenged on appeal, but concluded that each peremptory challenge excusing a black juror was exercised for a legitimate, nonracially motivated

TOMPKINS *v.* TEXAS

reason. The Court of Criminal Appeals affirmed, —— S. W. 2d —— (1987) but this Court now reverses with respect to three of the five jurors, holding that both state courts erred in deciding the factual issue of whether the prosecutor deliberately discriminated in using his peremptory challenges.

For several reasons, I disagree with the Court. As an initial matter, the majority fails to observe *Batson*'s admonition that since a claim of intentional discrimination poses an issue of fact which will "largely . . . turn on evaluation of credibility, a reviewing court ordinarily should give those findings great deference." 476 U. S., at 98, n. 21. Here, on remand six years after the conviction, the trial court held a hearing, heard evidence, and made its factual determinations, finding that none of the five jurors at issue was excused for racial reasons. With respect to the three jurors the Court now finds were wrongly excused, Thomas, Samuel, and Green, the trial judge found that Thomas was excused because the prosecutor was skeptical about her ability to follow the law on circumstantial evidence that the State intended to rely on; Samuel was excused because the prosecutor doubted his ability to understand the complexities of a capital case, not because he was black; and Green had frequently changed his mind about the death penalty and had vacillated with respect to his ability to follow the law of causation, and indicated that he might require evidence of premeditation. With respect to each of the three jurors, the trial court found that the "State's excusal . . . was neutral, relative, clear and legitimate as required by *Batson* and was not racially motivated." App. 47–49.

The Court of Criminal Appeals affirmed. Noting that it is the accused's burden to prove discrimination, the court quoted *Batson* to explain that when the prosecutor comes forward with a neutral explanation for its strikes, " '[t]he trial court then will have the duty to determine if the defendant has established purposeful discrimination.' " —— S. W. 2d,

TOMPKINS *v.* TEXAS

at —— (quoting *Batson*, 476 U. S., at 98). When such a neutral explanation is offered, the court said, an issue of fact is joined, and it is then the burden of the accused to persuade the trial judge by a preponderance of the evidence that the allegations of purposeful discrimination are true in fact. The court described its appellate function as follows:

> "Here, we are on much more familiar ground, for it is the sufficiency of evidence to support the proposition that we evaluate against a settled standard. Thus, where the accused has the ultimate burden to prove a factual allegation, such as purposeful discrimination in jury selection, by a preponderance of evidence, an appellate court must view the entire record in a manner favorable to the factfinder's determination and reverse only if no rational trier of fact could have failed to find his factual allegation true by a preponderance of evidence. . . . This Court and the courts of appeals are principally reviewing courts. We do not substitute our judgments of witnesses' credibility and evidentiary weight for those of the factfinder, but affirm those judgments whenever the record discloses sufficient evidence in their support." —— S. W. 2d, at ——.

The Court of Criminal Appeals then proceeded to examine each of the five jurors at issue and in each case "agree[d] with the trial judge that the prosecuting attorneys articulated at the hearing racially neutral explanations, which were both plausible and unambiguous, for exercising their peremptories on the five complained about black venirepersons." *Id.* at ——.

The majority holds that all of this is insufficient to satisfy *Batson*, despite the "great deference" due state-court findings of fact. It is first ruled that the standard of review regularly followed and articulated by the Texas Court of Criminal Appeals was too lax and deferred too much to the trial court. The Constitution is said to bar Texas' sufficiency

TOMPKINS *v.* TEXAS

of the evidence standard in favor of a clearly erroneous standard which would give appellate courts more room to find error in the trial courts' findings. As the majority itself recognizes, this is an extraordinary imposition on the state courts. Only "rarely and reluctantly" has the Court found cause to invalidate state procedural rules. See *Felder* v. *Casey*, 487 U. S. ——, —— (1988). Even if the Court had not proceeded with such evident gusto to invalidate the traditional standard of review used in Texas, what the Court does is quite unacceptable to me.

In the first place, the majority apparently believes that state trial courts will not follow *Batson* and cannot be trusted fairly to pass upon the credibility of the prosecutor and the reasons he offers for the use of peremptories, a view that I do not share. The majority also considers the sufficiency of the evidence standard to be toothless, but that is not an unusual standard to be used in reviewing factual determinations in criminal cases, including determinations of guilt. And in this very case, the Court of Criminal Appeals did not adopt the trial court's findings on juror Green but made its own finding. Furthermore, when in criminal cases coming from state courts it is claimed in this Court on direct appeal, or in collateral proceedings in a federal court, that the evidence of guilt is constitutionally insufficient, the standard to be used in deciding the issue is the very standard the court of appeals employed in this case. We have held in such cases that "the relevant question is whether, after viewing the evidence in the light most favorable to the prosecution, *any* rational trier of fact could have found the essential elements of the crime beyond a reasonable doubt." *Jackson* v. *Virginia*, 443 U. S., 307, 319 (1979) (emphasis in original). *Jackson* discarded the "no evidence" standard and adopted the rule just quoted. It went no further, however, and it is the *Jackson* standard that is now followed in federal courts when state-court judgments in criminal cases are challenged for insuffi-

TOMPKINS *v.* TEXAS

cient evidence.* If this standard is constitutionally sufficient in reviewing guilt determinations, I see nothing untoward in a state appellate court's use of this standard in reviewing factfindings such as are at issue in this case.

The majority's determination to force state appellate courts to expand their oversight of their trial courts will, of course, require this Court and federal courts in collateral proceedings to exercise a stricter standard in reviewing state-court *Batson* determinations. And if this category of findings is to be subject to such special review in the federal courts, it is difficult to predict where the trend initiated by today's decision will cease.

As I understand *Batson*, the accused has the burden throughout of proving deliberate discrimination. The prosecutor in response must do more than assert his good faith and absence of discriminatory intent. But it suffices if he puts forth a believable, neutral explanation for his strikes, and it will very likely not be believable if his explanation has no relation to the juror's anticipated performance as a juror in the kind of case before the court. In *Batson*, the Court emphasized that this was the extent of the prosecutor's duty. As the court below observed, the issue before the trial court is then essentially one of deciding the credibility of the prosecutor, and if the judge believes the prosecutor, he is also no doubt satisfied that there is a satisfactory basis for the strikes that have taken place. In this case, the trial court, after a hearing, found that with respect to each juror the reasons for striking were not only neutral but also relevant to the case. The majority now, however, insists not only that the prosecutor do more but also requires that the trial judge and the appellate courts second-guess reasons for removing jurors, even if these courts credit the prosecutor's honesty.

---

*See, *e. g.*, *Martin* v. *Foltz*, 773 F. 2d 711, 717 (CA6 1985), cert. denied 478 U. S. 1021 (1986); *United States* v. *Fairman*, 769 F. 2d 386, 393 (CA7 1985); *Machin* v. *Wainwright*, 758 F. 2d 1431, 1435 (CA11 1985); *Paullet* v. *Howard*, 634 F. 2d 117, 118 (CA3 1980).

TOMPKINS *v.* TEXAS

The prosecutor's use of his peremptories may be approved only after canvassing his action in terms of a long list of considerations that the majority specifies in its opinion; and if the strikes are approved, the trial court is constitutionally required to record its reasons for doing so in order that appellate review, on a cold record, of the trial court's factual determinations may be made, perhaps by judges sitting in Washington, D. C.

Even if one accepts the majority's new rule for overturning state courts' factual determinations, it is difficult to understand why the Court does not remand to permit the Texas court to apply the proper standard in the first instance. This is the Court's usual practice. Here, for all practical purposes, the Court's opinion settles this case and decides that each of the three jurors was stricken in violation of *Batson.* I disagree with respect to each juror. A prosecutor, without violating *Batson*, may strike jurors whom he in good-faith doubts will follow the rules about circumstantial evidence, jurors whom he in good faith doubts will be able to understand the facts and the instructions given them and jurors engaged in an occupation that in the prosecutor's experience makes their neutrality suspect. Judgments like this are what peremptories are all about. Rather than subject peremptories to the regime the Court imposes today, it would be more straightforward to hold that when a black is on trial in a criminal case, peremptory challenges by the prosecution are unconstitutional because they pose an unacceptable risk of racial discrimination in the selection of jurors.

With all due respect, I dissent.

1st DRAFT

SUPREME COURT OF THE UNITED STATES

No. 87-6405

PHILLIP D. TOMPKINS, PETITIONER *v.* TEXAS

ON WRIT OF CERTIORARI TO THE COURT OF CRIMINAL APPEALS OF TEXAS

[May ——, 1989]

JUSTICE BLACKMUN, concurring in part and dissenting in part.

My conclusions in this case are exactly the opposite of JUSTICE WHITE's and of those Justices who have joined him, for I would reverse the judgment of the Texas Court of Criminal Appeals on each of the two issues (lesser included offense and *Batson* violation) that are before us. I therefore join part II of the Court's opinion but dissent from part I.

I

In *Beck* v. *Alabama*, 447 U. S. 625, 637 (1980), this Court articulated a clear and simple rule: a defendant is entitled to have the jury instructed on a lesser included offense when the evidence, although establishing that "the defendant is guilty of a serious, violent offense . . . leaves some doubt with respect to an element that would justify conviction of a capital offense." By that rule, we adopted, as a matter of due process in capital cases, the nearly universal principle of law that the jury is "permitted to find the defendant guilty of any lesser offense necessarily included in the offense charged," if supported by evidence. *Id.*, at 633.

Today, without analysis or explanation, the majority replaces this basic requirement with a curious artifice. The majority reduces *Beck* to a rule that the jury need be given no more than *one* lesser included offense instruction, regardless of the number of elements of the capital crime that are reasonably in doubt, and regardless of the number of lesser included offenses that are reasonably supported by evidence. *Beck* is satisfied, we are now told, so long as the jury is given a "third option," falling "somewhere in between" execution and acquittal. *Ante*, at 7.

This holding, it seems to me, flies in the face of *Beck*'s positive requirement that a capital jury be given a *meaningful* choice between the extremes of acquittal and conviction on a capital charge where, under the evidence adduced at trial, one or more of the elements of the capital offense are in doubt. Far from serving the underlying purposes of *Beck*—that due process requires proper lesser included offense instructions in a capital case to ensure rationality and reliability in the determinations of guilt—the majority's "any-old-solitary-lesser-included-offense-instruction-will-do" rule invites a jury to disregard its legal duty and injects additional arbitrariness into the uniquely delicate process of deciding the fate of a capital defendant.

Because I can neither ignore the clear holding of *Beck* nor comprehend the legal basis for the standard the majority today applies, and because the facts of this case vividly demonstrate the perverse effects of the majority's rule on any semblance of rationality in the imposition of capital punishment, I dissent.

II

> "[D]eath is a different kind of punishment from any other which may be imposed in this country. . . . From the point of view of the defendant, it is different in both its severity and its finality. From the point of view of society, the action of the sovereign in taking the life of one of its citizens also differs dramatically from any other legitimate state action. It is of vital importance to the defendant and to the community that any decision to impose the death sentence be, and appear to be, based on reason rather than caprice or emotion." *Gardner* v.

TOMPKINS *v.* TEXAS

Florida, 430 U. S. 349, 357–358 (1977) (opinion of JUSTICE STEVENS for a plurality).

Among the safeguards designed to ensure that the death penalty is imposed only on the basis of reason is the requirement that the jury in the guilt phase of a capital trial be properly instructed on the applicable law. This Court in *Beck* recognized that in a capital case, where the defendant is undoubtedly guilty of some violent crime but may be innocent of the capital offense charged, jurors are hard pressed to follow their instructions when those instructions do not include lesser included offenses and the jury, therefore, is restricted to a choice between conviction of the capital offense and full acquittal.[1] Although we recognized the risk that the jury in that situation might well "'resolve its doubts in favor of conviction,'" 447 U. S., at 634, quoting *Keeble* v. *United States*, 412 U. S. 205, 213 (1973), that risk was not our sole concern. "In any particular case [the absence of a lesser included offense instruction] may favor the defendant or the prosecution .... But in every case [it] introduce[s] a level of uncertainty and unreliability into the factfinding process that cannot be tolerated in a capital case." 447 U. S., at 643. As a matter of due process, the Court held, a capital defendant "'is entitled to an instruction on a lesser included offense if the evidence would permit a jury rationally to find him guilty of the lesser offense and acquit him of the greater.'" *Id.*, at 635, quoting *Keeble*, 412 U. S., at 208.

The majority in the present case, however, claims that *Beck* is satisfied as long as the jury is "given a means to avoid a Hobson's choice between acquittal and capital murder." *Ante*, at 8. The means identified, and approved, is that the jury receive *some* lesser included offense intruction—some "'third option of finding that although the defendant had committed a grave crime, it was not so grave as to warrant capi-

[1] In *Beck* we invalidated an Alabama statute which prevented a trial court in a capital case from instructing the jury on any lesser included offense, regardless of evidentiary support. 447 U. S., at 628–629, and n. 3.

TOMPKINS *v.* TEXAS

tal punishment.'" *Ante*, at 7, quoting *Hopper* v. *Evans*, 456 U. S. 605, 609 (1982). This is the entirety of the majority's analysis of what due process requires in the capital context, and why. It is not hard to understand why the majority avoids any analysis of this point; with all respect, no analysis could possibly support it.

While concededly *Beck* itself did not specifically require that an instruction be given on every lesser included offense supported by the evidence (only one instruction was requested in *Beck*, so the question was not presented), I find it undeniable that the principles on which *Beck* rests require that *all* such instructions be given. Section I of the Court's opinion in *Beck* consists of a painstaking review of the almost universal practice in American common and statutory law of giving a lesser included offense instruction for each offense called for by the evidence.[2] 447 U. S., at 633–638. Furthermore, the values underlying *Beck*—the Constitution's special concern for rational deliberation in capital cases—are not vindicated, and indeed may be disserved, if a capital jury is given some mere noncapital alternative on which to rest its conclusion.

The problem we identified and supposedly cured in *Beck* exists any time the jury has not been instructed on the of-

---

[2] In *Beck* we relied on the standards articulated in *Keeble* v. *United States*, 412 U. S. 208 (1973), in formulating a constitutional rule. *Keeble* concerned the interpretation of a federal criminal statute, the Major Crimes Act of 1885, but based its requirement that a lesser included offense instruction be given under the Act on both statutory interpretation and the fact that serious due process issues would be raised if the Act were not interpreted to require the instruction. In *Beck* we also noted that the rule applicable in state courts is "that a defendant is entitled to a lesser included offense instruction when the evidence warrants it." 447 U. S., at 636. There is nothing in *Beck* that suggests that we did anything but incorporate the generally recognized principles of the doctrine of lesser included offense instructions as a matter of due process in capital cases. Indeed, in *Hopper* v. *Evans*, 456 U. S. 605, 612 (1982), we referred to *Keeble* as expressing "federal constitutional standards."

TOMPKINS *v.* TEXAS

fense which matches the facts as it has found them. Although it may very well be that, absent a proper instruction, the jury will likely choose whatever "intermediate position" it is offered rather than convict the defendant of the capital offense, the result is still a form of jury nullification, rather than adherence to the oath to follow the law. The jury still has been deprived of the choices it should have enjoyed, and the ultimate outcome still is capricious. Neither *Beck*, nor due process, should be read to make the procedure by which the jury determines guilt or innocence *more* arbitrary.

What due process requires is a set of instructions that includes those offenses on which a rational jury could find the defendant guilty while acquitting the defendant on the greatest offense. The instructions also should inform the jury about what types of facts are important, *instructing* them on the essential elements of the relevant offenses, and focusing on the major points of uncertainty. See n. 8, *infra*. Lesser included offense instructions ensure, to the fullest extent possible, that the jury stays true to its responsibility of applying the law on which it has been instructed to the facts it has found from the evidence presented.

The Court made clear in *Hopper* v. *Evans*, 456 U. S., at 611, that lesser included offense instructions are required to channel the jury's discretion "so that it may convict a defendant of *any* crime fairly supported by the evidence" (emphasis added). When a court fails to instruct a jury on a lesser included offense that the evidence reasonably supports, the jury's proper role is distorted; a jury that adheres to its oath may be deprived of the opportunity to consider the only offense that aligns with the facts as it has found them. The jury's ability to follow its proper role is tested too severely, and for no good reason, when such guidance is lacking because the instructions on the law are incomplete. To inject such caprice into the guilt phase of a capital trial utterly defeats *Beck*'s command of rationality.

TOMPKINS *v.* TEXAS

Although *Beck* used the phrase "third option," see 447 U. S., at 637, it used that phrase as a general reference to lesser included offense instructions, not as some newly created restrictive term of art. See also *Hopper*, 456 U. S., at 609. By focusing on two words that have no obvious content, the majority would ignore the due process concerns that animated *Beck*, and deprive that decision of much of its force.

III

The facts of this case, and the choices presented to the jury by the instructions, clearly reveal the threadbare quality of the majority's approach. The lesser included offense instructions petitioner requested went to two distinct elements of the charged crime of capital murder: the requirement that the murder be *intentional*, and the requirement that the murder be committed in the course of robbery or kidnaping. The bases for doubt regarding the former were categorically stronger than the latter, but only the latter instruction was given to the jury. By adopting a rule which permits trial judges to choose the weaker of available lesser included offense instructions as the "third option," the majority here has ignored the Court's admonition in *Beck* that "if the unavailability of a lesser included offense instruction enhances the risk of an unwarranted conviction, [the State] is constitutionally prohibited from withdrawing that option from the jury in a capital case." 447 U. S., at 638.

The majority correctly notes that the record in this case contains ample evidence of petitioner's involvement in the events leading to the death of Mary Diana Berry. The evidence that petitioner participated in either a robbery or a kidnaping of the victim, or both, is overwhelming.[3] None of

[3] Petitioner's use of Berry's automatic teller card to remove $1,000 from her account (shown by both eyewitness and photographic evidence), and his possession of her bank card, credit cards, and other items, see App. 84, could have left little doubt in a reasonable juror's mind that petitioner had been involved in robbing her. The fact that the victim's car was found abandoned, with its lights on and motor running, *id.*, at 83, suggests that

TOMPKINS *v.* TEXAS

the evidence presented suggested any motive other than robbery, or any circumstance other than abduction.[4]

On the other hand, the evidence concerning the details of the victim's subsequent death, and, specifically, the evidence concerning petitioner's criminal intent towards his victim, is much less clear. The circumstantial evidence supports several possibilities concerning petitioner's *mens rea*. Thus, petitioner may have killed Berry intentionally. A reasonable juror might have concluded that petitioner is a clever and depraved killer, who sought to make his intentional murder look more like a careless step in a scheme where death was not intended. Or a reasonable juror might have concluded that petitioner simply decided to use an unorthodox method of suffocating his victim by stuffing an overlarge gag in her mouth.

The evidence also suggests, however, that petitioner may not have intended to kill Berry, and that her death was the result of petitioner's recklessness or negligence. The victim was tied in a way which left some slack, and the tree to which she was tied was located in a field not far from the house of the person who located the body.[5] See App. 83. A reasonable juror certainly might have believed that peti-

---

she had been abducted against her will. In addition, there was no evidence that the victim knew petitioner or ever previously had encountered him, *id.*, at 84, and that she therefore would be likely to have accompanied him voluntarily.

[4] For example, there was no evidence that the victim had been beaten or sexually assaulted. See *id.*, at 82–84.

[5] In addition, the medical examiner determined that even in the extreme situation in which *no* air came through the cloth gag (a fact he was not able to ascertain), it would have taken at least three minutes after the gagging took place before the victim could have suffocated. *Id.*, at 84. It was therefore possible that the victim showed no sign upon her being gagged that she was unable to breathe, and that petitioner was unaware that the victim would be unable to breathe when he left her. For additional discussion of the manner in which the circumstantial evidence could support findings of recklessness or negligence, see the dissenting opinion of Judge Clinton in the Texas Court of Criminal Appeals. *Id.*, at 103–109.

TOMPKINS *v.* TEXAS

tioner bound and gagged Berry with the intent of returning to untie her once he had used her automatic teller card, or with no intent of returning, but with the sole aim of preventing her from calling out for or obtaining help for some period of time.

Despite the very real possibility that petitioner did not intend Berry's death, the trial court refused to instruct the jury on involuntary manslaughter and criminally negligent homicide, neither of which, under Texas law, requires an intent to kill.[6] Instead, the jury was instructed on two types of murder: (a) capital murder, which includes intentionally committing murder in the course of committing or attempting to commit kidnaping, burglary, robbery, aggravated sexual assault, or arson, Texas Penal Code Ann., § 19.03(a)(2) (1989), and (b) murder, which is not a capital crime, and which includes intentionally causing death. § 19.02. Each offense requires that the defendant act with the intent to cause the death of another.[7] Accordingly, the jury was

[6] Texas defines involuntary manslaughter as occurring when a person "recklessly causes the death of an individual." Texas Penal Code Ann. § 19.05(a)(1) (1989). "A person acts recklessly, or is reckless, with respect to circumstances surrounding his conduct or the result of his conduct when he is aware of but consciously disregards a substantial and unjustifiable risk that the circumstances exist or the result will occur. The risk must be of such a nature and degree that its disregard constitutes a gross deviation from the standard of care that an ordinary person would exercise under all the circumstances as viewed from the actor's standpoint." § 6.03(c).

A person commits criminally negligent homicide "if he causes the death of an individual by criminal negligence." § 19.07(a). "A person acts with criminal negligence, or is criminally negligent, with respect to circumstances surrounding his conduct or the result of his conduct when he ought to be aware of a substantial and unjustifiable risk that the circumstances exist or the result will occur. The risk must be of such a nature and degree that the failure to perceive it constitutes a gross deviation from the standard of care that an ordinary person would exercise under all the circumstances as viewed from the actor's standpoint." § 6.03(d).

[7] Although murder is defined in § 19.02 as "intentionally or knowingly" causing the death of an individual, here the trial court instructed the jury only as to intentional killing. See App. 37.

TOMPKINS v. TEXAS

given three choices: petitioner intended to kill the victim in the course of a robbery or a kidnaping; petitioner intended to kill the victim but was not engaged in robbery or kidnaping; or petitioner was not guilty of either charge, and should be acquitted.

It is inconceivable that this choice satisfies *Beck*. The directive of *Beck* is positive:

> "[W]hen the evidence unquestionably establishes that the defendant is guilty of a serious, violent offense—but leaves some doubt with respect to an element that would justify conviction of a capital offense—the failure to give the jury the 'third option' of convicting on a lesser included offense would seem inevitably to enhance the risk of an unwarranted conviction." 447 U. S., at 637.

The failure to instruct on manslaughter and criminally negligent homicide was clear error. A reviewing court must close its eyes, as does the majority, in order to ignore the fact that a jury, on the record in this case, could reasonably have concluded that petitioner acted recklessly, or negligently, but *without intent to kill*, in the events that led to Berry's death.

Yet the majority does more than close its eyes. In concluding that the lesser included offense instruction that was given actually satisfies *Beck*, the majority implicitly holds that a jury reasonably could have concluded that petitioner intended to kill Berry, but that no kidnaping or robbery took place, or that petitioner intended to kill Berry but was not involved in any kidnaping or robbery that did take place. But such a conclusion would be nothing other than jury nullification.

The majority appears to take solace in its belief that "if [the jury] found that petitioner had committed a serious, violent crime but did not believe he deserved to be executed for his act—they could have convicted him of noncapital murder," *ante*, at 7, and in the assumption that "[i]f these jurors had doubted petitioner's intent to kill yet balked at exoneration, it is highly unlikely that they would have convicted him of

TOMPKINS *v.* TEXAS

capital murder, the more serious of the two types of murder on which they were instructed," *ante*, at 8.[6] What the majority fails to explain (or justify) is that no reasonable juror could have believed that the evidence supported a conviction on noncapital intentional murder without also believing that the evidence supported conviction on capital murder.

The only element differentiating the two offenses is whether petitioner committed the murder in the course of a kidnaping or a robbery. No reasonable juror could have answered this question in the negative and, therefore, no reasonable juror could have voted for conviction on noncapital intentional murder without completely ignoring the overwhelming evidence on robbery and kidnaping. In other words, in order to reach this result the jury would be required to disregard its obligation to apply the law as it was instructed, and would have had to apply its own brand of justice, based on the jurors' personal views of what the defendant deserved. Accordingly, the only additional option given the jury, aside from a capital conviction or acquittal, was a

---

[6] To assume on the one hand that the jurors followed the trial court's instructions in reaching the verdict they returned, then to bolster that assumption by finding it more likely that the jurors, if not convinced that the State had proved all elements of the capital offense, would have refused to follow the instructions given and would have returned a verdict of non-capital murder which was not supported by the evidence, is something I cannot accept.

Indeed, the majority's post-hoc rationalization also ignores the fundamental and self-evident point that jury instructions are supposed to *instruct* the jury, not merely set the boundaries of its discretion. Instructions should serve to tell the jury what particular factual findings are essential to a finding of guilt, focusing their attention on what is really important. Here, the jury was not told that it could find lack of intent yet still convict of some serious offense, because the only instructions given required that intent be found. It is therefore more likely that a juror, convinced that petitioner tied the victim to a tree and stuffed the gag in her mouth, would fail to give adequate consideration to the question whether he acted with intent to kill.

TOMPKINS *v.* TEXAS

form of jury nullification.[9]

In short, the majority's approach endorses instructions that

> "plainly invit[e] the jurors to disregard their oaths and choose a verdict for a lesser offense whenever they feel the death penalty is inappropriate. There is an element of capriciousness in making the jurors' power to avoid the death penalty dependent on their willingness to accept this invitation to disregard the trial judge's instructions." *Roberts* v. *Louisiana*, 428 U. S. 325, 335 (1976) (plurality opinion).

It is disappointing that the majority embraces such a solution when simply requiring that appropriate lesser included offense instructions be given will make it far easier for jurors to follow the instructions they are given, and to return verdicts consistent with the facts as they find them.[10]

---

[9] Even if the decision of the trial judge to give the non-capital murder instruction requires us to assume that, as a matter of state law, the jury lawfully could have concluded that the murder was *not* committed in the course of robbery or kidnaping, there can be no doubt that the evidence in support of noncapital murder is extraordinarily weak. The inescapable conclusion is that the trial judge, by choosing as the sole "third option" the lesser included offense instruction the jury was least likely to accept as a reasonable alternative, increased the likelihood of an "unwarranted conviction," *Beck*, 447 U. S., at 638, in direct violation of *Beck*.

[10] The majority draws entirely too much comfort from the fact that the jury found, at the sentencing stage, that petitioner committed the murder "deliberately"—a finding the majority assures itself confirms that the jury would have convicted of intentional murder even if it had been offered instructions on negligent and reckless homicide. But several members of the Texas Court of Criminal Appeals have had occasion to note in other circumstances that a Texas jury might well have failed to see any difference between "intentional" and "deliberate." See *Lane* v. *State*, 743 S. W. 2d 617, 628–629 (1987); *Gardner* v. *State*, 730 S. W. 2d 675, 689, cert. denied, 484 U. S. 905 (1987). Having been forced by the absence of lesser included offense instructions on negligence and recklessness into finding "intent," the jury might well have thought it inconsistent and impermissible to decline to find "deliberateness."

TOMPKINS *v.* TEXAS

IV

Over the past two decades this Court has labored to ensure that the death penalty will be imposed only when appropriate, and only pursuant to procedures that assure a reliable determination of guilt and a reasoned sentencing decision. Today a substantial safeguard has been ignored, with the result that petitioner, undoubtedly guilty of a serious crime, faces execution after conviction by a jury which was not permitted to consider the possibility that he was innocent of a capital crime but guilty of one of two serious, noncapital, crimes amply supported by the evidence.

This result has a particularly bitter irony. Each appellate court to consider this case, including this one, has taken note of a confession not admitted into evidence. See App. 85, n. 7; *ante*, at 2. The written statement was given shortly after petitioner was arrested and one day after Berry's body was found. In the statement, petitioner admits that he tied Berry up so that he could use her automatic teller card and then claims that he found her dead when he returned to untie her. Although this court does not sit as a finder of fact, I am persuaded that the confession would have moved the jury had it been admitted. The Texas Court of Criminal Appeals apparently felt the same way. See App. 85, n. 7. The confession's plaintive tone and elaborate detail ring true. See *id.*, at 50–55.

That it seems highly likely that petitioner did not intend Berry's death reveals just how wrong the majority's decision is, and how much uncertainty still remains in the process by which capital punishment is imposed. Had the command of *Beck* been followed in this case, I have little doubt that petitioner would not be subject to a capital sentence and our society would not face the prospect of executing a man for a crime that almost certainly was not a capital crime under the statutes of Texas. Unfortunately, this probably is not the first time such a result has been achieved in the area of capital punishment. See *McCleskey* v. *Kemp*, 481 U. S. 279

TOMPKINS *v.* TEXAS

(1987); *Darden* v. *Wainwright*, 477 U. S. 168 (1986). I dissent.

4th DRAFT

SUPREME COURT OF THE UNITED STATES

No. 87-6405

PHILLIP D. TOMPKINS, PETITIONER *v.* TEXAS

ON WRIT OF CERTIORARI TO THE COURT OF CRIMINAL APPEALS OF TEXAS

[May ——, 1989]

JUSTICE STEVENS delivered the opinion of the Court.

A jury found petitioner guilty of an intentional killing in the course of a robbery and kidnaping and sentenced him to death. His case gives rise to two questions: (1) whether it was constitutional error for the trial judge to grant only one of petitioner's three requests for instructions on lesser included, noncapital offenses; and (2) whether the Court of Criminal Appeals of Texas erred when it affirmed the trial judge's determination that the prosecutors' use of peremptory challenges to exclude all blacks from the jury was based consistently on "neutral, relative, clear and legitimate" reasons and "was not racially motivated." [ ]

Early on the morning of January 27, 1981, the body of Mary Diana Berry, a 24-year-old hospital pharmacist, was found tightly bound to a tree near a remote road in the Houston area. A large wad of bedsheeting had been stuffed in her mouth, forcing her tongue deep into the rearmost part of her mouth and causing her to suffocate.

Berry had left work at about 11 p. m. on January 25. After an apparent collision with a car often driven by petitioner, Berry vanished, her car abandoned at the accident site. Two and one-half hours later, a night janitor at Berry's bank saw petitioner using an automatic teller card to withdraw $1,000 from her account; his testimony was corroborated by photographs taken by an automatic camera. When petitioner was apprehended a few days later, the bank card,

TOMPKINS *v.* TEXAS

credit cards, and certain other items belonging to Berry were in his possession. A severed electrical cord in the trunk of his car matched the cord that had been used to bind Berry's ankles. In short, the record contains ample circumstantial evidence of petitioner's involvement in the crime. A Texas grand jury charged him with capital murder.[1]

In a written confession, petitioner stated that he had tied and gagged Berry solely to keep her from escaping and seeking help while he used her bank card. That confession, however, was not admitted into evidence and petitioner did not testify regarding the incident; in fact, the defense rested without introducing any evidence on petitioner's behalf.[2] Petitioner's attorneys nevertheless argued that it was reasonable to infer that the binding and gagging of Berry—rather than, for instance, strangling or stabbing her—demonstrated that he did not intend to kill her.[3]

---

[1] The Texas capital murder statute provides:

"(a) A person commits an offense if he commits murder as defined under Section 19.02(a)(1) of this code and:

. . . . .

"(2) the person intentionally commits the murder in the course of committing or attempting to commit kidnapping, burglary, robbery, aggravated rape, or arson . . . .

. . . . .

"(c) If the jury does not find beyond a reasonable doubt that the defendant is guilty of an offense under this section, he may be convicted of murder or of any other lesser included offense." Tex. Penal Code Ann., Art. 19.03 (Vernon 1974).

[2] Petitioner did testify briefly during the State's case in chief in an unsuccessful attempt to establish that his companion at the time of the incident was his common-law wife and thus disqualified under state law from testifying against him. Tr. 924–930.

[3] Tr. 1012. Petitioner's attorneys urged the jury to find a lack of intent to kill based on a number of circumstances, among them that: Berry was left close enough to a house to permit quick discovery, *id.*, at 1014–1015, 1043; the gag did not cover Berry's nose and the bonds were loose enough to demonstrate a lack of intent to kill, *id.*, at 1011, 1048; and Berry had a respiratory problem that aggravated an otherwise nonlethal gag, *id.*, at 1049. Counsel further argued that the State's evidence failed to prove pe-

TOMPKINS v. TEXAS

To convict petitioner of capital murder the jury had to find both that he intentionally killed Berry and that he did so while engaged in robbing or kidnaping her.[4] Defense counsel asked that jurors be instructed that if they did not find that the State had proved capital murder, they could find petitioner guilty of any of three lesser, noncapital offenses. The judge gave the requested instruction on noncapital murder[5] but refused to instruct on either involuntary man-

---

titioner robbed or kidnaped Berry. *E. g., id.*, at 1012–1013, 1041–1043. "[S]omeone not on trial here who is much smarter and much meaner than Phillip Tompkins" was at fault, counsel suggested, and then laid the blame on petitioner's live-in female companion. *Id.*, at 1018–1021; see also *id.*, at 1047.

[4] The judge instructed the jury in part as follows:

"Before you would be warranted in convicting the defendant of capital murder, you must find from the evidence beyond a reasonable doubt not only that on the occasion in question the defendant was engaged in the commission or attempted commission of the felony offense of robbery and/or of kidnapping of Mary D. Berry, as defined in this charge, but also that during the commission of the robbery and/or kidnapping or attempted commission thereof, if any, the defendant suffocated Mary D. Berry by placing a cloth gag in her mouth with the intention of thereby killing her. Unless you find from the evidence beyond a reasonable doubt that the defendant, Phillip Daniel Tompkins, on said occasion, specifically intended to kill the said Mary D. Berry when he suffocated Mary D. Berry by placing a cloth gag in her mouth, if he so did, taking into consideration the foregoing instructions, you cannot convict him of the offense of capital murder." App. 36–37.

[5] Although the statute labels it "murder," we shall refer to the offense enumerated at Tex. Penal Code Ann., Art. 19.02(a)(1) (Vernon 1974), as "noncapital murder" to distinguish it from capital murder, Art. 19.03. The judge instructed petitioner's jury regarding noncapital murder as follows:

"If you do not so find beyond a reasonable doubt, or if you have a reasonable doubt thereof, you will acquit the defendant of capital murder and consider whether he is guilty of the lesser offense of murder.

"If you find from the evidence beyond a reasonable doubt that on or about the 26th day of January, 1981, in Harris County, Texas, the defendant, Phillip Daniel Tompkins, did intentionally cause the death of Mary D. Berry by suffocating her by placing a cloth gag in her mouth, and you have

TOMPKINS v. TEXAS

slaughter or criminally negligent homicide, neither of which requires an intent to kill. Having convicted petitioner of the capital offense, the jury, after a separate sentencing hearing, affirmatively answered the special questions that mandate a death sentence in Texas—in particular, that petitioner had acted "deliberately and with the reasonable expectation that . . . death . . . would result."[6] Thus, on two separate occasions, the jury found that petitioner intended to kill Berry.

On appeal petitioner argued that the refusal to instruct on involuntary manslaughter and criminally negligent homicide violated the Due Process Clause of the Fourteenth Amend-

---

a reasonable doubt as to whether the defendant was then and there engaged in the commission or attempted commission of robbery and/or kidnapping of Mary D. Berry at the time of the suffocating, if any, then you will find the defendant guilty of murder, but not capital murder.

"If you find from the evidence beyond a reasonable doubt that the defendant is either guilty of capital murder or murder, but you have a reasonable doubt as to which offense he is guilty of, then you should resolve that doubt in the defendant's favor, and in such event, you will find the defendant guilty of the lesser offense of murder." App. 37.

The judge also charged the jury that it might exonerate petitioner: "If you have a reasonable doubt as to whether the defendant is guilty of any offense, then you should acquit the defendant and say by your verdict not guilty." *Id.*, at 38.

The instructions the jury received on capital murder and noncapital murder were substantially similar to those petitioner requested. See *id.*, at 24–27.

[6] Tr. 205. Texas law provides:

"(b) On conclusion of the presentation of the evidence, the court shall submit the following . . . issues to the jury:

"(1) whether the conduct of the defendant that caused the death of the deceased was committed deliberately and with the reasonable expectation that the death of the deceased or another would result;

"(2) whether there is a probability that the defendant would commit criminal acts of violence that would constitute a continuing threat to society . . . .

. . . . .

"(e) If the jury returns an affirmative finding on each issue submitted under this article, the court shall sentence the defendant to death." Tex. Crim. Proc. Code Ann., Art. 37.071 (Vernon 1974).

TOMPKINS v. TEXAS

ment as construed in *Beck* v. *Alabama*, 447 U. S. 625 (1980).[7] The Court of Criminal Appeals rejected that argument because in this case, unlike *Beck*, the petitioner "did not testify or present any evidence from any source that he possessed only the intent to either rob or kidnap Berry." —— S. W. 2d ——, —— (1987). Although we do not agree with the Texas court's basis for distinguishing *Beck*, we conclude that no constitutional error occurred because the trial judge did instruct the jury on the lesser included offense of noncapital murder.

In *Beck* we considered the constitutionality of Alabama's unique statutory prohibition against giving any lesser included offense instructions in capital cases.[8] Beck had been accused of an intentional killing in the course of a robbery, a capital crime. His own testimony established that he had participated in a robbery in which his accomplice unexpectedly had struck and killed the victim. If that testimony was true, Beck was guilty of noncapital felony murder, but not of the capital crime of robbery-intentional killing. The Alabama statute, however, prohibited the court from charging the jury on that lesser included offense. Thus the jury faced "the choice of either convicting the defendant of the capital crime, in which case it [was] required to impose the death penalty, or acquitting him, thus allowing him to escape all penalties for his alleged participation in the crime." *Beck*, 447 U. S., at 628–629.

We held that Alabama's refusal to allow the jury to consider any verdict between the two extremes was unacceptable in a capital case. We explained:

> "While we have never held that a defendant is entitled to a lesser included offense instruction as a matter of due

[7] Petitioner also argued that he was entitled to those lesser included offense instructions as a matter of state law. We, of course, do not review the Texas court's rejection of that argument. Cf. *Beck* v. *Alabama*, 447 U. S., at 630, n. 5.

[8] See *id.*, at 628, n. 3; *id.*, at 630, n. 5; *id.*, at 635, and 636, n. 12.

TOMPKINS v. TEXAS

> process, the nearly universal acceptance of the rule in both state and federal courts establishes the value to the defendant of this procedural safeguard. That safeguard would seem to be especially important in a case such as this. For when the evidence unquestionably establishes that the defendant is guilty of a serious, violent offense—but leaves some doubt with respect to an element that would justify conviction of a capital offense—the failure to give the jury the 'third option' of convicting on a lesser included offense would seem inevitably to enhance the risk of an unwarranted conviction.
>
> "Such a risk cannot be tolerated in a case in which the defendant's life is at stake." *Id.*, at 637.

Thus Beck was entitled to have the jury instructed regarding not only capital murder and acquittal, but also one lesser included, noncapital offense suggested by the evidence at trial.

Petitioner interprets *Beck* to mean that the Constitution mandates lesser included offense instructions covering all possible permutations of juror determinations regarding elements of the capital crime. Contending that his jury, like the one in *Beck*, could have drawn conflicting inferences regarding his intent to kill, petitioner asserts that the trial court was required to give all requested unintentional homicide instructions.[9] The reason *Beck* ordered just one noncapital charge, he suggests, is that only one was requested.

Pretermitting this argument, the Court of Criminal Appeals attempted to distinguish *Beck* on the ground that there the defense had adduced evidence disputing intent to kill during its own case, whereas here petitioner rested without in-

---

[9] The dissent agrees with this interpretation of *Beck* and suggests that it is reinforced by the "almost universal practice" of American courts. See *post*, at ——. Neither petitioner nor the dissent, however, has cited a single appellate court case holding that the Constitution requires a judge to give multiple lesser included offense instructions. Moreover, it is noteworthy that petitioner's trial counsel did not request the court to instruct the jury on the lesser included offense of either kidnaping or robbery.

TOMPKINS *v.* TEXAS

troducing any evidence.[10] Our reasoning in *Beck* would have been the same, however, if the evidence had been received during the prosecutor's case in chief. A defendant in a capital case is not required to waive his privilege against self-incrimination to obtain the benefit of a constitutionally required lesser included offense instruction.[11]

Nevertheless we are not persuaded that the right to one such instruction recognized in *Beck* entails a constitutional right to have the jury instructed on *every* lesser included, noncapital offense that might be supported by the evidence. As we explained in *Hopper* v. *Evans*, 456 U. S. 605, 609 (1982):

> "Our opinion in *Beck* stressed that the jury was faced with a situation in which its choices were only to convict the defendant and sentence him to death or find him not guilty. The jury could not take a third option of finding that although the defendant had committed a grave crime, it was not so grave as to warrant capital punishment. We concluded that a jury might have convicted Beck but also might have rejected capital punishment if it believed Beck's testimony. On the facts shown in *Beck*, we held that the defendant was entitled to a lesser included offense instruction as a matter of due process."

In this case, unlike *Beck*, the jury was given "a third option of finding that although the defendant had committed a grave crime, it was not so grave as to warrant capital punishment." 456 U. S., at 609. Thus, these jurors never faced the dilemma posed in *Beck*. From the outset they were given three options. They could have convicted petitioner of capital murder if that was warranted. They could have acquit-

[10] Ironically, the Texas Court of Criminal Appeals stated: "It appears that had appellant's written confession been admitted into evidence, the issue that appellant presents might call for a conclusion different from the one [we reach]." —— S. W. 2d ——, —— n. 7 (1987).

[11] "No person . . . shall be compelled in any criminal case to be a witness against himself . . . ." U. S. Const., Amdt. 5.

TOMPKINS *v.* TEXAS

ted him if they decided that he had committed no crime. If their determination fell somewhere in between—if they found that petitioner had committed a serious, violent crime but did not believe he deserved to be executed for his act—they could have convicted him of noncapital murder.

On the record before us it is proper to presume that the jury followed the judge's instructions and was convinced beyond a reasonable doubt that petitioner did intend to kill Berry when he stuffed the gag and her tongue down her throat. The jury implicitly made such a finding when it returned the guilty verdict and expressly so found at the conclusion of the sentencing hearing.[12] If these jurors had doubted petitioner's intent to kill yet balked at exoneration, it is highly unlikely that they would have convicted him of capital murder, the more serious of the two types of murder on which they were instructed. Thus, on the facts of this case, petitioner was afforded the procedural safeguard mandated by our holding in *Beck*.

It may well be sound policy to instruct the jury on every lesser included offense supported by the evidence. But the Constitution requires no such rule. It mandates only that a jury be given a means to avoid a Hobson's choice between acquittal and capital murder. Because the instructions in this case afforded the jury such an option, they did not offend the Constitution.

On the second question presented by the certiorari petition, the Court is equally divided. Accordingly, the judgment of the Court of Criminal Appeals of Texas is affirmed.

So ordered.

---

[12] Petitioner does not question the sufficiency of the evidence supporting the capital murder conviction. It is therefore quite wrong for the dissent to conclude that petitioner "almost certainly" did not intend to kill his victim. See *post*, at ——. The dissent bases its gratuitous factual finding on petitioner's self-serving comment in a statement to police, which was not admitted into evidence. Nor was the comment subject to cross-examina-

TOMPKINS *v.* TEXAS

JUSTICE O'CONNOR took no part in the consideration or decision of this case.

tion, since petitioner elected not to testify about the crime. See *supra*, at n. 2.

Soon after the Stevens draft opinion of the Court in *Tompkins* v. *Texas* was circulated, Justice White sent around a draft opinion, reprinted on page 167, concurring in the affirmance on the jury instruction issue, but dissenting on the reversal on *Batson* grounds. Under the majority approach, White wrote, "[t]he Constitution is said to bar Texas' sufficiency of the evidence standard in favor of a clearly erroneous standard which would give appellate courts more room to find error in the trial courts' findings. . . . [T]his is an extraordinary imposition on the state courts." Even if "the Court had not proceeded with such evident gusto to invalidate the traditional standard of review used in Texas, what the Court does is quite unacceptable to me."

"As I understand *Batson*," the White draft stated, "the accused has the burden throughout of proving deliberate discrimination. The prosecutor in response must do more than assert his good faith and absence of discriminatory intent. But it suffices if he puts forth a believable, neutral explanation for his strikes. . . . In *Batson*, the Court emphasized that this was the extent of the prosecutor's duty."

In this case, "[t]he majority now, however, insists not only that the prosecutor do more but also requires that the trial judge and the appellate courts second-guess reasons for removing jurors, even if these courts credit the prosecutor's honesty." The majority is subjecting the trial court's judgment to "appellate review, on a cold record . . . by judges sitting in Washington, D.C."

Justice White concluded, "Rather than subject peremptories to the regime the Court imposes today, it would be more straightforward to hold that when a black is on trial in a criminal case, peremptory challenges by the prosecution are unconstitutional because they pose an unacceptable risk of racial discrimination in the selection of jurors. With all due respect, I dissent."

Justice Blackmun also circulated an opinion, reprinted on page 173, concurring in part and dissenting in part. However, he concurred on the *Batson* issue and dissented on the jury instruction holding.

Stevens's draft could have become a leading case on application of the *Batson* rule, had it come down as the *Tompkins* opinion of the Court. But the five-to-three majority in its favor became a four-to-four vote on the issue when Justice Kennedy, in the phrase of a law clerk memo to Justice Marshall, "jumped ship and voted to affirm on the *Batson* issue." Kennedy's switch was announced in a May 16, 1989, letter to Justice Stevens. "I tentatively voted at Conference," Kennedy noted, "to vacate the judgment of the Texas Court of Criminal Appeals and remand for further consideration of the trial court's findings on the *Batson* issue." Justice Kennedy had, however, now changed his mind. "As I understand *Batson*," Kennedy wrote, "where there is a prima facie case of discrimination in jury selection, the prosecution bears the burden of coming forward with a neutral, case-related explanation for its actions. In my view, the State has done so here, and the trial court's findings to support the State's showing are not clearly erroneous."

Kennedy's letter concluded, "Since the prosecutors' explanations for their use of peremptory challenges against black venirepersons are neutral, case-related, and supported by the evidence, I believe the trial court did not err in finding that no *Batson* violation was committed. For these reasons, I cannot join Part II of your opinion. My vote is to affirm the conviction."

As Marshall's law clerk's memo summarized it, "This means that . . . the vote will be 4–4" on the *Batson* issue. In addition, Justice Stevens had concluded that he had been wrong on the jury instruction issue. He had circulated a new draft opinion of the Court on May 17, 1989, reprinted on page 186, deleting the *Batson* discussion. Then, two days later, Justice Stevens sent a "Dear Chief" letter stating, "After further reflection, I have decided to change my vote on the [jury instruction] issue in this case." This meant a four-to-four division on that issue also. This led Justice Stevens to conclude, in his letter to the Chief Justice, "I am now persuaded that the best disposition of the entire case . . . is a simple affirmance by an equally divided Court." On June 5, 1989, the Justices issued a per curiam affirming the Texas court decision in *Tompkins* by an equally divided Court.

Justice Kennedy's switch in *Tompkins* made a difference in the application of *Batson*. On March 13, 1989, while the Justices were still considering *Tompkins*, Justice Stevens sent Justice Scalia a letter explaining his draft opinion of the Court. In it, he wrote, "I do think, however, that it is quite important that we give lower courts as much guidance as possible without taking a backward step that would deprive *Batson* of any real significance." From Stevens's point of view, just such a step was taken when the Court dealt with the issue again in the 1991 case of *Hernandez* v. *New York*.[5] This time Justice Kennedy announced the principal opinion. It substantially followed the approach of Justice White's draft *Tompkins* dissent. Instead of the stricter standard that would have been adopted under Stevens's draft *Tompkins* opinion of the Court, *Hernandez* stated the lesser holding that, as summarized by Stevens's *Hernandez* dissent, "a defendant's *Batson* challenge fails whenever the prosecutor advances a nonpretextual justification that is not facially discriminatory."[6]

This is true, according to *Purkett* v. *Elem*,[7] the most recent case on the matter, even where the prosecutor's reason is "silly or superstitious." Justice Stevens dissented in both *Hernandez* and *Purkett*. Had his stricter Tompkins standard retained its majority, both *Hernandez* and *Purkett* might have been decided differently.

Notes

1. 476 U.S. 79 (1986).
2. 380 U.S. 202 (1968).
3. *Batson* v. *Kentucky*, No. 84-6263 Conference Date: Dec. 13, 1985 (apparently a typed version of Justice Brennan's conference statement).
4. 490 U.S. 754 (1989).
5. 500 U.S. 352 (1991).
6. Id. at 376.
7. 115 S.Ct. 1769 (1995).

5

Patterson v. *McLean Credit Union (1989): Civil Rights in the Rehnquist Court*

It cannot be doubted that the constitutional line is being drawn farther to the right by the Rehnquist Court than it was by its immediate predecessors. The Chief Justice was well characterized by a *Newsweek* article as "The Court's Mr. Right."[1] According to the *New York Times*, "William H. Rehnquist is a symbol. People who have trouble naming all nine Supreme Court Justices quickly identify him as its doctrinaire, right-wing anchor. . . . Justice Rehnquist is the Court's most predictable conservative member, using his considerable intelligence, energy and verbal facility to shape the law to his vision."[2]

Rehnquist's vision in this respect has always been a clear one. He once noted that he joined the Court with a desire to counteract the Warren Court decisions.[3] "I came to the court," Rehnquist said, "sensing . . . that there were some excesses in terms of constitutional adjudication during the era of the so-called Warren Court." Some of that Court's decisions, the Justice went on, "seemed to me hard to justify. . . . So I felt that at the time I came on the Court, the boat was kind of keeling over in one direction. Interpreting my oath as I saw it, I felt that my job was to kind of lean the other way."[4]

Among the cases where Rehnquist has leaned the other way have been those involving civil rights. When Rehnquist was a law clerk to Justice Robert H. Jackson he wrote a memo on the *Brown* segregation case,[5] urging that the separate-but-equal doctrine, under which segregation had been upheld, was "right and should be affirmed."[6]

Justice Rehnquist stated in 1985 that his views had probably changed and that he accepted *Brown* as the law of the land.[7] But his votes in cases involving civil rights clearly place him in the right wing of the Court on civil rights issues.

What is not known outside the Marble Palace is that Chief Justice Rehnquist has urged even more extreme views within the Court than have appeared in his published opinions. A major part of contemporary civil rights litigation has been based upon laws enacted during Reconstruction. Among them is an 1866 statute that provides, in its second section (now 42 U.S.C. § 1982), "All citizens . . . shall have the same right, in every State and

Territory, as is enjoyed by white citizens thereof to inherit, purchase, lease, sell, hold and convey real and personal property." In the 1968 case of *Jones* v. *Alfred H. Mayer Co.*,[8] the Court held that section 1982 prohibits racial discrimination in the sale or rental of property. As such it forbids a private development company to refuse to sell a home to someone because he is black.

A 1976 case, *Runyon* v. *McCrary*,[9] dealt with section 1 of the 1866 law (now 42 U.S.C. § 1981). It provides that all persons "shall have the same right in every State and Territory to make and enforce contracts . . . as is enjoyed by white citizens." *Runyon* ruled that this statute prohibits racial discrimination in the making and enforcement of private contracts. The Court found that a private school's denial of admission on racial grounds violated the statute. The relationship the pupils' parents had sought to enter into was contractual in nature and by denying them the right to enter into the contract, the school had discriminated contrary to the statute.

In the 1989 case of *Patterson* v. *McLean Credit Union*,[10] the Court heard argument on "[w]hether or not the interpretation of § 1981 in *Runyon* v. *McCrary* . . . should be reconsidered." At the postargument conference, Chief Justice Rehnquist declared that *Runyon* was wrong and that Justice White was correct in his dissent in that case. Therefore, he urged, the Court should overrule *Runyon*.

The Chief Justice did not, however, stop with his recommendation to overrule *Runyon*. He also told the *Patterson* conference that the Court should overrule *Jones* v. *Alfred H. Mayer Co.* as well. The Rehnquist position in this respect was not a new one, though it was unknown outside the Court. The Chief Justice had written an April 7, 1987, letter to Justice White on a 1987 case involving section 1981[11] in which he stated, "I once again question the soundness of our opinion in *Jones* v. *Alfred H. Mayer Co.*, . . . which held that this class was protected not merely against state action but against action by other private individuals."

Justice Powell sent a letter two days later to Justice White, stating, "I . . . share the reservation expressed by the Chief Justice in his join note of April 7. In retrospect, I think our cases following *Jones* v. *Alfred H. Mayer Co.*, . . . misconstrued §§ 1981 and 1982." Justice O'Connor also wrote to Justice White that she "shared [the] reservations about the Court's construction" of the 1866 law.

After these notes were circulated, Justice Blackmun, who had authored the lower court opinion in the *Jones* case,[12] wrote to Justice White on April 13, 1987: "I am somewhat amused at the exchanges in the correspondence concerning *Jones* v. *Alfred H. Mayer Co.* . . . My amusement is due to my personal involvement in the case. If one just hangs on long enough, he may see almost anything happen."

Despite the last Blackmun comment, what did not happen was the overruling of either *Jones* or *Runyon*. *Jones* itself was not questioned in any published Court opinion and, in *Patterson* v. *McLean Credit Union*, the Court expressly refused to overrule *Runyon* v. *McCrary*. In *Patterson*, even the Justices who agreed with Rehnquist that *Runyon* had been wrongly decided, refused to go along with the Chief Justice and overrule that case. Their view was the one stated a few years earlier by Justice Powell in the April 9, 1987, letter quoted earlier : "[I]f the 'slate were clean' I would be inclined to agree with your view." The Powell letter "went on to say, however, that it was 'too late' to reexamine the prior precedents. John [Stevens] . . . also stated that he thought these precedents were 'incorrectly decided,' but he concluded that it would be inadvisable to overrule *Jones* and its progeny."

Perhaps the best statement of the reasons why *Jones* and *Runyon* should not be overruled is contained in the draft opinion of the Court prepared by Justice Brennan in the *Patterson* case, which is reprinted on p. 203. It is far more complete than the treatment of the subject in either the ultimate opinion of the Court or the final Brennan dissent in *Patterson*. It is a pity that it was never published, for it contains a discussion of stare decisis and the exceptions to its doctrine that merits comparison with the already classic analysis of stare decisis in the joint opinion of Justices O'Connor, Kennedy, and Souter in the 1992 case of *Planned Parenthood* v. *Casey*[13] (which, by the way, was the portion of the *Casey* opinion drafted by Justice Souter).

The Brennan draft starts with a typical judicial encomium to stare decisis: "[I]t serves important societal interests in fairness, stability, and predictability in the law . . . and in efficient judicial decisionmaking. Through adherence to *stare decisis*, 'we ensure that the law will not merely change erratically, but will develop in a principled and intelligible fashion.'"

Nevertheless, the Brennan draft goes on, "we have identified circumstances in which we will recognize an exception to that doctrine." That is so because "the alternative to a somewhat relaxed doctrine of *stare decisis* is stagnation, or at least an unsatisfactory resort to drawing ever finer lines of distinction." Stare decisis, however, remains the rule. "It remains . . . the heavy burden of a litigant urging that we overrule a precedent to demonstrate that it falls within the scope of [the] exceptions to *stare decisis*."

In *Patterson*, the Brennan draft states, "[c]onsiderations of *stare decisis* . . . require that we defer to our prior and now long-standing interpretation of § 1981, absent compelling reasons not to do so." There is no "special justification" for a departure from *Runyon*. To be sure, "[*s*]*tare decisis* will not save a statutory precedent that is without foundation." But *Runyon*'s interpretation of the statute, "though disputable, lies well outside these exceptions to *stare decisis* recognized for inadequately considered or patently unfounded decisions." Indeed, Justice Brennan affirms, the *Runyon* interpretation was "based upon a full and considered review of the statute's language and legislative history, assisted by careful briefing, and . . . this interpretation, though not inevitable, is by no means an implausible one."

The Brennan *Patterson* draft not only holds that stare decisis requires the reaffirmation of *Runyon*. It also goes out of its way (in more detail than in the published Brennan dissent) to find that *Jones* v. *Alfred H. Mayer* was correctly decided. The draft specifically agrees with *Jones* "that Congress said enough about the injustice of private discrimination, and the need to end it, to show that it did indeed intend the [1866] Civil Rights Act to sweep that far." In fact, the Brennan analysis leads the draft to state, "In sum, although *Jones* and *Runyon* both resolved what are assuredly close questions of statutory interpretation, we are unable to conclude that either the decision in *Jones* that . . . the 1866 Act was intended to reach private discrimination, or the decision in *Runyon* . . . was patently wrong and thus within the acknowledged exception to *stare decisis* that allows us to correct past errors." A contrary result would defeat the very goal of stare decisis. "The entire purpose of the policy of *stare decisis* . . . is to avoid the uncertainty that would result from our intermittent reconsideration of such questions. We do not believe our longstanding interpretation of § 1981 to prohibit private discrimination has been shown to be so dubious as to trigger an exception to this sound policy."

Finally, in a draft section paralleled by a shorter treatment in the final Brennan dissent, the Justice declares, "We are equally unpersuaded that *Runyon* v. *McCrary* falls within the exception to *stare decisis* for precedents that have proved 'outdated, . . . unworkable, or otherwise legitimately vulnerable to serious reconsideration.'" The draft notes that "[w]ith the passage of time, a statutory precedent sometimes becomes so problematic as to appear ripe for reconsideration. The Court has in those circumstances recognized an exception to the dictates of *stare decisis.*" The following examples are given: "The Court has overruled statutory precedents because the premises underlying a decision have been rendered untenable by subsequent congressional or judicial action . . . because a decision has come to appear inconsistent with another line of authority . . . and because experience has shown a precedent to be seriously at odds with congressional policy."

However, the Brennan draft states, "[n]one of these considerations is present here. On the contrary," the draft concludes, in language similar to that in Justice Brennan's published dissent,[14] "*Runyon* is entirely consonant with our society's deep commitment to the eradication of discrimination based on a person's race or the color of her skin. . . . In the past, this Court has overruled decisions antagonistic to our Nation's commitment to the ideal of a society in which a person's opportunities do not depend on her race, . . . and we decline now to abandon a statutory construction so in harmony with that ideal."

In *Patterson* v. *McLean Credit Union*, Chief Justice Rehnquist definitely lost his battle to have the Court overrule the *Jones* and *Runyon* cases. Despite this, he has generally prevailed in the civil rights cases decided by his Court. In accordance with Rehnquist's view, the Court has narrowed the scope of civil rights statutes in a number of decisions and has also limited the power of the states to enact such laws.

However, Chief Justice Rehnquist's approach almost lost him his Court in one important civil rights case—*Patterson* v. *McLean Credit Union* itself. At issue in *Patterson* was more than the question of whether *Runyon* v. *McCrary* should be overruled. Once the Court decided that *Runyon*'s holding should remain as governing law, it had to deal with the merits of the case. The petitioner, who had been employed by the respondent credit union for ten years, brought an action under section 1981 alleging that the respondent had harassed her, failed to promote her to an intermediate accounting clerk position, and discharged her, all because of her race. The lower courts ruled in favor of respondent. Certiorari was granted by an eight-Justice Court, with Justices Brennan, White, Marshall, and Stevens voting to grant, and the Chief Justice and Justices Blackmun, O'Connor, and Scalia to deny.

We have seen that Justice Brennan prepared a draft opinion of the Court in *Patterson*. That was true because the conference on October 14, 1988, voted by a bare majority to reverse (Justices Brennan, Marshall, Blackmun, and Stevens, were joined by Kennedy, who was only appointed after the cert vote). The Justices not only rejected the Chief Justice's plea to overrule *Runyon*; the conference majority also refused to accept his interpretation that racial harassment was not actionable under the statute. Three days later, Justice Brennan, senior in the majority, assigned the opinion to himself.

Justice Brennan circulated his draft opinion of the Court, reprinted on page 203, on December 3. We have already dealt with its discussion of the stare decisis issue. On the merits of the case, the draft found for the petitioner and vacated the decision of the lower courts. The key issue, as stated in the draft, was "whether a plaintiff may state a cause of action under § 1981 based upon allegations that her employer harassed her because of her race. The Court of Appeals held that claims of racial harassment, as opposed to allegations of discriminatory hiring, firing, or promotion, are not cognizable under § 1981, because racial harassment does not go to 'the very existence and nature of the employment contract,' . . . and hence cannot abridge the right to make and enforce contracts free of discrimination. We disagree."

The Brennan draft asserted "that in granting the freedmen the 'same right . . . to make and enforce contracts' as white citizens, Congress meant to encompass post-contractual conduct demonstrating that a freedman had not been accorded the right to enter a contract on the same terms as white persons." Hence, "the equal right to make and enforce contracts protected by § 1981 is not limited in scope to a right to overtly equal treatment at the time of entering into and ending a contractual relationship."

The draft finds that, "Racial harassment severe enough to amount to a breach of contract as a matter of state law is certainly cognizable . . . , for an employer's discriminatory failure to abide by the terms of a black employee's contract constitutes a denial of contractual opportunities as surely as does the initial offer of different employment terms to blacks and whites, or a race-based discharge." Nor need the "term breached by the racial harassment . . . be an explicit one." On the contrary, "it may be the implied covenant of good faith and fair dealing often supplied and given content by state law." Racial harassment that amounts to a breach of contract violates the statute, if it was racially motivated.

Nor, under the Brennan draft, is a breach of contract itself necessary. "Even if it does not breach an express or implied contract term, however, harassment is actionable . . . if it demonstrates that the employer has sought to evade the statute's strictures concerning contract formation." In such a case, where an employee makes a claim under the statute alleging racial harassment and alleges no breach of contract, the question is "whether in nature and extent the acts constituting harassment were sufficiently severe or pervasive as effectively to belie any claim that the contract was entered into in a racially neutral manner." Thus, "[w]here a black employee demonstrates that she has worked in conditions substantially different from those enjoyed by similarly situated white employees, and can show the necessary racial animus, a jury may infer that the black employee has not been afforded the same right to make an employment contract as white employees." When "the different contractual expectations are unspoken, but come clear during the course of employment as the black employee is subjected to substantially harsher conditions than her white co-workers," it cannot "be said that whites and blacks have had the same right to make an employment contract."

In *Patterson* itself, Justice Brennan's draft concludes, the petitioner's harassment claim came within the scope of the statute. "On the basis of the evidence at trial, the jury might have concluded that petitioner was subjected to such serious and extensive racial harassment as to have been denied the right to make an employment contract on the same basis as white employees of the credit union."

1st DRAFT

SUPREME COURT OF THE UNITED STATES

No. 87-107

BRENDA PATTERSON, PETITIONER *v.* McLEAN CREDIT UNION

ON WRIT OF CERTIORARI TO THE UNITED STATES COURT OF APPEALS FOR THE FOURTH CIRCUIT

[November ——, 1988]

JUSTICE BRENNAN delivered the opinion of the Court.

Respondent McLean Credit Union employed petitioner Brenda Patterson, a black woman, as a teller and file clerk for ten years, until it laid her off on July 19, 1982, and subsequently discharged her. Thereafter, petitioner commenced this action under 42 U. S. C. § 1981,[1] alleging that McLean had harassed her, failed to promote her to an intermediate accounting clerk position, and discharged her, all because of her race.[2] After hearing the evidence at trial, the District Court granted respondent's motion for a directed verdict with respect to Patterson's cause of action for racial harassment, ruling that harassment cannot form the basis for a separate claim under § 1981. The court then instructed the jury that in order to prevail on her promotion-discrimination claim, petitioner had to prove both that McLean failed to pro-

[1] Section 1981 provides:

"All persons within the jurisdiction of the United States shall have the same right in every State and Territory to make and enforce contracts, to sue, be parties, give evidence, and to the full and equal benefit of all laws and proceedings for the security of persons and property as is enjoyed by white citizens, and shall be subject to like punishment, pains, penalties, taxes, licenses, and exactions of every kind, and to no other."

[2] Petitioner also raised a pendent state-law claim for infliction of mental and emotional distress. The District Court directed a verdict for respondent on this claim, on the ground that petitioner had not alleged sufficiently extreme and outrageous treatment to recover under North Carolina law.

PATTERSON *v.* McLEAN CREDIT UNION

mote her because she was black, and that she was better qualified than the white employee who she claimed was promoted in her stead. The jury returned a verdict for respondent on both the promotion and discharge claims.

On appeal, petitioner challenged the dismissal of her racial harassment claim, and also the instructions given to the jury on her promotion-discrimination claim. The Court of Appeals for the Fourth Circuit affirmed. 805 F. 2d 1143. It held that while racial harassment might be probative of the discriminatory intent that must be shown in a § 1981 action, see *General Building Contractors Assn.* v. *Pennsylvania*, 458 U. S. 375 (1982), it was not cognizable as a discrete claim under § 1981, because harassment alone does not abridge the right "to make and enforce contracts." 805 F. 2d, at 1145–1146. The Court of Appeals also held that once respondent had advanced superior qualification as a reason for its promotion decision, petitioner could prevail only by proving that she in fact was better qualified, and hence that respondent's proffered reason was a pretext. *Id.*, at 1147. The court reasoned that an employer need not favor members of racial minorities when choosing among equally well-qualified individuals. *Ibid.*

We granted certiorari to consider whether § 1981 encompasses petitioner's claim of racial harassment in her employment, and whether the jury instruction given on her promotion-discrimination claim was erroneous. —— U. S. ——. After argument on these issues, however, we requested the parties to brief and argue an additional question: "Whether or not the interpretation of 42 U. S. C. § 1981 adopted by this Court in *Runyon* v. *McCrary*, 427 U. S. 160 (1976), should be reconsidered." —— U. S. ——. We decline today, for reasons of *stare decisis*, to revisit *Runyon*. Moreover, because we are persuaded that § 1981 encompasses petitioner's racial harassment claim, and that the District Court erred in instructing the jury as to petitioner's burden in proving her dis-

PATTERSON *v.* McLEAN CREDIT UNION

criminatory-promotion claim, we vacate the decision of the Court of Appeals and remand for further proceedings.

I

Twelve years ago, in deciding *Runyon* v. *McCrary*, this Court treated as already "well established" the proposition "that § 1 of the Civil Rights Act of 1866, 14 Stat. 27, 42 U. S. C. § 1981, prohibits racial discrimination in the making and enforcement of private contracts," as well as state-mandated inequalities, drawn along racial lines, in individuals' ability to make and enforce contracts. 427 U. S., at 168, citing *Johnson* v. *Railway Express Agency, Inc.*, 421 U. S. 454 (1975); *Tillman* v. *Wheaton-Haven Recreation Assn., Inc.*, 410 U. S. 431 (1973); and *Jones* v. *Alfred H. Mayer Co.*, 392 U. S. 409 (1968). Since deciding *Runyon*, we have upon a number of occasions treated as settled law its interpretation of § 1981 as extending to private discrimination. *Goodman* v. *Lukens Steel Co.*, —— U. S. —— (1987); *St. Francis College* v. *Al-Khazraji*, —— U. S. —— (1987); *General Building Contractors Assn.* v. *Pennsylvania*, *supra*; *Delaware State College* v. *Ricks*, 449 U. S. 250 (1980); *McDonald* v. *Santa Fe Trail Transp. Co.*, 427 U. S. 273 (1976). We have also reiterated our holding in *Jones* that § 1982 similarly applies to private discrimination in the sale or rental of real or personal property—a holding arrived at through an analysis of legislative history common to both § 1981 and § 1982. *Shaare Tefila Congregation* v. *Cobb*, —— U. S. —— (1987); *Sullivan* v. *Little Hunting Park, Inc.*, 396 U. S. 229 (1969). We may not lightly abandon such a long and consistent line of precedents.

"[T]he doctrine of *stare decisis* . . . demands respect in a society governed by the rule of law," *Akron* v. *Akron Center for Reproductive Health*, 462 U. S. 416, 419–420 (1983), for it serves important societal interests in fairness, stability, and predictability in the law, see, *e. g.*, *Boys Markets, Inc.* v. *Retail Clerks Union*, 398 U. S. 235, 240 (1970), and in efficient

PATTERSON *v.* McLEAN CREDIT UNION

judicial decisionmaking.[3] Through adherence to *stare decisis*, "we ensure that the law will not merely change erratically, but will develop in a principled and intelligible fashion." *Vasquez* v. *Hillery*, 474 U. S. 254, 265 (1986). This goal has long been thought sufficiently important to justify a practice of following even doubtful precedents. See *Burnet* v. *Coronado Oil & Gas Co.*, 285 U. S. 393, 406 (1932) (Brandeis, J., dissenting) ("*Stare decisis* is usually the wise policy, because in most matters it is more important that the applicable rule of law be settled than that it be settled right"); *Illinois Brick Co.* v. *Illinois*, 431 U. S. 720, 736–737 (1977).[4]

Nevertheless, this Court has recognized that "*stare decisis* is a principle of policy and not a mechanical formula" to be followed no matter what the consequences. *Helvering* v. *Hallock*, 309 U. S. 106, 119 (1940). We have thus acknowledged that the values served by *stare decisis* must sometimes "yield in favor of a greater objective." *Vasquez* v. *Hillery*, *supra*, at 266. In our efforts to determine "the golden mean between too much flexibility and too much rigidity" in our adherence to *stare decisis*, 12 W. Holdsworth, A History of English Law 160 (1938), we have identified circumstances in which we will recognize an exception to that doctrine, *e. g.*, *Patsy* v. *Florida Bd. of Regents*, 457 U. S. 496, 501 (1982), and we have overruled prior decisions when those circumstances clearly exist. It remains, however, the heavy burden of a litigant urging that we overrule a precedent to dem-

---

[3] "The labor of judges would be increased almost to the breaking point if every past decision could be reopened in every case, and one could not lay one's own course of bricks on the secure foundation of the courses laid by others who had gone before him." B. Cardozo, The Nature of the Judicial Process 149 (1921), quoted in *Runyon* v. *McCrary*, 427 U. S. 160, 190–191 (STEVENS, J., concurring).

[4] Cf. J. Kent, Commentaries *475–*477; W. Blackstone, Commentaries *69–*71. See also *Sheddon* v. *Goodrich*, 8 Ves. 481, 497, 32 Eng. Rep. 441, 447 (1803) ("better that the law should be certain than that every judge should speculate upon improvements").

PATTERSON *v.* McLEAN CREDIT UNION

onstrate that it falls within the scope of these exceptions to *stare decisis*.

This burden is particularly heavy, and our recognition of exceptions to *stare decisis* particularly spare, when we are confronted with a precedent, such as *Runyon* v. *McCrary*, that interprets a statute. The Court's readier willingness to overrule its constitutional precedents is attributable to the greater need for flexibility in responding to "changes in society or in the law," *Vasquez* v. *Hillery*, *supra*, at 266, that render prior interpretations of the Constitution outdated or unworkable. "[W]here correction through legislative action is practically impossible," *Burnet* v. *Coronado Oil & Gas Co.*, *supra*, at 407, the alternative to a somewhat relaxed doctrine of *stare decisis* is stagnation, or at least an unsatisfactory resort to drawing ever finer lines of distinction until the outdated precedent appears an isolated—but nevertheless "binding"—anomaly. But where "correction can be had by legislation," *ibid.*, this concern is absent, and the Court has repeatedly recognized that "considerations of *stare decisis* are at their strongest when this Court confronts its previous constructions of legislation." *Monell* v. *New York City Dept. of Social Services*, *supra*, at 714 (REHNQUIST, J., dissenting).[5]

Considerations of *stare decisis* therefore require that we defer to our prior and now long-standing interpretation of § 1981, absent compelling reasons not to do so. After reargument in this case, we are of the view that there is no "special justification," *Arizona* v. *Rumsey*, 467 U. S. 203, 212 (1984), for a departure from our decision in *Runyon* v.

[5] See also *Square D Co.* v. *Niagara Frontier Tariff Bureau*, 476 U. S. 409, 424 (1986); *NLRB* v. *Longshoremen*, 473 U. S. 61, 84 (1985); *Patsy* v. *Florida Bd. of Regents*, 457 U. S. 496, 517 (1982) (WHITE, J., concurring); *Illinois Brick Co.* v. *Illinois*, 431 U. S. 720, 736 (1977); *Edelman* v. *Jordan*, 415 U. S. 651, 671 and n. 14 (1974); *Monroe* v. *Pape*, 365 U. S. 167, 192 (1961) (Harlan, J., concurring); *Burnet* v. *Coronado Oil & Gas Co.*, 285 U. S. 393, 406–408 (1932) (Brandeis, J., dissenting).

PATTERSON *v.* McLEAN CREDIT UNION

McCrary that § 1981 reaches private acts of racial discrimination. *Runyon* did not plainly misconstrue § 1981; rather, it was based on a plausible reading of the provision's legislative history that has not been shown to be clearly mistaken by any new information or arguments advanced in the briefs filed in this case. Furthermore, far from being undermined by Congress' subsequent policy choices, *Runyon*'s view of the scope of § 1981 has been recognized and even built upon by Congress. Finally, this Court's interpretation of § 1981 in *Runyon* is in full harmony with our society's abhorrence of the injustice of race-based discrimination, and § 1981 has taken an important place in the panoply of protections against such discrimination.

A

Stare decisis will not save a statutory precedent that is without foundation. We do not owe a full measure of deference to a statutory interpretation arrived at without "documenting briefs and adequate arguments on both sides as foundation for due deliberation." *Monroe* v. *Pape*, 365 U. S. 167, 220 (1961) (Frankfurter, J., dissenting). Nor will we be bound by an interpretation if the Court "has never explored or analyzed in detail" its justifications. *Copperweld Corp.* v. *Independence Tube Corp.*, 467 U. S. 752, 766 (1984). In addition, even though a statutory precedent was based upon briefing, argument, and analysis, we have declined to follow it if factors have come to light that undermine the Court's prior considered view and very plainly show it to have been wrong. See, *e. g.*, *Griffin* v. *Breckenridge*, 403 U. S. 88, 95–96, 99–102 (1971); *Monroe* v. *Pape*, *supra*, at 192 (Harlan, J., concurring) (recognizing an exception to *stare decisis* where it appears "beyond doubt" that a statutory precedent "misapprehended the meaning of the controlling provision").

The Court's prior interpretation of § 1981, though disputable, lies well outside these exceptions to *stare decisis* recognized for inadequately considered or patently unfounded

PATTERSON *v.* McLEAN CREDIT UNION

decisions. Indeed, a survey of our cases demonstrates that the Court's interpretation of § 1981 has been based upon a full and considered review of the statute's language and legislative history, assisted by careful briefing, and that this interpretation, though not inevitable, is by no means an implausible one.

In *Jones* v. *Alfred H. Mayer Co.*, 392 U. S. 409 (1968), this Court considered whether § 1982, which provides that "[a]ll citizens of the United States shall have the same right, in every State and Territory, as is enjoyed by white citizens thereof to inherit, purchase, lease, sell, hold, and convey real and personal property," prohibits private discrimination on the basis of race, and if so, whether the statute is constitutional. The Court held, over two dissenting votes, that § 1982 bars private as well as public racial discrimination, and that the statute was a valid exercise of Congress' power under § 2 of the Thirteenth Amendment to identify the badges and incidents of slavery and to legislate to end them.

The Court began its careful analysis in *Jones* by noting the expansive language of § 1982, and observing that a black citizen denied the opportunity to purchase property as a result of discrimination by a private seller cannot be said to have the "same right" to purchase property as a white citizen. 392 U. S., at 420–421. Although Justice Harlan, in dissent, disagreed with the Court's broad interpretation of the word "right," he did not argue that the Court's view was plainly mistaken, but only that "there is an inherent ambiguity in the term 'right' as used in § 1982." *Id.*, at 452–453.[6] The Court also noted that in its original form § 1982 had been part of § 1

[6] "The 'right' referred to may either be a right to equal status under the law, in which case the statute operates only against state-sanctioned discrimination, or it may be an 'absolute' right enforceable against private individuals." *Jones* v. *Alfred H. Mayer Co.*, 392 U. S. 409, 453 (1968) (Harlan, J., dissenting).

PATTERSON *v.* McLEAN CREDIT UNION

of the Civil Rights Act of 1866,[7] and that § 2 of the 1866 Act provided for criminal penalties against any person who violated rights secured or protected by the Act "under color of any law, statute, ordinance, regulation, or custom." *Id.*, at 424–426. This explicit limitation upon the scope of § 2, to exclude criminal liability for private violations of § 1, strongly suggested that § 1 itself prohibited private discrimination, for otherwise the limiting language of § 2 would have been redundant. *Ibid.* Although the dissent thought a better explanation of the language of § 2 was that it "was carefully drafted to enforce all of the rights secured by § 1," *id.*, at 454, it is by no means obvious why the dissent's view should be regarded as the more accurate interpretation of the structure of the 1866 Act.[8]

---

[7] Act of April 9, 1866, c. 31, § 1, 14 Stat. 27. Section 1 provided:

"[C]itizens, of every race and color, without regard to any previous condition of slavery or involuntary servitude, . . . shall have the same right, in every State and Territory in the United States, to make and enforce contracts, to sue, be parties, and give evidence, to inherit, purchase, lease, sell, hold, and convey real and personal property, and to full and equal benefit of all laws and proceedings for the security of person and property, as is enjoyed by white citizens, and shall be subject to like punishment, pains, and penalties, and to none other, any law, statute, ordinance, regulation, or custom, to the contrary notwithstanding."

All members of the Court agreed in *Jones* that intervening revisions in the property clause of § 1—the reenactment of the 1866 Act in § 18 of the Voting Rights Act of 1870, Act of May 31, 1870, c. 114, § 18, 16 Stat. 144, the codification of the property clause in § 1978 of the Revised Statutes of 1874, and its recodification as 42 U. S. C. § 1982—had not altered its substance. *Jones*, 392 U. S., at 436–437 (opinion of the Court), 453 (dissent).

[8] In support of its view, the Court in *Jones* quoted from an exchange during the House debate on the civil rights bill. When Congressman Loan of Missouri asked the Chairman of the House Judiciary Committee why § 2 had been limited to those who acted under color of law, he was told, not that the statute had no application at all to those who had not acted under color of law, but that the limitation had been imposed because it was not desired to make "a general criminal code for the States." *Jones*, *supra*, at 425 n. 33, quoting Cong. Globe, 39th Cong., 1st Sess., 1120. Justice Harlan in dissent conceded that the Court's interpretation of this exchange as

PATTERSON *v.* McLEAN CREDIT UNION

The Court then engaged in a particularly thorough analysis of the legislative history of § 1 of the 1866 Act, *id.* at 422–437, which had been discussed at length in the briefs of both parties and their *amici.*[9] While never doubting that the prime targets of the 1866 Act were the Black Codes, in which the Confederate States imposed severe disabilities on the freedmen in an effort to replicate the effects of slavery, see, *e. g.*, 1 C. Fairman, Reconstruction and Reunion 1864–88, at 110–117 (1971) (discussing Mississippi's Black Codes), the Court concluded that Congress also had intended § 1 to reach private discriminatory conduct. The Court cited a bill (S.60) to amend the Freedmen's Bureau Act, introduced prior to the civil rights bill, and passed by both Houses during the 39th Congress (though it was eventually vetoed by President Johnson), as persuasive evidence that Congress was fully aware that any newly recognized rights of blacks would be as vulnerable to private as to state infringement. 392 U. S., at 423 and n. 30. The amendment would have extended the jurisdiction of the Freedmen's Bureau over all cases in the former Confederate States involving the denial on account of race of rights to make and enforce contracts or to purchase or lease property, "in consequence of any State or local law, ordinance, police, or other regulation, custom, *or prejudice.*" Cong. Globe, 39th Cong., 1st Sess., 209 (emphasis added). When the civil rights bill was subsequently introduced, Representative Bingham specifically linked it in scope to S.60. *Id.*, at 1292. See *Jones*, *supra*, at 424 n. 31.

The Court further noted that there had been "an imposing body of evidence [before Congress] pointing to the mistreatment of Negroes by private individuals and unofficial groups,

---

supporting a broader reading of § 1 was "a conceivable one." 392 U. S., at 470.

[9]See, *e. g.*, Brief for Petitioner 12–16, Brief for Respondents 7–24, Brief for United States as *Amicus Curiae* 28–35, 38–51, Brief for National Committee Against Discrimination in Housing as *Amicus Curiae* 9–39, in *Jones* v. *Alfred H. Mayer Co.*, O. T. 1967, No. 645.

mistreatment unrelated to any hostile state legislation." 392 U. S., at 427. This evidence included the comprehensive report of Major General Carl Schurz on conditions in the Confederate States, released some weeks before the civil rights bill was introduced. This report stressed that laws were only part of the problem facing the freedmen, who also encountered private discrimination and often brutality.[10] The congressional debates on the Freedmen's Bureau and civil rights bills show that legislators were well aware that the rights of former slaves were as much endangered by private action as by legislation. See *id.*, at 427–428 and nn. 37–40. To be sure, there is much emphasis in the debates on the evils of the Black Codes. But there are also passages that indicate that Congress intended to reach private discrimination that posed an equal threat to the rights of the freedmen. See *id.*, at 429–437. Senator Trumbull, for example, promised to introduce a bill aimed not only at "local legislation,"

[10] Report of C. Schurz, S. Exec. Doc. No. 2, 39th Cong., 1st Sess. (1865). The Schurz report is replete with descriptions of private discrimination. It notes, for example, that some planters had initially endeavored to maintain "the relation of master and slave, partly by concealing from [their slaves] the great changes that had taken place, and partly by terrorizing them into submission to their behests." *Id.*, at 15. It portrays as commonplace the use of "force and intimidation" to keep former slaves on the plantations. *Id.*, at 17, 18. See *Jones*, *supra*, at 428–429. See also Report of the Joint Committee on Reconstruction, 39th Cong., 1st Sess., pts. i–iv (1866). The Joint Committee on Reconstruction conducted hearings contemporaneously with Congress' consideration of the civil rights bill. In addition to uncovering numerous incidents of violence aimed at restraining southern blacks' efforts to exercise their new-won freedom, *e. g.*, *id.*, at pt. iii, p. 143, and whippings aimed simply at making them work harder, or handed out as punishment for a laborer's transgressions, *e. g.*, *id.*, at pt. iv, p. 83, these investigations identified pervasive forms of private discrimination plainly evidencing an intent on the part of employers not to offer the freedmen nondiscriminatory opportunities to contract. For example, employers often refused to pay freedmen more than a fraction of white laborers' wages, *e. g.*, *id.*, at pt. ii, pp. 12–13, 54–55, 234, and sometimes refused to contract at all with their former slaves, *e. g.*, Schurz Report, *supra*, at 16.

PATTERSON *v.* McLEAN CREDIT UNION

but at any "prevailing public sentiment" that blacks in the South "should continue to be oppressed and in fact deprived of their freedom." Cong. Globe, 39th Cong., 1st Sess., 77, quoted in *Jones*, *supra*, at 431.[11]

It is possible, as the dissent in *Jones* demonstrates, 392 U. S., at 454–473, to take the emphasis in the debates on the Black Codes as controlling, and to read all references to private action as aberrations or as mere background. But it is no less plausible to conclude, as the Court did after thorough analysis in *Jones*, that Congress said enough about the injustice of private discrimination, and the need to end it, to show that it did indeed intend the Civil Rights Act to sweep that far. In fact, Justice Harlan seems to have conceded that the Court's view of the scope of § 1982 was not implausible, for he stated in dissent only that the legislative history of the 1866 Act did not "overwhelmingly support the result reached by the Court," and that upon reading that same history, "a contrary conclusion may equally well be drawn." *Id.*, at 454. We certainly could not with confidence hold that the interpretation of § 1982 in *Jones* as prohibiting private discrimination in the sale or lease of property was unwarranted.

Because the language of both § 1981 and § 1982 appeared traceable to § 1 of the Civil Rights Act of 1866, the decision in *Jones* was naturally taken to indicate that § 1981 also prohibited private racial discrimination in the making and enforcement of contracts. Thus, in *Tillman* v. *Wheaton-Haven Recreational Assn., Inc.*, 410 U. S. 431, 440 (1973), the

[11] Senator Trumbull was speaking here of his Freedmen's Bureau bill, which was regarded as having the same scope as his later civil rights bill. See *supra*, at ——.

For other statements indicating that § 1 reached private conduct, see Cong. Globe, 39th Cong., 1st Sess., 1118 ("Laws barbaric and treatment inhuman are the rewards meted out by our white enemies to our colored friends. We should put a stop to this at once and forever") (Representative Wilson); *id.*, at 1152 (bill aimed at "the tyrannical *acts*, the tyrannical *restrictions*, and the tyrannical *laws* which belong to the condition of slavery") (emphasis added) (Representative Thayer).

PATTERSON *v.* McLEAN CREDIT UNION

Court held that "[i]n light of the historical interrelationship between § 1981 and § 1982," there was no reason to construe those sections differently as they related to a claim that a community swimming club denied property-linked membership preferences to blacks; and in *Johnson* v. *Railway Express Agency, Inc.*, 421 U. S. 454, 459–460 (1975), the Court stated "that § 1981 affords a federal remedy against discrimination in private employment on the basis of race." The Court only addressed the scope of § 1981 in any depth, however, in *Runyon* v. *McCrary*, 427 U. S. 160 (1976), where we held that § 1981 prohibited racial discrimination in the admissions policy of a private school. That issue was directly presented and fully briefed in *Runyon.*[12]

Although the Court in *Runyon* treated it as settled by *Jones*, *Tillman*, and *Johnson* that § 1981 prohibited private racial discrimination in contracting, it nevertheless discussed in detail the claim that § 1981 is narrower in scope than § 1982. The primary focus of disagreement between the majority in *Runyon* and JUSTICE WHITE's dissent, a debate renewed by the parties here, concerns the origins of § 1981. Section 1 of the 1866 Act was expressly reenacted by § 18 of the Voting Rights Act of 1870. Act of May 31, 1870, c. 114, § 18, 16 Stat. 144. Section 16 of the 1870 Act nevertheless also provided "[t]hat all persons within the jurisdiction of the United States shall have the same right in every State and Territory in the United States to make and enforce contracts . . . ." *Id.*, § 16, 16 Stat. 144. Section 1 of the 1866 Act, as reenacted by § 18 of the 1870 Act, was passed under Congress' Thirteenth Amendment power to identify and legislate against the badges and incidents of slavery, and, we held in *Jones*, applied to private acts of discrimination. The dissent in *Runyon*, however, argued that § 16 of the 1870 Act was

[12] See, *e. g.*, Brief for Petitioners 2, 6–11, Brief for Respondents 13–22, Brief for United States as *Amicus Curiae* 13–18, in *Runyon* v. *McCrary*, O. T. 1975, No. 75–62; Brief for Petitioner 17–59, in *Fairfax-Brewster School, Inc.* v. *Gonzales*, O. T. 1975, No. 75–66.

PATTERSON *v.* McLEAN CREDIT UNION

enacted solely under Congress' Fourteenth Amendment power to prohibit States from denying any person the equal protection of the laws, and could have had no application to purely private discrimination. See *Runyon, supra*, at 195–201 (WHITE, J., dissenting) (discussing the legislative history of § 16). But see *District of Columbia* v. *Carter*, 409 U. S. 418, 424 n. 8 (1973) (suggesting Congress may have the power to proscribe purely private conduct under § 5 of the Fourteenth Amendment). When all existing federal statutes were codified in the Revised Code of 1874, the Code included but a single provision prohibiting racial discrimination in the making and enforcement of contracts—§ 1977, which was identical to the current § 1981. The *Runyon* dissenters believed that this provision derived solely from § 16 of the 1870 Act, that the analysis of § 1 in *Jones* was hence of no application to § 1981, and that § 1981 could not be interpreted to prohibit private discrimination.

The Court concluded in *Runyon*, however, that § 1977 derived from *both* § 1 of the 1866 Act (as reenacted) and § 16 of the 1870 Act, and thus was to be interpreted, in light of the decision in *Jones*, as applying to private conduct. See also *General Building Contractors Assn.* v. *Pennsylvania*, 458 U. S. 375, 390 n. 17 (1982) ("§ 1981, because it is derived in part from the 1866 Act, has roots in the Thirteenth as well as the Fourteenth Amendment"). This result followed, the Court held, from the terms of the 1874 revision of the statutes. The revisers who prepared the codification had authority only to "revise, simplify, arrange, and consolidate" existing laws, to omit "redundant or obsolete" provisions, and to make suggestions for repeal. Act of June 27, 1866, 14 Stat. 74–75. See *Runyon, supra*, at 168 n. 8. The revisers made no recommendation that § 1 of the 1866 Act, as reenacted, be repealed, and obviously the broad 1866 provision, applying to private actors, was not made redundant or obsolete by § 16 of the 1870 Act, with its potentially narrower scope. Hence the *Runyon* Court thought it most plausible

PATTERSON *v.* McLEAN CREDIT UNION

that § 1977 was a consolidation of § 1 and of § 16. *Ibid.* The Court explained that a revisers' note printed alongside § 1977, indicating that it was derived from § 16, but not mentioning § 1 or its reenactment, had to be viewed in light of the terms of the codification as either inadvertent or an error, and declined "to attribute to Congress an intent to repeal a major piece of Reconstruction legislation on the basis of an unexplained omission from the revisers' marginal notes." *Ibid.*[13] Respondent has supplied no new information on

[13] Congress originally entrusted the revision of the laws to three Commissioners appointed under the Act of June 27, 1866, 14 Stat. 74–75. These Commissioners were instructed to draft side-notes indicating the source of each section of their revision, *id.*, at § 2, 14 Stat. 75, and they wrote the marginal note to what became § 1977 of the Revised Code, which referred as a source only to § 16 of the 1870 Act. See 1 Revision of the United States Statutes as Drafted by the Commissioners Appointed for that Purpose 947 (1872). Congress rejected the work of the Commissioners, however, precisely because members believed it to contain new legislation. See 2 Cong. Rec. 646 (1874). Congress then appointed Thomas Durant to review the Commissioners' work. See Act of March 3, 1873, § 3, 17 Stat. 580. "[W]herever the meaning of the law had been changed," Durant was "to strike out such changes." 2 Cong. Rec. 646 (1874). Durant reported that he had compared the Commissioners' revision with preexisting statutes, and that "wherever it has been found that a section contained any departure from the meaning of Congress as expressed in the Statutes at Large, such change has been made as was necessary to restore the original signification." Report to the Joint Committee on the Revision of the Laws 1 (1873). Durant's revision, H. R. 1215, 43d Cong., 1st Sess. (1874), which was put before Congress in the form of a bill, see 2 Cong. Rec. 819 (1874), contained no marginal notations. See *id.*, at 826–827, 1210. The Commissioners' reference to § 16 reappeared only after Congress authorized the Secretary of State to publish the Revised Statutes with marginal notations. See Act of June 20, 1874, c. 333, § 2, 18 Stat. (pt. 3) 113. Apparently, the Secretary simply lifted notations from the Commissioners' draft revision. Hence, insofar as Durant might have thought that the Commissioners had changed the law by referring only to § 16 as their source, and that this problem had been cured merely by the omission of the marginal note from his own draft, it seems strained to rely upon the later decision to restore the Commissioners' marginal notes as evidence that § 1977 derives solely from § 16. This is particularly so in light

PATTERSON *v.* McLEAN CREDIT UNION

reargument that convinces us that the Court's conclusion as to the dual origins of § 1981 was plainly mistaken.[14]

In sum, although *Jones* and *Runyon* both resolved what are assuredly close questions of statutory interpretation, we are unable to conclude that either the decision in *Jones* that § 1 of the 1866 Act was intended to reach private discrimination, or the decision in *Runyon* that § 1981 is in part derived from the 1866 Act, was patently wrong and thus within the acknowledged exception to *stare decisis* that allows us to correct past errors. We are not infrequently faced with difficult questions of statutory interpretation, where analysis of the language and legislative history of a provision may lead to more than one plausible conclusion as to its meaning. The entire purpose of the policy of *stare decisis* that we have adopted in statutory cases is to avoid the uncertainty that

---

of criticism directed in Congress to the accuracy of some of the Commissioners' side-notes. See 2 Cong. Rec. 828 (1874) (citing as an error a marginal note that was "not sufficently comprehensive" to reflect the provision's source) (Representative Lawrence).

[14] We find strong support for our prior holding that § 1981 is derived in part from the 1866 Act in the legislative history of the 1874 codification. Representative Lawrence, a member of the Joint Committee on the Revision of the Laws, specifically commented in the House upon the proposed revision of the 1866 and 1870 Acts. 2 Cong. Rec. 827–828 (1874). He noted that the plan of revision was "to collate in one title of 'civil rights' the statutes which declare them." *Id.*, at 827. After setting out § 1 and § 2 of the 1866 Act, and then § 16 and § 17 of the 1870 Act, Representative Lawrence stated that the revisers had "very properly not treated [the 1870 Act] as superseding the entire original act." *Id.*, at 828. Rather, they had "translat[ed] the sections I have cited from the acts of 1866 and 1870, so far as they relate to a declaration of existing rights," in the provisions that have now become § 1981 and § 1982. *Ibid.* There is no hint in this passage that any part of the 1866 Act would be lost in the revision, and indeed in other parts of his statement Representative Lawrence makes it plain that he understood the revisers' task to be that of presenting "the actual state of the law." *Id.*, at 826. See also *id.*, at 647–649 (general discussion on the aim of the revision to codify existing law without modification), and at 1210 ("we do not purpose to alter the law one jot or tittle") (Representative Poland).

would result from our intermittent reconsideration of such questions. We do not believe our long-standing interpretation of § 1981 to prohibit private discrimination has been shown to be so dubious as to trigger an exception to this sound policy.

B

We have justified our practice of according special weight to statutory precedents by reference to Congress' ability to undo statutory interpretations it believes erroneous. Congress has not overturned or otherwise undermined *Runyon*. On the contrary, Congress has considered and rejected an amendment that would have rendered § 1981 unavailable in most cases as a remedy for private employment discrimination—which is evidence of congressional acquiescence that "has been deemed to be something other than mere congressional silence and passivity." *Flood* v. *Kuhn*, 407 U. S. 258, 283 (1972). In addition, Congress has built upon our interpretation of § 1981 in enacting a statute that provides for the recovery of attorney's fees in § 1981 actions.

After the Court's decision in *Jones* v. *Alfred H. Mayer Co.*, Congress enacted the Equal Employment Opportunity Act of 1972, Pub. L. 92–261, 86 Stat. 103 (1972), amending Title VII of the Civil Rights Act of 1964, 42 U. S. C. § 2000e *et seq.* During Congress' consideration of this legislation—by which time there had been ample indication that § 1981 was being interpreted to apply to private acts of employment discrimination[15]—it was suggested that Title VII rendered

[15] The Court had remarked in *Jones* upon the close parallel between § 1981 and § 1982. 392 U. S., at 441 n. 78. Moreover, the lower federal courts already had begun to interpret § 1981 to reach private employment discrimination. See, *e. g.*, *Waters* v. *Wisconsin Steel Works*, 427 F. 2d 476 (CA7), cert. denied, 400 U. S. 911 (1970); *Sanders* v. *Dobbs Houses, Inc.*, 431 F. 2d 1097 (CA5 1970), cert. denied, 401 U. S. 948 (1971); *Young* v. *IT & T*, 438 F. 2d 757 (CA3 1971); *Caldwell* v. *National Brewing Co.*, 443 F. 2d 1044 (CA5 1971), cert. denied, 405 U. S. 916 (1972); *Boudreaux* v. *Baton Rouge Marine Contracting Co.*, 437 F. 2d 1011 (CA5 1971).

PATTERSON *v.* McLEAN CREDIT UNION

redundant the availability of a remedy for employment discrimination under provisions derived from the Civil Rights Act of 1866. Some concluded that Title VII should be made, with limited exceptions, the exclusive remedy for such discrimination. See H. R. Rep. No. 92–238, p. 66–67 (minority views). Senator Hruska proposed an amendment to that effect. 118 Cong. Rec. 3172 (1972). Speaking for his amendment, Senator Hruska stated his belief that under existing law private employment discrimination would give rise to a § 1981 claim. He complained specifically that without a provision making Title VII an exclusive remedy, "a black female employee [alleging] a denial of either a promotion or pay raise . . . because of her color," might "completely bypass" Title VII by filing "a complaint in federal court under the provisions of the Civil Rights Act of 1866 against . . . the employer." *Id.*, at 3368, 3369. In speaking against the Hruska amendment, Senator Williams, floor manager of the bill, stated that it was not the purpose of the bill "to repeal existing civil rights laws," and that to do so "would severely weaken our overall effort to combat the presence of employment discrimination." *Id.*, at 3371. He referred to § 1981 as an existing protection that should not be limited by the amendments to Title VII:

> "The right of individuals to bring suits in federal courts to redress individual acts of discrimination, including employment discrimination[,] was first provided by the Civil Rights Acts of 1866 and 1871, 42 U. S. C. sections 1981, 1983. It was recently stated by the Supreme Court in the case of Jones v. Mayer, that these acts provide fundamental constitutional guarantees. In any case, the courts have specifically held that title VII and

Section 1981 also had been held applicable to other forms of private discrimination. See, *e. g.*, *Scott* v. *Young*, 307 F. Supp. 1005 (ED Va.), aff'd, 421 F. 2d 143 (CA4 1969), cert. denied, 398 U. S. 929 (1970) (amusement park admissions policy); *Grier* v. *Specialized Skills*, 326 F. Supp. 856 (WDNC 1971) (admission to barber school).

> the Civil Rights Acts of 1866 and 1871 are not mutually exclusive, and must be read together to provide alternative means to redress individual grievances.
>
> Mr. President, the amendment of [Senator Hruska] will repeal the first major piece of civil rights legislation in this Nation's history. We cannot do that.
>
> . . . . .
>
> The peculiarly damaging nature of employment discrimination is such that the individual, who is frequently forced to face a large and powerful employer, should be accorded every protection that the law has in its purview, and that the person should not be forced to seek his remedy in only one place." *Id.*, at 3371–3372.[16]

The Hruska amendment failed to win passage on a tied vote, *id.*, at 3373, and the Senate later defeated a motion to reconsider the amendment by a vote of 50–37. *Id.*, at 3964–3965. Though the House initially adopted a similar amendment, 117 Cong. Rec. 31973, 32111 (1971), it eventually agreed with the Senate that Title VII should not preclude other remedies for employment discrimination. See H. R. Conf. Rep. No. 92–899 (1972). Thus, Congress in 1972 assumed that § 1981 reached private discrimination, and declined to alter its availability as an alternative to those remedies provided by Title VII. The Court in *Runyon* properly relied upon Congress' refusal to adopt an amendment that would have made § 1981 inapplicable to racially discriminatory actions by private employers, and concluded, as do we, that "[t]here could hardly be a clearer indication of congressional agreement with the view that § 1981 *does* reach private acts of racial discrimination." 427 U. S., at 174–175 (emphasis in original).

[16] See also 118 Cong. Rec. 3370 (Senator Javits) (opposing the Hruska amendment because it would "cut off . . . the possibility of using civil rights acts long antedating the Civil Rights Act of 1964 in a given situation which might fall, because of the statute of limitations or other provisions, in the interstices of the Civil Rights Act of 1964").

PATTERSON *v.* McLEAN CREDIT UNION

Events since our decision in *Runyon* confirm Congress' approval of our interpretation of § 1981. In 1976—shortly after *Runyon* had been decided, and well after the Court had indicated in *Tillman* and *Johnson* that § 1981 prohibits private discrimination—Congress reacted to the ruling in *Alyeska Pipeline Service Co.* v. *Wilderness Society*, 421 U. S. 240 (1975), that attorney's fees are not ordinarily recoverable absent statutory authorization, by enacting the Civil Rights Attorney's Fees Awards Act of 1976, Pub. L. No. 94–559, 99 Stat. 2641, 42 U. S. C. § 1988. A number of civil rights statutes, like § 1981, did not provide for the recovery of attorney's fees, and Congress heard testimony that the decision in *Alyeska Pipeline* might have a "devastating impact" on litigation under the civil rights laws. H. R. Rep. No. 94–1558, p. 3 (1976). Congress responded by passing an Act to permit the recovery of attorney's fees in civil rights cases, including those brought under § 1981.

Congress was well aware when it passed the 1976 Act that this Court had interpreted § 1981 to apply to private discrimination. The House Judiciary Committee report had expressly stated:

> "Section 1981 is frequently used to challenge employment discrimination based on race or color. *Johnson* v. *Railway Express Agency, Inc.*, 421 U. S. 454 (1975). Under that section the Supreme Court recently held that whites as well as blacks could bring suit alleging racially discriminatory employment practices. *McDonald* v. *Santa Fe Trail Transportation Co.*, [427 U. S. 273 (1975)]. Section 1981 has also been cited to attack exclusionary admissions policies at recreational facilities. *Tillman* v. *Wheaton-Haven Recreation Ass'n*, 410 U. S. 431 (1973)." H. R. Rep. No. 94–1558, *supra*, at 4 (footnotes omitted).

Congress recognized that § 1981, thus interpreted, overlaps significantly with Title VII, and expressed dissatisfaction that attorney's fees should be available under the latter but not the former statute. See S. Rep. No. 94–1011, p. 4 (1976) ("fees are now authorized in an employment discrimination suit brought under Title VII of the 1964 Civil Rights Act, but not in the same suit brought under 42 U. S. C. § 1981, which protects similar rights but involves fewer technical prerequisites to the filing of an action"). Congress' action in providing for attorney's fees in § 1981 actions, intending that successful § 1981 plaintiffs who could have brought their action under Title VII not be deprived of fees, and knowing that this Court had interpreted § 1981 to apply to private discrimination, goes beyond mere acquiescence in our interpretation of § 1981. Congress approved and even built upon our interpretation. Overruling *Runyon* would be flatly inconsistent with this expression of congressional intent. See *Bob Jones University* v. *United States*, 461 U. S. 574, 601–602 (1983); *Patsy* v. *Florida Bd. of Regents*, 457 U. S. 496, 501 (1982); *Apex Hosiery Co.* v. *Leader*, 310 U. S. 469, 488 (1940).

C

We are equally unpersuaded that *Runyon* v. *McCrary* falls within the exception to *stare decisis* for precedents that have proved "outdated, . . . unworkable, or otherwise legitimately vulnerable to serious reconsideration." *Vasquez* v. *Hillery*, 474 U. S. 254, 266 (1986).

With the passage of time, a statutory precedent sometimes becomes so problematic as to appear ripe for reconsideration. The Court has in those circumstances recognized an exception to the dictates of *stare decisis* and has overruled prior decisions in order "to bring [the Court's] opinions into agreement with experience and with facts newly ascertained." *Burnet* v. *Coronado Oil & Gas Co.*, 285 U. S. 393, 412 (1932) (Brandeis, J., dissenting). The Court has overruled statutory precedents because the premises underlying a decision have been rendered untenable by subsequent congressional or judicial action, *e. g.*, *Braden* v. *30th Judicial Circuit Court*, 410 U. S. 484, 497–499 (1973); because a decision has

PATTERSON *v.* McLEAN CREDIT UNION

come to appear inconsistent with another line of authority, *e. g.*, *Monell* v. *New York City Dept. of Social Services*, 436 U. S. 658, 696 (1978); and because experience has shown a precedent to be seriously at odds with congressional policy, *e. g.*, *Boys Markets, Inc.* v. *Retail Clerks Union*, 398 U. S. 235, 241 (1970). None of these considerations is present here.[17] On the contrary, *Runyon* is entirely consonant with our society's deep commitment to the eradication of discrimination based on a person's race or the color of her skin. See *Bob Jones University* v. *United States*, 461 U. S., at 593 ("every pronouncement of this Court and myriad Acts of Congress and Executive Orders attest a firm national policy to prohibit racial segregation and discrimination"). That commitment is the product of a national consensus that racial discrimination is incompatible with our best conception of our

---

[17] We do not perceive any inconsistency between Title VII's scheme for redressing employment discrimination and § 1981, as interpreted to prohibit private discrimination, including employment discrimination. The legislative history of the 1972 amendments to Title VII, see *supra*, at ——, shows that Congress was well aware of the overlap between Title VII and § 1981, and nevertheless chose to retain the latter as a remedy for employment discrimination. See *Johnson* v. *Railway Express Agency, Inc.*, 421 U. S. 454, 461 (1975). Moreover, we have previously noted that "the remedies available under Title VII and under § 1981, although related, and although directed to most of the same ends, are separate, distinct, and independent." *Ibid.* Section 1981 is not limited in scope to employment discrimination by businesses with 15 or more employees, cf. 42 U. S. C. § 2000e(b), and hence may reach the nearly 15% of the workforce not covered by Title VII. See Eisenberg & Schwab, The Importance of Section 1981, 73 Cornell L. Rev. 596, 602 (1988). Nor is a § 1981 plaintiff limited to recovering backpay: she may also obtain damages, including punitive damages in an appropriate case. *Johnson*, 421 U. S., at 460. Moreover, a § 1981 backpay award may also extend beyond the two-year limit of Title VII. *Ibid.* Other differences between the two statutes include the right to a jury trial under § 1981, but not Title VII; a different statute of limitations in § 1981 cases, see *Goodman* v. *Lukens Steel Co.*, —— U. S. —— (1987); and the availability under Title VII, but not § 1981, of administrative machinery designed to provide assistance in investigation and conciliation, see *Johnson*, *supra*, at 460.

communal life, and with each individual's rightful expectation that her full participation in the community will not be contingent upon her race. In the past, this Court has overruled decisions antagonistic to our Nation's commitment to the ideal of a society in which a person's opportunities do not depend on her race, *e. g.*, *Brown* v. *Board of Education*, 347 U. S. 483 (1954) (overruling *Plessy* v. *Ferguson*, 163 U. S. 537 (1896)), and we decline now to abandon a statutory construction so in harmony with that ideal.

II

Because we today reaffirm that § 1981 prohibits private racial discrimination, we must further decide the two issues on which certiorari was granted in this case. The first of these issues is whether a plaintiff may state a cause of action under § 1981 based upon allegations that her employer harassed her because of her race. The Court of Appeals held that claims of racial harassment, as opposed to allegations of discriminatory hiring, firing, or promotion, are not cognizable under § 1981, because racial harassment does not go to "the very existence and nature of the employment contract," 805 F. 2d, at 1145, and hence cannot abridge the right to make and enforce contracts free of discrimination. We disagree.

A

The legislative history of § 1981 makes clear that we must not take an overly narrow view of what it means to have the "same right to make and enforce contracts" as white citizens. The very same legislative history that supports our interpretation of § 1981 in *Runyon* also indicates that the 39th Congress intended, in the employment context, to go beyond protecting the freedmen from literal refusals to contract for their labor, efforts to force them to remain with their prior owners, and discriminatory decisions to discharge them. Section 1 of the Civil Rights Act was also designed to protect the freedmen from the imposition of working conditions that evidenced an intent on the part of the employer not to contract

PATTERSON *v.* McLEAN CREDIT UNION

on nondiscriminatory terms. See nn. 10 and 11, *supra.* Congress realized that, in the former Confederate States, employers were attempting to "adher[e], as to the *treatment of the laborers,* as much as possible to the traditions of the old system, *even where the relations between employers and laborers had been fixed by contract.*" Report of C. Schurz, S. Exec. Doc. No. 2, 39th Cong., 1st Sess., 19 (1865) (emphasis added). These working conditions included the use of the whip as an incentive to work harder—the commonplace result of an entrenched attitude reported by General Schurz, that "[y]ou cannot make the negro work without physical compulsion," *id.*, at 16—and the practice of handing out severe and unequal punishment for perceived transgressions. See *id.*, at 20 ("The habit [of corporal punishment] is so inveterate with a great many persons as to render, on the least provocation, the impulse to whip a negro almost irresistible"). Since such "acts of persecution" against *employed* freedmen, *ibid.*, were one of the 39th Congress' concerns in enacting the Civil Rights Act, it is clear that in granting the freedmen the "same right . . . to make and enforce contracts" as white citizens, Congress meant to encompass post-contractual conduct demonstrating that a freedman had not been accorded the right to enter a contract on the same terms as white persons.[18]

Our past decisions also indicate that the equal right to make and enforce contracts protected by § 1981 is not limited in scope to a right to overtly equal treatment at the time of entering into and ending a contractual relationship. In *Goodman* v. *Lukens Steel Co.*, —— U. S. —— (1987), we af-

[18] We note, in fact, that the equal right "to make and enforce contracts," interpreted in its narrowest and most literal sense, would not include even the right to be free from discriminatory discharge from employment. The legislative history of the Civil Rights Act shows that § 1981 is broader in scope, and, indeed, the lower federal courts have consistently and without question treated discriminatory discharges as within the provision's protection, as did the District Court and Court of Appeals in this case. See 805 F. 2d, at 1145.

firmed a decision that a union collective-bargaining agent was liable under § 1981. The union had followed "a policy of refusing to file grievable racial discrimination claims however strong they might be and however sure the [union] was that the employer was discriminating against blacks," and thereby had "intentionally discriminated against blacks seeking a remedy for disparate treatment based on their race." *Id.*, at ——. Of course, the union's violation of § 1981 in *Goodman* related only *indirectly* to the commencement of its relationship with the employees it represented, but *directly* to *the way in which the union carried out* its part of the bargain that it would represent employees. Analogously, we have interpreted the equal right protected by § 1982 "to inherit, purchase, lease, sell, hold, and convey real and personal property" not just as covering the rights to acquire and dispose of property, but also the "right . . . to *use* property on an equal basis with white citizens," *Memphis* v. *Greene*, 451 U. S. 100, 120 (1981) (emphasis added), and "not to have property interests *impaired* because of . . . race," *id.*, at 122 (emphasis added).[19]

B

Although § 1981 thus does not require a plaintiff to prove overt discrimination at the time of hiring or discharge, it is nevertheless clear that the statutory language imposes a limit upon the type of harassment claims that are cognizable under § 1981. Section 1981 cannot be construed as a general proscription of racial discrimination in all aspects of contractual relationships, for it expressly prohibits discrimination only in the making and enforcement of contracts. Racial ha-

[19] In *Shaare Tefila Congregation* v. *Cobb*, —— U. S. —— (1987), we reversed the dismissal of a claim by a Jewish congregation alleging that individuals were liable under § 1982 for spraying racist graffiti on the walls of the congregation's synagogue. Though our holding in that case was limited to deciding that Jews are a group protected by § 1982, our opinion nowhere hints that the congregation's vandalism claim might not be cognizable under the statute.

PATTERSON *v.* McLEAN CREDIT UNION

rassment severe enough to amount to a breach of contract as a matter of state law is certainly cognizable under § 1981, for an employer's discriminatory failure to abide by the terms of a black employee's contract constitutes a denial of contractual opportunities as surely as does the initial offer of different employment terms to blacks and whites, or a race-based discharge. The term breached by the racial harassment may be an explicit one, or it may be the implied covenant of good faith and fair dealing often supplied and given content by state law. See Restatement (Second) of Contracts § 205 and Comment *d* (1981). A plaintiff who claims that racial harassment violates § 1981 because it amounts to a breach of contract must prove both that the harassment amounted to a breach under state law, and that it was racially motivated.

Even if it does not breach an express or implied contract term, however, harassment is actionable under § 1981 if it demonstrates that the employer has sought to evade the statute's strictures concerning contract formation. The question in each case in which an employee makes a § 1981 claim alleging racial harassment and alleges no breach of contract is therefore whether in nature and extent the acts constituting harassment were sufficently severe or pervasive as effectively to belie any claim that the contract was entered into in a racially neutral manner. Where a black employee demonstrates that she has worked in conditions substantially different from those enjoyed by similarly situated white employees, and can show the necessary racial animus, a jury may infer that the black employee has not been afforded the same right to make an employment contract as white employees. Obviously, as respondent conceded at oral argument, Tr. of Oral Arg. of Feb. 29, 1987, at 30, if an employer offers a black and a white applicant for employment the same written contract, but then tells the black employee that her working conditions will be much worse than those of the white hired for the same job because "there's a lot of harassment going on in this work place and you have to agree to that," it would have

PATTERSON *v.* McLEAN CREDIT UNION

to be concluded that the white and black had not enjoyed an equal right to make a contract. We see no relevant distinction between that case and one in which the different contractual expectations are unspoken, but become clear during the course of employment as the black employee is subjected to substantially harsher conditions than her white co-workers. In neither case can it be said that whites and blacks have had the same right to make an employment contract.

The determination whether intentional racial harassment grounds a § 1981 claim must be made on a case-by-case basis after a consideration of all the circumstances. See *Nazaire* v. *Trans World Airlines, Inc.*, 807 F. 2d 1372, 1380 (CA7 1986), cert. denied, —— U. S. —— (1987). Where liability is predicated on breach of an express or implied contract term, a court entertaining a § 1981 harassment claim must be guided by state law regarding the existence of the alleged term and proof of breach. Where no breach of contract is alleged, a harassment claim is cognizable under § 1981 if the nature and degree of harassment show that the employment contract was not entered into on racially neutral terms. As in the Title VII context, see *Meritor Savings Bank* v. *Vinson*, 477 U. S. 57 (1986),[20] an isolated racial slur will not ground this sort of § 1981 harassment claim, but severe and

[20] In *Meritor Savings Bank* we addressed the question whether allegations of discriminatory workplace harassment state a claim under § 703 of Title VII, 42 U. S. C. § 2000e–2(a)(1), which prohibits discrimination "with respect to [an employee's] compensation, terms, conditions, or privileges of employment." We held that sexual harassment creating a hostile workplace environment may ground an action under Title VII. "[N]ot all workplace conduct that may be described as 'harassment' affects a 'term, condition, or privilege' of employment within the meaning of Title VII," however. 477 U. S., at 67. "For sexual harassment to be actionable it must be sufficiently severe or pervasive 'to alter the conditions of [the victim's] employment and create an abusive working environment.'" *Ibid.* Similarly, not all workplace conduct that may be described as racial harassment affects an employee's right to make contracts free of discrimination. But racial harassment of sufficent severity may impinge upon that right, as explained in the text, and is actionable under § 1981.

PATTERSON *v.* McLEAN CREDIT UNION

pervasive racial harassment may do so. See, *e. g.*, *Hunter* v. *Allis Chalmers Corp.*, 797 F. 2d 1417 (CA7 1986); *Vance* v. *Southern Bell Tel. & Tel. Co.*, 672 F. Supp. 1408, 1413 (MD Fla. 1987); *Nieto* v. *UAW, Local 598*, 672 F. Supp. 987, 991 (ED Mich. 1987).

C

Petitioner has never alleged that McLean's harassment amounted to a breach of contract under North Carolina law. Nevertheless, applying the standards set forth above, the evidence in this case brings petitioner's harassment claim firmly within the scope of § 1981. Petitioner testified at trial that during her ten years at McLean she was subjected to racial slurs; given more work than white employees and assigned the most demeaning tasks; passed over for promotion, not informed of promotion opportunities, and not offered training for higher-level jobs; denied wage increases routinely given other employees; and singled out for scrutiny and criticism. On the basis of the evidence at trial, the jury might have concluded that petitioner was subjected to such serious and extensive racial harassment as to have been denied the right to make an employment contract on the same basis as white employees of the credit union.

Robert Stevenson, the General Manager and later President of McLean, interviewed petitioner for a file clerk position in 1972. At that time he warned her that all those with whom she would be working were white women, and that they probably would not like working with a black. Tr. 1–19. In fact, however, petitioner testified that it was Stevenson and her supervisors who subjected her to racial harassment, rather than her co-workers. For example, petitioner testified that Stevenson told her on a number of occasions that "blacks are known to work slower than whites by nature," Tr. 1–87 to 1–88, 2–80 to 2–81, or, as he put it in one instance, that "some animals [are] faster than other animals." Tr. 1–83. Stevenson also repeatedly suggested that

PATTERSON *v.* McLEAN CREDIT UNION

a white would be able to do petitioner's job better than she could. Tr. 1–83.[21]

Despite petitioner's stated desire to "move up and advance" at McLean to an accounting or secretarial position, Tr. 1–22, she testified that she was offered no training for a higher-level job during her entire tenure at the credit union. Tr. 1–25. White employees were offered training, Tr. 1–93, including a white employee at the same level as petitioner but with less seniority. That less senior white employee was eventually promoted to an intermediate accounting clerk position. Tr. 1–48 to 1–49, 2–114 to 2–115. As with every other promotion-opportunity that occurred, petitioner was never informed of that opening. Tr. 1–46, 1–91 to1–92. During the ten years petitioner worked for McLean, white persons were repeatedly hired for more senior positions, without any notice of these job openings being posted, and without petitioner ever being informed of, let alone interviewed for, any of these opportunities. Tr. 1–93 to 1–97. Petitioner claimed to have received different treatment as to wage increases as well as promotion opportunities. Thus she testified that she had been denied a promised pay raise after her first six months at McLean, though white employees automatically received pay raises after six months. Tr. 1–84 to 1–85. See also Tr. 1–60 to 1–65 (denial of merit increase).

Petitioner testified at length about allegedly unequal work assignments given by Stevenson and her other supervisors, Tr. 1–27 to 1–28, 1–30, and detailed the extent of her work assignments. Tr. 1–31, 1–101 to 1–120, 2–18, 2–119 to 2–121. When petitioner complained about her workload, she was

[21] A former manager of data processing for McLean testified that when he recommended a black person for a position as a data processor, Stevenson criticized him, saying that he did not "need any more problems around here," that he would interview the person, but not hire him, and that he would then "search for additional people who are not black." Tr. 2–160 to 2–161.

PATTERSON *v.* McLEAN CREDIT UNION

given no help with it. Tr. 1–82 to 1–83. In fact, she was given more work, and was told she always had the option of quitting. Tr. 1–29. Petitioner claimed that she was also given more demeaning tasks than white employees, and was the only clerical worker who was required to dust and to sweep. Tr. 1–31. She was also the only clerical worker whose tasks were not reassigned during a vacation. Whenever white employees went on vacation, their work was reassigned; but petitioner's work was allowed to accumulate for her return. Tr. 1–37, 1–87.

Petitioner further claimed that Stevenson scrutinized her more closely and criticized her more severely than white employees. Stevenson, she testified, would repeatedly stare at her while she was working, although he would not do this to white employees. Tr. 1–38 to 1–39, 1–90 to 1–91. Stevenson also made a point of criticizing the work of white employees in private, or discussing their mistakes at staff meetings without attributing the error to a particular individual. But he would chastise petitioner and the only other black employee publicly at staff meetings. Tr. 1–40, 1–89 to 1–90, 2–72 to 2–73.

The defense introduced evidence at trial contesting each of these assertions by petitioner. But given the extent and nature of the evidence produced by Patterson, and the importance of credibility determinations in assigning weight to that evidence, we must conclude that petitioner made a showing of racial harassment severe and pervasive enough to have her § 1981 harassment claim decided by a jury.

III

Finally, the District Court plainly erred when it instructed the jury as to petitioner's burden in proving her claim that McLean violated § 1981 by failing to promote her, because she is black, to an intermediate accounting clerk position. The District Court instructed the jury that Patterson had to prove not only that she was denied a promotion because of

PATTERSON *v.* McLEAN CREDIT UNION

her race, but also that she was better qualified than the white employee who had allegedly received the promotion.[2] That instruction is inconsistent with the scheme of proof we have carefully designed, in analogous cases, "to bring the litigants and the court expeditiously and fairly to [the] ultimate question" of whether the defendant intentionally discriminated against the plaintiff. *Texas Dept. of Community Affairs* v. *Burdine*, 450 U. S. 248, 253 (1981).

As a preliminary matter, we note that the Court of Appeals distinguished between petitioner's claims of racial harassment and discriminatory promotion, stating that although the former did not give rise to a discrete § 1981 claim, "[c]laims of racially discriminatory . . . promotion go to the very existence and nature of the employment contract and thus fall easily within § 1981's protection." 805 F. 2d, at 1145. Respondent concedes that a discriminatory-promotion claim properly may be cognizable under § 1981, but argues that petitioner failed to make out a prima facie case that she was discriminatorily passed over for a promotion, because she did not prove that McLean was seeking applicants for the intermediate accounting clerk position, or that the white employee named to that position had in fact received a "promotion" from her prior job. We express no opinion on the merits of these claims, which the Court of Appeals found it unnecessary to address after it upheld the District Court's jury instructions. We do emphasize, however, that in order to prove in this context that she was denied the same right "to make and enforce contracts" as white citizens, petitioner must show that she was in fact denied an *available* promotion

[2] The District Court instructed the jury as follows:

"In order to carry her burden on [her contention that the defendant denied her a promotion because of her race], the plaintiff must establish (1) that a promotion was in fact given to [the white employee]; (2) that the plaintiff had expressed an interest in the promotion . . . ; and (3) that plaintiff was better qualified for the position received by [the white employee] than was [that employee]; and (4) that plaintiff was denied a promotion because of her race." Tr. 5–12. See also Tr. 5–12 to 5–14.

PATTERSON *v.* McLEAN CREDIT UNION

because of her race. Upon remand, the Court of Appeals should consider respondent's argument that petitioner failed to make out a prima facie case in this regard. If the court does find that petitioner has satified her initial burden, petitioner would then be entitled to a further remand so that the jury may be given accurate instructions as to her ultimate burden on her promotion-discrimination claim, for we are of the view that the District Court erred in describing that burden.

A § 1981 plaintiff must prove purposeful discrimination. *General Building Contractors Assn.* v. *Pennsylvania*, 458 U. S. 375, 391 (1982). Where the ultimate issue in a disparate-treatment action is whether the defendant intentionally discriminated against the plaintiff, a well-established framework of proof applies if the plaintiff offers only indirect evidence of discriminatory motive. See *McDonnell Douglas Corp.* v. *Green*, 411 U. S. 792 (1973) (Title VII); *Dister* v. *The Continental Group Inc.*, —— F. 2d —— (2d Cir. 1988) (discriminatory interference with right to benefits, in violation of § 510 of ERISA, 29 U. S. C. § 1140); *Loeb* v. *Textron, Inc.*, 600 F. 2d 1003 (1st Cir. 1979) (violation of the Age Discrimination in Employment Act, 29 U. S. C. § 621 *et seq.*)[23] We can discern no reason why this scheme of proof, carefully structured as a "sensible, orderly way to evaluate the evidence in light of common experience as it bears on the critical question of discrimination," *Furnco Constr. Corp.* v. *Waters*, 438 U. S. 567, 577 (1978), would not apply to claims of racial discrimination under § 1981. Indeed, the Court of Appeals held below that "[t]he disparate treatment proof scheme de-

[23] Similar frameworks are used for proof in other cases involving an ultimate question of purposeful action based on illegitimate motives. *E. g.*, *Mt. Healthy City School Dist.* v. *Doyle*, 429 U. S. 274 (1977) (refusal to rehire as retaliation for excercise of First Amendment rights); *Washington* v. *Davis*, 426 U. S. 229 (1976) (equal protection violation); *NLRB* v. *Transportation Management Corp.*, 462 U. S. 393 (1983) (discharge based on protected union activity).

PATTERSON *v.* McLEAN CREDIT UNION

veloped for Title VII actions in *McDonnell Douglas Corp.* v. *Green*, [*supra*,] and its progeny, may properly be transposed, as here, to the jury trial of a § 1981 claim." 805 F. 2d, at 1147.[24] The courts below erred, however, in identifying a § 1981 plaintiff's burden under that framework.

A black plaintiff claiming that an employment decision infringed her § 1981 right to make and enforce contracts on the same terms as white persons has the initial burden of establishing a prima facie case. This burden is not an onerous one. *Burdine*, *supra*, at 253. The plaintiff need only prove by a preponderence of the evidence that she applied for an available position for which she was qualified, see *supra*, at ——, that she was rejected, and that the employer either continued to seek applicants for the position, or, as allegedly occurred in this case, filled the position with a white employee. See *McDonnell Douglas*, *supra*, at 802; *Burdine*, *supra*, at 253. We have required at this stage proof only that a plaintiff was qualified for the position she sought, not proof that she was better qualified than other applicants. See *McDonnell Douglas*, *supra*, at 802; *Burdine*, *supra*, at 253 n. 6. Proof sufficient to make out a prima facie case raises a presumption that the employer acted for impermissible reasons, see *Furnco Constr. Corp.*, *supra*, at 577, which the employer may then rebut by articulating "some legitimate, nondiscriminatory reason for the employee's rejection." *McDonnell Douglas*, *supra*, at 802.

In this case, in addition to attacking petitioner's claim to have made out a prima facie case, the respondent introduced evidence tending to show that if it promoted a white employee over petitioner, it did so because the white employee was better qualified for the job. This evidence rebutted any

[24] Accord, *e.g*, *Lopez* v. *S.B. Thomas, Inc.*, 831 F. 2d 1184, 1188 (CA2 1987); *Smith* v. *Papp Clinic, P.A.*, 808 F. 2d 1449, 1451 (CA11 1987); *Wilmington* v. *J. I. Case Co.*, 793 F. 2d 909, 914 (CA8 1986); *Hamilton* v. *Rodgers*, 791 F. 2d 439, 442 (CA5 1986); *Carter* v. *Duncan-Huggins, Ltd.*, 234 U. S. App. D. C. 126, 727 F. 2d 1225, 1232 (CADC 1984).

PATTERSON *v.* McLEAN CREDIT UNION

presumption of discrimination raised by petitioner's prima facie case. Our cases make it clear, however, that a plaintiff must have the opportunity to introduce evidence to show that the employer's proffered reasons for its decision were not its true reasons. It is equally well-established that this evidence may take a variety of forms. *McDonnell Douglas*, *supra*, at 804–805; *Furnco Constr. Corp.*, *supra*, at 578. Though petitioner *might* have sought to prove that McLean's claim to have promoted a better-qualified applicant was not its true reason by showing she was in fact better qualified than the person promoted, the district court erred in instructing the jury that to succeed petitioner was *required* to make that showing. Such an instruction is much too restrictive, cutting off other methods of proving pretext plainly recognized in our cases. We suggested in *McDonnell Douglas*, for example, that a black plaintiff might be able to prove pretext by showing that the employer has promoted white employees who lack the qualifications the employer relies upon, or by proving the employer's "general policy and practice with respect to minority employment." 411 U. S., at 804–805. And, of particular relevance given petitioner's evidence of racial harassment and her allegation that respondent failed to train her for an accounting position because of her race, we suggested that evidence of the employer's past treatment of the plaintiff would be relevant to a showing that the employer's proffered legitimate reason was not its true reason. *Id.*, at 804. There are innumerable different ways in which a plaintiff seeking to prove intentional discrimination by means of indirect evidence may show that an employer's stated reason is pretextual and not its real reason. The plaintiff may not be forced to pursue any one of these in particular.[25]

[25] The Court of Appeals mistakenly held that the instruction requiring petitioner to prove her superior qualifications was necessary in order to protect the employer's right to choose among equally well-qualified applicants. As we stated in *Texas Dept. of Community Affairs* v. *Burdine*,

PATTERSON *v.* McLEAN CREDIT UNION

IV

In summary, the Court of Appeals erred in holding that petitioner's racial harassment claim is not cognizable under § 1981. It likewise erred in holding that petitioner could succeed in her promotion-discrimination claim only by proving that she was better qualified for the position of intermediate accounting clerk than the white employee who was in fact promoted. The judgment of the Court of Appeals is vacated, and the case is remanded for further proceedings consistent with this opinion.

It is so ordered.

450 U. S. 248, 259 (1981), "the employer has discretion to choose among equally qualified candidates, *provided the decision is not based upon unlawful criteria*" (emphasis added). Where a plaintiff proves that an employer's purported reasons for a promotion decision were all pretextual, the factfinder may infer that the employer's decision was *not* based upon lawful criteria; and, as we point out in the text, there are many ways in which a plaintiff can prove pretext other than by proving her superior qualifications.

1st DRAFT

SUPREME COURT OF THE UNITED STATES

No. 87-107

BRENDA PATTERSON, PETITIONER *v.* McLEAN CREDIT UNION

ON WRIT OF CERTIORARI TO THE UNITED STATES COURT OF APPEALS FOR THE FOURTH CIRCUIT

[January ——, 1989]

JUSTICE WHITE, concurring in part and dissenting in part.

I agree with the Court that our decision in *Runyon* v. *McCrary*, 427 U. S. 160 (1976), should not now be overruled. Though I dissented in *Runyon*, and continue to believe the Court was wrong in that case, no arguments have been presented here that merit reversing that decision, particularly in light of our rule "that considerations of *stare decisis* weigh heavily in the area of statutory interpretation." *Illinois Brick Co.* v. *Illinois*, 431 U. S. 720, 736 (1977). Consequently, I join Part I of the Court's opinion.

Moreover, I think it indisputable that the District Court erred in its instructions to the jury concerning petitioner's "discrimination in promotion" claim. While, as the Court acknowledges (*Ante*, at 30–31), there may be other reasons why the judgment for respondent on this claim should be affirmed, the decisions of the lower courts on the particular jury instruction before us must be reversed. Therefore, I join Part III of the Court's opinion as well.

I respectfully dissent, however, from the Court's holding in Part II. I do not believe that racial harassment, standing alone, states a claim under § 1981.

I

Section 1981's protection of civil rights is significant, but limited. Specifically, that law (in relevant part) guarantees

PATTERSON *v.* McLEAN CREDIT UNION

only that "[a]ll persons within the jurisdiction of the United States shall have the same right . . . to make and enforce contracts . . . as is enjoyed by white citizens." 42 U. S. C. § 1981. The law's most obvious feature is the restriction of its scope to forbidding discrimination in the "mak[ing] and enforce[ment]" of contracts alone. Where an alleged act of discrimination does not involve the impairment of these specific rights, § 1981 provides no relief.

If a party refuses to contract with another due to his or her race, or offers different contractual terms based on race, § 1981's prohibition against discrimination in the "making" of contracts, as that prohibition was construed in *Runyon* v. *McCrary*, *supra*, is clearly violated. But where the contract between the parties is untainted by racial considerations, and a plaintiff alleges a § 1981 violation in the enforcement of the contract, a different analysis is appropriate. In such instances, we ask first if the alleged act of discrimination was in contravention of some covenant of the contract between the parties. See, *e. g.*, *Goodman* v. *Lukens Steel*, —— U. S. ——, ——, 107 S. Ct. 2617, 2623 (1987). In *Goodman*, for example, we put special emphasis on the fact that a sweeping ban on racial discrimination had been included in the collective bargaining agreement between the employer and the union, as a basis for holding that the union had violated § 1981 by failing to pursue employees' race-related grievances concerning the employer's breach of this contractual term. A similar analysis explains our decision finding a viable claim under § 1981 in *McDonald* v. *Santa Fe Trail Transp. Co.*, 427 U. S. 273 (1976).

In this case, however, there is no allegation that a provision of the employment contract between the parties went unenforced for race-related reasons.[1] The Court acknowl-

[1] The Solicitor General, appearing here as *amicus curiae*, argues that such a breach of contract may have been present in this case. In the Solicitor General's view, racial harassment is actionable under § 1981 if the conduct violates an "implied covenant of good faith and fair dealing . . . .

PATTERSON *v.* McLEAN CREDIT UNION

edges this, *ante*, at 27, admitting that there has been no allegation in this case of discriminatory breach of contract, or even of harassment that would constitute a "constructive discharge" (which, in turn, would be a breach). Nonetheless, the Court permits petitioner to go to trial on her racial harassment claim because that harassment might "show that the employment contract was not entered into on racially neutral terms." *Ante*, at 26. As the Court summarizes its holding: "The question in each case in which an employee makes a § 1981 claim alleging racial harassment and alleges no breach of contract is therefore whether . . . the acts constituting harassment . . . effectively . . . belie any claim that the contract was entered into in a racially neutral manner." *Id.*, at 25.

---

where state law implies into contract[s] some such covenant." See Brief of United States 7. The Solicitor General suggests that because North Carolina law appears to imply such a covenant into employment contracts, petitioner's racial harassment claims—standing alone—should have been submitted to the jury for a determination whether respondent's conduct constituted a racially-based breach of this implied contractual term, and thereby, violated § 1981. *Id.*, at 7–8.

This view of the statute, however, would better be considered in the context of a case where a plaintiff is advancing such a claim, and where State law is more clearly supportive of such a theory than is true here. In this case, petitioner herself expressly rejected the notion that she would "have been able to stop the harassment . . . under State contract law," further conceding that she could have been terminated under North Carolina law "for any reason whatsoever, including the bad faith reason." See Tr. of Oral Arg. (Feb. 29, 1988) 6–7. This case is thus an odd vehicle for considering the Solicitor General's theory, and I withhold judgment on it.

I do note in passing, though, that Solicitor General's position here could be considered self-contradictory: while he accepts the view that racial harassment resulting in a breach of a State law implied covenant of fair dealing can give rise to a claim under § 1981, he rejects the conclusion that Title VII's prohibition on all discrimination in the "terms, conditions, or privileges of employment" creates an implied term in employment contracts likewise forbidding racial harassment. See Brief of United States as *Amicus Curiae* 20–21.

PATTERSON *v.* McLEAN CREDIT UNION

It is difficult to understand this holding. Either a contract contains, or does not contain, racially-discriminatory terms. This is a question of fact, to be determined by judge and jury. If the Court means to say that evidence of racial harassment may be helpful in showing that a divergence in contract terms among employees is explained by race, instead of some other racially-neutral explanation, I would agree.[2] For example, if a potential employee is offered (and accepts) a contract to do a job for less money than others doing like work, evidence of racial harassment in the workplace may, as the Court suggests, "show that the employment contract was not entered into on racially neutral terms" and "belie any claim" that the disparity is explained by racially neutral reasons. *Ante*, at 25–26. But the ultimate issue in such a case is—and must be—whether there has been intentional discrimination in the "making or enforcement" of the contract. Cf. *General Building Contractors Assn.* v. *Pennsylvania*, 458 U. S. 375, 388–391 (1982). Racial harassment may "show" that such discrimination exists, but—and this is critical—it is not *itself* such discrimination.

Thus, where there is no allegation that an employment contract contains racially-discriminatory terms, and no allegation that there has been racially-discriminatory enforcement of the employment contract, racial harassment is not actionable under § 1981. It makes no sense to say, as the Court does, that racial harassment may be actionable because it "belie[s] any claim that the contract was entered into in a racially neutral manner" if, *as a matter of fact*, there is no aspect of an employment contract that is the product of racial discrimination. I cannot express the appropriate principle any more clearly than the majority itself does: "Section 1981 cannot be construed as a general proscription of racial dis-

[2] This was the permissible use of evidence of racial harassment that the Fourth Circuit, in its decision below, envisioned for § 1981 cases. See 805 F. 2d 1143, 1145; see also, *e. g.*, *Carter* v. *Duncan-Huggins, Ltd.*, 727 F. 2d 1225, 1233 (CADC 1984).

PATTERSON *v.* McLEAN CREDIT UNION

crimination in all contractual relationships, for it expressly prohibits discrimination only in the making and enforcement of contracts." *Ante*, at 24. Unfortunately, in the course of the majority's analysis of this case, this succinct statement of the law was forgotten.

In this particular case, the Court properly considers petitioner's allegations of racial harassment to be relevant on remand, but confuses the reasons why this is so. For example, petitioner alleges that respondent refused to contract with her for a position as an accountant due to her race. The Court discusses aspects of this refusal in its recitation of the alleged acts of racial harassment that it deems actionable under § 1981. See *Ante*, at 28. It is more precise to say, however, that the acts of "racial harassment" that the Court discusses in this regard (*e. g.*, the failure to inform petitioner of accountant openings, the failure to train petitioner for these positions) are facts that would tend to prove a run-of-the-mill, race-based refusal to contract claim under § 1981. That is, if the allegations of racial harassment are true, Mrs. Patterson may be well on her way towards establishing that respondent refused to contract with her for an accounting position due to her race. Such a claim is clearly cognizable under § 1981. But—and this is where the Court errs in its analysis—this claim will ultimately turn on whether race-related reasons were the basis for respondent's refusal to contract with petitioner for the accounting job. If respondent can prove otherwise, than these "acts of racial harassment" are not actionable under the statute.

The same is true—only more so—for those acts that constituted harassment with an even more tenuous link to petitioner's claims that respondent refused to contract with her, or failed to enforce its contractual promises to her. See, *e. g.*, *Ante*, at 29 (discussing petitioner's claims that her supervisor "repeatedly stare[d] at her" and "criticized her more severely than white employees"). These acts may be probative of the ultimate question of whether respondent discriminated against petitioner in the making or enforcement of their employment contract (or a potential contract for petitioner to serve as an accountant). But if respondent carries the day on this ultimate question, then the acts alleged—standing alone—do not make out a claim under § 1981.

To hold otherwise, as the Court does, divorces the interpretation of § 1981 from the statute's language. The words of limitation in the statute guarantee equal rights only to "*make and enforce* contracts;" the Court's interpretation of the law—holding that it forbids all racially-discriminatory acts (beyond a certain threshold of egregiousness) by parties in a contractual relationship—renders irrelevant this limiting phrase, or at the least, rewrites it substantially. The Court's result might be understandable if it were true that only by such an unjustified interpretation of § 1981 would there be any federal limitation on the type obnoxious discriminatory conduct alleged here. As I suggest below, however, see *infra* Part II, that is simply not the case. Consequently, I cannot accept the Court's judicial alteration of this century-old civil rights law.

II

I agree with the Court that racial harassment is a serious social problem that should be arrested. And I agree that Mrs. Patterson's allegations of racial harassment—if proven—describe a working environment that is forbidden by Federal law. Where I part with the majority is in its view that § 1981 is the statute that erects this prohibition; instead, Title VII of the Civil Rights Act is the law that protects persons from the type of treatment Mrs. Patterson allegedly suffered.

While § 1981 provides only that all persons must be accorded equal rights to "make and enforce contracts," Title VII of the Civil Rights Act is more expansive, making it unlawful for an employer to "discriminate against any individual with respect to his compensation, terms, conditions, or privi-

PATTERSON *v.* McLEAN CREDIT UNION

leges of employment." 42 U. S. C. § 2000e–2(a)(1). Allegations of racial harassment are actionable under Title VII's prohibition against discrimination in the "terms, conditions, or privileges of employment." "[T]he EEOC has long recognized that harassment on the basis of race . . . is an unlawful employment practice in violation of § 703 of Title VII of the Civil Rights Act." See *EEOC Compliance Manual* § 615.7 (1982). While this Court has never had occasion to directly pass upon this interpretation of Title VII, the lower federal courts have uniformly upheld this view,[3] and we have implicitly approved it in a recent decision concerning sexual harassment, *Meritor Savings Bank* v. *Vinson*, 477 U. S. 57, 65–66 (1986).

Of course, the mere fact that Title VII provides relief for persons in petitioner's position does not mean that § 1981 necessarily fails to provide a remedy also. See *Johnson* v. *Railway Express Agency*, 421 U. S. 454, 460–461 (1975). But at the same time, the fact that egregious racial harassment of employees is forbidden by a clearly-applicable law (Title VII) lessens the need for this Court to twist the interpretation of another statute (§ 1981) to cover these same acts. In this particular case, we do not know for certain why Mrs. Patterson chose to pursue only remedies under § 1981, and not under the more clearly applicable Title VII. See 805 F. 2d 1143, 1144, n. *; Tr. of Oral Arg. (Feb. 29, 1988) 15–16; 23. But in any event, the availability of the latter should deter us from a tortuous construction of the former to cover this case.

III

In sum, due respect for our previous decisions interpreting § 1981, coupled with the events that have transpired (or not transpired) since our decision in *Runyon*, require that that

[3] See, *e. g.*, *Firefighters Institute for Racial Equality* v. *St. Louis*, 549 F. 2d 506, 514–515 (CA8), cert denied *sub nom.*, *Banta* v. *United States*, 434 U. S. 819 (1977); *Rogers* v. *EEOC*, 454 F. 2d 234 (CA5 1971), cert. denied., 406 U. S. 957 (1972).

PATTERSON *v.* McLEAN CREDIT UNION

decision be retained as the governing interpretation of § 1981. However, I cannot accept the view that acts of discrimination that do not result in inequality in the "making and enforcement of contracts" give rise to a cause of action under that statute. Thus, I join Parts I and III of the Court's opinion, but must dissent from Part II of the Court's holding.

1st DRAFT

SUPREME COURT OF THE UNITED STATES

No. 87-107

BRENDA PATTERSON, PETITIONER *v.* McLEAN CREDIT UNION

ON WRIT OF CERTIORARI TO THE UNITED STATES COURT OF APPEALS FOR THE FOURTH CIRCUIT

[May —, 1989]

JUSTICE KENNEDY, concurring in part and dissenting in part.

I agree with the Court's holding in Part I that our decision in *Runyon* v. *McCrary*, 427 U. S. 160 (1976), must not be overruled. I agree also with the Court's holding in Part III that the District Court erred in its instructions to the jury regarding the burden of proof on petitioner's promotion claim. I express no view, however, on whether petitioner's promotion claim is sufficient to state a cause of action under 42 U. S. C. § 1981 for failure to make a new contract, a determination which should be made initially by the District Court on remand. See Part II, *infra*. Finally, I do not agree with Part II of JUSTICE BRENNAN's opinion, but rather join with JUSTICE WHITE and THE CHIEF JUSTICE in concluding that racial harassment, standing alone, does not state a claim under § 1981. *Ante*, at 1 (opinion of WHITE, J.). Although I agree with much of JUSTICE WHITE's separate opinion as to the reach of § 1981, I do not believe that discriminatory conduct amounting to a breach of contract is independently actionable under that statute. See Part I, *infra*.

I

I agree with JUSTICE WHITE's basic approach to interpreting the scope of § 1981. That provision's "most obvious feature is the restriction of its scope to forbidding discrimination

PATTERSON *v.* McCLEAN CREDIT UNION

in the 'mak[ing] and enforc[ment]' of contracts alone. Where an alleged act of discrimination does not involve the impairment of these specific rights, § 1981 provides no relief." *Ante*, at 2 (opinion of WHITE, J.). As both JUSTICE WHITE and JUSTICE BRENNAN recognize, "[s]ection 1981 cannot be construed as a general proscription of racial discrimination in all aspects of contractual relationships, for it expressly prohibits discrimination only in the *making* and *enforcement* of contracts." *Ante*, at 24 (opinion of BRENNAN, J.); *ante*, at 4–5 (opinion of WHITE, J.) (emphasis added). See also *Jones* v. *Mayer Co.*, 392 U. S. 409, 436 (1968) (§ 1982, the companion statute to § 1981, was designed "to prohibit all racial discrimination, whether or not under color of law, *with respect to the rights enumerated therein*") (emphasis added); *Georgia* v. *Rachel*, 384 U. S. 780, 791 (1966) ("The legislative history of the 1966 Act clearly indicates that Congress intended to protect a limited category of rights.").

I disagree, however, with the dictum in JUSTICE WHITE's opinion, also found in JUSTICE BRENNAN's opinion, stating that § 1981 applies to racially-motivated conduct amounting to a "breach" of the terms or conditions of an employment contract. See *ante*, at 24–25 (opinion of BRENNAN, J.); *ante*, at 2–3 (opinion of WHITE, J.).[1] That position is inconsistent with JUSTICE WHITE's own caution that § 1981 should not be read to provide relief where the alleged act of discrimination does not impair the right either to "make" or to "enforce" a contract. Moreover, this dictum goes far beyond a fair reading of *Runyon* and unjustifiably would undermine in a significant way the detailed and carefully crafted procedures established by Congress for conciliation and resolution of claims covered by Title VII.

---

[1] It is plain that this aspect of JUSTICES BRENNAN's and WHITE's opinions is dictum, since both opinions recognize, as they must, that petitioner has never alleged that respondent's conduct amounted to a breach of contract. *Ante*, at 27 (opinion of BRENNAN, J.); *ante*, at 2 (opinion of WHITE, J.). See Part II, *infra*.

PATTERSON *v.* McCLEAN CREDIT UNION

Section 1981 reads as follows:

> All persons within the jurisdiction of the United States shall have the same right in every State and Territory to make and enforce contracts, to sue, be parties, give evidence, and to the full and equal benefit of all laws and proceedings for the security of persons and property as is enjoyed by white citizens, and shall be subject to like punishment, pains, penalties, taxes, licenses, and exactions of every kind, and to no other.

By its plain terms, the relevant provision in § 1981 protects two rights: "the same right . . . to make . . . contracts" and "the same right . . . to . . . enforce contracts." The first of these protections extends only to the formation (*i. e.*, "mak[ing]") of the contractual relation, and not to problems that may arise later from performance of the contract. The statute prohibits, when based on race, the refusal to enter into a contract with someone, as well as the offering or making of a contract on discriminatory terms. But the right to "make" contracts does not comfortably extend to conduct by the employer after the contractual relationship has been established, including breach of the terms of the contract or discriminatory working conditions. Such post-formation conduct does not involve the right to "make" a contract, but rather involves the performance of contractual relations already established and the conditions of continuing employment, matters more naturally governed by state contract law and Title VII. See *infra*, at ——.

Nor does § 1981's guarantee of "the same right . . . to . . . enforce contracts" cover conduct amounting to a breach of the terms of a nondiscriminatory contract or to discriminatory working conditions in the employment context. A guarantee of "the same right . . . to enforce . . . contracts as is enjoyed by white citizens" constitutes protection of a legal process, and of a right of access to legal process, that will address and resolve contract-law claims without regard to race. It covers discrimination that infects the legal process so as to prevent anyone, on the basis of race, from enforcing contract rights, whether this discrimination is attributable to a statute or simply to existing practices. It also covers wholly *private* efforts to impede access to the courts or obstruct nonjudicial methods of adjudicating disputes about the force of binding obligations, as well as discrimination by private entities, such as labor unions, in enforcing the terms of a contract. Thus, consistent with our holding in *Runyon* that § 1981 applies to private conduct, we have recognized that certain private entities such as labor unions, which bear explicit responsibilities to process grievances, press claims, and represent their membership in disputes over the terms of binding obligations that run from the employer to the employee, are subject to liability under § 1981 for racial discrimination in the enforcement of labor contracts. See *Goodman* v. *Lukens Steel Co.*, 482 U. S. —— (1987).

The dictum in the opinions of JUSTICES BRENNAN and WHITE assuming that § 1981 extends coverage to discriminatory conduct amounting to a breach of contract adds a third right to that provision's protections, one that is simply not in the statute. An allegation that the employer has for racial reasons breached an implied or express term of the contract does not state a claim for the impairment of either the right to "make" or the right to "enforce" a contract. It is obvious that such a claim is not encompassed in the first of these rights. Nor, moreover, is it correct to say that a claim that the employer's conduct amounts to a breach of contract alleges that the plaintiff's right to "enforce" his contract has been impaired. To the contrary, conduct amounting to a breach of contract under state law is precisely what the language of § 1981 does not cover. That is because, in such a case, the plaintiff is entirely free to enforce the terms of the contract in state court, and therefore cannot possibly assert, by reason of the breach alone, that he has been deprived of the same right to "enforce" contracts as is enjoyed by white citizens. This, of course, assumes that the plaintiff has not

PATTERSON *v.* McCLEAN CREDIT UNION

alleged also that either the state or a private actor has, for racial reasons, impaired his right to "enforce" the contract in state court or through some other dispute resolution process. The latter situation would constitute a § 1981 violation.

The only case discussed by JUSTICES BRENNAN and WHITE in support of the assumption that § 1981 applies to post-formation conduct amounting to a breach of contract is *Goodman* v. *Lukens Steel*, 482 U. S. —— (1987). That case does not support the proposition that conduct by an employer or union in violation of the employment contract is by itself actionable under § 1981. In *Goodman*, plaintiffs claimed that both their employer and unions had violated Title VII and § 1981 in a number of ways relating to the employer's discriminatory discharge of employees during the probationary period, as well as by racial harassment and discrimination in assignments, promotions, and incentive pay. See *id.*, at ——. The relevant issue before this Court was whether the unions were liable under § 1981. Although the courts below identified several different instances of conduct by the unions violating § 1981, see *id.*, at —— - ——, the Court focused the inquiry on one aspect of the unions' conduct:

> "As we understand it, there was no suggestion below that the Unions held any racial animus against or denigrated blacks generally. Rather, it was held that a collective-bargaining agent could not, without violating Title VII and § 1981, follow a policy of refusing to file grievable racial discrimination claims however strong they might be and however sure the agent was that the employer was discriminating against blacks. The Unions, in effect, categorized racial grievances as unworthy of pursuit and, while pursuing thousands of other legitimate grievances, ignored racial discrimination claims on behalf of blacks, knowing that the employer was discriminating in violation of the contract. Such conduct, the courts below concluded, intentionally discriminated against blacks seeking a remedy for disparate treatment

PATTERSON *v.* McCLEAN CREDIT UNION

> based on their race and violated both Title VII and § 1981." *Id.*, at ——.

The Court concluded:

> "The courts below, in our view, properly construed and applied Title VII and § 1981. Those provisions do not permit a union to refuse to file any and all grievances presented by a black person on the ground that the employer looks with disfavor on and resents such grievances." *Id.*, at ——.

These conclusions do not establish the proposition that § 1981 covers conduct by the employer amounting to a breach of contract. Rather, *Goodman* appears to be a straightforward application of *Runyon* to § 1981's protection of the right to enforce contracts. Just as *Runyon* held that it violates § 1981 for a private party to refuse to *make* a contract with another person based on race, *Goodman* establishes quite clearly that it is a violation of § 1981 for a private entity, such as a union, charged with protecting the contract rights of employees to refuse to *enforce* those rights against the employer. In that situation, the plaintiff has a § 1981 claim *not* merely because the employer or the union has breached the terms of the collective bargaining agreement, but rather because the union, whose direct responsibility it is to enforce the contract rights of employees, has deprived the plaintiff of his right to *enforce* his claims under the collective bargaining agreement.[3]

[3] This interpretation of *Goodman* is reinforced by the Court's explicit endorsement of the holdings of the courts below on this issue. See 482 U. S., at ——. The Court of Appeals in that case made clear that the unions' violation was predicated not on a mere breach of contract, but rather on its deprivation of the plaintiff's right to enforce his agreement with the employer. The Court of Appeals held:

"By shirking their responsibility for presenting grievances based on discrimination, the unions also violated the duty to *enforce* the collective bargaining agreement." *Goodman* v. *Lukens Steel Co.*, 777 F. 2d 113, 127 (CA3 1985) (emphasis added).

PATTERSON *v.* McCLEAN CREDIT UNION

The assumption of JUSTICES BRENNAN and WHITE that § 1981 applies to post-formation conduct by the employer amounting to a breach of contract appears to rest on a mistaken interpretation by some of the lower courts of one of our most significant § 1981 cases, *Johnson* v. *Railway Express Agency*, 421 U. S. 454 (1975). In that case, the plaintiff sued his employer and his union for racial discrimination under both § 1981 and Title VII of the Civil Rights Act of 1964, 42 U. S. C. § 2000e–5. The suit was based on plaintiff's claims of wrongful discharge and other related issues. The Court considered and resolved several questions about the proper limitations period for § 1981 claims, but antecedent to these questions was the larger question of whether § 1981 applied at all to contracts of employment. On this point, the Court said simply that "it is well settled among the Federal Courts of Appeals—and we now join them—that § 1981 affords a federal remedy against discrimination in private employment on

---

Similarly, the District Court held:

"[T]he evidence in this case proves far more than mere passivity on the part of the unions. The distinction to be observed is between a union which, through lethargy or inefficiency simply fails to perceive problems or is inattentive to their possible solution . . . and a union which, aware of racial discrimination against some of its members fails to protect their interest. A union which intentionally avoids asserting discrimination claims . . . is liable under both Title VII and § 1981[.]" *Goodman* v. *Lukens Steel Co.*, 580 F. Supp. 1114, 1160 (EDPa. 1984).

JUSTICE WHITE also cites, but does not discuss in detail, *McDonald* v. *Santa Fe Trail Transportation Co.*, 427 U. S. 273 (1976). This case surely does not hold that § 1981 applies to an employer's conduct amounting to breach of contract. In *McDonald*, the plaintiffs claimed that their employer had violated Title VII and § 1981 by firing them on the basis of their race and that their union had violated § 1981 by refusing, for race-related reasons, to represent them in grievance proceedings. The issue before the Court, however, was not whether § 1981 extended to a claim that either the employer or the union had breached its contractual obligations. Rather, the only issue the Court faced with respect to the § 1981 challenge was "whether § 1981 . . . affords protection from racial discrimination in private employment to white persons as well as nonwhites." 427 U. S., at 276.

the basis of race." 421 U. S., at 459–460. In an accompanying footnote the Court listed decisions by seven different Courts of Appeals that had adopted this view. *Id.*, at 459, n. 6.

The *Johnson* Court did not undertake to assess the allegations in the complaint, and did not say anything about which of those allegations might be actionable under § 1981 or which might not. Instead, the antecedent issue resolved by the Court was merely whether the term "contracts" in § 1981 includes *employment* contracts. An examination of the cases cited in the footnote confirms this fact. On the language of the statute itself that issue was an easy one. The Court was right to hold that § 1981 covers employment contracts. But the Court's summary statement "that § 1981 affords a federal remedy against discrimination in private employment on the basis of race" has been consistently misunderstood to be not simply a resolution of the narrow issue regarding types of contract covered, but a conclusion that § 1981 offers the same broad protections against employment discrimination as are found in Title VII, even though the language of Title VII is different and more comprehensive than the language of § 1981. *Compare* 42 U. S. C. § 2000e–5 *with* 42 U. S. C. § 1981. That interpretation of *Johnson* is erroneous, as that case merely construed the scope of the word "contracts," and had nothing whatsoever to do with exploring the meaning of the terms "make" and "enforce."

Interpreting § 1981 to cover discriminatory breach of contract is not only inconsistent with a fair reading of that provision, but it would also produce undesirable results.[9] First,

[9] The Solicitor General has urged us to conclude that the language of § 1981, especially the words "the same right," requires us to look outside § 1981, in particular to state law, for the obligations and covenants to be protected by the federal statute. Under this view, § 1981 has no actual substantive content, but instead mirrors only the specific protections that are afforded under the law of contracts of each state. In addition to being directly inconsistent with *Runyon*, which we today decline to overrule, this approach, which essentially provides that § 1981 applies *only* to con-

PATTERSON *v.* McCLEAN CREDIT UNION

because § 1981 covers all types of contracts, such an interpretation would federalize all state-law claims for breach of contract where racial animus is alleged. Although we must do so when Congress clearly directs, we should be and are normally "reluctant to federalize" matters traditionally covered by state common law. *Santa Fe Industries, Inc.* v. *Green*, 430 U. S. 462, 479 (1977); see also *Sedima S. P. R. L.* v. *Imrex Co.*, 473 U. S. 479, 507 (1985) (MARSHALL, J., dissenting). By specifically limiting § 1981 to the impairment of the rights to "make" and "enforce" contracts, Congress cannot be said clearly to have intended such a result with respect to breach of contract claims. It would, moreover, be no small paradox that under the interpretation of § 1981 offered by the dictum in the opinions of JUSTICES BRENNAN and WHITE, the more a state extends its own contract law to protect employees in general and minorities in particular, the greater would be the potential displacement of state law by § 1981. I do not think § 1981 need be read to produce such a peculiar result.

Second, and even more disruptive, this interpretation of § 1981 would emasculate in unnecessary scope the detailed and carefully crafted procedures for conciliation and resolution of Title VII claims. In Title VII, Congress set up an elaborate administrative procedure, implemented through the Equal Employment Opportunity Commission (EEOC), designed to assist in the investigation of claims of racial discrimination in the workplace and to work towards the resolution of these claims through conciliation rather than litigation. See 42 U. S. C. § 2000e–5(b). Only after these procedures have been exhausted, and the plaintiff has obtained a "right to sue" letter from the EEOC, may she bring a Title VII action in court. See 42 U. S. C. § 2000e–5(f)(1). Section 1981, by contrast, provides no such administrative review or opportunity for conciliation.

---

duct amounting to a breach of contract, suffers from all the maladies that I discuss here.

PATTERSON v. McCLEAN CREDIT UNION

Where conduct is covered by both § 1981 and Title VII, the detailed procedures of Title VII are rendered a dead letter, as the plaintiff is free to pursue a claim by bringing suit under § 1981 without resort to these procedures. I agree that, after *Runyon*, there is some necessary overlap between Title VII and § 1981, and that where the statutes actually do overlap we are not at liberty "to infer any positive preference for one over the other." *Johnson, supra*, at 461. However, I do believe that we should be reluctant to read an earlier statute broadly where the result would be to circumvent the detailed remedial scheme constructed in a later statute. See *United States* v. *Fausto*, —— U. S. —— (1988). By reading § 1981 not as a "general proscription of racial discrimination in all aspects of contractual relationships," see *ante*, at 24 (opinion of BRENNAN, J.); *ante*, at 4–5 (opinion of WHITE, J.), but as limited to the specific rights that it expressly protects—the right to make and enforce contracts, see *ante*, at 2 (opinion of WHITE, J.)—we would preserve the integrity of Title VII's procedures without sacrificing any significant breadth of coverage of the civil rights laws.[4] There would of course still be some overlap between the two statutes: specifically, a refusal to enter into an employment contract on the basis of race. Such a claim would be actionable under Title VII as a "refus[al] to hire" based on race, 42 U. S. C. § 2000e–2(a), and under § 1981 as an impairment of "the same right . . . to make . . . contracts as is enjoyed by white citizens, 42 U. S. C. § 1981. But this is precisely where it would make sense for Congress to provide for the overlap, for it is at this stage of the employee-employer relationship

[4] Unnecessary overlap between Title VII and § 1981 would also serve to upset the delicate balance between employee and employer rights struck by Title VII in other respects. For instance, a plaintiff in a Title VII action is limited to a recovery of backpay, whereas under § 1981 a plaintiff may be entitled to plenary compensatory damages, as well as punitive damages in an appropriate case. Both the employee and employer will be unlikely to agree to a conciliatory resolution of the dispute under Title VII if the employer can be found liable for much greater amounts under § 1981.

PATTERSON *v.* McCLEAN CREDIT UNION

that Title VII's mediation and conciliation procedures would be minimally effective, since there is not yet any employee-employer relationship to salvage.

II

These views lead to the following conclusions. First, both JUSTICE BRENNAN and JUSTICE WHITE agree that petitioner has not alleged that respondent's conduct amounted to a breach of contract. See *ante*, at 27 (opinion of BRENNAN, J.); *ante*, at 2 (opinion of WHITE, J.). Therefore, the discussion of whether petitioner would have a claim cognizable under § 1981 for harassment amounting to a breach of contract is *obiter dictum*. Second, I join with JUSTICE WHITE and THE CHIEF JUSTICE in concluding that racial harassment *itself* is not actionable under § 1981. See *ante*, at 1, 4 (opinion of WHITE, J.). As JUSTICE WHITE points out, correctly in my view, racial harassment may serve as evidence to show either that the contract was made on discriminatory terms or that the plaintiff's right to enforce her contractual rights has been impaired. See *ibid.* Thus, for example, evidence of racial harassment might be used to establish that employees were intimidated into not enforcing their contractual rights in court or elsewhere, but such racial harassment is not itself cognizable divorced from the more specific claim that the employee's right to enforce the contract was impaired. Finally, I agree with JUSTICE BRENNAN that the District Court erred in its instructions to the jury concerning petitioner's claim of discrimination in promotion, and that we should reverse and remand on that claim. A claim of discrimination in promotion may be actionable under § 1981, if the plaintiff is able to establish that the promotion amounted to an opportunity to enter into a new contractual relationship with the employer. Whether petitioner can allege such a claim should be decided, as an initial matter, by the District Court.

Justice Brennan's draft opinion in *Patterson* refused to limit section 1981 to the formation of a contract. Instead, it held that the statutory scope extended to conduct by the employer after the contract relation had been established, including a racially motivated breach of the contract's terms or the imposition of discriminatory working conditions. Had the draft come down as the opinion of the Court, it would have made for a broadside interpretation of the statute that could have made it a general proscription of racial discrimination in all aspects of contract relations. More specifically, the statute could prohibit all racial discrimination in employment, even that practiced long after the making of the employment contract.

That result was, however, avoided by the ultimate disposition of the *Patterson* case. Once again the conference majority did not hold. Of course, the Justices who had voted the other way at the conference did not join the Brennan opinion. Thus, Justice O'Connor sent a December 7, 1988, "Dear Bill" letter: "While I agree that *Runyon* v. *McCrary* should not be overruled, I do not think I agree with your treatment of the merits, and I will await further writing or circulate something myself in due course." O'Connor meant, of course, that she would wait for a dissent on the merits or, if none was forthcoming, draft one herself.

On January 12, 1989, Justice White circulated a draft opinion, reprinted on p. 237, which concurred in the decision not to overrule *Runyon*, but dissented on the merits. On the first point, White wrote, "Though I dissented in *Runyon*, and continue to believe the Court was wrong in that case, no arguments have been presented here that merit reversing that decision, particularly in light of our rule 'that considerations of *stare decisis* weigh heavily in the area of statutory interpretation.'"

On the merits, Justice White asserted, with regard to Justice Brennan's draft, "[i]t is difficult to understand this holding. Either a contract contains, or does not contain, racially-discriminatory terms." It follows that "the ultimate issue in such a case is—and must be—whether there has been intentional discrimination in the 'making or enforcement' of the contract. . . . Racial harassment may 'show' that such discrimination exists, but—and this is critical—it is not *itself* such discrimination." In a case such as this, the White draft concluded, "where there is no allegation that an employment contract contains racially-discriminatory terms, and no allegation that there has been racially-discriminatory enforcement of the employment contract, racial harassment is not actionable under § 1981."

The White draft was caustic in its condemnation of Justice Brennan's approach: "To hold otherwise, as the Court does, divorces the interpretation of § 1981 from the statute's language. The words of limitation in the statute guarantee equal rights only to '*make and enforce* contracts;' the Court's interpretation of the law—holding that it forbids all racially-discriminatory acts (beyond a certain threshold of egregiousness) by parties in a contractual relationship—renders irrelevant this limiting phrase, or at the least, rewrites it substantially. . . . Consequently, I cannot accept the Court's judicial alteration of this century-old civil rights law."

White's draft dissent made the *Patterson* decision process "boil like a pot." What happened was described by Justice Stevens, in a May 22, 1989, letter to Justice Brennan. "On December 5, 1988," Stevens wrote, "when I joined your proposed majority opinion, I thought your draft expressed a position on the racial harassment issue that had been adopted by four other Justices at Conference—indeed, the portion of your opinion discussing harassment that amounts to a breach of contract was also endorsed by Byron. . . . In the intervening months, further study has convinced at least three members of the present majority to modify their views—and, in one case, his vote. I have no quarrel with this process (having done so a number of times myself, this Term as well as in the past)."

In *Patterson*, the process described by Stevens took place after the White draft dissent was circulated. The key development occurred when Justice Kennedy sent around a draft dissent on April 17, reprinted on page 245, which began its discussion of the merits: "I agree with JUSTICE WHITE's basic approach to interpreting the scope of § 1981." This meant that Justice Kennedy had changed his conference vote on the case.

The Kennedy draft, however, took an even more restrictive view of the reach of section 1981—in effect adopting the confined conference view asserted by Chief Justice Rehnquist. "I disagree . . . ," stated the Kennedy draft, "with the dictum in JUSTICE WHITE's opinion, also found in JUSTICE BRENNAN's opinion, stating that § 1981 applies to racially-motivated conduct amounting to a 'breach' of the terms or conditions of an employment contract."

Kennedy's draft contained somewhat different language from his final opinion in the case. "By its plain terms," the draft points out, "the relevant provision in § 1981 protects . . . 'the same right . . . to make . . . contracts.'" The protection here "extends only to the formation (*i.e.*, 'mak[ing]') of the contractual relation, and not to problems that may arise later from performance of the contract. . . . But the right to 'make' contracts does not comfortably extend to conduct by the employer after the contractual relation ship has been established, including breach of the terms of the contract or discriminatory working conditions. Such post-formation conduct does not involve the right to 'make' a contract, but rather involves the performance of contractual relations already established and the conditions of continuing employment, matters more naturally governed by state contract law and Title VII."

"Nor," according to Justice Kennedy's draft, "does § 1981's guarantee of 'the same right . . . to . . . enforce contracts' cover conduct amounting to a breach of the terms of a nondiscriminatory contract or to discriminatory working conditions in the employment context. A guarantee of 'the same right . . . to enforce . . . contracts as is enjoyed by white citizens' constitutes protection of a legal process, and of a right of access to legal process, that will address and resolve contract-law claims without regard to race."

Both Brennan's draft opinion of the Court and White's draft dissent had interpreted the statute more broadly. Their language, asserts Kennedy, "assuming that § 1981 extends coverage to discriminatory conduct amounting to a breach of contract adds a third right to that provision's protections, one that is simply not in the statute. An allegation that the employer has for racial reasons breached an implied or express term of the contract does not state a claim for the impairment of either the right to 'make' or the right to 'enforce' a contract."

Nor, Justice Kennedy declares, can it be said "that a claim that the employer's conduct amounts to a breach of contract alleges that the plaintiff's right to 'enforce' his contract has been impaired. To the contrary, conduct amounting to a breach of contract under state law is precisely what the language of § 1981 does not cover."

The Kennedy draft thus rejected the holding of Brennan's draft opinion of the Court, as well as the assumption in Justice White's draft dissent, "that § 1981 applies to post-formation conduct by the employer amounting to a breach of contract." In fact, Justice Kennedy declares in his draft, "Interpreting § 1981 to cover discriminatory breach of contract is not only inconsistent with a fair reading of that provision, but it would also produce undesirable results."

Specifically, the Kennedy draft states, "[B]ecause § 1981 covers all types of contracts, such an interpretation would federalize all state-law claims for breach of contract where racial animus is alleged." This would go counter to one of the themes of Rehnquist Court jurisprudence—that, as summarized in Kennedy's draft, "we should be and are normally 'reluctant to federalize' matters traditionally covered by state common law."

In addition, Justice Kennedy asserts, "It would . . . be no small paradox that under the interpretation of § 1981 offered by the dictum in the opinions of JUSTICES BRENNAN and WHITE, the more a state extends its own contract law to protect employees in general and minorities in particular, the greater would be the potential displacement of state law by§ 1981. I do not think § 1981 need be read to produce such a peculiar result."

At any rate, the Kennedy draft dissent concludes, "I join with JUSTICE WHITE and THE CHIEF JUSTICE in concluding that racial harassment *itself* is not actionable under§ 1981." Even if "racial harassment may serve as evidence to show either that the contract was made on discriminatory terms or that the plaintiff's right to enforce her contractual rights has been impaired[,] . . . such racial harassment is not itself cognizable divorced from the more specific claim that the employee's right to enforce the contract was impaired."

Justice Kennedy's draft dissent meant that there was now a bare majority to hold for the employer on the claim that the alleged racial harassment violated section 1981. This was recognized by Justice Brennan himself, when he wrote on May 1, 1989, to the other Justices who had joined his draft *Patterson* opinion, "Dear Thurgood, John, and Harry: Tony's dissent leaves me without a Court on Part II of my opinion in this case, dealing with the harassment claim."

Though Kennedy's switch changed the *Patterson* result, the new majority was divided on the scope of the statute in such a case—with different views on the subject stated in the White and Kennedy draft dissents. The matter was, however, resolved when Justice White sent a May 17 note to Justice Kennedy: "Dear Tony, I am withdrawing my prior circulation in this case and have decided to join you. I shall circulate a few words of my own shortly."

Justice Kennedy could now issue his opinion as the opinion of the Court, which he announced on June 15, 1989. Justice Brennan had to redraft his opinion as one "concurring in part and dissenting in part." His emotion at losing his Court on the merits is shown by the language at the beginning of Brennan's dissenting redraft, as emphasized by me: "What the Court declines to snatch away with one hand, it *steals* with the other." The redraft refers to "*The Court's fine phrases about our commitment to the eradication of racial discrimination.*" However, it asserts, "[w]hen it comes to deciding whether a civil rights statute should be construed to further that commitment, *the fine phrases disappear*, replaced by a formalistic method of interpretation antithetical to Congress' vision of a society in which contractual opportunities are equal."[15] (The italicized phrases were eliminated in the published version of Brennan's dissent.)

Thus, *Patterson* came down as a victory for the more restricted Rehnquist interpretation of the civil rights statute. As in the *Webster* case discussed in the next chapter, however, the final outcome was brought about only by a vote switch—this time by Justice Kennedy. Had the switches not occurred, both *Webster* and *Patterson* would have been decided differently. Without a doubt, they would have been landmarks in Rehnquist Court jurisprudence, but they would have stood for exactly the opposite doctrines than those decisions stand for today.

Notes

1. *Newsweek*, July 23, 1979, p. 68.
2. *New York Times*, July 12, 1981, sect. 4, p. 22.
3. *New York Times*, February 28, 1988, sect. 4, p. 1.
4. *New York Times Magazine*, March 3, 1985, p. 33.
5. *Brown* v. *Board of Education*, 347 U.S. 483 (1954).
6. See Schwartz, *A History of the Supreme Court* 364 (1993).
7. *New York Times*, supra note 4, p. 32.
8. 392 U.S. 409 (1968).
9. 427 U.S. 160 (1976).
10. 491 U.S. 164 (1989).
11. *Saint Francis College* v. *Al-Khazraji*, 481 U.S. 604 (1987).
12. 379 F.2d 33 (8th Cir. 1967).
13. 112 S.Ct. 2791 (1992).
14. 491 U.S. at 191.
15. 2nd Draft, *Patterson* v. *McLean Credit Union*, from Justice Brennan, recirculated June 13, 1989.

6

Webster v. *Reproductive Health Services* (*1989*): *Roe and the Swinging Pendulum*

The Court's continued adherence to *Roe* v. *Wade*[1] graphically demonstrates the limitations on the Chief Justice's ability to make quantum changes in constitutional jurisprudence. There were few things about which William H. Rehnquist felt more strongly when he ascended to the Court's center chair than the decision in *Roe* v. *Wade*. In his lecture, quoted in the Introduction, Rehnquist noted that Chief Justice Hughes was willing to suppress his own views in the interest of securing a majority—"Except in cases involving matters of high principle." For Chief Justice Rehnquist, *Roe* v. *Wade* was emphatically such a case. Justice Rehnquist himself had been one of the two dissenters in *Roe* v. *Wade*.[2] Moreover, his dissent in *Roe* had been an unusually strong one, which compared the Court's decision to one of its most discredited decisions—that in the 1905 case of *Lochner* v. *New York*.[3]

The Court's *Roe* opinion was based upon two essential holdings: (1) "the right of privacy, however based, is broad enough to cover the abortion decision." It follows from this that there is a "fundamental right" to an abortion; (2) "Where certain 'fundamental rights' are involved, the Court has held that regulation limiting these rights may be justified only by a 'compelling state interest.'"[4]

Justice Rehnquist, in his dissent, pointed out what the Court had done in its *Roe* opinion. According to Rehnquist, "The Court eschews the history of the Fourteenth Amendment in its reliance on the 'compelling state interest' test." The strict scrutiny–compelling interest approach had been developed to deal with equal protection claims. Now, in *Roe*, the Court held that the compelling interest test should be used when a statute infringing upon fundamental rights was challenged on due process grounds. As the Rehnquist dissent put it, in *Roe*, "[T]he Court adds a new wrinkle to this test by transposing it from the legal considerations associated with the Equal Protection Clause of the Fourteenth Amendment to this case arising under the Due Process Clause of the Fourteenth Amendment."[5]

In a December 14, 1972, letter to Justice Blackmun, Justice Stewart had criticized the *Roe* opinion because the "dicta [in the Court's opinion were] so inflexibly 'legislative.'" In his *Roe* dissent, Justice Rehnquist gave voice to a similar animadversion: "[T]he Court's sweeping invalidation of any restrictions on abortion during the first trimester is impossible to justify . . . , and the conscious weighing of competing factors that the Court's opinion apparently substitutes for the established test is far more appropriate to a legislative judgment than to a judicial one."[6]

More than that, as pointed out, the Rehnquist dissent in *Roe* compared the decision there with one of the most discredited Supreme Court decisions. "While the Court's opinion," asserts Rehnquist, "quotes from the dissent of Mr. Justice Holmes in *Lochner* v. *New York* . . . , the result it reaches is more closely attuned to the majority opinion of Mr. Justice Peckham in that case." "As in *Lochner*," *Roe* requires "this Court to examine the legislative policies and pass on the wisdom of these policies."[7]

Certainly, there is danger that the importation of the compelling interest standard into the Due Process Clause will lead to a revival of the substantive due process approach that prevailed in what Justice Stewart termed, in a February 8, 1973, letter to Justice Lewis F. Powell, "the heyday of the Nine Old Men, who felt that the Constitution enabled them to invalidate almost any state laws they thought unwise."

From this point of view, there may be validity to the Rehnquist charge that *Roe* marked a return to the substantive due process approach followed in cases such as *Lochner* v. *New York*, when, as the Court put it in a 1963 case, "courts used the Due Process Clause 'to strike down state laws . . . because they may be unwise, improvident, or out of harmony with a particular school of thought.'"[8] According to Justice Rehnquist, the *Roe* adoption of the compelling interest standard in due process cases inevitably requires the Court once again to pass on the wisdom of legislative policies in deciding whether the particular interest put forward is or is not "compelling." As Rehnquist put it in a 1977 memorandum, "the phrase 'compelling state interest' really asks the question rather than answers it, unless we are to revert simply to what Holmes called our own 'can't helps.'"[9] Just as important, in Rehnquist's view, under the *Roe* approach, the determination of what are and what are not "fundamental rights" is also left to the unfettered discretion of the individual Justices.[10]

Justice Rehnquist continued to assert his opposition to *Roe* v. *Wade*, as well as efforts to expand its doctrine, in the Burger Court's later abortion cases. In particular, in 1980, he successfully fought efforts to hold that the right to abortion included a right to public funds for abortions for indigent women.[11] On November 12 of that year, Justice Blackmun wrote to Justice Marshall, "I fear that the forces of emotion and professed morality are winning some battles. The 'real world' continues to exist 'out there' and I earnestly hope that the 'war,' despite these adverse 'battles' will not be lost."

Justice Rehnquist saw things differently. As he explained it in a 1977 dissent, a decision such as *Roe* "placed [the Court] in the position of Adam in the Garden of Eden . . . subjected to the human temptation to hold that any law containing a number of imperfections [is unconstitutional] simply because those who drafted it could have made it a fairer or a better law." To

Rehnquist, *Roe* v. *Wade* was the Court's "original sin," which expelled it from the paradise of proper constitutional construction—in the phrase of his same dissent, "a cat-o'-nine-tails to be kept in the judicial closet as a threat to legislatures which may, in the view of the judiciary, get out of hand and pass 'arbitrary,' 'illogical,' or 'unreasonable' laws."[12]

In 1989, when *Webster* v. *Reproductive Health Services*[13] came before the Court, Chief Justice Rehnquist sensed that he at last had the opportunity to win the *Roe* v. *Wade* "war" and regain judicial paradise.

At issue in *Webster* was a Missouri law regulating abortions, which was characterized at the time as one of the most restrictive laws on the subject. It (1) specified that a physician, prior to performing an abortion on any woman twenty or more weeks pregnant, had to ascertain whether the fetus was "viable" by performing "such medical examinations and tests as are necessary to make a finding of [the fetus's] gestational age, weight, and lung maturity,"; (2) prohibited the use of public employees and facilities to perform or assist abortions not necessary to save the mother's life; and (3) made it unlawful to use public funds, employees, or facilities for the purpose of "encouraging or counseling" a woman to have an abortion not necessary to save her life.

The lower courts had ruled that these provisions violated the Court's decisions in *Roe* v. *Wade* and subsequent cases. The Justices who supported the right to abortion feared that, under the new Chief Justice, the majority would use the case to strike at the *Roe* decision. "Taking this case," a December 29, 1988, memo on *Webster* to Justice Marshall by his law clerk warned, "would pose a great threat that the majority on this Court would overrule or dramatically limit, Roe." Despite this, the Court voted on January 9, 1989, to take the case, with Justices Brennan, Marshall, and Blackmun voting the other way.

On April 28, two days after the oral argument, the Justices held their conference on the *Webster* case. Five of them voted to uphold the three restrictions in the Missouri law—the Chief Justice and Justices White, O'Connor, Scalia, and Kennedy. Justices Brennan, Marshall, and Blackmun voted to strike down the law. The position of Justice Stevens was not clear; Justice Marshall's docket book, for example, contains only the scrawl, "On and off" next to the initials "JPS" on a blue line page of notebook paper attached to his tally sheet (used to track a case from the time it comes to the Court to its final disposition).

Marshall's sketchy conference notes on *Webster* indicate that Chief Justice Rehnquist stated that he "disagrees with Roe v. Wade," but would "not overrule as such." As a *Washington Post* article points out, the phrase "as such" foreshadowed the debate among the Justices during the *Webster* decision process: the Chief Justice would maintain in his drafts that his opinion would not "revisit the holding of *Roe* . . . and we leave it undisturbed," while the dissenters declared that it would all but dismantle the *Roe* ruling.[14]

Since he was in the conference majority, Chief Justice Rehnquist could, of course, choose the writer of the *Webster* opinion. On May 1, 1989, he assigned the opinion to himself, following the tradition that the Chief Justice should prepare the opinions in important cases. In addition, there is no doubt that Rehnquist wanted the opportunity to strike what could be a mortal blow against *Roe* v. *Wade*.

On May 25, the Chief Justice circulated the first draft of his *Webster* opinion. It is reprinted on page 266 and was intended as the *Webster* opinion of the Court. After the conference vote, Rehnquist naturally assumed that he was writing for a majority of the Justices.

Rehnquist's draft squarely upheld the Missouri law's abortion restrictions. The prohibition on the use of public employees and facilities for the performance of abortions was ruled consistent with the Court's prior abortion decisions. "Nothing in the Constitution," declared the draft, "requires States to enter or remain in the business of performing abortions." States "need not commit any resources to facilitating abortions." Similarly, the draft held that the prohibition on the use of public funds for abortion counseling did not impermissibly burden the right to an abortion. "If, as we have held, Missouri's policy of not using public facilities and employees to perform or assist in abortions is constitutionally permissible, we see no reason why the State may not also refuse to fund any speech-related conduct intended to encourage abortions." (In his final opinion Rehnquist was to adopt Justice O'Connor's reasoning and avoid deciding the validity of this prohibition, holding that the controversy over it was moot).

The Chief Justice's draft also sustained the challenged law's requirement that a physician performing an abortion on a woman twenty weeks or more pregnant must first perform tests to determine if the fetus was "viable." This viability-testing provision was ruled valid as "promoting the State's interest in potential human life." Here the Rehnquist draft made a direct attack on the trimester analysis that was the foundation of the *Roe* decision. "We think," the draft declared, "that the doubt cast upon the Missouri statute . . . is not so much a flaw in the statute as it is a reflection of the fact that the rigid trimester analysis of the course of a pregnancy enunciated in *Roe* has resulted in subsequent cases . . . making constitutional law in this area a virtual Procrustean bed."

The draft recognized that, though stare decisis was "a cornerstone of our legal system," it should give way in a case involving "a prior construction of the Constitution that has proved 'unsound in principle and unworkable in practice.'" Such was the case here: "We think the *Roe* trimester framework falls into that category."

The Chief Justice called the *Roe* framework "rigid" and asserted that it "is hardly consistent" with a Constitution such as ours. Here the draft quoted the landmark 1937 opinion of Chief Justice Hughes in which he overruled the cases that had applied the doctrine of freedom of contract to strike down laws protecting labor, on the ground that freedom of contract was not contained in the Constitution.[15] Similarly, the *Webster* draft pointed out, "The key elements of the *Roe* framework—trimesters and viability—are not found in the text of the Constitution or in any place else one would expect to find a constitutional principle. Since the bounds of the inquiry are essentially indeterminate, the result has been a web of legal rules that have become increasingly intricate, resembling a code of regulations rather than a body of constitutional doctrine."

Instead of the *Roe* framework, the Rehnquist draft offered a new test for the abortion restriction at issue: whether it "reasonably furthers the state's interest in protecting potential human life." This was, of course, a far less restrictive review standard than the "compelling interest" test that *Roe* required abortion restrictions to pass—at least during the first and second trimesters of pregnancy.

At the end of his draft opinion, the Chief Justice noted that the Court had been urged to "overrule our decision in *Roe* v. *Wade.*" The draft ostensibly declined the invitation, saying of *Roe* that "we leave it undisturbed." All that the draft opinion did was to state, "To the extent indicated in our opinion, we modify and narrow *Roe.*"

The Rehnquist disclaimer could not mask the lethal effect his opinion would have on *Roe* v. *Wade*—particularly in its substitution of the less restrictive test of "reasonably further[ing] the state's interest in protecting potential human life" for *Roe*'s compelling interest test. In effect, the Rehnquist draft was returning review of abortion restrictions to the same rational basis test that is used in reviewing economic classifications. That test is, however, an extremely deferential one. All it requires is that the classification at issue have a reasonable basis in fact and that it "rest upon some ground of difference having a fair and substantial relation to [the] object of the legislation."[16] The Court need determine only that the particular classification had been the product of a rational legislative choice.[17] Under the rational basis test, "it is only the individious discrimination, the wholly arbitrary act, which cannot stand."[18] Almost all laws emerge untouched from mere rationality scrutiny: "[T]hat test . . . ," says Justice Marshall, "when applied as articulated, leaves little doubt about the outcome; the challenged legislation is always upheld."[19]

Over the years, however, the Court developed a stricter level of scrutiny that was applied in certain cases. In such instances, the mere showing that a law was rationally related to a legitimate governmental objective was not enough to sustain a challenged classification. In those cases, the test of mere rationality gave way to one under which the classification was held to be denial of equal protection unless justified by a "compelling" governmental interest.[20] As Justice Brennan pointed out in a March 5, 1990, "Dear Chief" letter, this test is "a strict scrutiny test which requires that the restriction be narrowly tailored to serve a compelling state interest."

If virtually all laws emerge untouched from rational basis scrutiny, the opposite is true of laws subject to strict scrutiny. "If a statute is subject to strict scrutiny," Justice Marshall tells us, "the statute always, or nearly always, . . . is struck down."[21] Or, as Justice Rehnquist succinctly stated to the conference in a 1982 case,[22] "Strict [scrutiny] means nothing passes; rational [basis] means everything does."

What the compelling interest test means in practice was also pointed out in a February 8, 1973, letter from Justice Stewart to Justice Powell. "Application of the so-called 'compelling state interest' test automatically results, of course, in striking down the state statute under attack. . . . There is hardly a statute on the books that does not result in treating some people differently from others. There is hardly a statute on the books, therefore, that an ingenious lawyer cannot attack. . . . If he can persuade a court that [strict scrutiny][23] is involved, then the state cannot possibly meet its resulting burden of proving that there was a compelling state interest in enacting the statute exactly as it was written."

1st DRAFT

SUPREME COURT OF THE UNITED STATES

No 88-605

WILLIAM L. WEBSTER, ATTORNEY GENERAL OF MISSOURI, ET AL., APPELLANTS *v.* REPRODUCTIVE HEALTH SERVICES ET AL.

ON APPEAL FROM THE UNITED STATES COURT OF APPEALS FOR THE EIGHTH CIRCUIT

[May ——, 1989]

CHIEF JUSTICE REHNQUIST delivered the opinion of the Court.

This appeal concerns the constitutionality of a Missouri statute regulating the performance of abortions. The United States Court of Appeals for the Eighth Circuit struck down several provisions of the statute on the ground that they violated this Court's decision in *Roe* v. *Wade*, 410 U. S. 113 (1973), and cases following it. We noted probable jurisdiction, 488 U. S. —— (1989), and now reverse.

I

In June 1986, the Governor of Missouri signed into law Missouri Senate Committee Substitute for House Bill No. 1596 (hereinafter Act or statute), which amended existing state law concerning unborn children and abortions.[1]

[1] After *Roe* v. *Wade*, the State of Missouri's then-existing abortion regulations, see Mo. Rev. Stat. §§ 559.100, 542.380, and 563.300 (1969), were declared unconstitutional by a three-judge federal court. This Court summarily affirmed that judgment. *Danforth* v. *Rodgers*, 414 U. S. 1035 (1973). Those statutes, like the Texas statute at issue in *Roe*, made it a crime to perform an abortion except when the mother's life was at stake. 410 U. S., at 117–118, and n. 2.

In June 1974, the State enacted House Committee Substitute for House Bill No. 1211, which imposed new regulations on abortions during all stages of pregnancy. Among other things, the 1974 Act defined "viabil-

WEBSTER *v.* REPRODUCTIVE HEALTH SERVICES

The Act consisted of 20 provisions, five of which are now before the Court. The first provision, or preamble, contains "findings" by the state legislature that "[t]he life of each human being begins at conception," and that "unborn children have protectable interests in life, health, and well-being." Mo. Rev. Stat. §§ 1.205.1(1), (2) (1986). The Act further requires that all Missouri laws be interpreted to provide unborn children with the same rights enjoyed by other persons, subject to the Federal Constitution and this Court's precedents. § 1.205.2. Among its other provisions, the Act

---

ity," § 2(2); required the written consent of the woman prior to an abortion during the first 12 weeks of pregnancy, § 3(2); required the written consent of the woman's spouse prior to an elective abortion during the first 12 weeks of pregnancy, § 3(3); required the written consent of one parent if the woman was under 18 and unmarried prior to an elective abortion during the first 12 weeks of pregnancy, § 3(4); required a physician who performs an abortion to exercise professional care to "preserve the life and health of the fetus" regardless of the stage of pregnancy and, if he should fail that duty, deemed him guilty of manslaughter and made him liable for damages, § 6(1); prohibited the use of saline amniocentesis, as a method of abortion, after the first 12 weeks of pregnancy, § 9; and required certain recordkeeping for health facilities and physicians performing abortions, §§ 10, 11. In *Planned Parenthood of Central Missouri* v. *Danforth*, 428 U. S. 52 (1976), the Court upheld the definition of viability, *id.*, at 63–65, the consent provision in § 3(2), *id.*, at 65–67, and the recordkeeping requirements. *Id.*, at 79–81. It struck down the spousal consent provision, *id.*, at 67–72, the parental consent provision, *id.*, at 72–75, the prohibition on abortions by amniocentesis, *id.*, at 75–79, and the requirement that physicians exercise professional care to preserve the life of the fetus regardless of the stage of pregnancy. *Id.*, at 81–84.

In 1979, Missouri passed legislation that, *inter alia*, required abortions after 12 weeks to be performed in a hospital, Mo. Rev. Stat. § 188.025 (Supp. 1979); required a pathology report for each abortions performed, § 188.047; required the presence of a second physician during abortions performed after viability, § 188.030.3; and required minors to secure parental consent or consent from the Juvenile Court for an abortion, § 188.028. In *Planned Parenthood Assn. of Kansas City, Mo., Inc.* v. *Ashcroft*, 462 U. S. 476 (1983), the Court struck down the second-trimester hospitalization requirement, *id.*, at 481–482, but upheld the other provisions described above. *Id.*, at 494.

requires that, prior to performing an abortion on any woman whom a physician has reason to believe is 20 or more weeks pregnant, the physician ascertain whether the fetus is viable by performing "such medical examinations and tests as are necessary to make a finding of the gestational age, weight, and lung maturity of the unborn child." § 188.029. The Act also prohibits the use of public employees and facilities to perform or assist abortions not necessary to save the mother's life, and it prohibits the use of public funds, employees, or facilities for the purpose of "encouraging or counseling" a woman to have an abortion not necessary to save her life. §§ 188.205, 188.210, 188.215.

In July 1986, five health professionals employed by the State and two nonprofit corporations brought this class action in the United States District Court for the Western District of Missouri to challenge the constitutionality of the Missouri statute. Plaintiffs, appellees in this Court, sought declaratory and injunctive relief on the ground that certain statutory provisions violated the First, Fourth, Ninth, and Fourteenth Amendments to the Federal Constitution. App. A9. They asserted violations of various rights, including the "privacy rights of pregnant women seeking abortions"; the "woman's right to an abortion"; the "righ[t] to privacy in the physician-patient relationship"; the physician's "righ[t] to practice medicine"; the pregnant woman's "right to life due to inherent risks involved in childbirth"; and the woman's right to "receive . . . adequate medical advice and treatment" concerning abortions. *Id.*, at A17–A19.

Plaintiffs filed this suit "on their own behalf and on behalf of the entire class consisting of facilities and Missouri licensed physicians or other health care professionals offering abortion services or pregnancy counseling and on behalf of the entire class of pregnant females seeking abortion services or pregnancy counseling within the State of Missouri." *Id.*, at A13. The two nonprofit corporations are Reproductive Health Services, which offers family planning and gyneco-

WEBSTER v. REPRODUCTIVE HEALTH SERVICES

logical services to the public, including abortion services up to 22 weeks "gestational age,"[2] and Planned Parenthood of Kansas City, which provides abortion services up to 14 weeks gestational age. *Id.*, at A9–A10. The individual plaintiffs are three physicians, one nurse, and a social worker. All are "public employees" at "public facilities" in Missouri, and they are paid for their services with "public funds," as those terms are defined by Mo. Rev. Stat. § 188.200 (1986). The individual plaintiffs, within the scope of their public employment, encourage and counsel pregnant women to have nontherapeutic abortions. Two of the physicians perform abortions. App. A54–A55.

Several weeks after the complaint was filed, the District Court temporarily restrained enforcement of several provisions of the Act. Following a three-day trial in December 1986, the District Court declared seven provisions of the Act unconstitutional and enjoined their enforcement. 662 F. Supp. 407 (WD Mo. 1987). These provisions included the preamble, Mo. Rev. Stat. § 1.205 (1986); the "informed consent" provision, which required physicians to inform the pregnant woman of certain facts before performing an abortion, § 188.039; the requirement that post-16-week abortions be performed only in hospitals, § 188.025; the mandated tests to determine viability, § 188.029; and the prohibition on the use of public funds, employees, and facilities to perform or assist nontherapeutic abortions, and the restrictions on the use of public funds, employees, and facilities to encourage or counsel women to have such abortions, §§ 188.205, 188.210, 188.215. *Id.*, at 430.

The Court of Appeals for the Eighth Circuit affirmed, with one exception not relevant to this appeal. 851 F. 2d 1071 (1988). The Court of Appeals determined that Missouri's declaration that life begins at conception was "simply an

[2] The Act defines "gestational age" as the "length of pregnancy as measured from the first day of the woman's last menstrual period." Mo. Rev. Stat. § 188.015(4) (1986).

impermissible state adoption of a theory of when life begins to justify its abortion regulations." *Id.*, at 1076. Relying on *Colautti* v. *Franklin*, 439 U. S. 379, 388–389 (1979), it further held that the requirement that physicians perform viability tests was an unconstitutional legislative intrusion on a matter of medical skill and judgment. 851 F. 2d, at 1074–1075. The Court of Appeals invalidated Missouri's prohibition on the use of public facilities and employees to perform or assist abortions not necessary to save the mother's life. *Id.*, at 1081–1083. It distinguished our decisions in *Harris* v. *McRae*, 448 U. S. 297 (1980), and *Maher* v. *Roe*, 432 U. S. 464 (1977), on the ground that "'[t]here is a fundamental difference between providing direct funding to effect the abortion decision and allowing staff physicians to perform abortions at an existing publicly owned hospital.'" 851 F. 2d, at 1081, quoting *Nyberg* v. *City of Virginia*, 667 F. 2d 754, 758 (CA8 1982), appeal dism'd, 462 U. S. 1125 (1983). The Court of Appeals struck down the provision prohibiting the use of public funds for "encouraging or counseling" women to have nontherapeutic abortions, for the reason that this provision was both overly vague and inconsistent with the right to an abortion enunciated in *Roe* v. *Wade*. 851 F. 2d, at 1077–1080. The court also invalidated the hospitalization requirement for 16-week abortions, *id.*, at 1073–1074, and the prohibition on the use of public employees and facilities for abortion counseling, *id.*, at 1077–1080, but the State has not appealed those parts of the judgment below. See Juris. Statement I–II.[3]

II

Decision of this case requires us to address four sections of the Missouri Act: (a) the preamble; (b) the prohibition on the use of public facilities or employees to perform abortions; (c) the prohibition on public funding of abortion counseling; and

[3]The State did not appeal the District Court's invalidation of the Act's "informed consent" provision to the Court of Appeals, 851 F. 2d, at 1073, n. 2, and it is not before us.

(d) the requirement that physicians conduct viability tests prior to performing abortions. We address these *seriatim.*

A

The Act's preamble, as noted, sets forth "findings" by the Missouri legislature that "[t]he life of each human being begins at conception," and that "[u]nborn children have protectable interests in life, health, and well-being." Mo. Rev. Stat. §§ 1.205.1(1), (2) (1986). The Act then mandates that state laws be interpreted to provide unborn children with "all the rights, privileges, and immunities available to other persons, citizens, and residents of this state," subject to the Constitution and this Court's precedents. § 1.205.2.[4] In invalidating the preamble, the Court of Appeals relied on this Court's dictum that "'a State may not adopt one theory of when life begins to justify its regulation of abortions.'" 851 F. 2d, at 1075–1076, quoting *Akron* v. *Akron Center for Re-*

---

[4] Section 1.205 provides in full:

"1. The general assembly of this state finds that:

"(1) The life of each human being begins at conception;

"(2) Unborn children have protectable interests in life, health, and well-being;

"(3) The natural parents of unborn children have protectable interests in the life, health, and well-being of their unborn child.

"2. Effective January 1, 1988, the laws of this state shall be interpreted and construed to acknowledge on behalf of the unborn child at every stage of development, all the rights, privileges, and immunities available to other persons, citizens, and residents of this state, subject only to the Constitution of the United States, and decisional interpretations thereof by the United States Supreme Court and specific provisions to the contrary in the statutes and constitution of this state.

"3. As used in this section, the term 'unborn children' or "unborn child' shall include all unborn child or *[sic]* children or the offspring of human beings from the moment of conception until birth at every stage of biological development.

"4. Nothing in this section shall be interpreted as creating a cause of action against a woman for indirectly harming her unborn child by failing to properly care for herself or by failing to follow any particular program of prenatal care."

WEBSTER *v.* REPRODUCTIVE HEALTH SERVICES

productive Health, Inc., 462 U. S. 416, 444 (1983), citing *Roe* v. *Wade*, 410 U. S., at 159–162. It rejected Missouri's claim that the preamble was "abortion-neutral," and "merely determine[d] when life begins in a nonabortion context, a traditional state prerogative." 851 F. 2d, at 1076. The court thought that "[t]he only plausible inference" from the fact that "every remaining section of the bill save one regulates the performance of abortions" was that "the state intended its abortion regulations to be understood against the backdrop of its theory of life." *Ibid.*[6]

The State contends that the preamble itself is precatory and imposes no substantive restrictions on abortions, and that appellees therefore do not have standing to challenge it. Brief for Appellants 21–24. Appellees, on the other hand, insist that the preamble is an operative part of the Act intended to guide the interpretation of other provisions of the Act. Brief for Appellees 19–23. They maintain, for example, that the preamble's definition of life may prevent physicians in public hospitals from dispensing certain forms of contraceptives, such as the intrauterine device. *Id.*, at 22.

In our view, the Court of Appeals misconceived the meaning of the *Akron* dictum, which was only that a State could not "justify" an abortion regulation otherwise invalid under *Roe* v. *Wade* on the ground that it embodied the State's view about when life begins. Certainly the preamble does not by its terms regulate abortion or any other aspect of appellees' medical practice. The Court has emphasized that *Roe* v. *Wade* "implies no limitation on the authority of a State to make a value judgment favoring childbirth over abortion."

---

[6] Judge Arnold dissented from this part of the Court of Appeals' decision, arguing that Missouri's declaration of when life begins should be upheld "insofar as it relates to subjects other than abortion," such as "creating causes of action against persons other than the mother" for wrongful death or extending the protection of the criminal law to fetuses. 851 F. 2d, at 1085 (opinion concurring in part and dissenting in part).

WEBSTER *v.* REPRODUCTIVE HEALTH SERVICES

Maher v. *Roe*, 432 U. S., at 474. The preamble can be read simply to express that sort of value judgment.

We think the extent to which the preamble's language might be used to interpret other state statutes or regulations is something that only the courts of Missouri can definitively decide. State law has offered protections to unborn children in tort and probate law, see *Roe* v. *Wade*, *supra*, at 161–162, and § 1.205.2 can be interpreted to do no more than that. What we have, then, is much the same situation that the Court confronted in *Alabama State Federation of Labor* v. *McAdory*, 325 U. S. 450 (1945). As in that case:

> "We are thus invited to pass upon the constitutional validity of a state statute which has not yet been applied or threatened to be applied by the state courts to petitioners or others in the manner anticipated. Lacking any authoritative construction of the statute by the state courts, without which no constitutional question arises, and lacking the authority to give such a controlling construction ourselves, and with a record which presents no concrete set of facts to which the statute is to be applied, the case is plainly not one to be disposed of by the declaratory judgment procedure." *Id.*, at 460.

It will be time enough for federal courts to address the meaning of the preamble should it be applied to restrict the activities of appellees in some concrete way. Until then, this Court "is not empowered to decide . . . abstract propositions, or to declare, for the government of future cases, principles or rules of law which cannot affect the result as to the thing in issue in the case before it." *Tyler* v. *Judges of Court of Registration*, 179 U. S. 405, 409 (1900). See also *Valley Forge Christian College* v. *Americans United for Separation of Church and State, Inc.*, 454 U. S. 464, 473 (1982).[6] We

[6] Appellees also claim that the legislature's preamble violates the Missouri Constitution. Brief for Appellees 23–26. But the considerations discussed in the text make it equally inappropriate for a federal court to pass upon this claim before the state courts have interpreted the statute.

WEBSTER *v.* REPRODUCTIVE HEALTH SERVICES

therefore need not pass on the constitutionality of the Act's preamble.

B

Section 118.210 provides that "[i]t shall be unlawful for any public employee within the scope of his employment to perform or assist an abortion, not necessary to save the life of the mother," while § 188.215 makes it "unlawful for any public facility to be used for the purpose of performing or assisting an abortion not necessary to save the life of the mother."[7] The Court of Appeals held that these provisions contravened this Court's abortion decisions. 851 F. 2d, at 1082–1083. We take the contrary view.

As we said earlier this Term in *DeShaney* v. *Winnebago County Dept. of Social Services*, 489 U. S. ——, —— (1989), "our cases have recognized that the Due Process Clauses generally confer no affirmative right to governmental aid, even where such aid may be necessary to secure life, liberty, or property interests of which the government itself may not deprive the individual." In *Maher* v. *Roe*, *supra*, the Court upheld a Connecticut welfare regulation under which Medicaid recipients received payments for medical services related to childbirth, but not for nontherapeutic abortions. The Court rejected the claim that this unequal subsidization of childbirth and abortion was impermissible under *Roe* v. *Wade*. As the Court put it:

> "The Connecticut regulation before us is different in kind from the laws invalidated in our previous abortion decisions. The Connecticut regulation places no obstacles—absolute or otherwise—in the pregnant woman's path to an abortion. An indigent woman who desires an

[7] The statute defines "public employee" to mean "any person employed by this state or any agency or political subdivision thereof." Mo. Rev. Stat. § 188.200(1) (1986). "Public facility" is defined as "any public institution, public facility, public equipment, or any physical asset owned, leased, or controlled by this state or any agency or political subdivisions thereof." § 188.200(2).

WEBSTER *v.* REPRODUCTIVE HEALTH SERVICES

> abortion suffers no disadvantage as a consequence of Connecticut's decision to fund childbirth; she continues as before to be dependent on private sources for the service she desires. The State may have made childbirth a more attractive alternative, thereby influencing the woman's decision, but it has imposed no restriction on access to abortions that was not already there. The indigency that may make it difficult—and in some cases, perhaps, impossible—for some women to have abortions is neither created nor in any way affected by the Connecticut regulation." 432 U. S., at 474.

Relying on *Maher*, the Court in *Poelker* v. *Doe*, 432 U. S. 519, 521 (1977), held that the city of St. Louis committed "no constitutional violation . . . in electing, as a policy choice, to provide publicly financed hospital services for childbirth without providing corresponding services for nontherapeutic abortions."

More recently, in *Harris* v. *McRae*, 448 U. S. 297 (1980), the Court upheld "the most restrictive version of the Hyde Amendment," *id.*, at 325, n. 27, which withheld from States federal funds under the Medicaid program to reimburse the costs of abortions, "except where the life of the mother would be threatened if the fetus were carried to term." *Ibid.* As in *Maher* and *Poelker*, the Court required only a showing that Congress' authorization of "reimbursement for medically necessary services generally, but not for certain medically necessary abortions" was rationally related to the legitimate governmental goal of encouraging childbirth. 448 U. S., at 325.

The Court of Appeals distinguished these cases on the ground that "[t]o prevent access to a public facility does more than demonstrate a political choice in favor of childbirth; it clearly narrows and in some cases forecloses the availability of abortion to women." 851 F. 2d, at 1081. The court reasoned that the ban on the use of public facilities "could prevent a woman's chosen doctor from performing an abortion because of his unprivileged status at other hospitals or because a private hospital adopted a similar anti-abortion stance." *Ibid.* It also thought that "[s]uch a rule could increase the cost of obtaining an abortion and delay the timing of it as well." *Ibid.*

We think that this analysis is much like that which we rejected in *Maher*, *Poelker*, and *McRae*. As in those cases, the State's decision here to use public facilities and staff to encourage childbirth over abortion "places no governmental obstacle in the path of a woman who chooses to terminate her pregnancy." *McRae*, 448 U. S., at 315. Just as Congress' refusal to fund abortions in *McRae* left "an indigent woman with at least the same range of choice in deciding whether to obtain a medically necessary abortion as she would have had if Congress had chosen to subsidize no health care costs at all," *id.*, at 317, Missouri's refusal to allow public employees to perform abortions in public hospitals leaves a pregnant woman with the same choices as if the State had chosen not to operate any public hospitals at all. The challenged provisions only restrict a woman's ability to obtain an abortion to the extent that she chooses to use a physician affiliated with a public hospital. This circumstance is more easily remedied, and thus considerably less burdensome, than indigency, which "may make it difficult—and in some cases, perhaps, impossible—for some women to have abortions" without public funding. *Maher*, 432 U. S., at 474. Having held that the State's refusal to fund abortions does not violate *Roe* v. *Wade*, it strains logic to reach a contrary result for the use of public facilities and employees. If the State may "make a value judgment favoring childbirth over abortion and . . . implement that judgment by the allocation of public funds," *Maher*, *supra*, at 474, surely it may do so through the allocation of other public resources, such as hospitals and medical staff.

The Court of Appeals sought to distinguish our cases on the additional ground that "[t]he evidence here showed that

WEBSTER *v.* REPRODUCTIVE HEALTH SERVICES

all of the public facility's costs in providing abortion services are recouped when the patient pays." 851 F. 2d, at 1083. Absent any expenditure of public funds, the court thought that Missouri was "expressing" more than "its preference for childbirth over abortions," but rather was creating an "obstacle to exercise of the right to choose an abortion [that could not] stand absent a compelling state interest." *Ibid.* We disagree.

"Constitutional concerns are greatest," we said in *Maher, supra*, at 476, "when the State attempts to impose its will by the force of law; the State's power to encourage actions deemed to be in the public interest is necessarily far broader." Nothing in the Constitution requires States to enter or remain in the business of performing abortions. Nor, as appellees suggest, do private physicians and their patients have some kind of constitutional right of access to public facilities for the performance of abortions. Brief for Appellees 46–47. Indeed, if the State does recoup all of its costs in performing abortions, and no state subsidy, direct or indirect, is available, it is difficult to see how any procreational choice is burdened by the State's ban on the use of its facilities or employees for performing abortions.[8]

Maher, *Poelker*, and *McRae* all support the view that the State need not commit any resources to facilitating abortions, even if it can turn a profit by doing so. In *Poelker*, the suit was filed by an indigent who could not afford to pay for an abortion, but the ban on the performance of nontherapeutic abortions in city-owned hospitals applied whether or not the pregnant woman could pay. 432 U. S., at 520; *id.*, at 524

---

[8] A different analysis might apply if a particular State had socialized medicine and all of its hospitals and physicians were publicly funded. This case might also be different if the State barred doctors who performed abortions in private facilities from the use of public facilities for any purpose. See *Harris* v. *McRae*, 448 U. S. 297, 317, n. 19 (1980).

WEBSTER *v.* REPRODUCTIVE HEALTH SERVICES

(BRENNAN, J., dissenting).[9] The Court emphasized that the Mayor's decision to prohibit abortions in city hospitals was "subject to public debate and approval or disapproval at the polls," and that "the Constitution does not forbid a State or city, pursuant to democratic processes, from expressing a preference for normal childbirth as St. Louis has done." *Id.*, at 521. Thus we uphold the Act's restrictions on the use of public employees and facilities for the performance or assistance of nontherapeutic abortions.

C

The Missouri Act makes it "unlawful for any public funds to be expended . . . for the purpose of encouraging or counseling a woman to have an abortion not necessary to save her life." Mo. Rev. Stat. § 188.205. A threshold question is whether this provision reaches primary conduct, or whether it is simply an instruction to the State's fiscal officers not to allocate funds for abortion counseling. We accept, for purposes of decision, the State's claim that § 188.200 "is not directed at the conduct of any physician or health care provider, public or private," but "is directed solely at those persons responsible for expending public funds." Brief for Appellants 43.[10] The Court of Appeals held that this provision was "void for vagueness and violative of the right to privacy." 851 F. 2d, at 1077.[11] Appellees claim that the

[9] The suit in *Poelker* was brought by the plaintiff "on her own behalf and on behalf of the entire class of pregnant women residents of the City of St. Louis, Missouri, desiring to utilize the personnel, facilities and services of the general public hospitals within the City of St. Louis for the termination of pregnancies." *Doe* v. *Poelker*, 497 F. 2d 1063, 1065 (CA8 1974).

[10] While the Court of Appeals did not address this issue, the District Court thought that the definition of "public funds" in Mo. Rev. Stat. § 188.200 "certainly is broad enough to make 'encouraging or counseling' unlawful for anyone who is paid from" public funds as defined in § 188.200. 662 F. Supp. 407, 426 (WD Mo. 1987).

[11] The Court of Appeals did not consider the "encouraging and counseling" language of § 188.205 separately from § 188.210 and § 188.215. It instead held "that the ban on using public funds, employees, and facilities to

WEBSTER *v.* REPRODUCTIVE HEALTH SERVICES

dispute over funding for abortion counseling is now moot. Brief for Appellees 31–35. We disagree and turn to the merits.[12]

Missouri's prohibition on the use of public funds for abortion counseling does not impose any criminal penalties and can be enforced only through injunctive action. Mo. Rev. Stat. § 188.220. We have recognized that the Constitution is more tolerant of vagueness in laws that impose civil rather than criminal penalities, "because the consequences of imprecision are qualitatively less severe." *Village of Hoffman Estates* v. *Flipside, Hoffman Estates, Inc.*, 455 U. S. 489, 499 (1982); see *Winters* v. *New York*, 333 U. S. 507, 515 (1948). It follows that our tolerance should be, and is, equally great where noncompliance results only in the loss of

---

encourage and counsel a woman to have an abortion is an unacceptable infringement of the women's fourteenth amendment right to choose an abortion after receiving the medical information necessary to exercise the right knowingly and intelligently." 851 F. 2d, at 1079. In a separate opinion, Judge Arnold argued that Missouri's prohibition violated the First Amendment because it "sharply discriminate[s] between kinds of speech on the basis of their viewpoint: a physician, for example, could discourage an abortion, or counsel against it, while in a public facility, but he or she could not encourage or counsel in favor of it." *Id.*, at 1085.

[12] It is true that the State has not appealed the Court of Appeal's invalidation of those parts of Mo. Rev. Stat. § 188.210 and § 188.215 that forbid public employees from counseling women to have nontherapeutic abortions and forbid public facilities from being used for that purpose. See Juris. Statement I–II. However, appellees' argument that the funding ban no longer affects them "adversely," Brief for Appellees 32, confuses mootness with standing. See *Allen* v. *Wright*, 468 U. S. 737, 751 (1984). In any case, the plaintiff class certified by the District Court included "pregnant women seeking abortion services or pregnancy counseling within Missouri," 851 F. 2d, at 1073, n. 1, and appellees' complaint alleged that the funding ban "interfere[s] unconstitutionally with the privacy rights of pregnant women seeking abortions or seeking professional advice and assistance as to their pregnancies." App. A17. Thus appellees' complaint alleged that the funding ban concretely injured an identifiable group of persons in the certified class, and we may reach the merits of this issue.

WEBSTER *v.* REPRODUCTIVE HEALTH SERVICES

public funding. The State maintains—and we accept for purposes of decision—that § 188.205 was intended

> "to prohibit the expenditure of public funds for the identified *purpose* of affirmatively advocating to a particular woman that she undertake an abortion procedure not necessary to save her life. The statute does not prohibit the use of public funds to provide information regarding abortions or to inform a woman of options she may have to cope with an unwanted pregnancy." Brief for Appellants at 42.

Section 188.205 "may not satisfy those intent on finding fault at any cost, [but it is] set out in terms that the ordinary person exercising common sense can sufficiently understand and comply with." *Civil Service Comm'n* v. *Letter Carriers*, 413 U. S. 548, 579 (1973). As was true in *United States* v. *Harriss*, 347 U. S. 612, 618 (1954), "[t]he general class of cases to which [§ 188–205] is directed is plainly within [its] terms, [and it] will not be struck down as vague, even though marginal cases could be put where doubts might arise."

We do not agree with appellees' claim that this provision impermissibly burdens the right to an abortion recognized in *Roe* v. *Wade*. Brief for Appellees 43–44. If, as we have held, Missouri's policy of not using public facilities and employees to perform or assist in abortions is constitutionally permissible, we see no reason why the State may not also refuse to fund any speech-related conduct intended to encourage abortions. As we said in *Harris* v. *McRae*, 438 U. S., at 317, "a refusal to fund a protected activity, without more, cannot be equated with the imposition of a 'penalty' on that activity." See also *Buckley* v. *Valeo*, 424 U. S. 1, 93–95 (1976) (upholding statute providing federal funds only to candidates who enter primary campaigns). In *Regan* v. *Taxation With Representation of Washington*, 461 U. S. 540, 549 (1983), where we upheld Congress' decision to grant a tax exemption only to those nonprofit organizations that do not engage in substantial lobbying, we stated that "a legislature's

WEBSTER v. REPRODUCTIVE HEALTH SERVICES

decision not to subsidize the exercise of a fundamental right does not infringe the right, and thus is nōt subject to strict scrutiny." See *Lyng* v. *International Union, UAW*, —— U. S. ——, —— (1988).

We therefore uphold the constitutionality of § 188.205.

D

Section 188.029 of the Missouri Act provides:

> "Before a physician performs an abortion on a woman he has reason to believe is carrying an unborn child of twenty or more weeks gestational age, the physician shall first determine if the unborn child is viable by using and exercising that degree of care, skill, and proficiency commonly exercised by the ordinarily skillful, careful, and prudent physician engaged in similar practice under the same or similar conditions. In making this determination of viability, the physician shall perform or cause to be performed such medical examinations and tests as are necessary to make a finding of the gestational age, weight, and lung maturity of the unborn child and shall enter such findings and determination of viability in the medical record of the mother." [13]

As with the preamble, the parties disagree over the meaning of this statutory provision. The State emphasizes the language of the first sentence, which speaks in terms of the physician's determination of viability being made by the standards of ordinary skill in the medical profession. Brief for Appellants 32–35. Appellees stress the language of the second sentence, which prescribes such "tests as are necessary" to make a finding of gestational age, fetal weight, and lung maturity. Brief for Appellees 26–30.

[13] The Act's penalty provision provides that "any person who contrary to the provisions of sections 188.010 to 188.085 knowingly performs . . . any abortion or knowingly fails to perform any action required by [these] sections . . . shall be guilty of a class A misdemeanor." Mo. Rev. Stat. § 188.075.

WEBSTER *v.* REPRODUCTIVE HEALTH SERVICES

The Court of Appeals read § 188.029 as requiring that after twenty weeks "doctors *must* perform tests to find gestational age, fetal weight, and lung maturity." 851 F. 2d, at 1075, n. 5. The court indicated that the tests needed to determine fetal weight at 20 weeks are "unreliable and inaccurate" and would add $125 to $250 to the cost of an abortion. *Ibid.* It also stated that "amniocentesis, the only method available to determine lung maturity, is contrary to accepted medical practice until 28–30 weeks of gestation, expensive, and imposes significant health risks for both the pregnant women and the fetus." *Ibid.*

We must first determine the meaning of § 188.029 under Missouri law. Our usual practice is to defer to the lower court's construction of a state statute, but we believe the Court of Appeals has "fallen into plain error" in this case. *Frisby* v. *Schultz*, 487 U. S. ——, —— (1988); see *Brockett* v. *Spokane Arcades, Inc.*, 472 U. S. 491, 500, n. 9 (1985). "'In expounding a statute, we must not be guided by a single sentence or member of a sentence, but look to the provisions of the whole law, and to its object and policy.'" *Philbrook* v. *Glodgett*, 421 U. S. 707, 713 (1975), quoting *United States* v. *Heirs of Boisdore*, 8 How. 113, 122 (1849). See *Chemehuevi Tribe of Indians* v. *Federal Power Comm'n*, 420 U. S. 395, 402–403 (1975); *Kokoszka* v. *Belford*, 417 U. S. 642, 650 (1974). The Court of Appeals' interpretation also runs "afoul of the well-established principle that statutes will be interpreted to avoid constitutional difficulties." *Frisby*, 487 U. S., at ——.

We think the viability-testing provision makes sense only if the second sentence is read to require only those tests that are useful to making subsidiary findings as to viability. If we construe this provision to require a physician to perform those tests needed to make the three specified findings *in all circumstances*, including when the physician's reasonable professional judgment indicates that the tests would be irrelevant to determining viability or even dangerous to the mother and the fetus, the second sentence of § 188.029 would conflict with the first sentence's *requirement* that a physician apply his reasonable professional skill and judgment. It would also be incongruous to read this provision, especially the word "necessary,"[14] to require the performance of tests irrelevant to the expressed statutory purpose of determining viability. It thus seems clear to us that the Court of Appeals' construction of § 188.029 violates well-accepted canons of statutory interpretation used in the Missouri courts. See *State* v. *Stilley*, 337 S. W. 2d 934, 939 (Mo. 1960) ("The basic rule of statutory construction is to first seek the legislative intention, and to effectuate it if possible, and the law favors constructions which harmonize with reason, and which tend to avoid unjust, absurd, unreasonable or confiscatory results, or oppression"); *Bell* v. *Mid-Century Insurance Co.*, 750 S. W. 2d 708, 710 (Mo. App. 1988) ("Interpreting the phrase literally would produce an absurd result, which the legislature is strongly presumed not to intend").

Appellees claim that the statute, even construed as we have chosen to construe it, conflicts with language in *Roe* v. *Wade* and cases following it. Brief for Appellees 28. The Court of Appeals construed § 188.029 more broadly than we do and, as so construed, thought it conflicted with language in *Colautti* v. *Franklin*, 439 U. S. 379, 388–389 (1979). 851 F. 2d, at 1074.

The viability-testing provision of the Missouri Act is concerned with promoting the State's interest in potential human life rather than in maternal health. Section 188.029 creates what is essentially a presumption of viability at 20 weeks, which the physician must rebut with tests indicating that the fetus is not viable prior to performing an abortion.

---

[14] See Black's Law Dictionary 928 (5th ed. 1985) ("Necessary. This word must be considered in the connection in which it is used, as it is a word susceptible of various meanings. It may import absolute physical necessity or inevitability, or it may import that which is only convenient, useful, appropriate, suitable, proper, or conducive to the end sought.").

WEBSTER *v.* REPRODUCTIVE HEALTH SERVICES

It also directs the physician's determination as to viability by specifying consideration, if feasible, of gestational age, fetal weight, and lung capacity. The District Court found that "the medical evidence is uncontradicted that a 20-week fetus is *not* viable," and that "23½ to 24 weeks gestation is the earliest point in pregnancy where a reasonable possibility of viability exists." 662 F. Supp., at 420. But it also found that there may be a 4-week error in estimating gestational age, *id.*, at 421, which supports testing at 20 weeks.

In *Roe* v. *Wade*, the Court recognized that the State has "important and legitimate" interests in protecting maternal health and in the potentiality of human life. 410 U. S., at 162. During the second trimester, the State "may, if it chooses, regulate the abortion procedure in ways that are reasonably related to maternal health." *Ibid.* After viability, when the State's interest in potential human life was held to become compelling, the State "may, if it chooses, regulate, and even proscribe, abortion except where it is necessary, in appropriate medical judgment, for the preservation of the life or health of the mother." *Id.*, at 165.

In *Colautti*, *supra*, upon which appellees rely, the Court held that a Pennsylvania statute regulating the standard of care to be used by a physician performing an abortion of a possibly viable fetus was void for vagueness. 439 U. S., at 390–401. But in the course of reaching that conclusion, the Court reaffirmed its earlier statement in *Planned Parenthood of Central Missouri* v. *Danforth*, 428 U. S. 52, 64 (1976), that "the determination of whether a particular fetus is viable is, and must be, a matter for the judgement of the responsible attending physician." 439 U. S. at 396. To the extent that § 188.029 regulates the method for determining viability, it undoubtedly does superimpose state regulation on the medical determination of whether a particular fetus is viable. The District Court thought it unconstitutional for this reason. 622 F. Supp., at 423. To the extent that the viability tests increase the cost of what are in fact second-

WEBSTER *v.* REPRODUCTIVE HEALTH SERVICES

trimester abortions, their validity may also be questioned under the Court's holding in *Akron*, 462 U. S., at 434–435, that a requirement that second trimester abortions must be performed in hospitals was invalid because it substantially increased the expense of those procedures.

We think that the doubt cast upon the Missouri statute by these cases is not so much a flaw in the statute as it is a reflection of the fact that the rigid trimester analysis of the course of a pregnancy enunciated in *Roe* has resulted in subsequent cases like *Colautti* and *Akron* making constitutional law in this area a virtual Procrustean bed. Statutes specifying elements of informed consent to be provided abortion patients, for example, were invalidated if they were thought to "structure . . . the dialogue between the woman and her physician." *Thornburgh* v. *American College of Obstetricians & Gynecologists*, 476 U. S. 747, 763 (1986). As the dissenters in *Thornburgh* pointed out, such a statute would have been sustained under any traditional standard of judicial review, *id.*, at 802 (WHITE, J., dissenting), or for any other surgical procedure except abortion. *Id.*, at 783 (Burger, C. J., dissenting).

Stare decisis is a cornerstone of our legal system, but it has less power in constitutional cases, where, save for constitutional amendments, this Court is the only body able to make needed changes. See *United States* v. *Scott*, 437 U. S. 82, 101 (1978). We have not refrained from reconsideration of a prior construction of the Constitution that has proved "unsound in principle and unworkable in practice." *Garcia* v. *San Antonio Metropolitan Transit Authority*, 469 U. S. 528, 546 (1985); see *Solorio* v. *United States*, —— U. S. ——, —— (1987); *Erie R. R.* v. *Tompkins*, 304 U. S. 64, 74–78 (1938). We think the *Roe* trimester framework falls into that category.

In the first place, the rigid *Roe* framework is hardly consistent with the notion of a Constitution cast in general terms, as ours is, and usually speaking in general principles,

WEBSTER *v.* REPRODUCTIVE HEALTH SERVICES

as ours does. Chief Justice Hughes, speaking for the Court in *West Coast Hotel, Co.* v. *Parrish*, 300 U. S. 379 (1937), in which the Court overruled its earlier decision in *Adkins* v. *Children's Hospital*, 261 U. S. 525 (1923), said:

> "In each case the violation alleged by those attacking minimum wage regulation for women is deprivation of freedom of contract. What is this freedom? The Constitution does not speak of freedom of contract. It speaks of liberty and prohibits the deprivation of liberty without due process of law. In prohibiting that deprivation the Constitution does not recognize an absolute and controllable liberty. Liberty in each of its phases has its history and connotation. But the liberty safeguarded is liberty in a social organization which requires the protection of law against the evils which menace the health, safety, morals and welfare of the people." *West Coast Hotel, supra,* at 391.

The key elements of the *Roe* framework—trimesters and viability—are not found in the text of the Constitution or in any place else one would expect to find a constitutional principle. Since the bounds of the inquiry are essentially indeterminate, the result has been a web of legal rules that have become increasingly intricate, resembling a code of regulations rather than a body of constitutional doctrine.[15] As JUSTICE WHITE has put it, the trimester framework has left this Court to serve as the country's "*ex officio* medical board with powers

[15] For example, the Court has held that a State may require that certain information be given to a woman by a physician or his assistant, *Akron* v. *Akron Center for Reproductive Health, Inc.*, 462 U. S. 416, 448 (1983), but it may not require that such information be furnished to her only by the physician himself. *Id.*, at 449. Likewise, a State may require that abortions in the second trimester be performed in clinics, *Simopoulos* v. *Virginia*, 462 U. S. 506 (1983), but it may not require that such abortions be performed only in hospitals. *Akron, supra,* at 437–439. We no longer think these distinctions are of any constitutional import in view of our abandonment of the trimester framework.

WEBSTER *v.* REPRODUCTIVE HEALTH SERVICES

to approve or disapprove medical and operative practices and standards throughout the United States." *Planned Parenthood of Central Missouri* v. *Danforth*, 428 U. S. 52, 99 (1976) (concurring in part and dissenting in part). Cf. *Garcia*, 469 U. S., at 547.

In the second place, we do not see why the State's interest in protecting potential human life should come into existence only at the point of viability, and that there should therefore be a rigid line allowing state regulation after viability but prohibiting it before viability. "[T]he State's interest, if compelling after viability, is equally compelling before viability." *Thornburgh*, 476 U. S., at 795 (WHITE, J., dissenting); see *id.*, at 828 (O'CONNOR, J., dissenting) (State has compelling interest in ensuring maternal health and in protecting potential human life, and those interests exist 'throughout pregnancy'") (citation omitted).

The tests that § 188.029 requires the physician to perform are designed to determine viability. The State here has chosen viability as the point at which its interest in potential human life must be safeguarded. See Mo. Rev. Stat. § 188.030 ("No abortion of a viable child shall be performed unless necessary to preserve the life or health of the woman"). It is true that the tests in question increase the expense of abortion, and regulate the discretion of the physician in determining the viability of the fetus. Since the tests will undoubtedly show in many cases that the fetus is not viable, the tests will have been performed for what were in fact second-trimester abortions. But we are satisfied that the requirement of these tests reasonably furthers the state's interest in protecting potental human life, and we therefore hold § 188.029 to be constitutional.

III

Both appellants and the United States as *Amicus Curiae* have urged that we overrule our decision in *Roe* v. *Wade*. Brief for Appellants 12–18; Brief for United States as *Ami-*

cus Curiae 8–24. The facts of the present case, however, differ from those at issue in *Roe*. Here, Missouri has determined that viability is the point at which its interest in potential human life must be safeguarded. In *Roe*, on the other hand, the Texas statute criminalized the performance of *all* abortions, except when the mother's life was at stake. 410 U. S., at 117–118. This case therefore affords us no occasion to revisit the holding of *Roe*, which was that the Texas statute unconstitutionally infringed the right to an abortion derived from the Due Process Clause, *id.*, at 164, and we leave it undisturbed. To the extent indicated in our opinion, we modify and narrow *Roe* and succeeding cases.

Because none of the challenged provisions of the Missouri Act conflict with the Constitution, the judgment of the Court of Appeals is

Reversed.

Supreme Court of the United States
Washington, D. C. 20543

CHAMBERS OF
JUSTICE JOHN PAUL STEVENS

May 30, 1989

Re: 88-605 - Webster v. Reproductive Health Services

Dear Chief:

Parts I, II(A), II(B), and II(C) of your opinion are extremely persuasive. Although I continue to have some doubts about Parts II(A) and II(C), and therefore shall await other writing, I may be able to join these portions of what you have written.

Part II(D) is a different story. I know I will not join it, but you may nevertheless be interested in my initial reaction to it.

First, I think your construction of the plain language in the second sentence of §188.029 is untenable. Moreover, it is a little out of character for you to be adopting Missouri's version of the Holy Trinity doctrine when the Court of Appeals has given the statute a different reading.

Second, you make no attempt to explain how the testing requirement actually satisfies your newly minted standard of "reasonably further[ing] the state's interest in protecting potential human life" (p. 22). You cite to no evidence or findings of misdiagnosis by prudent physicians who make viability determinations in the exercise of their reasonable professional judgment. You do acknowledge that the tests will often be useless, but fail to explain how they will ever be useful.

Third, you make no attempt to explain or justify your new standard. If a simple showing that a state regulation "reasonably furthers the state interest in protecting potential human life" is enough to justify an abortion regulation, the woman's interest in making the abortion decision apparently is given no weight at all. A tax on abortions, a requirement

-2-

that the pregnant woman must be able to stand on her head for fifteen minutes before she can have an abortion, or a criminal prohibition would each satisfy your test. Because the test really rejects Roe v. Wade in its entirety, I would think that it would be much better for the Court, as an institution, to do so forthrightly rather than indirectly with a bombshell first introduced at the end of its opinion.

Fourth, it seems to me that your rejection of the trimester analysis in Roe v. Wade tends to undermine the basis for your validation of special tests to determine viability. If it is correct that the state interest in preserving potential life remains the same throughout the pregnancy, the viability determination is really of no relevance to the state. Thus, your somewhat gratuitous rejection of the trimester approach emphasizes the fact that you are prepared to uphold a testing requirement even though the results of the test are completely irrelevant to any state interest. They do further the state's interest in protecting potential human life because they place an additional burden on the abortion decision, but the same result could be accomplished by requiring tests of the woman's knowledge of Shakespeare or American history.

As you know, I am not in favor of overruling Roe v. Wade, but if the deed is to be done I would rather see the Court give the case a decent burial instead of tossing it out the window of a fast-moving caboose.

Respectfully,

The Chief Justice

Copies to the Conference

1st DRAFT

SUPREME COURT OF THE UNITED STATES

No. 88-605

WILLIAM L. WEBSTER, ATTORNEY GENERAL OF MISSOURI, ET AL., APPELLANTS *v.* REPRODUCTIVE HEALTH SERVICES ET AL.

ON APPEAL FROM THE UNITED STATES COURT OF APPEALS FOR THE EIGHTH CIRCUIT

[June ——, 1989]

JUSTICE BLACKMUN, dissenting.

Today, a bare majority of this Court disserves the people of this Nation, and especially the millions of women who have lived and come of age in the 16 years since the decision in *Roe* v. *Wade*, 410 U. S. 113 (1973), recognized that the constitutionally guaranteed right to privacy encompasses a woman's right, with her responsible physician, to choose whether or not to terminate a pregnancy. *Id.*, at 153. To those women, and to all others, this Court owes an essential duty of explanation—a duty of candor and forthrightness, a duty to interpret the Constitution and our past decisions in a reasoned and honest fashion. The majority mocks this duty. At every level of its review, from its effort to read the real meaning out of the Missouri statute to its evisceration of precedents and its deafening silence about the fundamental constitutional protections that it jettisons, the majority labors to obscure what is at stake in this monumental case and to cloak what it actually has decided.

Let there be no misunderstanding: the two isolated dissenters in *Roe*, after all these years, now have prevailed, with the assent of the Court's newest Members, in rolling back that case and in returning the law of procreative freedom to the severe limitations that generally prevailed before January 22, 1973. With feigned restraint, the majority

WEBSTER *v.* REPRODUCTIVE HEALTH SERVICES

states that this case presents no occasion to "revisit the holding of *Roe*," and that, accordingly, *Roe* and its progeny are merely "modif[ied] and narrow[ed]," but not overruled. *Ante*, at 23. This disclaimer is totally meaningless. The majority opinion is filled with winks, and nods, and knowing glances to those who would do away with *Roe* explicitly, but turns a stone face to anyone in search of what the majority conceives as the scope of a woman's right under the Due Process Clause to terminate a pregnancy free from the coercive and brooding influence of the State. The simple truth is that *Roe* no longer survives, and that the majority provides no substitute for its protective umbrella.

I rue this day. I rue the violence that has been done to the liberty and equality of women. I rue the violence that has been done to our legal fabric and to the integrity of this Court. I rue the inevitable loss of public esteem for this Court that is so essential. I dissent.

I

The majority parades through the four challenged sections of the Missouri statute *seriatim*. I shall not do this, but shall relegate most of my comments as to those sections to the margin.[1] Although I disagree with the majority's consider-

[1] Contrary to the majority, I do not see how the preamble, § 1.205, realistically may be construed as "abortion-neutral." It declares that "[t]he life of each human being begins at conception" and that "[u]nborn children have protectable interests in life, health, and well-being." Mo. Rev. Stat. §§ 1.205.1(1) and (2) (1986). By the preamble's specific terms, these declarations apply to all of Missouri's laws which, in turn, are to be interpreted to protect the rights of the unborn to the fullest extent possible under the Constitution of the United States and the decisions of this Court. § 1.205.2. As the Court of Appeals concluded, the Missouri Legislature "intended its abortion regulations to be understood against the backdrop of its theory of life." 851 F. 2d 1071, 1076 (CA8 1988). I agree with the Solicitor General's acknowledgment that this backdrop places "a burden of uncertain scope on the performance of abortion by supplying a general principle that would fill in whatever interstices may be present in existing

WEBSTER *v.* REPRODUCTIVE HEALTH SERVICES

ation of §§ 1.205, 188.205. 188.210, and 188.215, and am especially disturbed by its misapplication of our past decisions in upholding Missouri's ban on the performance of abortions at

---

abortion precedents." Brief for United States as *Amicus Curiae* on behalf of appellants 8, n. 5.

In my view, a State may not expand indefinitely the scope of its abortion regulations by creating interests in fetal life that are limited solely by reference to the decisional law of this Court. Such a statutory scheme, whose scope is dependent on the uncertain and disputed limits of our holdings, will have the unconstitutional effect of chilling the exercise of a woman's right to terminate a pregnancy and of burdening the freedom of health professionals to provide abortion services. In this case, moreover, because the preamble defines fetal life as beginning upon "the fertilization of the ovum of a female by a sperm of a male," § 188.015(3), the provision also unconstitutionally burdens the use of contraceptive devices, such as the IUD and the "morning after" pill, which may operate to prevent pregnancy only after conception as defined in the statute. See Brief for Association of Reproductive Health Professionals, et al., as *Amici Curiae* 30–39.

With respect to § 188.205, the majority provides no reason to second-guess the District Court's judgment that the provision makes it unlawful for anyone paid from public funds to encourage or counsel a woman to procure an abortion. 662 F. Supp. 407, 426 (WD Mo. 1987). So construed, § 188.205 violates not only a woman's right to receive medical information necessary to the informed exercise of her abortion rights, 851 F. 2d, at 1079, but also, as Judge Arnold concluded, the First Amendment's prohibition on regulations that discriminate on the basis of viewpoint. *Id.*, at 1085. Even assuming, however, that the majority has construed § 188.205 correctly, I would not uphold it in this case. If, as the majority asserts, *ante*, at 13–15, § 188.205 does not reach the conduct of physicians or health care providers, and if the provision does not prohibit the use of public funds to provide information regarding abortions, then the majority, through its statutory construction, has granted appellees all the relief they seek. Because, under the majority's construction, § 188.205 has no adverse effect on the original plaintiffs in this case, its discussion of the provision's validity constitutes a purely advisory opinion on a matter of constitutional law, and, as such, is an inappropriate exercise of the judicial power.

The majority upholds §§ 188.210 and .215 on the ground that the constitutionality of these provisions follows from our holdings in *Maher* v. *Roe*, 432 U. S. 464 (1977), *Poelker* v. *Doe*, 432 U. S. 519 (1977), and *Harris* v. *McRae*, 448 U. S. 297 (1980). There were strong dissents in all of those cases.

WEBSTER *v.* REPRODUCTIVE HEALTH SERVICES

"public facilities," the majority's discussion of these provisions is merely prologue to its consideration of the statute's viability-testing requirement, § 188.029—the only section of

---

Whatever one may think of *Maher*, *Poelker*, and *Harris*, however, they most certainly do not control this case, where the State not only has withdrawn from the business of abortion, but has taken affirmative steps to assure that abortions are not performed by *private* physicians in *private* institutions. Specifically, by defining "public facility" as "any public institution, public facility, public equipment, or any physical asset owned, leased, or controlled by this state or any agency or political subdivision thereof," § 188.200, the Missouri statute prohibits the performance of abortions in institutions that in all pertinent respects are private, yet are located on property owned, leased, or controlled by the government. Thus, under the statute, no abortion may be performed at Truman Medical Center in Kansas City—where, in 1985, 97 percent of all Missouri hospital abortions at 16 weeks or later were performed—even though the Center is a private hospital, staffed primarily by private doctors, and administered by a private corporation: the Center is located on ground leased from a political subdivision of the State.

The sweeping scope of Missouri's "public facility" provision sharply distinguishes this case from *Maher*, *Poelker*, and *Harris*. In one of those cases, it was said: "The State may have made childbirth a more attractive alternative . . . but it . . . imposed no restriction on access to abortion that was not already there." *Maher*, 432 U. S., at 474. Missouri's public facility ban, by contrast, goes far beyond merely offering incentives in favor of childbirth (as in *Maher* and *Harris*), or a straightforward disassociation of state-owned institutions and personnel from abortion services (as in *Poelker*). Here, by defining as "public" every health-care institution with some connection to the State, no matter how attenuated, Missouri has brought to bear the full force of its economic power and control over essential facilities to discourage its citizens from exercising their constitutional rights, even where the State itself could never be understood as authorizing, supporting, or having any other positive association with the performance of an abortion. See R. Dworkin, The Great Abortion Case, New York Review of Books, June 29, 1989, p. 49.

The difference is critical. Even if the State may decline to subsidize or to participate in the exercise of a woman's right to terminate a pregnancy, and even if a State may pursue its own abortion policies in distributing public benefits, it may not affirmatively constrict the availability of abortions by defining as "public" that which in all meaningful respects is private. With the certain knowledge that a substantial percentage of private

WEBSTER *v.* REPRODUCTIVE HEALTH SERVICES

the Missouri statute that the majority construes as implicating *Roe* itself. There, tucked away at the end of its opinion, the majority works a radical reversal of the law of abortion; and there, primarily, I direct my attention.

In the majority's view, the viability-testing provision imposes a burden on second-trimester abortions as a way of furthering the State's interest in protecting the potential life of the fetus. Since under the *Roe* framework, the State may not fully regulate abortion in the interest of potential life (as opposed to maternal health) until the third trimester, the majority finds it necessary, in order to save the Missouri testing provision, to throw out *Roe*'s trimester framework and, in a footnote, partially to overrule Justice Powell's opinion for the Court in *Akron* v. *Akron Center for Reproductive Health, Inc.*, 462 U. S. 416 (1983). *Ante*, at 19–22, and n. 15. In flat contradiction to *Roe*, 410 U. S., at 163, the majority concludes that the State's interest in potential life is compelling before viability, and upholds the testing provision because it "reasonably furthers" that state interest. *Ante*, at 22.

A

At the outset, I note that in its haste to limit abortion rights, the majority compounds the errors of its holding by needlessly reaching out to decide constitution questions that are not actually presented. The conflict between § 188.029 and *Roe*'s trimester framework, which purportedly drives the majority to reconsider our past decisions, is a contrived conflict: the product of an aggressive misreading of the

health-care providers will fall under the public facility ban, see Brief for National Association of Public Hospitals as *Amicus Curiae* 10–11, Missouri does not "leav[e] a pregnant woman with the same choices as if the State had not chosen to operate any public hospitals at all," *ante*, at 11; rather, the public facility ban leaves the pregnant woman with far fewer choices, or, for those too sick or too poor to travel, perhaps no choice at all. This aggressive and shameful infringement on the right of women to obtain abortions in consultation with their chosen physicians, unsupported by any state interest, much less a compelling one, violates the command of *Roe*.

viability-testing requirement and a needlessly wooden application of the *Roe* framework.

The majority's reading of § 188.029 is irreconcilable with the plain language of the statute and is in derogation of this Court's settled view that "'district courts and courts of appeal are better schooled in and more able to interpret the laws of their respective States.'" *Frisby* v. *Schultz*, 487 U. S. —, — (1988) (slip op. 7), quoting *Brockett* v. *Spokane Arcades, Inc.*, 472 U. S. 491, 499–500 (1985). Abruptly setting aside the construction of § 188.029 adopted by both the District Court and Court of Appeals as "plain error," the majority reads the viability-testing provision as requiring only that before a physician may perform an abortion on a woman who he believes to be carrying a fetus of 20 or more weeks gestational age, the doctor must determine whether the fetus is viable and, as part of that exercise, must, to the extent feasible and consistent with sound medical practice, conduct tests necessary to make findings of gestational age, weight, and lung maturity. *Ante*, at 17–19. But the majority's reading of the provision, according to which the statute requires the physician to perform tests only in order to determine *viability*, ignores the statutory language explicitly directing that "the physician *shall* perform or cause to be performed such medical examinations and tests as are *necessary to make a finding of the gestational age, weight, and lung maturity* of the unborn child and *shall* enter such findings" in the mother's medical record. § 188.029 (emphasis added). The statute's plain language requires the physician to undertake whatever tests are necessary to determine gestational age, weight, and lung maturity, regardless of whether these tests are necessary to a finding of viability, and regardless of whether the tests subject the pregnant woman or the fetus to additional health risks or add substantially to the cost of an abortion.

Had the majority read the statute as written, it would have had no cause to reconsider the *Roe* framework. As properly construed, the viability-testing provision does not pass constitutional muster under even a rational-basis standard, the least restrictive level of review applied by this Court. See *Williamson* v. *Lee Optical Co.*, 348 U. S. 483 (1955). By mandating tests to determine fetal weight and lung maturity for every fetus thought to be more than 20 weeks gestational age, the statute requires physicians to undertake procedures, such as amniocentesis, that, in the situation presented, have no medical justification, impose significant additional health risks on both the pregnant woman and the fetus, and bear no rational relation to the State's interest in protecting fetal life.[2] As written, § 188.029 is an arbitrary imposition of discomfort, risk, and expense, furthering no discernible interest except to make the procurement of an abortion as arduous and difficult as possible. Thus, were it not for the majority's tortured effort to avoid the plain import of § 188.029, it could have struck down the testing provision as patently irrational irrespective of the *Roe* framework.[3]

The majority eschews this straightforward resolution, only to precipitate a constitutional crisis. Far from avoiding constitutional difficulty, the majority engineers a dramatic retrenchment in our jurisprudence by exaggerating the con-

[2] The District Court found that "the only method to evaluate [fetal] lung maturity is by amniocentesis," a procedure that "imposes additional significant health risks for both the pregnant woman and the fetus." 662 F. Supp. 407, 422 (WD Mo. 1987). Yet the medical literature establishes that to require amniocentesis for all abortions after 20 weeks would be contrary to sound medical practice and, moreover, would be useless for the purpose of determining lung maturity until no earlier than between 28 and 30 weeks gestational age. *Ibid*; see also Brief for American Medical Association, et al., as *Amici Curiae* 41. Thus, were § 188.029 read to require a finding of lung maturity, it would require physicians to perform a highly intrusive procedure of risk that would yield no result relevant to the question of viability.

[3] I also agree with the Court of Appeals, 851 F. 2d, at 1074–1075, that, as written, § 188.029 is contrary to this Court's decision in *Colautti* v. *Franklin*, 439 U. S. 379, 388–389 (1979).

flict between its untenable construction of § 188.029 and the *Roe* trimester framework.

No one contests that under the *Roe* framework the State, in order to promote its interest in potential human life, may regulate and even proscribe non-therapeutic abortions once the fetus becomes viable. *Roe*, 410 U. S., at 164–165. If, as the majority appears to hold, the testing provision simply requires a physician to use appropriate and medically sound tests to determine whether the fetus is actually viable when the estimated gestational age is greater than 20 weeks (and therefore within what the District Court found to be the margin of error for viability, *ante*, at 19), then I see little or no conflict with *Roe*.[4] Nothing in *Roe*, or any of its progeny, holds that a State may not effectuate its compelling interest in the potential life of a viable fetus by seeking to ensure that no viable fetus is mistakenly aborted because of the inherent lack of precision in estimates of gestational age. A requirement that a physician make a finding of viability, one way or the other, for every fetus that falls within the range of possible viability does no more than preserve the State's recognized authority. Although, as the majority correctly points out, such a testing requirement would have the effect of imposing additional costs on second-trimester abortions where the tests indicated that the fetus was not viable, these costs would be merely incidental to, and a necessary accommodation of, the State's unquestioned right to prohibit non-therapeutic abortions after the point of viability. In short,

[4] The majority never states precisely its construction of § 188.029. I base my synopsis of the majority's views mainly on its assertion that the entire provision must be read in light of its requirement that the physician act only in accordance with reasonable professional judgment, *ante*, at 18, and that the provision imposes no requirement that a physician perform irrelevant or dangerous tests. *Id.*, at 17–18. To the extent that the majority may be reading the provision to require tests other than those that a doctor, exercising reasonable professional judgment, would deem necessary to a finding of viability, the provision bears no rational relation to a legitimate governmental interest, and cannot stand.

the testing provision, as construed by the majority, is consistent with the *Roe* framework and could be upheld effortlessly under current doctrine.[6]

How ironic it is, then, and disingenuous, that the majority scolds the Court of Appeals for adopting a construction of the statute that fails to avoid constitutional difficulties. *Ante*, at 17. By distorting the statute, the majority manages to avoid invalidating the testing provision on what should have been noncontroversial constitutional grounds; having done so, however, the majority rushes headlong into a much deeper constitutional thicket, brushing past an obvious basis for upholding § 188.029 in search of a pretext for scuttling the trimester framework. Evidently, from the majority's perspective, the real problem with the Court of Appeals' construction of § 188.029 is not that it raised a constitutional difficulty, but that it raised the wrong constitutional difficulty—

[6] The cases cited by the majority are not to the contrary. As noted by the majority, in both *Colautti* v. *Franklin*, 439 U. S. 379, 388–389 (1979), and *Planned Parenthood of Central Mo.* v. *Danforth*, 428 U. S. 52 (1976), we stressed that the determination of viability is a matter for the judgment of the responsible attending physician. But § 188.029, at least as construed by the majority, is consistent with this requirement. The provision does nothing to remove the determination of viability from the purview of the attending physician; it merely instructs the physician to make a finding of viability using tests to determine gestational age, weight, and lung maturity when such tests are feasible and medically appropriate.

I also see no conflict with the Court's holding in *Akron* that the State may not impose "a heavy, *and unnecessary*, burden on women's access to a relatively inexpensive, and otherwise accessible, and safe abortion procedure." 462 U. S., at 438 (emphasis added). In *Akron*, we invalidated a city ordinance requiring that all second-trimester abortions be performed in acute-care hospitals on the ground that such a requirement was not medically necessary and would double the cost of abortions. *Id.*, at 434–439. By contrast, the viability determination at issue in this case (as read by the majority), is necessary to the effectuation of the State's compelling interest in the potential human life of viable fetuses and applies not to all second-trimester abortions, but instead only to that small percentage of abortions performed on fetuses estimated to be of more than 20 weeks gestational age.

WEBSTER *v.* REPRODUCTIVE HEALTH SERVICES

one not implicating *Roe*. The majority has remedied that, traditional canons of construction and judicial forbearance notwithstanding.

B

Having set up the conflict between § 188.029 and the *Roe* trimester framework, the majority summarily discards *Roe*'s analytic core as "'unsound in principle and unworkable in practice.'" *Ante*, at 20, quoting *Garcia* v. *San Antonio Metropolitan Transit Authority*, 469 U. S. 528, 546 (1985). This is so, the majority claims, because the key elements of the framework do not appear in the text of the Constitution, because the framework more closely resembles a regulatory code than a body of constitutional doctrine, and because under the framework the State's interest in potential human life is considered compelling only after viability, when, in fact, that interest is equally compelling throughout pregnancy. *Ante*, at 21–22. The majority does not bother to explain these alleged flaws in *Roe*. Bald assertion masquerades as reasoning. The object, quite clearly, is not to persuade, but to prevail.

1

The majority opinion is far more remarkable for the arguments that it does not advance than for those that it does. The majority does not even mention, much less join, the true jurisprudential debate underlying this case: whether the Constitution includes an "unenumerated" general right to privacy as recognized in many of our decisions, most notably *Griswold* v. *Connecticut*, 381 U. S. 479 (1965), and *Roe*, and, more specifically, whether and to what extent such a right to privacy extends to matters of childbearing and family life, including abortion. See, *e. g.*, *Eisenstadt* v. *Baird*, 405 U. S. 438 (1972) (contraception); *Loving* v. *Virginia*, 388 U. S. 1 (1967) (marriage); *Skinner* v. *Oklahoma ex re. Williamson*, 316 U. S. 535 (1942) (procreation); *Pierce* v. *Society of Sisters*, 268 U. S. 510 (1925) (childrearing). These are questions of unsurpassed significance in this Court's interpretation of the Constitution, and mark the battleground upon which this case was fought, by the parties, by the Solicitor General as *amicus* on behalf of petitioners, and by an unprecedented number of *amici*. On these grounds, abandoned by the majority, the Court should decide this case.

But rather than arguing that the text of the Constitution makes no mention of the right to privacy, the majority complains that the critical elements of the *Roe* framework—trimesters and viability—do not appear in the Constitution and are, therefore, somehow inconsistent with a Constitution cast in general terms. *Id.*, at 21. Were this a true concern, we would have to abandon most of our constitutional jurisprudence. As the majority well knows, or should know, the "critical elements" of countless constitutional doctrines nowhere appear in the Constitution's text. The Constitution makes no mention, for example, of the First Amendment's "actual malice" standard for proving certain libels, see *New York Times* v. *Sullivan*, 376 U. S. 254 (1964), or of the standard for determining when speech is obscene. See *Miller* v. *California*, 413 U. S. 15 (1973). Similarly, the Constitution makes no mention of the rational-basis test, or the specific verbal formulations of intermediate and strict scrutiny by which this Court evaluates claims under the Equal Protection Clause. The reason is simple. Like the *Roe* framework, these tests or standards are not, and do not purport to be, rights protected by the Constitution. Rather, they are judge-made methods for evaluating and measuring the strength and scope of constitutional rights or for balancing the constitutional rights of individuals against the competing interests of government.

With respect to the *Roe* framework, the general constitutional principle, indeed the fundamental constitutional right, for which it was developed is the right to privacy, see, *e. g.*, *Griswold* v. *Connecticut*, 381 U. S. 479 (1965), a species of "liberty" protected by the Due Process Clause, which under our past decisions safeguards the right of women to exercise some control over their own role in procreation. As we recently reaffirmed in *Thornburgh* v. *American College of Obstetricians and Gynecologists*, 476 U. S. 747 (1986), few decisions are "more basic to individual dignity and autonomy" or more appropriate to that "certain private sphere of individual liberty" that the Constitution reserves from the intrusive reach of government than the right to make the uniquely personal, intimate, and self-defining decision whether to end a pregnancy. *Id.*, at 772. It is this general principle, the "'moral fact that a person belongs to himself and not others nor to society as a whole,'" *id.*, at 777, n. 5 (STEVENS, J., concurring), quoting Fried, Correspondence, 6 Phil. & Pub. Aff. 288–289 (1977), that is found in the Constitution. See *Roe*, 410 U. S., at 152–153. The trimester framework simply defines and limits that right to privacy in the abortion context to accommodate, not destroy, a State's legitimate interest in protecting the health of pregnant women and in preserving potential human life. *Id.*, at 154–162. Fashioning such accommodations between individual rights and the legitimate interests of government, establishing benchmarks and standards with which to evaluate the competing claims of individuals and government, lies at the the very heart of constitutional adjudication. To the extent that the trimester framework is useful in this enterprise, it is not only consistent with constitutional interpretation, but necessary to the wise and just exercise of this Court's paramount authority to define the scope of constitutional rights.

2

The majority next alleges that the result of the trimester framework has "been a web of legal rules that have become increasingly intricate, resembling a code of regulations rather that a body of constitutional doctrine." *Ante*, at 21. Again, if this were a true and genuine concern, we would have to abandon vast areas of our constitutional jurisprudence. The majority complains that under the trimester

WEBSTER *v.* REPRODUCTIVE HEALTH SERVICES

framework the Court has distinguished between a city ordinance requiring that second-trimester abortions be performed in clinics and a state law requiring that these abortions be performed in hospitals, or between laws requiring that certain information be furnished to a woman by a physician or his assistant and those requiring that such information be furnished by the physician exclusively. *Ibid.*, at n. 15, citing *Simopoulos* v. *Virginia*, 462 U. S. 506 (1983), and *Akron, supra.* Are these distinctions any finer, or more "regulatory," than the distinctions we have often drawn in our First Amendment jurisprudence, where, for example, we have held that a "release time" program permitting public-school students to leave school grounds during school hours to receive religious instruction does not violate the Establishment Clause, even though a release-time program permitting religious instruction on school grounds does violate the Clause? Compare *Zorach* v. *Clauson*, 343 U. S. 306 (1952), with *McCollum* v. *Board of Education*, 333 U. S. 203 (1948). Our Fourth Amendment jurisprudence recognizes factual distinctions no less intricate. Just this Term, for example, we held that while an aerial observation from a helicopter hovering at 400 feet does not violate any reasonable expectation of privacy, such an expectation of privacy would be violated by a helicopter observation from an unusually low altitude. *Florida* v. *Riley*, 488 U. S. —, — (1989) (O'CONNOR, J., concurring in the judgment) (slip op. 4). Similarly, in a Sixth Amendment case, the Court held that although an overnight ban on attorney-client communication violated the constitutionally guaranteed right to counsel, *Geders* v. *United States*, 425 U. S. 80 (1976), that right was not violated when a trial judge separated a defendant from his lawyer during a 15-minute recess after the defendant's direct testimony. *Perry* v. *Leeke*, 488 U. S. — (1989).

That numerous constitutional doctrines result in narrow differentiations between similar circumstances does not mean that this Court has abandoned adjudication in favor of regula-

WEBSTER *v.* REPRODUCTIVE HEALTH SERVICES

tion. Rather, these careful distinctions reflect the process of constitutional adjudication itself, which is often highly fact-specific, requiring such determinations as whether state laws are "unduly burdensome" or "reasonable" or bear a "rational" or "necessary" relation to asserted state interests. In a recent due process case, THE CHIEF JUSTICE wrote for the Court: "[M]any branches of the law abound in nice distinctions that may be troublesome but have been thought nonetheless necessary: 'I do not think we need trouble ourselves with the thought that my view depends upon differences of degree. The whole law does so as soon as it is civilized.'" *Daniels* v. *Williams*, 474 U. S. 327, 334 (1986), quoting *Le Roy Fibre Co.* v. *Chicago, M. & St. P.R. Co.*, 232 U. S. 340, 354 (1914) (Holmes, J., partially concurring).

These "differences of degree" fully account for our holdings in *Simopoulos*, *supra*, and *Akron*, *supra*, which the majority today partially overrules. Those decisions rest on this Court's reasoned and accurate judgment that hospitalization and doctor-counselling requirements unduly burdened the right of women to terminate a pregnancy and were not rationally related to the State's asserted interest in the health of pregnant women, while Virginia's *substantially less restrictive* regulations were not unduly burdensome and did rationally serve the State's interest.[6] That the Court exercised its best judgment in evaluating these markedly dif-

[6] The difference in the *Akron* and *Simopoulos* regulatory regimes is stark. The Court noted in *Akron* that the city ordinance requiring that all second-trimester abortions be performed in acute-care hospitals undoubtedly would have made the procurement of legal abortions difficult and often prohibitively expensive, thereby driving the performance of abortions back underground where they would not be subject to effective regulation. Such a requirement obviously did not further the city's asserted interest in maternal health. *Id.*, at 420, n. 1. On the other hand, the Virginia law at issue in *Simopoulos*, by permitting the performance of abortions in licensed out-patient clinics as well as hospitals, did not similarly constrict the availability of legal abortions and, therefore, did not undermine its own stated purpose of protecting maternal health.

WEBSTER *v.* REPRODUCTIVE HEALTH SERVICES

ferent statutory schemes no more established the Court as an "'*ex officio* medical board,'" *ante*, at 22, quoting *Planned Parenthood of Central Mo.* v. *Danforth*, 428 U. S. 52, 99 (1976) (opinion of WHITE, J., concurring in part and dissenting in part), than our decisions involving religion in the public schools establish the Court as a national school board, or our decisions concerning prison regulations establish the Court as a bureau of prisons. See *Thornburgh* v. *Abbott*, 490 U. S. ——, (1989) (adopting different standard of First Amendment review for incoming as opposed to outgoing prison mail). If, in delicate and complicated areas of constitutional law, our legal judgments "have become increasingly intricate," *ante*, at 21, it is not, as the majority contends, because we have overstepped our judicial role. Quite the opposite: the rules are intricate because we have remained conscientious in our duty to do justice carefully, especially when fundamental rights rise or fall with our decisions.

3

Finally, the majority announces that the trimester framework cannot stand because the State's interest in potential life is compelling throughout pregnancy, not merely after viability. *Ante*, at 22. In so doing, the majority refers to the dissents in *Thornburgh* v. *American College of Obstetricians and Gynecologists*, *supra*, and in *Akron*, *supra*, but here, having now prevailed, the majority does not deem it necessary to explain, to support, or to justify the essential premises of its position. The opinion contains not one word of rationale for its view of the State's interest. This "it-is-so-because-we-say-so" jurisprudence constitutes nothing other than an exercise of brute force; reason, much less persuasion, has no place.

In answering the majority's claim that the State's interest in the fetus is uniform and compelling throughout pregnancy, I could not improve upon what JUSTICE STEVENS has written:

> "I should think it obvious that the State's interest in the protection of an embryo—even if that interest is defined as 'protecting those who will be citizens' . . . —increases progressively and dramatically as the organism's capacity to feel pain, to experience pleasure, to survive, and to react to its surroundings increases day by day. The development of a fetus—and pregnancy itself—are not static conditions, and the assertion that the government's interest is static simply ignores this reality. . . . [U]nless the religious view that a fetus is a 'person' is adopted . . . there is a fundamental and well-recognized difference between a fetus and a human being; indeed, if there is not such a difference, the permissibility of terminating the life of a fetus could scarcely be left to the will of the state legislatures. And if distinctions may be drawn between a fetus and a human being in terms of the state interest in their protection—even though the fetus represents one of 'those who will be citizens'—it seems to me quite odd to argue that distinctions may not also be drawn between the state interest in protecting the freshly fertilized egg and the state interest in protecting the 9-month-gestated, fully sentient fetus on the eve of birth. Recognition of this distinction is supported not only by logic, but also by history and by our shared experiences." *Thornburgh*, 476 U. S., at 778–779 (footnotes omitted). See also *Roe*, 410 U. S., at 129–147.

For my own part, I remain convinced, as six other Members of this Court 16 years ago were convinced, that the *Roe* framework, and the viability standard in particular, fairly, sensibly, and effectively functions to safeguard the constitutional liberties of pregnant women while recognizing and accommodating the State's interest in potential human life. The viability line reflects the biological facts and truths of fetal development; it marks that threshold moment prior to which a fetus cannot survive separate from the woman and cannot reasonably and objectively be regarded as a subject of rights or interests distinct from, or paramount to, those of the pregnant woman. At the same time, the viability standard takes account of the undeniable fact that as the fetus evolves into its postnatal form, and as it loses its dependence on the uterine environment, the State's interest in the fetus' potential human life, and in fostering a regard for human life in general, becomes compelling. As a practical matter, because viability follows "quickening"—the point at which a woman feels movement in her womb—and because viability occurs no earlier than 23Æ weeks gestational age, it establishes an easily applicable standard for regulating abortion while providing a pregnant woman ample time to exercise her fundamental right with her responsible physician to terminate her pregnancy.[7] Although I have stated previously for a majority of this Court that "[c]onstitutional rights do not always have easily ascertainable boundaries," to seek and establish those boundaries remains the special responsibility of this Court. *Thornburgh*, 476 U. S., at 771. In *Roe*, we discharged that responsibility as logic and science compelled.

---

[7] Notably, the majority does not advance the now-familiar catch-phrase criticism of the *Roe* framework that because the point of viability will recede with advances in medical technology, *Roe* "is clearly on a collision course with itself." See *Akron*, 462 U. S., at 458 (dissenting opinion). This critique has no medical foundation. As the medical literature and the *amicus* briefs filed in this case conclusively demonstrate, "there is an 'anatomic threshold' for fetal viability of about 23–24 weeks gestation." Brief for American Medical Association, et al., as *Amici Curiae* 7. Prior to that time, the crucial organs are not sufficiently mature to provide the mutually sustaining functions that are prerequisite to extrauterine survival, or viability. Moreover, "no technology exists to bridge the development gap between the three-day embryo culture and the 24th week of gestation." Fetal Extrauterine Survivability, Report to the New York State Task Force on Life and Law 10 (1988). Nor does the medical community believe that the development of any such technology is possible in the foreseeable future. *Id.*, at 12. In other words, the threshold of fetal viability is, and will remain, no different from what it was at the time *Roe* was decided. Predictions to the contrary are pure science fiction. See Brief for A Group of American Law Professors as *Amici Curiae* 23–25.

WEBSTER v. REPRODUCTIVE HEALTH SERVICES

The new majority today advances not one reasonable argument as to why our judgment in that case was wrong and should be abandoned.

C

Having contrived an opportunity to reconsider the *Roe* framework, and then having discarded that framework, the majority casually upholds the testing provision because it "reasonably furthers the State's interest in protecting potential human life." *Ante*, at 22. In keeping with the rest of its opinion, the majority makes no attempt to explain or to justify this newly minted standard, either in the abstract or as applied in this case. But the meaning of the standard is clear enough: for all practical purposes, *Roe* is overruled.[9]

The "reasonably furthers" standard completely disregards the irreducible minimum of *Roe*: the Court's recognition that a woman has a limited fundamental constitutional right to decide whether to terminate a pregnancy. That right receives absolutely no recognition in the majority's written opinion. Since the State's interest in potential life is ultimately served only if abortion is abolished, every hindrance to a woman's ability to obtain an abortion reasonably furthers the State's interest in potential life. Indeed, the more severe the hindrance, the more the State's interest is furthered. A tax on abortions or a criminal prohibition would both satisfy the majority's standard. So, for that matter, would a requirement that a pregnant woman memorize and recite today's majority opinion before seeking an abortion.

---

[9] Writing for the Court in *Akron*, Justice Powell observed the same phenomenon, though in hypothetical response to the dissent in that case: "In sum, it appears that the dissent would uphold virtually any abortion regulation under a rational-basis test. It also appears that even where heightened scrutiny is deemed appropriate, the dissent would uphold virtually any abortion-inhibiting regulation because of the State's interest in preserving potential human life. . . . This analysis is wholly incompatible with the existence of the fundamental right recognized in *Roe* v. *Wade*." 462 U. S., at 420–421, n. 1.

WEBSTER *v.* REPRODUCTIVE HEALTH SERVICES

The majority pretends that *Roe* survives, explaining that the facts of this case differ from those in *Roe*: here, Missouri has chosen to assert its interest in potential life only at the point of viability, whereas, in *Roe*, Texas had asserted that interest from the point of conception, criminalizing all abortions, except where the life of the mother was at stake. *Ante*, at 23. This, of course, is a distinction without a difference. The majority has repudiated every principle for which *Roe* stands; in good conscience, it cannot possibly believe that *Roe* lies "undisturbed" merely because this case does not call upon the Court to reconsider the Texas statute, or one like it. If the Constitution permits a State to enact any statute that reasonably furthers its interest in potential life, and if that interest arises as of conception, why would the Texas statute fail to pass muster? One suspects that the majority agrees. It is impossible to read the majority's penultimate paragraph without recognizing its implicit invitation to every State to enact more and more restrictive abortion laws, and to assert their interest in potential life as of the moment of conception. All of these laws will satisfy the majority's non-scrutiny, until sometime down the line, the new regime of old dissenters and new appointees will summon the courage to say what will have been true from this time forth: that *Roe* is no longer good law.

D

Thus, "not with a bang, but a whimper," the majority discards a landmark case of the last generation, and casts into darkness the hopes and visions of every woman in this country who had come to believe that the Constitution guaranteed her the right to exercise some control over her unique ability to bear children. The majority does so either oblivious or insensitive to the fact that millions of women, and their families, have ordered their lives around the right to reproductive choice, and that this right has become vital to the full participation of women in the economic and political walks of American life. With today's decision, the way is now clear once again for government to force upon women the physical labor and specific and direct medical and psychological harms that may accompany carrying a fetus to term. The way is now clear again for the State to conscript a woman's body and to force upon her a "distressful life and future." *Roe*, 410 U. S., at 153.

The result, as we know from experience, see Cates & Rocket, Illegal Abortions in the United States: 1972–1974, 8 Family Planning Perspectives 86, 92 (1976), will be that every year hundreds of thousands of women, in desperation, will defy the law, and place their health and safety in the unclean and unsympathetic hands of back-alley abortionists, or they will attempt to perform abortions upon themselves, with disastrous results. Every year, many women, especially poor and minority women, will die or suffer debilitating physical trauma, all in the name of enforced morality or religious dictates or the lack of compassion, as it may be.

Of the aspirations and settled understandings of American women, of the inevitable and brutal consequences of what it is doing, the tough-approach majority utters not a word. This silence is callous. It is also profoundly destructive of this Court as an institution. To overturn a constitutional decision is a rare and grave undertaking. To overturn a constitutional decision that secured a fundamental personal liberty to millions of persons is unprecedented in our 200 years of constitutional history. Although the doctrine of *stare decisis* applies with somewhat diminished force in constitutional cases generally, *ante*, at 20, even in ordinary constitutional cases "any departure from *stare decisis* demands special justification." *Arizona* v. *Rumsey*, 467 U. S. 203, 212 (1984). See also *Vasquez* v. *Hillary*, 474 U. S. 254, 266 (1986) ("the careful observer will discern that any detours from the straight path of *stare decisis* in our past have occurred for articulable reasons, and only when the Court has felt obliged 'to bring its opinions into agreement with experience and with facts newly ascertained,'" quoting *Burnet* v. *Coronado*

WEBSTER *v.* REPRODUCTIVE HEALTH SERVICES

Oil & Gas Co., 285 U. S. 393, 412 (1932) (Brandeis, J., dissenting)). This requirement of justification applies with unique force where, as here, the Court's abrogation of precedent destroys people's firm belief, based on past decisions of this Court, that they possess an unabridgeable right to undertake certain conduct.[9]

As discussed at perhaps too great length above, the majority makes no serious attempt to carry "the heavy burden of persuading . . . that changes in society or in the law dictate" the abandonment of *Roe* and its numerous progeny, *Vasquez*, 474 U. S., at 266, much less the greater burden of explaining the abrogation of a fundamental personal freedom. Instead, the majority pretends that it has left *Roe* standing, and refuses even to discuss the real issue underlying this case: whether the Constitution includes an unenumerated right to privacy that encompasses a woman's right to decide whether to terminate a pregnancy. To the extent that the majority

[9] Cf. *South Carolina* v. *Gathers*, —— U. S. ——, —— (1989) (SCALIA, J., dissenting) ("the respect accorded prior decisions increases, rather than decreases, with their antiquity, as the society adjusts itself to their existence, and the surrounding law becomes premised on their validity").

Moreover, as Justice Powell wrote for the Court in *Akron*, *supra*, "There are especially compelling reasons for adhering to *stare decisis* in applying the principles of *Roe* v. *Wade*. That case was considered with special care. It was first argued during the 1971 Term, and reargued—with extensive briefing—the following Term. The decision was joined by THE CHIEF JUSTICE and six other Justices. Since *Roe* was decided in January 1973, the Court repeatedly and consistently has accepted and applied the basic principle that a woman has a fundamental right to make the highly personal choice whether or not to terminate her pregnancy." 462 U. S., at 420, n. 1. See, *e. g.*, *Planned Parenthood of Central Mo.* v. *Danforth*, 438 U. S. 52 (1976); *Bellotti* v. *Baird*, 428 U. S. 132 (1976); *Beal* v. *Doe*, 432 U. S. 438 (1977); *Maher* v. *Roe*, 432 U. S. 464 (1977); *Colautti* v. *Franklin*, 439 U. S. 379 (1979); *Bellotti* v. *Baird*, 443 U. S. 622 (1979); *Harris* v. *McRae*, 448 U. S. 297 (1980); *Akron* v. *Akron Center for Reproductive Health, Inc.*, 462 U. S. 416 (1983); *Thornburgh* v. *American College of Obstetricians and Gynecologists*, 476 U. S. 747 (1986).

WEBSTER *v.* REPRODUCTIVE HEALTH SERVICES

does criticize the *Roe* framework, these criticisms are pure *ipse dixit.*

This comes at a cost. The doctrine of *stare decisis* "permits society to presume that bedrock principles are founded in the law rather than in the proclivities of individuals, and thereby contributes to the integrity of our constitutional system of government, both in appearance and in fact." *Id.*, at 265–266. Today's decision involves the most politically divisive domestic legal issue of our time. By refusing to explain or to justify its revolutionary revision in the law of abortion, and by refusing to abide not only by our precedents, but also by our canons for reconsidering those precedents, the majority invites charges of cowardice and illegitimacy to our door. I cannot say that these are undeserved.

II

With *Roe*'s passing, a political revolution in the law takes hold. The pendulum swings, as it always has, and we move a very long step backward. But that pendulum will swing again one day, or perhaps the advance of scientific knowledge will solve the vexing problem of abortion in another way. In the meantime, though, the liberty of women to control their own destinies, despite our Bill of Rights, will be subject to the vicissitudes of political controversy. In a Nation that cherishes liberty, this should not be.

I dissent.

1st DRAFT

SUPREME COURT OF THE UNITED STATES

No. 88-605

WILLIAM L. WEBSTER, ATTORNEY GENERAL OF MISSOURI, ET AL., APPELLANTS *v.* REPRODUCTIVE HEALTH SERVICES ET AL.

ON APPEAL FROM THE UNITED STATES COURT OF APPEALS FOR THE EIGHTH CIRCUIT

[June —, 1989]

JUSTICE O'CONNOR, concurring in part and concurring in the judgment.

I concur in Parts I, II–A, and II–B of the Court's opinion. Nothing in the record before us or the opinions below indicates that the preamble to Missouri's abortion regulation statute will affect a woman's decision to have an abortion. I agree that appellees' suggestions to the contrary are simply too hypothetical to support the use of declaratory judgment procedures in this case. Similarly, it seems to me to follow directly from our previous decisions concerning state or federal funding of abortions, *Harris* v. *McRae*, 448 U. S. 297 (1980), *Maher* v. *Roe*, 432 U. S. 464 (1977), and *Poelker* v. *Doe*, 432 U. S. 519 (1977), that appellees' facial challenge to the constitutionality of Missouri's ban on the utilization of public facilities and the participation of public employees in the performance of abortions not necessary to save the life of the mother, Mo. Rev. Stat. §§ 188.210, 188.215, cannot succeed. Given Missouri's definition of "public facility" as "any public institution, public facility, public equipment, or any physical asset owned, leased, or controlled by this state or any agency or political subdivision thereof," Mo. Rev. Stat. § 188.200(2), there may be conceivable applications of the ban on the use of public facilities that would be unconstitutional. Appellees and amici suggest that the State could try to en-

WEBSTER *v.* REPRODUCTIVE HEALTH SERVICES

force the ban against private hospitals using public water and sewage lines, or against private hospitals leasing state-owned equipment or state land. See Brief for Appellees 49–50; Brief for National Association of Public Hospitals as *Amicus Curiae* 9–12. Whether some or all of these or other applications of § 188.215 would be constitutional need not be decided here. *Maher*, *Poelker*, and *McRae* stand for the proposition that some quite straightforward applications of the Missouri ban on the use of public facilities for performing abortions would be constitutional and that is enough to defeat appellees' assertion that the ban is facially unconstitutional. "A facial challenge to a legislative Act is, of course, the most difficult challenge to mount successfully, since the challenger must establish that no set of circumstances exists under which the Act would be valid. The fact that the [relevant statute] might operate unconstitutionally under some conceivable set of circumstances is insufficient to render it wholly invalid, since we have not recognized an 'overbreadth' doctrine outside the limited context of the First Amendment." *United States* v. *Salerno*, 481 U. S. 739, 745 (1987).

In its analysis of Missouri's "encouraging or counseling" provision, Mo. Rev. Stat. § 188.205, see *ante*, at 13–16, and Missouri's "determination of viability" provision, Mo. Rev. Stat. § 188.029, see *ante*, at 16–23, however, I believe the Court has proceeded in a manner unnecessary to deciding the questions at hand.

I

As the Court notes, § 188.205 of the Missouri Revised Statutes makes it "unlawful for any public funds to be expended . . . for the purposes of encouraging or counseling a woman to have an abortion." Distinct prohibitions against encouraging and counseling appear in two succeeding sections of the Missouri Act. Section 188.210 makes it "unlawful for a doctor, nurse or other health care personnel, a social worker, a counselor or persons [sic] of similar occupation who is a public employee within the scope of his public employment to en-

WEBSTER *v.* REPRODUCTIVE HEALTH SERVICES

courage or counsel a woman to have an abortion not necessary to save her life." Section 188.215 makes it "unlawful for any public facility to be used . . . for the purpose of encouraging or counseling a woman to have an abortion not necessary to save her life." Despite Missouri's argument throughout this litigation that § 188.205 "is not directed at the conduct of any physician or health care provider, public or private," Brief for Appellants 43, the Court of Appeals below did not distinguish the reach of § 188.205 from that of § 188.210 and § 188.215. Rather, that court struck down all three of these "encouraging or counseling" provisions as unconstitutionally vague and as "an unacceptable infringement of the woman's fourteenth amendment right to choose an abortion . . . ." 851 F. 2d 1071, 1079 (1988).

Before us today is only the Court of Appeals' determination that the "encouraging or counseling" provision in § 188.205—the public funding provision—is unconstitutional. Missouri has chosen not to appeal the judgment of the Court of Appeals finding the "encouraging or counseling" provisions of § 188.210 or § 188.215 unconstitutional. I agree with the Court that we should accept the State's assertion as to the reach of § 188.205. See *ante*, at 13. To accept what was implicit in the Court of Appeals' decision and explicit in the District Court's decision, see *ante*, at 13 n. 10—that § 188.205 reaches the speech of health professionals and makes the expression of particular medical advice unlawful—would render superfluous the prohibition directed to public employees contained in § 188.210 and, at the same time, create a serious question of First Amendment law. Cf. *Thornburgh* v. *American College of Obstetricians & Gynecologists*, 476 U. S. 747, 830 (1986) (dissenting opinion); *Akron* v. *Akron Center for Reproductive Health, Inc.*, 462 U.S 416, 472, n. 16 (1983) (dissenting opinion). As we observed only last Term in another case raising First Amendment questions, where a statute is "readily subject to a narrowing construction that avoids constitutional difficulties," we will not defer to a con-

WEBSTER *v.* REPRODUCTIVE HEALTH SERVICES

struction of a state statute given by lower federal courts that does not avoid these difficulties. *Frisby* v. *Schultz*, 487 U. S. —, — (1988).

Having agreed with the State that § 188.205 "is directed solely at those persons responsible for expending public funds," Brief for Appellants 43, the Court nevertheless rejects appellees' suggestion that this interpretation of § 188.205 dissipates any controversy that may otherwise have existed between the parties over that statutory provision. *Ante*, at 13–14 & n. 12. It is, of course, true that a plaintiff class such as the one certified by the District Court below to include "pregnant females," 662 F. Supp. 407, 411 (WD Mo. 1987), *could* be adverse to the State over its prohibition on the public funding of abortion counseling services whether or not the prohibition affects what health professionals can actually say. Such a prohibition clearly inhibits to some degree pregnant women's access to assistance in deciding whether to have an abortion, thereby generating an injury sufficient to support Article III standing. See *McRae*, *supra*, at 297 (pregnant women have standing to challenge Hyde Amendment limiting use of federal funds to reimburse cost of abortions under Medicaid program); *Maher*, *supra*, at 464 (pregnant women have standing to challenge state regulations limiting state Medicaid benefits for abortions).

Whether this plaintiff class *is* adverse to the State over § 188.205, as the Court has properly interpreted it, depends on the actual substance of the plaintiffs' (appellees here) original complaint and on the plaintiffs' continuing desire to seek redress for the injury originally alleged in their complaint. If either of these prerequisites is absent, an actual and ongoing controversy between the litigants sufficient to support our jurisdiction under Art. III, § 2 of the Constitution does not exist. In my opinion both prerequisites are missing.

The Court, by selective quotation of the original complaint, asserts that appellees did in fact seek redress for Missouri's prohibition on the public funding of abortion counseling serv-

WEBSTER *v.* REPRODUCTIVE HEALTH SERVICES

ices interpreted to affect solely the conduct of the State's fiscal officers. See *ante*, at 14, n. 12. Reading the relevant portion of the complaint in context, however, reveals that appellees challenged the "encouraging or counseling" portion of § 188.205 only because they believed that it, like the similar portions of § 188.210 and § 188.215, directly prohibited health professionals from giving certain medical advice:

> "[Sections 188.205, 188.210, and 188.215] are unconstitutional as creating situations of gross professional malpractice for 'public employees' forbidden to advise properly their patients and clients. By eliminating abortion (which is a recognized medical alternative to an unwanted or medically undesirable pregnancy) from the full range of options available for discussion, encouragement, counseling, performance and assistance between a health care professional and his or her patient or client is [sic] to regulate unconstitutionally the practice of medicine and the rights of free speech and association and to interfere unconstitutionally with the privacy rights of pregnant women seeking abortions or seeking professional advice and assistance as to their pregnancies." Complaint ¶25.

I think it difficult to read this portion of the complaint as a constitutional challenge to the prohibition on state funding of abortion counseling. Aside from challenging the "perform or assist" prohibitions in all three provisions, the complaint only charges the unconstitutionality of state-imposed limitations on the substance of medical advice public employees may provide and state limitations on the use of public facilities for the provision of that advice. Section 188.205, as interpreted, imposes neither of these limitations.

Even assuming the Court has correctly read appellees' complaint, the Court ignores the stance appellees have taken here. They now assert that, on the State's interpretation of § 188.205, "there is no longer a case or controversy as to the public funds provision . . . ." Brief for Appellees 34. Plaintiffs are masters of their complaints and remain so at the appellate stage of a litigation. See *Caterpillar, Inc.* v. *Williams*, 482 U. S. 386, 398–399 (1987). For appellees to argue that there is no longer a case or controversy between them and the State amounts to a decision no longer to seek a declaratory judgment that § 188.205 is unconstitutional and accompanying injunctive relief. In so doing, appellees have rendered moot the fourth question on which certiorari was granted. See *Deakins* v. *Monaghan*, —— U. S. ——, —— (1988).

Under these circumstances, I believe we are without jurisdiction to decide the merits of the mooted controversy. *Sosna* v. *Iowa*, 419 U. S. 393, 402 (1975). Rather, it is our practice to vacate the judgment below with directions to the District Court to dismiss the relevant portion of the complaint. *Deakins*, *supra*, at ——; *United States* v. *Munsingwear, Inc.*, 340 U. S. 36, 39–40 (1950). Moreover, "[b]ecause this case was rendered moot in part by [appellees'] willingness permanently to withdraw their equitable claims from their federal action, a dismissal with prejudice is indicated." *Deakins*, *supra*, at ——. That is the disposition I think appropriate in this portion of the case now before us. I should note, however, that the interpretation of § 188.205 offered by the State and adopted by the Court and myself is not binding on the Supreme Court of Missouri which has the final word on the meaning of that State's statutes. *Virginia* v. *American Booksellers Ass'n, Inc.*, —— U. S. ——, —— (1988); *O'Brien* v. *Skinner*, 414 U. S. 524, 531 (1974). Should it happen that § 188.205, as ultimately interpreted by the Missouri Supreme Court, does prohibit publicly employed health professionals from giving specific medical advice to pregnant women, "the vacation and dismissal of the complaint that has become moot 'clears the path for future relitigation of the issues between the parties,' should subsequent events rekindle their controversy." *Deakins*, *supra*, at ——, quoting *Munsingwear*, *supra*, at 40. Until such

WEBSTER *v.* REPRODUCTIVE HEALTH SERVICES

events make their appearance and give rise to relitigation, I believe we and all federal courts are without jurisdiction to hear the merits of this moot dispute.

No other member of the Court, however, shares the view that we are without jurisdiction to decide the constitutionality of § 188.205 and the Court is evenly divided on the merits of the question. Under circumstances such as these, where the Court is threatened with the inability to reach a decision and where I substantially agree with an approach taken on the merits, I will accept the determination that the Court does have jurisdiction. See *United States* v. *Jorn*, 400 U. S. 470, 488 (1971) (statement of Black and BRENNAN, JJ.); *Screws* v. *United States*, 325 U. S. 91, 134 (1945) (addendum by Rutledge, J.). I therefore also concur in Part II–C of the Court's opinion. The Court has interpreted § 188.205 so that it does not impose any restrictions on the advice a health professional may give a patient. This interpretation avoids what I would otherwise consider a serious First Amendment issue. It is with that understanding that I concur.

II

I also agree with the Court that it was plain error for the Court of Appeals to interpret the second sentence of Mo. Rev. Stat. § 188.029 as meaning that "doctors *must* perform tests to find gestational age, fetal weight and lung maturity." 851 F. 2d, at 1075, n. 5 (emphasis in original). When read together with the first sentence of § 188.029—which requires a physician to "determine if the unborn child is viable by using and exercising that degree of care, skill, and proficiency commonly exercised by the ordinary skillful, careful, and prudent physician engaged in similar practice under the same or similar conditions"—it would be contradictory nonsense to read the second sentence as requiring a physician to perform viability examinations and tests in situations where it would be careless and imprudent to do so. The Court is quite correct: "the viability-testing provision makes sense

WEBSTER *v.* REPRODUCTIVE HEALTH SERVICES

only if the second sentence is read to require only those tests that are useful to making subsidiary findings as to viability," *ante*, at 17, and, I would add, only those examinations and tests that it would not be imprudent or careless to perform in the particular medical situation before the physician.

Unlike the Court, I do not understand these viability testing requirements to conflict with any of the Court's past decision concerning state regulation of abortion. Therefore, there is no necessity to accept the State's invitation to reexamine the constitutional validity of *Roe* v. *Wade*, 410 U. S. 113 (1973). Where there is no need to decide a constitutional question, it is a venerable principle of this Court's adjudicatory processes not to do so for "[t]he Court will not 'anticipate a question of constitutional law in advance of the necessity of deciding it.'" *Ashwander* v. *Tennessee Valley Authority*, 297 U. S. 288, 346 (1936) (Brandeis, J., concurring), quoting *Liverpool, New York and Philadelphia S. S. Co.* v. *Commissioners of Emigration*, 113 U. S. 33, 39 (1885). Neither will it "formulate a rule of constitutional law broader than is required by the precise facts to which it is to be applied." *Ibid.* Quite simply, "[i]t is not the habit of the Court to decide questions of a constitutional nature unless absolutely necessary to a decision of the case." *Burton* v. *United States*, 196 U. S. 283, 295 (1905). No reason is offered for departing from this "fundamental rule of judicial restraint," *Three Affiliated Tribes of the Fort Bethold Reservation* v. *Wold Engineering*, 467 U. S. 138, 157 (1984), and I would not do so in a case of such constitutional moment. When the constitutional invalidity of a State's abortion statute actually turns on the constitutional validity of *Roe* v. *Wade*, there will be time enough to reexamine *Roe*. And to do so carefully.

In assessing § 188.029 it is especially important to recognize that appellees did not appeal the District Court's ruling that the first sentence of § 188.029 is constitutional. 662 F. Supp., at 420–422. There is, accordingly, no dispute between the parties before us over the constitutionality of the

WEBSTER *v.* REPRODUCTIVE HEALTH SERVICES

"presumption of viability at 20 weeks," *ante*, at 18, created by the first sentence of § 188.029. If anything might arguably conflict with the Court's previous decisions concerning the determination of viability, I would think it is the introduction of this presumption. The Court, see *ante*, at 19, refers to a passage from *Planned Parenthood of Central Missouri* v. *Danforth*, 428 U. S. 53, 64 (1976): "The time when viability is achieved may vary with each pregnancy, and the determination of whether a particular fetus is viable is, and must be, a matter for the judgment of the responsible attending physician." The 20-week presumption of viability in the first sentence of § 188.029, it could be argued (though, I would think, unsuccessfully), restricts "the judgment of the responsible attending physician," by imposing on that physician the burden of overcoming the presumption. This presumption may be a "superimpos[ition of] state regulation on the medical determination of whether a particular fetus is viable," *ante*, at 19, but, if so, it is a restriction on the physician's judgment that is not before us. As the Court properly interprets the second sentence of § 188.029, it does nothing more than delineate means by which the unchallenged 20-week presumption of viability may be overcome if those means are useful in doing so and can be prudently employed. Contrary to the Court's suggestion, see *ante*, at 19–20, the District Court did not think the second sentence of § 188.029 unconstitutional for this reason. Rather, both the District Court and the Court of Appeals thought the second sentence to be unconstitutional precisely because they interpreted that sentence to impose state regulation on the determination of viability that it does not impose.

I do not think the second sentence of § 188.029, as interpreted by the Court, imposes a degree of state regulation on the medical determination of viability that in any way conflicts with prior decisions of this Court. As the Court recognizes, the requirement that, where not imprudent, physicians perform examinations and tests useful to making subsidiary findings to determine viability "promot[es] the State's interest in potential life rather than in maternal health." *Ante*, at 18. No decision of this Court has held that the State may not directly promote its interest in potential life when viability is possible. Quite the contrary. In *Thornburgh*, *supra*, the Court considered a constitutional challenge to a Pennsylvania statute requiring that a second physician be present during an abortion performed "when viability is possible." 476 U. S., at 769–770. For guidance, the Court looked to the earlier decision in *Planned Parenthood Assn. of Kansas City, Missouri, Inc.* v. *Ashcroft*, 462 U. S. 476 (1983), upholding a Missouri statute requiring the presence of a second physician during an abortion performed after viability. *Id.*, at 482–486 (opinion of Powell, J.); *id.*, at 505 (opinion concurring in the judgment in part and dissenting in part). The *Thornburgh* majority struck down the Pennsylvania statute merely because the statute had no exception for emergency situations and not because it found a constitutional difference between the State's promotion of its interest in potential life when viability is possible and when viability is certain. 476 U. S., at 770–771. Despite the clear recognition by the *Thornburgh* majority that the Pennsylvania and Missouri statutes differed in this respect, there is no hint in the opinion of the *Thornburgh* Court that the State's interest in potential life differs depending whether it seeks to further that interest post-viability or when viability is possible. Thus, all nine members of the *Thornburgh* Court appear to have agreed that it is not constitutionally impermissible for the State to enact regulations designed to protect the State's interest in potential life when viability is possible. See *id.*, at 811 (WHITE, J., dissenting); *id.*, at 832 (dissenting opinion). That is exactly what Missouri has done in § 188.029.

Similarly, the basis for reliance by the District Court and the Court of Appeals below on *Colautti* v. *Franklin*, 439 U. S. 379 (1979), disappears when § 188.029 is properly interpreted. In *Colautti* the Court observed:

WEBSTER *v.* REPRODUCTIVE HEALTH SERVICES

> "Because this point [of viability] may differ with each pregnancy, neither the legislature nor the courts may proclaim one of the elements entering into the ascertainment of viability—be it weeks of gestation or fetal weight or any other single factor—as the determinant of when the State has a compelling interest in the life or health of the fetus. Viability is the critical point." *Id.*, at 388–389.

The courts below, on the interpretation of § 188.029 rejected here, found the second sentence of that provision at odds with this passage from *Colautti.* See 851 F. 2d, at 1074; 662 F. Supp., at 423. On this Court's interpretation of § 188.029 it is clear that Missouri has not substituted any of the "elements entering into the ascertainment of viability" as "the determinant of when the State has a compelling interest in the life or health of the fetus." All the second sentence of § 188.029 does is to require, when not imprudent, the performance of "those tests that are useful in making *subsidiary* findings as to viability." *Ante*, at 17 (emphasis added). Thus, consistent with *Colautti*, viability remains the "critical point" under § 188.029.

Finally, and rather half-heartedly, the Court suggests that the marginal increase in the cost of an abortion created by Missouri's viability testing provision may make § 188.029, even as interpreted, suspect under this Court's decision in *Akron*, 462 U. S., at 434–439, striking down a second-trimester hospitalization requirement. See *ante*, at 20. I dissented from the Court's opinion in *Akron* because it was my view that, even apart from *Roe*'s trimester framework which I continue to consider problematic, see *Thornburgh, supra*, at 828 (dissenting opinion), the *Akron* majority had distorted and misapplied its own standard for evaluating State regulation of abortion which the Court had applied with fair consistency in the past: that, pre-viability, "a regulation imposed on a lawful abortion is not unconstitutional unless it unduly burdens the right to seek an abortion." *Akron, supra,* at 453 (dissenting opinion) (internal quotes omitted).

It is clear to me that requiring the performance of examinations and tests useful to determining whether a fetus is viable, when viability is possible, and when it would not be medically imprudent to do so, does not impose an undue burden on a woman's abortion decision. On this ground alone I would reject the suggestion that § 188.029 as interpreted is unconstitutional. More to the point, however, just as I see no conflict between § 188.029 and *Colautti* or any decision of this Court concerning a State's ability to give effect to its interest in potential life, I see no conflict between § 188.029 and the Court's opinion in *Akron*. The second-trimester hospitalization requirement struck down in *Akron* imposed, in the majority's view, "a heavy, and unnecessary, burden," 462 U. S., at 438, more than doubling the cost of "women's access to a relatively inexpensive, otherwise accessible, and safe abortion procedure." *Ibid.*; see also *id.*, at 434. By contrast, the cost of examinations and tests that could usefully and prudently be performed when a woman is 20–24 weeks pregnant to determine whether the fetus is viable would only marginally if at all increase the cost of an abortion. See Brief for American Association of Prolife Obstetricians and Gynecologists, *et al.* as *Amici Curiae* 3 ("At twenty weeks gestation, an ultrasound examination to determine gestational age is standard medical practice. It is routinely provided by the plaintiff clinics. An ultrasound examination can effectively provide all three designated findings of sec. 188.029"); *id.* at 22 ("A finding of fetal weight can be obtained from the same ultrasound test used to determine gestational age"); *id.* at 25 ("There are a number of different methods in standard medical practice to determine fetal lung maturity at twenty or more weeks gestation. The most simple and most obvious is by inference. It is well known that fetal lungs do not mature until 33–34 weeks gestation. . . . If an assessment of the gestational age indicates that the child is less than thirty-three weeks, a general finding can be made that the fetal lungs are not mature. This finding can then be used by the physician in making his determination of viability under section 188.029"); cf. Brief for American Medical Association, *et al.* as *Amici Curiae* 42 (no suggestion that fetal weight and gestational age cannot be determined from the same sonogram); *id.* at 43 (another clinical test for gestational age and, by inference, fetal weight and lung maturity, is an accurate report of the last menstrual period), citing Smith, Frey & Johnson, *Assessing Gestational Age*, 33 Am. Fam. Physician 215, 219 (1986).

Moreover, the examinations and tests required by § 188.029 are to be performed when viability is possible. This feature of § 188.029 distinguishes it from the second-trimester hospitalization requirement struck down by the *Akron* majority. As the Court recognized in *Thornburgh*, the State's compelling interest in potential life post-viability renders its interest in determining the critical point of viability equally compelling. See *supra*, p. ——. Under the Court's precedents, the same cannot be said for the *Akron* second-trimester hospitalization requirement. As I understand the Court's opinion in *Akron*, therefore, the Court's suggestion today that *Akron* casts doubt on the validity of § 188.029, even as the Court has interpreted it, is without foundation and cannot provide a basis for reevaluating *Roe*. Accordingly, because the Court of Appeals misinterpreted Mo. Rev. Stat. § 188.029, and because, properly interpreted, § 188.029 is not inconsistent with any of this Court's prior precedents, I would reverse the decision of the Court of Appeals.

In sum, I concur in Parts I, II–A, II–B, and II–C of the Court's opinion and concur in the judgment of Part II–D.

1st DRAFT

SUPREME COURT OF THE UNITED STATES

No. 88-605

WILLIAM L. WEBSTER, ATTORNEY GENERAL OF MISSOURI, ET AL., APPELLANTS *v.* REPRODUCTIVE HEALTH SERVICES ET AL.

ON APPEAL FROM THE UNITED STATES COURT OF APPEALS FOR THE EIGHTH CIRCUIT

[June 29, 1989]

JUSTICE SCALIA, concurring in part and concurring in the judgment.

I join Parts I, II–A, II–B, and II–C of the opinion of THE CHIEF JUSTICE. As to Part II–D, I share JUSTICE BLACKMUN's view, *post*, at 18, that it effectively would overrule *Roe* v. *Wade*, 410 U. S. 113 (1973). I agree that should be done, but would do it more explicitly. Since today we contrive to avoid doing it, and indeed to avoid almost any decision of national import, I need not set forth my reasons, some of which have been well recited in dissents of my colleagues in other cases. See, *e. g.*, *Thornburgh* v. *American College of Obstetricians & Gynecologists*, 476 U. S. 747, 786–797 (1986) (WHITE, J., dissenting); *Akron* v. *Akron Center for Reproductive Health, Inc.*, 462 U. S. 416, 453–459 (1983) (O'CONNOR, J., dissenting); *Roe* v. *Wade*, *supra*, at 172–178 (REHNQUIST, J., dissenting); *Doe* v. *Bolton*, 410 U. S. 179, 221–223 (1973) (WHITE, J., dissenting).

The outcome of today's case will doubtless be heralded as a triumph of judicial statesmanship. It is not that, unless it is statesmanlike needlessly to prolong this Court's self-awarded sovereignty over a field where it has little proper business since the answers to most of the cruel questions posed are political and not juridical—a sovereignty which therefore quite properly, but to the great damage of the Court, makes it the

WEBSTER *v.* REPRODUCTIVE HEALTH SERVICES

object of the sort of organized public pressure that political institutions in a democracy ought to receive.

JUSTICE O'CONNOR's assertion, *ante*, at 8, that a "'fundamental rule of judicial restraint'" requires us to avoid reconsidering *Roe* cannot be taken seriously. By finessing *Roe* we do not, as she suggests, *ante*, at 8, adhere to the strict and venerable rule that we should avoid "'decid[ing] questions of a constitutional nature.'" We have not disposed of this case on some statutory or procedural ground, but have decided, and could not avoid deciding, whether the Missouri statute meets the requirements of the United States Constitution. The only choice available is whether, in deciding that constitutional question, we should use *Roe* v. *Wade* as the benchmark, or something else. What is involved, therefore, is not the rule of avoiding constitutional issues where possible, but the quite separate principle that we "will not 'formulate a rule of constitutional law broader than is required by the precise facts to which it is to be applied.'" *Ante*, at 8. The latter is a sound general principle, but one often departed from when good reason exists. Just this Term, for example, in an opinion authored by JUSTICE O'CONNOR, despite the fact that we had already held a racially based set-aside unconstitutional because unsupported by evidence of identified discrimination, which was all that was needed to decide the case, we went on to outline the criteria for properly tailoring race-based remedies in cases where such evidence is present. *Richmond* v. *J. A. Croson Co.*, —— U. S. ——, —— - —— (1989) (slip op., at 30–33). Also this Term, in an opinion joined by JUSTICE O'CONNOR, we announced the constitutional rule that deprivation of the right to confer with counsel during trial violates the Sixth Amendment even if no prejudice can be shown, despite our finding that there had been no such deprivation on the facts before us—which was all that was needed to decide the case. *Perry* v. *Leeke*, —— U. S. ——, —— - ——(1989) (slip op., at 5–8); see *id.*, at —— (KENNEDY, J., concurring in part). I have not identified with certainty the first instance of our deciding a case on broader constitutional grounds than absolutely necessary, but it is assuredly no later than *Marbury* v. *Madison*, 1 Cranch 137 (1803), where we held that mandamus could constitutionally issue against the Secretary of State, although that was unnecessary given our holding that the law authorizing issuance of the mandamus by this Court was unconstitutional.

The Court has often spoken more broadly than needed in precisely the fashion at issue here, announcing a new rule of constitutional law when it could have reached the identical result by applying the rule thereby displaced. To describe two recent opinions that JUSTICE O'CONNOR joined: In *Daniels* v. *Williams*, 474 U. S. 329 (1986), we overruled our prior holding that a "deprivation" of liberty or property could occur through negligent governmental acts, ignoring the availability of the alternative constitutional ground that, even if a deprivation had occurred, the state's post-deprivation remedies satisfied due process, see *id.*, at 340–343 (STEVENS, J., concurring in the judgment). In *Illinois* v. *Gates*, 462 U. S. 213 (1983), we replaced the preexisting "two-pronged" constitutional test for probable cause with a totality-of-the-circumstances approach, ignoring the concurrence's argument that the same outcome could have been reached under the old test, see *id.*, at 267–272 (WHITE, J., concurring in the judgment). It is rare, of course, that the Court goes out of its way to *acknowledge* that its judgment could have been reached under the old constitutional rule, making its adoption of the new one unnecessary to the decision, but even such explicit acknowledgment is not unheard-of. See *Commonwealth Edison Co.* v. *Montana*, 453 U. S. 609 (1981); *Perez* v. *Campbell*, 402 U. S. 637 (1970). For a sampling of other cases where the availability of a narrower, well-established ground is simply ignored in the Court's opinion adopting a new constitutional rule, though pointed out in separate opin-

WEBSTER *v.* REPRODUCTIVE HEALTH SERVICES

ions of some Justices, see *Michelin Tire Corp.* v. *Wages*, 423 U. S. 276 (1976); *Pointer* v. *Texas*, 380 U. S. 400 (1965); *Mapp* v. *Ohio*, 367 U. S. 643 (1961). It would be wrong, in any decision, to ignore the reality that our policy not "to formulate a rule of constitutional law broader than is required by the precise facts" has a frequently applied good-cause exception. But it seems particularly perverse to convert the policy into an absolute in the present case, in order to place beyond reach the inexpressibly "broader-than-was-required-by-the-precise-facts" structure established by *Roe* v. *Wade*.

The real question, then, is whether there are valid reasons to go beyond the most stingy possible holding today. It seems to me there are not only valid but compelling ones. Ordinarily, speaking no more broadly than is absolutely required avoids throwing settled law into confusion; doing so today preserves a chaos that is evident to anyone who can read and count. Alone sufficient to justify a broad holding is the fact that our retaining control, through *Roe*, of what I believe to be, and many of our citizens recognize to be, a political issue, continuously distorts the public perception of the role of this Court. We can now look forward to another Term with cartsfull of mail from the public, and streetsfull of demonstrators, urging us—their unelected and life-tenured judges who have been awarded those extraordinary, undemocratic characteristics precisely in order that we might follow the law despite the popular will—to follow the popular will. Indeed, I expect we can look forward to even more of that than before, given our indecisive decision today. And if these reasons for taking the unexceptional course of reaching a broader holding are not enough, then consider the nature of the constitutional question we avoid: In most cases, we do no harm by not speaking more broadly than the decision requires. Anyone affected by the conduct that the avoided holding would have prohibited will be able to challenge it himself, and have his day in court to make the argument.

WEBSTER *v.* REPRODUCTIVE HEALTH SERVICES

Not so with respect to the harm that many States believed, pre-*Roe*, and many may continue to believe, is caused by largely unrestricted abortion. That will continue to occur if the States have the constitutional power to prohibit it, and would do so, but we skillfully avoid telling them so. Perhaps those abortions should occur. That is surely an arguable question, the question that reconsideration of *Roe* v. *Wade* entails. But what is not at all arguable, it seems to me, is that we should decide now and not insist that we be run into a corner before we grudgingly yield up our judgment. The only sound reason for the latter course is to prevent a change in the law—but to think that desirable begs the question to be decided.

It was an arguable question today whether § 188.029 of the Missouri law contravened this Court's understanding of *Roe* v. *Wade*,* and I would have examined *Roe* rather than

*That question, compared with the question whether we should reconsider and reverse *Roe*, is hardly worth a footnote, but I think JUSTICE O'CONNOR answers that incorrectly as well. In *Roe*, we said that "the physician [has the right] to administer medical treatment according to his professional judgment up to the points where important state interests provide compelling justifications for intervention." We have subsequently made clear that it is also a matter of medical judgment when viability (one of those points) is reached. "The time when viability is achieved may vary with each pregnancy, and the determination of whether a particular fetus is viable is, and must be, a matter for the judgment of the responsible attending physician." *Parenthood of Central Missouri* v. *Danforth*, 428 U. S. 52, 64 (1976). Section 188.029 conflicts with the purpose and hence the fair import of this principle because it will sometimes require a physician to perform tests that he would not otherwise have performed to determine whether a fetus is viable. It is therefore a legislative imposition on the judgment of the physician, and one that increases the cost of an abortion.

JUSTICE O'CONNOR would nevertheless uphold the law because it "does not impose an undue burden on the woman's abortion decision." *Ante*, at 11. This conclusion is supported by the observation that the required tests impose only a marginal cost on the abortion procedure, far less of an increase than the cost-doubling hopitalization requirement invalidated in *Akron* v. *Akron Center for Reproductive Health, Inc.*, 462 U. S. 416,

WEBSTER *v.* REPRODUCTIVE HEALTH SERVICES

examining the contravention. Given the Court's newly contracted abstemiousness, what will it take, one must wonder, to permit us to reach that fundamental question? The result of our vote today is that we will not reconsider that prior opinion, even if most of the Justices think it is wrong, unless we have before us a statute that in fact contradicts it—and even then (under our newly discovered "no-broader-than-necessary" requirement) only minor problematical aspects of *Roe* will be reconsidered, unless one expects State legislatures to adopt provisions whose compliance with *Roe* cannot even be argued with a straight face. It thus appears that the mansion of constitutionalized abortion-law, constructed overnight in *Roe* v. *Wade*, must be disassembled door-jamb by door-jamb, and never entirely brought down, no matter how wrong it may be.

Of the four courses we might have chosen today—to reaffirm *Roe*, to overrule it explicitly, to overrule it *sub silentio*, or to avoid the question—the last, the one we have chosen, is the least responsible. On the question of the constitutional-

---

453–459 (1983). *Ante*, at 12. The fact that the challenged regulation is less costly than what we struck down in *Akron* tells us only that we cannot decide the present case on the basis of that earlier decision. It does not tell us whether the present requirement is an "undue burden," and I know of no basis for determining that this particular burden (or any other for that matter) is "due." One could with equal justification conclude that it is not. To avoid the question of *Roe* v. *Wade*'s validity, with the attendant costs that this will have for the Court and for the principles of self-governance, on the basis of a standard that offers "no guide but the Court's own discretion," *Baldwin* v. *Missouri*, 281 U. S. 586, 596 (1930) (Holmes, J., dissenting), merely adds to the irrationality of what we do today.

Similarly irrational is the new concept that JUSTICE O'CONNOR introduces into the law in order to achieve her result, the notion of a State's "interest in potential life when viability is possible." *Ante*, at 10. Since "viability" means the mere *possibility* (not the certainty) of survivability outside the womb, "possible viability" must mean the possibility of a possibility of survivability outside the womb. Perhaps our next opinion will expand the third trimester into the second even further, by approving State action designed to take account of "the chance of possible viability."

WEBSTER *v.* REPRODUCTIVE HEALTH SERVICES

ity of § 188.029, I concur in the judgment of the Court and strongly dissent from the manner in which it has been reached.

At the end of his *Webster* draft opinion of the Court, we saw, Chief Justice Rehnquist disclaimed any intention to overrule *Roe* v. *Wade*. The disclaimer could, however, scarcely disguise the potentially fatal effect that the Rehnquist opinion might have upon *Roe* v. *Wade*. Though the Chief Justice received memos on May 30 from Justices White and Kennedy joining his opinion, other Justices indicated dissatisfaction with the draft. The day after the draft was circulated, on May 26, Justice Blackmun sent around a memo, "I shall be writing something in this case." This foreshadowed a dissent by the author of the *Roe* opinion, as well as a joinder in it by Justices Brennan and Marshall, who wrote on May 30 that they would wait to see the Blackmun opinion.

On the same day, Justice Stevens, who had been undecided at the conference, sent a two-page letter to the Chief Justice, reprinted on p. 289, in which he challenged the Rehnquist repudiation of *Roe*. A year earlier, in a May 27, 1988, letter to Justice O'Connor, Justice Stevens himself had indicated that he disagreed with the Court's creation of different review standards. "As you know," Stevens wrote, "I have always had difficulty with the Court's 'tiered' analysis of equal protection issues. When we say, for example, that a classification affecting fundamental rights, such as the right to vote, is 'valid only if necessary to achieve a compelling governmental purpose,' I wonder whether we really mean that there must be a compelling—and not just a sensible—reason for setting the voting age at 18 rather than 17 or 19."

Despite the view thus expressed, the Stevens letter to the Chief Justice took strong issue with the reasonableness test stated in Rehnquist's draft of the opinion of the Court in *Webster*. Justice Stevens objected to what he termed "your newly minted standard of 'reasonably further[ing] the state's interest in protecting potential human life.'" He complained, "[Y]ou make no attempt to explain or justify your new standard."

Under the new review standard, Justice Stevens wrote, "[i]f a simple showing that a state regulation 'reasonably furthers the state interest in protecting potential human life' is enough to justify an abortion regulation, the woman's interest in making the abortion decision apparently is given no weight at all."

In addition, Justice Stevens asserted, the Rehnquist test would uphold virtually all abortion restrictions. He gave the following illustrations: "A tax on abortions, a requirement that the pregnant woman must be able to stand on her head for fifteen minutes before she can have an abortion, or a criminal prohibition would each satisfy your test." In fact, Stevens went on, "the same result could be accomplished by requiring tests of the woman's knowledge of Shakespeare or American history."

Justice Stevens wrote that the test in the Rehnquist draft "really rejects *Roe* v. *Wade* in its entirety" and it did so without acknowledging its fatal effect. "I would think," his letter declared, "that it would be much better for the Court, as an institution, to do so forthrightly rather than indirectly with a bombshell first introduced at the end of its opinion." As this passage indicates, Justice Stevens strongly objected to the manner in which the Chief

Justice had accomplished his "somewhat gratuitous rejection of the trimester approach."

Stevens's letter clearly indicated that its author would not join the Rehnquist draft. "As you know," the letter mockingly concluded, "I am not in favor of overruling *Roe* v. *Wade*, but if the deed is to be done I would rather see the Court give the case a decent burial instead of tossing it out the window of a fast-moving caboose."

Justice Blackmun followed up his May 26 memo indicating that he would write separately with a draft dissenting opinion, which he circulated on June 21. Blackmun's draft, reprinted on page 291, was a passionate dissent that mourned what he termed "*Roe*'s passing." "The simple truth," the draft dissent declared, "is that *Roe* no longer survives. . . . [T]he majority discards a landmark case of the last generation, and casts into darkness the hopes and visions of every woman in this country who had come to believe that the Constitution guaranteed her the right to exercise some control over her unique ability to bear children."

The opening paragraph set the tone of the Blackmun draft: "Today, a bare majority of this Court disserves the people of this Nation, and especially the millions of women who have lived and come of age in the 16 years since the decision in *Roe* v. *Wade* . . . recognized that the constitutionally guaranteed right to privacy encompasses a woman's right, with her responsible physician, to choose whether or not to terminate a pregnancy. To those women, and to all others, this Court owes an essential duty of explanation—a duty of candor and forthrightness, a duty to interpret the Constitution and our past decisions in a reasoned and honest fashion. The majority mocks this duty. At every level of its review, from its effort to read the real meaning out of the Missouri statute to its evisceration of precedents and its deafening silence about the fundamental constitutional protections that it jettisons, the majority labors to obscure what is at stake in this monumental case and to cloak what it actually has decided."

Justice Blackmun referred to the "feigned restraint" of the Rehnquist draft when it stated that *Roe* was not overruled. "This disclaimer," Blackmun asserted, "is totally meaningless." Instead, the draft dissent declared, "The simple truth is that *Roe* no longer survives, and . . . the majority provides no substitute for its protective umbrella."

The Blackmun language was unusually strong: "I rue this day. I rue the violence that has been done to the liberty and equality of women. I rue the violence that has been done to our legal fabric and to the integrity of this Court. I rue the inevitable loss of public esteem for this Court that is so essential. I dissent."

The draft dissent was caustic in its reaction to the review standard stated in the Chief Justice's draft opinion. "There," Justice Blackmun wrote, "tucked away at the end of its opinion, the majority works a radical reversal of the law of abortion." What the Rehnquist draft had done was "to throw out *Roe*'s trimester framework." In its stead, "[i]n flat contradiction to *Roe*, the majority concludes that the State's interest in potential life is compelling before viability, and upholds the testing provision because it 'reasonably furthers' that state interest."

Blackmun complained that the Rehnquist opinion did not explain why *Roe* was wrong: "The majority does not bother to explain [the] alleged flaws in *Roe*. Bald assertion masquerades as reasoning. The object, quite clearly, is not to persuade, but to prevail." Later, after analyzing *Roe* and its reasoning, Blackmun asserted, "The new majority today advances not one reasonable argument as to why our judgment in that case was wrong and should be abandoned."

The draft dissent referred again to the Rehnquist review standard, saying, "[T]he majority casually upholds the testing provision because it 'reasonably furthers the State's interest in protecting potential human life.' In keeping with the rest of its opinion, the majority makes no attempt to explain or to justify this newly minted standard, either in the abstract or as applied in this case. But the meaning of the standard is clear enough: for all practical purposes, *Roe* is overruled."

Justice Blackmun used and adapted the mocking examples in the Stevens letter: "A tax on abortions or a criminal prohibition would both satisfy the majority's standard. So, for that matter, would a requirement that a pregnant woman memorize and recite today's majority opinion before seeking an abortion."

The Rehnquist test, Blackmun urged, would uphold virtually all abortion restrictions. "It is impossible," declared the Blackmun draft, "to read the majority's penultimate paragraph without recognizing its implicit invitation to every State to enact more and more restrictive abortion laws, and to assert their interest in potential life as of the moment of conception. All of these laws will satisfy the majority's non-scrutiny, until sometime down the line, the new regime of old dissenters and new appointees will summon the courage to say what will have been true from this time forth: that *Roe* is no longer good law."

Blackmun categorized the Rehnquist opinion's result as a "revolutionary revision in the law of abortion." Indeed, declared Blackmun, "With *Roe*'s passing, a political revolution in the law takes hold." Under the Rehnquist draft opinion of the Court, the Blackmun dissent asserted, "[t]he pendulum swings, as it always has, and we move a very long step backward." Justice Blackmun stated that the pendulum would swing again one day. "In the meantime, though," his draft dissent concluded, "the liberty of women to control their own destinies, despite our Bill of Rights, will be subject to the vicissitudes of political controversy. In a Nation that cherishes liberty, this should not be."

As soon as Justices Brennan and Marshall read Justice Blackmun's draft, they sent memos joining it. Brennan's memo called Blackmun's opinion "magnificent."

The next day, June 22, Chief Justice Rehnquist circulated a scheduling memorandum that told the Justices that he would announce the *Webster* decision on June 29–then designated as the final day of the Court's term. The

June 22 memo indicated that the Chief Justice believed that he still retained his majority for what the Blackmun dissent had termed the "deceptive" overruling of *Roe*.

On June 23, however, Justice O'Connor circulated the opinion reprinted on page 313. It was headed, "JUSTICE O'CONNOR, concurring in part and concurring in the judgment." The O'Connor opinion indicated for the first time that the *Webster* majority was not holding.

In her draft, Justice O'Connor concurred in the Rehnquist opinion in its refusal to strike down the challenged statute's public funding provision as well as the provision prohibiting use of public funds, employees, or facilities for abortion "encouraging or counseling" (though she dealt with the latter provision on the ground of mootness, rather than on the merits, as the Rehnquist draft had done–an approach that, we saw, the Chief Justice was to follow in his final *Webster* opinion).

However, the O'Connor draft categorically refused to agree with the portion of the Rehnquist draft repudiating *Roe* v. *Wade* and concurred only in the judgment upholding the "viability" test provision of the Missouri law. "Unlike the Court," Justice O'Connor wrote, "I do not understand these viability testing requirements to conflict with any of the Court's past decisions concerning state regulation of abortion." That being the case, "there is no necessity to accept the . . . invitation to reexamine the constitutional validity of *Roe* v. *Wade*." In such a case, the Court should follow the "venerable principle" that a constitutional question should not be decided "unless absolutely necessary to decision of the case." Referring to the Rehnquist draft, O'Connor wrote, "No reason is offered for departing from this 'fundamental rule of judicial restraint,' . . . and I would not do so in a case of such constitutional moment. When the constitutional invalidity of a State's abortion statute actually turns on the constitutional validity of *Roe* v. *Wade*, there will be time enough to reexamine *Roe*. And to do so carefully."

Justice O'Connor contended that the viability test requirement could be upheld "even apart from *Roe*'s trimester framework which I continue to consider problematic,"—she had written "outmoded" in the typed draft of her opinion, but now replaced it with the less pejorative "problematic." Either way, she concluded, "It is clear to me that requiring the performance of examinations and tests useful to determining whether a fetus is viable, when viability is possible, and when it would not be medically imprudent to do so, does not impose an undue burden on a woman's abortion decision. On this ground alone I would reject the suggestion that § 188.029 as interpreted is unconstitutional."

In O'Connor's view, this meant that this case "cannot provide a basis for reevaluating *Roe*." On this—the crucial aspect of the Rehnquist draft—the Chief Justice's opinion had now apparently lost its majority.

On June 26, the Rehnquist draft received a further blow. Justice Scalia circulated a short opinion, reprinted on page 326, "concurring in part and concurring in the judgment." The Scalia draft agreed with Justice Blackmun that the Rehnquist opinion "effectively would overrule *Roe* v. *Wade*." Scalia wrote, "I think that should be done, but would do it more explicitly." The Rehnquist draft was "finessing *Roe*" and on this Justice Scalia refused to go along. "I concur in the judgment of the Court," the Scalia opinion concluded, "and strongly dissent from the manner in which it has been reached."

Assaulted from the left (by the Blackmun draft dissent, joined by Justices Brennan and Marshall), the center (Justice O'Connor), and the right (Justice Scalia), Chief Justice Rehnquist now struggled to secure a majority. First, he sought to answer the Blackmun dissent. A third Rehnquist draft, circulated June 26, conceded, "Our holding today will allow some governmental regulation of abortion that would have been prohibited." On the other hand, the Chief Justice asserted, Blackmun's warning that the states "will treat our holding today as an invitation to enact abortion regulation reminiscent of the dark ages not only misreads our holding but does scant justice to those who serve in such bodies and the people who elect them."

On June 27, Chief Justice Rehnquist sent around a fourth draft designed to attract Justice O'Connor. Rehnquist incorporated some of the points in O'Connor's draft—particularly, as indicated, her refusal to rule on the viability testing provision because of mootness. "Sandra has indicated that she had no objection to such modest plagiarism," Rehnquist wrote in his covering memo.

The Rehnquist fourth draft still was headed "the opinion of the Court"—indicating that the Chief Justice had not yet given up his hope of getting a majority behind his opinion. The draft also contained the June 29 scheduled announcement date—another suggestion that Rehnquist thought that the decision process was nearing its end.

But the Chief Justice could not reconstitute his majority. A Rehnquist memo to the Justices postponed the *Webster* announcement until July 3. Then, on June 28, Justice O'Connor circulated a new draft that was the first opinion referring to the Rehnquist opinion as a plurality opinion, rather than that of the Court or of a majority. The same day, the final Blackmun dissent was sent around. It changed the word "majority" to "plurality" some forty-five times.

Now Justice Blackmun abandoned his draft's alarmist tone. In his final draft, Blackmun wrote that the plurality opinion did not make "a single, even incremental, change in the law of abortion." The Blackmun final dissent retained much of his sharp draft language, but he deleted the words, "*Roe* no longer survives." And, instead of the passage beginning, "I rue the day," he now wrote, "I fear for the future. I fear for the liberty and equality of the millions of women who have lived and come of age in the 16 years since *Roe* was decided. I fear for the integrity of, and public esteem for, this Court."

The Blackmun dissent's conclusion also deleted the phrase about the "revolution" created by "*Roe*'s passing" and the Court's "very long step backward." Instead, his final dissent concluded, "For today, at least, the law of abortion stands undisturbed. For today, the women of this Nation still retain the liberty to control their destinies. But the signs are evident and very ominous, and a chill wind blows."

By this point, even Chief Justice Rehnquist recognized that his opinion's "wind" would not blow away *Roe* v. *Wade*. On June 29, the Chief Justice circulated his fifth and last draft. Recognizing reality, he finally headed the draft, "CHIEF JUSTICE REHNQUIST announced the judgment of the Court . . . and an opinion with respect to" the portions that challenged *Roe*, in which Justices White and Kennedy joined. The Rehnquist opinion was thus announced on July 3 only as the opinion of a plurality. In his published opinion, the Chief Justice had to modify his earlier draft statement that "we modify and narrow *Roe*." Instead, the final plurality opinion concluded, "[t]o the extent indicated in our opinion, we would modify and narrow *Roe*." As handed down, the Rehnquist *Webster* opinion concluded, not, as the earlier drafts had done, that it narrowed *Roe* (or, as the Blackmun draft dissent had asserted, that it overruled *Roe*), but that the plurality would do so if a later case gave it the opportunity.

Notes

1. 410 U.S. 113 (1973).
2. The other was Justice White.
3. 198 U.S. 45 (1905).
4. 410 U.S. at 155.
5. Id. at 173.
6. Ibid.
7. Id. at 174.
8. *Ferguson* v. *Skrupa*, 372 U.S. 726, 731 (1963).
9. Re: No. 76-811 *Regents of the University of California* v. *Allen Bakke*, Memorandum to the Conference, Nov. 11, 1977.
10. Compare Rehnquist, J., dissenting in *Weber* v. *Aetna Casualty & Surety Co.*, 406 U.S. 164, 179 (1972).
11. *Harris* v. *McCrae*, 448 U.S. 297 (1980).
12. *Trimble* v. *Gordon*, 430 U.S. 762, 779 (1977).
13. 492 U.S. 90 (1989).
14. *Washington Post*, May 23, 1993, p. A1.
15. *West Coast Hotel Co.* v. *Parrish*, 300 U.S. 379, 391 (1937).
16. *Reed* v. *Reed*, 404 U.S. 71, 76 (1971).
17. *Alexander* v. *Fioto*, 430 U.S. 634, 640 (1977).
18. *New Orleans* v. *Dukes*, 427 U.S. 298, 303–304 (1976).
19. Marshall, J., dissenting, in *Massachusetts Board of Retirement* v. *Murgia*, 427 U.S. 307, 319 (1976).
20. See Harlan, J., dissenting, in *Shapiro* v. *Thompson*, 394 U.S. 618, 658 (1969).
21. Marshall, J., supra note 19.
22. *Cabell* v. *Chavez-Salido*, 454 U.S. 432 (1982).
23. The original reads "fundamental interest."

7

Hodgson v. *Minnesota (1990)*: *Roe* Reaffirmed

Before Justice O'Connor refused to go along, Chief Justice Rehnquist's draft opinion of the Court in *Webster* v. *Reproductive Health Services*[1] was the low point for *Roe* v. *Wade*[2] in Supreme Court jurisprudence. Indeed, had the Rehnquist draft retained a majority, it is difficult to disagree with the assertion in Justice Blackmun's draft *Webster* dissent that *Roe* would no longer have survived. In particular, under the Rehnquist draft's new test for an abortion restriction—whether it "reasonably furthers the state's interest in protecting potential human life"—the *Roe* decision would have been virtually eviscerated.

Since Rehnquist was rebuffed in *Webster*, *Roe* has not only survived but been strongly confirmed, despite the efforts of Chief Justice Rehnquist the other way. But it was, to paraphrase what the Duke of Wellington once said of Waterloo, a close-run thing. Had Justice O'Connor joined the Rehnquist draft opinion of the Court in *Webster*, *Roe* would have been relegated to the limbo of discarded decisions.

The abortion issue came before the Court again a year after *Webster* in the 1990 case of *Hodgson* v. *Minnesota*.[3] A Minnesota law provided that no abortion should be performed on a woman under eighteen years of age until at least forty-eight hours after both of her parents had been notified. It further provided that the notice requirement should be effective unless the pregnant minor obtained a court order permitting the abortion to proceed—what the Justices were to term a "judicial bypass procedure."

The case confronted Chief Justice Rehnquist with a virtual Hobson's choice. This time he realized that he definitely did not have the votes for another *Webster*-like attempt. The only alternative was to forego repeating his *Webster* effort, but that meant leaving the leadership role in *Hodgson* to others—notably Justices Stevens, O'Connor, and Kennedy. Unpalatable though that choice might be to a Chief Justice who felt as he did about *Roe* v. *Wade*, it was the only practical course open to Rehnquist.

The postargument *Hodgson* conference took place on December 1, 1989. A bare majority voted to uphold both provisions of the challenged law (Justices Brennan, Marshall, Blackmun, and Stevens voting the other way). As in

Webster, Justice O'Connor was again to be the key Justice in the case; her votes made it possible for the final decision to come down as it did.

After the conference, there was an interchange between Justices Stevens and O'Connor. The latter had urged, in a memo, that (as explained in a Stevens letter to the Chief Justice on December 7, 1989) "an otherwise unconstitutional parental consent requirement can be saved by a satisfactory judicial bypass procedure [and that] leads inexorably to the conclusion that a bypass will also save an invalid two-parent notification requirement." Justice Stevens wrote, "I am persuaded that the conclusion does not follow."

The Court had previously upheld a *one*-parent consent requirement if the state provided an "alternate procedure," such as a judicial bypass option.[4] Stevens's letter expressed agreement with such a result. "In my judgment," the letter stated, "a single parent consent requirement for any surgical procedure performed on a minor is perfectly reasonable as a general rule, but it constitutes an undue burden if it does not contain an escape hatch for the exceptional case—*e.g.*, a Christian Scientist who will not permit a ruptured appendix to be removed to save a child's life. The absolute veto cannot stand without some form of state authorized bypass."

This was not the case, according to Justice Stevens, with the two-parent notification requirement at issue in *Hodgson*. "It seems to me . . . ," Stevens wrote in his letter, "that a two-parent notification requirement for any surgical procedure would not survive a rational basis test because it is counterproductive in broken family cases and is wholly unnecessary in the ideal family in which, as a practical matter, notice to either parent would constitute notice to both. A child who has one parent's consent to any form of surgery should not be compelled to go to court to obtain relief from a statute that is unconstitutional because it is irrational as applied in most cases."

After she had read Stevens's letter, Justice O'Connor spoke to its author and was apparently convinced by him. On December 8, O'Connor wrote to the Chief Justice about "John's views." "[I]f I understand his approach correctly," O'Connor stated, "I think I can agree with it. This leads me to change my vote to reverse in 88-1125 and still to affirm in 88-1309." This meant that O'Connor was now voting to strike down both provisions of the Minnesota law.

Before O'Connor's switch, Justices Brennan, Marshall, Blackmun, and Stevens had been in dissent and Justice Brennan, the senior among them, had written, "Would you, Harry [Blackmun], take on the dissent?" With O'Connor's changed vote, there was a bare majority to invalidate both of the statute's challenged provisions. Presumably because he had been the catalyst in the construction of the new majority, the opinion was now assigned by Brennan to Justice Stevens.

On February 7, 1990, Justice Stevens circulated the draft opinion of the Court reprinted on page 342. It ruled that both the notice and judicial bypass provisions of the Minnesota law were invalid. As in his December 7 letter, Stevens drew a distinction between a one-parent consent requirement and a statute requiring notice to *both* parents. "We now conclude," the Stevens draft declared, "that the requirement of notice to both of the pregnant minor's parents is not reasonably related to legitimate state interests and that both parts of the statute are unconstitutional."

In the Stevens opinion, the constitutional objection to the two-parent notice requirement was not removed by the judicial bypass option. As the draft put it, "A judicial bypass that is designed to handle exceptions from a reasonable general rule, and thereby preserve the constitutionality of that rule, is quite different from a requirement that a minor—or a minor and one of her parents—must apply to a court for permission to avoid the application of a rule that is not reasonably related to legitimate state goals." The requirement that the bypass procedure must be invoked to avoid the two-parent notice requirement "represents no less of an unjustified governmental intrusion into the family's decisional process" than the notice requirement itself.

1st DRAFT

SUPREME COURT OF THE UNITED STATES

Nos. 88-1125 AND 88-1309

JANE HODGSON, ET AL., PETITIONERS
88-1125 v.
MINNESOTA ET AL.

MINNESOTA, ET AL., PETITIONERS
88-1309 v.
JANE HODGSON ET AL.

ON WRITS OF CERTIORARI TO THE UNITED STATES COURT OF APPEALS FOR THE EIGHTH CIRCUIT

[February ——, 1990]

JUSTICE STEVENS delivered the opinion of the Court.

A Minnesota statute, Minn. Stat. § 144.343(2)–(7) (1989), provides, with certain exceptions, that no abortion shall be performed on a woman under 18 years of age until at least 48 hours after both of her parents have been notified. In subdivisions 2–4 of the statute the notice is mandatory unless (1) the attending physician certifies that an immediate abortion is necessary to prevent the woman's death and there is insufficient time to provide the required notice; (2) both of her parents have consented in writing; or (3) the woman declares that she is a victim of parental abuse or neglect, in which event notice of her declaration must be given to the proper authorities. The United States Court of Appeals for the Eighth Circuit, sitting en banc, unanimously held this provision unconstitutional. In No. 88-1309, we granted the State's petition to review that holding.

Subdivision 6 of the same statute provides that if a court enjoins the enforcement of subdivision 2, the same notice requirement shall be effective unless the pregnant woman obtains a court order permitting the abortion to proceed. By a

HODGSON *v.* MINNESOTA

vote of 7–3, the Court of Appeals upheld the constitutionality of subdivision 6. In No. 88–1125, we granted the plaintiffs' petition to review that holding. We now conclude that the requirement of notice to both of the pregnant minor's parents is not reasonably related to legitimate state interests and that both parts of the statute are unconstitutional.

I

The parental notice statute was enacted in 1981 as an amendment to the Minors' Consent to Health Services Act. The earlier statute, which remains in effect as subdivision 1 of § 144.343 and as § 144.346, had modified the common law requirement of parental consent for any medical procedure performed on minors. It authorized "any minor" to give effective consent without any parental involvement for the treatment of "pregnancy and conditions associated therewith, venereal disease, alcohol and other drug abuse."[1] The statute, unlike others of its age,[2] applied to abortion services.

The 1981 amendment qualified the authority of an "unemancipated minor"[3] to give effective consent to an abortion

---

[1] Subdivision 1 of § 144.343 presently provides:

"Any minor may give effective consent for medical, mental and other health services to determine the presence of or to treat pregnancy and conditions associated therewith, venereal disease, alcohol and other drug abuse, and the consent of no other person is required."

The statute permits the health professional treating the minor to notify parents only when a failure to do so would jeopardize the minor's health. § 144.346.

[2] See Haw. Rev. Stat. § 577A, 577A2 (1971); Mo. Rev. Stat. § 431.062 (1971). See generally Pilpel & Zuckerman, Abortion and the Rights of Minors, in Abortion, Society and the Law 275, 279–280 (1973) (J. Walbert & J. Butler eds.).

[3] Although there is no statutory definition of emancipation in Minnesota, see *Streitz* v. *Streitz*, 363 N. W. 2d 135, 137 (Minn. Ct. App. 1985), we have no reason to question the State's representation that Minn. Stat. §§ 144.341 and 141.342 apply to the minor's decision to abort. Brief for Respondents in No. 88–1125, at p. 2, n. 2. Those sections provide that a minor who is

HODGSON v. MINNESOTA

by requiring that either her physician or an agent notify "the parent" personally or by certified mail at least 48 hours before the procedure is performed.[4] The term "parent" is defined in subdivision 3 to mean "both parents of the pregnant woman if they are both living." No exception is made for a divorced parent, a noncustodial parent, or a biological parent who never married or lived with the pregnant woman's mother. The statute does provide, however, that if only one parent is living, or "if the second one cannot be located through reasonably diligent effort," notice to one parent is sufficient.[5] It also makes exceptions for cases in which emergency treatment prior to notice "is necessary to prevent

---

living separate and apart from her parents or who is either married or has borne a child may give effective consent to medical services without the consent of any other person.

The notification statute also applies to a woman for whom a guardian or conservator has been appointed because of a finding of incompetency. § 144.343(2). This portion of the statute is not challenged in this case.

[4] Subdivision 2 provides:

"Notwithstanding the provisions of section 13.02, subdivision 8, no abortion operation shall be performed upon an unemancipated minor . . . . until at least 48 hours after written notice of the pending operation has been delivered in the manner specified in subdivisions 2 to 4.

"(a) The notice shall be addressed to the parent at the usual place of abode of the parent and delivered personally to the parent by the physician or an agent.

"(b) In lieu of the delivery required by clause (a), notice shall be made by certified mail addressed to the parent at the usual place of abode of the parent with return receipt requested and restricted delivery to the addressee which means postal employee can only deliver the mail to the authorized addressee. Time of delivery shall be deemed to occur at 12 o'clock noon on the next day on which regular mail delivery takes place, subsequent to mailing."

[5] Subdivision 3 provides, in part:

"For purposes of this section, 'parent' means both parents of the pregnant woman if they are both living, one parent of the pregnant women if only one is living or if the second one cannot be located through reasonably diligent effort, or the guardian or conservator if the pregnant woman has one."

HODGSON *v.* MINNESOTA

the woman's death," both parents have already given their consent in writing, or the proper authorities are advised that the minor is a victim of sexual or physical abuse.[6] The statute subjects a person performing an abortion in violation of its terms to criminal sanctions and to civil liability in an action brought by any person "wrongfully denied notification."[7]

Subdivision 6 authorizes a judicial bypass of the two-parent notice requirement if subdivision 2 is ever "temporarily or

---

[6] Subdivision 4 provides:

"No notice shall be required under this section if:

"(a) The attending physician certifies in the pregnant woman's medical record that the abortion is necessary to prevent the woman's death and there is insufficient time to provide the required notice; or

"(b) The abortion is authorized in writing by the person or persons who are entitled to notice; or

"(c) The pregnant minor woman declares that she is a victim of sexual abuse, neglect, or physical abuse as defined in section 626.556. Notice of that declaration shall be made to the proper authorities as provided in section 626.556, subdivision 3."

Under Minn. Stat. § 626.556, if the minor declares that she is the victim of abuse, the notified physician or physician's agent must report the abuse to the local welfare or law enforcement agency within twenty-four hours, § 626.556(3)(a), (3)(e), whereupon the welfare agency "shall immediately conduct an assessment and offer protective social services for purposes of preventing further abuses, safeguarding and enhancing the welfare of the abused or neglected minor, and preserving family life whenever possible." § 626.556(10)(a). If the agency interviews the victim, it must notify the parent of the fact of the interview at the conclusion of the investigation unless it obtains a court order. § 626.556(10)(c). Individuals who are subjects of the investigation have a right of access to the record of the investigation. § 626.556(11).

[7] Subdivision 5 provides:

"Performance of an abortion in violation of this section shall be a misdemeanor and shall be grounds for a civil action by a person wrongfully denied notification. A person shall not be held liable under this section if the person establishes by written evidence that the person relied upon evidence sufficient to convince a careful and prudent person that the representations of the pregnant woman regarding information necessary to comply with this section are bona fide and true, or if the person has attempted with reasonable diligence to deliver notice, but has been unable to do so."

permanently" enjoined by judicial order. If the pregnant minor can convince "any judge of a court of competent jurisdiction" that she is "mature and capable of giving informed consent to the proposed abortion," or that an abortion without notice to both parents would be in her best interest, the court can authorize the physician to proceed without notice. The statute provides that the bypass procedure shall be confidential, that it shall be expedited, that the minor has a right to court-appointed counsel, and that she shall be afforded free access to the court "24 hours a day, seven days a week." An order denying an abortion can be appealed on an expedited basis, but an order authorizing an abortion without notification is not subject to appeal.[8]

---

[8] Subdivision 6 provides:

"If subdivision 2 of this law is ever temporarily or permanently restrained or enjoined by judicial order, subdivision 2 shall be enforced as though the following paragraph were incorporated as paragraph (c) of that subdivision; provided, however, that if such temporary or permanent restraining order or injunction is ever stayed or dissolved, or otherwise ceases to have effect, subdivision 2 shall have full force and effect, without being modified by the addition to the following substitute paragraph which shall have no force or effect until or unless an injunction or restraining order is again in effect.

"(c) (i) If such a pregnant woman elects not to allow the notification of one or both of her parents or guardian or conservator, any judge of a court of competent jurisdiction shall, upon petition, or motion, and after an appropriate hearing, authorize a physician to perform the abortion if said judge determines that the pregnant women is mature and capable of giving informed consent to the proposed abortion. If said judge determines that the pregnant woman is not mature, or if the pregnant woman does not claim to be mature, the judge shall determine whether the performance of an abortion upon her without notification of her parents, guardian or conservator would be in her best interests and shall authorize a physician to perform the abortion without such notification if said judge concludes that the pregnant woman's best interests would be served thereby.

"(ii) Such a pregnant woman may participate in proceedings in the court on her own behalf, and the court may appoint a guardian ad litem for her. The court shall, however, advise her that she has a right to court appointed counsel, and shall, upon her request, provide her with such counsel.

HODGSON *v.* MINNESOTA

The statute contains a severability provision, but it does not include a statement of its purposes. The Minnesota Attorney General has advised us that those purposes are apparent from the statutory text and that they "include the recognition and fostering of parent-child relationships, promoting counsel to a child in a difficult and traumatic choice, and providing for notice to those who are naturally most concerned for the child's welfare."[9] The District Court found that the primary purpose of the legislation was to protect the well-being of minors by encouraging them to discuss with their parents the decision whether to terminate their pregnancies.[10] It also found that the legislature was motivated by a

"(iii) Proceedings in the court under this section shall be confidential and shall be given such precedence over other pending matters so that the court may reach a decision promptly and without delay so as to serve the best interests of the pregnant woman. A judge of the court who conducts proceedings under this section shall make in writing specific factual findings and legal conclusions supporting the decision and shall order a record of the evidence to be maintained including his own findings and conclusions.

"(iv) An expedited confidential appeal shall be available to any such pregnant woman for whom the court denies an order authorizing an abortion without notification. An order authorizing an abortion without notification shall not be subject to appeal. No filing fees shall be required of any such pregnant woman at either the trial or the appellate level. Access to the trial court for the purposes of such a petition or motion, and access to the appellate courts for purposes of making an appeal from denial of the same, shall be afforded such a pregnant woman 24 hours a day, seven days a week."

[9] Brief for Cross-Petitioner State of Minnesota in No. 88–1309 (hereinafter Minn. Br.), p. 4; see also *id.*, at 8–9.

[10] "The Minnesota legislature had several purposes in mind when it amended Minn. Stat. § 144.343 in 1981. The primary purpose was to protect the well-being of minors by encouraging minors to discuss with their parents the decision whether to terminate their pregnancies. Encouraging such discussion was intended to achieve several salutory results. Parents can provide emotional support and guidance and thus forestall irrational and emotional decision-making. Parents can also provide information concerning the minor's medical history of which the minor may not be aware. Parents can also supervise post-abortion care. In addition, par-

HODGSON *v.* MINNESOTA

desire to deter and dissuade minors from choosing to terminate their pregnancies.[11] The Attorney General, however, disclaims any reliance on this purpose.[12]

II

This litigation was commenced on July 30, 1981, two days before the effective date of the parental notification statute. The plaintiffs include two Minnesota doctors who specialize in obstetrics and gynecology, four clinics providing abortion and contraceptive services in metropolitan areas in Minnesota, six pregnant minors representing a class of pregnant minors, and the mother of a pregnant minor. Plaintiffs alleged that the statute violated the Due Process and Equal Protection Clauses of the Fourteenth Amendment and various provisions of the Minnesota Constitution.

Based on the allegations in their verified complaint, the District Court entered a temporary restraining order enjoining the enforcement of subdivision 2 of the statute. After a hearing, the court entered a preliminary injunction which still remains in effect. App. 31. The District Court refused, however, to rule on the validity of the judicial bypass

---

ents can support the minor's psychological sequelae that may attend the abortion procedure." App. to Pet. for Cert. in No. 88-1125, pp. 24a-25a.

[11] The District Court's finding 59 reads as follows:

"The court finds that a desire to deter and dissuade minors from choosing to terminate their pregnancies also motivated the legislature. Testimony before a legislative committee considering the proposed notification requirement indicated that influential supporters of the measure hoped it 'would save lives' by influencing minors to carry their pregnancies to term rather than aborting." *Id.*, p. 25a.

[12] "The court also found that a desire to dissuade minors from choosing to terminate their pregnancies also motivated the legislature. Finding 59, Hodgson Appendix 25a. This finding was based on no more than the testimony before a legislative committee of some supporters of the act who hope it 'would save lives.' There is no direct evidence, however, that this was the motive of any legislator." Minn. Br., at p. 4, n. 2.

HODGSON v. MINNESOTA

procedure in advance of trial.[33]

In 1986, after a five-week trial, the District Court concluded that both the two-parent notification requirement and the 48-hour waiting period were invalid. It further concluded that the definition of the term "parent," which is carried over into the notification requirement, was not severable from the remainder of the statute. The court declared the entire statute unconstitutional and enjoined the defendants from enforcing it.

A three-judge panel of the Court of Appeals affirmed. 827 F. 2d 1191 (1987). The court first held that a compulsory notification requirement is invalid if it does not provide the pregnant minor with the option of an alternative court procedure in which she can demonstrate either her maturity or that performance of an abortion without notification would be in her best interests. App. to Pet. for Cert. 62a. Second, relying heavily on the findings of the District Court concerning the impact of a two-parent notice requirement on families in which the parents are divorced, separated, or unmarried, the panel also concluded that the unconstitutional notification requirement could not be saved by the judicial bypass. The court reasoned that a mature minor and her custodial parent are in a better position than a court to determine whether notifying the noncustodial parent would be in the child's best interests and that they should not be forced to submit to a "Hobson's choice" between an unconstitutional notice requirement and a burdensome court bypass.[34] The panel fur-

[33] On January 23, 1985, the court granted partial summary judgment in favor of defendants on several of the plaintiffs' claims, but reserved ruling on the constitutionality of subdivision 6 as applied until after trial.

[34] "Where the underlying notification provision is unconstitutional because with respect to children of broken families it fails to further the state's significant interests, however, a mature minor or minor whose best interests are contrary to notifying the non-custodial parent is forced to either suffer the unconstitutional requirement or submit to the burdensome court bypass procedure. Such a Hobson's choice fails to further any significant interest. Just as there must be a constitutional judicial alterna-

HODGSON *v.* MINNESOTA

ther held that the two-parent notice requirement was not severable.[15]

The panel opinion was vacated and the Court of Appeals reheard the case en banc. 853 F. 2d 1452 (1988). The court unanimously and summarily rejected the State's submission that the two-parent notice requirement was constitutional without any bypass procedure. *Id.*, at 1456–1457. The majority concluded, however, that subdivision 6 of the statute was valid. It agreed with the District Court that the development of a full factual record may demonstrate that a facially valid statute is "unconstitutional in operation," *id.*, at 1459, and that "the detailed factual findings concerning the general difficulties of obtaining an abortion in Minnesota and the trauma of the bypass procedure, compared to its effectiveness, raise considerable questions about the practical wisdom of this statute." *Ibid.* In the majority's opinion, however, those questions were for the legislature to consider because the statute served valid state interests: the interest in "'encouraging an unmarried pregnant minor to seek the

---

tive to a notice requirement, so there must be a constitutional notice or consent alternative to the court bypass.

"The second reason for our conclusion that the court bypass procedure does not save the two-parent notification requirement is that where the parents are divorced, the minor and/or custodial parent, and not a court, is in the best position to determine whether notifying the non-custodial parent would be in the child's best interests. In situations where the minor has a good relationship with the non-custodial parent but the custodial parent does not, there is nothing to prevent the minor from consulting with the non-custodial parent if she so desires. The minor and custodial parent, however, by virtue of their major interest and superior position, should alone have the opportunity to decide to whom, if anyone, notice of the minor's abortion decision should be given." *Id.*, at 68a–69a (citations omitted).

[15] The panel did not reach the question of the constitutionality or severability of the mandatory 48-hour waiting period. A concurring judge agreed with the panel that a requirement that a pregnant minor seeking an abortion notify a noncustodial parent could not withstand constitutional scrutiny and was not saved by a court bypass procedure. *Id.*, at 72a.

HODGSON *v.* MINNESOTA

help and advice of her parents in making the very important decision whether or not to bear a child,' "[16] as well as the independent interest of the parents in the upbringing of their children.[17]

After noting that the State did not challenge the District Court's findings, *id.*, at 1462, the court concluded that these findings placed undue emphasis on one parent and no parent households. For even though the two-parent notice requirement may not further the interests of the pregnant minor in such cases, the rights of "best-interest" and mature minors were nevertheless protected by the bypass procedure. More importantly, "as applied to all pregnant minors, regardless of their family circumstances, the District Court did not consider whether parental and family interests (as distinguished from the interests of the minor alone) justified the two-parent notice requirement." *Id.*, at 1463. The court wrote:

> "The district court enjoined the entire statute because of the impact of the two-parent notice requirement primarily upon one group of pregnant minors, without considering the effect of the bypass, or the parental and family interests which have been recognized by the Supreme Court. In concentrating upon the impact of the statute on the pregnant minor not living with both parents, and on the mature or non best-interest pregnant minor, the district court gave only limited consideration to the 50% or more pregnant minors who live with both parents and to pregnant minors who are immature and whose best interests may require parental involve-

---

[16] *Id.*, at 1460, quoting from Justice Powell's opinion in *Bellotti* v. *Baird*, 443 U. S. 622, 640–641 (1979) *(Bellotti II)*.

[17] The court also suggested that the statute furthered the "state interest in providing an opportunity for parents to supply essential medical and other information to a physician," 853 F. 2d, at 1461, but the State has not argued here that that interest provides an additional basis for upholding the statute.

> ment. The district court's determination that an undue burden on the one group renders the statute unconstitutional for all is contrary to the Supreme Court's decision that a notice-consent/bypass procedure plainly serves important state interests and is narrowly drawn to protect only those interests. . . . Considering the statute as a whole and as applied to all pregnant minors, the two-parent notice requirement does not unconstitutionally burden the minor's abortion right." *Id.*, at 1464–1465 (citation omitted).

The Court of Appeals also rejected the argument that the 48-hour waiting period imposed a significant burden on the minor's abortion right, finding that the waiting period could run concurrently with the scheduling of an appointment for the procedure. Accordingly, the court reversed the judgment of the District Court without reaching the question of severability.[18]

In dissent, two members of the court criticized the majority for ignoring "the evidence amassed in a five-week trial," for relying on the judicial bypass procedure "to uphold an unconstitutional two-parent notice requirement," and for creating "a new right, apparently of constitutional dimension, for non-custodial parents to receive notice of their minor children's activities." *Id.*, at 1466. One of the dissenters joined a third dissenter in expressing the opinion that "a single-parent notification requirement would withstand constitutional challenge." *Id.*, at 1472.

III

There is a natural difference between men and women: only women have the capacity to bear children. A woman's decision to beget or to bear a child is a component of her lib-

[18] The court also rejected the argument that the statute violated the Equal Protection Clause by singling out abortion as the only pregnancy-related medical procedure requiring notification. *Id.*, at 1466. The equal protection challenge is not renewed here.

HODGSON *v.* MINNESOTA

erty that is protected by the Due Process Clause of the Fourteenth Amendment to the Constitution. See *Carey* v. *Population Servs. International*, 431 U. S. 678, 685, 687 (1977); *Cleveland Board of Education* v. *LaFleur*, 414 U. S. 632, 639–640 (1974); *Roe* v. *Wade*, 410 U. S. 113, 152–153 (1973); *id.*, at 168–170 (Stewart, J., concurring); *Eisenstadt* v. *Baird*, 405 U. S. 438, 453 (1972); *Griswold* v. *Connecticut*, 381 U. S. 479, 502–503 (1965) (WHITE, J., concurring in judgment). That Clause, as interpreted in those cases, protects the woman's right to make such decisions independently and privately, see *Whalen* v. *Roe*, 429 U. S. 589, 598–600, & n. 23 (1977), free of unwarranted governmental intrusion.

> "Moreover, the potentially severe detriment facing a pregnant woman, see *Roe* v. *Wade*, 410 U. S., at 153, is not mitigated by her minority. Indeed, considering her probable education, employment skills, financial resources, and emotional maturity, unwanted motherhood may be exceptionally burdensome for a minor. In addition, the fact of having a child brings with it adult legal responsibility, for parenthood, like attainment of the age of majority, is one of the traditional criteria for the termination of the legal disabilities of minority. In sum, there are few situations in which denying a minor the right to make an important decision will have consequences so grave and indelible." *Bellotti II*, 443 U. S., at 642.

As we stated in *Planned Parenthood of Missouri* v. *Danforth*, 428 U. S. 52, 74 (1976), the right to make this decision "do[es] not mature and come into being magically only when one attains the state-defined age of majority." Thus, the constitutional protection against unjustified state intrusion into the process of deciding whether or not to bear a child extends to pregnant minors as well as adult women.

In cases involving abortion, as in cases involving the right to travel or the right to marry, the identification of the constitutionally protected interest is merely the beginning of the

HODGSON *v.* MINNESOTA

analysis. State regulation of travel and of marriage is obviously permissible even though a State may not categorically exclude nonresidents from its borders, *Shapiro* v. *Thompson*, 394 U. S. 618, 631 (1969), or deny prisoners the right to marry, *Turner* v. *Safly*, 482 U. S. 78, 94–99 (1987). But the regulation of constitutionally protected decisions, such as where a person shall reside or whom he or she shall marry, must be predicated on legitimate state concerns other than disagreement with the choice the individual has made. Cf. *Turner* v. *Safly*, *supra*; *Loving* v. *Virginia*, 388 U. S. 1, 12 (1967). In the abortion area, it is settled that the State has no obligation to spend its own money, or use its own facilities, to subsidize nontherapeutic abortions for minors or adults. See, *e. g.*, *Maher* v. *Roe*, 432 U. S. 464 (1977); cf. *Webster* v. *Reproductive Health Services*, — U. S. —, — (1989) (plurality opinion); *id.*, at — (O'CONNOR, J., concurring in part and concurring in judgment). A State's value judgment favoring childbirth over abortion provides adequate support for decisions involving such allocation of public funds, but not for simply substituting a state decision for an individual decision that a woman has a right to make for herself. Otherwise, the interest in liberty protected by the Due Process Clause would be a nullity. A state policy favoring childbirth over abortion is not in itself a sufficient justification for overriding the woman's decision or for placing "obstacles—absolute or otherwise—in the pregnant woman's path to an abortion." *Maher*, *supra*, at 474; see also *Harris* v. *McRae*, 448 U. S. 297, 315–316 (1980).

In these cases the State of Minnesota does not rest its defense of this statute on any such value judgment. Indeed, it affirmatively disavows that state interest as a basis for upholding this law.[39] Moreover, it is clear that the state judges who have interpreted the statute in over 3,000 decisions implementing its bypass procedures have found no legislative

[39] See *supra* n. 12.

HODGSON *v.* MINNESOTA

intent to disfavor the decision to terminate a pregnancy. On the contrary, in all but a handful of cases they have approved such decisions.[20] Because the Minnesota statute unquestionably places obstacles in the pregnant minor's path to an abortion, the State has the burden of establishing its constitutionality. The Minnesota statute cannot be sustained if the obstacles it imposes are not reasonably related to legitimate state interests. Cf. *Turner* v. *Safly*, 482 U. S., at 97; *Carey* v. *Population Servs. International*, 431 U. S. 678, 704 (1977) (opinion of Powell, J.); *Doe* v. *Bolton*, 410 U. S. 179, 194–195, 199 (1974).

IV

The Court has considered the constitutionality of statutes providing for parental consent or parental notification in six abortion cases decided during the last fourteen years.[21] Although the Massachusetts statute reviewed in *Bellotti I* and *Bellotti II* required the consent of both parents, and the Utah statute reviewed in *Matheson* required notice to both parents, none of the opinions in any of those cases focused on the possible significance of making the consent or the notice requirement applicable to both parents instead of just one. In contrast, the arguments in this case, as well as the extensive findings of the District Court, are directed primarily at that distinction. It is therefore appropriate to summarize these findings before addressing the constitutionality of the 48-

[20] The District Court found:

"During the period for which statistics have been compiled, 3,573 bypass petitions were filed in Minnesota courts. Six petitions were withdrawn before decision. Nine petitions were denied and 3,558 were granted." Finding No. 55, App. to Pet. for Cert. 23a.

[21] *Planned Parenthood of Missouri* v. *Danforth*, 428 U. S. 52, 72–75 (1976); *Bellotti* v. *Baird*, 428 U. S. 132 (1976) (*Bellotti I*); *Bellotti* v. *Baird*, 443 U. S. 622 (1979); *H. L.* v. *Matheson*, 450 U. S. 398 (1981); *Akron* v. *Akron Center for Reproductive Health*, 462 U. S. 416, 439–442 (1983); and *Planned Parenthood Assn.* v. *Ashcroft*, 462 U. S. 476, 490–493 (1983); *id.*, at 505 (O'Connor, J., concurring in judgment in part and dissenting in part).

hour waiting period or the two-parent notification requirement, particularly since none of the findings has been challenged in either this Court or the Court of Appeals.

Approximately one out of every two marriages ends in divorce. App. to Pet. for Cert. 29a. Unrebutted evidence indicates that only 50% of minors in the State of Minnesota reside with both biological parents. *Ibid*; App. 125–126. This conclusion is substantially corroborated by a study indicating that 9% of the minors in Minnesota live with neither parent and 33% live with only one parent. App. to Pet. for Cert. 29a.[22]

The District Court found—on the basis of extensive testimony at trial—that the two-parent notification requirement had particularly harmful effects on both the minor and the custodial parent when the parents were divorced or separated. Relations between the minor and absent parent were not reestablished as a result of the forced notification thereby often producing disappointment in the minor "when an anticipated reestablishment of her relationship with the absent parent d[id] not occur." Moreover, "[t]he reaction of the custodial parent to the requirement of forced notification is often one of anger, resentment and frustration at the intrusion of the absent parent," and fear that notification will threaten the custody rights of the parent or otherwise promote intra-family violence. Tragically, those fears were often realized:

> "Involuntary involvement of the second biological parent is especially detrimental when the minor comes from an abusive, dysfunctional family. Notification of the mi-

[22] The figures are not dissimilar to those throughout the Nation. See, *e. g.*, Brief for *Amici Curiae* American Psychological Assn., et. al., in Nos. 88–1125, 88–1309, at pp. 12–13 ("It is estimated that by age 17, 70 percent of white children born in 1980 will have spent at least some time with only one parent, and 94 percent of black children will have lived in one-parent homes") (citing Hofferth, Updating Children's Life Course, 47 J. Marriage and Fam. 93, 93 (1985)).

HODGSON *v.* MINNESOTA

nors can take advantage of the exception for a minor who declares that she is a victim of sexual or physical abuse because of the obligation to report the information to the authorities and the attendant loss of privacy. See Findings 46 and 47, *id.*, at 21a.[34] This concern about family violence helps to explain why the District Court found that in many instances the requirement that both parents be notified actually impairs family communication. Minors who otherwise would inform one parent were unwilling to do so when such notification likely would also involve the parent in the torturous ordeal of explaining to a court why the second parent should not be notified. The court found:

> "Minors who ordinarily would notify one parent may be dissuaded from doing so by the two-parent requirement. A minor who must go to court for authorization in any event may elect not to tell either parent. In these instances, the requirement that minors notify both

on these statistics, state official suggest that the 'battering' of women by their partners 'has come to be recognized as perhaps the most frequently committed violent crime in the state' of Minnesota. These numbers do not include incidents of psychological or sexual abuse, low-level physical abuse, abuse of any sort of the child of a batterer, or those incidents which are not reported. Many minors in Minnesota live in fear of violence by family members; many of them are, in fact, victims of rape, incest, neglect and violence. It is impossible to accurately assess the magnitude of the problem of family violence in Minnesota because members of dysfunctional families are characteristically secretive about such matters and minors are particularly reluctant to reveal violence or abuse in their families. Thus the incidence of such family violence is dramatically underreported." *Id.*, at 80a.

[34] "Minors who are victims of sexual or physical abuse often are reluctant to reveal the existence of the abuse to those outside the home. More importantly, notification to government authorities creates a substantial risk that the confidentiality of the minor's decision to terminate her pregnancy will be lost. Thus, few minors choose to declare they are victims of sexual or physical abuse despite the prevalence of such abuse in Minnesota, as elsewhere." *Id.*, at 21a.

biological parents actually reduces parent-child communication." *Id.*, at 31a.[25]

The great majority of bypass petitions are filed in the three metropolitan counties in Minnesota, where courts schedule bypass hearings on a regular basis and have in place procedures for hearing emergency petitions. *Id.*, at 18a. Courts in the non-metropolitan areas are acquainted with the statute and, for the most part, apply it conscientiously, but a number of counties are served by judges who are unwilling to hear bypass petitions. *Id.*, at 18a–19a. Aside from the unavoidable notification of court officials, the confidentiality of minors has been maintained. *Id.*, at 20a.

During the period between August 1, 1981 and March 1, 1986, 3,573 judicial bypass petitions were filed in Minnesota courts. All but 15 were granted.[26] The judges who adjudicated over 90% of these petitions testified; none of them identified any positive effects of the law.[27] The court experience

---

[25] As one of the guardians ad litem testified, "We have had situations reported to me by my other guardians as well as teenagers that I talked to myself who have said that they will consider telling one parent, usually mom, sometimes dad, but since they would have to go to court anyway, because they are absolutely sure they don't want the other parent to know, they don't tell either one." App. 239 (Testimony of Susanne Smith).

[26] See *supra* n. 20.

[27] One testified that minors found the bypass procedure "a very nerve-racking experience" finding 60, App. to Pet. for Cert. 25a; another testified that the minor's level of apprehension is twice what I normally see in court." *Ibid.* A Massachusetts judge who heard similar petitions in that State expressed the opinion that "going to court was 'absolutely' traumatic for minors . . . at a very difficult time in their lives." *Ibid.* One judge stated that he did not "perceive any useful public purpose to what I am doing in these cases" and that he did not "see anything that is being accomplished that is useful to anybody." Testimony of Gerald C. Martin, A–488–489.

The public defenders and guardians ad litem gave similar testimony. See Testimony of Cynthia Daly (public defender) App. 187 (bypass "was another hoop to jump through and a very damaging and stress-producing procedure that didn't do any good"); Testimony of Susanne Smith App. 234

HODGSON *v.* MINNESOTA

produced fear, tension, anxiety, and shame among minors, causing some who were mature, and some whose best interests would have been served by an abortion, to "forgo the bypass option and either notify their parents or carry to term." Finding 44 *id.*, at 20a. Among parents who supported their daughters in the bypass proceedings, the court experience evoked similar reactions.[38]

Scheduling petitions in the Minnesota court typically required minors to wait only two or three days for hearings. The District Court found, however, that the statutory waiting period of 48 hours was frequently compounded by a number of other factors that "commonly" created a delay of 72 hours, *id.*, at 22a, and, "in many cases" a delay of a week or more in effecting a decision to terminate a pregnancy. *Id.*, at 23a. A delay of that magnitude increased the medical risk associated with the abortion procedure to "a statistically significant degree." Finding 43 *id.*, at 20a. While recognizing that a mandatory delay following the notice to a minor's par-

---

(guardian ad litem) ("The teenagers that we see in the guardian's office are very nervous, very scared. Some of them are terrified about court processes. They are often exhausted. . . . They are upset about and tell us that they are upset about the fact that they have to explain very intimate details of their personal lives to strangers. They talk about feeling that they don't belong in the court system, that they are ashamed, embarrassed and somehow that they are being punished for the situation they are in"); Testimony of Heather Sweetland (public defender) A–585 ("Most of the women that are my clients in these hearings are scared . . . Some of them will relax slightly but the majority of them are very nervous").

Doctor Hodgson, one of the plaintiffs in this case, testified that when her minor patients returned from the court process, "some of them are wringing wet with perspiration. They're markedly relieved, many of them . . . They—they dread the court procedure often more than the actual abortion procedure. And it—it's frequently necessary to give them a sedative of some kind beforehand." App. 468.

[38] According to the testimony at trial, parents who participated in the bypass procedure—many of whom had never before been in court—were "real upset" about having to appear in court, App. 167, and were "angry, they were worried about their kid and they were nervous too." App. 186.

ent served the State's interest in protecting pregnant minors, the court found that that interest could be served by a shorter waiting period. *Id.*, at 49a.

At least 37 witnesses testified to the issue whether the statute furthered the State's interest in protecting pregnant minors. Only two witnesses testified that a two-parent notification statute did minors more good than harm; neither of these witnesses had direct experience with the Minnesota statute. Summarizing its findings on the question whether the statute as a whole furthered the State's interests, the District Court wrote:

> "Of the remaining witnesses who spoke to the issue whether Minn. Stat. § 144.343 effectuates the State's interest in protecting pregnant minors, all but four of these are personally involved in the statute's implementation in Minnesota. They are judges, public defenders, guardians ad litem, and clinic counselors. None of these witnesses testified that the statute has a beneficial effect upon the minors whom it affects. Some testified the law has a negligible effect upon intra-family communication and upon the minors' decision-making process. Others testified the statute has a deleterious effect on the well-being of the minors to whom it applies because it increases the stress attendant to the abortion decision without creating any corresponding benefit. Thus five weeks of trial have produced no factual basis upon which this court can find that Minn. Stat. § 144.343(2)–(7) on the whole furthers in any meaningful way the State's interest in protecting pregnant minors or assuring family integrity." *Id.*, at 40a–41a.

Focusing specifically on the statutory requirement that both parents be notified, the District Court concluded:

> "The court finds that this requirement places a significant burden upon pregnant minors who do not live with both parents. Particularly in these cases, notification of

HODGSON v. MINNESOTA

an abusive, or even a disinterested, absent parent has the effect of reintroducing that parent's disruptive or unhelpful participation into the family at a time of acute stress. Similarly, the two-parent notification requirement places a significant obstacle in the path of minors in two parent homes who voluntarily have consulted with one parent but not with the other out of fear of psychological, sexual, or physical abuse toward either the minor or the notified parent. In either case, the alternative of going to court to seek authorization to proceed without notifying the second parent introduces a traumatic distraction into her relationship with the parent whom the minor has notified. The anxiety attending either option tends to interfere with and burden the parent-child communication the minor voluntarily initiated with the custodial parent.

. . . . .

"Indeed, 20 to 25% of minors seeking judicial authorization to proceed with an abortion without parental notification are accompanied to court by one parent or at least have obtained the approval of one parent. In these cases the necessity either to notify the second parent despite the agreement of both the minor and the notified parent that such notification is undesirable, or to obtain a judicial waiver of the notification requirement, distracts the minor and her parent and disrupts their communication. Thus the need to notify the second parent or to make a burdensome court appearance actively interferes with the parent-child communication voluntarily initiated by the child, communication assertedly at the heart of the State's purpose in requiring notification of both parents. In these cases, requiring notification of both parents affirmatively discourages parent-child communication." *Id.*, at 46a–47a.

HODGSON *v.* MINNESOTA

V

Three separate but related interests—the interest in the welfare of the pregnant minor, the interest of the parents, and the interest of the family unit—are relevant to our consideration of the constitutionality of the 48-hour waiting period and the two-parent notification requirement.

The State has a strong and legitimate interest in the welfare of its young citizens, whose immaturity, inexperience, and lack of judgment may sometimes impair their ability to exercise their rights wisely. See *Bellotti* v. *Baird*, 443 U. S. 622, 634–639 (1979) (opinion of Powell, J.); *Prince* v. *Massachusetts*, 321 U. S. 158, 166–167 (1944).[a] That interest, which justifies state-imposed requirements that a minor obtain his or her parent's consent before undergoing an operation, marrying, or entering military service, see *Parham* v. *J. R.*, 442 U. S. 584, 603–604 (1979); *Planned Parenthood of Missouri* v. *Danforth*, 428 U. S. 52, 95 (1976) (WHITE, J., dissenting); *id.*, at 102–103 (dissenting opinion), extends also to the minor's decision to terminate her pregnancy. Although the Court has held that parents may not exercise "an absolute, and possibly arbitrary, veto" over that decision, *Danforth*, 428 U. S., at 74, it has never challenged a State's reasonable judgment that the decision should be made after notification to and consultation with a parent. See *Ohio* v. *Akron Center for Reproductive Health*, *post*; *Akron* v. *Akron Center for Reproductive Health*, 462 U. S. 416, 428, n. 10, 439 (1983); *H. L.* v. *Matheson*, 450 U. S. 398, 409–410 (1981);

[a] "Properly understood . . . the tradition of parental authority is not inconsistent with our tradition of individual liberty; rather, the former is one of the basic presuppositions of the latter. Legal restrictions on minors, especially those supportive of the parental role, may be important to the child's chances for the full growth and maturity that make eventual participation in a free society meaningful and rewarding." *Bellotti II*, 443 U. S., at 638–639 (opinion of Powell, J.).

See also *Stanford* v. *Kentucky*, —— U. S. ——, —— (1989) (BRENNAN, J., dissenting); *Thompson* v. *Oklahoma*, —— U. S. ——, ——, n. 23 (1988) (plurality opinion).

HODGSON *v.* MINNESOTA

Bellotti II, 443 U. S., at 640–641 (opinion of Powell, J.); *Danforth*, 428 U. S., at 75. As Justice Stewart, joined by Justice Powell, pointed out in his concurrence in *Danforth*:

> "There can be little doubt that the State furthers a constitutionally permissible end by encouraging an unmarried pregnant minor to seek the help and advice of her parents in making the very important decision whether or not to bear a child." 428 U. S., at 91.

Parents have an interest in controlling the education and upbringing of their children but that interest is "a counterpart of the responsibilities they have assumed." *Lehr* v. *Robertson*, 463 U. S. 248, 257 (1983); see also *Parham*, 442 U. S., at 602 (citing 1 W. Blackstone, Commentaries *447; 2 J. Kent, Commentaries on American Law *190); *Pierce* v. *Society of Sisters*, 268 U. S. 510, 535 (1925). The fact of biological parentage generally offers a person only "an opportunity . . . to develop a relationship with his offspring." *Lehr*, 463 U. S., at 262; see also *Caban* v. *Mohammed*, 441 U. S. 380, 397 (1979) (Stewart, J., dissenting). But the demonstration of commitment to the child through the assumption of personal, financial or custodial responsibility may give the natural parent a stake in the relationship with the child rising to the level of a liberty interest. See *Stanley* v. *Illinois*, 405 U. S. 645, 651 (1972); *Lehr*, 463 U. S., at 261; *Michael H.* v. *Gerald D.*, —— U. S. ——, —— (1989) (WHITE, J., dissenting); cf. *Caban*, 441 U. S., at 393, n. 14. But see *Michael H.*, —— U. S., at —— (plurality opinion).

While the State has a legitimate interest in the creation and dissolution of the marriage contract, see *Sosna* v. *Iowa*, 419 U. S. 393, 404 (1975); *Maynard* v. *Hill*, 125 U. S. 190, 205 (1888), the family has a privacy interest in the upbringing and education of children and the intimacies of the marital relationship which is protected by the Constitution against undue state interference. See *Wisconsin* v. *Yoder*, 406 U. S. 205, 233–234 (1972); *Griswold* v. *Connecticut*, 381 U. S. 479, 495–496 (1965) (Goldberg, J., concurring); *Poe* v. *Ull-*

man, 367 U. S. 497, 551–552 (1961) (Harlan, J., dissenting); *Gilbert* v. *Minnesota*, 254 U. S. 325, 335–336 (1920) (Brandeis, J., dissenting); see also *Michael H.* v. *Gerald D.*, — U. S. —, — (1989) (O'CONNOR, J., concurring in part); *Roberts* v. *United States Jaycees*, 468 U. S. 609, 618–620 (1984); *Cleveland Board of Education* v. *LaFleur*, 414 U. S. 632, 639–640 (1974). The family may assign one parent to guide the children's education and the other to look after their health.[30] "The statist notion that governmental power should supersede parental action in all cases because some parents abuse and neglect children is repugnant to American tradition." *Parham*, 442 U. S., at 603. We have long held that there exists a "private realm of family life which the state cannot enter." *Prince* v. *Massachusetts*, 321 U. S. 158, 166 (1944). Thus, when the government intrudes on choices concerning the arrangement of the household, this Court has carefully examined the "governmental interests advanced and the extent to which they are served by the challenged regulation." *Moore* v. *East Cleveland*, 431 U. S. 494, 499 (1977) (plurality opinion); *id.*, at 507, 510–511 (BRENNAN, J., concurring); see also *Meyer* v. *Nebraska*, 262 U. S. 390, 399–400 (1923).

A natural parent who has demonstrated sufficient commitment to his or her children is thereafter entitled to raise the children free from undue state interference. As JUSTICE WHITE explained in his opinion for the Court in *Stanley* v. *Illinois*, 405 U. S. 645 (1972):

> "The Court has frequently emphasized the importance of the family. The rights to conceive and to raise one's children have been deemed 'essential' *Meyer* v. *Nebraska*, 262 U. S. 390, 399 (1923), 'basic civil rights of man,' *Skinner* v. *Oklahoma*, 316 U. S. 535, 541 (1942),

[30] Under common law principles, one parent has authority to act as agent for the other in matters of their child's upbringing and education. See Spencer, Law of Domestic Relations 432 (1911); Reeve's Domestic Relations 295 (1816).

HODGSON *v.* MINNESOTA

and '[r]ights far more precious . . . than property rights,' *May* v. *Anderson*, 345 U. S. 528, 533 (1953). 'It is cardinal with us that the custody, care and nurture of the child reside first in the parents, whose primary function and freedom include preparation for obligations the state can neither supply nor hinder.' *Prince* v. *Massachusetts*, 321 U. S. 158, 166 (1944). The integrity of the family unit has found protection in the Due Process Clause of the Fourteenth Amendment, *Meyer* v. *Nebraska, supra*, at 399, the Equal Protection Clause of the Fourteenth Amendment, *Skinner* v. *Oklahoma, supra*, at 541, and the Ninth Amendment, *Griswold* v. *Connecticut*, 381 U. S. 479, 496 (1965) (Goldberg, J., concurring)." 405 U. S., at 651.[a]

VI

We think it is clear that a requirement that a minor wait 48 hours after notifying a single parent of her intention to get an abortion would reasonably further the legitimate state interest of ensuring that the minor's decision is knowing and intel-

[a] "Certainly the safeguarding of the home does not follow merely from the sanctity of property rights. The home derives its pre-eminence as the seat of family life. And the integrity of that life is something so fundamental that it has been found to draw to its protection the principles of more than one explicitly granted Constitutional right." *Poe* v. *Ullman*, 367 U. S., at 551–552 (Harlan, J., dissenting).

Far more than contraceptives, at issue in *Poe* and *Griswold*, marital communications have been privileged from undue interference by the State. See, *e. g.*, *Stein* v. *Bowman*, 13 Pet. 209, 223 (1840) ("This rule is founded upon the deepest and soundest principles of our nature. Principles which have grown out of those domestic relations, that constitute the basis of civil society; and which are essential to the enjoyment of that confidence which should subsist between those who are connected by the nearest and dearest relations of life. To break down or impair the great principles which protect the sanctities of husband and wife, would be to destroy the best solace of human existence"); II Best, The Principles of the Law of Evidence 994–995 (1876); 1 Greenleaf on Evidence 286–287 (1866); I Phillips on Evidence 69–80 (1849).

ligent. We have held that when a parent or another person has assumed "primary responsibility" for a minor's well-being, the State may properly enact "laws designed to aid discharge of that responsibility." *Ginsberg* v. *New York*, 390 U. S. 629, 639 (1968). To the extent that subdivision 2 of the Minnesota statute requires notification of only one parent, it does just that. The brief waiting period provides the parent the opportunity to consult with his or her spouse and a family physician, and it permits the parent to inquire into the competency of the doctor performing the abortion, discuss the religious or moral implications of the abortion decision, and provide the daughter needed guidance and counsel in evaluating the impact of the decision on her future. See *Zbaraz* v. *Hartigan*, 763 F. 2d 1532, 1552 (CA7 1985) (Coffey, J., dissenting), *aff'd by an equally divided Court*, —— U. S. —— (1987).

The 48-hour delay imposes only a minimal burden on the right of the minor to decide whether or not to terminate her pregnancy. Although the District Court found that scheduling factors, weather, and the minor's school and work commitments may combine, in many cases, to create a delay of a week or longer between the initiation of notification and the abortion, App. to Pet. for Cert. 22a–23a, there is no evidence that the 48-hour period itself is unreasonable or longer than appropriate for adequate consultation between parent and child. The statute does not impose any period of delay once the parents or a court, acting in loco parentis, express their agreement that the minor is mature or that the procedure would be in her best interest. Indeed, as the Court of Appeals noted and the record reveals,[a] the 48-hour waiting period may run concurrently with the time necessary to make

[a] The record contains the telephone training manual of one clinic which contemplates that notification will be made on the date the patient contacts the clinic to arrange an abortion so that the appointment can be scheduled for a few days later. Since that clinic typically has a one to two day backlog, App. 146–147, the statutory waiting period creates little delay.

HODGSON *v.* MINNESOTA

an appointment for the procedure, thus resulting in little or no delay.[*]

VII

It is equally clear that the requirement that *both* parents be notified, whether or not both wish to be notified or have assumed responsibility for the upbringing of the child, does not reasonably further any legitimate state interest. The usual justification for a parental consent or notification provision is that it supports the authority of a parent who is presumed to act in the minor's best interest and thereby assures that the minor's decision to abort is knowing, intelligent and deliberate. That interest is fully served by a requirement that the minor notify one parent who can then seek the counsel of his or her mate or any other party, when such advice and support is needed to help the child make a difficult decision. Of course, in the ideal family setting, notice to either parent would normally constitute notice to both. But in many families it would not. In those cases there is no reason to question one parent's judgment that notice to the other parent would not assist the minor or to presume that the parent who has assumed parental duties is incompetent to make decisions regarding the health and welfare of the child. By

---

[*] *Akron* v. *Akron Center for Reproductive Health*, 462 U. S. 416, 449 (1984), upon which the plaintiffs rely, is not to the contrary. There we invalidated a provision that required that mature women, capable of consenting to an abortion, wait 24 hours after giving consent before undergoing an abortion. The only legitimate state interest asserted was that the "woman's decision be informed." *Id.*, at 450. We decided that "if a woman, after appropriate counseling, is prepared to give her written informal consent and proceed with the abortion, a State may not demand that she delay the effectuation of that decision." *Id.*, at 450–451. By contrast, in this case, the State asserts a legitimate interest in protecting minor women from their own immaturity. As we explain in the text, the right of the minor to make an informed decision to terminate her pregnancy is not defeated by the 48-hour waiting period. It is significant that the statute does not impose a waiting period if a substitute *competent* decisionmaker—a parent or court—gives affirmative consent to the abortion.

decreeing otherwise, the two-parent notification provision requires the participation in the decisionmaking process of a person whose advice is not wanted and, presumptively, does not further advance the child's best interest.

The record reveals that in the thousands of dysfunctional families affected by this statute, the two-parent notice requirement proved positively harmful to the minor and her family. The testimony at trial established that this requirement, ostensibly designed for the benefit of the minor, resulted in major trauma to the child, and often to a parent as well. In some cases, the parents were divorced and the second parent did not have custody or otherwise participate in the child's upbringing. App. 244–245; *id.*, at 466; *id.*, at 115. In these circumstances, the privacy of the parent and child was violated, even when they suffered no other physical or psychological harm. In other instances, however, the second parent had either deserted or abused the child, *id.* 462, 464, had died under tragic circumstances, *id.*, at 120–121, or was not notified because of the considered judgment that notification would inflict unnecessary stress on a parent who was ill. *Id.*, at 204, 465.[34] In these circumstances, the stat-

[34] The most common reason for not notifying the second parent was that that parent was a child or spouse-batterer, *id.*, at 204, and notification would have provoked further abuse. For example, Judge Allen Oleisky, whose familiarity with the Minnesota statute is based on his having heard over 1000 petitions from minors, *id.*, at 154, testified that battering is a frequent crime in Minnesota, that parents seek an exemption from the notification requirement because they have been battered or are afraid of assault, and that notification of the father would "set the whole thing off again in some cases." *Id.*, at 166–167. See also *id.*, at 237; *id.*, at 245; *id.*, at 339.

That testimony is confirmed by the uncontradicted testimony of one of plaintiffs' experts that notice of a daughter's pregnancy "would absolutely enrage [a batterer]. It would be much like showing a red cape to a bull. That kind of information just plays right into his worst fears and his most vulnerable spots. The sexual jealousy, his dislike of his daughter going out with anybody else, would make him very angry and would probably

HODGSON *v.* MINNESOTA

ute was not merely irrelevant but actually counterproductive. The focus on notifying the second parent distracted both the parent and minor from the minor's imminent abortion decision.

The State does not rely primarily on the best interests of the minor in defending this statute. Rather, it argues that, in the ideal family, the minor should make her decision only after consultation with both parents who should naturally be concerned with the child's welfare and that the State has an interest in protecting the independent right of the parents "to determine and strive for what they believe to be best for their children." Minn. Br. 26. Neither of these reasons can justify the two-parent notification requirement. Full communication among all members of a family may well be desirable but cannot be decreed by the State. The State has no more interest in requiring family members to talk with one another than it has in requiring them to live together. In *Moore* v. *East Cleveland*, 431 U. S. 494 (1977), we invalidated a zoning ordinance which "slic[ed] deeply into the family itself," *id.*, at 498, permitting the city to "standardiz[e] its children—and its adults—by forcing all to live in certain narrowly defined family patterns." *Id.*, at 506. Although the ordinance was supported by state interests other than the state interest in substituting its conception of family life for the family's own view, the ordinance's relation to those state interests was too "tenuous" to satisfy constitutional standards. By implication, a state interest in standardizing its children and adults, making the "private realm of family life" conform to some state-designed ideal, is not a legitimate state interest at all. See also *Meyer* v. *Nebraska*, 262 U. S. 390, 399 (1923) (right to establish a home and bring up children may not be interfered with by legislative action which is

---

create severe abuse as well as long term communication difficulties." *Id.*, at 194 (Testimony of Lenore Walker).

without "reasonable relation to some purpose within the competency of the State to effect").[38]

Nor can any state interest in protecting a parent's interest in shaping a child's values and lifestyle overcome the liberty interests of a minor acting with the consent of a single parent or court. See *Bellotti II*, 443 U.S. 622 (1979); *Bellotti I*, 428 U.S. 132 (1976); *Planned Parenthood of Missouri* v. *Danforth*, 428 U. S. 52 (1976). In *Danforth*, the majority identified the only state interest in requiring parental consent as that in "the safeguarding of the family unit and of parental authority" and held that that state interest was insufficient to support the requirement that mature minors receive parental consent. The Court summarily concluded that "[a]ny independent interest that a parent may have in the termination of the minor daughter's pregnancy is no more weighty than the right of privacy of the competent minor mature enough to have become pregnant." 428 U. S., at 75. It necessarily follows that the combined force of the separate interest of one parent and the minor's privacy interest must outweigh the separate interest of the second parent. Indeed, no Member of the Court took issue with the Court's holding that the parent's separate interest could not outweigh the minor's privacy right and none of the dissenting Justices placed any reliance on the notion that the parent has an independent inter-

---

[38] Communications between would-be parents themselves were implicated in *Planned Parenthood of Missouri* v. *Danforth*, 428 U. S. 52 (1976), in which we examined a statute that required spousal consent prior to the performance of an abortion. The statute was justified, by analogy to regulations governing the adoption of children, artificial insemination, and the disposition of an interest in real property, as a permissible protection of the father's *independent* interest in the expectancy of parental rights, see *id.*, at 68; see also *id.*, at 90 (Stewart, J., concurring); *id.*, at 93 (WHITE, J., dissenting), a right that in theory is greater than the *joint* interest in the upbringing of a child. We nonetheless noted that in the ideal family the decision to terminate a pregnancy would be concurred in by both the wife and her husband and held that the state regulation of the wife's right to abortion was unduly burdensome.

HODGSON *v.* MINNESOTA

est in the abortion decision that is worthy of protection. See *id.*, at 94–95 (WHITE, J., concurring in part and dissenting in part); *id.*, at 102–103 (opinion concurring in part and dissenting in part).

In *Bellotti I* and *Bellotti II*, we also identified the difference between parental interests and the child's best interest. Although the District Court invalidated the Massachusetts statute there under review on the grounds that it permitted a parent or the court, acting in loco parentis, to refuse consent based on the parent's own interests, the state Attorney General argued that the parental right consisted "'exclusively of the right to assess independently, for their minor child, what will serve that child's best interest.'" 428 U. S., at 144. Because we believed that the Attorney General's interpretation "would avoid or substantially modify the federal constitutional challenge," *id.*, at 148, we ordered the District Court to certify the state law question to the Supreme Judicial Court of Massachusetts. *Id.*, at 151–152. On review in this Court for the second time, after the Supreme Judicial Court stated unambiguously that the "good cause" standard required the judge to grant consent to an abortion found to be in the minor's best interest, 443 U. S., at 630, 644, we confirmed that such a construction satisfied "some of the concerns" about the statute's constitutionality, *id.*, at 644, and thereby avoided "much of what was objectionable in the statute successfully challenged in *Danforth*." *Id.*, at 645. Indeed, the constitutional defects that Justice Powell identified in the statute—its failure to allow a minor who is found to be mature and fully competent to make the abortion decision independently and its requirement of parental consultation even when an abortion without notification would be in the minor's best interests—are predicated on the assumption that the State may not require a parent's intrusion into the abortion decision when parental involvement would not be in the best interest of the child. 443 U. S., at 651.

HODGSON *v.* MINNESOTA

The Minnesota two-parent notification requirement is an oddity among state and federal consent provisions governing the health, welfare and education of children. A minor desiring to enlist in the armed services or the Reserve Officers' Training Corps (ROTC) need only obtain the consent of "his parent or guardian." 10 U. S. C. § 505(a); 2104(b)(4); 2107(2)(4). The consent of "*a* parent or guardian" is also sufficient to obtain a passport for foreign travel from the United States Department of State, 22 CFR § 51.27 (1988), and to participate as a subject in most forms of medical research. 45 CFR §§ 46.404, 46.405 (1988). In virtually every State, the consent of one parent is enough to obtain a driver's license or operator's permit. The same may be said with respect to the decision to submit to any medical or surgical procedure other than an abortion.[38] Indeed, the only other Minnesota statute that the State has identified which requires two-parent consent is that authorizing the minor to change his name. Tr. of Oral Arg. 30, 32; Reply Brief of Minn. in 88–1309, p. 5 (citing Minn. Stat. § 259.10). These statutes provide testimony to the unreasonableness of the Minnesota two-parent notification requirement and to the ease with which the State can adopt less burdensome means to protect the minor's welfare. Cf. *Clark* v. *Jeter*, 486 U. S. 456, 464 (1988).

We therefore reject the plaintiffs' argument in No. 88–1125 that a 48-hour bypass is necessarily unconstitutional but hold that subdivision 2 of § 144.343 violates the Constitution insofar as it requires two-parent notification. We thus affirm the judgment of the Court of Appeals in No. 88–1309.

---

[38] See, *e. g.*, Brief for *Amici Curiae* American Psychological Assn. in Nos. 88–1125, 88–1309, at p. 6, n. 8 (state law typically allows a minor parent—whatever her age—to consent to the health care of her child); Brief of the American College of Obstetricians and Gynecologists, et al., as *Amici Curiae* in No. 88–1309 ("In areas that do not deal with sexuality or substance abuse, states require, at most, a single parent's consent before performing medical procedures on a minor").

HODGSON *v.* MINNESOTA

VIII

The question which remains is whether the constitutional objection to the two-parent notice requirement is removed by the judicial bypass option provided in subdivision 6 of the Minnesota statute. A majority of the Court has previously held that a statute requiring one parent's consent to a minor's abortion will be upheld if the State provides an "alternate procedure whereby a pregnant minor may demonstrate that she is sufficiently mature to make the abortion decision herself or that, despite her immaturity, an abortion would be in her best interests." *Planned Parenthood Assn.* v. *Ashcroft*, 462 U. S. 476, 491 (1983) (opinion of Powell, J.); *id.*, at 505 (opinion of O'CONNOR, J.). Indeed, in *Bellotti II*, four Members of the Court expressed the same opinion about a statute requiring the consent of both parents. See 443 U. S., at 643–644. As we shall explain, however, neither of those precedents controls our decision today.

In *Bellotti II*, eight Members of the Court joined the judgment holding the Massachusetts statute unconstitutional. Thus, the Court did not *hold* that the judicial bypass set forth in that statute was valid; it held just the opposite. Moreover, the discussion of the minimum requirements for a valid judicial bypass in Justice Powell's opinion was joined by only four Members of the Court. Indeed, neither the arguments of the parties, nor any of the opinions in the case, considered the significant difference between a statute requiring the involvement of *both* parents in the abortion decision and a statute that merely requires the involvement of one. Thus, while we adhere to the relevant legal standards articulated in Justice Powell's opinion, the doctrine of *stare decisis* does not require that those standards be applied to a statute that mandates the involvement of both parents.

Unlike *Bellotti II*, the judgment in *Ashcroft* sustained the constitutionality of the statute containing a judicial bypass as an alternative to the requirement of *one* parent's consent to a minor's abortion. The distinctions between notice and consent and between notification of both parents rather than just one arguably constitute a sufficient response to an argument resting on *stare decisis*. Further analysis is necessary, however, because, at least on the surface, the consent requirement would appear to be more onerous than a requirement of mere notice.

The significance of the distinction between a statute requiring the consent of one parent and a statute requiring notice to both parents must be tested by the relationship of the respective requirements to legitimate state interests. We have concluded that the State has a strong and legitimate interest in providing a pregnant minor with the advice and support of a parent during the decisional period. A general rule requiring the minor to obtain the consent of one parent reasonably furthers that interest. An exception from the general rule is necessary to protect the minor from an arbitrary veto that is motivated by the separate concerns of the parent rather than the best interest of the child. Cf. *Parham* v. *J. R.*, 442 U. S. 584, 604–608 (1979). But the need for such an exception does not undermine the conclusion that the general rule is perfectly reasonable—just as a rule requiring the consent of either parent for any other medical procedure would surely be reasonable if an exception was made for those emergencies in which, for example, a parent might deny life saving treatment to a child on religious grounds. See *id.*, at 602–603.

For reasons that we have already set forth at length, a rule requiring consent or notification of both parents is not reasonably related to the state interest in giving the pregnant minor the benefit of parental advice. The State has not called our attention to, nor are we aware of, any other medical situation in Minnesota or elsewhere in which the provision of treatment for a child has been conditioned on notice to, or consent by, both parents rather than just one. Indeed, the fact that one-parent consent is the virtually uniform rule for any other activity which affects the minor's health, safety or

HODGSON *v.* MINNESOTA

welfare emphasizes the aberrant quality of the two-parent notice requirement.

A judicial bypass that is designed to handle exceptions from a reasonable general rule, and thereby preserve the constitutionality of that rule, is quite different from a requirement that a minor—or a minor and one of her parents—must apply to a court for permission to avoid the application of a rule that is not reasonably related to legitimate state goals. A requirement that a minor acting with the consent of *both* parents apply to a court for permission to effectuate her decision clearly would constitute an unjustified official interference with the privacy of the minor and her family. The requirement that the bypass procedure must be invoked when the minor and one parent agree that the other parent should not be notified represents no less of an unjustified governmental intrusion into the family's decisional process. When the parents are living together and have joint custody over the child, the State has no legitimate interest in the communication between father and mother about the child. "[W]here the parents are divorced, the minor and/or custodial parent, and not a court, is in the best position to determine whether notifying the non-custodial parent would be in the child's best interests." App. to Pet. for Cert. at 69a. We therefore agree with the panel's conclusion that the "minor and custodial parent, however, by virtue of their major interest and superior position, should alone have the opportunity to decide to whom, if anyone, notice of the minor's abortion decision should be given. *See id.* Accordingly, we conclude that the unconstitutional notice provisions in Minn. Stat. Ann. § 144.343(2)–(7) are not saved by the presence in the statute of an alternative court bypass procedure." *Ibid.*

IX

The District Court and the three-judge panel of the Court of Appeals both held that the two-parent notification requirement is not severable from the remainder of the statute. It

HODGSON *v.* MINNESOTA

is not our practice to review the construction of a state statute that has been embraced by both the District Court and the Court of Appeals. See *Bishop* v. *Wood*, 426 U. S. 341, 346 (1976). In this case, however, the panel opinion was vacated and the en banc opinion of the Court of Appeals did not reach the question of severability because it sustained subdivision 7 of § 144.343. In this circumstance, rather than addressing the merits of the severability question ourselves, we leave that issue open for such consideration as the Court of Appeals deems appropriate on remand. Accordingly, in No. 88–1125, the judgment is reversed and the case is remanded for further proceedings consistent with this opinion.

It is so ordered.

1st DRAFT

SUPREME COURT OF THE UNITED STATES

Nos. 88-1125 AND 88-1309

88-1125 JANE HODGSON, ET AL., PETITIONERS
v.
MINNESOTA ET AL.

88-1309 MINNESOTA, ET AL., PETITIONERS
v.
JANE HODGSON ET AL.

ON WRITS OF CERTIORARI TO THE UNITED STATES COURT OF APPEALS FOR THE EIGHTH CIRCUIT

[June ——, 1990]

JUSTICE O'CONNOR, concurring, concurring in the judgment, and dissenting.

I join all but Parts III and VIII of the Court's opinion. While I agree with some of the central points made in Part III, I cannot join the broader discussion. I agree that the Court has characterized "[a] woman's decision to beget or to bear a child [as] a component of her liberty that is protected by the Due Process Clause of the Fourteenth Amendment to the Constitution." *Ante*, at 12. See, *e. g.*, *Carey* v. *Population Services International*, 431 U. S. 678, 685, 687 (1977); *Griswold* v. *Connecticut*, 381 U. S. 479, 502–503 (1965) (WHITE, J., concurring). This Court extended that liberty interest to minors in *Bellotti* v. *Baird*, 443 U. S. 622, 642 (1979) *(Bellotti II)*, and *Planned Parenthood of Central Missouri* v. *Danforth*, 428 U. S. 52, 74 (1976), albeit with some important limitations: "[P]arental notice and consent are qualifications that typically may be imposed by the State on a minor's right to make important decisions. As immature minors often lack the ability to make fully informed choices that take account of both immediate and long-range consequences,

HODGSON *v.* MINNESOTA

a State reasonably may determine that parental consultation often is desirable and in the best interest of the minor." *Bellotti II*, *supra*, at 640–641; see also *H. L.* v. *Matheson*, 450 U. S. 398, 423 (1981) (STEVENS, J., concurring); cf. *Thompson* v. *Oklahoma*, 108 S. Ct. 2687, 2692–2695 (1988) ("Inexperience, less education, and less intelligence make the teenager less able to evaluate the consequences of his or her conduct while at the same time he or she is much more apt to be motivated by mere emotion or peer pressure than is an adult"); *Stanford* v. *Kentucky*, 109 S. Ct. 2969, 2988 (1989) (BRENNAN, J., dissenting) ("[M]inors are treated differently from adults in our laws, which reflects the simple truth derived from communal experience, that juveniles as a class have not the level of maturation and responsibility that we presume in adults and consider desirable for full participation in the rights and duties of modern life").

It has been my understanding in this area that "[i]f the particular regulation does not 'unduly burde[n]' the fundamental right, then our evaluation of that regulation is limited to our determination that the regulation rationally relates to a legitimate state purpose." *Akron* v. *Akron Center for Reproductive Health*, 462 U. S. 416, 453 (1983) (O'CONNOR, J., dissenting); see also *Webster* v. *Reproductive Health Services*, 109 S. Ct. 3040, 3063 (1989) (O'CONNOR, J., concurring). It is with that understanding that I agree with the Court's statement that the "statute cannot be sustained if the obstacles it imposes are not reasonably related to legitimate state interests. Cf. *Turner* v. *Safley*, 482 U. S., at 97; *Carey* v. *Population Services Internationa* 431 U. S., at 704 (opinion of Powell, J.); *Doe* v. *Bolton*, 410 U. S. 179, 194–195, 199 (1973)." *Ante*, at 15.

I agree with the Court that Minnesota has offered no sufficient justification for its interference with the family's decisionmaking processes created by subdivision 2—two-parent notification. Subdivision 2 is the most stringent notification statute in the country. See *ante*, at 3 n. 5. The only other

HODGSON *v.* MINNESOTA

state that defines the generic term "parents," see, *e. g.*, Tenn. Code Ann. 36–1–201, Tit. III (6) (Supp. 1989) (adoption statute) ("'Parents' means either the singular or plural of the word 'parent'"); see also *ante*, at 15 n. 23, as "both parents" is Arkansas, and that statute provides for numerous exceptions to the two-parent notification requirement and permits bypassing notification where notification would not be in the best interests of the minor. See Ark. Code §§ 20–16–802, 804, 808 (Supp. 1989).

The Minnesota exception to notification for minors who are victims of neglect or abuse is, in reality, a means of notifying the parents. As the Court points out, see *ante*, at 5 n. 7, to avail herself of the neglect or abuse exception, the minor must report the abuse. A report requires the welfare agency to immediately "conduct an assessment." Minn. Stat. § 662.556(10)(a) (1988). If the agency interviews the victim, it must notify the parent of the fact of the interview; if the parent is the subject of an investigation, he has a right of access to the record of the investigation. §§ 626.556 (10)(c); 626.556(11); see also Oral Argument Transcript, at 19 ("[I]t turns out that the reporting statute in Minnesota requires that after it's reported to the welfare department, the welfare department has to do an assessment and tell the parents about the assessment. This could all be done in a time frame even before the abortion occurs"). The combination of the abused minor's reluctance to report sexual or physical abuse, see *ante*, at 18 n. 26, with the likelihood that invoking the abuse exception for the purpose of avoiding notice will result in notice, makes the abuse exception less than effectual.

Minnesota's two-parent notice requirement is all the more unreasonable when one considers that only half of the minors in the state of Minnesota reside with both biological parents. See *ante*, at 16. A third live with only one parent. *Ibid.* Given its broad sweep and its failure to serve the purposes asserted by the State in too many cases, I join the Court's striking of subdivision 2. I cannot join, however, the

Court's conclusion that subdivision 6—two-parent notification plus judicial bypass—fails to pass constitutional muster.

In a series of cases, this Court has explicitly approved judicial bypass as a means of tailoring a parental consent provision so as to avoid unduly burdening the minor's limited right to obtain an abortion. See *Bellotti* v. *Baird*, 428 U. S. 132, 147–148 (1976); *Planned Parenthood of Missouri* v. *Danforth*, 428 U. S. 52 (1976); *Bellotti* v. *Baird*, 443 U. S. 622, 642–644 (1979). In *Danforth*, the Court stated that the

> "primary constitutional deficiency lies in [the notification statute's] imposition of an absolute limitation on the minor's right to obtain an abortion. . . . [A] materially different constitutional issue would be presented under a provision requiring parental consent or consultation in most cases but providing for prompt (i) judicial resolution of any disagreement between the parent and the minor, or (ii) judicial determination that the minor is mature enough to give an informed consent without parental concurrence or that abortion in any event is in the minor's best interest. Such a provision would not impose parental approval as an absolute condition upon the minor's right but would assure in most instances consultation between the parent and child." 428 U. S., at 90–91.

Subdivision 6 passes constitutional muster because the interference with the internal operation of the family required by subdivision 2 simply does not exist where the minor can avoid notifying one or both parents by use of the bypass procedure.

1st DRAFT

SUPREME COURT OF THE UNITED STATES

Nos. 88-1125 AND 88-1309

JANE HODGSON, ET AL., PETITIONERS
88-1125 *v.*
MINNESOTA ET AL.

MINNESOTA, ET AL., PETITIONERS
88-1309 *v.*
JANE HODGSON ET AL.

ON WRITS OF CERTIORARI TO THE UNITED STATES COURT OF APPEALS FOR THE EIGHTH CIRCUIT

[March ——, 1990]

JUSTICE MARSHALL, concurring in the judgment in part and dissenting in part.

I concur in the Court's judgment that Minnesota's two-parent notification requirement is unconstitutional. I cannot join any part of the Court's opinion, however, because even in striking down portions of the statute, the Court eschews the strict scrutiny we have applied to governmental restrictions on procreative freedom for more than two decades. See, *e. g.*, *Griswold* v. *Connecticut*, 381 U. S. 479, 485 (1965); *id.*, at 497–498 (Goldberg, J., concurring). Instead, the Court inexplicably employs language suggesting a more relaxed standard. By asking only whether the statute's restrictions on abortion are "reasonably related to legitimate state interests," *ante*, at 2, the Court continues its steady erosion of a woman's fundamental constitutional right to control her reproductive destiny without interference from the State.

I also concur in the Court's judgment that the availability of the judicial bypass option does not save the two-parent notification requirement. I do not join part VIII of the Court's opinion, however, because I do not think resolution of this question depends on whether the notification requirement is "a reasonable general rule." *Id.*, at 35. Instead, the bypass procedure cannot save the notification requirement because the bypass itself is unconstitutional both on its face and as applied.

I dissent from the Court's decision in part VI that the *one*-parent notification and 48-hour delay requirements, when coupled with a judicial bypass procedure, are constitutional. *Id.*, at 26–27, and n. 33. At the very least, this scheme substantially burdens a woman's right to privacy without advancing a compelling state interest. More significantly, in some instances it usurps a young woman's control over her own body by giving either a parent or a court the power effectively to veto her decision to have an abortion.

I

This Court has consistently held since *Roe* v. *Wade*, 410 U. S. 113 (1973), that the constitutional right of privacy "is broad enough to encompass a woman's decision whether or not to terminate her pregnancy." *Id.*, at 153. We have also repeatedly stated that "[a] woman's right to make that choice freely is fundamental." *Thornburgh* v. *American College of Obstetricians and Gynecologists*, 476 U. S. 747, 772 (1986). Accord *Akron* v. *Akron Center for Reproductive Health, Inc.*, 462 U. S. 416, 420, n. 1 (1983); *Roe, supra*, at 155. As we reiterated in *American College of Obstetricians and Gynecologists, supra*, "Few decisions are more personal and intimate, more properly private, or more basic to individual dignity and autonomy, than a woman's decision—with the guidance of her physician and within the limits specified in *Roe*—whether to end her pregnancy." *Id.*, at 772. Accordingly, we have subjected state laws limiting that right to the most exacting scrutiny, requiring a State to show that such a law is narrowly drawn to serve a compelling interest. *Roe, supra*, at 155; *Akron Center for Reproductive Health, supra*,

HODGSON *v.* MINNESOTA

at 427. Only such strict judicial scrutiny is sufficiently protective of a woman's right to make the intensely personal decision whether to terminate her pregnancy.

Roe remains the law of the land. See *Webster* v. *Reproductive Health Servs.*, —— U. S. ——, —— (1989) (plurality opinion); *id.*, at —— (O'CONNOR, J., concurring in part and concurring in the judgment); *id.*, at —— (BLACKMUN, J., concurring in part and dissenting in part). Accordingly, to be constitutional, state restrictions on abortion must meet the rigorous test set forth above. It is therefore deeply disturbing that the Court uses language that suggests a more relaxed standard of review,[1] as though a woman's right to control her own body were no more important than an optician's freedom to fit customers' eyeglasses without a prescription, see *Williamson* v. *Lee Optical of Oklahoma, Inc.*, 348 U. S. 483, 488 (1955). Cf. *American College of Obstetricians and Gynecologists*, *supra*, at 775 (STEVENS, J., concurring) ("[T]he freedom from unwarranted governmental intrusion into individual decisions in matters of childbearing . . . comes to this Court with a momentum for respect that is lacking when appeal is made to liberties which derive merely from shifting economic arrangements") (citation omitted).

II

I agree with the Court's conclusion in part VII of its opinion that the two-parent notification requirement is unconstitutional. As the Court holds, that requirement would not withstand even a relaxed level of scrutiny because it does not

[1] See, *e. g.*, *ante*, at 2 ("We now conclude that the requirement of notice to both of the pregnant minor's parents is not reasonably related to legitimate state interests"); *id.*, at 14 ("The Minnesota statute cannot be sustained if the obstacles it imposes are not reasonably related to legitimate state interests"); *id.*, at 26 (stating that requirement of 48-hour delay after notifying one parent "would reasonably further the legitimate state interest of ensuring that the minor's decision is knowing and intelligent"); *id.*, at 27 (holding that two-parent notification requirement "does not reasonably further any legitimate state interest").

reasonably further any legitimate state interest. *Ante*, at 27. Therefore, the requirement surely fails to satisfy the strict scrutiny applicable to a burden on a fundamental right.

III

I strongly disagree, however, with the Court's conclusion in part VI of its opinion that the State may constitutionally force a minor woman to choose between notifying one parent and then waiting 48 hours before proceeding with an abortion, and disclosing her intimate affairs to a judge and asking that he grant her permission to have an abortion.[2] First, the one-parent notification and delay requirements significantly restrict a young woman's right to reproductive choice. I base my conclusion not on my intuition about the needs and attitudes of young women, but on a sizable and impressive collection of empirical data documenting the effects of parental notification statutes and of delaying an abortion. Second, the burdensome restrictions are not narrowly tailored to serve any compelling state interest. Finally, for the reasons discussed in part IV, *infra*, the judicial bypass procedure does not save the notice and delay requirements.

A

As the Court acknowledges, neither the scope of a woman's privacy right nor the magnitude of a law's burden is diminished because a woman is a minor, *ante*, at 12–13; rather, a woman's minority status affects only the nature of the State's

[2] The statute provides for one-parent notification where only one parent is living or where the second parent "cannot be located through reasonably diligent effort." Minn. Stat. § 144.343(3) (1988). I read part VI of the Court's opinion as upholding the one-parent notification requirement in these instances. The Court's logic would appear to extend to a hypothetical statute that requires only one-parent notification. Such a statute, however, is not before us, as the Court expressly declines to decide whether the Minnesota provision defining "parent" as "both parents" in most instances is severable from the rest of the Minnesota statute. *Ante*, at 36.

HODGSON *v.* MINNESOTA

interests. Yet the Court upholds the one-parent notification requirement without considering its effects on a minor woman's exercise of her right to privacy. In fact, many of the burdens recognized by the Court as resulting from the two-parent notification requirement also flow from the one-parent notification requirement.

A substantial proportion of pregnant minors voluntarily consult with a parent regardless of the existence of a notification requirement. See, *e. g.*, Torres, Forrest, and Eisman, Telling Parents: Clinic Policies and Adolescents' Use of Family Planning and Abortion Services, 12 Family Planning Perspectives 284, 287, 288, 290 (1980) (51% of minors discussed abortion with parents in the absence of a parental consent or notification requirement). Minors 15 years old or younger are even more likely voluntarily to discuss the abortion decision with their parents. *Id.*, at 290 (69% of such minors voluntarily discuss abortion with parents). For these women, the notification requirement by itself does not impose a significant burden. But for those young women who would choose not to inform their parents, the burden is evident: the notification requirement destroys their right to avoid disclosure of a deeply personal matter. Cf. *Whalen* v. *Roe*, 429 U. S. 589, 599–600 (1977).

A notification requirement can also have severe physical and psychological effects on a young woman. First, forced notification of one parent can be just as traumatic as notification of both parents, depending on the nature of the woman's relationship with her parents. Cf. *ante*, at 28–29. The disclosure of a daughter's intention to have an abortion often leads to a family crisis, characterized by severe parental anger and rejection. Osofsky and Osofsky, Teenage Pregnancy: Psychosocial Considerations, 21 Clinical Obstetrics and Gynecology 1161, 1164–1165 (1978). The impact of any notification requirement is especially devastating for minors who live in fear of physical, psychological, or sexual abuse. See, *e. g.*, Clary, Minor Women Obtaining Abortions: A

Study of Parental Notification in a Metropolitan Area, 72 American J. of Pub. Health 283, 284 (1982) (finding that many minors chose not to inform parents voluntarily because of fear of negative consequences such as physical punishment or other retaliation). See also Tr. 911 (testimony of Dr. Elissa Benedek) (stating that usually minors accurately predict parental reaction to news about daughters' pregnancies). Cf. *ante*, at 16–17. Certainly, child abuse is not limited to families with two parents.

Second, the prospect of having to notify a parent causes many young women to delay their abortions, thereby increasing the health risks of the procedure. See Cates, Schulz, and Grimes, The Risks Associated with Teenage Abortion, 309 New England J. of Medicine 621, 623 (1983) (finding that for women 19 years old and younger, the number of deaths per 100,000 abortions was 0.2 for the first 8 weeks of pregnancy, 0.6 for weeks 9–12, 3.4 for weeks 13–16, and 7.8 for week 17 and after). See also *H. L.* v. *Matheson*, 450 U. S. 398, 439 (1981) (MARSHALL, J., dissenting). The risks posed by this delay are especially significant because adolescents already delay seeking medical care until relatively late in their pregnancies, when risks are higher. See 1 National Research Council, Risking the Future: Adolescent Sexuality, Pregnancy and Childbearing 114 (C. Hayes ed. 1987).

In addition, a notification requirement compels many minors to travel to a State without such a requirement for an abortion to avoid notifying a parent. Cartoof and Klerman, Parental Consent for Abortion: Impact of the Massachusetts Law, 76 American J. of Pub. Health 397, 399 (1986) (finding that 1/3 of minors seeking abortions traveled outside of State to avoid Massachusetts's parental notice requirement). Other women may resort to the horrors of self-abortion or illegal abortion rather than tell a parent. Torres, Forrest, and Eisman, *supra*, at 288 (9% of minors attending family planning clinics said they would have a self-induced or an illegal abortion rather then tell a parent); *H. L.* v. *Mathe-*

HODGSON *v.* MINNESOTA

a minor's fear of notifying her parent. Moreover, the 48-hour delay burdens the rights of all minors, including those who would voluntarily consult with their parents.[4] The Court's assertion that the 48-hour delay "imposes only a minimal burden," *ante*, at 26, callously ignores the increased health risks and costs that this delay entails. The District Court specifically found as a matter of fact that "[d]elay of any length in performing an abortion increases the statistical risk of mortality and morbidity." 648 F. Supp. 756, 765 (D Minn 1986). Even a brief delay can have a particularly detrimental impact if it pushes the abortion into the second trimester, when the operation is substantially more risky and costly. *Ibid.* See also C. Teitze & S. Henshaw, Induced Abortion: A World Review 1986, pp. 103–104, 110 (6th ed. 1986). Moreover, the District Court found that the 48-hour delay "frequently is compounded by scheduling factors such as clinic hours, transportation requirements, weather, a minor's school and work commitments, and sometimes a single parent's family and work commitments," often resulting in an effective delay of a week or more. 648 F. Supp., at 765.[5] The increased risk caused by a delay of that magnitude, the District Court found, is statistically significant at any point in the pregnancy. *Ibid.* Certainly no pregnant woman facing these heightened risks to her health would dismiss them as "minimal."[6]

---

[4] As the Court notes, *ante*, at 26, the 48-hour delay does not apply if a parent or court consents to the abortion.

[5] Although these other factors would constrain a young woman's ability to schedule an abortion even in the absence of the 48-hour delay requirement, the addition of the immutable statutory delay reduces both the woman's and the clinic's scheduling flexibility and thus can exacerbate the effect of the other factors. For instance, a woman might contact a clinic on Monday and find that her schedule and the clinic's allow for only a Tuesday appointment for that week. Without the 48-hour delay requirement, the woman could be treated the next day; with the statutory delay, however, the woman would be forced to wait a week.

[6] The Court concludes that the 48-hour delay requirement actually results in "little or no delay" because the statutory period "may run con-

C

Because the one-parent notification and delay requirements burden a young woman's right freely to decide whether to terminate her pregnancy, the State must show that these requirements are justified by a compelling state interest and are closely tailored to further that interest. The main purpose of the notification requirement is to "protect the well-being of minors by encouraging minors to discuss with their parents the decision whether to terminate their pregnancies" *Id.*, at 766. The 48-hour delay, in turn, is designed to provide parents with adequate time to consult with their daughters. *Ante*, at 26. As the Court states, such consultation is intended to ensure that the minor's decision is "knowing and intelligent." *Ibid.* I need not determine whether the State's interest ultimately outweighs young women's privacy interests, however, because the strictures here are not closely tailored to further the State's asserted goal.

For the many young women who would voluntarily consult with a parent before having an abortion, see *supra*, at —, the notification and delay requirements are superfluous, and so do not advance the State's interest. The requirements affect only those women who would not otherwise notify a parent. But compelled notification is unlikely to result in productive consultation in families in which a daughter does not

---

currently with the time necessary to make an appointment for the procedure." *Ante*, at 27. See also 853 F. 2d 1452, 1465 (CA8 1988) (en banc). The Court bases this conclusion on the testimony of the co-administrator of one abortion clinic that a one or two-day scheduling backlog was typical. *Ante*, at 26, n. 32. "One or two days," however, obviously means that the backlog is not necessarily 48 hours. Furthermore, that witness also stated that if "a woman says that she must be seen on a particular day our policy is that we will always see her." App. 147. But because of the mandated 48-hour delay, the clinic cannot honor a woman's request for an abortion until at least two full days have elapsed. The testimony therefore is hardly sufficient to justify ignoring the District Court's factual finding with regard to the effects of the delay requirement.

HODGSON *v.* MINNESOTA

feel comfortable consulting her parents about intimate or sexual matters. See Melton, Legal Regulation of Adolescent Abortion: Unintended Effects, 42 American Psychologist 79, 81 (1987) (stating that in many families, compelled parental notification is unlikely to result in meaningful discussion about the daughter's predicament); Tr. 1357–1358 (testimony of Dr. Steven Butzer) (stating that involuntary disclosure is disruptive to family and has "almost universally negative" effects, in accord with minor's expectations). Moreover, in those families with a history of child abuse, a pregnant minor forced to notify a parent is more likely to be greeted by physical assault or psychological harrassment than open and caring conversation about her predicament. See Tr. 316 (testimony of Dr. Lenore Walker) (stating that forced notification in dysfunctional families is likely to sever communication patterns and increase the risk of violence); *H. L.* v. *Matheson*, 450 U. S., at 446 (MARSHALL, J., dissenting). Forced notification in such situations would amount to punishing the daughter for the lack of a stable and communicative family environment, when the blame for that situation surely lies principally, if not entirely, with the parents. Parental notification in the less-than-ideal family, therefore, would not lead to an informed decision by the minor.[7]

[7] The State also asserts that the requirements permit parents to provide doctors with relevant information about their daughters' medical history and "to assist with ensuring that proper after-care procedures are followed." Brief of Cross-Petitioners 34–36. See also *ante*, at 26 (delay period "permits the parent to inquire into the competency of the doctor performing an abortion"). If these are actual state interests, it seems peculiar that the State does not try to facilitate similar parental involvement in minors' treatment for pregnancy and childbirth, see *infra*, at ——, which pose far greater risks to the minor's health than abortion, see *supra*, at ——. In any event, compelled notification is unlikely to result in helpful parental involvement in those families in which a parent reacts to the news of the daughter's predicament by rejecting or abusing the young woman. See *supra*, at ——.

HODGSON *v.* MINNESOTA

The State also claims that the statute serves the interest of protecting parents' independent right "to shape the[ir] child[ren]'s values and life style[s]" and "to determine and strive for what they believe to be best for their children." Brief for Cross-Petitioners 26. If this is so, the statute is surely underinclusive, as it does not require parental notification where the minor seeks medical treatment for pregnancy, venereal disease, or alcohol and other drug abuse. See Minn. Stat. § 144.343(1). Are we to believe that Minnesota parents have no interest in their children's well-being in these other contexts?

In any event, parents' right to direct their children's upbringing is a right *against* state interference with family matters. See, *e. g.*, *Prince* v. *Massachusetts*, 321 U. S. 158, 166 (1944) (noting that this Court's decisions "have respected the private realm of family life which the state cannot enter"). See also *Wisconsin* v. *Yoder*, 406 U. S. 205, 232 (1972); *Pierce* v. *Society of Sisters*, 268 U. S. 510, 534–535 (1925). Yet, ironically, the State's requirements here affirmatively interfere in family life by trying to force families to conform to the State's archetype of the ideal family. Cf. *Moore* v. *East Cleveland*, 431 U. S. 494, 506 (1977) ("[T]he Constitution prevents [the state] from standardizing its children—and its adults—by forcing all to live in certain narrowly defined family patterns"); *ante*, at 29. It is a strange constitutional alchemy that would transform a limitation on state power into a justification for governmental intrusion into family interactions. Moreover, as a practical matter, "state intervention is hardly likely to resurrect parental authority that the parents themselves are unable to preserve." *H. L.* v. *Matheson*, *supra*, at 448 (MARSHALL, J., dissenting). See also *Planned Parenthood of Central Mo.* v. *Danforth*, 428 U. S. 52, 75 (1976) (finding it unlikely that parental veto power over abortion "will enhance parental authority or control where the minor and the nonconsenting parent are so

HODGSON *v.* MINNESOTA

fundamentally in conflict and the very existence of the pregnancy has already fractured the family structure").

Even if the State's interest is construed as merely the *facilitation* of the exercise of parental authority, the notification and delay requirements are not narrowly drawn. Parental authority is not limitless. Certainly where parental involvement threatens to harm the child, the parent's authority must yield. *Prince* v. *Massachusetts*, *supra*, at 169–170; *H. L.* v. *Matheson*, 450 U. S., at 449 (MARSHALL, J., dissenting). Yet the notification and delay requirements facilitate the exercise of parental authority even where it may physically or psychologically harm the child. See *supra*, at ——.

Furthermore, the exercise of parental authority in some instances will take the form of obstructing the minor's decision to have an abortion. A parent who objects to the abortion, once notified, can exert strong pressure on the minor, in the form of stern disapproval, withdrawal of financial support, or physical or emotional abuse, to block her from getting an abortion. See *Bellotti II*, 443 U. S., at 647 (plurality opinion) ("[M]any parents hold strong views on the subject of abortion, and young pregnant minors, especially those living at home, are particularly vulnerable to their parents' efforts to obstruct . . . an abortion"). See also *H. L.* v. *Matheson*, *supra*, at 438–439 (MARSHALL, J., dissenting). In such circumstances, the notification requirement becomes, in effect, a consent requirement. As discussed below, *infra*, at ——, the State may not permit any person, including a parent, to veto a woman's decision to terminate her pregnancy. Because the notification and delay requirements effectively give parents the opportunity to exercise an unconstitutional veto in some situations, those requirements are not narrowly tailored to the state's interest in facilitating *legitimate* exercises of parental authority.

HODGSON *v.* MINNESOTA

IV

The one-parent notification and 48-hour delay requirements, then, do not satisfy the strict scrutiny applicable to laws restricting a woman's constitutional right to have an abortion. The judicial bypass procedure cannot salvage those requirements because that procedure itself is unconstitutional. For this same reason, the bypass cannot save the two-parent notification requirement.

A

The State argues that the bypass procedure saves the notification and delay requirements because it provides an alternative way to obtain a legal abortion for minors who would be harmed by those requirements. This Court has upheld a one-parent consent requirement where the State provided an alternative judicial procedure "'whereby a pregnant minor [could] demonstrate that she [was] sufficiently mature to make the abortion decision herself or that, despite her immaturity, an abortion would be in her best interests.'" *Planned Parenthood Assn. of Kansas City, Inc.* v. *Ashcroft*, 462 U. S. 476, 491 (1983) (opinion of Powell, J.) (quoting *Akron Center for Reproductive Health*, 462 U. S., at 439–440).

I continue to believe, however, that a judicial bypass procedure of this sort is itself unconstitutional because it effectively gives a judge "an absolute veto over the decision of the physician and his patient." *Planned Parenthood Assn. of Kansas City, supra*, at 504 (BLACKMUN, J., concurring in part and dissenting in part); see also *Bellotti II*, 443 U. S., at 655 (STEVENS, J., concurring in the judgment) ("The provision of an absolute veto to a judge . . . is to me particularly troubling. . . . It is inherent in the right to make the abortion decision that the right may be exercised without public scrutiny and in defiance of the contrary opinion of the sovereign or other third parties") (footnote omitted); *Planned Parenthood of Central Mo., supra*, at 74 ("[T]he State does not

HODGSON *v.* MINNESOTA

have the constitutional authority to give a third party an absolute, and possibly arbitrary, veto over the decision of the physician and his patient to terminate the patient's pregnancy, regardless of the reason for withholding the consent"). No person may veto *any* minor's decision, made in consultation with her physician, to terminate her pregnancy. An "immature" minor has no less right to make decisions regarding her own body than a mature adult.

Minnesota's bypass provision allows a judge to authorize an abortion if he determines either that a woman is sufficiently mature to make the decision on her own or, if she is not sufficiently mature, that an abortion without parental notification would serve her best interests. Minn. Stat. § 144.343(6). Of course, if a judge refuses to authorize an abortion, a young woman can then reevaluate whether she wants to notify a parent. But many women will carry the fetus to term rather than notify a parent. See *supra*, at ——. Other women may decide to inform a parent but then confront parental pressure or abuse so severe as to obstruct the abortion. For these women, the judge's refusal to authorize an abortion effectively constitutes an absolute veto.

The constitutional defects in any provision allowing someone to veto a woman's abortion decision are exacerbated by the vagueness of the standards contained in this statute. The statute gives no guidance on how a judge is to determine whether a minor is sufficiently "mature" and "capable" to make the decision on her own. See Minn. Stat. § 144.343(6)(c)(i) (judge shall authorize abortion if he "determines that the pregnant woman is mature and capable of giving informed consent to the proposed abortion"). Cf. Lewis, *supra*, at 84, 87 (noting the absence of a judicial standard for assessing maturity). The statute similarly is silent as to how a judge is to determine whether an abortion without parental notification would serve an immature minor's "best interests." § 144.343(6)(c)(i) (judge shall authorize abortion for immature minor without notification "if said judge concludes that the pregnant woman's best interests would be served thereby"). Is the judge expected to know more about the woman's medical needs or psychological makeup than her doctor? Should he consider the woman's financial and emotional status to determine the quality of life the woman and her future child would enjoy in this world? Neither the record nor the Court answers such questions. As JUSTICE STEVENS wrote in *Bellotti II*, the best interest standard "provides little real guidance to the judge, and his decision must necessarily reflect personal and societal values and mores whose enforcement upon the minor—particularly when contrary to her own informed and reasonable decision—is fundamentally at odds with privacy interests underlying the constitutional protection afforded her decision." 443 U. S., at 655–656 (STEVENS, J., concurring in the judgment). It is difficult to conceive of any reason, aside from a judge's personal opposition to abortion, that would justify a finding that an immature woman's best interests would be served by forcing her to endure pregnancy and childbirth against her will.

B

Even if I did not believe that a judicial bypass procedure was facially unconstitutional, the experience of Minnesota's procedure in operation demonstrates that the bypass provision before us cannot save the parental notification and delay requirements. This Court has addressed judicial bypass procedures only in the context of facial challenges. See *Planned Parenthood Assn. of Kansas City*, 462 U. S., at 490–493 (opinion of Powell, J.); *Akron Center for Reproductive Health*, 462 U. S., at 439–442; *Bellotti II*, 443 U. S., at 643–644 (plurality opinion). The Court has never considered the actual burdens a particular bypass provision imposes on a woman's right to choose an abortion. Such consideration establishes that, even if judges authorized every abortion sought by petitioning minors, Minnesota's judicial bypass is

HODGSON *v.* MINNESOTA

far too burdensome to remedy an otherwise unconstitutional statute.

The District Court found that the bypass procedure imposed significant burdens on minors. First, "scheduling practices in Minnesota courts typically require minors to wait two or three days between their first contact with the court and the hearing on their petitions. This delay may combine with other factors to result in a delay of a week or more." 648 F. Supp., at 763. As noted above, *supra*, at ——, a delay of only a few days can significantly increase the health risks to the minor; a week-long delay inevitably does. Furthermore, in several counties in Minnesota, no judge is willing to hear bypass petitions, forcing women in those areas to travel long distances to obtain a hearing. *Ibid.*; Donovan, Judging Teenagers: How Minors Fare When They Seek Court-Authorized Abortions, 15 Family Planning Perspectives 259, 264 (1983) (50% of Minnesota minors utilizing bypass were not residents of city in which court was located); Melton, *supra*, at 80 ("In Minnesota, where judges in rural counties have often recused themselves from participation in the abortion hearings, minors sometimes have to travel a round-trip of more than 500 miles for the hearing"). The burden of such travel, often requiring an overnight stay in a distant city, is particularly heavy for poor women from rural areas. Furthermore, a young woman's absence from home, school, or work during the time required for such travel and for the hearing itself can jeopardize the woman's confidentiality. See *ibid.*

The District Court also found that the bypass procedure can be extremely traumatic for young women.

> "The experience of going to court for a judicial authorization produces fear and tension in many minors. Minors are apprehensive about the prospect of facing an authority figure who holds in his hands the power to veto the decision to proceed without notifying one or both parents. Many minors are angry and resentful at

HODGSON *v.* MINNESOTA

> being required to justify their decision before complete strangers. Despite the confidentiality of the proceeding, many minors resent having to reveal intimate details of their personal and family lives to these strangers. Finally, many minors are left feeling guilty and ashamed about their lifestyle and their decision to terminate their pregnancy. Some mature minors and some minors in whose best interests it is to proceed without notifying their parents are so daunted by the judicial proceeding that they forego the bypass option and either notify their parents or carry to term.
>
> "Some minors are so upset by the bypass proceeding that they consider it more difficult than the medical procedure itself. Indeed the anxiety resulting from the bypass proceeding may linger until the time of the medical procedure and thus render the latter more difficult than necessary." 648 F. Supp., at 763–764.[8]

Yet, despite the substantial burdens imposed by these proceedings, the bypass is, in effect, a "rubber stamp," *id.*, at 766 (testimony of Honorable William Sweeney); only an extremely small number of petitions are denied, *id.*, at 765. See also Melton, *supra*, at 80 ("Available research indicates that judicial bypass proceedings are merely pro forma. Although they represent substantial intrusion on minors' privacy and take up significant amounts of court time, there is no evidence that they promote more reasoned decision mak-

[8] Dr. Hodgson testified that some minors dread the court procedure so much that they become "wringing wet with perspiration" and frequently require a sedative beforehand. App. 468. One judge who has heard a significant number of bypass petitions testified that the court experience is "very nervewracking" for young women. 648 F. Supp. 756, 766 (D Minn 1986). Another testified that pregnant minors' "level of apprehension is twice what I normally see in court. . . . You see all the typical things that you would see with somebody under incredible amounts of stress, answering monosyllabically, tone of voice, tenor of voice, shaky, wringing of hands, you know, one young lady had her—her hands were turning blue and it was warm in my office." *Ibid.*

HODGSON *v.* MINNESOTA

ing or screen out adolescents who may be particularly immature or vulnerable. . . . The hearings typically last less than 15 minutes. . . . Despite the complex issues involved (maturity and the best interests of the minor), experts are rarely if ever called to testify"). The judges who have adjudicated over 90% of the bypass petitions between 1981 and 1986 could not identify any positive effects of the bypass procedure. See 648 F. Supp., at 766; *ante*, at 18–19, and n. 27. The large number of women who undergo the bypass process do not receive any sort of counseling from the court—which is not surprising, given the court's limited role and lack of expertise in that area. The bypass process itself thus cannot serve the state interest of promoting informed decision-making by all minors. If the State truly were concerned about ensuring that all minors consult with a knowledgeable and caring adult, it would provide for some form of counseling rather than for a judicial procedure in which a judge merely gives or withholds his consent.[9]

Thus, regardless of one's view of the facial validity of a bypass procedure, Minnesota's procedure in practice imposes an excessive burden on young women's right to choose an

[9] Maine, for example, requires that a minor obtain the consent of a parent, guardian, or adult family member; undergo a judicial bypass; *or* receive counseling from the physician or a counselor according to specified criteria. See Me. Rev. Stat. Ann., Tit. 22, § 1597–A (1989). Wisconsin requires abortion providers to encourage parental notification unless they determine that the minor has a valid reason for not notifying her parents. Wisc. Stat. § 146.78 (Supp. 1988). In the latter situation, the provider must encourage—but not require—the minor to notify "another family member, close family friend, school counselor, social worker or other appropriate person." § 146.78(5)(c). I express no opinion on the constitutionality or efficacy of these schemes, but raise them only as examples of alternatives that seem more closely related than a judicial bypass procedure to the goal of ensuring that the minor's decision is informed.

In any event, most abortion clinics already provide extensive counseling. See 1 National Research Council, *supra*, at 191–192 (90% of abortion clinics routinely provide counseling for all first-abortion patients, and all clinics make counseling available to all patients on request).

abortion. Cf. *Bellotti II*, 443 U. S., at 655 (STEVENS, J., concurring in the judgment) ("[T]he need to commence judicial proceedings in order to obtain a legal abortion would impose a burden at least as great as, and probably greater than, that imposed on the minor child by the need to obtain the consent of a parent"). Furthermore, the process does not serve the State's interest of ensuring that minors' decisions are informed. Surely, then, a State could not require that *all* minor women seeking an abortion obtain judicial approval.[10] The Court's holding that the burdensome bypass procedure saves the State's burdensome notification and delay requirements thus strikes me as the equivalent of saying that two wrongs make a right. I cannot accept such a novel judicial calculus.

V

The Court today strikes down an irrational and vastly overbroad requirement that a pregnant minor either notify both her parents of her decision to obtain an abortion or obtain the approval of a judge. With that decision I agree. At the same time, though, the Court upholds a requirement that a minor wait 48 hours after notifying one parent of her decision, unless she submits to the onerous judicial bypass procedure. From that decision I vehemently dissent. This scheme forces a young woman in an already dire situation to choose between two fundamentally unacceptable alternatives: notifying a possibly dictatorial or even abusive parent and justifying her profoundly personal decision in an intimidating judicial proceeding to a black-robed stranger. For such a woman, this dilemma is more likely to result in trauma and pain than in an informed and voluntary decision.

[10] Indeed, the State conceded in oral argument before the Eighth Circuit, sitting en banc, that a judicial approval provision by itself would be unconstitutional. See 853 F. 2d, at 1469 (Lay, C. J., dissenting).

As it turned out, the Stevens draft opinion in *Hodgson* could not hold its majority. Justice Stevens circulated redrafts of his opinion, including a draft circulated on June 7, still headed "JUSTICE STEVENS delivered the opinion of the Court." In the copy I have, someone has crossed out "delivered the opinion" and penned in "announced the judgment." The change was made official, when a sixth draft was circulated on June 16, with its printed heading, "JUSTICE STEVENS announced the judgment of the Court."

The change occurred because, on June 11, Justice O'Connor sent around an opinion, reprinted on p. 377, concurring in part and dissenting in part. As explained in her covering memo, "At the end of the day, I am back where I started. I agree with John [Stevens] that subdivision 2, the 2-parent notification, is invalid. But I agree with Tony [Kennedy] that subdivision 6, the 2-parent notification plus judicial bypass, passes constitutional muster."

The Court was now fragmented. Four Justices (the Chief Justice and Justices White, Scalia, and Kennedy) held that two-parent notification was constitutional, with or without bypass; four Justices (Justices Brennan, Marshall, Blackmun and Stevens) held that two-parent notification was unconstitutional, with or without bypass; one Justice (Justice O'Connor) held that two-parent notification was unconstitutional without judicial bypass, but constitutional with bypass.

With the Court thus split, Justice Kennedy sent around a June 13 Memorandum to the Conference that informed the Justices that, because of the division, "John and I propose issuing a *per curiam* opinion along the lines of the one attached. The separate opinions would then be opinions concurring and dissenting from the judgement announced in the *per curiam*." The attached one-paragraph per curiam stated, "For reasons stated in separate opinions that follow, the judgment of the Court of Appeals in its entirety is affirmed." (The lower court had invalidated the two-parent notice requirement and upheld the judicial bypass alternative.)

At the conference on June 14, there was opposition to the issuance of a per curiam. The next day, Justice Stevens, who had joined with Justice Kennedy on the per curiam suggestion, sent a Memorandum to the Conference revoking the idea. "After giving further consideration to the proposed use of a per curiam in this case . . . ," the memo began, "I have now concluded that I will not be able to join such a disposition."

If a per curiam were used, Justice Stevens pointed out, it "would constitute the only opinion for the Court and therefore what I regard as two unfortunate consequences would ensue. First, what would otherwise be my opinion for the Court in No. 88-1309, (drafted pursuant to Bill Brennan's assignment) would be converted into an opinion concurring in part and dissenting in part from the PC. Secondly, the headnote for the PC would be meaningless and there would be no syllabus in the U.S. Reports." In particular, use of a per curiam would deprive any other opinion that was issued of the status of a Court opinion.

As it turned out, when *Hodgson* came down, Justice Stevens announced the judgment of the Court and his opinion striking down the two-parent notification provision (a holding agreed to by five Justices), and Justice Kennedy issued an opinion upholding the judicial bypass provision (a holding also agreed to by five Justices). The bare majority for both holdings was supplied by Justice O'Connor's vote.

While the Court appeared hopelessly fragmented on *Hodgson*, Justice Brennan sent a June 13, 1990, letter to Justice Marshall urging him to join as much of the Stevens opinion as possible. "I think," Brennan wrote, "it is important for John to get as much support as possible, now that Sandra has for the first time joined us in holding invalid a law regulating abortion."

O'Connor's final posture was the crucial element of the *Hodgson* decision. It meant that there was no real possibility of overruling *Roe* v. *Wade*. Hence, Justice Stevens could conclude, in a June 18 letter on *Hodgson*'s effect, "that whatever else may have happened, it is still the law that a woman's decision in favor of an abortion is a part of her liberty that is protected by the Due Process Clause, and as long as that is true the fact that a State may disapprove of abortion is not a sufficient reason for interfering with that basic liberty."

The same point was made by Justice Marshall when he wrote in his *Hodgson* opinion, concurring in part and dissenting in part, "*Roe* remains the law of the land."[5] In the first draft of his opinion, reprinted on p. 381, Marshall had taken issue with Stevens's then draft opinion of the Court on language that he interpreted as indicating a less strict standard of review than that required by *Roe* v. *Wade*. The passages that Justice Marshall objected to from the draft (which is reprinted starting on page 342) were the following: "We now conclude that the requirement of notice to both of the pregnant minor's parents is not reasonably related to legitimate state interests"; "The Minnesota statute cannot be sustained if the obstacles it imposes are not reasonably related to legitimate state interests"; the statement that requirement of a 48-hour delay after notifying one parent "would reasonably further the legitimate state interest of ensuring that the minor's decision is knowing and intelligent"; and the position that the two-parent notification requirement "does not reasonably further any legitimate state interest."

Marshall's draft declared, "It is therefore deeply disturbing that the Court uses language that suggests a more relaxed standard of review, as though a woman's right to control her own body were no more important than an optician's freedom to fit customers' eyeglasses without a prescription, see *Williamson* v. *Lee Optical of Oklahoma, Inc.*, 348 U.S. 483, 488 (1955)." This passage does not appear in the final Marshall *Hodgson* opinion, although the relaxed review standard language against which it was directed remained in the final *Hodgson* opinion issued by Justice Stevens.

In 1987, in a comment on Chief Justice Rehnquist, Justice Marshall said, "He has no problems, wishy-washy, back and forth. He knows exactly what he wants to do, and that's very important as a chief justice."[6]

There is no doubt that William H. Rehnquist has been a stronger Court head than his predecessor. However, as the *Webster* and *Hodgson* cases show, he, too, has not always been able to impose his will upon the often prima donnaish individuals who make up the Court. There were few things on which Rehnquist felt more deeply than the need to overrule *Roe* v. *Wade*. Yet we saw that he was unable to accomplish his goal of casting *Roe* into limbo in the *Webster* case and did not really try again the next term in *Hodgson* v. *Minnesota*. *Hodgson*, indeed, with Justice O'Connor's first vote to strike down a law regulating abortion, has proved the Thermidor for the would-be Rehnquist "revolution" (to use the term in Justice Blackmun's draft *Webster* dissent) in abortion law.

Since *Hodgson*, the Court has strongly reaffirmed *Roe*. In the 1992 case of *Planned Parenthood* v. *Casey*,[7] Chief Justice Rehnquist renewed his *Webster* effort to inter *Roe*, but he was again able to secure only four votes. Justice O'Connor, once more the key vote, not only remained true to her *Webster-Hodgson* posture, but joined in writing an opinion that specifically rejected the invitation to overrule *Roe* v. *Wade*. On the contrary, the joint opinion of Justices O'Connor, Kennedy, and David H. Souter declared, "the essential holding of *Roe* v. *Wade* should be retained and once again reaffirmed. . . . [T]he woman's right to terminate her pregnancy before viability is the most central principal of *Roe* v. *Wade*. It is a rule of law and a component of liberty we cannot renounce."[8]

Justice Blackmun delivered a poignant separate *Casey* opinion in which he stressed that *Roe* still survived by only one vote and how "I fear for the darkness as four Justices anxiously await the single vote necessary to extinguish the light."[9] However, with the replacement of Justice White (always a consistent supporter of the Chief Justice's effort to overrule *Roe* v. *Wade*) by Justice Ruth Bader Ginsburg, *Roe* appears as secure for the forseeable future as so controversial a decision can be.

Notes

1. Supra Chapter 6.
2. 410 U.S. 113 (1973).
3. 497 U.S. 417 (1990).
4. *Kansas City* v. *Ashcroft*, 462 U.S. 476 (1983).
5. 497 U.S. at 463.
6. *New York Times*, December 13, 1987, p. 37.
7. 112 S.Ct. 2791 (1992).
8. Id. at 2804, 2817.
9. Id. at 2844.

8

General Motors Corporation v. *United States (1990): Administrative Deadlines—Mandatory or Directory?*

The mills of administrative justice grind slowly. In all too many administrative agencies the goal of dispensing speedy and inexpensive justice has proved to be a will-o'-the-wisp. Every student of the agencies has complained of the cumbersome and overtechnical nature of their adjudicatory process. A federal statute, the Administrative Procedure Act, empowers the courts to "compel agency action . . . unreasonably delayed."[1] This has not, however, resolved the problem of administrative delay.

The problem is strikingly demonstrated by *Heckler* v. *Day*,[2] where the Supreme Court rebuffed judicial efforts to eliminate delay in Social Security disability cases. The Court itself has referred to the hardship imposed by the torpidity of the administrative process in those cases.[3] The record in the *Day* case showed that the situation had not improved since the court's animadversion in this respect. The two named plaintiffs had had their disability benefits terminated. Day was forced to wait 167 days for a reconsideration determination; he then received a hearing before an administrative law judge 173 days after his hearing request. A second plaintiff waited 215 days for a reconsideration determination and was given a hearing 65 days after his hearing request. Plaintiffs brought a class action for declaratory and injunctive relief from the delays, contending that the delays they had experienced violated their statutory right to a hearing within a reasonable time.

The lower courts agreed with this contention and issued an injunction, requiring the Secretary of Health and Human Services in the future to issue reconsideration determinations within 90 days of requests for reconsideration, to conduct hearings within 90 days of requests for hearings, and to pay interim benefits to any claimant who did not receive a reconsideration determination or hearing within 180 days of the request for reconsideration or who did not receive a hearing within ninety days of the hearing request.

The Supreme Court reversed this decision, holding that it was not appropriate for a federal court to prescribe deadlines for agency adjudication of disability claims and to order payment of interim benefits in the event of noncompliance. In the Court's view, "[I]t would be an unwarranted judicial intrusion into this pervasively regulated area for federal courts to issue injunctions imposing deadlines with respect to future disability claims."[4]

The gap left by cases such as *Heckler* v. *Day* has led legislatures to attempt to deal with the problem of administrative delay by laws providing specific time limits within which various administrative steps must be taken. Thus, a statute may require that agency hearings be held within a stated time or that the administrative law judge enter findings, conclusions, and an order within a specified number of days. But the courts generally hold that such time limits are directory, not mandatory, and refuse to invalidate agency action merely because the limits have been violated.[5]

During Chief Justice Rehnquist's first term, the Supreme Court gave its imprimatur to the case law on the matter. In *Brock* v. *Roadway Express*,[6] the agency regulations expressly allowed only a total delay of six months during the issuing of the preliminary order, the holding of the postdeprivation hearing, the issuing of the administrative law judge's opinion, and the issuing of the final order of the Secretary. In addition, the statute provided that "the Secretary of Labor shall issue a final order within one hundred and twenty days." In line with the case law already mentioned, the Court interpreted the time requirements as merely "directory in nature," rather than mandatory. The Court so held even though, in the *Brock* case, the administrative law judge did not even submit a recommended decision for over seven months, and a nineteen-month period then elapsed before the Secretary announced the final decision. Well might Justice Brennan declare that "this cavalier treatment of a statutory imperative" was of "dubious validity."[7]

The Court's toothless approach to what Justice Stevens, in a *Brock* dissent, termed "this apparently routine and unjustified delay"[8] despite a statutory time limit would have been changed had Justice Blackmun's draft opinion of the Court come down as the final opinion in *General Motors Corporation* v. *United States*.[9] That case arose under the Clean Air Act. The statute provided for federal and state programs to deal with the problem of air pollution. As stated in the opinion of the Court, "The [act and amendments to it] specified a detailed timetable for Federal and State action to accomplish this objective. They required the EPA Administrator, within 30 days of the passage of the Amendments, to promulgate national ambient air quality standards (NAAQS). . . . Within nine months thereafter, each State was to submit a state implementation plan (SIP) to implement, maintain, and enforce the NAAQS. . . . As the final step in this start-up phase of the program, EPA was to act on a proposed SIP within four months: 'The Administrator shall, within four months after the date required for submission of a plan under paragraph (1), approve or disapprove such plan or any portion thereof.'"

In 1980, EPA approved Massachusetts' proposed SIP governing certain emissions from automobile-painting operations. The SIP permitted General Motors to meet emissions limits in stages, but required full compliance by December 31, 1985. In June 1985, General Motors sought an extension of that deadline until summer 1987. Massachusetts approved the revision and submitted it to EPA on the day before the existing SIP's deadline, but EPA did not reject it until September 1988.

The question before the Court was whether the statute imposed a four-month deadline on EPA review of a SIP revision. The lower courts held that it did. At the conference on the case, the Justices were sharply divided on the issue. Justice Blackmun, to whom the case was assigned, circulated a May 30, 1990, Memorandum to the Conference, in which he wrote, "You may recall that when this case was discussed at Conference, we were divided—and, I think, undecided—on the 4-month issue. On further study, I have concluded that the 4-month requirement does apply to a SIP revision."

In accordance with the conclusion thus expressed, Justice Blackmun prepared the draft opinion of the Court reprinted on p. 405. Part III of the draft dealt with the deadline issue—"whether the Act imposes a 4-month deadline on EPA review of a proposed SIP revision." It begins by noting that "Congress imposed a strict time constraint on EPA's review of an original SIP, requiring final action within four months after the State submitted its plan." Section 110(a)(2), which imposed the deadline for EPA approval of an original SIP, is quoted.

Justice Blackmun then points out, "Anticipating that the States would have to revise SIPs periodically, Congress provided for such revisions in § 110(a)(3)." Under that section, "[t]he Administrator shall approve any revision of an implementation plan . . . if he determines that it meets the requirements of [§ 110(a)(2)]." According to the Blackmun draft, as claimed by the petitioner, "the reference to § 110(a)(2) was intended to incorporate both the substantive and procedural requirements of that provision." This "indicates to us that Congress intended to incorporate the 4-month time provision. . . . There is no indication in the statute that Congress intended to carve out that one provision pertaining to the 4-month deadline, nor is there any suggestion that Congress regarded the expeditious approval of a SIP revision to be any less important than the expeditious approval of an original SIP."

Hence, the Blackmun draft concludes, "[w]e hold, as did the Court of Appeals in this case, that the 4-month deadline also applies to EPA's review of a state-submitted revision of a SIP." Such a conclusion is compelled both by the language and structure of the statute. "Because Congress plainly wrote that assumption into the statute itself, because we must read the statute as a whole, and because the statute would have no intelligible meaning were we to rule otherwise, we hold that the statute requires EPA to take final action on a SIP revision within four months of its submission."

Such an interpretation, Justice Blackmun declares, gives effect to "Congress' intent in the Clean Air Act . . . to establish a federal-state partnership for the control of air pollution." EPA was to establish the NAAQS, while the states were to have the primary responsibility for assuring air quality. "Only if EPA promptly reviews the state-submitted SIP revision can the State, in turn, perform its congressionally intended role as the primary implementer and enforcer of its air-quality-control measures."

1st DRAFT

SUPREME COURT OF THE UNITED STATES

No. 89-369

GENERAL MOTORS CORPORATION, PETITIONER *v.* UNITED STATES

ON WRIT OF CERTIORARI TO THE UNITED STATES COURT OF APPEALS FOR THE FIRST CIRCUIT

[May ——, 1990]

JUSTICE BLACKMUN delivered the opinion of the Court.

This case concerns a Clean Air Act enforcement action by the Environmental Protection Agency (EPA) against petitioner General Motors Corporation (GMC). We are asked to decide whether the 4-month time limit on EPA review of an original state implementation plan (SIP) also applies to its review of a SIP revision, and whether, if EPA fails to complete its review of a SIP revision in a timely manner, EPA is prevented from enforcing an existing SIP during the interval between the end of the 4-month period and the time the agency finally rules on the revision.

I

What is known as the Clean Air Act, 77 Stat. 392, became law on December 17, 1963. Twenty years ago, Congress enacted the Clean Air Act Amendments of 1970, 84 Stat. 1676, a comprehensive national program that made the States and the Federal Government partners in the struggle against air pollution. The threats to human health were regarded as urgent, and the 1970 Amendments were designed to result in the expeditious establishment of programs to deal with the problem. The Amendments specified a detailed timetable for Federal and State action to accomplish this objective. They required the EPA Administrator, within 30 days of the passage of the Amendments, to promulgate national ambient air quality standards (NAAQS). § 109(a)(1), 42 U. S. C. § 7409(a)(1). Within nine months thereafter, each State was required to submit a state implementation plan (SIP) to implement, maintain, and enforce the NAAQS. § 110(a)(1), 42 U. S. C. § 7410(a)(1). As the final step in this start-up phase of the program, EPA was required to act on a proposed SIP within four months: "The Administrator shall, within four months after the date required for submission of a plan under paragraph (1), approve or disapprove such plan or any portion thereof." § 110(a)(2), as amended, 42 U. S. C. § 7410(a)(2). The Administrator was directed to approve the SIP if he determined that it was adopted after reasonable notice and hearing and that it met various substantive requirements, including emissions limitations, devices for monitoring air-quality data, and enforcement mechanisms.

The integrated timetable established by the 1970 Amendments reflected the urgency of establishing air-pollution controls. But the Amendments also recognized that local needs and control strategies could evolve over time, and that SIPs would have to change as well. The States therefore were authorized to propose SIP revisions, and the EPA Administrator was directed to approve any such proposed revision "if he determines that it meets the requirements of paragraph (2) and has been adopted by the State after reasonable notice and public hearings." § 110(a)(3), 42 U. S. C. § 7410(a)(3)(A).

The 1970 Amendments also specified certain enforcement mechanisms. The Act empowered EPA to order compliance with an applicable implementation plan, § 113(a), 42 U. S. C. § 7413(a), and to seek injunctive relief against a source violating the plan or an EPA order, § 113(b), as amended, 42 U. S. C. § 7413(b). In addition, Congress prescribed criminal penalties for knowing violations of plans and orders, § 113(c), 42 U. S. C. § 7413 (c), and authorized citizen suits for injunctions against violators, in the absence of Government enforcement, § 304, as amended, 42 U. S. C. § 7604.

GENERAL MOTORS CORP. v. UNITED STATES

Congress further amended the Clean Air Act by the Clean Air Act Amendments of 1977. 91 Stat. 685. It added to the Act the concept of a "nonattainment area"—an area where air quality falls short of the NAAQS. § 171(2), 42 U. S. C. § 7501(2). The deadline for attainment of the primary NAAQS in a nonattainment area was December 31, 1982. §§ 172(a)(1), 42 U. S. C. § 7502(a)(1). Further extensions were permitted for "photochemical oxidants" (ozone) or carbon monoxide, but only if the State demonstrated that attainment was not possible before 1983 "despite the implementation of all reasonably available measures" and that attainment would be achieved "as expeditiously as practicable, but not later than December 31, 1987." § 172(a)(2), 42 U. S. C. § 7502(a)(2).

II

A

The entire Commonwealth of Massachusetts is a nonattainment area for NAAQS with respect to ozone. See 40 CFR § 81.322, p. 126 (1989). Petitioner GMC owns and operates an automobile assembly plant in Framingham, Mass. The plant's painting operation is a source of volatile organic compounds that contribute to ozone. In 1980, EPA approved Massachusetts' proposed nonattainment area SIP governing volatile organic compound emissions from automobile-painting operations. The SIP permitted GMC to meet emissions limits in stages, but required full compliance by December 31, 1985. In 1981, EPA published a policy statement suggesting that new technology in automobile-painting operations might justify deferral of industry compliance until 1986 or 1987. 46 Fed. Reg. 51386. Three years later, in November 1984, GMC sought an extension from the December 31, 1985, compliance date imposed by the existing SIP, not for the new technology, but rather for additional time to install emission controls on its existing lines. App. 38. In June 1985, GMC proposed converting to the new technology and requested a summer 1987 deadline. *Id.*, at 41. The

GENERAL MOTORS CORP. v. UNITED STATES

Commonwealth approved the revision and submitted the proposal to EPA on December 30, 1985, one day before the existing SIP compliance deadline. *Id.*, at 50.

GMC began construction of a new painting facility but continued to operate its existing plant. On August 14, 1986, EPA sent GMC a Notice of Violation informing GMC that it was in violation of the applicable SIP. *Id.*, at 75. Approximately one year later, on August 17, 1987, respondent filed an enforcement action under § 113(b) of the Act, 42 U. S. C. § 7413(b), alleging violations of the existing SIP's 1985 deadline. On September 4, 1988, the agency made its final decision to reject the revision. 53 Fed. Reg. 36011.

B

The District Court construed § 110(a)(3) as imposing a 4-month time limit on EPA review of a SIP revision, App. 123–124, and concluded that when EPA failed to complete its review within four months, it was barred from enforcing the existing SIP during the interval between the end of the 4-month period and the time EPA finally acted on the revision. *Id.*, at 125. Because EPA had not issued a Notice of Noncompliance until well after the 4-month period had elapsed and, at the time of the court's ruling, had yet to make a final decision on the Commonwealth's SIP revision, summary judgment was entered for GMC.

The Court of Appeals for the First Circuit reversed that judgment and remanded the case for further proceedings. 876 F. 2d 1060 (1989). The Court of Appeals agreed with the District Court that the Act imposed a 4-month deadline on EPA review of a SIP revision, but concluded that the failure to meet that deadline did not preclude EPA from enforcing the existing SIP.

Reasoning that an enforcement bar was too drastic a remedy for agency delay, the court concluded that the appropriate remedies for agency inaction were those provided by the Act itself: a suit to compel agency action under § 304(a)(2), or

GENERAL MOTORS CORP. v. UNITED STATES

a request pursuant to § 113(b), 42 U. S. C. 7413(b), for reduction or elimination of penalties during the period in which unreasonable agency delay resulted in prejudice. 876 F. 2d, at 1067–1068. We granted certiorari because of a disagreement among the Circuits as to whether EPA is barred from enforcing an existing SIP if the agency fails to take action on a proposed SIP revision within four months.[1] —— U. S. —— (1989).

III

We first address whether the Act imposes a 4-month deadline on EPA review of a proposed SIP revision. To ensure clear statements of pollution-control requirements and to hasten compliance with state-determined source-specific limitations, Congress imposed a strict time constraint on EPA's review of an original SIP, requiring final action within four months after the State submitted its plan. § 110(a)(2), 42 U. S. C. § 7410(a)(2). We hold, as did the Court of Appeals in this case, that the 4-month deadline also applies to EPA's review of a state-submitted revision of a SIP.

Section 110(a)(2), which applies to EPA's approval of an original SIP, established a detailed list of requirements governing EPA review:

> "The Administrator shall, within four months after the date required for submission of a plan . . . approve or disapprove such plan . . . if he determines that it was adopted after reasonable notice and hearings and that [it satisfies certain substantive requirements specified in subparagraphs (A)–(K)]."

Anticipating that the States would have to revise SIPs periodically, Congress provided for such revisions in § 110(a)(3). This latter provision does not contain a separate list of requirements. It simply states:

[1] See *e. g.*, *American Cyanamid Co. v. U. S. Environmental Protection Agency*, 810 F. 2d 493 (CA5 1987); *Duquesne Light Co. v. EPA*, 225 U. S. App. D. C. 290, 698 F. 2d 456 (1983).

GENERAL MOTORS CORP. v. UNITED STATES

> "The Administrator shall approve any revision of an implementation plan . . . if he determines that it meets the requirements of [§ 110(a)(2)] and has been adopted by the State after reasonable notice and public hearings."

Petitioner contends that the reference to § 110(a)(2) was intended to incorporate both the substantive and procedural requirements of that provision. Brief for Petitioner 13. Petitioner relies on what it sees as clear congressional intent that the States were to play an integral role in determining how best to improve the Nation's air quality. Petitioner argues that, by exercising a "pocket veto" over a SIP revision, EPA has given itself a power that it does not have under the Act. *Id.*, at 18–19.

EPA, on its part, maintains that the word "it" in § 110(a)(3) refers to a SIP revision and that § 110(a)(3) can fairly be read to incorporate only the substantive standards from § 110(a)(2). Brief for United States 16. EPA points out that Congress was specific about other deadlines in the Act and stresses that there is no realistic possibility that EPA can take final action on a SIP revision within four months. *Id.*, at 16–17, n. 14, and 20–21. As long as the agency is under a general duty under the Administrative Procedure Act to act "within a reasonable time," and as long as a remedy exists under that Act for agency action "unreasonably delayed," 5 U. S. C. §§ 555 and 706(1), a 4-month deadline is unnecessary. Brief for United States 19–20, 23–24.

The Court of Appeals said, 876 F. 2d, at 1066, that the question "admittedly is" a close one. We, however, agree with that court and the District Court, and with all the other Courts of Appeals that have addressed the issue,[8] that peti-

[8] See *United States* v. *Alcan Foil Products Division*, 889 F. 2d 1513, 1518 (CA6 1989), cert pending, No. 89–1104; *American Cyanamid*, 810 F. 2d, at 495; *Council of Commuter Organizations* v. *Thomas*, 799 F. 2d 879, 888 (CA2 1986); *Duquesne Light*, 225 U. S. App. D. C., at 305, 698 F. 2d, at 471; *General Motors Corp.* v. *E. P. A.*, 871 F. 2d 495 (CA5 1989). Cf. *United States* v. *National Steel Corp.*, 767 F. 2d 1176, 1183, n. 1 (CA6

GENERAL MOTORS CORP. v. UNITED STATES

tioner's reading of the Act is the correct one and that the Act imposes a 4-month deadline on EPA review of a SIP revision. The statutory language, expressly incorporating "the requirements of" § 110(a)(2), indicates to us that Congress intended to incorporate the 4-month time provision. EPA's reading of the statute—that every provision of § 110(a)(2) is incorporated in § 110(a)(3), with the exception of the 4-month rule—seems strained. Indeed, in other cases EPA itself has interpreted § 110(a)(3) to incorporate procedural elements of paragraph (2). See *Public Service Co. of Indiana* v. *United States Environmental Protection Agency*, 682 F. 2d 626, 631–632 (CA7 1982) (§ 110(a)(3)(A) permits partial approval of a SIP revision), cert. denied, 459 U. S. 1127 (1983). There is no indication in the statute that Congress intended to carve out that one provision pertaining to the 4-month deadline, nor is there any suggestion that Congress regarded the expeditious approval of a SIP revision to be any less important than the expeditious approval of an original SIP.

Moreover, the Clean Air Act elsewhere assumes that EPA review of a SIP revision within four months is required. In one provision added by the 1977 Amendments, § 110(g)(1), 42 U. S. C. § 7410(g)(1), Congress expressly granted to state governors the authority to issue temporary emergency suspensions of parts of a SIP for which a proposed revision had been submitted and "which [EPA] has not approved or disapproved under this section within the *required four month period*" (emphasis added). EPA argues that § 110(g)(1) is irrelevant to the meaning of §§ 110(a)(3) and (2) because subsection (g) was enacted in the 1977 Amendments to the Clean Air Act and subsections (a)(2) and (3) were enacted in the 1970 Amendments. Brief for United States 19. We are not persuaded. The statutory reference to "the required four month period" demonstrates that Congress, in 1977, interpreted the 1970 Amendments as having imposed a time

1985), and the Sixth Circuit's discussion of that footnote in *Alcan Foil*, *supra*, at 1517.

GENERAL MOTORS CORP. v. UNITED STATES

limit on a revised SIP determination. While such language in a subsequent amendment does not compel us to recognize the 4-month time limit, language in amendments of a statute by a later Congress often deserves some weight. This particular statutory language is neither a *post hoc* rationalization found in subsequent legislative history nor a coincidental wording of an entirely separate statutory provision. We read the several provisions of this statute as a whole, regardless of the enactment dates of its individual sections. See *Pennsylvania* v. *Union Gas Co.*, —— U. S. ——, ——, n. 2 (1989) (slip op. 4–5) (reading a statute and later amendments together to inform our understanding of other definitional sections); *Clark* v. *Uebersee Finanz-Korp.*, 332 U. S. 480, 488 (1947) (Court's task "is to give all of it [Trading With the Enemy Act and later amendments]—1917 to 1941—the most harmonious, comprehensive meaning possible"). The only way we can give any satisfactory meaning to § 110(g)(1) is to hold that there is a 4-month deadline imposed on EPA review of a SIP revision. Congress, in 1977, drafted a statute that explicitly incorporated an assumption as to what the 1970 Congress required, *i. e.*, that a revision, as well as an original SIP, be reviewed by EPA within four months of submission. Because Congress plainly wrote that assumption into the statute itself,[8] because we must read the statute as a whole, and because the statute would have no intelligible meaning were we to rule otherwise, we hold that the statute requires

[8] Although subsequent "legislative history" is not probative with reqard to the intent of an earlier Congress, see *Gwaltney of Smithfield, Ltd.* v. *Chesapeake Bay Foundation, Inc.*, 484 U. S. 49, 63, n. 4 (1987) (refusing to rely on conflicting legislative history of amendments passed after the Court of Appeals had issued its opinion), amendments of a statute by a later Congress, when the act as amended is the applicable law, may be probative of the meaning of another section of the statute. See *Markham* v. *Cabell*, 326 U. S. 404, 411 (1945) ("[T]he normal assumption is that where Congress amends only one section of a law, leaving another untouched, the two were designed to function as an integrated whole. We should give each as full a play as possible.").

GENERAL MOTORS CORP. v. UNITED STATES

EPA to take final action on a SIP revision within four months of its submission.

We might add that this interpretation is reinforced by the structure of the Act. Congress' intent in the Clean Air Act was to establish a federal-state partnership for the control of air pollution. Under this approach, the Federal Government, through EPA, establishes the NAAQS, while the States have the "primary responsibility for assuring air quality," 42 U. S. C. § 7407(a), when it comes to determining the source-specific emission limits necessary to achieve the national standards. EPA's basic role and obligation is set forth in the statute, which states that the Administrator "shall approve any revision" if it meets the requirements of § 110(a)(2). Only if EPA promptly reviews the state-submitted SIP revision can the State, in turn, perform its congressionally intended role as the primary implementer and enforcer of its air-quality-control measures.

IV

This conclusion requires that we next consider whether EPA's failure to take final action on a SIP revision within the 4-month period bars the United States from enforcing an existing SIP until EPA issues a final decision on the proposed revision. Because the statute does not reveal any congressional intent to bar enforcement of an existing SIP if EPA fails to act on a proposed SIP revision within the 4-month period, we agree with the Court of Appeals that such an enforcement action is not barred.

The language of the Clean Air Act plainly states that EPA may bring an action for penalties or injunctive relief whenever a person is in violation of any requirement of an "applicable implementation plan." § 113(b)(2), 42 U. S. C. § 7413(b)(2). There can be little or no doubt that the existing SIP remains the "applicable implementation plan" even after the State has submitted a proposed revision. The statute states: "For purposes of this chapter, an applicable imple-

GENERAL MOTORS CORP. v. UNITED STATES

mentation plan is the implementation plan, or most recent revision thereof, which has been approved under [§ 110(a), 42 U. S. C. § 7410(a)] or promulgated under [110(c), 42 U. S. C. § 7410(c)] and which implements the requirements of this section." § 110(d), 42 U. S. C. § 7410(d). Both this Court and the Courts of Appeals have recognized that the approved SIP is the applicable implementation plan during the time a SIP revision proposal is pending. See, *e. g.*, *Train* v. *Natural Resources Defense Council, Inc.*, 421 U. S. 60, 92 (1975); *United States* v. *Alcan Foil Products Division*, 889 F. 2d 1513, 1519 (CA6 1989), cert. pending, No. 89–1104; *United States* v. *Wheeling-Pittsburgh Steel Corp.*, 818 F. 2d 1077, 1084 (CA3 1987); *Duquesne Light* v. *EPA*, 225 U. S. App. D. C. 290, 305, 698 F. 2d 456, 471 (1983). The commentators agree with this conclusion. See D. Currie, Air Pollution § 8.07, n. 14 (Supp. 1990); 1 W. Rodgers, Jr., Environmental Law: Air and Water § 3.39(c) (1986 and Supp. 1988).

There is nothing in the statute that limits EPA's authority to enforce the "applicable implementation plan" solely to those cases where EPA has met a 4-month deadline with respect to review of SIP revisions. Moreover, we find it significant that Congress expressly enacted an enforcement bar elsewhere in the statute. See § 113(d)(10); 42 U. S. C. § 7413(d)(10) ("During the period of the order . . . no Federal enforcement action pursuant to this section and no action under section 304 of this Act shall be pursued against such owner. . . ."). The fact that Congress explicitly enacted an enforcement bar similar to the one proposed by petitioner in one section of the statute, but failed to do so in the section at issue in this case reinforces our refusal to import such a bar here. See *Russello* v. *United States*, 464 U. S. 16, 23 (1983).[4]

---

[4] Our conclusion is further supported by the language of § 110(g), 42 U. S. C. § 7410(g), discussed above. Section 110(g) grants certain authority to a State's governor to suspend the existing SIP after four months. As the Court of Appeals discerned, 876 F. 2d, at 1069, n. 6, there would

GENERAL MOTORS CORP. v. UNITED STATES

We note that other statutory remedies are available when EPA delays action on a SIP revision.[8] Although these statutory remedies may not appear to be so strong a deterrent to EPA delay as would an enforcement bar, these are the remedies that Congress has provided in the statute.[9] Cf. *Brock* v. *Pierce County*, 476 U. S.253, 260 (1986) ("We would be most reluctant to conclude that every failure of an agency to observe a procedural requirement voids subsequent agency action, especially when important public rights are at stake. When, as here, there are less drastic remedies available for failure to meet a statutory deadline, courts should not assume that Congress intended the agency to lose its power to act" (footnote omitted)). In the absence of a specific provision suggesting that Congress intended to create an enforcement bar, we decline to infer one.

The judgment of the Court of Appeals is affirmed.

It is so ordered.

---

have been no reason for Congress to add that section if the existing SIP automatically became unenforceable after some period of EPA delay. The existence of this explicit exception indicates that in all other circumstances the existing SIP remains in effect.

[8] As the Court of Appeals observed, the statutory remedies for EPA inaction include a suit to compel agency action under § 304(a)(2), 42 U. S. C. 7604(a)(2), and a request pursuant to § 113(b), 42 U. S. C. 7413(b), for reduction or elimination of penalties during any period in which unreasonable agency delay results in prejudice. 876 F. 2d, at 1067–1068.

[9] The Commonwealth of Massachusetts, the State whose interests are involved here, in a brief joined by 12 other States, asserts that its interest is better served by preserving EPA's ability to enforce the Act. See Brief for Massachusetts, et al., as *Amici Curiae* 10–12.

1st DRAFT

SUPREME COURT OF THE UNITED STATES

No. 89-369

GENERAL MOTORS CORPORATION, PETITIONER v. UNITED STATES

ON WRIT OF CERTIORARI TO THE UNITED STATES COURT OF APPEALS FOR THE FIRST CIRCUIT

[May ——, 1990]

JUSTICE SCALIA, concurring in the judgment.

I concur in the judgment of the Court, and join Parts I, II and IV of the Court's opinion, except to the extent Part IV refers to the conclusion reached in Part III. I disagree with Part III of the opinion, holding that the Clean Air Act requires the Environmental Protection Agency (EPA) to process within four months proposed revisions to state implementation plans (SIPs). In my view, neither the language nor the structure of the Act supports that conclusion.

Petitioner points to three provisions of the Act that it claims establish a four-month deadline for processing proposed SIP revisions. First, it relies on section 110(a)(2), 84 Stat. 1680, 42 U. S. C. § 7410(a)(2). As the Court recounts, that section is part of the detailed timetable established by the 1970 Amendments, designed to put in place quickly a nationwide program reducing air pollution. *Ante*, at 1–2. I do not understand petitioner to claim that section 110(a)(2), by itself, imposes a four-month deadline on processing of proposed SIP revisions. Such a position would be untenable, since this section applies only to the EPA's action on the original proposed SIPs.

Petitioner relies, however, upon the reference to section 110(a)(2) in section 110(a)(3)(A), which provides:

> "The Administrator shall approve any revision of an implementation plan applicable to an air quality control

GENERAL MOTORS CORP. v. UNITED STATES

> region if he determines that it meets the requirements of paragraph (2) [*i. e.*, § 110(a)(2), 42 U. S. C. § 7410(a)(2)] and has been adopted by the State after reasonable notice and public hearings." 42 U. S. C. § 7410(a)(3).

The Court agrees with petitioner's contention that this subparagraph "expressly incorporat[es] 'the requirements of' § 110(a)(2)," including the four-month deadline. *Ante*, at 7.

That seems to me quite wrong. The requirements referred to are evidently the requirements listed in subparagraphs (A) through (K) of paragraph (2)—since otherwise it would have been unnecessary *add* in subparagraph (3)(A) the requirement that the plan have been "adopted by the State after reasonable notice and public hearings." That precise requirement is already contained in paragraph (2), but in the prologue rather than subparagraphs (A)–(K). Even assuming, however, that all of paragraph (2) was referred to as "requirements," no conceivable interpretation of the text could incorporate the four-month deadline. Subparagraph (3)(A) does not incorporate requirements in general, but requirements *for the plan*. Approval may be granted only if "it [the SIP] meets the requirements of paragraph (2)"—not if "he [the Administrator] complies with the requirements of paragraph (2)." The four-month deadline is not remotely a requirement that the *plan* must meet, but rather is a requirement that the Administrator must meet when making his determination under paragraph (2). No language of subparagraph (3)(A) imposes a similar requirement, either expressly or by incorporation. Words have no meaning if we are to interpret statutes in this fashion. I may also note (though this point seems to me so clear as not to require further confirmation) that the very next subparagraph of the Act, § 110(a)(3)(B), requires approval of a certain type of SIP revisions, if the revision "complies with paragraph (2) of this subsection," and then immediately adds that "[t]he Administrator shall approve or disapprove any revision no later than three months after its submission." Giving the Court's interpretation to the former phrase, it seems exceedingly strange to incorporate by reference a four-month deadline and then immediately reduce it to three. It also seems exceedingly implausible that, if *all* SIP revisions were subject to a four-month deadline by virtue of subparagraph 110(a)(3)(A), it would have been thought necessary to add a special provision with the effect of shortening the deadline by only a single month.

Petitioner's final contention is that section 110(g), 42 U. S. C. § 7410(g), imposes the four-month limitation. That section provides:

> "(1) In the case of any State which has adopted and submitted to the Administrator a proposed plan revision which the State determines—
>
> > (A) meets the requirements of this section, and
> >
> > (B) is necessary (i) to prevent the closing for one year or more of any source of air pollution, and (ii) to prevent substantial increases in unemployment which would result from such closing, and
>
> which the Administrator has not approved or disapproved under this section *within the required four month period*, the Governor may issue a temporary emergency suspension of the part of the applicable implementation plan for such State which is proposed to be revised with respect to such source. . . .
>
> (2) A temporary emergency suspension issued by a Governor under this subsection shall remain in effect for a maximum period of four months . . . ." 42 U. S. C. § 7410(g) (emphasis added).

According to petitioner, section 110(g) on its own terms "requir[es]" the Administrator to process proposed revisions within a "four month period." The Court agrees, though with some hesitation, observing that the language "deserves some weight," *ante*, at 8, and holding that "there is a 4-month

GENERAL MOTORS CORP. v. UNITED STATES

deadline" because "Congress, in 1977, drafted a statute that explicitly incorporated an assumption as to what the 1970 Congress required," *ibid.*

This is certainly petitioner's strongest claim, but I would reject it. Section 110(g) does not, by its terms, *require* the Administrator to take any action. It merely authorizes the Governor to suspend the existing SIP if action by the Administrator has not occurred. True, it *presupposes* that some "four month period" is "required"—and I think we must pretend that that erroneous presupposition is correct in order to make this section function as Congress intended. But that pretense does not have to be extended beyond this section to the entire Act. The very most one can assert to be required is that we impose a four-month deadline upon the Administrator with respect to the limited class of emergency-action SIP revisions defined in § 110(g). (One problem with this is that nothing in § 110(g) requires the State to identify at the time of submission those revisions that belong to the emergency-action class—though perhaps the Administrator could impose such a requirement by regulation, or perhaps States could be expected to make the identification voluntarily, since it is in their interest to obtain prompt EPA action.) In fact, I think giving effect to the obvious intent of § 110(g) requires even less distortion than that—to-wit, merely that the Governor be permitted to implement the plan if the Administrator has not acted within four months, but without imposing any legal requirement that the Administrator do so. But there is absolutely no justification whatever for preventing the mistake from frustrating the intended effect of § 110(g) by causing it to frustrate the clearly intended effect of the remainder of the Act—converting the mistaken assumption, in other words, into an amendment by inadvertence. The implications of such an amendment are absurd. No one even remotely familiar with the requirements of administrative action under this legislation would think it reasonable to impose an absolute, four-month deadline on all SIP revision approvals, even when no emergency situation such as that described in § 110(g) exists.

Finally, Congress's general intent "to establish a federal-state partnership for the control of air pollution," *ante*, at 9, does not suffice to read a four-month deadline into the statute where the language will not bear it.

To hold that the EPA is not subject to a general four-month deadline is not to hold that it is subject to no time constraints. It cannot unreasonably delay in processing proposed SIP revisions since, like all agencies, it must conform to the Administrative Procedure Act's requirement that it act "within a reasonable time . . . to conclude a matter presented to it." 5 U. S. C. § 555(b). Petitioner's alternative claim is that the delay in this case violated that provision. For the reasons stated by the Court in Part IV with respect to the (erroneously found) deadline violation, I would conclude that even if an APA violation did occur it would not bar the agency from enforcing the preexisting SIP.

After he had received Justice Blackmun's draft opinion of the Court, Justice Scalia sent a May 30, 1990, "Dear Harry" letter in which he differed with the Blackmun assessment of the conference vote in the Justice's May 30 memo. It will be recalled that Justice Blackmun had written that the conference was "undecided—on the 4-month issue." The Scalia letter disagreed. "My record of the Conference discussion," it stated, "was that a majority opposed (with varying degrees of conviction) imposition of a four-month deadline. (The Chief, Bill, John, Sandra, Tony and I.)"

Justice Scalia's letter also noted, "I attach (in typed form, since the printing office is backed up) my proposed concurrence explaining why that vote was correct." The next day Justice Scalia circulated a printed draft of his concurrence, which is reprinted on p. 416. His draft declared, "I disagree with Part III of the opinion, holding that the Clean Air Act requires the Environmental Protection Agency (EPA) to process within four months proposed revisions to state implementation plans (SIPs). In my view, neither the language nor the structure of the Act supports that conclusion."

According to Justice Scalia's draft, "No one even remotely familiar with the requirements of administrative action under this legislation would think it reasonable to impose an absolute, four-month deadline on all SIP revision approvals." Nor is the Blackmun assertion that the deadline is consistent with the structure of the statute supported. In the Scalia view, "Congress's general intent 'to establish a federal-state partnership for the control of air pollution,' does not suffice to read a four-month deadline into the statute where the language will not bear it."

Scalia concludes that the petitioner's claim, supported by the Court, that the statute "establish[es] a four-month deadline for processing proposed SIP revisions . . . seems . . . quite wrong."

Scalia's draft concurrence was the catalyst that led to the final *General Motors* decision that there was no binding four-month deadline applicable to the SIP revision. On June 1, Justice Brennan wrote to Justice Blackmun that he did not join Part III of his draft opinion of the Court. "I find," Brennan stated, "that I am still persuaded by the position written up by Nino with respect to the 4-month requirement." Similar letters were sent to Justice Blackmun by Justices Stevens, O'Connor, and Kennedy and the Chief Justice.

In his May 30 memo, Justice Blackmun had noted, with regard to his draft's conclusion on the four-month issue, "Some of you may disagree. If a majority does, I shall have to revise that portion of the opinion."

Now, after he had received the refusals to join Part III of his draft, Justice Blackmun sent around a June 6 Memorandum to the Conference: "In my letter of May 30, which accompanied the proposed draft of the opinion in this case was circulated [*sic*], I stated that if a majority disagreed on the 4-month issue, I would revise that portion of the opinion. All the votes are now in, and they seem to be 6-to-3 against the 4-month requirement."

Because of this, Justice Blackmun wrote, "I therefore am circulating a new draft"—with a new Part III, holding that EPA was not bound by the four-month deadline. The revised Part III, which is the version that appears in the final *General Motors* opinion, was adapted from the Scalia draft concurrence. When Justice Scalia read it, he wrote to Justice Blackmun on June 11, "I would be pleased to join your opinion. (My concurrence is of course withdrawn.)" The others also joined and the *General Motors* opinion came down as a unanimous opinion.

In noting the majority against the four-month deadline in his June 6 letter, Justice Blackmun wrote, "I could go along with this, for I do not feel strongly about the point." Yet the point decided in *General Motors* does involve an important administrative law issue—that of whether a statutory time limit for administrative agencies is mandatory or only directory.

In *General Motors*, Blackmun's draft opinion of the Court would have treated the administrative time limit as a "statutory imperative," rather than a mere hortatory declaration without binding effect. The final *General Motors* opinion rejects this approach and reaffirms the rule that administrative time limits are not mandatory. Under it the statement by a federal court may come to serve as a description of all too many administrative cases: "Perhaps inspired by *Jarndyce* v. *Jarndyce*, the fabled interminable litigation of Dickens' *Bleak House*, the Interstate Commerce Commission has been presiding over this continuing saga for the last ten years, now in its sixth epoch."[10]

Notes

1. 5 U.S.C. § 706(c).
2. 467 U.S. 104 (1984).
3. *Mathews* v. *Eldridge*, 424 U.S. 319 (1976).
4. 467 U.S. at 119.
5. *Brock* v. *Pierce County*, 476 U.S. 253 (1986).
6. 481 U.S. 252 (1987).
7. Id. at 271.
8. Id. at 278, n. 7.
9. 496 U.S. 530 (1990).
10. *Arizona Elec. Power Co-op* v. *United States*, 816 F.2d 1366, 1368 (9th Cir. 1987).

9

United States v. *France (1991)*: *Magistrates' Powers and Delayed Decisions*

The case of *United States* v. *France*[1] well illustrates how the decision rendered by the Court may not reflect the actual decision process or the efforts devoted by the Justices to the case. The case also shows that the Justices' inability to decide the issue before them may lead only to postponement of a decision on the matter, particularly where the case itself proved an unsuitable vehicle for resolving the issue.

The ever-increasing workload of the federal courts led Congress to set up the federal magistrate judges system in 1968. Federal magistrates act as adjuncts to the federal district courts, relieving the district judges of duties that they would otherwise have to perform. In a number of cases, the Supreme Court has had to deal with the question of what authority federal magistrates may exercise, both under the Federal Magistrates Act and the requirements of Article III of the Constitution.[2] *United States* v. *France* was one of these cases.

The Federal Magistrates Act grants district courts authority to assign to magistrates certain described functions as well as "such additional duties as are not inconsistent with the Constitution and laws of the United States." In the 1989 case of *Gomez* v. *United States*,[3] the Court held that the statute did not allow a magistrate to select the jury in a felony trial over the defendant's objection. In the *France* case, the defendant had been convicted of assaulting her husband with a firearm on a military base and sentenced to five years in prison. Without objection from either party, a magistrate presided during the selection of the jury. The defendant's objection to one question asked by the prosecutor was sustained, but otherwise the defendant made no objection to the conduct of the jury selection or to the qualification of any of the jurors. As Justice Stevens stated in his draft opinion of the Court, the issue was "whether the defendant's express or implied consent warrants a different result" from that reached in *Gomez*. The lower court had ruled that it did not.

The conference in *France* voted to permit the magistrate to conduct the voir dire in the defendant's trial. The opinion was assigned to Justice Stevens, who had also written the opinion in *Gomez*. He soon circulated the draft opinion of the Court reprinted on p. 426. The draft contains a fuller discussion of the governing principles in such a case than the *Peretz* opinion did later in 1991,[4] where the *France* issue was finally decided.

According to Stevens's draft in the *France* case, the *Gomez* case "yielded three propositions that guide our present inquiry." The first was "that a magistrate 'exceeds his jurisdiction,' by selecting a jury 'despite the defendant's objection.'" But *Gomez* "did not resolve the quite different question whether a judge may authorize a magistrate to conduct the *voir dire* if the parties consent."

The second proposition stated by Stevens's draft was that, "as Congress expanded the express authority of magistrates to perform tasks that had traditionally been the exclusive province of Article III judges, it repeatedly conditioned the exercise of the magistrate's authority on the consent of the litigants."

The third proposition in Stevens's draft was based upon the importance of magistrates in the federal judicial system. As the draft puts it, "[A]lthough the jurisdiction that a federal judge may delegate to a magistrate is neither limited to the kind of ministerial tasks that can be performed by a 'supernotary' nor coextensive with the authority of the District Court itself, Congress intended the magistrate to play an integral and important role in the federal judicial system." In particular, the duty "to select juries in felony trials . . . is certainly comparable to other functions that magistrates may perform with the consent of the parties."

The propositions just stated lead Stevens to "conclude that the Magistrates Act's 'additional duties' clause permits a magistrate to preside over jury selection in a felony trial provided the parties consent." Nor, according to the draft, "is there any constitutional infirmity in the delegation of jury selection to a magistrate absent the litigants' objection." The analysis here is essentially similar to that contained in the opinion of the Court that Justice Stevens was to issue in the *Peretz* case.[5]

Stevens's *France* draft then repeats the point that the conduct of the voir dire was similar to other duties performed by magistrates: "[S]upervising jury selection in felony trials is certainly a function of comparable importance to presiding over misdemeanor trials and serving as special master in civil cases, responsibilities the statute expressly entrusts to magistrates provided the litigants consent."

Hence, the Stevens draft concludes, supervision of the voir dire is one of the duties that may be delegated to magistrates. "The Act evinces a congressional belief that magistrates are well qualified to handle matters of similar importance to jury selection but conditions their jurisdiction to accept such responsibilities on the consent of the parties." Such a result fully protects defendant's rights. "If a defendant perceives any threat of injury from the absence of an Article III judge in the jury selection process, she need only decline to consent to the magistrate's supervision to ensure that a judge conduct the voir dire."

At the end of his draft, Justice Stevens applies his interpretation of the "additional duties" clause to the *France* case, where the defendant neither consented nor objected to the magistrate's conduct of the voir dire. His conclusion is that preservation of the right to have the district judge supervise the jury selection "depends upon its affirmative exercise." Consequently, "no error was committed because respondent's failure to object constituted implied consent to the magistrate's actions."

On the contrary, in a case such as this, "Given the tactical considerations that might prompt a defense counsel to prefer a particular magistrate to a particular district judge, as long as the defendant has the right to insist on having the Article III judge preside, it is appropriate to construe the failure to assert that right as tantamount to express consent to the performance of the task by the magistrate."

7th DRAFT

SUPREME COURT OF THE UNITED STATES

No. 89-1363

UNITED STATES, PETITIONER *v.* DARLINA K. FRANCE

ON WRIT OF CERTIORARI TO THE UNITED STATES COURT OF APPEALS FOR THE NINTH CIRCUIT

[January ——, 1991]

JUSTICE STEVENS delivered the opinion of the Court.

The Federal Magistrates Act grants district courts authority to assign magistrates certain described functions as well as "such additional duties as are not inconsistent with the Constitution and laws of the United States."[1] In *Gomez* v. *United States*, 490 U. S. —— (1989), we held that those "additional duties" do not encompass the selection of a jury in a felony trial without the defendant's consent. In this case, we consider whether the defendant's express or implied consent warrants a different result.

I

Respondent was convicted of various offenses for assaulting her husband with a firearm on a military base in Hawaii and was sentenced to prison for five years. App. 56-57.[2] Without objection from either party, a magistrate presided during the selection of the jury. Respondent's objection to one question asked by the prosecutor was sustained, but oth-

[1] Pub. L. 90-578, 82 Stat. 1108, as amended, 28 U. S. C. § 636(b)(3).

[2] Respondent was convicted of assault with a deadly weapon, in violation of 18 U. S. C. § 113(a), assault resulting in serious bodily injury, in violation of 18 U. S. C. § 113(f), and use of a firearm in relation to a crime of violence, in violation of 18 U. S. C. § 924(c). The conviction under § 924(c) carried with it a five-year mandatory prison term with no possibility of parole or probation.

UNITED STATES *v.* FRANCE

erwise respondent made no objection to the conduct of the *voir dire* or to the qualification of any of the jurors. *Id.*, at 4–54.

While respondent's appeal from her convictions was pending in the Court of Appeals for the Ninth Circuit, we decided *Gomez.* Based on that decision, respondent argued that the conduct of the *voir dire* in her case was plain error. The Ninth Circuit agreed that the magistrate had improperly participated in the *voir dire* and reversed respondent's convictions. See *United States* v. *France*, 886 F. 2d 223 (CA9 1989). The Court of Appeals read our decision in *Gomez* to establish that the Magistrates Act does not permit a magistrate to conduct a felony trial *voir dire* even if the defendant does not object to the magistrate's participation. *Id.*, at 227. The Court of Appeals further held that the absence of a contemporaneous objection did not bar consideration of respondent's *Gomez* claim because an objection would have been futile in light of previous Ninth Circuit holdings permitting magistrates to conduct the *voir dire* in felony trials. *Id.*, at 227–228.[3]

We granted certiorari to review the Ninth Circuit's interpretation of our opinion in *Gomez.* —— U. S. —— (1990).[4]

---

[3] Contemporaneous objection to trial court errors is required by Federal Rule of Criminal Procedure 51, which provides:

"Exceptions to rulings or orders of the court are unnecessary and for all purposes for which an exception has heretofore been necessary it is sufficient that a party, at the time the ruling or order of the court is made or sought, makes known to the court the action which that party desires the court to take or that party's objection to the action of the court and the grounds therefor; but if a party has no opportunity to object to a ruling or order, the absence of an objection does not thereafter prejudice that party."

[4] The Courts of Appeals are divided over whether *Gomez* requires reversal of convictions of defendants who failed to object to a magistrate conducting their *voir dire.* The First Circuit has followed the Ninth Circuit's holding that reversal is required. See *United States* v. *Martinez-Torres*, Nos. 87-2006, 87-2007, 87-2008 (CA1, Aug. 20, 1990) (en banc). The other circuits have disagreed. See *United States* v. *Wey*, 895 F. 2d 429

UNITED STATES *v.* FRANCE

Because the Ninth Circuit mistakenly read *Gomez* to preclude a magistrate's supervision of *voir dire* with the defendant's consent, we now reverse.

II

Our opinion in *Gomez* recounted the gradual congressional enlargement of the jurisdiction of federal magistrates. Adhering to the interpretive approach adopted in earlier cases, we rejected a literal reading of the "additional duties" clause of the Act and instead sought to deduce its meaning in light of the structure and purpose of the overall statutory scheme.[5] Our review of the Federal Magistrates Act as enacted in 1968 and amended in 1976 and 1979 yielded three propositions that guide our present inquiry.

First, our review led us to conclude only that a magistrate "exceeds his jurisdiction," by selecting a jury "despite the defendant's objection." *Gomez* v. *United States*, 490 U. S., at ——. This conclusion was based on our analysis of the statutory authority of the official, rather than on any uncertainty

(CA7 1990); *United States* v. *Vanwort*, 887 F. 2d 375 (CA2 1989), cert. denied *sub nom. DaSilva* v. *United States*, 495 U. S. —— (1990); *United States* v. *Mang Sun Wong*, 884 F. 2d 1537 (CA2 1989), cert. denied, 493 U. S. —— (1990); *Government of Virgin Islands* v. *Williams*, 892 F. 2d 305 (CA3 1989).

[5] "The Federal Magistrates Act provides that a 'magistrate may be assigned such additional duties as are not inconsistent with the Constitution and laws of the United States.' 28 USC § 636(b)(3). Read literally and without reference to the context in which they appear, these words might encompass any assignment that is not explicitly prohibited by statute or by the Constitution.

. . . . .

"When a statute creates an office to which it assigns specific duties, those duties outline the attributes of the office. Any additional duties performed pursuant to a general authorization in the statute reasonably should bear some relation to the specified duties. Thus in *United States* v. *Raddatz*, 447 U. S. 667, 674–676 (1980); *Mathews* v. *Weber*, 423 U. S. 261 (1976); and *Wingo* v. *Wedding*, 418 U. S. 461 (1974), we interpreted the Federal Magistrates Act in light of its structure and purpose." *Gomez* v. *United States*, 490 U. S. ——, ——, —— (1989).

UNITED STATES *v.* FRANCE

about the power of the federal court to hear and decide a case that fell plainly within its subject-matter jurisdiction. Because the error in *Gomez* stemmed from the official's lack of authority, harmless-error analysis was inappropriate, even though the defendant had alleged no specific prejudice. *Ibid.* *Gomez*, however, did not resolve the quite different question whether a judge may authorize a magistrate to conduct the *voir dire* if the parties consent. Unlike the question we answered in *Gomez*, over which there was a conflict in the Courts of Appeals, see *id.*, at —— and n. 7, those courts had uniformly rejected challenges to a magistrate's authority to conduct the *voir dire* when no objection to his performance of this duty had been raised in the trial court.[6]

Second, as Congress expanded the express authority of magistrates to perform tasks that had traditionally been the exclusive province of Article III judges, it repeatedly conditioned the exercise of the magistrate's authority on the consent of the litigants.[7] Thus, in 1968 when magistrates were empowered to try "minor offenses," the exercise of that jurisdiction in any specific case was conditioned upon the defendant's express written consent. See *id.*, at ——. Similarly, the 1976 Amendment provided that a magistrate could be designated as a special master in any civil case but only with the consent of the parties. *Id.*, at ——. And in 1979, when Congress enlarged the magistrate's criminal jurisdiction to encompass all misdemeanors, the exercise of that authority

[6] See, *e. g.*, *United States* v. *Ford*, 824 F. 2d 1430 (CA5 1987); *United States* v. *DeFiore*, 720 F. 2d 757 (CA2 1983), cert. denied *sub nom.* *Coppola* v. *United States*, 466 U. S. 906 (1984); *United States* v. *Rivera-Sola*, 713 F. 2d 866 (CA1 1983); *Haith* v. *United States*, 342 F. 2d 158 (CA3 1965).

[7] The legislative history of the statute also emphasizes the crucial nature of the presence or absence of the litigants' consent. See H. R. Rep. No. 96–287, p. 20 (1979) ("Because of the consent requirement, magistrates will be used only as the bench, bar, and litigants desire, only in cases where they are felt by all participants to be competent").

UNITED STATES *v.* FRANCE

was subject to the defendant's consent. As we explained in *Gomez:*

> "A critical limitation on this expanded jurisdiction is consent. As amended in 1979, the Act states that 'neither the district judge nor the magistrate shall attempt to persuade or induce any party to consent to reference of any civil matter to a magistrate.' 93 Stat. 643, 28 U. S. C. § 636(c)(2). In criminal cases, the Government may petition for trial before a district judge. 'Defendants charged with misdemeanors can refuse to consent to a magistrate and thus effect the same removal,' S. Rep. No. 96–74, p. 7 (1979), for the magistrate's criminal trial jurisdiction depends on the defendant's specific, written consent." *Id.*, at ——.

Third, although the jurisdiction that a federal judge may delegate to a magistrate is neither limited to the kind of ministerial tasks that can be performed by a "supernotary" nor coextensive with the authority of the District Court itself, Congress intended the magistrate to play an integral and important role in the federal judicial system. See *id.*, at —— (citing H. R. Rep. No. 96–287, p. 5 (1979)). The specific grants of authority to magistrates clearly establish the importance of that role in the present system.[8] Although our

[8] "It can hardly be denied that the system created by the Federal Magistrates Act has exceeded the highest expectations of the legislators who conceived it. In modern federal practice, federal magistrates account for a staggering volume of judicial work. In 1987, for example, magistrates presided over nearly half a million judicial proceedings. *See* S. Rep. No. 100–293, 100th Cong., 2d Sess. 7, *reprinted in* 1988 U. S. Code Cong. & Admin. News 5564. As a recent Senate Report noted, '[i]n particular, magistrates [in 1987] conducted over 134,000 preliminary proceedings in felony cases; handled more than 197,000 references of civil and criminal pretrial matters; reviewed more than 6,500 social security appeals and more than 27,000 prisoner filings; and tried more than 95,000 misdemeanors and 4,900 civil cases on consent of the parties.' *Id.* at 5565. Given the bloated dockets that district courts have now come to expect as

UNITED STATES *v.* FRANCE

review of other provisions of the Act convinced us that Congress did not authorize magistrates to select juries in felony trials over the defendant's objection, that duty is certainly comparable to other functions that magistrates may perform with the consent of the parties.

With these propositions in mind, we conclude that the Magistrates Act's "additional duties" clause permits a magistrate to preside over jury selection in a felony trial provided the parties consent. In reaching this result, we are assisted by the reasoning of the Court of Appeals for the Third Circuit, which, following our decision in *Gomez*, addressed the question whether the rationale of that opinion applied when the defendant had not objected to the magistrate's conduct of the *voir dire*. See *Government of Virgin Islands* v. *Williams*, 892 F. 2d 305, 308–309 (CA3 1989). After noting that we had carefully left that question open,[9] Chief Judge Gibbons first decided that authorization of a magistrate to conduct a felony trial *voir dire* is "'not inconsistent with the Constitution and laws of the United States' .... 28 U. S. C. § 636(b)(3)." See *id.*, at 310–311.

As the Third Circuit noted, no statute prohibits federal magistrates from conducting *voir dire* when a defendant con-

---

ordinary, the role of the magistrate in today's federal judicial system is nothing less than indispensable." *Government of Virgin Islands* v. *Williams*, 892 F. 2d, at 308.

[9] "The Court did not, however, reach the question presented in this case: whether the Federal Magistrates Act permits a magistrate to preside over the selection of a jury when a defendant consents. In *Gomez*, the Court framed the issue as 'whether presiding at the selection of a jury in a felony trial *without the defendant's consent*' is an additional duty within the meaning of the Federal Magistrates Act. *Id.* at 2239 (emphasis added); *see also id.* at 2248 (rejecting the government's harmless error analysis on the grounds that it 'does not apply in a felony case in which, *despite the defendant's objection* and without any meaningful review by a district judge, an officer exceeds his jurisdiction by selecting a jury'). *Gomez* thus left open the question whether a defendant's consent makes a difference as to whether a district court may assign voir dire to a magistrate." *Government of Virgin Islands* v. *Williams*, 892 F. 2d, at 308–309.

UNITED STATES *v.* FRANCE

sents. Cf. 28 U. S. C. § 1334(c) (explicitly proscribing delegation of bankruptcy appeals to a magistrate). Nor is there any constitutional infirmity in the delegation of jury selection to a magistrate absent the litigants' objection. In *Gomez*, we suggested, but did not decide, that a criminal defendant may have a constitutional right in a felony trial to demand the presence of an Article III judge at *voir dire*. *Gomez*, 490 U. S., at —— and n. 9, —— n. 25. We need not resolve that question now, however, to determine that a defendant has no constitutional right to have an Article III judge preside at jury selection if the defendant has raised no objection to the judge's absence.

We have previously held that litigants may waive their right to have an Article III judge preside over a civil trial. See *Commodity Futures Trading Comm'n* v. *Schor*, 478 U. S. 833, 848 (1986). The most basic rights of criminal defendants are similarly subject to waiver. See, *e. g.*, *United States* v. *Gagnon*, 470 U. S. 522, 528 (1985) (absence of objection constitutes waiver of right to be present at all stages of criminal trial); *Levine* v. *United States*, 362 U. S. 610, 619 (1960) (failure to object to closing of courtroom is waiver of right to public trial); *Segurola* v. *United States*, 275 U. S. 106, 111 (1927) (failure to object constitutes waiver of Fourth Amendment right against unlawful search and seizure); *United States* v. *Figueroa*, 818 F. 2d 1020, 1025 (CA1 1987) (failure to object results in forfeiture of claim of unlawful post-arrest delay); *United States* v. *Bascaro*, 742 F. 2d 1335, 1365 (CA11 1984) (absence of objection is waiver of double jeopardy defense), cert. denied, 472 U. S. 1017 (1985); *United States* v. *Coleman*, 707 F. 2d 374, 376 (CA9) (failure to object constitutes waiver of Fifth Amendment claim), cert. denied, 464 U. S. 854 (1983). See generally *Yakus* v. *United States*, 321 U. S. 414, 444 (1944) ("No procedural principle is more familiar . . . than that a . . . right may be forfeited in criminal as well as civil cases by the failure to make timely

UNITED STATES *v.* FRANCE

assertion of the right . . ."). Just as the Constitution affords no protection to a defendant who waives these fundamental rights, so it gives no assistance to a defendant who fails to demand the presence of an Article III judge at the selection of her jury.

We also do not believe that the structural principles behind Article III are implicated here. The "ultimate decision" whether to invoke the magistrate's assistance is made by the district court, subject of course to veto by the parties. *United States* v. *Raddatz*, 447 U. S. 667, 683 (1980). Because "the entire process takes place under the district court's total control and jurisdiction," *id.*, at 681, there is no danger that use of the magistrate involves a "congressional attempt[] 'to transfer jurisdiction [to non-Article III tribunals] for the purpose of emasculating' constitutional courts, *National Insurance Co.* v. *Tidewater Co.*, 337 U. S. 582, 644 (1949) (Vinson, C. J., dissenting) . . . ." *Commodity Futures Trading Comm'n* v. *Schor*, 478 U. S. at 850.[10]

[10] Although the dissent contends that *United States* v. *Raddatz*, 447 U. S., at 682, suggests that *de novo* review is necessary to protect the structural aspect of Article III, *post*, at 16 and n. 5, *Raddatz* holds to the contrary. Title 28 U. S. C. § 636(b)(1), the constitutionality of which the Court upheld in *Raddatz*, provides for *de novo* review *only* when a party objects to the magistrate's findings or recommendations. Thus, *Raddatz* establishes that to the extent "de novo review is required to satisfy Article III concerns, it need not be exercised unless requested by the parties." *United States* v. *Peacock*, 761 F. 2d 1313, 1318 (CA9) (Kennedy, J.), cert. denied, 474 U. S. 847 (1985). Because as the dissent points out, the "parties may *not* waive Article III's structural guarantee," *post*, at 15, the Court necessarily concluded in *Raddatz* that *de novo* review is not critical to Article III's separation-of-powers function. We agree that *de novo* review is not necessary to protect the separation of powers when, as is the case here, judicial duties are delegated to adjuncts, the authority of which may be invoked only at the behest of an Article III Court, and the officers of which are appointed, and subject to removal by, an Article III Court. See *United States* v. *Raddatz*, 447 U. S., at 685 (BLACKMUN, J., concurring).

The Court in *Raddatz* properly considered the availability of *de novo* review upon request to be a significant protection for Article III's *personal*

UNITED STATES *v.* FRANCE

A magistrate's supervision of *voir dire* with the parties' consent not only satisfies the statute's literal requirement that a magistrate's "additional duties" be consistent with the laws and the Constitution but also passes the functional test we endorsed in *Gomez* to determine intended "additional duties." As we discussed above, the presence or absence of consent is crucial to the statutory division between permissible and impermissible duties. Furthermore, supervising jury selection in felony trials is certainly a function of comparable importance to presiding over misdemeanor trials and serving as special master in civil cases, responsibilities the statute expressly entrusts to magistrates provided the litigants consent.

We share the confidence expressed by the Third Circuit in *Williams* that this reading of the additional duties clause strikes the balance Congress intended between the interests of the criminal defendant and the policies that undergird the Federal Magistrates Act. 892 F. 2d, at 311. The Act is designed to relieve the district courts of certain subordinate duties that often distract the courts from more important matters.[11] Our reading of the "additional duties" clause will permit the courts, with the litigants' consent, to "continue innovative experimentations" in the use of magistrates to im-

---

guarantee, because a magistrate may perform duties under § 636(b)(1) *even if a party objects*. Because a magistrate may *not* supervise *voir dire* if the defendant objects, *de novo* review is not necessary to protect any personal Article III right that might exist here.

[11] See, *e. g.*, H. R. Rep. No. 94–1609, p. 7 (1976) (magistrate is to "assist the district judge in a variety of pretrial and preliminary matters thereby facilitating the ultimate and final exercise of the adjudicatory function at the trial of the case"); S. Rep. No. 92–1065, p. 3 (1972) (magistrates "render valuable assistance to the judges of the district courts, thereby freeing the time of those judges for the actual trial of cases"); H. R. Rep. No. 1629, 90th Cong., 2d Sess., p. 12 (1968) (purpose of Act is "to cull from the ever-growing workload of the U. S. district courts matters that are more desirably performed by a lower tier of judicial officers").

UNITED STATES *v.* FRANCE

prove the efficient administration of the courts' dockets. See H. R. Rep. No. 94-1609, p. 5 (1976).[12]

At the same time, the requirement that a criminal defendant consent to the additional duty of jury selection protects a defendant's interest in requesting the presence of a judge at all critical stages in her felony trial.

> "If a criminal defendant, together with his attorney, believes that the presence of a judge best serves his interests during the selection of the jury, then *Gomez* preserves his right to object to the use of a magistrate. Where, on the other hand, the defendant is indifferent as to whether a magistrate or a judge should preside, then it makes little sense to deny the district court the opportunity to delegate that function to a magistrate, particularly if such a delegation sensibly advances the court's interest in the efficient regulation of its docket." *Government of Virgin Islands* v. *Williams*, 892 F. 2d, at 311.

In sum, the structure and purpose of the Magistrates Act convince us that supervision of *voir dire* in a felony proceeding is an additional duty that may be delegated to a magistrate under § 636(b)(3) if the litigants consent.[13] The Act evinces a congressional belief that magistrates are well qualified to handle matters of similar importance to jury selection

[12] See, *e. g.*, *United States* v. *Peacock*, 761 F. 2d, at 1319 ("There may be sound reasons . . . to allow the magistrate to assist [in *voir dire*], as was done in this case. [E]ach of the . . . circuits in the federal system[ ] has been instructed to improve its efficiency in juror utilization. . . . The practice of delegating *voir dire* to a magistrate may assist the district courts in accomplishing this objective").

[13] We noted in *Gomez* that the legislative history of the Act nowhere listed supervision, without a defendant's consent, of a felony trial *voir dire* as a potential magistrate responsibility. We did call attention, however, to a Committee Report that referred to a "letter suggest[ing] that a magistrate selected juries only *with* consent of the parties." *Gomez* v. *United States*, 490 U. S., at ——, n. 30 (emphasis added) (citing H. R. Rep. No. 94-1609, p. 9 (1976)).

UNITED STATES *v.* FRANCE

but conditions their jurisdiction to accept such responsibilities on the consent of the parties. If a defendant perceives any threat of injury from the absence of an Article III judge in the jury selection process, she need only decline to consent to the magistrate's supervision to ensure that a judge conduct the *voir dire.*[14]

III

We must still decide whether, given this interpretation of the "additional duties" clause, the magistrate's presiding at the selection of respondent's jury was permissible. Although respondent did not object, neither did she expressly consent to the magistrate's supervision of the *voir dire.* App. 4–54. Indeed, she now argues that the magistrate's participation was plain error and that, in any event, it would have been futile for her counsel to object because it was the settled practice in the United States District Court for the District of Hawaii to delegate this function to magistrates and that practice had been twice expressly upheld by the Court of Appeals for the Ninth Circuit. In response, the Government argues that any error was waived because no

---

[14] We do not qualify the portion of our opinion in *Gomez* that explained why jury selection is an important function, the performance of which may be difficult for a judge to review with infallible accuracy. See 490 U. S., at ——. We are confident, however, that defense counsel can sensibly balance these considerations against other concerns in deciding whether to object to a magistrate's supervision of *voir dire.* We stress, in this regard, that defendants may waive the right to judicial performance of other important functions, including the conduct of the trial itself in misdemeanor and civil proceedings. Like jury selection, these duties require the magistrate to "observe witnesses, make credibility determinations, and weigh contradictory evidence," *id.* at ——, n. 27, and therefore present equivalent problems for judicial oversight. The dissent's distress at the difficulties of effective judicial review of consented-to magistrate jury selection, *post,* at 10, is thus unwarranted, for a defendant has the power to avoid the need for any judicial review by simply declining to consent. The dissent's concomitant "regret[ ]" at our silence regarding the appropriate "standard of review" is equally unwarranted. That issue was neither briefed nor argued and is not before us in this case.

UNITED STATES v. FRANCE

timely objection was made as required by Rule 51 of the Federal Rules of Criminal Procedure,[15] and further that the error cannot be considered "plain error" within the meaning of Rule 52(b)[16] because respondent has demonstrated no prejudice. In our view of the case, however, no error was committed because respondent's failure to object constituted implied consent to the magistrate's actions.[17]

The error that occurred in *Gomez*—assignment to a magistrate of supervision over jury selection despite the defendant's objection—simply did not occur in this case. Accordingly, the question before us is not whether respondent waived her right to complain of an error committed by the trial court; rather the question is whether she waived her right to insist on having the trial judge conduct the *voir dire*. Because we are satisfied that the preservation of that right depends upon its affirmative exercise, we conclude that there was no error in this case.[18]

---

[15] See n. 3, *supra*.

[16] Federal Rule of Criminal Procedure 52(b) provides:

"*Plain Error*. Plain errors or defects affecting substantial rights may be noticed although they were not brought to the attention of the court."

[17] Because we hold that no error was committed, we express no opinion on the question whether, or under what circumstances, a court of appeals can properly reverse convictions based on errors to which the defendant made no objection in the district court, and which are not "plain" under Federal Rules of Criminal Procedure 52(b). See, *e. g.*, *Singleton* v. *Wulff*, 428 U. S. 106, 121 (1976); *Grosso* v. *United States*, 390 U. S. 62, 70–71 (1968). Cf. *Osborne* v. *Ohio*, 495 U. S. ——, —— (1990). We also do not suggest that, as a general matter, a trial error ceases to exist when a defendant fails to object. We hold only that the absence of the defendant's objection is the crucial factor in determining whether supervision of jury selection qualifies as an "additional dut[y]" under 28 U. S. C. § 636(b)(3). Thus, our holding neither endorses nor questions the proposition that an appellate court may sometimes exercise its discretion to excuse the failure to object to an error because objection would have been futile. See, *e. g.*, *Guam* v. *Yang*, 850 F. 2d 507, 512 n. 8 (CA9 1988); *United States* v. *Byers*, 740 F. 2d 1104, 1109 n. 6 (D. C. Cir. 1984); *United States* v. *Scott*, 425 F. 2d 55, 57–58 (CA9 1970) (en banc).

[18] We recognize that in several situations in which the Act explicitly empowers magistrates to perform duties only with the litigants' consent, Con-

UNITED STATES *v.* FRANCE

The case was tried by a visiting district judge who did not regularly sit in the District of Hawaii. App. 6. In earlier cases, defense counsel had objected, without success, to the use of a magistrate to conduct the *voir dire*. Brief for Respondent 3–4. We therefore presume that counsel knew that there was a substantial legal basis for believing that the defendant had a right to have the trial judge preside. It is true that the earlier objections had been overruled, *ibid.*, and that the Court of Appeals for the Ninth Circuit had twice upheld the magistrate's jurisdiction despite such objections. See *United States* v. *Peacock*, 761 F. 2d 1313 (CA9), cert. denied, 474 U. S. 847 (1985); *United States* v. *Bezold*, 760 F. 2d 999 (CA9 1985), cert. denied, 474 U. S. 1063 (1986). It nevertheless is equally true that counsel may well have preferred to have the local magistrate, rather than the visiting judge, preside in this case because counsel was familiar with the magistrate's practice and unfamiliar with the practice of the visiting judge. Indeed, the magistrate did sustain respondent's objection to one question proposed by the prosecutor and asked an additional question of the venire at respondent's request. App. 47–49.

Whether or not this speculation is reasonable in this particular case, it is surely true that in this class of cases defense counsel will sometimes prefer to have a magistrate rather than the trial judge preside at the *voir dire*. Counsel could reasonably believe that a magistrate would conduct a more thorough *voir dire* than a district judge, who may be preoccupied with other responsibilities. In a particular instance, counsel might conclude that the magistrate's view of juror qualifications would be more favorable to the defendant than

gress required express consent. As we explain below, however, the tactical reasons a defendant might possess for withholding an objection to a magistrate's supervision of *voir dire* make it appropriate to view a failure to object as equivalent to consent. Cf. *United States* v. *Busche*, No. 89-3539 (CA7, Oct. 16, 1990). The dissent does not, and indeed cannot, identify any language in the Act that prohibits this sensible interpretation, despite the dissent's citation to language requiring express consent in other contexts, *post*, at 4.

UNITED STATES *v.* FRANCE

the district judge's view or that the magistrate might be more willing to permit counsel to ask questions of the venire. Given the tactical considerations that might prompt a defense counsel to prefer a particular magistrate to a particular district judge, as long as the defendant has the right to insist on having the Article III judge preside, it is appropriate to construe the failure to assert that right as tantamount to express consent to the performance of the task by the magistrate. The general policy that is implemented by Federal Rule of Criminal Procedure 51 fully supports this conclusion.

The judgment of the Court of Appeals is reversed.

It is so ordered.

JUSTICE SOUTER took no part in the consideration or decision of this case.

5th DRAFT

SUPREME COURT OF THE UNITED STATES

No. 89-1363

UNITED STATES, PETITIONER *v.* DARLINA K. FRANCE

ON WRIT OF CERTIORARI TO THE UNITED STATES COURT OF APPEALS FOR THE NINTH CIRCUIT

[January ——, 1991]

JUSTICE MARSHALL, with whom JUSTICE WHITE and JUSTICE BLACKMUN join, and with whom JUSTICE SCALIA joins as to Parts I and II, dissenting.

The Court's decision today hinges on a crucial premise: that respondent "consented" to the Magistrate's selection of the jury at her felony trial. The premise is false. What the majority calls "consent" is nothing more than respondent's silence. Faced with a Magistrate's assumption of jury selection duties—duties that the supervising federal court had expressly (though erroneously) found to lie within the Magistrate's powers—respondent did not raise an objection. Indeed, in view of Circuit precedent, any objection would have been futile. I cannot understand how mere silence in such circumstances can be construed as consent.

Perhaps sensing the difficulty of the transformation it seeks to effect, the majority tries to blur the distinction—assuring us, for example, that silence can "impl[y]" consent, *ante*, at 11, or that silence is "tantamount to express consent," *ante*, at 13. Such definitions may pass muster in other circumstances, but they are unacceptable here. The unalterable fact is that a magistrate's supervision of felony jury selection violates the Federal Magistrates Act, and that violation cannot be cured by a defendant's mere acquiescence in the practice. Because the majority's equation of silence with "consent" runs contrary to criminal procedure practice

UNITED STATES *v.* FRANCE

and is at odds with the structure of the Federal Magistrates Act, I cannot accept it.

I also cannot accept the majority's underlying conclusion that consent of any sort, express or implied, can authorize a magistrate to conduct felony jury selection. In *Gomez* v. *United States*, 490 U. S. 858 (1990), we held that the Federal Magistrates Act does not authorize magistrates to supervise jury selection at a felony trial. Our reasoning in *Gomez* makes clear that the absence or presence of consent is irrelevant to the Act's prohibition upon magistrate felony jury selection. Only this construction of the Federal Magistrates Act, moreover, avoids the troubling question whether magistrate felony jury selection is consistent with Article III of the Constitution—a question the majority fails to answer in a manner consistent with our precedents. I respectfully dissent.

I

The Federal Magistrates Act provides that "[a] magistrate may be assigned such additional duties as are not inconsistent with the Constitution and laws of the United States." 28 U. S. C. § 636(b)(3). In *Gomez*, we concluded that the "additional duties" clause does not authorize a magistrate to conduct jury selection at a felony trial. We granted certiorari in this case to consider whether the Court of Appeals erred when it applied *Gomez*, despite respondent's failure to object at trial to the Magistrate's supervision of jury selection.

By imaginatively reconstructing *Gomez*, the majority avoids answering this question. According to the majority, our holding in *Gomez* establishes that the Federal Magistrates Act bars magistrate jury selection only when the defendant fails to consent to this procedure. *Ante*, at 9. The majority then asserts that "respondent's failure to object constituted *implied consent*" to magistrate jury selection in this case. *Ante*, at 11 (emphasis added). Consequently, the Court of Appeals had no cause to apply *Gomez*, because the

UNITED STATES *v.* FRANCE

Magistrate's supervision of jury selection gave rise to no error at all. *Ante*, at 11–12, n. 17.

Thus, the majority's analysis injects two new questions into this case: first, whether a failure to object can constitute consent to a magistrate's supervision of felony jury selection; and, second, whether a party's consent creates statutory authority for a magistrate to engage in this function under the Federal Magistrates Act. In my view, the clear answer to both questions is "no."

II

I cannot accept the majority's equation of respondent's failure to object to magistrate *voir dire* with "consent" to this procedure. This formulation is contrary to criminal procedural law in general and to the structure of the Federal Magistrates Act in particular.

It is true, as the majority notes, that a criminal defendant can waive many "basic" procedural guarantees. *Ante*, at 7. But we do not ordinarily premise such waiver on a bare failure to object to a trial procedure that contravenes such a right. See, *e. g.*, *Johnson* v. *Zerbst*, 304 U. S. 458, 464–465 (1938) (presumption against waiver of right to counsel); *Barker* v. *Wingo*, 407 U. S. 514, 525 (1972) (noting that courts will not "presum[e] waiver of a fundamental right from inaction" (footnote omitted)). Even when a failure to object *does* constitute waiver, courts do not say—as the majority does here—that the defendant has "consented" to the procedure in such a manner as to render it free from underlying error. If this were the law, the "plain error" rule, see Fed. Rule Crim. Proc. 52(b), and related error-preservation doctrines, see *Singleton* v. *Wulff*, 428 U. S. 106, 121 (1976), would have no function. Thus, with regard to *none* of the "basic" criminal rights adverted to by the majority, *ante*, at 7, will a court treat a mere failure to object as immunizing the procedure in question from review altogether. *United States* v. *Crawford*, 906 F. 2d 1531, 1533–1534 (CA11 1990) (engaging in plain-error review of alleged denial of Fifth

UNITED STATES v. FRANCE

Amendment right against self-incrimination); *United States* v. *Orr*, 864 F. 2d 1505, 1508 (CA10 1988) (engaging in plain-error review of alleged denial of Fourth Amendment right against unlawful search); *United States* v. *Figueroa*, 818 F. 2d 1020, 1025 (CA1 1987) (engaging in plain-error review of alleged denial of right of defendant arrested without warrant to be brought before magistrate without unnecessary delay); *United States* v. *Kupau*, 781 F. 2d 740, 743 (CA9) (engaging in plain-error review of alleged denial of right to be present at all stages of criminal trial), cert. denied, 479 U. S. 823 (1986); *United States* v. *Jefferson*, 714 F. 2d 689, 706–707 (CA7 1983) (engaging in plain-error review of alleged denial of right not to be subject to double jeopardy); cf. *Hutchins* v. *Garrison*, 724 F. 2d 1425, 1431 (CA4 1983) (finding that review of right-to-open-trial claim is precluded only if court finds "'an intentional relinquishment of a known right or privilege'" (quoting *Johnson* v. *Zerbst*, *supra*, at 464)), cert. denied, 464 U. S. 1065 (1984).

The equation of a defendant's failure to object with consent is particularly inappropriate in the setting of the Federal Magistrates Act. The Act imposes strict conditions for finding that a party has consented to a magistrate's assumption of trial duties. For example, although a magistrate may conduct a misdemeanor trial when the defendant consents, the Act requires that such consent be *in writing*. See 18 U. S. C. § 3401(b); see also 28 U. S. C. § 636(a)(3) (incorporating requirements of 18 U. S. C. § 3401 into the Federal Magistrates Act). The procedural safeguard of a written waiver "'show[s] a statutory intent to preserve trial before the district judge as the principal—rather than an elective or alternative—mode of proceeding in minor offense cases.'" *Gomez* v. *United States*, *supra*, at 872, n. 24, n. 24 (quoting 114 Cong. Rec. 27342 (1968) (remarks of Rep. Poff)).

The Federal Magistrates Act also permits a magistrate to try a civil matter when the parties consent. See 28 U. S. C. § 636(c)(1). Here, too, the Act demands that a party's consent be express. See § 636(c)(2) ("If a magistrate is designated to [try a civil case,] . . . the clerk of court shall . . . notify the parties of their right to consent to the exercise of such jurisdiction. *The decision of the parties shall be communicated* to the clerk of court" (emphasis added)).

It is hard to imagine that Congress would take such care to assure that parties do not silently waive the right to a have a district judge preside at a misdemeanor or civil trial, and yet take no care to avoid inadvertent waiver of the right to have a district judge preside at a crucial stage of a felony trial. But that is precisely the implausible intention that the majority attributes to Congress by holding that a mere failure to object constitutes "consent" to a magistrate's supervision of felony jury selection.

The majority seeks to skirt this incongruity by asserting that implied consent is warranted in this context because "defense counsel will sometimes prefer to have a magistrate rather than trial judge preside at jury selection." *Ante*, at 13. Given this possibility, the majority contends, "it is appropriate to construe" a failure to object to magistrate supervision of felony jury selection *"as tantamount to express consent* to the performance of the task by the magistrate." *Ibid.* (emphasis added). Yet civil and misdemeanor trials present this exact same possibility. Even though a party to a civil or misdemeanor trial "will sometimes prefer to have a magistrate rather than a trial judge preside," the Federal Magistrates Act requires something more definitive than silence to communicate such a preference. Thus, the majority's speculation as to defense counsel's preferences cannot form the basis for inferring that Congress would have allowed consent in felony cases to be expressed less affirmatively than in misdemeanor or civil trials.[1]

[1] The majority stresses that no language in the Act "prohibit[s]" its "sensible" equation of silence with consent. *Ante*, at 12 n. 18. In *Gomez*, however, we stressed that the Federal Magistrates Act must be interpreted not only in light of its language but "in light of its structure and its

UNITED STATES *v.* FRANCE

Once it is recognized that a failure to object to magistrate jury selection does not constitute consent to that procedure, there is no difficulty in concluding that the Court of Appeals had the discretion to reach the merits of respondent's claim under *Gomez*. To be sure, Rule 52(b) of the Federal Rules of Criminal Procedure, which authorizes a court to take account of a "plain error" not objected to at trial, contains the negative implication that other unobjected-to errors may *not* be considered. This reflects longstanding and universal understanding. See, *e. g.*, *United States* v. *Wey*, 895 F. 2d 429, 430 (CA7 1990), cert. denied, —— U. S. —— (1990); *United States* v. *Brodie*, 276 U. S. App. D. C. 328, 333, 871 F. 2d 125, 130 (1989). The prohibition implied in Rule 52(b), however, is not absolute, since it must be reconciled with 28 U. S. C. §2106, which authorizes courts of appeals to make such disposition of lower court judgments "as may be just under the circumstances." We have interpreted this provision to permit review of unobjected-to errors in certain narrow contexts other than plain error. For example, in *Grosso* v. *United States*, 390 U. S. 62 (1968), we excused the failure to object when the claim pressed on appeal relied upon post-trial Supreme Court decisions that were wholly "novel" in light of prior precedent. See *id.*, at 70–72. See also *Wood* v. *Georgia*, 450 U. S. 261, 265, n. 5 (1981); *Anderson* v. *United States*, 417 U. S. 211, 217, n. 5 (1974); *United States* v. *Byers*, 239 U. S. App. D. C. 1, 29, and n. 53, 740 F. 2d 1104, 1132, and n. 53 (CADC 1984) (Robinson, J., concurring).

The contexts in which a court may invoke §2106 to supersede the negative implication of Rule 52(b) are narrow and limited, but I think they include the present case. Here, an objection by respondent to magistrate supervision of jury

purpose." *Gomez* v. *United States*, 490 U. S. 858, 864 (1989). The majority makes no attempt to square its treatment of silence as consent with the Act's structure, which requires express consent for a magistrate's assumption of misdemeanor or civil trial duties.

UNITED STATES *v.* FRANCE

selection would have been contrary to firmly established Ninth Circuit precedent and practice. See *United States* v. *France*, 886 F. 2d 223, 227 (CA9 1989) (citing *United States* v. *Peacock*, 761 F. 2d 1313 (CA9), cert. denied, 474 U. S. 874 (1985); *United States* v. *Bezold*, 760 F. 2d 999 (CA9 1985), cert. denied, 474 U. S. 1063 (1986)). While respondent's conviction was pending on direct appeal, we issued our decision in *Gomez*, which rejected these circuit precedents. The Court of Appeals chose to entertain respondent's *Gomez* claim, applying a circuit rule allowing it to overlook a failure to raise an objection that would have been foreclosed by a "solid wall" of contrary circuit precedent and practice. See *Guam* v. *Yang*, 850 F. 2d 507, 512, n. 8 (CA9 1988) (en banc); *United States* v. *Scott*, 425 F. 2d 55, 57–58 (CA9 1970) (en banc). While I do not suggest that such a circuit rule is mandatory, it is certainly a permissible application of the discretion conferred by § 2106.

The Government contends that even though, under the pre-*Gomez* Ninth Circuit precedent, the district judge was not required (when faced with an objection) to supervise jury selection himself, he might voluntarily have done so—so that in one sense an objection would not necessarily have been futile. For purposes of establishing the permissible application of § 2106, however, I think the futility of a legal objection must be assessed on the basis of apparent legal entitlement under circuit precedent and practice, rather than on the basis of possible judicial grace. A court of appeals may choose to accept the latter as a basis for not exercising its § 2106 discretion, but I cannot say that it eliminates the discretion entirely.

III

Even if a failure to object could be treated as "consent" in this context, the majority's result still is wrong. It is clear from the reasoning in *Gomez* that the prohibition on magistrate jury selection in felony cases stems from a *jurisdictional* allocation of judicial functions between district judges

UNITED STATES *v.* FRANCE

and magistrates. Because this jurisdictional division under the Act was designed to serve the interests of the judicial system, not merely those of individual parties, a defendant's consent, no matter how express, cannot invest a magistrate with the power to conduct felony jury selection. Cf. *Insurance Corp. of Ireland* v. *Compagnie des Bauxites de Guinee*, 456 U. S. 694, 702 (1982) (because subject-matter jurisdiction serves systemic interest of limiting federal judicial power, "no action of the parties can confer subject-matter jurisdiction upon a federal court").

A

The majority locates the source of a magistrate's authority to conduct consented-to felony jury selection in the Act's "additional duties" clause, which states that "[a] magistrate may be assigned such additional duties as are not inconsistent with the Constitution and laws of the United States." 28 U. S. C. § 636(b)(3). Whether the additional duties clause authorizes a magistrate to conduct jury selection in a felony trial is a conventional issue of statutory interpretation. In *Gomez*, we held that "[t]he absence of a specific reference to jury selection in the statute, or indeed, in the legislative history, persuades us that Congress did not intend the additional duties clause to embrace this function." *Gomez* v. *United States*, 490 U. S., at 875–876 (footnote omitted). In my view, the existence of a defendant's consent occasions no modification or qualification of that conclusion.

In *Gomez*, we rejected a literal reading of the additional duties clause that would have authorized magistrates to exercise *any* power not expressly prohibited by federal statute or the Constitution. See *id.*, at 864–865. Relying on precedent and legislative history, we emphasized that the additional duties clause is to be read according to Congress' intention that magistrates "handle subsidiary matters[, thereby] enabl[ing] district judges to concentrate on trying cases." *Id.*, at 872.

UNITED STATES *v.* FRANCE

> "If district judges are willing to experiment with the assignment to magistrates of other functions in aid of the business of the courts, *there will be increased time available to judges for the careful and unhurried performance of their vital and traditional adjudicatory duties*, and a consequent benefit to both efficiency and the quality of justice in the Federal courts." H. R. Rep. No. 94–1609, p. 12 (1976) (emphasis added) (1976 amendments to Federal Magistrates Act); accord, S. Rep. No. 371, 90th Cong., 1st Sess., 26 (1967) (Federal Magistrates Act of 1968).[2]

We identified two reasons in *Gomez* for inferring that Congress intended jury selection in felony trials to be one of the "vital and traditional adjudicatory duties" retained by district judges rather than delegated to magistrates. First, we noted that Congress felt it necessary to define expressly a magistrate's limited authority to conduct misdemeanor and civil trials. See 28 U. S. C. §§636(a)(3), 636(c). We concluded that "th[is] carefully defined grant of authority to conduct trials of civil matters and of minor criminal cases" constituted "an implicit withholding of the authority to preside at a felony trial." *Gomez* v. *United States*, *supra*, at 872. And in light of the traditional judicial and legislative understand-

[2]This theme pervades the Act's legislative history. See, *e. g.*, S. Rep. No. 96–74, p. 3 (1979) (1979 amendments to Federal Magistrates Act) ("In enacting the Federal Magistrates Act in 1968, the Congress clearly intended that the magistrate should be a judicial officer whose purpose was to assist the district judge to the end that the judge could have more time to preside at the trial of cases"); H. R. Rep. No. 94–1609, p. 6 (1976) (same); S. Rep. 94–625, p. 6 (1976) (1976 amendments to Federal Magistrates Act) ("Without the assistance furnished by magistrates . . . the judges of the district courts would have to devote a substantial portion of their available time to various procedural steps rather than to the trial itself"); see also S. Rep. No. 371, 90th Cong., 1st Sess., 9 (1967) (Federal Magistrates Act is intended "to cull from the ever-growing workload of the U. S. district courts matters that are more desirably performed by a lower tier of judicial officers").

UNITED STATES *v.* FRANCE

ing that jury selection is an essential component of a felony trial,[8] we determined that Congress' intention to deny magistrates the authority to preside at felony trials should extend to jury selection. See *id.*, at 871–872.

In my view, this structural inference is affected not at all by a defendant's consent. Indeed, as I have pointed out, consent of the parties is a necessary condition of a magistrate's statutory authority to preside at a civil or misdemeanor trial. See 18 U. S. C. § 3401(b); 28 U. S. C. § 636(c)(1). Thus, to hold, as the majority does, that a magistrate may likewise conduct jury selection in a felony trial so long as the defendant consents is to treat the magistrate's authority in this part of the felony trial as perfectly coextensive with his authority in civil and misdemeanor trials—the reading of the Act that *Gomez* categorically rejected.

The second basis for our conclusion in *Gomez* that Congress intended felony jury selection to be nondelegable was Congress' failure expressly to provide for judicial review of magistrate jury selection in felony cases. The Federal Magistrates Act provides two separate standards of judicial review: "clearly erroneous or contrary to law" for magistrate resolution of nondispositive matters, see 28 U. S. C. § 636(b)(1)(A), and "*de novo*" for magistrate resolution of

[8] As we have observed, "'"[W]here the indictment is for a felony, the trial commences at least from the time when the work of empanelling the jury begins."'" *Gomez* v. *United States*, *supra*, at 873 (1990) quoting *Lewis* v. *United States*, 146 U. S. 370, 374 (1892), quoting *Hopt* v. *Utah*, 110 U. S. 574, 578 (1884). Jury selection procedures are inexorably tied to the felony trial, as we have recognized, because of the crucial rights that these procedures safeguard. "Jury selection is the primary means by which a court may enforce a defendant's right to be tried by a jury free from ethnic, racial, or political prejudice, or predisposition about the defendant's culpability." *Gomez* v. *United States*, *supra*, at 873 (citations omitted). We discerned Congress' recognition of this understanding from its passage of the Speedy Trial Act, 18 U. S. C. § 3161, and from its placement of rules relating to juries and jury selection in a chapter of the Federal Rules of Criminal Procedure entitled "Trial." See *Gomez* v. *United States*, *supra*, at 873, citing Fed. Rules Crim. Proc. 23 and 24.

UNITED STATES *v.* FRANCE

dispositive matters, see § 636(b)(1)(B)–(C). We deemed Congress' failure to identify *any* standard of judicial review for jury selection in felony trials as persuasive evidence that Congress intended that magistrates not perform this function. *Gomez* v. *United States*, *supra*, at 873–874.

Again, I fail to see how a defendant's consent to a magistrate's exercise of such authority can alter this inference. Congress said no more about the standard of review for consented-to magistrate jury selection than it did about the standard for unconsented-to magistrate jury selection. Nor does the majority say anything today about the appropriate standard of review for consented-to magistrate jury selection.

The majority's silence is regrettable. In *Gomez*, we recognized that jury selection is most similar to the functions identified as "dispositive matters," for which the Act prescribes a *de novo* review standard. 490 U. S., at 873. We expressed "serious doubts," however, as to whether any review could be meaningfully conducted. *Id.*, at 874.

> "To detect prejudices, the examiner—often, in the federal system, the court—must elicit from prospective jurors candid answers about intimate details of their lives. The court further must scrutinize not only spoken words but also gestures and attitudes of all participants to ensure the jury's impartiality. But only words can be preserved for review; no transcript can recapture the atmosphere of the *voir dire*, which may persist throughout the trial." *Id.*, at 874–875 (citations omitted).

We likewise concluded that reexamination of individual jurors by the district judge would not be feasible because "as a practical matter a second interrogation might place jurors on the defensive, engendering prejudices irrelevant to the facts adduced at trial." *Id.*, at 875, n. 29. These difficulties in providing for effective review of magistrate jury selection

UNITED STATES *v.* FRANCE

were central to our construction of the Act in *Gomez*, yet they go completely unmentioned today.[4]

B

The majority purports to distill "three propositions" from our decision in *Gomez* that allegedly deprive that decision of any force in the present case. These three propositions, in addition to placing a revisionist gloss on *Gomez*, lend no support to the view that conducting consented-to jury selection is one of a magistrate's "additional duties" under the Federal Magistrates Act.

First, according to the majority, we concluded in *Gomez* that a Magistrate exceeded his jurisdiction only because the Magistrate selected a felony jury over the defendant's objection. See *ante*, at 3. Although it asserts that this factor was essential to our analysis, the majority fails to explain how an objection has any bearing on the power of a magistrate to conduct felony jury selection. As I have already indicated, the reasoning behind our conclusion in *Gomez* that Congress did not endow magistrates with jurisdiction to preside over felony jury selection had nothing to do with the defendant's objection to such jurisdiction.

---

[4] Because the defendant can eliminate the need for judicial review altogether by simply declining to consent to magistrate jury selection, the majority finds no cause for "distress at the difficulties of effective judicial review." *Ante*, at 11 n. 14. This contention misses the point. Insofar as the Federal Magistrates Act insists that magistrate functions be subject to judicial review, the impossibility of effective review is reason not to construe the additional duties clause as authorizing magistrates to conduct felony jury selection, regardless of whether the parties consent. Cf. *Gomez* v. *United States*, *supra*, at 874–875. The majority also dismisses its failure to articulate a standard for judicial review on the ground that the issue "is not before us in this case." *Ante*, at 11, n. 14. Again, the majority misses the point. This issue *is* before us insofar as the difficulty of articulating such a standard counsels against reading the additional duties clause to authorize consented-to magistrate felony jury selection. Cf. *id.*, at 873–874.

UNITED STATES *v.* FRANCE

Second, the majority notes that Congress has expanded magistrates' specifically enumerated powers by allowing them to serve as special masters and to conduct civil and misdemeanor trials, provided that the parties consent. See *ante*, at 4–5. The fact that Congress imposed this condition of consent on magistrates' exercise of expressly provided authority, however, does not prove that Congress also authorized magistrates to conduct trial duties not expressly enumerated in the Federal Magistrates Act—such as supervision of felony jury selection. At most, these specifically enumerated grants of trial authority suggest that *if* Congress had intended to confer on magistrates authority to conduct felony jury selection, it *would have* predicated that authority on the parties' consent. Indeed, as I have already discussed, see *supra*, at ——, construing the Act as authorizing magistrates to conduct consented-to jury selection in felony cases merely because the Act authorizes consented-to jurisdiction in civil and misdemeanor cases is to draw an inference from Congress' silence precisely opposite to the inference we drew in *Gomez*.

Moreover, the additional duties clause contains no language conditioning a magistrate's authority under that clause on the parties' consent. This silence is evidence that Congress did not intend consent to affect the scope of a magistrate's power under that provision. See *General Motors Corp.* v. *United States*, 496 U. S. ——, —— (1990) (Congress' inclusion of time limitations in some provisions of a statute suggests that its omission of a time limitation from another provision of the same statute was intentional); *Russello* v. *United States*, 464 U. S. 16, 23 (1983) ("'[W]here Congress includes particular language in one section of a statute but omits it in another section of the same Act, it is generally presumed that Congress acts intentionally and purposely in the disparate inclusion or exclusion'" (citation omitted)). Thus, the majority errs in concluding that jury

UNITED STATES *v.* FRANCE

selection can become an "additional duty" of a magistrate when the parties consent, but not otherwise.

Finally, the majority justifies its construction of the additional duties clause by noting that "Congress intended the magistrate to play an integral and important role in the federal judicial system." *Ante*, at 5. Taken literally, such a rationale admits of no limits, and for this reason it cannot function as a legitimate basis for construing the scope of a magistrate's permissible "additional duties." As in *Gomez*, we must give content to the additional duties clause by looking to Congress' intention that magistrates be delegated administrative and other quasi-judicial tasks in order to free Article III judges to conduct trials, most particularly *felony* trials. See *supra*, at 8–9, and n. 2. By creating jurisdiction for magistrates to preside over a "critical stage" of the felony trial, see *Gomez* v. *United States*, 490 U. S., at ——,, merely because a defendant fails to request a judge, the majority completely misapprehends both Congress' conception of the appropriate role to be played by magistrates and our analysis in *Gomez*.[6]

[6] In *Gomez*, we noted that Committee Reports accompanying the 1976 and 1979 amendments to the Magistrates Act contained charts cataloging magistrate functions. Although we did not place extensive reliance on these charts, we found it relevant, in determining Congress' understanding of the permissible scope of magistrate duties, that not one of the charts mentioned jury selection. See *Gomez* v. *United States*, 490 U. S., at 875–876, and n. 30 (citing H. R. Rep. No. 96–287, pp. 4–5 (1979); S. Rep. No. 96–74, at 3; H. R. Rep. No. 94–1609, at 7; S. Rep. No. 94–625, at 5). Needless to say, the charts also contain no mention of jury selection where the parties have consented to magistrate supervision.

The majority responds to the absence of any reference by Congress itself to magistrates' conducting felony jury selection by stating that in *Gomez* we took notice of a House Committee Report that "'referred'" to a letter from a district judge mentioning jury selection as a duty judges in that district assigned to magistrates. *Ante*, at 10, n. 13. While the majority observes that the letter "'suggest[ed] that a magistrate selected juries . . . with consent of the parties,'" *Gomez* v. *United States*, *supra*, at 875–876, n. 30, it neglects to record other salient facts we noted about this letter.

UNITED STATES *v.* FRANCE

IV

I have outlined why I believe the only defensible construction of the Federal Magistrates Act is that jury selection in a felony trial can never be one of a magistrate's "additional duties"—regardless of whether a defendant consents to this function. But even if I believed that mine was only one of two "reasonable" interpretations, I would still reject the majority's construction of the Act because it needlessly raises a serious constitutional question: whether jury selection by a magistrate—even when a defendant consents—is consistent with Article III.

It is well established that we should "avoid an interpretation of a federal statute that engenders constitutional issues if a reasonable alternative interpretation poses no constitutional question." *Gomez* v. *United States*, *supra*, at 864, (citing cases); accord, *e. g.*, *Commodity Futures Trading Comm'n* v. *Schor*, 478 U. S. 833, 841 (1986); *Ashwander* v. *TVA*, 297 U. S. 288, 348 (1936) (Brandeis, J., dissenting). This principle operates with particular force when an Article III question is at stake. Cf. *Northern Pipeline Construction Co.* v. *Marathon Pipe Line Co.*, 458 U. S. 50, 90 (1982) (REHNQUIST, J., concurring in judgment) ("Particularly in an area of constitutional law such as that of 'Art. III Courts,' with its frequently arcane distinctions and confusing precedents, rigorous adherence to the principle that this Court should decide no more of a constitutional question than is absolutely necessary accords with both our decided cases and

First, the letter was the "lone reference" in the entire legislative history to such authority. 490 U. S., at 875, n. 30. Second, the letter suggested that magistrate jury selection took place "*perhaps only in civil trials*." *Id.*, at 876, n. 30 (emphasis added). Finally, as we pointed out in *Gomez*, "[the letter] displays little concern about the validity of such assignments: 'How can we do all of this? We just do it. It's not necessary that we find authority in black and white before we give something to the magistrate. . . . Sure we might get shot down once in a while by an appellate court. So what?'" *Ibid.* (citation omitted).

UNITED STATES *v.* FRANCE

with sound judicial policy"). Although this principle guided our analysis in *Gomez*, see *Gomez* v. *United States*, *supra*, at 864, it is all but forgotten today.

The majority not only needlessly creates a constitutional issue by accepting magistrate supervision of magistrate felony jury selection but also resolves this issue in an entirely unsatisfactory manner. The majority notes that because Article III guarantees individuals an impartial adjudicator, parties may waive their Article III protections. *Ante*, at 7, citing *Schor*, *supra*, at 848. From this, the majority concludes that respondent's failure to object to the Magistrate's supervision of jury selection constituted such a waiver, thereby eliminating any Article III problems.

This analysis misses a key step. As we explained in *Schor*, Article III's protections have two distinct dimensions. First, Article III "safeguard[s] litigants' 'right to have claims decided before judges who are free from potential domination by other branches of government.'" *Schor*, *supra*, at 848, quoting *United States* v. *Will*, 449 U. S. 200, 218 (1980). Second, Article III "serves as 'an inseparable element of the constitutional system of checks and balances'" by preserving "the role of the Judicial Branch in our tripartite system" of government. *Schor*, *supra*, at 850, quoting *Northern Pipeline*, *supra*, at 58. Although, as the majority notes, parties may waive their personal guarantee of an independent Article III adjudicator, *Schor*, *supra*, at 848, parties may *not* waive Article III's structural guarantee.

> "Article III, § 1, safeguards the role of the Judicial Branch in our tripartite system by barring congressional attempts to 'transfer jurisdiction [to non-Article III tribunals] for the purpose of emasculating' constitutional courts . . . . To the extent that this structural principle is implicated in a given case, *the parties cannot by consent cure the constitutional difficulty* for the same reason that the parties by consent cannot confer on federal courts subject-matter jurisdiction beyond the limitations imposed by Article III, § 2. When these Article III

UNITED STATES *v.* FRANCE

> limitations are at issue, notions of consent and waiver cannot be dispositive because the limitations serve institutional interests that the parties cannot be expected to protect." 478 U. S., at 850–851 (emphasis added) (citations omitted).

In *Gomez*, we recognized and attempted to accommodate "abiding concerns regarding the constitutionality of delegating felony trial duties to magistrates." See *Gomez* v. *United States*, 490 U. S., at 863. Because jury selection is "a critical stage" of the felony trial, see *id.*, at 873, there is a serious question, as several courts of appeals have noted, whether allowing a magistrate to conduct felony jury selection "impermissibly intrude[s] on the province of the judiciary," *Schor*, *supra*, at 851–852. See *United States* v. *Trice*, 864 F. 2d 1421, 1426 (CA8 1988), cert. dism'd, 491 U. S. 914 (1989); *United States* v. *Ford*, 824 F. 2d 1430, 1434–1435 (CA5 1987) (en banc), cert. denied, 484 U. S. 1034 (1988).

Indeed, this problem admits of no easy solution. Our decision in *United States* v. *Raddatz*, 447 U. S. 667 (1980), suggests that delegation of Article III powers to a magistrate is permissible "so long as the ultimate decision is made by the district court." *Id.*, at 683. In *Schor*, we likewise emphasized the availability of *de novo* judicial review in upholding the performance of core Article III powers by an Article I tribunal. See 478 U. S., at 853. But this means of satisfying the Constitution is not available here. For, as I have noted, *supra*, at 9, the Federal Magistrates Act does not expressly provide for judicial review of felony jury selection, and in *Gomez* we expressed "serious doubts" whether such review was even possible. See *Gomez* v. *United States*, *supra*, at 874.[*]

[*] The majority contends that magistrate jury selection raises no Article III structural difficulties, because "'the entire process takes place under the district court's total supervision and control.'" *Ante*, at 8, quoting *United States* v. *Raddatz*, 447 U. S. 667, 681 (1980). However, as *Raddatz* and *Schor* underscore, the requirement of "the district court's total supervision and control" must include the availability of meaningful judicial

UNITED STATES *v.* FRANCE

Because it completely ignores the teachings of *Raddatz* and *Schor*, the majority's analysis of the Article III difficulty posed by its construction of the Federal Magistrates Act raises the question whether these decisions remain good law. This consequence is particularly unfortunate, because, as I have set forth above, the most coherent reading of the Federal Magistrates Act avoids these problems entirely.

I dissent.

---

review of the magistrate's actual rulings at jury selection. The majority does not show how this can be accomplished, and *Gomez* strongly suggests that it cannot.

The majority attempts to deflect this point by reconstructing our decision in *Raddatz*. In the majority's view, because the Court in *Raddatz* recognized that *de novo* review is performed only when requested by one of the parties, and because the parties cannot waive structural components of Article III, it follows that the *Raddatz* Court "necesssarily concluded" that *de novo* review is not a condition of adjudication by magistrates. *Ante*, at 8 n. 10. This reasoning not only ignores what the Court actually said in *Raddatz*. See *United States* v. *Raddatz*, *supra*, at 683 ("[A]lthough the [Federal Magistrates Act] permits the district court to give to the magistrate's proposed findings of fact and recommendations 'such weight as [their] merit commands and the sound discretion of the judge warrants,' that delegation does not violate Art. III *so long as the ultimate decision is made by the district court*" (emphasis added) (citation omitted)); *id.*, at 685 (BLACKMUN, J., concurring) (identifying availability of judicial review as relevant to the conclusion that magistrate determination of suppression motion satisfies Article III). It also misapprehends the function of judicial review in our Article III jurisprudence. Our decisions require only that *de novo* review be *available* when core Article III powers are delegated to a non-Article III adjudicator, see *Commodity Future Trading Comm'n* v. *Schor*, 478 U. S. 833, 853 (1986), not that such review be exercised *sua sponte*. We did not establish in *Schor*, for example, that an Article III court must review an Administrative Law Judge's adjudication of state common-law claims even when both parties are satisfied with the judge's decision. Indeed, if an Article III court were automatically obliged to perform *de novo* review in all cases, there would be no point in establishing a non-Article III adjudicatory scheme in the first place. Thus, it is only a scheme providing *de novo* review *upon request* that cannot be waived by the parties consistent with Article III. The majority makes no effort to explain how an Article III court could meaningfully respond to such a request here.

As it turned out, the Stevens draft opinion of the Court in *United States* v. *France* could not retain a majority. On December 28, 1990, Justice Scalia wrote to Justice Stevens, "I am sorry to say that I at least would be unable to join [an] opinion that construed the statute as you do in Part II of your latest draft. I do not believe *Gomez* permits that construction, and I am not certain that, if it did, the construction would be constitutional."

Next came the draft dissent by Justice Marshall, reprinted on p. 440, which disagreed with both the Stevens interpretation of the "additional duties" clause and the holding that defendant had impliedly consented to assignment of the jury selection to the magistrate. "The Court's decision today," the Marshall draft begins, "hinges on a crucial premise: that respondent 'consented' to the Magistrate's selection of the jury at her felony trial. The premise is false. What the majority calls 'consent' is nothing more than respondent's silence. . . . I cannot understand how mere silence in such circumstances can be construed as consent."

The equation of silence with consent, Justice Marshall asserts, is contrary to normal criminal procedure practice, as well as the structure of the Federal Magistrates Act. "It is hard to imagine that Congress would take such care to assure that parties do not silently waive the right to a [*sic*] have a district judge preside at a misdemeanor or civil trial, and yet take no care to avoid inadvertent waiver of the right to have a district judge preside at a crucial stage of a felony trial."

In addition, the Marshall draft goes on, "I also cannot accept the majority's underlying conclusion that consent of any sort, express or implied, can authorize a magistrate to conduct felony jury selection." In Justice Marshall's view, "the absence or presence of consent is irrelevant to the Act's prohibition upon magistrate felony jury selection." That is true because "the prohibition on magistrate jury selection in felony cases stems from a *jurisdictional* allocation of judicial functions between district judges and magistrates. Because this jurisdictional division under the Act was designed to serve the interests of the judicial system, not merely those of individual parties, a defendant's consent, no matter how express, cannot invest a magistrate with the power to conduct felony jury selection."

The Marshall draft dissent rejects the three propositions upon which the Stevens draft opinion of the Court relied—which Marshall characterizes as "placing a revisionist gloss on *Gomez*." First, the Marshall draft states, the *Gomez* holding "that Congress did not endow magistrates with jurisdiction to preside over felony jury selection had nothing to do with the defendant's objection to such jurisdiction."

Nor was the fact that Congress has expanded magistrates' powers by allowing them to serve as special masters and to conduct civil misdemeanor trials, provided that the parties consent, relevant. "The fact that Congress imposed this condition of consent on magistrates' exercise of expressly provided authority, however, does not prove that Congress also authorized magistrates to conduct trial duties not expressly enumerated in the Federal Magistrates Act—such as supervision of felony jury selection." Similarly, the fact that "Congress intended the magistrate to play an integral and important role in the federal judicial system" does not justify the Stevens draft holding. Indeed, Marshall's draft asserts, "[t]aken literally, such a rationale admits of no limits, and for this reason it cannot function as a legitimate basis for construing the scope of a magistrate's permissible 'additional duties.'"

Justice Marshall's draft dissent gives a categorical answer to what he terms the two questions presented in the case: "[F]irst, whether a failure to object can constitute consent to a magistrate's supervision of felony jury selection; and, second, whether a party's consent creates statutory authority for a magistrate to engage in this function under the Federal Magistrates Act. In my view, the clear answer to both questions is 'no.'"

Justice Scalia wrote to Justice Marshall, "I fully agree with your analysis of the consent issue in this case, and would like to join parts I and II of your opinion." Justices White and Blackmun sent letters to Justice Marshall joining his whole draft dissent. Since the *France* Court was an eight-Justice Court (Justice Souter, just appointed, did not participate in the case), the Justices were now equally divided in the case.

At this point, Justice Stevens tried to save what he considered the main holding of his draft opinion of the Court—that in Part II upholding magistrates' authority to conduct the voir dire where the defendant consents. Stevens wrote to Chief Justice Rehnquist on December 28, 1990, "Before a decision is made concerning the possible reassignment or reargument of this case, I would like to suggest the possibility of a per curiam disposition adopting the construction of the statute set forth in Part II of my circulating opinion and Thurgood's analysis of the consent issue. Such a disposition would affirm the judgment of the Ninth Circuit, but would allow magistrates to preside at jury selections in the future with the party's consent."

Stevens's suggestion was not accepted, and he then proposed setting the case for reargument. He circulated proposed questions for the reargument similar to those stated in the order granting certiorari in the *Peretz* case. On January 15, 1991, however, Justice Marshall wrote to Justice Stevens rejecting Stevens's proposal. "I believe," the Marshall letter said, "that there is a significant risk that reargument in this case will *not* afford us a certain opportunity to address the most important question raised by our current circulating opinion drafts. Like you, I am most concerned with the question whether a defendant's express consent invests a magistrate with authority to conduct felony *voir dire.* But because respondent merely failed to object and did not expressly consent to this function, this case presents a poor vehicle for addressing that question. Indeed, it is possible upon reargument that a majority of the Court will adopt my view that a mere failure to object cannot be equated with 'consent.' In that event, we still will not have occasion to address the effect of express consent upon magistrate felony *voir dire* under the Federal Magistrate Act. This would result in a waste of time and resources for both us and the litigants."

In his December 28 letter, Justice Stevens had stated, "I think it would be most unfortunate to leave open the question whether a conviction is invalid when the magistrate selects the jury with the express consent of the parties."

Justice Marshall agreed. His January 15 letter pointed out that the Court was then holding *Peretz* v. *United States* for decision after the *France* case was to be decided. *Peretz*, Marshall wrote, "would be a proper vehicle for determining whether magistrate *voir dire* is permissible when the defendant expressly consents. Unlike respondent in this case, the defendant in *Peretz* did expressly consent to magistrate *voir dire*, as both parties have acknowledged."

Marshall's letter to Stevens suggested a different disposition of the *France* case. "As an alternative to your proposal, then, I would recommend disposing of this case promptly—either by outright affirmance or by affirmance by an equally divided Court—and then inviting the parties in *Peretz* to address the . . . questions set forth in your memorandum of January 11, 1991."

On January 15, Justice Stevens wrote to Chief Justice Rehnquist, "Thurgood's proposal is certainly reasonable." The next day, another Stevens letter went to the Chief Justice: "Upon further reflection, I am persuaded that we should adopt Thurgood's suggestion to grant this case and to affirm *United States* v. *France*, No. 89-1363, by an equally divided court."

Stevens's letters led to acceptance of Justice Marshall's suggestion. On January 22, 1991, the Court issued a per curiam drafted by the Chief Justice in which an equally divided court upheld the decision of the lower court overturning the defendant's conviction on the ground that a magistrate judge presiding over selection of the felony jury constituted reversible error, despite defendant's failure to object.[6] As a report by the Administrative Office of the U.S. Courts puts it, "Since the Court was equally divided, it issued no written opinion and its decision is of little precedential value."[7]

In accordance with Justice Marshall's suggestion, the Court also issued a January 22 order granting certiorari in the *Peretz* case, limited to the questions drafted by Justice Stevens—in particular, whether "a magistrate [may] conduct the *voir dire* in a felony trial if the defendant consents."[8] *Peretz* differed from *France* because, as Justice Marshall's January 15 letter pointed out, "the defendant in *Peretz* did expressly consent to magistrate *voir dire*."

On June 27, 1991, the Court did decide *Peretz* v. *United States*,[9] holding, by a bare majority, that a magistrate could conduct the voir dire in a felony trial where the defendant had expressly consented. The draft opinion of the Court circulated by Justice Stevens had, as the Justice summarized it in his June 5 "Dear Chief" letter, "include[d] two rationales for the result: first, that the statute authorizes a magistrate to conduct the *voir dire* in a felony trial if the defendant consents; and second, that even if the statute did not do so, the defendant's consent in this case resulted in a waiver."

"These two paths," the Stevens letter explained, "were both included because there was some uncertainty at Conference on which to choose." However, Justice Stevens went on, "Now that five of us have agreed to the first approach, the second argument seems superfluous. I therefore propose to delete the second argument from the opinion."

The final *Peretz* opinion was limited to the first rationale noted in the

Stevens letter, holding that the Magistrates Act permits a magistrate to supervise jury selection in a felony trial where the defendant expressly consents. Stevens's *Peretz* opinion is a truncated version of his draft opinion of the Court in *United States* v. *France*. The same is true of Justice Marshall's *Peretz* dissent.[10]

The *Peretz* case did not wholly resolve the problem presented in *France*. *Peretz* held only that express consent would permit a magistrate to supervise a felony voir dire. Still left open is the question of whether the same is true where defendant merely fails to object. While *Peretz* was pending, *Lopez-Pena* v. *United States*[11] came to the Court. As explained in a January 24, 1991, Memorandum to the Conference from Stevens, "If we decide in *Peretz* that the Magistrates Act allows a magistrate to conduct the *voir dire* if a defendant consents, this case will present the question whether failure to object is sufficient to constitute consent under the Act." However, the day after *Peretz* was decided, on June 28, 1991, the Court denied certiorari in *Lopez-Pena*.[12] The question that was left open by the affirmance of *France* by an equally divided Court on whether a defendant's failure to object is, as Stevens's *France* draft put it, "tantamount to express consent to the performance of the task by the magistrate," remains undecided.

Notes

1. 498 U.S. 335 (1991).
2. See Administrative Office of the U.S. Courts, *A Constitutional Analysis of Magistrate Judge Authority* 1–2 (1993).
3. 490 U.S. 858 (1989).
4. *Peretz* v. *United States*, 501 U.S. 923 (1991).
5. Ibid.
6. Supra note 1.
7. Supra note 2, at 60.
8. 498 U.S. 1066 (1991).
9. Supra note 4.
10. 501 U.S. at 940.
11. 501 U.S. 1249 (1991).
12. Ibid.

10

Ford Motor Credit Co. v. *Department of Revenue (1991): A Tax Case Switch*

The 1991 case of *Ford Motor Credit Co.* v. *Department of Revenue*[1] well illustrates the often tortuous Supreme Court decision process. In that case, the judicial mountain truly labored, and all that it brought forth was the mouse of an affirmance by an equally divided Court.

At issue in *Ford Motor Credit* was one of the most difficult constitutional questions—that of the power of the states to tax interstate commerce. Florida taxed intangible personal property, such as accounts receivable and shares of stock, at one-tenth of one percent of the assessed value of the property. The tax was imposed on "any person, regardless of domicile, who owns or has management, custody, or control of intangible property that has acquired a business situs in this state." Ford Motor Credit Co. (FMCC) was a Delaware corporation that provided financing in Florida for dealers and consumers to purchase Ford automobiles. Could the Florida tax be imposed on FMCC without unconstitutionally burdening interstate commerce?

At the conference on the case, the Justices voted six to two to uphold the tax, with Justice O'Connor not participating. However, in a December 7, 1990, Memorandum to the Conference Justice Blackmun noted, "According to my notes, the Conference discussion on this case was indecisive and tentative, and the voting was far from firm." As summarized by Blackmun, "Thurgood and Tony were to reverse. Sandra is 'out.' John would affirm for lack of standing. Nino 'did not understand' John's explanation and would affirm by refusing to apply the internal consistency test [to be discussed later] to property taxes; if, however, that test does apply, he would reverse. David leaned toward affirmance so long as there was as yet no actual imposition of a duplicative tax. . . . The Chief initially passed, stating that he had been in dissent in this area, but, after the discussion, leaned toward affirmance. Byron stated that he 'never did understand' the internal consistency test and was inclined, 'some way or another,' to affirm."

Chief Justice Rehnquist had assigned the opinion to Justice Blackmun, but Blackmun added to the confusion by changing his vote. As his memo explained it, "After again reviewing the Court's recent cases, I have come to the conclusion that we cannot affirm here without overruling established precedent. I have not understood my assignment as being one to overrule. Thus, the proposed opinion is to reverse."

The Blackmun memo was accompanied by the draft opinion of the Court, printed on page 464. The draft invalidated the tax. It stated the governing rule in such a case as follows: "In reviewing a state tax alleged to violate the Commerce Clause, this Court has upheld the tax if it 'is applied to an activity with a substantial nexus with the taxing State, is fairly apportioned, does not discriminate against interstate commerce, and is fairly related to the services provided by the State.' . . . If the challenged tax fails any one of these four conditions, the tax is unconstitutional."

The apportionment requirement, Justice Blackmun went on, ensures "that each State is permitted to tax only its fair share of an interstate transaction." The Court has not required any specific apportionment formula. "Instead . . . we have held that a tax is fairly apportioned if it is internally and externally consistent." In this case, the Blackmun draft stated, "we conclude that the tax challenged here is not internally consistent." Justice Blackmun explained that "[a] tax is internally consistent if no multiple taxation would result from every other State's imposing an identical tax."

According to the draft, "Florida's intangible tax scheme fails this test. . . . If every State were to adopt the Florida tax, Company A, an entity domiciled in Florida but owning intangible property with a business situs in Georgia, would pay two taxes on the same intangible property—a domiciliary tax to Florida and a business situs tax to Georgia. This inevitable multiple taxation renders the Florida intangible tax scheme internally inconsistent."

More than that, the draft explained, "[i]f one extends the hypothetical somewhat, it demonstrates that the Florida tax scheme discriminates against interstate commerce. Under the challenged tax, Company B, domiciled in Georgia and doing business exclusively in Georgia, would be subject only to a single tax on a loan made on a car sale in Georgia, while Company A would be subject to the double tax noted above on the same car loan. Thus, the intangibles tax disadvantages an interstate business competing with a wholly intrastate entity for the same market."

1st DRAFT

SUPREME COURT OF THE UNITED STATES

No. 88–1847

FORD MOTOR CREDIT COMPANY, INC., APPELLANT *v.* DEPARTMENT OF REVENUE, STATE OF FLORIDA

ON APPEAL FROM THE DISTRICT COURT OF APPEAL OF FLORIDA, FIRST DISTRICT

[December ——, 1990]

JUSTICE BLACKMUN delivered the opinion of the Court.

In this appeal ~~petitioner~~ appellant claims that Florida's intangible property tax scheme unconstitutionally discriminates against interstate commerce. We agree and reverse the Florida District Court of Appeal's judgment upholding the tax.

I

Appellant Ford Motor Credit Company (FMCC), a wholly owned subsidiary of Ford Motor Company (Ford), is a Delaware corporation with its principal place of business in Dearborn, Mich. FMCC is authorized to do business in Florida. In 1980, 1981, and 1982, the tax years at issue, FMCC maintained branch offices in Florida through which FMCC provided financing for dealers to purchase automobiles from Ford and for consumers to purchase automobiles from Ford dealers. FMCC also engaged in commercial, industrial, real estate, consumer loan, and lease financing in Florida and other States.

During the years in question, Florida taxed intangible personal property, including loans, accounts receivable, and shares of stock, at the rate of one mill—one-tenth of one percent—of the assessed value of the property. Florida imposed the tax on all intangible property owned by a domiciliary corporation, regardless of business situs, see *Florida Steel Corp.* v. *Dickinson*, 328 So. 2d 418, 419 (Fla. 1976), and

FORD MOTOR CREDIT *v.* FLORIDA REVENUE DEPT.

on "any person, regardless of domicile, who owns or has management, custody, or control of intangible property that has acquired a business situs in this state." Fla. Stat. § 199.052(1) (1983). The statute described property with a business situs in Florida as:

> "All bills, notes or accounts receivable, obligations, or credits, wheresoever situated, arising out of, or issued in connection with, the sale, leasing, or servicing of real or personal property in the state . . . . Sales of tangible personal property are in this state if the property is delivered or shipped to a purchaser within this state . . . ." § 199.112(1).

In 1983, appellee Florida Department of Revenue audited FMCC's returns for the years 1980–1982 and, following an assessment and formal administrative hearing, issued a final order determining that FMCC owed approximately $2.5 million in intangible property taxes, penalties, and interest.* At the administrative hearing, FMCC challenged the assessment on several grounds, including an argument that the Florida intangible property tax unconstitutionally burdened interstate commerce. FMCC argued that if every State were to adopt Florida's "business situs" and "domiciliary" tax provisions, a taxpayer would be taxed on intangible property both by its domiciliary State and by whichever State was the "business situs" of the same intangible property. Citing this Court's decision in *Container Corp.* v. *Franchise Tax Bd.*, 463 U. S. 159, 169–170 (1983), FMCC asserted that this potential for duplicate taxation rendered the taxing scheme "internally inconsistent," in violation of the Commerce Clause of the United States Constitution. In its final order, the Department acknowledged FMCC's contention that the Florida

*The amount in controversy has not been paid, so there is no question here concerning the refund of taxes. Florida has been protected by the posting of a bond. See Fla. Stat. § 72.011(3)(b) (1989).

tax on intangible property was unconstitutional but determined that it had no jurisdiction to rule on that contention.

The Florida District Court of Appeal affirmed the Department's final order. 537 So. 2d 1011 (1988). The court rejected FMCC's contention that more than one State could not constitutionally tax the same intangible property, reasoning that "since [FMCC] has extended its activities regarding its intangibles to Florida and has availed itself of the benefits of the laws of several states with regard to this property, those several states, including Florida, may each impose a tax on such intangible property." *Id.*, at 1012, citing *State Tax Comm'n* v. *Aldrich*, 316 U. S. 174 (1942), and *Curry* v. *McCanless*, 307 U. S. 357 (1939). The court declined to apply the "internal consistency" test to the Florida taxing scheme, stating that this Court has applied this test only to franchise and excise taxes and never to the kind of property tax challenged here. 537 So. 2d, at 1012–1013. The Supreme Court of Florida denied a petition for discretionary review. 542 So. 2d 988 (1989).

We noted probable jurisdiction. —— U. S. —— (1990).

II

In reviewing a state tax alleged to violate the Commerce Clause, this Court has upheld the tax if it "is applied to an activity with a substantial nexus with the taxing State, is fairly apportioned, does not discriminate against interstate commerce, and is fairly related to the services provided by the State." *Complete Auto Transit, Inc.* v. *Brady*, 430 U. S. 274, 279 (1977). If the challenged tax fails any one of these four conditions, the tax is unconstitutional. In this case, FMCC contends that the Florida intangibles tax violates the second and third conditions of the *Complete Auto* test.

A

We have stated that the rationale behind the apportionment requirement is that each State is permitted to tax only

FORD MOTOR CREDIT *v.* FLORIDA REVENUE DEPT.

its fair share of an interstate transaction. See, *e. g.*, *Goldberg* v. *Sweet*, 488 U. S. 252, 261 (1989); *Container Corp.* v. *Franchise Tax Bd.*, 463 U. S., at 169–170. Instead of requiring a specific apportionment formula—a task properly reserved to a State's legislature—we have held that a tax is fairly apportioned if it is internally and externally consistent. *Goldberg*, 488 U. S., at 261; *Armco Inc.* v. *Hardesty*, 467 U. S. 638, 644 (1984); *Container Corp.*, 463 U. S., at 169–170. Because we conclude that the tax challenged here is not internally consistent, we need not address its external consistency.

A tax is internally consistent if no multiple taxation would result from every other State's imposing an identical tax. *Id.*, at 169. In assessing the potential for multiple taxation, "the internal consistency test focuses on the text of the challenged statute and hypothesizes a situation where other States have passed an identical statute." *Goldberg*, 488 U. S., at 261. We have held that a party challenging the internal consistency of a taxing scheme is not required to demonstrate actual multiplicity of taxation. See *Armco Inc.*, 467 U. S., at 644.

Florida's intangible tax scheme fails this test. As noted, Florida taxes 100 percent of the intangibles owned by a Florida domiciliary and also taxes all of a nondomiciliary's intangibles that have a business situs in Florida. If every State were to adopt the Florida tax, Company A, an entity domiciled in Florida but owning intangible property with a business situs in Georgia, would pay two taxes on the same intangible property—a domiciliary tax to Florida and a business situs tax to Georgia. This inevitable multiple taxation renders the Florida intangible tax scheme internally inconsistent and thus violative of the second condition of the *Complete Auto* test. Appellee Department urges us to apply the internal consistency test differently by imagining that only Florida's business situs tax has been adopted by all States. This misreads the internal consistency test, which examines

FORD MOTOR CREDIT *v.* FLORIDA REVENUE DEPT.

whether a State's taxation of a given class of transactions or a certain type of value (here, intangible property) is fairly apportioned.

B

If one extends the hypothetical somewhat, it demonstrates that the Florida tax scheme discriminates against interstate commerce. Under the challenged tax, Company B, domiciled in Georgia and doing business exclusively in Georgia, would be subject only to a single tax on a loan made on a car sale in Georgia, while Company A would be subject to the double tax noted above on the same car loan. Thus, the intangibles tax disadvantages an interstate business competing with a wholly intrastate entity for the same market and fails the third condition of *Complete Auto:* the disparate tax burden it generates "has a forbidden impact on interstate commerce because it exerts an inexorable hydraulic pressure on interstate businesses to ply their trade within the State that enacted the measure rather than 'among the several States.' U. S. Const., Art. I, § 8, cl. 3." *American Trucking Assns., Inc.* v. *Scheiner*, 483 U. S. 266, 286–287 (1987).

III

The Florida District Court of Appeal did not conclude that the challenged tax was internally consistent. As noted, the court declined to apply the "internal consistency" test to the intangible property tax on the grounds that this Court never had applied the test to this kind of tax and that this Court had suggested in earlier opinions that multiple taxation of intangibles did not violate the Due Process Clause. 537 So. 2d, at 1012–1013. We hold this rationale to be an insufficient basis for upholding the challenged tax.

Although this Court has not had cause before now to apply the internal consistency test to an intangible property tax, there is nothing in the test itself that suggests we should exempt an intangibles tax from such scrutiny, and neither the Florida court nor appellee has offered any persuasive reason

FORD MOTOR CREDIT *v.* FLORIDA REVENUE DEPT.

for doing so. This Court has held that the *Complete Auto* standard applies to any tax that "substantially affect[s] interstate commerce," even if it attaches only to a " 'local' or intrastate activity." *Commonwealth Edison Co.* v. *Montana*, 453 U. S. 609, 615, 616 (1981). As has been demonstrated above, the Florida taxing scheme inevitably disadvantages an entity that conducts business beyond the borders of its domiciliary State. The logical result of this burden is that businesses subject to the tax would be disinclined to expand operations to other States. We conclude, therefore, that the tax on intangibles, like the severance taxes at issue in *Commonwealth Edison*, "'may substantially affect interstate commerce, and this effect is the proper focus of Commerce Clause inquiry." *Id.*, at 616.

We also reject the Florida court's conclusion that this Court's decisions in *Aldrich* and *Curry* render the internal consistency test inapplicable to taxes on intangible property. Each of those cases concerned due process challenges to the multiple taxation of intangibles. In particular, the Court had to decide whether a nondomiciliary State was empowered to tax intangible property with which it had some connection. In each case, the Court stated that the Fourteenth Amendment did not preclude taxation of these intangibles by the owner's domicile and by any other State "which has extended benefits or protection, or which can demonstrate 'the practical fact of its power' or sovereignty as respects the [intangible property] . . . ." *Aldrich*, 316 U. S., at 181–182 (citation omitted); see *Curry*, 307 U. S., at 367–368. Indeed, the Court's sole inquiry in both *Curry* and *Aldrich* was whether the nondomiciliary State had established a sufficient nexus with the intangible property to justify taxing that property.

The Florida District Court of Appeal acknowledged that *Curry* and *Aldrich* were not Commerce Clause cases, but attempted to minimize this distinction by noting that this Court "'has indicated that taxes which satisfy the due process clause

FORD MOTOR CREDIT *v.* FLORIDA REVENUE DEPT.

generally will satisfy the commerce clause." 537 So. 2d, at 1012. Whatever the merit of that generalization, we note that none of the cases supplying the vague language the court cites for this proposition addressed a tax scheme alleged to generate the potential for multiple taxation that we find violative in the present case. See *Ott* v. *Mississippi Valley Barge Line Co.*, 336 U. S. 169, 174 (1949) (noting that the challenged tax posed "no risk of multiple taxation" and that there was "no claim . . . that [the] tax discriminate[d] against interstate commerce"); *Ford Motor Co.* v. *Beauchamp*, 308 U. S. 331 (1939); *Pacific Telephone & Telegraph Co.* v. *Tax Comm'n*, 297 U. S. 403 (1936).

We decline to attribute to *Curry* and *Aldrich* a breadth of analysis that is not evident from the text of the opinions. The Court in those cases did not examine whether the taxes at issue were properly apportioned or whether the challenged taxes discriminated against interstate commerce. They cannot control our analysis of this case and manifestly do not preclude our conclusion that the Florida intangibles tax is internally inconsistent and therefore violates the Commerce Clause. The judgment of the Florida District Court of Appeal is therefore reversed.

It is so ordered.

JUSTICE O'CONNOR took no part in the consideration and decision of this case.

1st DRAFT

SUPREME COURT OF THE UNITED STATES

No. 88–1847

FORD MOTOR CREDIT COMPANY, INC., APPELLANT *v.* DEPARTMENT OF REVENUE, STATE OF FLORIDA

ON APPEAL FROM THE DISTRICT COURT OF APPEAL OF FLORIDA, FIRST DISTRICT

[February ——, 1991]

JUSTICE STEVENS delivered the opinion of the Court.

Florida's taxation of intangible property imposes a heavier burden on resident taxpayers engaged in interstate commerce than on non-residents. The question we decide today is whether a non-resident taxpayer, who claims that the tax violates the Commerce Clause of the Federal Constitution, has standing to challenge the constitutionality of the tax for this reason.

I

Florida imposes an annual tax on the full value of intangible personal property[1] that is either owned by a Florida domiciliary or that has a business situs in Florida.[2] Appellant, Ford Motor Credit Company (FMCC), is engaged primarily in the business of financing the wholesale and retail sale of vehicles manufactured by its parent, Ford Motor

[1] According to Fla. Stat. § 199.023(1) (1983), "intangible personal property" means "[a]ll personal property which is not in itself intrinsically valuable but derives its chief value from that which it represents . . . ."

[2] Florida law defines "business situs" to include accounts receivable "arising out of, or issued in connection with, the sale, leasing, or servicing of . . . personal property in the state . . . it being the legislative intent to provide that such intangibles shall be assessable regardless of where they are kept, approved as to their creation, or paid . . . ." Fla. Stat. § 199.112(1) (1983).

FORD MOTOR CREDIT *v.* FLORIDA REVENUE DEPT.

Company.[3] FMCC is a Delaware corporation with its principal place of business in Dearborn, Michigan. It is authorized to transact business in Florida and maintains branch offices in the State, where it services loans secured by vehicles sold to Florida residents. There is no longer any dispute that the intangible assets subject to Florida's tax, consisting of Florida accounts receivable,[4] have a business situs in Florida. App. to Juris. Statement 13.

The Florida statute taxes intangible personal property, including loans and accounts receivable, at the rate of one mill per dollar of assessed value.[5] The tax is imposed on "any person, regardless of domicile, who owns or has management, custody, or control of intangible property that has acquired a business situs in this state." Fla. Stat. § 199.052(1) (1983). It is undisputed that FMCC is such a "person." It is also undisputed that FMCC's intangibles with a taxable situs in Florida are taxed at the same rate as those owned by Florida domiciliaries. App. 18.

The constitutionality of the tax is called into question because the Florida Supreme Court has held that the tax applies to all intangible property owned by a domiciliary corporation, regardless of its business situs. See *Florida Steel Corp.* v. *Dickinson*, 328 So. 2d 418, 419 (1976). Thus, for example, a Florida finance company doing business in Michigan or Delaware must pay a tax to Florida on its receivables in those States, whereas FMCC is not subject to any intangible property tax on its Delaware or Michigan receivables because neither of those States taxes intangible property. The

[3] FMCC is also engaged in commercial, industrial, and real estate financing, consumer loan financing, and leasing company financing in Florida and in other States. App. 4.

[4] Most of the accounts receivable at issue here arose out of sales of automobiles delivered to or located in Florida and involved debtors residing in Florida. *Ibid.*

[5] Another way of describing the rate is one tenth of one percent. Thus, a loan with a balance of $1000 on January 1 would be assessed a tax of $1.

FORD MOTOR CREDIT *v.* FLORIDA REVENUE DEPT.

extraterritorial reach of the Florida statute thus disfavors resident companies competing with non-resident companies.

During the years 1980–1982, FMCC filed corporate tax returns and paid the intangible property tax. App. 4.[6] In 1983, appellee Department of Revenue audited those returns and assessed a deficiency of approximately $1.2 million in intangible property taxes for the tax years 1980–1982, plus interest and penalties. App. to Juris. Statement 10. FMCC filed a timely protest and challenged the assessment on various grounds, including the contention that the tax imposed an unconstitutional burden on interstate commerce. The Division of Administrative Hearings rejected that argument, claiming that it lacked jurisdiction to rule on the constitutional issue, and entered appellee's recommended order. *Id.*, at 13.

The Florida District Court of Appeal affirmed. In response to the argument that the Florida scheme exposed FMCC to the risk of multiple taxation on the same intangibles in violation of the "internal consistency" test articulated in *Container Corp.* v. *Franchise Tax Board*, 463 U. S. 159, 169 (1983), the Court of Appeal first stated that the tax had only an indirect effect on interstate commerce, App. to Juris. Statement 4, and then noted that this Court had not applied the internal consistency test to property taxes, and therefore, it declined to extend the test to Florida's intangible property tax. *Id.*, at 5. The Florida Supreme Court denied a petition for discretionary review, 542 So. 2d 988 (1989), and we noted probable jurisdiction of FMCC's appeal. —— U. S. —— (1990).

II

A state tax does not violate the Commerce Clause if it "is applied to an activity with a substantial nexus with the taxing State, is fairly apportioned, does not discriminate against interstate commerce, and is fairly related to the services pro-

[6] The parties stipulated to all relevant facts. See App. 2–12.

FORD MOTOR CREDIT *v.* FLORIDA REVENUE DEPT.

vided by the State." *Complete Auto Transit, Inc.* v. *Brady*, 430 U. S. 274, 279 (1977). In this case, it is clear that FMCC's accounts receivable that have a business situs in Florida have an adequate "nexus with the taxing state," and there is no claim that the tax is not fairly related to the services provided to FMCC by Florida. Moreover, insofar as the tax applies to FMCC's intangibles with a Florida situs, it does not discriminate against interstate commerce. Appellant's main argument is that the tax is not fairly apportioned because it fails the "internal consistency" test.

The internal consistency test was first articulated in a case involving the question whether California had taxed a disproportionate share of the income of a unitary business headquartered in Illinois.[7] In that context, we explained:

---

[7]The test, though first enunciated in *Container Corp.*, has its roots in earlier cases. *See, e. g.*, *Pullman's Palace Car Co.* v. *Pennsylvania*, 141 U. S. 18, 26 (1891) (upholding State's mileage-based apportionment mechanism on the ground that if it "were adopted by all the States through which these cars ran, the company would be assessed upon the whole value of its capital stock, and no more"); *Western Live Stock* v. *Bureau of Revenue*, 303 U. S. 250, 260 (1938) (upholding New Mexico's gross receipts tax on local sales of advertising space in journal published in state, but circulating in state and out of state, because it was "not one which in form or substance can be repeated by other states in such manner as to lay an added burden on the interstate distribution of the magazine"); *Halliburton Oil Well Cementing Co.* v. *Reily*, 373 U. S. 64, 72 (1963) (invalidating state tax because "[i]f similar unequal tax structures were adopted in other States," those engaged in "multistate activities" of assembling items in one State for use in others would be penalized in comparison with those who assembled items and used them in the same State). Justice Goldberg, in his dissent in *General Motors Corp.* v. *Washington*, 377 U. S. 436 (1964), anticipated the test when he observed that "an out-of-state firm manufacturing goods in a State having the same taxation provisions as does Washington would be subjected to two taxes on interstate sales to Washington customers." *Id.*, at 460. Such a "threat of duplicative taxation" could "discourage the development of multistate business operations," thus "inhibit[ing] the realization of a free and open economy unencumbered by local tariffs and protective devices." *Ibid.* His rationale was subsequently adopted by the Court in *Armco Inc.* v. *Hardesty*, 467 U. S. 638, 642 (1984), and in

FORD MOTOR CREDIT *v.* FLORIDA REVENUE DEPT.

> "Having determined that a certain set of activities constitute a 'unitary business,' a State must then apply a formula apportioning the income of that business within and without the State. Such an apportionment formula must, under both the Due Process and Commerce Clauses, be fair. See *Exxon Corp.* [v. *Wisconsin Dept. of Revenue*, 447 U. S. 207,] 219, 227–228 [(1980)]; *Moorman Mfg. Co.* [v. *Bair*], 437 U. S. [267,] 272–273 [(1978)]; *Hans Rees' Sons, Inc.* [v. *North Carolina ex rel. Maxwell*], 283 U. S. [123,] 134 [(1931)]. The first, and again obvious, component of fairness in an apportionment formula is what might be called internal consistency—that is, the formula must be such that, if applied by every jurisdiction, it would result in no more than all of the unitary business' income being taxed." *Container Corp.* v. *Franchise Tax Board*, 463 U. S. 159, 169 (1983).

In two later cases, we applied this test to tax statutes that were facially discriminatory against the complaining taxpayer. Thus, in *Armco Inc.* v. *Hardesty*, 467 U. S. 638 (1984), we sustained an Ohio manufacturer's challenge to West Virginia's gross receipts tax on the business of selling tangible property at wholesale because it exempted local manufacturers. And in *Tyler Pipe Industries, Inc.* v. *Washington State Department of Revenue*, 483 U. S. 232 (1987), we held that Washington's manufacturing tax was invalid because it was assessed only on products that were sold to out-of-state purchasers. In both of these cases, we established that application of the internal consistency test does not require the taxpayer to show actual discriminatory impact from other States.[6] See *id.*, at 247 ("As we explained in *Armco*,

---

Tyler Pipe Industries, Inc. v. *Washington Department of Revenue*, 483 U. S. 232, 240–248 (1987).

[6] One commentator has noted that were we to require other States to implement taxing schemes that resulted in multiple taxation before we

FORD MOTOR CREDIT *v.* FLORIDA REVENUE DEPT.

our conclusion that a tax facially discriminates against interstate commerce need not be confirmed by an examination of the tax burdens imposed by other States" . . .).

In *American Trucking Assns., Inc.* v. *Scheiner*, 483 U. S. 266 (1987), over the dissent of JUSTICE O'CONNOR who regarded the use of the internal consistency test as appropriate only in cases involving a facially discriminatory tax, see *id.*, at 303, the Court applied the test in a different context. We noted that Pennsylvania's vehicle registration fee and fuel consumption taxes readily satisfied the test, see *id.*, at 282–283, but that the State's flat taxes imposed a heavier burden on out-of-state businesses that competed in an interstate market than it imposed on Pennsylvania's own residents. We explained:

> "The precise issue is therefore more subtle: do the methods by which the flat taxes are assessed discriminate against some participants in interstate commerce in a way that contradicts the central purpose of the Commerce Clause? We find dispositive those of our precedents which make it clear that the Commerce Clause prohibits a State from imposing a heavier tax burden on out-of-state businesses that compete in an interstate market than it imposes on its own residents who also engage in commerce among States.

---

were willing to address the claim, the practical consequences would be undesirable:

"Taxpayers would face uncertainties in determining their state tax liabilities, states would face uncertainties in predicting state tax collections, and compliance and administration difficulties would be exacerbated. Finally, even if otherwise unacceptable, there is something unseemly about determining state tax liabilities 'on a first-come-first-tax basis.' Given the fundamental concerns underlying the commerce clause, it would be perverse indeed to constitutionalize a rule rewarding beggar-thy-neighbor state tax policies with state tax collections depending on who won the race to the taxpayer's door." Hellerstein, *Is 'Internal Consistency' Foolish?: Reflections on an Emerging Commerce Clause Restraint on State Taxation*, 87 Mich. L. Rev. 138, 170 (1988) (footnotes omitted).

FORD MOTOR CREDIT *v.* FLORIDA REVENUE DEPT.

"The way in which a tax levied on participants in interstate commerce is measured and assessed bears directly on whether it implicates central Commerce Clause values. The method of assessing the marker and axle taxes in this case on Pennsylvania-based vehicles and on other vehicles establishes that the State is not treating the two types of vehicles with an even hand." 483 U. S., at 282 (footnote omitted).

. . . . .

"The unapportioned flat taxes, however, penalize some travel within the free trade area. Whether the full brunt, or only a major portion, of their burden is imposed on the out-of-state carriers, their inevitable effect is to threaten the free movement of commerce by placing a financial barrier around the State of Pennsylvania. To pass the 'internal consistency' test, a state tax must be of a kind that, 'if applied by every jurisdiction, there would be no impermissible interference with free trade.' *Armco Inc.* v. *Hardesty*, 467 U. S., at 644. If each State imposed flat taxes for the privilege of making commercial entrances into its territory, there is no conceivable doubt that commerce among the States would be deterred." *Id.*, at 284 (footnote omitted).

Finally, in *Goldberg* v. *Sweet*, 488 U. S. 252 (1989), we found that the Illinois tax on interstate communications passed the internal consistency test and was constitutional. We pointed out that "the central purpose behind the apportionment requirement is to ensure that each State taxes only its fair share of an interstate transaction." *Id.*, at 260–261. We summarized the test as follows:

"To be internally consistent, a tax must be structured so that if every State were to impose an identical tax, no multiple taxation would result. [*Container Corp.* v. *Franchise Tax Bd.*,] 463 U. S., at 169. Thus, the internal consistency test focuses on the text of the challenged

FORD MOTOR CREDIT *v.* FLORIDA REVENUE DEPT.

statute and hypothesizes a situation where other States have passed an identical statute. We conclude that the Tax Act is internally consistent, for if every State taxes only those interstate phone calls which are charged to an in-state service address, only one State would tax each interstate telephone call." *Id.*, at 261.

FMCC correctly argues that Florida's entire intangible property taxing scheme, including both the tax on all of a resident's receivables and the tax on a non-resident's receivables with a Florida situs, is not internally consistent. For if every State were to replicate Florida's scheme, finance companies would be taxed twice on their out-of-state receivables—once by their home State and once by the situs State—whereas their in-state receivables would be taxed only once.

Nevertheless, none of the foregoing authorities is directly applicable to FMCC's attack on the Florida tax on its receivables with a Florida situs. Florida is not taxing more than its fair share of any FMCC transaction, cf. *Goldberg, supra.* Nor does Florida impose any greater burden on FMCC or on any other out-of-state company than it imposes on its own residents, cf. *American Trucking Assns., supra.* More importantly, unlike the taxpayers in *Armco* and *Tyler Pipe, supra*, FMCC is not the victim of any discrimination apparent on the face of the statute. And, of course, the *Container* case is inapplicable because this case does not involve apportionment of the income of a unitary business.

If the Florida tax applied only to intangibles with a Florida situs, it not only would pass the internal consistency test, but also would be constitutional. The constitutional issue that is now presented is a direct consequence of Florida's failure to exempt intangible property with an out-of-state situs from the tax imposed on residents. For a period of over thirty-five years, the Florida courts assumed that the statute should be construed to contain a "foreign business situs ex-

FORD MOTOR CREDIT *v.* FLORIDA REVENUE DEPT.

emption" because they believed that there might be a federal "constitutional barrier to the taxation of intangibles by both the state of domicile and the state of commercial activity." *Florida Steel Corp.* v. *Dickerson*, 328 So. 2d 418, 419 (Fla. 1976). Only after the Florida Supreme Court, relying on this Court's decision in *State Tax Commission* v. *Aldrich*,[9] was satisfied that there was no constitutional infirmity in the taxation of the same intangibles by two States, did it conclude that residents could be taxed on their out-of-state holdings. *Ibid.*

In this case, Florida contends that there is no constitutional requirement that property taxes must pass the internal consistency test. Moreover, it argues that there are justifications for imposing taxes on residents that do not automatically apply to non-residents.[10] Residents presumably derive more benefits from the government that their taxes support than do non-residents. Moreover, a state tax that disfavors a State's own residents and favors non-residents does not raise the same concerns that motivated our decisions in the

[9] 316 U. S. 174, 181 (1942) (Due Process Clause does not prohibit "taxation of intangibles by more than one State").

[10] In support of its argument that domicile is a legitimate basis for double taxation, appellee relies on *Curry* v. *McCanless*, 307 U. S. 357 (1939), in which we stated:

"The taxpayer who is domiciled in one state but carries on business in another is subject to a tax there measured by the value of the intangibles used in his business. *New Orleans* v. *Stempel*, 175 U. S. 309; *Bristol* v. *Washington County*, 177 U. S. 133; *State Board of Assessors* v. *Comptoir National*, 191 U. S. 388; *Metropolitan Life Ins. Co.* v. *New Orleans*, 205 U. S. 395; *Liverpool & L. & G. Ins. Co.* v. *Board*, 221 U. S. 346; *Wheeling Steel Corp.* v. *Fox*, 298 U. S. 193; cf. *Blodgett* v. *Silberman*, [277 U. S. 1]; *Baldwin* v. *Missouri*, [281 U. S. 586]. But taxation of a corporation by a state where it does business, measured by the value of the intangibles used in its business there, does not preclude the state of incorporation from imposing a tax measured by all its intangibles. *Cream of Wheat Co.* v. *Grand Forks*, [253 U. S. 325,] 329; see *Fidelity & Columbia Trust Co.* v. *Louisville*, 245 U. S. 54." *Id.*, at 368 (footnote omitted).

FORD MOTOR CREDIT *v.* FLORIDA REVENUE DEPT.

cases applying the internal consistency test.[11]

This is not to say, however, that the Florida tax on out-of-state intangibles is valid. As FMCC argues, it inevitably deters Florida businesses from acquiring intangible property with an out-of-state situs (or encourages them to transact business through otherwise unnecessary subsidiaries) and may well have an adverse effect on the interstate flow of capital. If invalid, this aspect of the statutory scheme might be entirely unenforceable, or perhaps might be saved by allowing Florida residents a credit for any intangible property tax paid to the State where its foreign intangibles are located.[12] In this case, however, we do not have a resident taxpayer before us. We must, therefore, decide whether a non-resident, such as FMCC, has standing to avoid the application of the

[11] Of course, this does not mean that a state tax that discriminates among a State's residents by disfavoring those who engage in interstate commerce is valid. See *Tyler Pipe Industries, Inc.* v. *Washington Dept. of Revenue*, 483 U. S. 232, 240–248 (1987) (invalidating manufacturing tax that discriminated between in-state manufacturers that sold at wholesale in state and those that sold at wholesale out of state); *Bacchus Imports, Ltd.* v. *Dias*, 468 U. S. 263 (1984) (invalidating tax exemption for locally produced alcoholic beverages in case brought by local wholesalers); *Boston Stock Exchange* v. *State Tax Commission*, 429 U. S. 318, 333–334 (1977) (invalidating securities transfer tax that discriminated against those state residents who sold out of state rather than in state).

[12] See *Tyler Pipe Industries* v. *Washington State Dept. of Revenue*, 483 U. S., at 245, n. 13 ("Many States provide tax credits that alleviate or eliminate the potential multiple taxation that results when two or more sovereigns have jurisdiction to tax parts of the same chain of commercial events"); *Goldberg* v. *Sweet*, 488 U. S., at 264 ("To the extent that other States' telecommunications taxes pose a risk of multiple taxation, the credit provision contained in the Tax Act operates to avoid actual multiple taxation"); *D. H. Holmes Co.* v. *McNamara*, 486 U. S. 24, 31 (1988) ("The . . . taxing scheme is fairly apportioned, for it provides a credit against its use tax for sales taxes that have been paid in other States"). Similarly, in *American Trucking Assns., Inc.* v. *Scheiner*, 483 U. S., at 282–283, the reciprocity among States with respect to registration fees avoided a multiple tax burden on interstate trucks, and acted, in effect, as a credit.

FORD MOTOR CREDIT *v.* FLORIDA REVENUE DEPT.

tax to its Florida intangibles because the statute arguably discriminates against Florida domiciliaries.

III

If the litigant before us were a Florida domiciliary challenging Florida's power to impose a tax on out-of-state intangibles that were being, or could also be,[13] taxed by another State, we would be forced to decide whether the internal consistency test should be applied to the taxation of intangible property and, if so, whether the State's power to tax its own residents nevertheless justified a second tax on those intangibles. Cf. *Curry* v. *McCanless*, 307 U. S. 357 (1939).[14] We have not yet decided either of these constitutional questions, and it is our settled practice to avoid the premature resolution of such issues. See *Rescue Army* v. *Municipal Court*, 331 U. S. 549, 568–569 (1947); *Ashwander* v. *TVA*, 297 U. S. 288, 346–348 (1936) (Brandeis, J., concurring).

Ordinarily "a litigant must assert his or her own legal rights and interests, and cannot rest a claim to relief on the legal rights or interests of third parties." *Powers* v. *Ohio*, —— U. S. —— (1991) [slip op., at 9]. Although this general

[13] The Florida domiciliary need not wait until another State *actually* imposes a tax that results in multiple taxation of its out-of-state intangibles. See *Armco Inc.* v. *Hardesty*, 467 U. S., at 645, n. 8 ("'The immunities implicit in the Commerce Clause and the potential taxing power of a State can hardly be made to depend, in the world of practical affairs, on the shifting incidence of the varying tax laws of the various States at a particular moment'") (quoting *Freeman* v. *Hewit*, 329 U. S. 249, 256 (1946)).

[14] See n. 10 *supra*. The holding in *Curry* v. *McCanless* was limited to the Due Process Clause. With respect to the Commerce Clause question raised by FMCC, Chief Justice Stone's observation in *Northwest Airlines, Inc.* v. *Minnesota*, 322 U. S. 292, 318 (1944) may have more bearing: "[T]he taxation of intangibles of interstate carriers is subject to the rule of apportionment wherever the tax without it would subject the commerce to the burden of multiple state taxation." However, Chief Justice Stone was writing in dissent, and the case involved a State's taxation of tangible property. Our only point here is that the issue has not yet been squarely and definitively resolved.

FORD MOTOR CREDIT *v.* FLORIDA REVENUE DEPT.

rule is not applied absolutely, none of the limited exceptions to this rule is present here.[16] Thus, even if a resident taxpayer could persuade us that Florida has no power to tax its out-of-state receivables, or that any such tax must allow a credit for taxes paid to the situs State, neither that argument nor that remedy is available to FMCC.

FMCC is a non-resident taxpayer and its intangibles with a Florida situs are unquestionably subject to Florida's taxing jurisdiction. If only one State may tax those intangibles, it is clearly Florida, rather than the domiciliary State, that may do so. "The ancient maxim which assigns to tangibles, as well as intangibles, the situs of the owner for purposes of taxation has its foundation in the protection which the owner receives from the government of his residence, and the exception to the principle is based upon the theory that if the owner, by his own act, gives to such property a permanent location elsewhere, the situs of the domicile must yield to the actual situs and resulting dominion of another government." *Southern Pacific Co.* v. *Kentucky*, 222 U. S. 63, 68 (1911). Indeed, the Florida Supreme Court's interpretation of its own statute has made it clear that if constitutional concerns require any exemption from the statute's coverage, it is the out-of-state intangibles owned by Florida residents that would be exempted. See *Florida Steel Corp., supra.*

FMCC's challenge to the Florida tax must rest on its application to FMCC. At present, FMCC is treated no less favorably than any other taxpayer, resident or non-resident, that owns intangibles with a Florida situs. The tax on domiciliaries' out-of-state receivables causes FMCC no harm

[16] In deciding whether a party can assert the rights or interests of third parties, the Court considers "the relationship of the litigant to the person whose right he seeks to assert" and whether "the relationship between the litigant and the third party may be such that the former is fully, or very nearly, as effective a proponent of the right as the latter." *Singleton* v. *Wulff*, 428 U. S. 106, 114–115 (1976). Another consideration "is the ability of the third party to assert his own right." *Id.*, at 116.

FORD MOTOR CREDIT *v.* FLORIDA REVENUE DEPT.

and the invalidation of that aspect of the tax would provide it no benefit. The entire basis for its potential harm rests on the possibility that Michigan might enact a similar statute, thereby subjecting FMCC to double taxation on its Florida intangibles. But if that should happen, and if FMCC's constitutional arguments are valid, then it would have standing to challenge the application of Michigan's tax to its Florida assets and its challenge would prevail.

Arguably a logical application of the internal consistency test should provide every taxpayer with immunity from the imposition of any tax that does not pass the test. It seems to us in this case, however, that such a result would provide FMCC with a windfall and would not forestall any realistic threat to interstate commerce. On the face of the statute, Florida's tax does not discriminate against FMCC or impose any barrier to out-of-state concerns desiring access to the Florida market. To the extent that Florida has elected to discriminate against its own residents, FMCC has no standing to vindicate their rights. The strength of the attack a resident may make on the statute and the fashioning of an appropriate remedy if such an attack should succeed must be considered in litigation brought by a different taxpayer.

The judgment of the District Court of Appeal is affirmed.

It is so ordered.

JUSTICE O'CONNOR took no part in the consideration and decision of this case.

1st DRAFT

SUPREME COURT OF THE UNITED STATES

No. 88–1847

FORD MOTOR CREDIT COMPANY, INC., APPELLANT *v.* DEPARTMENT OF REVENUE, STATE OF FLORIDA

ON APPEAL FROM THE DISTRICT COURT OF APPEAL OF FLORIDA, FIRST DISTRICT

[April ——, 1991]

JUSTICE BLACKMUN, dissenting.

I

The majority acknowledges, as it must, that Florida's scheme for taxing intangible property is internally inconsistent. *Ante*, at 8. This conclusion follows inescapably from the structure of the tax: Florida taxes 100 percent of the intangibles owned by a Florida resident and also taxes all of a nonresident's intangibles that have a business situs in Florida. If every State were to enact the Florida tax, an entity domiciled in Florida but owning intangible property with a business situs in Delaware would pay two taxes on the same intangible property—a resident tax to Florida and a business situs tax to Delaware. Similarly, a Delaware business owning intangible property located in Florida would also pay two taxes on the Florida property. Such inevitable multiple taxation renders the Florida scheme internally inconsistent, and therefore unconstitutional. See *Goldberg* v. *Sweet*, 488 U. S. 252, 261 (1989).

The majority declines, nevertheless, to invalidate Florida's tax because it rules that appellant lacks standing. I believe this conclusion rests on faulty logic and diverges from this Court's prior decisions in the area. Moreover, although the majority's result gives the appearance of judicial restraint, the constitutional finding that underlies today's decision in-

FORD MOTOR CREDIT *v.* FLORIDA REVENUE DEPT.

trudes further upon the States' taxing authority than any of this Court's prior holdings. In order to conclude that appellant has no standing, the majority must first find that Florida can, or at least should, cure the constitutional defect in its tax law in only one way. Indeed, the majority flatly asserts that the internal inconsistency of Florida's tax is "a direct consequence of Florida's failure to exempt [out-of-state property] from the tax imposed on residents," *ante*, at 8, and suggests that the proper method of solving this problem is for Florida to give its residents a tax credit for any intangible property taxes paid to States in which their foreign intangibles have a business situs. Based upon this identification of specific harm and remedy, the majority not surprisingly concludes that FMCC is not the proper party to challenge the Florida tax. After all, because FMCC is not a Florida resident whose foreign intangibles are subject to the objectionable tax, FMCC would not benefit from the tax credit that the Court suggests would heal the Florida tax's constitutional infirmity.

This analysis is sound, however, only if one accepts the Court's starting point. I conclude that nothing in our Commerce Clause jurisprudence gives this Court the authority to prefer one portion of Florida's intangibles tax to another and that the Court errs in doing so. The challenged tax is internally inconsistent because Florida taxes *both* its residents' intangible property with a foreign situs *and* nonresidents' intangible property with a business situs in Florida. Thus, it makes just as much sense to say that the scheme's internal inconsistency derives from Florida's taxation of intangible property with a business situs in Florida as it does to say that the Florida tax scheme's constitutional infirmity rests in the taxation of a Florida resident's out-of-state intangibles.

If one acknowledges that the Florida tax's constitutional deficiency is caused by the State's decision to tax intangibles based upon business situs *and* domicile, it follows that for purposes of standing to attack the scheme as internally inconsistent, Ford Motor Credit Company (FMCC) is in a position no different, and no less strong, from that of the Florida resident whom the majority names as the proper party to raise the challenge. Both FMCC and the Florida resident are harmed by the *risk* of double taxation of intangible property with a business situs outside their respective domiciliary States.

Florida may eliminate this risk—and thus the tax's internal inconsistency—by altering either the business situs or the domicile component of the tax. As the majority suggests, the State could elect to provide its residents with a credit for the business situs taxes they pay to other States. Significantly, however, Florida also could remedy the scheme's internal inconsistency by forgoing the taxation of nonresidents' intangible property with a Florida business situs. This latter route would exempt FMCC and fully satisfy the majority's apparent concern that FMCC is seeking a remedy from which it will not benefit. See, *ante*, at 10–11.

Nor may one plausibly contend that FMCC lacks standing because Florida is not *compelled* to remedy the offensive tax in a way that will affect FMCC's tax liability. The fallacy of such reasoning is self-evident. Because Florida may always meet a taxpayer's attack on the internal inconsistency of the intangibles tax by modifying its tax in a way that does not affect that taxpayer's liability, it is impossible to hold that FMCC lacks standing on this ground without concluding that no taxpayer—including the Florida resident whom the majority believes to be the proper plaintiff in a suit of this kind—has standing to challenge the internally inconsistent scheme. This cannot be a correct application of the consistency test—a prophylactic rule permitting the assertion of hypothetical harm as a means of rooting out a tax scheme that impermissibly burdens interstate commerce.

I am similarly unpersuaded by the majority's conclusion that FMCC also lacks standing because business situs taxes are preferable to taxes based on the taxpayer's domicile.

FORD MOTOR CREDIT *v.* FLORIDA REVENUE DEPT.

Ante, at 12. This Court has never held that a State may not tax property based upon the property owner's domicile. Further, this Court has

> "'long held that the Constitution imposes no single [apportionment] formula on the States,' [*Container Corp. of America* v. *Franchise Tax Bd.*, 463 U. S. 159 164 (1983)], and therefore [has] declined to undertake the essentially legislative task of establishing a 'single constitutionally mandated method of taxation.' *Id.*, at 171; see also *Moorman Mfg. Co.* v. *Bair*, 437 U. S. 267, 278–280 (1978). Instead, we determine whether a tax is fairly apportioned by examining whether it is internally and externally consistent. [*American Trucking Assns., Inc.* v. *Scheiner*, 483 U. S. 266, 285 (1987)]; *Armco Inc.* v. *Hardesty*, 467 U. S. 638, 644 (1984); *Container Corp.*, *supra*, at 169–170." *Goldberg* v. *Sweet*, 488 U. S., at 261.

I would not disturb this sound approach. Having concluded that Florida's intangibles tax is internally inconsistent, I would allow the Florida Legislature to remedy this deficiency in the manner it deems appropriate. Contrary to the majority's suggestion, *ante*, at 12, I do not think that this Court may surmise from past enactments that the Florida Legislature would always favor the business situs component of the intangibles tax. Divination of this kind is both unreliable and inappropriate.

Finally, I cannot accept the majority's suggestion that the Florida scheme poses no "realistic threat to interstate commerce." *Ante*, at 13. Under the internal consistency test, if every State were to enact the challenged tax, a wholly intrastate company would pay only one tax on its intangibles, while a company doing business in more than one State would pay a double tax. Thus, the disparate burden the intangibles tax generates "has a forbidden impact on interstate commerce because it exerts an inexorable hydraulic pressure on interstate businesses to ply their trade within the

State that enacted the measure rather than 'among the several States.' U. S. Const., Art. I, §8, cl. 3." *Scheiner*, 483 U. S., at 286–287.

It bears reemphasis that the internal consistency test is simply one method of ensuring that a tax on interstate commerce is fairly apportioned and that "the central purpose behind the apportionment requirement is to ensure that each State taxes only its fair share of an interstate transaction." *Goldberg* v. *Sweet*, 488 U. S., at 260–261. Because Florida's tax on intangibles fails the internal consistency test, Florida clearly is taxing more intangibles than is constitutionally permitted. The majority offers no persuasive reason why FMCC—one of the taxpayers caught within this net that is cast too broadly—should not be able to challenge the Florida tax.

II

Inasmuch as I would allow FMCC to challenge the tax, I must examine briefly the arguments offered by respondent in support of the Florida District Court of Appeal's judgment in this case.

As noted, the Court of Appeal did not conclude that the challenged tax was internally consistent. Instead, the court declined to apply the internal consistency test to its intangible property tax on the grounds that this Court had applied the test only to franchise and excise taxes and that this Court had suggested in earlier opinions that multiple taxation of intangibles did not violate the Commerce Clause. 537 So. 2d 1011, 1012–1013 (1988). I cannot accept this rationale for upholding the challenged tax.

Although this Court has not had cause before now to apply the internal consistency test to an intangible property tax, there is nothing in the test itself that suggests that an intangibles tax should be exempt from such scrutiny, and neither the Florida court nor appellee has offered any persuasive reason for such an exemption. This Court has held that the Commerce Clause analysis set out in *Complete Auto*

FORD MOTOR CREDIT *v.* FLORIDA REVENUE DEPT.

Transit, Inc. v. *Brady*, 430 U. S. 274, 279 (1977), applies to any tax that "substantially affect[s] interstate commerce," even if it attaches only to a "'local' or intrastate activity." *Commonwealth Edison Co.* v. *Montana*, 453 U. S. 609, 615, 616 (1981). As has been demonstrated above, the Florida taxing scheme inevitably disadvantages an entity that conducts business beyond the borders of its domiciliary State. The logical result of this burden is that businesses subject to the tax would be disinclined to expand operations to other States. I conclude, therefore, that the tax on intangibles, like the severance taxes at issue in *Commonwealth Edison*, "may substantially affect interstate commerce, and this effect is the proper focus of Commerce Clause inquiry." *Id.*, at 616.

I also cannot accept the Florida court's conclusion that this Court's decisions in *State Tax Comm'n* v. *Aldrich*, 316 U. S. 174 (1942), and *Curry* v. *McCanless*, 307 U. S. 357 (1939), render the internal consistency test inapplicable to taxes on intangible property. Those cases concerned due process challenges to the multiple taxation of intangibles. In particular, the Court had to decide whether a nondomiciliary State was empowered to tax intangible property with which it had some connection. In each case, the Court stated that the Fourteenth Amendment did not preclude taxation of these intangibles by the owner's domiciliary State and by any other State "which has extended benefits or protection, or which can demonstrate 'the practical fact of its power' or sovereignty as respects the [intangible property] . . . ." *Aldrich*, 316 U. S., at 181–182 (citation omitted); see *Curry*, 307 U. S., at 367–368. Indeed, the Court's sole inquiry in both *Curry* and *Aldrich* was whether the nondomiciliary State had established a sufficient nexus with the intangible property to justify taxing that property.

The Florida District Court of Appeal acknowledged that *Curry* and *Aldrich* were not Commerce Clause cases, but attempted to minimize this fact by noting that this Court

FORD MOTOR CREDIT *v.* FLORIDA REVENUE DEPT.

"has indicated that taxes which satisfy the due process clause generally will satisfy the commerce clause." 537 So. 2d, at 1012. Whatever the merit of that generalization, none of the cases supplying the vague language the court cited for this proposition addressed a tax scheme alleged to generate the potential for multiple taxation that is unconstitutional in the present case. See *Ott* v. *Mississippi Valley Barge Line Co.*, 336 U. S. 169, 174 (1949) (noting that the challenged tax posed "no risk of multiple taxation" and that there was "no claim . . . that [the] tax discriminate[d] against interstate commerce"); *Ford Motor Co.* v. *Beauchamp*, 308 U. S. 331 (1939); *Pacific Telephone & Telegraph Co.* v. *Tax Comm'n*, 297 U. S. 403 (1936).

I decline to attribute to *Curry* and *Aldrich* a breadth of analysis that is not evident from the text of the opinions. This Court in those cases did not examine whether the taxes at issue were properly apportioned or whether the challenged taxes discriminated against interstate commerce. They cannot control the analysis of this case and manifestly do not preclude the conclusion that the Florida intangibles tax is internally inconsistent and therefore is in violation of the Commerce Clause.

I respectfully dissent.

The Blackmun *Ford Motor Credit* draft was the first Supreme Court opinion to apply the internal consistency test to an intangible property tax. But the draft itself was not to come down as the opinion of the Court, since it was contrary to the conference vote. As Chief Justice Rehnquist put it in his December 7, 1990, letter to Blackmun, "[Y]our proposed opinion in this case has come out to 'reverse,' rather than to 'affirm,' which as you point out in your memo of December 7th was the tentative Conference vote." Because of this, the Chief Justice reassigned the case to Justice Stevens on January 4, 1991.

Justice Stevens circulated a new draft opinion of the Court on February 26, which affirmed the state court decision upholding the tax. It is reprinted on page 471. The Stevens draft, like the one Justice Blackmun had prepared, recognized that the Florida tax "is not internally consistent. For if every State were to replicate Florida's scheme, finance companies would be taxed twice on their out-of-state receivables—once by their home State and once by the situs State—whereas their in-state receivables would be taxed only once."

Nevertheless, the Stevens draft did not conclude from this that the tax was invalid. Florida had argued "that there is no constitutional requirement that property taxes must pass the internal consistency test." Justice Stevens did not deal with this argument. Instead, his draft followed the view stated by him at the conference—that FMCC, a nonresident, did not have standing to avoid the application of the tax to its Florida intangibles because the statute arguably discriminated against Florida domiciliaries. As the draft concluded, "To the extent that Florida has elected to discriminate against its own residents, FMCC has no standing to vindicate their rights. The strength of the attack a resident may make on the state and the fashioning of an appropriate remedy if such an attack should succeed must be considered in litigation brought by a different taxpayer."

On March 20, 1991, Justice Blackmun wrote to Justice Stevens that he could not join his opinion and would be circulating a dissent. On April 2, Blackmun sent around the draft dissent reprinted on page 484, which was quickly joined by Justices Marshall and Kennedy. The Blackmun draft dissent urged that, so far as standing was concerned, FMCC "is in a position no different, and no less strong, from that of the Florida resident whom the majority names as the proper party to raise the challenge." The draft dissent also repeated (though in shorter form) the holding in the Blackmun draft opinion of the Court "that the Florida intangibles tax is internally inconsistent and therefore is in violation of the Commerce Clause."

However, on May 9, the Court's decision to affirm the tax unraveled, as Justice Souter changed his vote. In a letter on that date to Justices Blackmun and Stevens, Souter wrote, "Because John's opinion comes out to where I hoped to be when we voted on this, I feel a little bit of a rotter in joining Harry's dissent. But so I believe I must do." Though the Souter explanation was ambivalent, the Justice had definitely switched his vote. This made for a four-to-four division. This was pointed out in a May 9, note to the Chief Justice from Justice Scalia, who wrote, "I had intended to write a few words separately but since it now appears that the decision below will be affirmed by an equally divided Court it would be a waste of time to circulate anything."

The next day, May 10, Justice Stevens wrote to Chief Justice Rehnquist, "Since David and Nino have now voted, and since I have established such an enviable record at writing majority opinions that end up in a tie, cf. *United States* v. *France*, I propose that we enter the attached order on Monday."

The order mentioned by Justice Stevens was a per curiam drafted by the Justice which affirmed the decision upholding the Florida tax by an equally divided Court. (Parenthetically, as we saw in Chapter 9, the *France* case referred to in the Stevens letter was another 1991 case in which Justice Stevens had also written a draft opinion of the Court, only to see his majority disappear, with the case likewise ultimately decided without opinion by an equally divided Court.)

Had the Blackmun draft opinion of the Court come down as the *Ford Motor Credit* opinion, it would have answered the question of whether the internal consistency test applies to intangible property. As it turned out, however, the vote switches in the case prevented the question from being answered. Therefore, the lacuna in this highly technical area of constitutional law that would have been filled by the Blackmun opinion still remains.

Note

1. 500 U.S. 172 (1991).